Property, Piracy and Punishment

Property, Piracy and Punishment

Hugo Grotius on War and Booty in *De iure praedae* – Concepts and Contexts

Edited by

Hans W. Blom

BRILL

LEIDEN • BOSTON
2009

Cover illustration: Leiden, University Library, ms. BPL 917, fol. 7r (detail). This and the other illustrations in this volume are from the ms. of *De iure praedae* and are printed with permission of Leiden University Library.

Originally published as Volumes 26 (2005), 27 (2006) and 28 (2007) of Brill's journal *Grotiana.*

This book is printed on acid-free paper.

Library of Congress Cataloging-in-Publication Data

Property, piracy and punishment : Hugo Grotius on war and booty in De iure praedae : concepts and contexts / edited by Hans W. Blom.
p. cm.
Includes index.
"Originally published as Volumes 26 (2005), 27 (2006) and 28 (2007) of Brill's journal Grotiana."
ISBN 978-90-04-17513-6 (hardback : alk. paper) 1. Grotius, Hugo, 1583-1645. De jure praedae commentarius--Congresses. 2. Prize law--Congresses. I. Blom, H. W. II. Title.

KZ6600.P76 2009
343.09'6--dc22

2009003129

ISBN 978 90 04 17513 6

Contents

Introduction

Hans W. Blom
Faculty of Social Sciences, Erasmus University Rotterdam
blom@fsw.eur.nl

Abstract
In this introduction, the meaning and relevance of the study of *De iure praedae*, as one of the juvenilia of Grotius, is discussed and the contending approaches are described. A survey of the volume is provided.

Keywords
De iure praedae, Grotius's juvenilia, rival paradigms, piracy, privateering, just war, NIAS

In this volume the papers of a conference on *De iure praedae* are collected, that took place in June 2005, at the Netherlands Institute for Advanced Study in the Humanities and Social Sciences (NIAS). The conference concluded the work of a NIAS Theme Group.[1] This publication, and also the preparation of a web-based edition of *De iure praedae* are among the outcomes of this year at NIAS. The interest for, and study of Hugo Grotius and Grotiana is rising, both in span and detail. This volume of Grotiana aims to testify that. The Netherlands Institute for Advanced Study deserves gratitude for supporting the initiative of the Grotiana Foundation, in generously facilitating the Theme Group on *De iure praedae* during the academic year 2004-2005.

De Iure Praedae, One of Grotius's Juvenilia

De iure praedae, largely written in 1604-1606, was rediscovered in 1864 and published four years later. Yet it will be only in the twentieth century that it is

[1] See http://www.nias.knaw.nl/en/news_forthcoming_activities/grotius/ for the conference. The Theme Group consisted of Hans Blom and Laurens Winkel (convenors), Peter Borschberg, Martine van Ittersum, Henk Nellen, Jan Waszink and George Wright.

to be seriously studied. The 1868 essay of Robert Fruin in *De Gids* notwithstanding,[2] growing attention for this text coincides with a more recently increased interest in the early writings of Grotius, and their subsequent publication. Discussion of *De iure praedae* also coincides with changing paradigms in the study of Grotius. The concern for his juvenilia is witnessed by editions of the poetry, early manuscripts, historical and church-political works,[3] drawing attention to the topicality of Grotius's writings, but also demanding a view on their interconnections. In an exemplary study, Peter Haggenmacher gave an example of precisely this, in his 1983 book on the sources of *De iure praedae* and *De iure belli ac pacis*.[4]

A few years before, Wolfgang Fikentscher had published an essay on 'fides' as the foundation of Grotius's law of nations.[5] Fikentscher defends the thesis that the Grotian natural law differs from that of the Spanish Scholastics in Grotius's foundation of natural law in the notion of trust.

> Instead of the Scholastic deduction from an Aristotelian conceived Nature, Grotius puts the free and equal action of the faithful. The autonomy of personhood, reflecting sovereignty on the level of states, and the autonomous fides that obliges sovereignty are absent in the catholic law of nations of the Late Scholastics, but provide the foundation to the Grotian law of nations.[6]

According to Fikentscher, who in his protestant interpretation relies heavily on Fruin, Grotius was driven to develop his notion of trust because of the 'universal priesthood of the reformation'. Grotius – so Fikentscher – also attempted to transcend the toleration discussion and free it from religious contention by moving to trust instead of conscience.

---

[2] Robert Fruin, 'Een onuitgegeven werk van Hugo de Groot', *De Gids*, 32 (1868), 1-37, 215-254.

[3] *The poetry of Hugo Grotius. De dichtwerken van Hugo Grotius*, ed by B.L. Meulenbroek et al. (Assen: Van Gorcum, 1970 –); *Meletius, sive de iis quae inter Christianos conveniunt epistola*, ed. by G. H. M. Posthumus Meyjes (Leiden: Brill, 1988); *De republica emendanda*, ed. by Arthur Eyffinger et al., *Grotiana*, 5 (1984), 66-121; *Commentarius in Theses XI*, ed. by P. Borschberg (Berne: Lang, 1994).

[4] *Grotius et la doctrine de la guerre juste* (Paris: Presses Universitaires de France, 1983).

[5] W. Fikentscher, *De fide et perfidia. Der Treuegedanke in den "Staatsparallelen" des Hugo Grotius aus heutiger Sicht* (München: Bayerischen Akademie der Wissenschaften, 1979).

[6] Op. cit., pp. 63-4: 'Was das grotianische Völkerrecht vom Völkerrecht der spanischen Scholastiker unterscheidet, ist seine Begründung auf den Treuegedanken. An die Stelle der scholastischen Deduktion aus der aristotelisch begriffenen Natur tritt bei Grotius das gleichberechtigte, freie Handeln der Getreuen. Die Autonomie der Persönlichkeit, der im Leben der Staaten deren Souveränität entspricht, und die autonomen und souveränitätsverbindende fidesdies sind die Elemente, die dem katholischen Völkerrecht der Spätscholastik fehlen, und auf denen das grotianische Völkerrecht ruht.'

For the present context, Fikentscher's argument is relevant in that it draws attention to the fact that this concept of fides even precedes *De iure praedae* and is first developed in the likewise manuscript *Parallelon* (1601-1602).[7] The essay of Fikentscher has arguably not received the attention it deserves, also being the first major publication on the *Parallelon* to appear after its publication by Meerman in 1803. By coincidence, Fikentscher prepared his essay at NIAS in 1971-72 while working on his book on comparative legal methodology.

The rediscovery of the manuscript of *De iure praedae* also made it evident that *Mare liberum* (1609) was a reworked chapter of the original manuscript of *De iure praedae*, or better phrased, it was a reworked chapter *inside* this manuscript, thus highlighting the complicated nature of the re-discovered manuscript as both a finished manuscript and a work in progress. Its first publication did not make this visible, since H. G. Hamaker – on the basis of an argument from authorial intent – had decided to take the latest version of the manuscript as the text that Grotius had wanted to write. He thereby did not account for the fact that the reworking of chapter 12 was undertaken with a view to its publication in 1609, and hence represents a different 'intended text' from the chapter 12 as it originally belonged to *De iure praedae*. Fruin, who immediately noticed the connection between chapter 12 and *Mare liberum*, opines that 'in the edition of Mr. Hamaker according to the autograph, the text for the first time is published in complete exactness. Moreover, it appears for the first time unabridged and in its authentic setting of the whole argument of the author'.[8] Fruin says too little and too much here. Martine van Ittersum studied – in a critical exchange with Fruin – the historical circumstances of *De iure praedae*. Like Fruin she locates the text squarely within the pursuits of the VOC, unlike Fruin she objects to the idea that the text is a theoretical achievement.[9]

[7] *Hugonis Grotii, Batavi, Parallelon rerumpublicarum liber tertius: De moribus ingenioque populorum Atheniensium, Romanorum, Batavorum = Vergelijking der gemeenebesten door Hugo de Groot*, Derde boek: Over de zeden en den inborst der Athenienseren, Romeinen en Hollanderen / ed. from the Ms., tr. into Dutch, and annot. by Johan Meerman; with index by J. Brill, 4 vols (Haarlem: Loosjes, 1801-03).

[8] 'de uitgaaf van den Heer Hamaker naar het handschrift de tekst voor het eerst met volkomen juistheid verschijnt. Hij verschijnt tevens voor het eerst volledig en in zijn oorspronkelijk verband met het geheele betoog van den schrijver', Fruin, 'Een onuitgegeven werk', p. 224.

[9] Martine Julia van Ittersum, *Profit and Principle. Hugo Grotius, Natural Rights Theories and the Rise of Dutch Power in the East Indies, 1595-1615* (Leiden: Brill, 2006).

Contending Interpretations

As a text, *Mare liberum* has been well-known for its role in the debate that connected Grotius to Selden and Hobbes, on the extent of dominium. Students of Hobbes, therefore, were bound to have an interest in *De iure praedae* as well. Hobbes-studies have become a major field of research, i.a. because of the importance allotted to contract theory by modern welfare economics, and by implication, modern political science.[10] Grotius obtained an important share in that heightened interest. Richard Tuck started in 1979 with *Natural right theories* a series of publications in which the early Grotius became increasingly important, claiming i.a. that *De iure praedae* can help us understand the radical nature of *De iure belli ac pacis* in its 1625 version, showing the important differences with the more canonical 1631 edition. Reinhard Brandt had published his *Eigentumstheorien von Grotius bis Kant* in 1974.[11] Books about this topic followed, such as Buckle, Horne.[12] Moreover, students of the Scottish Enlightenment have pointed out the importance of Grotius for the innovative teaching at the university in Glasgow, and later in Edinburgh, contributing as will be argued below to the Grotian Tradition.[13]

Yet Haggenmacher and Tuck propagate different routes to arrive at their revisionist positions, and they express important disagreements. Theirs is also a shadow of what Henk Nellen in another context recognised: 'that Grotius in the twentieth century sometimes also was a catalyst that set fire to hidden animosities, promoted factions and reinvigorated existing controversies'.[14] Nellen was referring to controversies around C. van Vollenhoven and

[10] The late Jean Hampton wrote an exemplary study in this category: *Hobbes and the social contract tradition* (Cambridge: Cambridge University Press, 1986).

[11] Reinhard Brandt, *Eigentumstheorien von Grotius bis Kant*, Problemata 31 (Stuttgart: Frommann-Holzboog, 1974).

[12] Stephen Buckle, *Natural law and the theory of property. Grotius to Hume* (Oxford: Clarendon Press, 1991); T. A. Horne, *Property rights and poverty. Political argument in Britain, 1605-1834* (Chapel Hill: University of North Carolina Press, 1990).

[13] See i.a. John Cairns, 'Importing our lawyers from Holland. Netherlands influences on Scots law and lawyers in the eighteenth century', in: *Scotland and the Low Countries, 1124-1994*, The Mackie monographs 3, ed. by Grant G. Simpson (East Linton: Tuckwell, 1996), pp. 136-153; for the work of James Moore on Grotius in Schotland, see most recently: *Natural rights on the threshold of the Scottish Enlightenment. The writings of Gershom Carmichael*, Natural law and Enlightenment classics, ed. by James Moore and Michael Silverthorne, texts tr. from the Latin by Michael Silverthorne, forew. by James Moore (Indianapolis, IN: Liberty Fund, 2002).

[14] Henk Nellen, '"Het Leidse haylichje" Hugo Grotius in de twintigste eeuw', *Jaarboek van de Maatschappij der Nederlandse Letterkunde 1994-1995* (Leiden: Maatschappij der Nederlandse Letterkunde, 1996), 37-64 (p. 39).

C. J. H. van Eijsinga concerning 'het Leidse heylichje' – the 'Leiden Saint' – as one of the opponents, the Utrecht professor Gerretson, ironically called the object of their veneration. The discussion then was about the meaning of Grotius for modern international law; the discussion between Haggenmacher and Tuck is about the intellectual origins, and also the reception, of Grotius's oeuvre.

Apart from disagreement about the title of *De iure praedae* – Tuck prefers to call it *De Indis*, because Grotius at least twice used this or a similar term to refer to his manuscript – the interpretations differ also concerning the general trend of interpretation. Tuck set out on a path sketched by Michel Villey, about the origins of the modern concept of subjective rights. His last book wants to reinforce Grotius as a precursor of Hobbesian Epicureanism and Kantian realism, and set him apart from the 'sorry comforters' of eighteenth-century natural law.[15] Other intellectual historians consider the pivotal eighteenth-century – and authors like Adam Smith or David Hume – in terms of what some have called the Grotian Tradition.[16]

Peter Haggenmacher is a historian of legal thought as much as he studies modern international law. No Grotian Quest for him, since he has clearly declared that Grotius may have worked on the law of war and peace, yet was in no way the Father of International Law, as some have called him, nor in any way interested in developing a theory of that field. And as a student of the law of war and peace Grotius is clearly taking position within the available Scholastic framework. It is Haggenmacher's achievement to have indicated these connections with utmost clarity, and his book would merit translation into English. Yet the Grotian Quest had a role to play in the wider field of International Relations, as Roelofsen has explained.[17]

In recent years this essentially contested image of Grotius has given rise to a new twist, one that is best understood as post-colonial criticism. Reviving the criticism, not to say the anger, that Jean-Jacques Rousseau expressed against

---

[15] Job 16.2; Georg Cavallar, 'Lauter "leidige Tröster"? Kants Urteil über die Völkerrechtslehren von Grotius, Pufendorf und Vattel', *Allgemeine Zeitschrift für Philosophie*, 30 (2005), 271-91; B. Orend, *War and International Justice* (Waterloo: Wilfrid Laurier Press, 2000), chapter 2:'Kant's Just War Theory' (pp. 41-61).

[16] Tradition is here taken in a literal sense, as that what has been 'traditus'. I distinguish it from the Grotian Quest, which is an ideological revivalist program. Tradition and Quest can co-exist in the work of one author, see e.g. Edward Keene, *Beyond the Anarchical Society: Grotius, Colonialism and Order in World Politics* (Cambridge: Cambridge University Press, 2002).

[17] C.G. Roelofsen, 'Grotius and the 'Grotian Heritage' in International Law and International Relations. The Quatercentenary and its Aftermath (circa 1980-1990)', *Grotiana*, 11 (1990), 6-28.

the author of *De iure belli ac pacis*, the post-colonial critic sees Grotius as a White Man, who not only justifies slavery,[18] but, moreover, was the 'idéologue' of these barbarous colonisers, the V.O.C. For this position, *De iure praedae* is ideal material. But still it is material with a lot of complications.

First of all, the manuscript is a clean copy that has been revised; at some places very extensively, at others only ephemerally, or not at all. The most extensive reworking is chapter 12, that prepared *Mare liberum*, but that is not the only one. Part of the NIAS Theme Group activities was to chart these reworkings, because the publication of 1868 – on which all further editions have been based – does not indicate the revisions and only presents the final version. On the one hand, a web-based edition is being prepared that will show all additions and deletions and will also allow reading the text in its 'pristine' form. Since the manuscript is an autograph, and forms part of a larger collection of Grotius's autographs, comparison of these papers, by substance and by technical characteristics of the paper used (watermarks, quality) provides further information for dating the writing and revision (e.g. some of the revisions are on inserted paper, that can be related to other paper in the manuscript collection).

The post-colonial critic looks at Grotius as a spindoctor of the V.O.C., as the Karl Rove of Oldenbarnevelt, but spin doctors don't normally go so far as to develop a brand new theory of natural law – or at least, that is what Barbeyrac and his likes in the eighteenth century believed that Grotius had been doing –, or introduce a concept of divided sovereignty as Edward Keene argues in *Beyond the Anarchical Society*. The spin doctor and the theorist sit uncomfortably together, yet they might be accommodated by emphasising the ad hoc nature of the theorist. It is here that the post-colonial critic joins forces with the Scholastic interpretation, with a difference though: in the new vision, Grotius is no longer interested in Scholastic doctrine per se, but only 'pinched' whatever suited him and the case of his patrons. The theoretical argument in *De iure praedae*, on the post-colonial critic's reading is just the necessary support for colonial aggression in Asia. It is bad conscience turned into abstract talk.

Suspiciously absent – or almost; see the articles of George Wright and Guus van Nifterik – in the studies on *De iure praedae* in this volume are considerations of the Grotian Tradition in a broad sense. In the understanding of Knud Haakonssen, 'Grotius's legacy was rich and varied, and both he himself and his ideas became European phenomena in several fields, including

[18] However, see Gustaaf van Nifterik, 'Grotius on "slavery" ', *Grotiana*, 22/23 (2001/2002), 243-254, for a critical discussion of that view.

philosophy'.[19] Tuck's argument that the Grotius of *De iure praedae* and *De iure belli ac pacis* (1st edn 1625, not the later editions of 1631 ff) is close to Hobbes, and that Hobbes was a reader of the 1625 edition, is a detail in a larger discussion about how to summarize best this legacy. *De iure praedae* as a starting point for a tradition. However, *De iure praedae* was just not publicly available in the high days of modern natural law thought. It had to work indirectly, through *Mare liberum* and *De iure belli ac pacis*. And thus we need a more detailed understanding of the relationship between these works.

Robert Feenstra has argued – and we find this argument echoed in the contributions of Benjamin Straumann and Laurens Winkel – that not only the classification of the just causes of war derives from fundamental distinctions in Roman law, but that this classification also provides the backbone to *De iure belli ac pacis*.[20] Now one might argue by taking his 'justae causae' from the classification of individual actions under Roman law, that Grotius was in need of a set of additional concepts: among which most importantly: sovereignty, dominium and natural liberty. Here he could fall back on his previous studies as a historian of the States of Holland (1601): elaborating on the major treatises justifying the Dutch Revolt, among which most importantly the exchange between Vranck and Leicester on the nature of sovereignty.[21]

De Iure Praedae and Booty

In the process, the description of Grotius is now becoming much more solid and detailed. The *Briefwisseling* has been completed, its contents are being prepared for internet publication. In the shifting positioning and alliances of Grotian Origins, Tradition, Quest and Critique, our understanding of this enigmatic figure in early-modern intellectual life is certainly becoming more complete and versatile, permitting to locate Grotius within a much wider range of argument and debate. To a considerable extent this is due to the study of *De iure praedae*.

---

[19] Knud Haakonssen, *Natural law and moral philosophy. From Grotius to the Scottish Enlightenment* (Cambridge, Cambridge University Press, 1996), p. 30.

[20] R. Feenstra, 'La systématique du droit dans l'oeuvre de Grotius', in *La sistematica giuridica. Storia, teoria e problemi attuali* (Rome: Istituto della Enciclopedia Italiana, 1991) pp. 333–343; repr. in R. Feenstra, *Legal Scholarship and Doctrines of Private Law, 13th–18th Centuries* (Aldershot: Ashgate, 1996).

[21] See also Richard Tuck, *Philosophy and government 1572-1651* (Cambridge: Cambridge University Press. 1993); Henk Nellen, *Hugo de Groot. Een leven in strijd om de vrede, 1583-1645* (Amsterdam: Balans, 2007), p. 56ff.

The title of this work refers to the law of prize and booty, and it is remarkable that relatively limited attention generally is paid to what exactly this law is about.[22] It seems as if, by embedding the law of booty within a more general law of war and peace, the former has disappeared behind the latter. For sure, Haggenmacher has carefully enumerated the use Grotius made of previous ideas on the topic. Yet Kempe argues, by condemning the Portuguese as pirates and brigands, Grotius was putting his new legal framework to the harshest test he could possibly have had. Since for Grotius – Kempe continues – those who act unlawful nevertheless are not *outside* the law, but *under* the law, just punishment is the Portugueses' due share.

Here the by no means new, yet highly pointed statement of Grotius – 'a just war is execution of justice' (*De iure praedae*, VII, p. 66) – obtains a covering role in the argument. The statement should be read in combination with the Grotian interpretation of 'vim vi repellere', i.e. the claim that where justice cannot be obtained, war is justified.[23] The connection between prize and just war, and between just war and the European state system are thus the wider context of *De iure praedae*.[24]

Along these lines, one returns to *De iure belli ac pacis*, full circle from the juvenilia. Maybe this is another support for the thesis that Grotius happened to publish only those juvenilia that turned out to have some relevance in his later life, and therefore that most of the juvenilia ended up being reworked for some further goal. The *Parallelon*, of which only the third book has survived – in the manuscript published by Meerman – on this reading then presumably has consisted of yet two other books, of which the first ended up being published as *De antiquitate*, and the other has been resumed in the *Annales et historiae*. The manuscript of *De iure praedae*, interestingly, had two of those afterlives: one quite visibly in *Mare liberum*, the other less visibly in *De iure belli ac pacis*. Maybe the fact that Grotius at some point had lost track of the manuscript explains its survival.[25]

---

[22] See C.G. Roelofsen, 'Grotius and State Practice of his day', *Grotiana*, 10 (1989), 3-46, repr. in Idem, *Studies in the History of International Law, law. Practice and doctrine in particular with regard to the law of naval warfare in the Low Countries from circa 1450 until the early 17th century* (Utrecht: [s.n.], 1991); Idem, 'Early Dutch Prize Laws: Some Thoughts on a case before the Court of Holland and the Grand Council of Mechelen (1477-1482)', *Netherlands international law review*, 29 (1980), 218-226; repr. in Idem, *Studies*, pp. 1-10.

[23] *Mare liberum*, XIII, p. 75: *Quod autem in iudicio obtineretur, id ubi iudicium haberi non potest, iusto bello vindicatur.*

[24] See also R. C. H. Lesaffer, 'The Grotian Tradition Revisited: Change and Continuity in the History of International Law', *British Yearbook of International Law*, ed. by J. Crawford and V. Lowe (Oxford: Oxford University Press, 2002), pp. 103-139.

[25] Pace Fruin, 'Een onuitgegeven werk', p. 236.

It has been remarked that Grotius's eirenic character received an ironic twist as precisely he was requested to defend warfare in Europe and beyond – he helped Barnevelt to urge France continue the war with Spain, he defended Heemskerk's piracy and in 1635 his then Swedish masters require him to defend the war with France. Fikentscher thinks that Grotius was able to combine both thanks to his presupposition of a universal rule of law, more in particular his law of nations built upon trust and good faith.[26] Ambiguities are certainly present in the various attempts to understand the relationship of juvenilia to the 'mature' work. Jan and Annie Romein, in a rampant psychologism, want Grotius to be encapsulated in his prodigy childhood:

> And thus he matured too early, became a child prodigy. ... Not only his soul, worse it must have damaged his mind, to be at such an early age so saturated, and from a remnant of natural reaction have refused to continue accepting new impressions, the proximate cause in our opinion of his deeply entrenched conservatism. *Ruit hora* he chooses as his motto. Time flies. He who drank the cup of time too early, he couldn't have chosen a better one. [etc.][27]

One doesn't have to adhere to an extreme position like the above to recognise that the juvenilia of Grotius are worthy of research in their own right. Not just as a historical document, but also as the expression of the creative capabilities of towering intellect.

This Volume

For sure, *De iure praedae* is approached from different angles and perspectives, and that reflects in the contributions to this volume. The articles are presented

---

[26] Fikentscher, *De fide et perfidia*, p. 65: 'Grotius könnte diese drei seiner inneren Einstellung zuwiderlaufenden Arbeiten mit dem guten juristischen Gewissen, dem er zeitlebens Treu zu bleiben suchte, nur übernehmen, wenn er auch den Krieg und die kriegsführenden Nationen einer weltweiten Rechtsordnung unterstellte, eben seinem auf Treue und Glauben gründenden Völkerrecht'.

[27] 'En zo werd hij te vroeg rijp, werd hij een wonderkind ... En niet alleen zijn ziel, erger misschien nog moet het zijn geest geschaad hebben, omdat deze op zó jeugdige leeftijd reeds zó verzadigd, juist uit een rest van natuurlijke reactie geweigerd moet hebben, nieuwe indrukken te blijven opnemen - de laatste oorzaak, komt ons voor, van zijn diep geworteld conservatisme. *Ruit hora* kiest hij zich tot lijfspreuk. De tijd vervliegt. Hij die de beker van de tijd te vroeg had leeggedronken, had er zich waarlijk geen betere kunnen kiezen. De tijd vervliegt. Hoe kon het hem anders voorkomen, die zonder strijd overwinnaar verklaard was op het toernooiveld des geestes op een leeftijd waarop anderen nog strijd moeten voeren om er toegelaten te worden; hem wiens baan daardoor voltrokken leek op het punt, waar anderen haar beginnen?', Jan Romein en Annie Romein-Verschoor, *Erflaters van onze beschaving. Nederlandse gestalten uit zes eeuwen*, 12th edn (Amsterdam: Querido, 1977; 1st edn 1938-40), pp. 231-256 (pp. 235-6).

in an order that brings out the conversational character. A short overview now follows.

Biography

Henk Nellen describes the world to which Grotius belonged, Peter Borschberg the world he did not belong to, and to a large extent was even ignorant of. The world of humanism that shows itself in its epistolary form in the *Briefwisseling*, is a starting point for an essay in which Nellen wants to give a biographical characteristic of Grotius, the eirenic classicist who yet always was asked to defend the wars of others. Writing in defence of Dutch action in the Asian theatre, explains Borschberg, did not entail a wide or accurate understanding of that world and its maritime functioning. Grotius repeated what captains wrote to their company.

Henk Nellen confronts the issue of the personality of Grotius as it transpires in his correspondence. It allows a considered opinion on the special place of the juvenilia in the compass of a scholar's life. Discussions of his and his friends' readings and writings are an important element in the *Briefwisseling*, and there is also reference to *De iure praedae* and its context. As he mentions in a letter to Lingelsheim, Grotius was convinced to have done something new in his presentation of the law of booty and prize – he considered that the only part of the commentary to be published.[28] As Peter Borschberg amply argues, indeed the 'historical part' of *De iure praedae* does not stand out as an innovation, or represent what some scholars have claimed to be the reflection of a thorough study of Asian trading practices. Yet, the political developments in the years to follow and a request from Zeeland to once again underline the importance and rightfulness of the VOC's dealings in the East made Grotius rewrite chapter 12 of *De iure praedae*, and had it rushed to the press in 1609. Irony – and also the intricacies of this combination in one humanist of the roles of scholar and political consultant – made that the publication of these new methods had to wait till 1625.

Sources

In a more general sense, the study of the sources of Grotius is present in many of the contributions to this volume. Next to the Roman legal sources that Winkel, Scattola, and Straumann discuss, the theological origins are analysed

[28] BW, I, p. 72.

by Franco Todescan and Petra-Silke Bergjan. Todescan brings to bear his previous studies of the theological 'roots' of Grotius on his comparison of the systemic aspects of *De iure praedae* and *De iure belli ac pacis*. Mark Somos discusses Grotius's tinkering with sources, in his use of the Bible as a text in *De iure praedae*. Jon Miller analyses the interconnections between *De iure praedae*, the *Stobaeus*, and *De iure belli ac pacis*, in order to better define Grotius's Stoicism in the first text.

The humanist Grotius was certainly more at home in the world of classical writing. As a humanist, he was a legal humanist too. That is where Winkel finds the roots of the juridical self-understanding in *De iure praedae* and its later development in *De iure belli ac pacis*. The word 'regula' probably stems from a new interest in Byzantine Roman law among humanists. The contents of the 'regulae' and 'leges' of the dogmatica in *De iure praedae* is discussed also by Merio Scattola and Franco Todescan. Scattola takes up the issue of whether a war can be just from both sides – ex utraque parte –, as this topic is crucial in the development of modern political thought. Asking for the meaning of the allegedly 'new method' Grotius presents in *De iure praedae*, Scattola discusses both Grotius's departure from Scholastic positions on just war, and the methodological arguments for the peculiar voluntarism typical of this first design of *De iure belli ac pacis*. It leaves no doubt why Grotius was considering that the dogmatic part of *De iure praedae* merited publication. But, as with most of his early writings, Grotius only published after having had an occasion for a complete reworking of the original text, i.c. *De iure belli ac pacis*. Something like that did not occur with his literary and philosophical pursuits. Yet they were part and parcel of Grotius's early intellectual life. As Jon Miller shows, his interest in classical philosophy, in particular Stoic philosophy, is wide-ranging. Studying his *Stobaeus* helps understand the way in which Grotius understood Stoic philosophy in *De iure praedae* and afterwards. The Fathers of the Church had a similar fascination for Grotius. While he will use them profusely in his *Pietas Ordinum*, his interest in theological issues did not rise only then. Silke-Petra Bergjan studies the use Grotius made of these writers of the early Church and highlights his attempts at historical contextualisation as an instrument of interpretation. As a well-trained humanist, Grotius was acutely aware of the importance of supporting his arguments with authoritative support, or even better, cloak his arguments in the language of these authorities. Silke-Petra Bergjan discusses the use of the Fathers of the Church in the juvenilia of Grotius. She draws attention to both the content and the style of patristic citations, first and foremost in *Ordinum pietas*, and also in *De iure praedae*, emphasising the historical turn that Grotius brings to the material, in discussing the opinions of the Fathers on church and state, church institutions and practices. Grotius reflects here preferences of the legal humanists of the *mos gallicus*, by qualifying e.g. Deuteronomy 20.1 to 23.9 as a historically conditioned argument.

Theology

It is noteworthy that in *De iure praedae* Grotius distinguishes philosophy, theology and civil law as separate approaches to the issues of war and booty, and prioritises them in this order. Mark Somos discusses the extent to which his lack of trust in theology as the moral basis for just war theory shows in *De iure praedae*, in particular in his use of the Bible, whereas Joris van Eijnatten presents one of the well-known Calvinist uses of the Bible in providing moral guidance to merchants and mariners in re war. A greater contrast is barely possible. Although the Calvinist minister of van Eijnatten's story is not a zealous warmonger, and is certainly indebted to Erasmus, Grotius comes up with a deconstruction of the Biblical texts that leave little space for Biblical guidance. Somos takes seriously the critical comments by Welwod, and extensively documents Grotius's method in this respect.

Joris van Eijnatten takes up the issue of the extent to which theological – and in particular Calvinist – engagement with just war theory led to significantly different results from early-modern natural law approach. Analysing the moral advises to maritime merchants and their crews by the Zeeland minister and theologian Godfried Udemans, van Eijnatten shows that in practical substance the Calvinist attitude to war was not very different from that of Grotius. Van Eijnatten thereby not only falsifies the hypothesis of J.T. Johnson of the Calvinist prevalence of a doctrine of 'holy war', he also shows that – for all the theological conflicts between Remonstrants and Counterremonstrants – Dutch Protestants were more united in their notion of just war than the commentators think who emphasise that when Grotius developed his version of it, he did so as an Arminian. 'In the *Spiritual helm*, then, religious purpose is not a motive by and of itself, but one consideration among others.' (p. 211)

It is commonplace in Grotius studies to consider the Biblical references that Grotius adduces e.g. in *De iure belli ac pacis* and also in *De iure praedae* as being on a par with the classical quotations, i.e. as additional support of the thesis developed from contemporary debate. Somos asks in his contribution the simple question: what is the use that Grotius makes of the Bible in *De iure praedae*? To that purpose Somos compares Grotius's use to that of the tradition, both Catholic and Protestant, to conclude that Grotius comes up with interpretations of the topical Bible places that go against all previous understanding. Somos elaborates this fact as a subterfuge to deny the Bible any relevance in the actual debate on just war, just as Grotius had announced in the first chapter of *De iure praedae*. One of the core passages in this article is Deut. 20, where God commands his people to take spoils and kill and wage war without proper declaration.

Textual Matters

But what about the text of *De iure praedae* itself? Jan Waszink looks at the autograph manuscript of *De iure praedae*, and makes a case for documenting and studying the changes Grotius made to the first draft, whereas Martine van Ittersum discusses the use Grotius made of the manuscript when he rewrote its chapter XII in preparing Mare liberum. Waszink explores the first, and to this date only, edition of the Ms. by H. G. Hamaker, and points out some of its debateable aspects. Both Waszink and van Ittersum were part of the NIAS research group in 2004-5, and the new boost of attention to *De iure praedae* shows that modern history of ideas requires co-operation across specialisations and prejudices. Van Ittersum documents that Grotius used the Ms. in order to have a fast way to get *Mare liberum* composed and ready for the press. Grotius just blotted down in the margin of chapter 12 a list of contents for the new text, and started adjusting the chapter to his pressing needs. This procedure can be reconstructed in part by also looking at the watermarks of the paper used, which allows with the necessary caution to also surmise the dating of other additions and deletions in the Ms. Providing an accessible (internet) edition of the Ms. including the additions and deletions is now well under way.

World Orders

Grotius is an attractive author for many different intellectual pursuits. Franco Todescan has studied Grotius's use of the Scholastics for many years, and gives here an English compendium of his views. Eric Wilson is a more recent student of Grotius, and approaches him from a different perspective and with a different method. While Wilson sees Grotius as the ideologue of emerging world capitalism, and uses Derrida to demonstrate this, Todescan is interested in a different kind of modernity. Todescan – who published a volume of essays under the title *Etiamsi daremus* –, searches *De iure praedae* for the preparation of *De iure belli ac pacis*, and finds it in the subtle voluntarism that paves the way for the distinction of utmost importance, that between the primary and secondary law of nations. Todescan argues that this distinction allows Grotius to define the relationship between natural law and civil law. According to Todescan, *De iure praedae* argues theologically from the will of God and develops the legal scaffold deductively, whereas in the later work Grotius follows the naturalism of the *appetitus societatis*.

Subjective Rights

What the precise nature of these innovations might be is a bone of contention among Grotius scholars. Although there is no doubt that subjective rights and modern liberty have something to do with it, less agreement exists as to historical background and Wirkungsgeschichte. Consequently, the old debate about the 'modernity' of Grotius has not been stopped by the availability of *De iure praedae*. Straumann and Wright want to tackle the issue of subjective rights, the first by showing the Roman legal background of the concept of natural rights that Grotius develops; the latter by criticising the political program that supposedly is behind Richard Tuck's understanding of subjective rights in Grotius. Straumann wants Roman (and thus Grotian) origins to the modern notion of liberty; Wright wants to see Grotius also as the precursor of Rousseau, Hegel and Marx.

Straumann makes a very precise point about the origins of the rights that Grotius introduced in *De iure praedae* and that in *Mare liberum* and its sequel, the defence against Welwod, would develop into subjective rights.

Straumann draws wider conclusions, in his critique of Benjamin Constant and the connected argument about the 'two concepts of liberty' that distinguishes ancient and modern freedom, by stating that the 'modern' liberty in reality has its origins in the Roman legal actions that Grotius had discovered in the Digest, and explicitly translated as subjective rights. Constant thus misconstrued the history of the modern concept of liberty, argues Straumann.

George Wright disagrees here in his discussion of 'context' in Quentin Skinner and Richard Tuck by arguing that it is politically backward-looking and restrictive to praise modern subjective rights. Wright demands Rousseau and Hegel and Marx as part of the canon of modern liberty. Along these lines, Wright joins the critique of Tuck's historical understanding of subjective rights by Perez Zagorin and others.

Piracy and Punishment

The concluding two contributions analyse two concepts that are central to *De iure praedae*: piracy and punishment. It seems almost forgotten that these are the central notions in the commentary, even if other concerns are claiming our contemporary attention. The distinction of piracy and privateering and its role in the wider argument is the topic of the article by Michael Kempe, in which he develops the reasoning of Grotius in a direction opposite to what customary is done. Kempe does not start from Grotius's notion of (natural) law, just war, or his relation to the Scholastics in general, but asks the precise question how Grotius understood privateering and its illegal companion, piracy. Kempe argues that the latter is as important in Grotius's reasoning as is the former, and that the achievement as a treatise in legal theory can just as well be reconstructed from this side.

Gustaaf van Nifterik in a comparable way studies in great detail Grotius's understanding of punishment and the justification of the state's right to punish. The analysis leads van Nifterik to important other texts of Grotius, up to *De iure belli ac pacis*, that in combination show how Grotius struggled to come to an adequate understanding.

Acknowledgements

The conference, on which this volume is based, was made possible by financial support from the Netherlands Institute for Advanced Study in the Humanities and Social Sciences (NIAS), the Netherlands Organisation for Scientific Research (NWO), the M.A.O.C. Gravin van Bylandt Stichting, and the Grotiana Foundation. At various stages and in various ways, this research has benefited immensely from the help of the Leiden University Library and in particular its section Westerse Handschriften, the repository of the Ms. of *De iure praedae*. The reproductions in this volume of some of its pages are only one of its many effects.

Hugo Grotius's Political and Scholarly Activities in the Light of his Correspondence

Henk J.M. Nellen*
Senior Researcher, Huygens Institute, The Hague
e-mail: Henk.Nellen@huygensinstituut.knaw.nl

Abstract
The 7725 letters of Hugo Grotius's correspondence of the years 1594 to 1645 reflect the highlights and drawbacks of an eventful career. Some important gradual developments and abiding features in the letters will be pointed out. In this way Grotius's political and scholarly activities can be analysed from the perspective of the correspondence.

Keywords
correspondence, patriotism, publishing activities, tolerance, religious latitudinarianism, eclecticism

Introduction

In the period between 1594 and 1645, the famous humanist and lawyer Hugo Grotius exchanged approximately 7725 letters with 396 correspondents. The list of addressees contains 263 names, as against 287 of those writing to Grotius. At a rough estimate, one might say that only half of the letters that were actually exchanged have found their way into our hands. The number of letters written by Grotius (4270) is considerably greater than that of the letters he received (2669): 61.5% compared to 38.5%.[1] In recent years, I have studied

* I wish to thank my colleague George Wright for correcting my English.

[1] See for the numerical data H.J.M. Nellen, 'The correspondence of Hugo Grotius', *Les grands intermédiaires culturels de la République des Lettres. Etudes de réseaux de correspondances du XVIe au XVIIIe siècles*, ed. Chr. Berkvens-Stevelinck et al. (Paris: Champion, 2005), pp. 127-164 (p. 131). For the calculation of these percentages only the correspondences consisting of 10 or more letters have been taken into account. Alphabetically arranged lists of senders and addressees in *Briefwisseling van Hugo Grotius*, ed. P.C. Molhuysen, B.L. Meulenbroek, P.P. Witkam, H.J.M. Nellen and C.M. Ridderikhoff, 17 vols, Rijks Geschiedkundige Publicatiën, Grote Serie (The Hague 1928-2001) [= BW], XVII, pp. 625-636.

most of these letters, and will now try to describe the image of Grotius's scholarly activities that emerges from his correspondence.

Grotius was a controversial scholar who developed and promoted bold, even audacious ideas across a broad spectrum of disciplines. As a humanist, he advocated a return to the sources, although surely he must have realised that his research often shed light on views that infringed Christian belief and morals. As a politician he dedicated himself to theology and in the process evoked the ire of the theologians. In turn, his ideas on church-state relationships roused the anger of princes, prelates, and politicians alike. In the course of his life, Grotius had to cope with many tensions between his official duties, scholarly activities, inner convictions and, last but not least, the maintenance of his own reputation. Towards the end of his life, he wrote a letter in which he referred to the twin role he had to play: he worked toward the reunification of the churches for the greater public good and juxtaposed this divine mandate to individual care for one's office, family or personal occupations. He expressed his sincere hope to fulfil both tasks equally well, but glossed over any possible points of friction.[2] Grotius upheld a façade that is hardly transparent. But when one takes the time and effort to trawl the letters, it becomes increasingly manifest that even a scholar and statesman of his stature was confronted with many troublesome dilemmas. It is the task of this paper to see how he rose to the challenge. It goes without saying that my description will be both general and incomplete. In order to master an overwhelming mass of information, I will proceed as follows. First, I will sketch some gradual developments; after that I will go into the more lasting elements which might be detected in Grotius's convictions.

Gradual Developments

Patriotism

Until 1618 the letters attest to a fervent patriotism. Grotius supports the interests of Holland in publications like *Mare liberum* (1609), *De antiquitate* (1610) and *Poemata collecta* (1617). After 1618, however, the correspondence is dominated by his struggle for official rehabilitation and return from exile.

---

[2] BW, XIV, no. 6112, to H. Appelboom, 28 February 1643: 'Didici ... a sapientibus plerisque nostrum duas impositas esse personas, alteram communem a Deo, alteram peculiarem a principibus, parentibus aut dilectu proprio. Velim utranque bene implere.'

Grotius then holds a neutral position towards the fatherland. In 1635 he refuses to take up the pen against John Selden, the English lawyer who had opposed his *Mare clausum* to *Mare liberum*. In the meantime, Grotius had entered the Swedish service as ambassador, stationed in Paris. Although he still valued his *Mare liberum*, he was loath to defend the freedom of the seas, because he would inevitably thwart the Swedish goal of achieving dominance in the Baltic Sea.[3] After 1637, Grotius wrote many letters, in which he distanced himself from the old fatherland. He compared Holland to a ship. He wanted to follow its course through a turbulent sea for the only reason that he had some friends on board.[4] Now he disavowed publications like *De antiquitate*, arguing that in his early youth he had been blinded by love for the fatherland.[5] He no longer wanted to be associated with the *Poemata collecta*, because he felt estranged from the dignitaries he had extolled in his occasional poetry. He was also afraid that its martial and erotic undertones would work against him.[6] Self-consciously he compared himself to Augustine who, at the end of his life, had denounced many erroneous convictions in his *Retractationes*.[7]

Church Unity

Before 1618 Grotius envisaged his ideal of church unity within the framework of the Protestant churches. He tried to settle internal dissensions within the Reformed Church of the Republic, promoted the Church of England as a model and appealed to Lutherans to join in. On that point, however, Grotius left the Roman Catholics out of his scheme. Here and there, the correspondence yields proof that he considered the inclusion of Rome as an ideal that

---

[3] BW, VI, no. 2450, to W. de Groot, 24 January 1636: 'Ego, cum Suedia multum teneat orae maritimae, quid aliud praestare possum quam silentium?'; BW, VIII, no. 3085, to L. Camerarius, 20 May 1637.

[4] BW, XV, no. 6638, to N. van Reigersberch, 9 January 1644.

[5] BW, XIV, no. 6051, to W. de Groot, 24 January 1643: 'Quae autem ex Antiquitate reipublicae Batavicae obiiciuntur, ea nolo tueri omnia. Excessi enim modum studio in eam rempublicam in qua versabar, et multa talia aetas in nobis decoquit.'

[6] BW, X, no. 4280, to W. de Groot, 3 September 1639; BW, XVI, no. 7186, to W. de Groot, 10 December 1644 (p. 217 and notes 12-13). See also BW, V, no. 1961, to W. de Groot, 16 December 1634, with a reference to a poem in *De dichtwerken van Hugo Grotius / The poetry of Hugo Grotius*, ed. by B.L. Meulenbroek, A. Eyffinger, E. Rabbie, 7 vols (Assen: van Gorcum, 1970-), I.4a/b (ed. E. Rabbie, 1992), pp. 320-324; BW, XIV, no. 6342, note 10.

[7] BW, XII, no. 5084, to W. de Groot, 2 March 1641; BW, XII, no. 5303, to W. de Groot, 3 August 1641; BW, XIV, no. 6166, to W. de Groot, 11 April 1643.

could materialize only in the very long run.[8] After the fall of Oldenbarnevelt, Grotius stuck to a neutral position as far as church unity was concerned. As Swedish ambassador in Paris, he abided by the official policy of his adoptive fatherland where, from 1593 onwards, Lutheranism was the state religion. Very characteristically he kept his distance from the Scot John Durie, who advocated the unification of the Protestant Churches in Sweden, Germany and England. Citing the motto 'Near is my coat, but nearer is my skin', Grotius unambiguously informed the Swedish chancellor Axel Oxenstierna that he was prepared to favour Durie's efforts only as far as Swedish interests would allow.[9] After 1637, however, he opened up and began his public life as a conciliator. He hoped to achieve unity between Roman Catholics and moderate Protestants by fighting the prejudices against Roman Catholics in particular. In a short, but very controversial treatise, *De Antichristo* (1640), he countered the traditional identification of Papacy and Antichrist on exegetical grounds: the passages on the Antichrist, for example in 2 Thessalonians 2:3, referred to contemporary events, in particular the abuse of power and moral decay in the Roman Empire. In another pamphlet he also discussed passages from the Bible in order to prove that good works were required in order to reach salvation.[10] In his view, the essential doctrine of faith and good works had been preserved in the Western churches. Among these institutions, the Church of Rome was entitled to primacy, and therefore the adherents of all other confessions had to ally themselves with Rome, provided that the Pope would cooperate with secular authorities to stamp out traditional excesses like idolatry and simony.[11] Grotius even expressed his ideas in his letters to his Swedish superiors. In a long letter addressed to Johan Oxenstierna, plenipotentiary at the peace conference in Munster-Osnabruck, he pleaded for church unity. If the Swedish Lutheran Church would associate with Rome, both the

---

[8] See for example BW, I, nos. 219 and 224, to Isaac Casaubon, 7 January and 7 February 1612.

[9] BW, VIII, nos. 3248, 3313 and 3372, letters dated on 12 September, 24 October and 5 December 1637. In the first letter Grotius wrote: 'Ego nunc contentus ero eius propositum hactenus commendare, quatenus id neque regni Suedici neque ecclesiarum eius tranquillitati obstiturum iudicabitur. Nam tunica propior pallio.'

[10] *Commentatio de Antichristo* and *De fide et operibus* (Amsterdam: Blaeu, 1640) [*TMD*, 1100 and 1109]; also in: Hugo Grotius, *Opera omnia theologica*, 3 vols (Amsterdam: Blaeu, 1679) [*TMD*, 919]; repr. Stuttgart: Frommann, 1972), [= *OTh*], III, pp. 455-474 and 513-532, esp. 521-524. *TMD* = J. ter Meulen and P.J.J. Diermanse, *Bibliographie des écrits imprimés de Hugo Grotius* (The Hague: Nijhoff 1950).

[11] BW, XIV, nos. 6444, 6479, 6516 and 6532, to W. de Groot, 26 September, 17 October, 7 and 14 November 1643.

universal church and Sweden itself would profit greatly.[12] The outcome of Grotius's campaign for unity is well known: the enterprise aroused only scorn and vehement pamphlets. 'By undertaking many things, I have accomplished nothing'. These famous, but presumably apocryphal last words might certainly be applied to his struggle for church unity.[13]

Abiding Features

Propaganda Strategies

Throughout the correspondence, Grotius distinguished himself as a propagandist. Let me start with four introductory remarks. The negative reception of *Ordinum pietas* in 1613 was a traumatic experience for Grotius. Afterwards he tried to avoid direct confrontation with his adversaries. In books like *De satisfactione* (1617), *Disquisitio an pelagiana sint* (1622), *De iure belli ac pacis* (1625), *De imperio* (1647) and exegetical treatises such as *De antichristo* he deliberately abstained from factual references to contemporary religious and political issues. Of course, he did not keep out of current disputes in his apology, the *Verantwoordingh* (1622), but even in this polemical tract he held his pen in order to spare his main antagonist, Prince Maurice.[14] Only at the end of his life did he permit himself to launch sharp attacks against adversaries like André Rivet and Johan de Laet.

In the second place, it should be noted that Grotius's ideas and arguments were determined by the aim he had in mind. In order to achieve this aim he collected citations that had to fit as material in his line of reasoning. He did not bother too much about the original context of these citations; he did not strive for an unbiased treatment of sources.[15]

---

[12] BW, XVI, no. 7176, dated 3 December 1644: 'Quodsi aliquando regnum Suediae salva ea reformatione, quae non in subtilibus controversiis et disputationibus scholasticis, sed in rebus solidis consistit, in sedis romanae communionem restitui possit, videor inde mihi prospicere magnum bonum ecclesiae universali, magna autem rei Suedicae incrementa.'

[13] Jean Le Clerc, *Sentimens de quelques théologiens de Hollande...* (Amsterdam: Mortier, 1711), p. 402.

[14] BW, XVII, no. 763A, Grotius's letter of dedication to the government of Holland (pp. 204-205 and 208).

[15] Cf. Hugo Grotius, *De imperio summarum potestatum circa sacra*, ed., tr. and com. by H.-J. van Dam. Studies in the History of Christian Thought, 102 (Leiden: Brill, 2001), [= *De imperio*], Introduction, pp. 4-6.

In the third place, it has to be emphasized that Grotius learned to know the value of propaganda at an early age. This becomes clear from the aforementioned occasional poetry on heroic deeds, marriages and funerals of celebrities. In particular, the combination of poem and illustration was very much sought after: poetry had a great propagandistic value when it appeared together with engravings. Printing firms asked for pointed Latin epigrams that explained military events, biblical scenes or townscapes, and Grotius generously supplied the presses with material.[16]

In the fourth place, I should stress that Grotius succeeded as a propagandist because he had a ready pen. Whether he wrote in Latin, Dutch or French made no difference. His style was always clear, succinct and eloquent. How then does Grotius the propagandist appear in his correspondence? He constantly shows his involvement in the lay-out, printing and distribution of his works. Furthermore, he attached great importance to the translation of his texts into different languages. Illustrative examples are his *De antiquitate*, *Ordinum pietas*, *Apologeticus* (*Verantwoordingh*) and *De veritate* (1627), publications that saw the light in two, three or more languages in order to reach as many readers as possible. Grotius despised the *Gazette de France*, the state-controlled newspaper, but at the same time he availed himself of this medium to publish statements in support of the Swedish cause.[17] Grotius was also a propagandist in so far as he promoted the edition of books by others. These were mostly pamphlets justifying the Remonstrant cause. It will surprise no one if I say that many passages in the correspondence concern negotiations with printers. I shall dwell very briefly on four aspects: numbers of copies produced, working relations with printers, author's wages and printing privileges.

The correspondence yields scarce information on the numbers of copies produced. The first issue of the *Verantwoordingh*, Grotius's defence of Oldenbarnevelt's policy, published in Holland, comprised 1500 copies.[18] After this first impression, six other editions saw the light in a short space of time. In the same year, 700 copies of the Latin translation *Apologeticus* were printed.[19] This was done by Nicolas Buon in Paris who, some years later, was to procure the *editio princeps* of *De iure belli ac pacis* as well. Grotius suspected Buon of reprinting the *Apologeticus* secretly. In this way he avoided giving Grotius his

16 A. Eyffinger, *Grotius poeta. Aspecten van Hugo Grotius' dichterschap* (The Hague 1981), pp. 56-58.

17 BW, XV, no. 7022, to J. Oxenstierna, 27 August 1644.

18 BW, II, no. 814, from W. de Groot, 10 January 1623.

19 BW, II, no. 800, to G.M. Lingelsheim, 19 November 1622.

presentation copies, and he could also keep the price high, telling his customers again and again that the copies on the shelves were the last ones of the entire issue.[20] The first edition of *De antichristo* from 1640 had only 500 copies. The printer, Johan Blaeu, underestimated the market for this highly controversial treatise, but a reprint appeared very soon.[21] Grotius's magnum opus, the *Annotationes in libros Evangeliorum* (1641), was printed in an edition of 1200 copies.[22]

The correspondence is full of complaints on the troubled working relations with printers. During his exile in France, Grotius published many works in Holland. He mistrusted the Leiden printers because of their close ties with the university's Faculty of Theology. His arch enemy Daniel Heinsius held the firm of the Leiden Elzeviers in the palm of his hand.[23] Grotius looked for a printer he could trust. Eventually his choice fell on Johan Blaeu in Amsterdam.[24] Grotius held Blaeu in high esteem. He considered him to be a kindred spirit, but at the same time the relationship is marked by a great distance between the scholar and the craftsman. Grotius shunned any contact through letter writing and gave instructions via intermediaries, like his brother Willem de Groot and his friend Gerardus Joannes Vossius. Only one letter by Blaeu has been preserved[25] and this document evokes many questions. The geographical distance and the complicated negotiations soon proved to be serious handicaps. Grotius repeatedly complained about the results. In his letters he contributed to the stereotypical image of the printer, who was bent on profits only, neglected the wishes of his authors and carried out all assignments with proverbial slowness. Grotius felt exploited. He had done the scholarly work, while the printer lined his purse. This reproach is not totally off the mark.[26]

As far as I know Grotius was not paid for his books, although he wrote some bestsellers.[27] At the most, he received payment *in natura*, that is, he agreed on

---

[20] BW, III, no. 1277, to J. Wtenbogaert, 23 June 1628: '... seggende altijd dat het de leste waeren'.

[21] *TMD*, 1100 and 1101; BW, XI, no. 4572, from W. de Groot, 25 March 1640.

[22] BW, XII, no. 5066, from W. de Groot, 18 February 1641.

[23] H.J.M. Nellen, *Hugo de Groot. Een leven in strijd om de vrede (1583-1645)*, (Amsterdam: Balans, 2007), pp. 498-499, and the letters mentioned there in notes 136-137.

[24] It was the poet P.C. Hooft, who once had recommended the founder of the printing house, Willem Jansz Blaeu, to Grotius. See BW, I, no. 487, from P.C. Hooft, 29 November 1616.

[25] BW, X, no. 4006, from J. Blaeu, 7 March 1639.

[26] BW, V, no. 2091, to W. de Groot, 11 May 1635: 'Magni facio Blavium, sed trico est, ut video, nec tempora observat.' See also BW, XII, nos. 5168, 5257, 5400, etc.

[27] Cf. BW, VIII, no. 3135, to W. de Groot, 26 June 1637. While living in Paris as an exile, Grotius never received any wages. As ambassador he refused to negotiate on a remuneration. See also BW, VIII, no. 3256, addressed to the same correspondent and dated 18 September 1637.

a certain number of presentation copies he could sell himself to benefit his own purse. Such an agreement took place when *De iure belli ac pacis* appeared. Nicolas Buon gave Grotius 200 copies, 60 of which had been printed on first quality paper. Half of the copies on this special paper were delivered with a binding; 12 of these were even bound in such an elegant way that the books could be presented to distinguished acquaintances of the author, such as the king of France.[28] In order to gain some money, Grotius decided to sell some of the 200 copies: in September 1625, he organized the transportation of 72 copies to Holland, to be offered for sale in bookshops in Amsterdam, Leiden and other cities.[29] For books like the *Historia Gotthorum* and the *Annales*, which were only published posthumously, in 1655 and 1657, he did not demand any payment. One hundred well-bound copies, printed on excellent paper, would suffice. As he explained, he had a reason for demanding this high number. He was not keen on material gain, but at the same time he abhorred sacrificing money for the publication of his own books, which could be prevented only if he was offered these books, to be distributed among his friends: 'tantus est eorum quibus debeo numerus'.[30] Blaeu distinguished between money-making bestsellers and unsaleable books for the happy few. *De iure belli ac pacis*, and the pamphlets against André Rivet belonged to the first category, the *Anthologia Graeca* (1795-1822), an edition meant for scholars with knowledge of classical Greek, to the second. Grotius preferred a luxurious lay-out for the *Anthologia*, but Blaeu was not very keen on this project. He feared his competitor Johannes Janssonius would skim off the market by publishing a cheap reprint. In that case Blaeu would have great difficulty in selling the copies of his own expensive edition. The same had happened before, when he published *De iure belli ac pacis*,[31] but now the loss might be much greater as the *Anthologia Graeca* was not a popular book.[32]

The competition between Blaeu and Janssonius leads us to the problem of printing privileges. The authorities would grant a privilege for a certain time and for the region over which they possessed jurisdiction, in order to

[28] BW, III, no. 1338, to W. de Groot, 16 November 1628.

[29] BW, II, no. 991, from J. de Groot, 11 July 1625; BW, II, no. 992, 18 July 1625 and other letters exchanged between Hugo and Willem de Groot, in particular BW, II, no. 1008, dated 5 September 1625.

[30] BW, VIII, no. 3338, to G.J. Vossius, 10 November 1637.

[31] Cf. *TMD*, 567 (ed. 1631) and 568 (ed. 1632). See also BW, XII, no. 5380, from W. de Groot, 23 September 1641: 'Tum et hoc nosti, homines nostros ad rem faciendam attentos non libenter uti maioribus characteribus propter magnitudinem expensarum et metum, ne ab aliis minori forma imprimantur libri.'

[32] BW, IX, no. 3414, from G.J. Vossius, 6 January 1638.

protect the printer against reprints by others. The privilege guaranteed the printer's sales and profits. After 1618, Grotius did not succeed in obtaining privileges for the books he published in Holland. This even applies to the *Inleiding tot de Hollandsche rechts-geleertheyd*, a useful juridical handbook, which was printed for the first time in The Hague in 1631. Immediately after the first edition, four cheap versions followed.[33] The *Annotationes in libros Evangeliorum* were also published without a privilege. Blaeu, however, was spared the damage of a reprint, presumably because competing firms like Janssonius considered a reprint of this voluminous work too great a financial risk. The Annotations on the Old Testament were published by Sébastien Cramoisy in Paris. Like Blaeu, this printer did not succeed in obtaining a privilege from the French government. In order to preclude competition, Cramoisy embarked on an association with Blaeu. According to the title-page, the Dutch printer took over a part of the issue to sell it on his own account in his Amsterdam bookshop.[34]

Care for the (Post) Classical Legacy

As a humanist Grotius promoted the publication of all sources from classical and early-Christian times. He wanted to publish a treatise of the neo-Platonist Porphyry, 'Against the Christians', saying that there was no poison so lethal that medical science could not extract a curative substance from it.[35] The discovery, collation and emendation of texts was a daily activity for Grotius and his scholarly friends. He was delighted with the news that Nicolas Rigault was about to publish his edition of Tertullian. In the same period, in 1633, the English scholar Patrick Young published a letter in Oxford by Pope Clemens I to the Corinthians. 'From all four corners of the world,' Grotius wrote, 'these early-Christian relics must be gathered, because they strongly reflect the splendour of apostolic instruction. Later corruption of the text is not a sufficient cause for discarding these sources. What is necessary is the expertise of a master craftsman, who is able to separate the dross from the pure material'.[36]

---

[33] *TMD*, 757-761.

[34] H. Grotius, *Annotata ad Vetus Testamentum*, 3 vols (Lutetiae Parisiorum, sumptibus Sebastiani Cramoisy, regis et reginae architypographi, et Gabrielis Cramoisy, via Iacobaea, sub Ciconiis. MDCXLIV. Prostant Amsterdami, apud Iohannem Blaeu), [*TMD*, 1137].

[35] BW, III, no. 1217, to Lucas Holstenius, 2 February 1628: 'Ego ita censeo nullum esse tam pestilens venenum, unde non ars medica aliquid salubre possit educere.' See also BW, V, nos. 1747 and 1754.

[36] BW, V, no. 1844, to Jean Des Cordes, 1 June 1633: 'Quaerenda sunt per omnes recessus ista primi saeculi multum de apostolico auro retinentis fragmenta, nec abiicienda statim, si quid

Dogmatic Minimalism

With respect to dogma Grotius was a minimalist. He tried to reduce belief to a minimum of rules. The best way to ward off dissension and internal strife was to stick to the terminology of the Bible. Through the ages the scholastic distinctions regarding the Trinity had given occasion to fierce debates and polemics, also among Protestants. As a consequence the dividing lines between the confessions had been sharpened. Accusations of Arianism, Nestorianism and Eutychianism went back and forth. Grotius appealed to the famous rule of Vincent of Lérins, who stated that the believer was obliged to respect only the essential rules and these rules could be boiled down to what in the history of the church everybody, everywhere and always had considered to be the truth ('quod ubique, quod semper, quod ab omnibus'). Grotius was very broad-minded in this respect, because he acknowledged that in the early Christian church, no two theologians held the same opinions on the non-essential rules of faith. Even so, the ideal of the old church was more than a vague illusion to him, as he was convinced that in the first three centuries a *communis opinio* had prevailed regarding the intricate problem of grace and free will.[37] The Anglican Church came close to the ideal of the old church, since it did not indulge in the excesses of the Reformation on the Continent.[38]

Tolerance

Grotius championed a broad consensus inside the state-controlled church, on the basis of the creed of the old church. He rejected polemics and dogmatic precision and stressed practical piety. He based the interpretation of the Bible on philological and historical principles instead of confessional prejudices. His exegetical method is diametrically opposed to that of most of his seventeenth-century colleagues, who worked the other way around: they studied and explained the Bible driven by the ambition to confirm dogmatic views which

forte allevit adultera manus, sed quod in metallis fieri solet, periti artificis manu separanda scoria a materia puriore.'

[37] BW, IV, no. 1502, to N.van Reigersberch, 16 May 1630 (p. 205), to be compared with a passage in the Amsterdam oration, *Verhael van de heeren ...*, The Hague 1616 (*TMD*, 844). I consulted the edition of 1622 (*TMD*, 845), here pp. 6 and 11. See also BW, XIII, no. 5646 and BW, XIV, no. 6389.

[38] Cf. Hugo Grotius, *Ordinum Hollandiae ac Westfrisiae pietas*, ed., tr. and com. by E. Rabbie, Studies in the History of Christian Thought, 66 (Leiden: Brill, 1995), 188-189 (p. 232) and *TMD*, 971, remarque 3. See also G.H.M. Posthumus Meyjes, 'Hugo Grotius as an irenicist', *The world of Hugo Grotius (1583-1645). Proceedings of the international colloquium ... Rotterdam 6-9 April 1983* (Amsterdam: APA, 1984), pp. 59-60.

had been established in fierce confessional controversies. Grotius's tolerance went together with the conviction that in the Bible truth had not always been stated unequivocally. In case a believer wanted to prove the truth, he often could do no more than try to convince the unbeliever.[39] Grotius abhorred schismatic movements. Believers who were excommunicated had to suffer their lot with resignation.[40]

Supremacy of the Secular Authorities

A presbytery was a 'ministerium' (service), not a 'potestas' (power). Misled by blind devotion, many princes neglected their task and gave too much room to religious factions. The care for the church, however, was the most important part of their office. In many places the body politic was harmed by an ongoing dispute between secular and ecclesiastical authorities over areas of competence.[41] The rebelliousness of the theologians, the 'imprudentia theologorum' caused turmoil, popular uprising and civil war in Bohemia, France, England and Holland. The preachers misused the great influence they had over the churchgoers. The essence of many letters before and after 1618 is that the government should repress the preachers severely. Grotius pointed out that armed insurrections against kings had to be rejected, even in cases where these kings persecuted their subjects.[42] He abhorred the theories of the Monarchomachs.[43] He was wont to refer to the consequences of the intolerance of the Calvinist preachers during the first years of the Dutch Revolt. Eventually, the Flemish provinces had been forced to a reconciliation with the king of Spain, merely because preachers in towns like Ghent conducted a reign of terror and tried to establish branches of the

[39] BW, V, no. 1946 (p. 270), to G.J. Vossius, 12 August 1634, in answer to no. 1930 (pp. 252-253).

[40] See the aforementioned letters published in BW, XIV, nos. 6444, 6479, 6516 and 6532 (*supra*, note 11).

[41] Cf. BW, X, no. 3951 (pp. 62-63), to A. Oxenstierna, 29 January 1639. See also BW, VI, no. 2207 (p. 121), to P. Holing, 1 August 1635: 'Illud vero ubique christianis inculcandum censeo non esse quamvis probabili religionis obtentu sumenda arma adversus eos qui imperii habenas tenent.'

[42] BW, IV, no. 1386 (dispute of competence), BW, IV, nos. 1395 and 1417 (influence through preaching), BW, IV, no. 1601 (Grotius pleads for severe repression of recalcitrant preachers in Holland), BW, V, no. 1748 (in the small towns in particular, the preachers held the magistracy on a leash). See also BW, III, nos. 1047 and 1062.

[43] BW, XIV, no. 6516, to W. de Groot, 7 November 1643; *De imperio*, III. 6-8, and pp. 670-677.

Geneva regime everywhere. Even his wife Maria subscribed to this view of the Dutch Revolt.[44]

Rejection of Ardent Pacifism

Grotius was not a pacifist. As a diplomat, he endorsed Swedish politics that aimed at making the Baltic a Swedish inland sea. The outbreak of the Swedish-Danish war, as reported in the correspondence, is very remarkable. In December 1643, Sweden launched a completely unexpected attack on Holstein and Jutland. The Danish authorities referred to *De iure belli ac pacis*. Here Grotius had defended the proposition that, according to the law of nations at least, a war should be announced in an official notification. As an ambassador, however, Grotius justified the attack not as a war, but as a legitimate quartering of troops in an area that was tributary to the enemy.[45] At this point of his career, Grotius seems to have forgotten that once, in his annotations on Matthew, he had allowed himself a digression on just wars. This passage, in fact *De iure belli ac pacis* in a greatly reduced size, recommended justice, prudence and charity, especially to Christians who felt called upon to start a war.[46]

Religion often served to ignite, disguise or fuel political conflicts.[47] Adequate government interference, combined with dogmatic tolerance, had to defuse religious controversy. In addition to that, Grotius tried to keep conflicts under control by stipulating a general and supranational natural right. Even God had to comply with this right, since He himself had endowed human nature with it.[48] On the basis of this natural right, it was possible to decide whether

---

[44] BW, III, no. 1161, from M. van Reigersberch, [18] July [1627].

[45] BW, XV, no. 6726, from W. de Groot, 22 February 1644, and no. 6861, to A. Oxenstierna, 14 May 1644. Cf. H. Grotius, *De iure belli ac pacis libri tres ... Curavit B.J.A. de Kanter-Van Hettinga Tromp* (Leiden: Brill, 1939) [*TMD*, 617]; repr. with 'annotationes novae', ed. by R. Feenstra et al. (Aalen: Scientia Verlag, 1993), III. 3, 5-7 (pp. 648-653). In BW, XV, no. 6861 Grotius remarks: 'Quod de indictione belli etiam mea, quae non tanti est, auctoritate a Danis adfertur, facile solvitur: hibernorum captiones in locis imperii hostilis et qui hostibus tributa pendat, nihil aliud esse quam consequentiam belli pridem suscepti; uti eo more bellantes omnes, usum Daniae regem, usos Gallos ... Regem vero Daniae cum id quod belli iure factum erat ultum ivit totis Daniae viribus, naves hostiliter capiendo, milites oppugnando, novum sic inchoasse bellum non Germanicum amplius, sed Danicum. Quare ipsius fuisse id nobis indicere.'

[46] *OTh*, II. 1, pp. 65-71, ad Matthaeum 5: 40.

[47] BW, XII, no. 5312, to I. Jasky, 9 August 1641: 'Verum est bella ferme omnia seculi nostri per religionis dissidia nasci aut ali.'

[48] Cf. BW, IX, no. 3586, to W. de Groot, 21 May 1638: 'Deo liberum erat hominem non condere. Condito homine, id est natura ratione utente et ad societatem eximiam conformata, necessario probat actiones tali naturae consentaneas, contrarias improbat. At multa alia non necessario aut iubet aut punit, sed quia ita ipsi visum.'

a war was justified. According to a letter dating from 1637, he had written *De iure belli ac pacis* with two goals in mind: to convince authorities of the necessity to abstain from cruelty in warfare and to introduce young lawyers to the science of law.[49]

Eclecticism

When writing on politics and religion, Grotius demonstrated great versatility in filching from other sources what he deemed fit to suit his arguments. As has been pointed out before, he constructed his arguments with all kinds of evidence without bothering too much about the context of the citations. He was an annotator, a collector of sources, for whom revision often only meant the addition of newly found historical evidence. It is dangerous, therefore, to look for a dominant philosophy in his line of thought.[50] Grotius must be considered as a Christian-humanist who saw Christianity as the perfection of pagan and classical civilisation. Of course, he was prepared to draw from the legacy of ancient philosophy to the extent it corroborated and underpinned Christian belief. Without any doubt, Grotius contributed much to the spread of Stoic ideas. In *De iure belli ac pacis*, Prolegomena 6-7, he refers to 'appetitus societatis' and 'oikeiosis' as the basis for justice and rights in human society. This is Stoic terminology,[51] but one has to bear in mind that Grotius derived his 'Stoicism' from other authors, Cicero in the first place, who took a biased position towards this philosophy. In *De iure praedae* he already speaks of the 'communis totius humanitatis necessitudo', a phrase that does not differ very much from the Christian idea of love for one's neighbour. Grotius made use of the terms 'appetitus societatis' and 'oikeiosis' in order to corroborate and enliven his argumentation. In this way he embellished his thought without adding

[49] BW, VIII, no. 3376, to J. Frischmann, 10 December 1637. Frischmann studied law. He was a pupil of Matthias Bernegger in Strasburg. See also BW, IV, no. 1633, to J. Crellius, 10 May 1631.

[50] Cf. BW, V, no. 1906, to H. Conring, 1634, on the importance of Aristotle's writings. Anyone who tried to make a name by criticizing this philosopher brought himself into general contempt. Although Aristotle had erred, his texts deserved to be studied in their original form by the youth. In his letters Grotius repeatedly gave the highest praise to Aristotle, 'philosophorum acutissimus' and 'summus docendi artifex'. Cf. BW, XVII, no. 8A (p. 14) and BW, I, no. 402 (pp. 384-385).

[51] L.C. Winkel, 'Les origines antiques de l'*appetitus societatis* de Grotius', *Tijdschrift voor Rechtsgeschiedenis* 68 (2000), pp. 393-403; B. Straumann, 'Oikeiosis and appetitus societatis. Hugo Grotius' Ciceronian argument for natural law and just war', *Grotiana* 24/25 (2003-2004), pp. 41-66 (p. 45 note 12).

anything new to it. Yet it also falls into line with the baptised version of Stoicism in favour with many of his contemporaries.[52]

Grotius was the first to acknowledge this way of working. On the 1st of January 1636 he sent a New Year's message or 'strena' to his brother-in-law Nicolaes van Reigersberch. He expatiated on his own personal motto 'hora ruit', without mentioning it explicitly. Grotius indulged in this digression because he was inspired by the curious story of an Englishman from Shropshire, Thomas Parr, who reached the exceptionally advanced age of 152 years. Grotius enjoyed the story, particularly because Parr had committed adultery when he was more than 100 years old.[53] The antiquarian Thomas Howard, count of Arundel, presented Parr as an object of interest – a 'remarkable piece of antiquity' – to the court in polluted London, where the old man had to give up his usual diet consisting of green cheese, onions, coarse bread, buttermilk and mild ale (cider only on special occasions), with the inevitable consequence that he died soon afterwards, in November 1635. Grotius linked this story[54] to some proverbs that pleaded for a virtuous life. It was important not to lead a long but a virtuous life. He cited such Stoics as Chrysippus, Cicero and Seneca, and introduced these citations with the sentence: 'Why not add something from the Stoics as well, not because I always follow the school of the Stoics, but because I am used to pinching the best things from everywhere. 'Quid si et de Stoicis addam quaedam, non quod semper posticam sequar, sed quod undique optima excerpam.' The text in the *Briefwisseling* gives 'posticam' (backdoor), but, when I checked the original manuscript in the University Library of Leiden, I discovered that in this place one must read 'Porticum'.[55] I do not want to discuss here how Grotius dealt with Stoic philosophy in his works. It is certain, however, that in many letters and works he opposed the deterministic view of a fixed fate, which precluded human responsibility or lowered God to the cause of evil and sin. He polemically compared the doctrine of predestination with the 'fatalis necessitas' of the Stoics. This he did

52 Cf. Hugo Grotius, *De jure praedae commentarius*. Ex auctoris codice descripsit et vulgavit H.G. Hamaker (The Hague: Nijhoff, 1868), p. 39. See also *ibidem*, p. 13: 'Haec est illa hominum inter se cognatio, illa mundi civitas, quam tot tantisque praeconiis veteres philosophi nobis commendant, praesertim Stoici, quorum sententiam etiam Cicero exsequitur ...'.

53 BW, VI, no. 2405, to P. Schmalz, 20 December 1635. Grotius thought the advanced age of Parr very exceptional. Therefore he informed his brother Willem (BW, VI, no. 2362, dated 23 November 1635) about the age not in figures, but in characters: '... scribam non numeris, sed plenis literis nequid de sensu dubites.'

54 On Thomas Parr, see K. Thomas in: *Oxford Dictionary of National Biography*, vol. 42 (Oxford: OUP, 2004), pp. 852-854.

55 BW, VI, no. 2421, text on the basis of Leiden, University Library, MS Pap. 2.

in so many letters that his conviction can certainly be labelled as constant.[56] Yet he was equally intrigued by the limits of man's freedom, as for instance is evident from his collection of sentences of the philosophers on fate and free will.[57]

As becomes clear from the above overview, Grotius's scholarly activities are strongly reflected in his voluminous correspondence. The letter offered him an expedient means to supervise the publication of his works, to comment on recent developments in state and church, and to establish and maintain friendships. The correspondence is a source that adds much to the information contained in his books. In order to describe his activities as a scholar, I made an arbitrary choice that easily could have turned out otherwise, since the correspondence contains many interesting and informative letters that enable us to follow Grotius in his workaday life, with both abiding features and new developments.

---

[56] BW, I, no. 221 (pp. 194-195), to A. Walaeus, 11 January 1612; BW, I, no. 308, to I. Casaubon, 12 December 1613 (Zeno, mentioned in this letter, is not the Byzantine Emperor, as the editor assumes, but Zeno of Citium, the founder of the Stoic school); BW, I, no. 312, to F. Sandius, 27 January 1614; BW, I, no. 409, to J.A. de Thou, 5 June 1615. See also Hugo Grotius, *Meletius sive de iis quae inter christianos conveniunt epistola*, ed., tr. and com. by G.H.M. Posthumus Meyjes. Studies in the History of Christian Thought, 40 (Leiden: Brill, 1988), p. 83.

[57] See Hugo Grotius, *Philosophorum sententiae de fato et de eo quod in nostra est potestate* (Paris: Camusat, 1648), [*TMD*, 523], reprinted in *OTh*, III, pp. 377-453.

Grotius, Maritime Intra-Asian Trade and the Portuguese Estado da Índia: Problems, Perspectives and Insights from *De iure praedae*

Peter Borschberg[1]
Associate Professor, Department of History, National University of Singapore
e-mail: hispb@nus.edu.sg

A piratica, qua gaudent pleraeque gentes,
abhorrent Nostrorum animi…[2]

Abstract
The present article explores the historical sections of Grotius's *De iure praedae Commentarius* (chapters 11 through 16) bearing the following fundamental but very important questions in mind: What did Grotius actually know about the Portuguese Estado da Índia at the time of drafting the treatise between 1604 and 1606/8? What did he know about the Luso-Asian trading regime or Asian trading practices at large? Using the published correspondence of Grotius, archival documentation, manuscript fragments as well as unpublished reading notes and drafts, a case will be made that he had in fact few sources at his fingertips. This insight serves fundamentally to refute older assumptions, expounded notably by Robert Fruin and C.H. Alexandrowicz, that the young Grotius conducted independent research in the VOC company archives, or had immersed himself with Asian maritime codes or commercial practices.

Keywords
Hugo Grotius, Mare Liberum, De iure praedae, Estado da India, Dutch East India Company, Asian trade

[1] This paper contains insights gained before and after the June 2005 Grotius colloquium at the Netherlands' Institute for Advanced Studies (NIAS) in Wassenaar. My special gratitude is extended to Martine van Ittersum for the many hours we spent in the National Archives in The Hague and the Dousa Kamer at Leiden University Library conducting extensive research on B.P.L. 917, the autograph manuscript of *De iure praedae*. I would also like to specially thank Henk Nellen for critically commenting on the drafts of the present article and also for generously sharing his deep and vast knowledge of Grotius'ss correspondence with me.

[2] Hugo Grotius, *Parallelon rerumpublicarum liber tertius: De moribus ingenioque populorum Atheniensium, Romanorum, Batavorum*, ed. by Johan Meerman, 4 vols (Haarlem: Loosjes, 1801-03), see I.3.6, p. 101.

The Manuscript of *De iure praedae* and its Title

It is now an academic commonplace to treat Hugo Grotius's *De iure praedae commentarius* as a commissioned response to the seizure of the Portuguese-flagged carrack. Sadly, however, many researchers begin to seriously disagree after this very basic insight. They part company over who actually commissioned the work. Some researchers think it was the Grand Pensionary *(landsadvocaat)* Johan van Oldenbarnevelt, while a far larger group point fingers at the directors of the United Dutch East India Company (VOC) in Amsterdam.[3] There is also substantial disagreement over authorial intention: Exactly what kind of a 'response' is this treatise? Is it a legal brief? Is it a court petition *(pledooi voor het groote proces)* or a *Gelegenheitsschrift* (treatise of occasion) as Fruin has also called it?[4] Should *De iure praedae* be classified under the general rubric 'patriotic literature' along with others pieces Grotius wrote in the first decade of the seventeenth century, such as for example the *Annales et Historiae de Rebus Belgicis* (Annals and Histories of the Low Countries) and *De Antiquitate Reipublicae Batavorum* (On the Antiquity of the Dutch Republic)?[5] Or should *De iure praedae* just be deemed an early piece of VOC 'propaganda'?[6]

Consensus is also wanting with regard to the work's proper title. *De iure praedae commentarius* is not the name given to the work by its twenty-one year old author Grotius, but by the auctioneers at Martinus Nijhoff, the nineteenth century librarians at Leiden University Library and also by H. G. Hamaker,

---

[3] Exactly who commissioned the work from Grotius remains uncertain. Based on Grotius's correspondence, some authors claim it was the VOC directors, while others opine that it was Oldenbarnevelt who earlier 'defended a similar case'. Concerning the latter position, see Jan den Tex, *Oldenvarnevelt,* 5 vols (Haarlem: Tjeenk Willink, 1960-1972), specifically IV, p. 172. Fruin wishes to see a link between the writing of *De iure praedae* and Grotius's earlier output as a legal counsel while the 'Sta. Catarina incident' was pending before the Admiralty Court. See 'Een onuitgegeven werk', in *Fruin's Verspreide Geschriften*, ed. by P. J. Blok, P. L. Muller and S. Muller Fzn? 11 vols (The Hague: Nijhoff, 1900-05), III, p. 391.

[4] Ibid., p. 372.

[5] Hugo Grotius, *Annales et Historiae de Rebus Belgicis* (Amsterdam: Blaeu, 1657), published posthumously, completed around 1612, and *De Antiquitate Reipublicae Batavicae* (Leiden: Raphelengius, 1610). For the modern critical edition of the text in English, see *The Antiquity of the Batavian Republic*, ann. by Petrus Scriverius, ed. and intr. by Jan H. Waszink, Bibliotheca Latinitatis Novae (Assen: Van Gorcum, 2000).

[6] Borschberg, 'Grotius' Theory of Trans-Oceanic Trade Regulation: Revisiting Mare Liberum (1609)', *Institute for International Law and Justice Working Paper*, History and Theory of International Law Series, New York University Hauser School of Law, 14 (revised text of August 2006), esp. p. 9; M. J. van Ittersum, *Profit and Principle: Hugo Grotius, Natural Rights Theories and the Rise of Dutch Power in the East Indies*, 1595–1615 (Leiden: E. J. Brill, 2006), esp. pp. 486ff.

the first editor of the Latin text.[7] In his correspondence, Grotius refers to it in a generally vague and descriptive manner, calling it *De Rebus Indicanis* (On the Affairs of the Indies) on at least two occasions.[8] Some academics like the political theorist Richard Tuck opine that such authentic references, including *De Indis* (his preferred title), are probably the closest modern scholarship can get to an original title for the work, especially because it was employed by Grotius himself.[9] But admittedly, Tuck's views are not widely accepted, and a distinct majority of researchers, rightly or wrongly, continue to employ the nineteenth century title. For the sake of simplicity, and as a means of forestalling any confusion among my readers, I will abide by accepted convention and in the course of my paper refer to this work as *De iure praedae commentarius* or in English as *Commentary on the Law of Prize and Booty*.[10] In the context of the present exposé I will also accept its established dates of composition, namely October 1604 to the autumn of 1606, with some revisions made and marginal source references added to parts of the text in later years, especially 1608 and early 1609.[11] Such amendments

---

[7] See the annotated auction catalogue of 1864, L. J. Noordhoff, *Beschrijving van het zich in Nederland bevindende en nog onbeschreven gedeelte der papieren afkomstig van Huig de Groot welke in 1864 te 's-Gravenhage zijn geveilt* (Groningen: Noordhoff, 1953); also Fruin, 'Een onuitgegeven werk', p. 367, 'No. 72 werd Aldus beschreven: *H. Grotii opus de jure Praedae in XVI capita divisum* 280 pag. – Mscr. autographe inédit. Seulment une partie du chapitre XII a été publié en 1609, sous le titre *Mare Liberum*'; Hugo Grotius, *De jure praedae commentarius,* ed. by H.G. Hamaker (The Hague: Nijhoff, 1868) [= *IPC*].

[8] See esp. the editorial comment by Philip Molhuysen in *Briefwisseling van Hugo Grotius,* ed. by P.C. Molhuysen and others, 17 vols. (The Hague, 1928-2001) [= BW], I.148, p. 129n6 '... zoals Grotius indertijd "de Jure Praedae" "de Rebus Indicanis" noemde', that is '... just as Grotius at the time called his "De Jure Praedae" "De Rebus Indicanis".'

[9] The question of the 'proper title' for *De iure praedae* has been raised by Tuck, especially his *Philosophy and Government, 1572-1651* (Cambridge: CUP, 1993), and also in *The Rights of War and Peace. Political Thought and the International Order from Grotius to Kant* (Oxford: OUP, 1999). See also below, note 12.

[10] The most commonly used English translation is *De Jure Praedae Commentarius. Commentary on the Law of Prize and Booty. A Translation of the Original Manuscript of 1604,* tr. by G. L. Williams and W. H. Zeydel (Oxford: Clarendon Press, 1950). This edition contains several errors that have been corrected in *Commentary on the Law of Prize and Booty,* ed. and intr. by Martine van Ittersum (Indianapolis: Liberty Fund, 2006) [= *Commentary*]. All subsequent references in this article will be to the 2006 edition.

[11] Concerning the dating of *De iure praedae,* see the authoritative Jacob ter Meulen and P. J. J. Diermanse, *Bibliographie des écrits imprimés de Hugo Grotius* (The Hague: Nijhoff, 1950), p. 304, Borschberg, *Commentarius in Theses XI. An Early Treatise on Sovereignty, the Just War and the Legitimacy of the Dutch Revolt* (Bern: Lang, 1994), pp. 16-17, and the article by Willem J. M. van Eysinga, 'Quelques observations au sujet du Mare Liberum et du De Iure Praedae de Grotius', *Grotiana,* 9 (1941-42), 72-75.

were made amongst others to chapter XII that was separately published as *Mare liberum* or *The Free Sea* in 1609.[12]

Grotius, Archival Research, and Asian Maritime Customs

In the present article I do not wish to engage in the debate over the supposed nature or authorial intention of Grotius's early oeuvre as whole, not least since I have already brought my findings to paper in some earlier publications.[13] The question I address in this paper concerns the sources used by Grotius for drafting and completing the second part of the manuscript, commonly known as the *pars historica* or the 'historical section' of *De iure praedae.* This spans chapters XI through XVI.[14] For the record, the *pars historica* also includes the text of the aforementioned *Mare liberum.*[15]

Most of what is known about the background and historical context of *De iure praedae* was brought to print in a lengthy piece of the Leiden professor of national history Robert Fruin. In 1868 he published in the Dutch periodical *De Gids* an article entitled *Een onuitgegeven werk van Hugo de Groot* that was

---

[12] *Mare liberum, sive de iure quod Batavis competit in rebus Indicanis,* (Leiden: Raphelengius, 1609); this first edition was anonymous and did not bear the name of Grotius as author. – The most commonly used English translation remains *Mare Liberum, The Freedom of the Seas, or, The Right which Belongs to the Dutch to Take Part in the East Indian Trade,* translated by Ralph van Deman Magoffin, ed. and intr. by James Brown Scott (New York: OUP, 1916). See also *The Free Sea,* tr. by Richard Hakluyt; ed. and intr. by David Armitage (Indianapolis: Liberty Fund, 2004) which is far superior to the translation of Magoffin. The initial dating of *De iure praedae* was set by Robert Fruin as approximately October 1604-1605. The date of completion was revised back to about the autumn of 1606 as a result of supplementary evidence published in 1928. In a letter to Heidelberg-based councilllor Georg Michael Lingelsheim, Grotius announces that he has 'finished' his work on the Indies affairs, but casts doubt over whether to publish the whole book or only the parts pertaining to the law of prize and booty. See *BW*, I.86, 1 November 1606, p. 72 and its translation into English in *Commentary*, p. 552: 'The little treatise on Indian affairs [opusculum de Rebus Indicanis] is complete: but I do not know whether it should be published as it was written or only those parts which pertain to the universal law of war and booty. Many indeed have dealt with this subject both old and new. But I believe that new light can be thrown on the matter with a fixed order of teaching, the right proportion of divine and human law mixed together with the dictates of philosophy.' Grotius also calls it 'de rebus Indicis opusculum' in a second letter to Lingelsheim, dated 1 November 1606, see *BW*, I.86, p. 72.

[13] Borschberg, 'Grotius' Theory of Trans-Oceanic Trade Regulation', pp. 8ff., 47ff.

[14] The *Pars Historica* or historical part of *De iure praedae* derives its title from two words *sequuntur historica* scribbled at the top of the page marking the beginning of chapter XI. The first part of the work, widely known as the *pars dogmatica* or 'theoretical section', spans chapters I through X.

[15] See note 12.

translated into English and brought into print as *An Unpublished Work of Hugo Grotius.*[16] Fruin's exposé has long established itself as something of a critical historical introduction to the text which is lacking in the first Latin edition prepared by Hamaker. But Fruin's research – conducted almost one and a half centuries ago – is not without its questionable assumptions and false conclusions. Some of these have been identified and corrected in the important study by Van Ittersum entitled *Profit and Principle. Hugo Grotius, Natural Rights Theories and the Rise of Dutch Power in the East Indies, 1595-1615.* I refer to this excellent work for further reference on the importance and historic reception of Fruin's article.

Though doubtlessly a seminal study, the Leiden professor's publication proves problematic in several instances. Most unfortunately, some of his false or baseless assumptions have been accepted by the scholarly community as commonplaces or – worse still – as unassailable truths. *De iure praedae,* as a whole, explores the theoretical and historical grounds for attacking and seizing the Portuguese carrack *Sta. Catarina* on February 25, 1603.[17] Following the footsteps of Grotius, Fruin misidentified the location of this act of hostility as the Strait of Malacca,[18] whereas in fact it took place between the Hook of Barbukit (now Malaysia) and Singapore's eastern seaboard. This clearly places the event in the Singapore Straits.[19]

---

[16] Fruin, 'Een onuitgegeven werk', pp. 443-445; 'An unpublished work of Hugo Grotius. Translated from an essay in Dutch (1868),' contained in *Bibliotheca Visseriana,* 5, Leiden: E. J. Brill, 1925, pp. 3ff. In the present article I will be citing from 'Een onuitgegeven werk', the Dutch-language version printed in *Fruin's Verspreide Geschriften*. See also Van Ittersum, *Profit and Principle,* p. 4.

[17] Peter Borschberg, 'The Seizure of the Sta. Catarina off Singapore: Dutch Freebooting, the Portuguese Empire and Intra-Asian Trade at the Dawn of the Seventeenth Century', *European Encounters and Clashes in the South China Sea,* ed. by Rui Manuel Loureiro (Macao: Instituto Cultural de Macau, 2004; Special Issue of *Revista de Cultura / Review of Culture,* International Edition, 11 (2004)), 11-25. This article is available on-line from the Instituto Cultural de Macao at the following website: www.icm.gov.mo. See also Borschberg, 'The Seizure of the Sta. Catarina Revisited: The Portuguese Empire in Asia, VOC Politics and the Origins of the Dutch-Johor Alliance (c.1602-1616)', *Journal of Southeast Asian Studies,* 33 (2002), 31-62; Martine van Ittersum, 'Hugo Grotius in Context: Van Heemskerk's Capture of the Santa Catarina and its Justification in De Jure Praedae (1604-1606)', *Asian Journal of Social Science,* 31 (2003), 511-548; Van Ittersum, *Profit and Principle,* pp. xix, 35.

[18] The claim is found both in *De iure praedae* as well as in the *Annales et historiae.* See also Henk Nellen, *Hugo de Groot. Een leven in strijd om de vrede, 1583-1648,* (Amsterdam: Uitgeverij Balans, 2007), p. 82.

[19] Borschberg, 'Hugo Grotius, East India Trade and the King of Johor', *Journal of Southeast Asian Studies,* 30 (1999), 226; Charles Ralph Boxer, *Fidalgos in the Far East, 1550-1770. Fact and Fancy in the History of Macao* (The Hague: Nijhoff, 1948), p. 50; Dirk van der Cruysse, *Louis XIV et le Siam* (Paris: Fayard, 1991), pp. 57-60; *Commentary,* p. xiii. – Just as some period

Fruin also erred when he singled out as central concern of *De iure praedae* the supposed need to mollify the pacifist concerns of the Dutch East India Company's (VOC) Mennonite shareholders. For sure, the early VOC had its Mennonite shareholders, and concerns were voiced about the recourse to violence, either in offensive prize taking against Iberian shipping or even in self-defence. But disgruntled Mennonite shareholders can hardly be the targeted audience of *De iure praedae.* Fruin's claim would hardly seem problematic, had it not been repeated and even amplified in a number of key publications of more recent decades.[20] Van Ittersum has convincingly rebuffed once and for all the centrality of the 'Mennonite shareholder theses' with ample evidence dredged in the National Archives of the Netherlands in The Hague (formerly known as the Algemeen Rijksarchief).[21] Yet there is one additional aspect of Fruin's article that requires explicit rebuttal here, and that concerns his assumptions about the sources to which Grotius had access when writing *De iure praedae.*

> Hugo de Groot took on himself the writing of such a treatise. I cannot assure that he had been incited to this by the [VOC] directors; I've not been able to find any proof of this. In a letter to his brother [Willem] dating from a later period, he admits to have stood in close relationship with the Company. And there can be no doubt that he made use of the archives of the United Company and of its predecessors[22] when writing his piece.[23]

Fruin's assumption about Grotius supposed 'archival research' activities would probably seem innocuous if it had not been taken on and developed further by Charles H. Alexandrowicz in his *Introduction to the History of the*

---

publications, such as the rare pamphlet by Richard Schilders, Grotius wrongly placed the *Sta. Catarina* incident in the Strait of Malacca. For this error, see the *Corte ende sekere Beschryvinghe vant veroveren der rijcke ende gheweldighe krake, comende uytet gheweste van China, door den Admirael Jacobus Heemskercke* … (Ghedruckt na de copy van Middelborch by Richard Schilders, 1604). A copy of this rare pamphlet can be found in Amsterdam University Library. The copy consulted by Fruin belongs to the Bibliotheca Thysiana in Leiden.

[20] See for example Richard Tuck in *The Cambridge History of Political Thought 1450-1700*, ed. by J. H. Burns and M. A. Goldie (Cambridge: CUP, 1991), p. 504.

[21] Ittersum, *Profit and Principle*, pp. 113f., 118-119, pp. 167ff.

[22] These corporate 'predecessors' are known in Dutch as the *voorcompagniën,* a group of regional trading firms engaged in the Indies trade.

[23] Fruin, 'Een onuitgegeven werk', p. 403, 'Het schrijven van zulk een betoog nam Hugo de Groot op zich. Ik kan niet verzekeren dat hij er door de bewindhebbers to aangezocht is; geen bewijs daarvan heb ik kunnen ontdekken. Maar dat hij tot de Companie in nauwe betrekking heeft gestaan, zegt hij zelf in een brief aan zijn broeder van latere dagteekening. En dat hij de archieven der Vereenigde Companie en van haar voorganster bij het schrijven van zijn verhandling heeft gebruikt, lijdt geen twijfel.' Translation into English, P.B.

Law of Nations in the East Indies, published in 1967, just shy of a full century after Fruin's original article. The following two excerpts from Alexandrowicz are classic examples of how unproven or assumed positions can become accepted truths:

> When Grotius studied the facts of the case of the *Santa Catharina,* which led to the writing of the treatise *De iure praedae*, he acquired from the relevant documents and sources first-hand knowledge of the problems of the East Indies and the habits and laws of its peoples and rulers.
>
> ... It is therefore possible to assume that Grotius in formulating his doctrine of the freedom of the sea found himself encouraged by what he learned from the study of Asian maritime custom ... [A] brief analysis of various passages of Grotius' *Mare Liberum* may confirm the correctness of the above assumption.[24]

Not only was it now assumed that Grotius had gained access to, or even studied in, the VOC archives (that presumably included the holdings of its corporate predecessors), he now was seen to have studied the habits and laws of Asian rulers, nay even delved into Asian maritime custom? Is that true? Is there any evidence to support this claim? Is it sufficient to simply defer to the published chapter of *Mare liberum* as a pool of evidence for the 'correctness of the above assumption'? The reader may already surmise that my answer to the latter is negative. With the 'Alexandrowicz thesis' I have arrived at the very heart of my exposé. In the present context I shall pose a very basic but also important question: What did Grotius know at the time of writing *De iure praedae?* Specifically, I am interested to probe what Grotius knew about Asian customs and princes and the intra-Asian maritime trading regime at large. I will specifically focus my attention also on the role of the Portuguese *Estado da Índia* within the Asian maritime trading regime.

Early Materials from Grootenhuys

Which source materials – published or unpublished – did Grotius actually have at his disposal while drafting *De iure praedae*? Where better than to search for answers in Grotius's expansive and learned correspondence. As is widely accepted, the young humanist was asked to write a piece justifying the seizure of the *Sta. Catarina*. It is highly unlikely that the treatise was meant to influence the decision of the court, as the Amsterdam Admiralty Board had adjudicated the *Sta. Catarina* and its cargo legal prize on 9 September, 1604, and first

[24] Alexandrowicz, *Introduction*, p. 65.

evidence of Grotius working on the manuscript of *De iure praedae* dates from a later period, namely mid-October that year.[25] In other words, the Dutch humanist had begun drafting his treatise around the time, or even after, the verdict on the *Sta. Catarina* incident was cast by the Admiralty Board.[26] Of special interest to my investigations are pieces of correspondence that underscore two facets of Grotius's toiling on the manuscript: the piece was most probably commissioned by the directors of the VOC in Amsterdam, and those directors arranged to 'feed' Grotius with materials for the completion of his task.[27]

Attention is now drawn to two letters written by Jan ten Grootenhuys[28] dating from the second half of October 1604. These can be found in their original Latin in the first volume of Grotius's *Briefwisseling* or 'Correspondence' as well as in English translation in the 2006 English-language edition of *De iure praedae*.[29] In the first letter, dated 15 October 1604, Grootenhuys wrote:

> At last, oh most learned of men, we send you the Indian Reports which you have been expecting for a long time. These reports were taken from the captains of the ships themselves, who had to confirm them under oath as well. You will clearly understand from them what the Portuguese have attempted against each of the voyages for the purpose of destroying our men. In addition, you will derive from them countless proofs of perfidy, tyranny and hostility suitable to your apology. We trust that your apology, begun so feliticiously, will be completed in a short while thanks to your attentiveness. The letters of Peter Plancius, the privateering commissions and other documents if necessary will be delivered to you at the first opportunity, as will those that your affection should subsequently demand from us, you to whom we offer every service with the greatest pleasure.[30]

---

[25] See below, note 29.

[26] See also Borschberg, 'Grotius' Theory of Trans-Oceanic Trade Regulation', p. 5.

[27] Ibid., p. 7.

[28] Jan was the younger brother of VOC director Arendt ten Grootenhuys and had studied together with Grotius at the States' College in Leiden. See also Ittersum, *Profit and Principle*, pp. 24-25; *Commentary*, p. xv. He is reported by Van Ittersum to have been on close or 'intimate terms' with him in the first decade of the seventeenth century. See Van Ittersum, *Profit and Principle*, p. 295 note 6. Arendt ten Grootenhuys served on the board of directors of the 'Old East India Company' (Oude O. I. C.) together with Pieter Plancius. See: Jan Parmentier, Karel Davids and John Everaert, *Peper, Plancius en Porselein. De reis van het schip Swarte Leeuw naar Atjeh en Bantam* (Zutphen: Walburg Pers, 2003), p. 80, note 9.

[29] See *BW*, I.53 and I.54, pp. 44-5. *Commentary*, pp. 545-547.

[30] *Commentary*, pp. 545-546. For the original Latin text, see BW, I.53, pp. 44-45. See also Van Ittersum, *Profit and Principle*, p. 26.

On the dorso of this letter Grotius noted as received:

> Privateering commissions
> The verdict of the Admiralty court
> The edict of the Estates of Holland
> Obtain from Plancius the titles of such books on Portuguese trade in the East Indies as may be purchased here.[31]

This first surviving letter of Grootenhuys reveals a number of important aspects about the commissioned nature and the working habits of the young Dutch humanist. In broad terms, one can say that by mid-October Grotius had already started writing on his treatise. The letter of Grootenhuys served as a reminder that there was some urgency about completing the project, and that Grotius would be given access to more documentation if he so desired. Importantly, the letter also served to reinforce the the parameters pegged by the VOC directors: Grotius was to highlight the perfidity, tyranny and hostility of the Portuguese in the East Indies, and underscore their countless misdeeds against Dutch traders. Grootenhuys may have called the work in progress an *apologia* or 'apology', but the anti-Iberian tone and thrust desired of the work is nothing less than propaganda.

Given the nature of the materials either forwarded or promised, one is very tempted to concluded that in October 1604 Grotius was toiling on the historical section of *De iure praedae* (chapters X-XVI).[32] It is uncertain how long Grootenhuys had kept Grotius waiting for the 'Indian reports' – the wording may very well just be a baroque pose of gallantry or courtesy.

Of special interest to the present exposé are the reports confirmed under oath mentioned by Grootenhuys. These documents, bound together in a single volume as the 'Book treating of the cruel, treasonous and hostile procedures of the Portuguese in the East Indies', presently belong to the National Archives in The Hague. They were identified, transcribed, discussed and published by the Dutch historian Coolhaas in 1965 as *Een bron van het historische gedeelte van Hugo de Groots 'De iure praedae'*, that is 'A source of the historical part of Hugo Grotius's *De iure praedae*.'[33] As the study of Coolhaas is academically outstanding as well as exhaustive, suffice it to observe here that this 'Book ... of the Portuguese in the East Indies' can be deemed little more than the embittered and vindictive carping of interviewees who earlier suffered at the

---

[31] *Commentary*, p. 547.

[32] These observations also coincide with the claims of Van Ittersum, *Profit and Principle*, p. 27.

[33] Published in the *Bijdragen en Mededelingen van het Historisch Genootschap*, 79 (1965), 415-540.

hands of the *Estado da Índia's* officers. This collection of affidavits supplied Grotius with some concrete historical examples and evidently also the anti-Lusitanian tone that contributed meaningfully to the shape and rhetorical objective of the *pars historica,* especially chapter XI.[34]

Grootenhuys promised more documents, and judging from the notes jotted down by Grotius on the original letter of 15 October, as well as from the second letter of Grootenhuys dating from 20 October, 1604, these were indeed received. In the latter we read:

> We hope that you have received those documents pertaining to the Indies trade that I recently sent to you. For the present we enclose the edict of the Estates of Holland, and the sworn statement of Mr. Apius, along with the verdict of the Amsterdam Admiralty, court. The day after tomorrow, God willing, we will send you the rest, wherein I will write to you at length.[35]

Again, on the dorso, Grotius noted as received:

> the placard of the Estates General
> edict
> the instructions mentioned by them
> ....
> Of Amsterdam
> ....
> Map of the East Indies
> The location of the carrack's capture and a description of its seizure
> Placards and extracts from the instructions with regard to the prize
> Plancius' memorandum
> Map of the East Indies[36]

From the two letters of Grootenhuys and the notes recorded by Grotius on their dorso, the nature of the materials 'fed' to the young humanist were of a dual nature: first, affidavits outlining the personal and harrowing experiences of officers and ships' mates who had sailed and returned from the Indies. Second, official documentation pertaining specifically to the *Sta. Catarina* incident, as well as Dutch privateering activities in general. The latter fundamentally confirmed the *Sta. Catarina* incident as a lawful act of prize taking and also endorsed attacks on Spanish and Portuguese targets as legitimate acts

---

[34] At the auction of 1864, chapter XI of *De iure praedae* was identified as a distinct and separate piece by its own right. It was also sold separately from the main text (lot 72) as lot 11, entitled '*H. Grotius, De bello Batavorum cum Lusitanis, imprimis de rebus per Indiam gestis dissertation,* 48 pag. – Mscr. autographe inédit. Il parait que ce traité a été destiné primitivement pour fair partie de l'ouvrage décrit sous le No. 72.' See also Van Ittersum, *Profit and Principle,* p. 27.

[35] *Commentary,* p. 547. For the original Latin text of the letter, see BW, I.54, p. 45.

[36] Ibid.

of war. These official documents include specifically: the Edict of the States-General, the Decree of the States of Holland of 1 September, 1604, and the Verdict of the Amsterdam Admiralty Board of 9 September, 1604, adjudicating the *Sta. Catarina* case as good prize.[37] Suffice it to observe here that the intricate theory behind the concept of the just war, and the taking of prize as lawful acts within the context of a just war, was subsequently worked out by Grotius in the *pars dogmatica* or 'theoretical part' of *De iure praedae.*

Of special interest to the present exposé are the affidavit of Apius, the letters and the memorandum of Plancius, the map(s) of the East Indies and a question reserved for the Dutch cleric Petrus Plancius (Pieter Platevoet).

Martin Apius was one of the members of Admiral Van Neck's crew taken prisoner by the Portuguese in Macao. Seventeen of his mates were executed in the Luso-Chinese enclave, but Apius was brought to Goa where he was cross-examined by officers of the *Estado da Índia,* and later set free. His affidavit was filed on his return to the Netherlands.[38] As is known, the execution of seventeen mates of Van Neck's crew triggered the decision of Jakob van Heemskerk and his *breede raad* (naval council) to attack Portuguese mercantile shipping off the coast of the Malay Peninsula,[39] and the name of Martin Apius is also found in the main text of *De iure praedae.*[40] This first package of documents dispatched to Grotius in mid-October 1604 also finds a strong echo in the *pars historica* (chapters XI through XVI).

The entry 'location of the carrack's capture and a description of its seizure' probably refer to a document, or several documents, such as significantly the *Discourse ende Advertisment* as well as a notarized testimony of Jakob van Heemskerk dated 27 August, 1603. Copies of both manuscripts are preserved in the National Archives in The Hague and yield important information on the supposed Portuguese harassment of Johor at the open of the seventeenth century, the events leading up to the seizure of the *Sta. Catarina,* and the course of events off the Hook of Barbukit near the Johor River estuary.[41] Aspects of this information were incorporated into the historical section of *De iure praedae.*[42] Of special significance in this context are the developments

[37] English translations of all these documents can be found in *Commentary*, pp. 503-516.

[38] A copy of the testimony of Apius found among Grotius's papers was sold at the 1864 auction.

[39] Borschberg, *The Santa Catarina Incident of 1603*, p. 14; Van Ittersum, *Profit and Principle*, pp. 19-20.

[40] *Commentary*, pp. 279ff.; Parmentier, Davids and Everaert, *Peper, Plancius en Porselein*, pp. 58-59.

[41] Coolhaas, *Een bron*, pp. 528-529.

[42] Borschberg, *Grotius, East India Trade*, p. 231.

immediately leading up to the seizure of the *Sta. Catarina,* as well as the presence of Johor royalty aboard Heemskerk's flagship *Witte Leeuw* during the exchange of fire with the Portuguese carrack on 25 February, 1603.[43]

A Question for Pieter Plancius

Evidence gleaned from the two letters of Grootenhuys from October 1604 point at the existence of 'letters' as well as a 'memorandum' of Peter Plancius. As observed by Philip Molhuysen, editor of the first volume of the Grotian *Briefwisseling,* Plancius was *bekend door zijn studiën over the zeevaart* that is 'known for his studies on navigation'.[44] But he is today celebrated for his work on astronomy and especially also geography.[45]Acknowledged as one of the founding fathers of cartography in the Dutch Republic, Plancius was an avid collector of travelogs of Spanish and Portuguese voyages, and incorporated information mined from these into his cartographic creations. Plancius served with Arendt ten Grootenhuys on the board of directors of one of the *voorcompagniën,* a regional trading firm that was merged into the VOC in 1602.[46] He drew an estimated one hundred maritime charts, many of which were used during the early voyages of the Dutch to the East Indies. Plancius, in other words was a pioneer and an acknowledged expert on the geography of, and maritime navigation to, the East Indies.[47] This expertise provides the immediate context for understanding the question jotted down by Grotius – evidently intended as a reminder for himself - 'Te vraghen aen Plancius om de namen derghene dye in den Portugese handel in Oostindie hebben geschreven om hyer te becomen', that is 'obtain from Plancius the titles of such books on Portuguese trade in the East Indies as may be available here'. We will return to that request in just a short while, after engaging with some thoughts on the map(s) of the East Indies passed on to the Dutch humanist for the fulfilment of his commission.

What remains shrouded in mystery is the map, or possibly two maps, forwarded to Grotius by Grootenhuys in October 1604. To discuss possible

---

[43] On the significance of this argument, see Borschberg, *Grotius, East India Trade,* p. 234.

[44] BW, I.53, p. 44n2.

[45] For a comprehensive account of Plancius' life and works, see J. Keuning, *Petrus Plancius: theoloog en geograaf 1552-1622* (Amsterdam: Van Kampen, 1946).

[46] See above note 28.

[47] Concerning the significance of Plancius during the early Dutch voyages to the East Indies, see Parmentier, Davids and Everaert, *Peper, Plancius en Porselein,* pp. 43ff.

specimens is really nothing more than speculation. Certain is that Plancius prepared scores of maps for VOC and fundamentally based his charts on Cornelis Claesz. Another source of cartographical information might have been Pieter Bertius, a friend and correspondent of Grotius in this period. He is known to have published maps depicting the Malay Peninsula, then commonly referred to in Dutch circles as 'Malakka' after the great trading emporium situated on its western coast. Judging from a number of internal arguments of *De iure praedae,* such as Grotius's misplacement of the *Sta. Catarina* incident, and also in view of his occasional penchant for Ptolemaic geographic nomenclature (which doubtlessly stemmed from his familiarity with the Greek and Roman classical sources), it seems plausible that he was working with specimens such as Claesz, Plancius, or Bertius. But as said, this is just speculation. The former two maps were widely available at the time, and a copy of Claesz can be found, among other places, inserted in Jan Huyghen van Linschoten's widely consulted and readily available *Reysgeschrift* of 1595. There is no firm evidence in *De iure praedae* that Grotius actually consulted the *Reysgeschrift,* and indeed, much the same can be said for Linschoten's *Itinerario* published one year later in 1596. Admittedly, a copy of the latter was confiscated from Grotius's private library in 1618,[48] but it is not certain when Grotius consulted the work, let alone purchased his personal copy.

With these deliberations I am placed in a position to answer the question concerning the books available in the Netherlands on the Portuguese India. There is no record that Grotius ever lodged his request, and even if he did, it appears to have remained unfulfilled or negative. This is because there is not a single Portuguese source cited or even mentioned throughout the completed manuscript of *De iure praedae* that even as much as alludes to the *Estado da Índia* or the maritime intra-Asian trading regime. Nor are there, to the best of my knowledge, any surviving reading notes from such sources that were prepared by Grotius. Portuguese materials touching on the East Indies were difficult to obtain in the Netherlands, partially because of Portugal's policies of secrecy, but also because there were genuinely few printed sources that could have been successfully mined for writing *De iure praedae.*

---

[48] The list of books confiscated from Grotius's library in 1618 can be found in Philip C. Molhuysen, 'De bibliotheek van Hugo de Groot in 1618', *Mededelingen der Koninklijke Nederlandsche Akademie van Wetenschappen* n.r. 6 (1943), 45-63. For the modern critical text version, see Jan Huyghen van Linschoten, *Itinerario. Voyage ofte Schipvaert van Jan Huygen van Linschoten naer Oost ofte Portugaels Indien, 1579-1592,* and *Reys-geschrift vande navigatiënder Portugaloysers,* ed. by Hans Kern, (vols 1-3) and J. C. M. Warnsinck (vols 4-5) (The Hague: Nijhoff, 1939).

As mentioned, the most readily available source to Grotius would have been Linschoten's *Itinerario* and *Reysgeschrift* which incorporate and reproduce in translation materials of Portuguese origin. Another accessible source would have been (the first volume of) Ramusio's *Delle Navigazioni e Viaggi* first published in Venice in 1550.[49] Among the more interesting testimonies included in the *Viaggi* is the *Suma Oriental* of the early sixteenth century Portuguese apothecary and diplomat Tomé Pires. This was published by Ramusio without providing the name of the author and in a text version so abridged that it is difficult to recognize the treatise for what it really is. The full text of Pires was published in English translation by the Hakluyt Society in London in 1944.[50] Still, a closer comparison of the full text with Ramusio's rendition will quickly reveal that the best information about the nature of pre-colonial Southeast Asia and the early Luso-Asian trading regime around the Straits of Malacca and across the Indonesian Archipelago is wanting.[51] It has been surmised that Ramusio was working with a transcript heavily censored by the Portuguese authorities.[52]

---

[49] It appears under the heading 'Sommario di Tutti li Regni, Città, e Popoli Orientali', in Ramusio's *Viaggi,* vol. 1 (Venice, 1550), fols. 349-63. Concerning Ramusio's addition of the *Suma Oriental* to his *Viaggi*, see especially Biblioteca Nacional de Lisboa: Rui Manuel Loureiro, *O Manuscrito de Lisboa da "Soma Horiemtall" de Tomé Pires* (unpublished doctoral dissertation, University of Lisbon, 1994), p. 31; See also his 'O Sudeste Asiático na Suma Oriental de Tomé Pires', *Revista de Cultura* 4 (2003), 107-123 (109-110), together with Ramusio's testimony of how difficult it was to obtain even an imperfect or corrupted copy of the manuscript while he was in Lisbon.

[50] Tomé Pires, *The Suma Oriental of Tome Pires. An Account of the East from the Red Sea to Japan. Written in Malacca and India in 1512-1515*, ed. by Armando Cortesão, 2 vols (London: Hakluyt Society, 1944). Facsimile editions of this important work are also available from AES Publishers in Delhi, 1990. For modern text-critical aspects of Pires' *Suma,* see Rui Manuel Loureiro, *O Manuscrito de Lisboa da 'Suma Oriental' de Tomé Pires (Contribuição para uma Edição Crítica)* (Macao: Instituto Português do Oriente, 1996), (especially the introduction); 'A malograda embaixada de Tomé Pires a Pequim', *Portugal e a China – Conferências no II Curso Livre de História das Relações entre Portugal e a China (Séculos XVI-XIX)*, ed. by Jorge M. dos Santos Alves (Lisbon: Fundação Oriente, 1999), pp. 39-55; 'O Sudeste Asiático na Suma Oriental de Tomé Pires', pp. 107-123.

[51] On the primordial significance of Pires as a source on the nature of trade in the pre-colonial period and the early Luso-Asian trading regime, see: Marie-Antoinette Petronella Meilink-Roelofsz, *Asian Trade and European Influence in the Indonesian Archipelago between 1500 and about 1630* (The Hague: Nijhoff, 1962), p. 1; Rui Manuel Loureiro, 'Sixteenth Century Iberian Accounts of Indonesia. A Preliminary Survey', *Indonesia-Portugal. Five Hundred Years of Historical Relationship*, ed. by Ivo Carneiro de Sousa and R. Z. Leirissa (Lagos: CEPESA, 2001), p. 23.

[52] See Rui Manuel Loureiro, *O Manuscrito de Lisboa*, pp. 33-43.

For the Lack of Portuguese Sources: Vitoria, the 'School of Salamanca' and the Alexandrine Bulls of 1493

Without useful published sources explaining Asian customs or mechanisms of the Luso-Asian trading regime at his fingertips, Grotius resorted instead to materials on the Spanish conquest of the Americas. The *Brevísima Relación* of Bartolomé las Casas was of course translated into several European languages, including Dutch, before and shortly after the turn of the seventeenth century.[53] The treatise was given a title – and richly adorned with engraved images - that sought to underscore the tyrannical nature of Spanish rule in the Americas, and implicitly also in the (Spanish) Low Countries.[54]

Concerns about the advent of the Spaniards in the New World and the impact of early colonisation on its native peoples were openly vented by a group of sixteenth century Spanish Dominicans whom modern scholars have collectively dubbed the 'School of Salamanca'. Grotius was doubtlessly inspired by their writings when drafting his *De iure praedae* and incorporated many references to their works both in the *pars dogmatica* (chapters I through X) as well as in the *pars historica* (chapters XI through XVI).[55] This is especially true of the works of two Spanish clerics, Diego de Covarrubias y Leyva and Francisco de Vitoria.[56] It further transpires that Grotius had received from the VOC directors a copy of Vitoria's *Relectiones XII* published in Lyon in 1557.[57] Supporting this claim are testimonies from Grotius's *Briefwisseling* dating the early 1640s. In May 1643 while rummaging through his books,[58] Grotius retrieved the copy of Vitoria's *Relectiones* which he claimed Grootenhuys had passed on to him long time ago. He expressed his intention to return the copy of Vitoria to its rightful

[53] See the *Seer cort verhael vande destructie van d'Indien vergeradert deurden Bischop Don Fray Bartholome de las Casas* (s.l.: 1578).

[54] See *Den Spieghel Vande Spaensche Tyrannie beeldelijken afgemaelt, leest breederen in-hout door het schrijven van den E. Bisschop van Chiapa in nieu Spaengien, ghenaemt Don Fray Bartolome de las Casas, van S. Dominicus Orden, aen den grootmaechtigen Coninck van Spaengien Philips de tweede* (Amsterdam: Cornelis Claesz, 1609).

[55] Borschberg, *Grotius, East India Trade*, p. 237; Van Ittersum, *Profit and Principle*, p. 328-329 n38.

[56] For a comprehensive selection of his works, see Diego de Covarrubias y Leyva, *Opera Omnia quae hactenus extant*, 2 vols (Frankfurt/M.: Ex Officina Nicolai Bassaei, Impensis Sigismundi Feierabend, 1573).

[57] Francisco de Vitoria, *Relectiones Theologicae XII* (Lyon: Iacobus Boyerius, 1557).

[58] Interestingly, the copy of Vitoria's *Relectiones* is not featured in the list of books confiscated from Grotius's library in 1618. See: Molhuysen, 'De bibliotheek van Hugo de Groot'.

owner.[59] Based on such epistolary testimony, two conclusions are warranted in the present context: First, the long acknowledged impact of the Salmantino on Grotius's early thought on war, peace and trade can be partially explained by the fact that Grootenhuys forwarded to Grotius a copy of Vitoria at a relatively early stage of drafting *De iure praedae*. Second, in the evident absence of Portuguese sources on the Luso-Asian trading regime, Grotius appears to have based his argument on Spanish authors such as Vitoria, and transposed the principles from the New World to the Asian scenario.[60] Such parallels could hardly be warranted, not least because the early European colonial powers – and that includes the Dutch as much as the Portuguese – treated Asian princes in principle as full members of the international community and family of rulers, as sovereigns co-equal to their counterparts in Europe. Grotius himself drafted a letter on behalf of the VOC for the Sultan of Tidor in 1606 or early 1607, beseeching him to unite with the company against the Iberian enemy and other possible (European) competitors in the East Indies trade.[61] Other draft treaties found among Grotius's papers preserved at the National Archives in The Hague include letters or treaties addressed to the 'Emperor of Borneo' (that is the Sultan of Brunei who used to control much of Borneo Island), the Sultan of Siau,[62] and the Sultan of Ternate.[63] In *De iure praedae* he expressly holds the Sultan of Johor to be a rightful overlord, implicitly equal to his sovereign counterpart in Europe and rightfully exercising full public authority.[64] Grotius was himself painfully aware of the serious problems raised by his transposition of principles from the New World to Southeast Asia as is wonderfully evidenced from a short deleted comment found in chapter II of *De iure praedae*'s autograph manuscript. The Dutchman wrote: *Alia enim*

[59] See the letter of Grotius to P. Spiring Silvercrona, dat. 9 May, 1643, BW, XIV.6205, p. 252: 'Nuper dum libros recenseo, invenio inter eos Relectiones Fr. Victoriae; nescio an datas mihi, an commodatas olim a domino Grotenhusio, praetore nunc Amstelodamensi. Eum librum remittam ei …', see also the letter of Grotius to his brother Willem, 27 June, 1643, BW, XIV.6282, p. 360: 'Rogo memineris de libro Fr. Victoriae, quem nescio dominus Grotenhusius mihi donarit aut commodarit. Libens ei aut illum librum aut quem voluerit eius loco remittam.'

[60] Borschberg, 'Grotius' Theory of Trans-Oceanic Trade Regulation', p. 24. Concerning Grotius's use of Vitoria in the early seventeenth century, see also: Van Ittersum, *Profit and Principle,* pp. 327-328, 329n38; Hans Thieme, 'Natürliches Privatrecht Spätscholastik', *Zeitschrift der Savigny-Stiftung für Rechtsgeschichte,* Germanistische Abteilung, 70 (1953), 235-236, 262-266.

[61] *Commentary*, pp. 553-555.

[62] Siau is an island to the north-northeast of Sulawesi, in the border area between modern Indonesia and the Philippines.

[63] Borschberg, *Grotius, East India Trade*, p. 229.

[64] *Commentary*, p. 432, 'There is in India a kingdom called Johore, which has long been considered a sovereign principality…'

India, alia Americana ratio est that is 'The case of the East Indies and the Americas are different'.[65] Truth has been spoken here, they were very different indeed, especially with regard to the treatment of (and treaties with) native rulers, the conduct of trade, and missionisation.[66]

Although Grotius echoes many arguments from Vitoria, there are also noteworthy deviations, and two such instances merit further exploration here. The first concerns the pattern of arguments taken on from Vitoria. Grotius follows the Salmantino professor in examining possible scenarios for Spain's just and unjust conquest of the New World. He takes on the arguments about the humanity and equality of the native Americans, the extant of influence exerted by the pope over the faithful who have accepted him as the Vicar of Christ on earth, and of course the issue of apostolic concession (papal donation). The point Grotius fails to take on from Vitoria is the argument dismissing the universal authority of the Holy Roman Emperor.[67] Given that the Dutch Republic remained formally a part of the Holy Roman Empire until the Peace of Westphalia in 1648, this issue may have been deemed too sensitive.

The second pattern concerns the infidelity of the native peoples of the New World and its impact on their exercise of *dominium*. This is a very important argument that, when transposed to the East Indies, served Grotius to underscore the independence and genuine sovereignty of the rulers of Southeast Asia. As a subset to this argument, he shared with Vitoria (but not other Salmantino doctors, such as notably Domingo de Soto) the idea of a *ius communicandi* that is a natural and inalienable 'right of communication'.[68] However, the Dutch humanist significantly expanded this *ius communicandi*, developed by Vitoria as a right to preach the Gospel to the peoples of the New World, into a far more comprehensive entitlement that significantly also entails the right to conduct trade and access emporia via the high seas. While assuming a prominent place within the context of his argument, especially in chapter XII (*Mare liberum*), Grotius betrays his minimal knowledge of the *Estado da Índia* and the Luso-Asian trading regime at large. His heavy reliance on Vitoria together

---

[65] Alexandrowicz, *Introduction*, p. 47n1.

[66] Unlike the Spaniards, the Portuguese generally dropped their religious biases in order to maximize trading profits and preserve peace with neighboring Asian overlords. For a synopsis of the specifically Southeast Asian context see the very useful article by John Villiers, 'Doing Business with the Infidel: Merchants, Missionaries and Monarchs in Sixteenth Century Southeast Asia', in *Maritime Asia. Profit Maximisation, Ethics and Trade Structure, c. 1300-1800*, ed. by Karl A. Sprengard and R. Ptak (Wiesbaden: Harrassowitz, 1994).

[67] Borschberg, 'Grotius' Theory of Trans-Oceanic Trade Regulation', p. 25.

[68] Concerning the differences in the position of Vitoria and De Soto, see also Borschberg, 'Grotius' Theory of Trans-Oceanic Trade Regulation', p. 27.

with the projection of principles from the New World to the Asian scenario, are also evidenced by his exclusive reliance on the bulls of Pope Alexander VI issued in 1493 in favour of the Spanish and Portuguese crowns.[69]

The Alexandrine bulls issued on the return of Christopher Columbus to Europe following his first voyage of discovery to the New World form an important pillar in Spain's moral and legal claims to the Americas. As such, they do not stake out Portugal's claims in the East, but rather define the 'border' between Spanish and Portuguese claims in the Atlantic, and define the Eastern perimeter of Spain's fresh claims to the Americas. By contrast, the Lusitanian crown based its claims of apostolic concession on a series of bulls issued after the conquest of Ceuta in 1415, as the Portuguese began to progressively explore the Western coastline of the African continent (and in the process also sanctioned the reintroduction of the slave trade). In this context, the bulls promulgated by Popes Martin V, Eugene IV and Nicholas V are of noteworthy historical significance.[70] The Alexandrine bulls of 1493 marked not the beginning, but rather the beginning of the end of such papal donations. In any case for Portugal the Alexandrine bulls only really defined its 'Western boundary' with Spain in the Atlantic.[71] The Lusitanian crown's claims in Africa and Asia – and indeed to the vast open high seas surrounding these great continents – were tenuously staked out in earlier acts of apostolic concession that were confirmed and augmented in the early sixteenth century following the conquest of Malacca and the Spice Islands (Moluccas).[72] It is against the backdrop of these important colonial acquisitions that historians should also place the papal donations in favour of Portugal stipulated in the bull of Medici Pope Leo X of November 1514.[73]

---

[69] On this point see also Borschberg, *Grotius, East India Trade*, pp. 236, 237, 238, 242; pp. 7, 15, 26. – Concerning Vitoria's *ius communicandi* in general, see Karl-Heinz Ziegler, 'Völkerrechtliche Aspekte der Eroberung Lateinamerikas', *Zeitschrift für Neuere Rechtsgeschichte*, 23 (2001), pp. 9, 20ff. and more extensively in Isabel Trullo Pérez, *Francisco de Vitoria : il diritto alla comunicazione e i confini della socialità umana* (Turin: Giappichelli, 1997).

[70] See also Borschberg, *Grotius, East India Trade* (1999), p. 239. For a short general background and overview of the papal donations in favour of Portugal in the fifteenth century, see also: John M. Hobson, *The Eastern Origins of Western Civilisation* (Cambridge: CUP, 2004), pp. 135-137.

[71] For English translations of these key documents, see: *The Philippine Islands, 1493-1898*, ed. by Emma H. Blair and James A. Robertson, 55 vols (Cleveland: Clark, 1903-1909). See ibid. I, pp. 105-111 for the bull *Inter Caetera* of 4 May 1493, and pp. 111-114 for the extension of the Apostolic Grant (Revision of the original line of demarcation contained in the bull *Inter Caetera* of May 1493) dated 25 September, 1493.

[72] See also Jan Somers, *De VOC als volkenrechtelijke actor* (Deventer: Gouda Quint, 2001), pp. 30-34 for a useful summary of Portugal's legal claims in the East Indies.

[73] Blair and Robertson, *The Philippine Islands*, I, pp. 136-138, for the bull of Leo X dated 3 November, 1504 which repeats and extends the Apostolic grants of the fifteenth century.

It is clear that Grotius ignores entirely almost all apostolic concessions made in favor of the Lusitanian crown. In *De jure praedae* (and implicitly *Mare liberum*) he also fails to drop but a single reference to the treaties signed at Tordesillas (1494) and Saragossa (1529) that privately settled competing claims for *dominium* between Spain and Portugal.[74] Vitoria had no need to mention them, as they were only ephemeral to his argument. In his *De Indiis Recenter Inventis* (Relection on the Indies Recently Discovered), the question is not focused on 'who can claim what' by discovery, apostolic concession or conquest. The Salmantino theologian was first and foremost concerned with moral and religious issues, questions surrounding Christian charity as well as select problems associated with the missionisation of the Amerindians in the New World.

As for Grotius's deference to other authors of the School of Salamanca, one needs to evaluate marginal references in the manuscript of *De jure praedae* with the greatest possible caution. With an eye cast specifically on chapter XII *(Mare liberum),* not all references are the fruit of his own labour, as the Dutchman was known to 'lift' whole clusters of references from other sources, such as notably from Vitoria or Covarrubias.[75] This raises a number of questions as to how deeply familiar he really was at that time with the works of the Salmantino theologians. As late as 1618 the Dutch humanist privately conceded in a letter: *Dominicanorum vix legi quenquam* that is 'I have hardly read any of the Dominicans', a clear confession that, apart from Vitoria and Covarrubias, he had hardly perused any of the writings of the Spanish late scholastics.[76]

It is clear that in the early stages of drafting *De iure praedae* Grotius was being 'fed' with more material pertaining to the *Sta. Catarina* incident, the *Estado da Índia's* activities, and the maritime Luso-Asian trading regime at large. Of special interest to Grotius's knowledge of the *Estado da Índia* and the Intra-Asian trading regime are a series of documents listed at the end of the autograph manuscript of *De iure praedae* owned by Leiden University Library. He noted: 'A copy of each of the following documents will be appended'.[77] The list includes items already familiar to us from the two letters

[74] Ibid., pp. 115-129 for the Treaty of Tordesillas and pp. 222-239 for the Treaty of Saragossa.

[75] Borschberg, 'Grotius' Theory of Trans-Oceanic Trade Regulation', p. 8.

[76] BW, I.567, p. 611; Borschberg, 'Grotius' Theory of Trans-Oceanic Trade Regulation', p. 27. The question may legitimately arise as to whether the Roman Inquisitor Sylvester Mazzolini de Prierio, whose *Summa Sylvestrinae* is cited in *De iure praedae,* should also be included among the 'Dominicans' generally speaking. A closer scrutiny of the dictionary-like *Summa* and of Grotius's references thereunto shows that he only looked up select key terms and expressions important to the argument of *De iure praedae.*

[77] *Commentary*, p. 497.

of Grootenhuys: The edict of the Dutch States General of 1599, the verdict of the Admiralty Board of 1604, and the Decree of the States of Holland of September 1604. Certain documents have until now not been mentioned, such as for example the 'excerpt from a letter of the Bishop of Malacca to the King', the letter from the 'Senate of Malacca', two letters addressed to Jacob van Heemskerk, and a letter of the 'Commander of the captured vessel to Heemskerk'.[78] With the exception of the bishop's letter, all of the documents concerned deal with specifics of the '*Sta. Catarina* incident': The Captain-Major *(capitão-mór)* of Malacca, Fernão d'Albuquerque, a man of great ancestry, conceded to Heemskerk the carrack as 'valid prize of war' and thanked the Dutch admiral for keeping his word and bringing all survivors of the captured carrack safely to the Portuguese enclave. A message with a similar content of gratitude stemmed from Malacca's 'Senate'. There is a separate request of Albuquerque to intervene with the Sultan of Johor to free some Christian hostages. And finally the broken and financially broken captain Sebastião Serrão, a *casado* of Goa, humbly beseeched Heemskerk for a piece of cloth from which to sew new clothes. These 'situational letters' have very little to offer on the *Estado da Índia* or the Intra-Asian trading regime.[79]

Of some interest to the present exposé, however, is the letter of Dom João Ribeiro Gaio, the Bishop of Malacca, addressed to King Philip of Spain and Portugal dated 30 April, 1600. According to Van Ittersum, the original Portuguese transcript together with a translation of the letter into Dutch has been lost. A copy of the notarized Dutch translation of 1604, however, was sold to Frederick Muller at the Martinus Nijhoff auction of Grotius's manuscripts and personal papers in 1864. A copy of the letter prepared by Muller and written in his hand is preserved at Leiden University Library. The text was earlier published as an appendix in the English translation of *De iure praedae* published in 1950.[80] To the modern reader, the letter of Bishop Ribeiro Gaio is as interesting as it must have been to a Dutch audience in the early seventeenth century. It provides a snapshot of the dissatisfactions felt by the Portuguese on the arrival of the first competitors from northern Europe. The epistolary report is intrinsically designed as a wake-up call for King Philip III of Spain (who also ruled as Philip II of Portugal), explaining that the setbacks experienced against the Dutch and some Asian allies 'arise from a gross neglect of these southern regions on the part of the *Estado da India*'.

---

[78] For their incorporation into the text of chapter XII of *De iure praedae* (*Mare liberum*) see for example *Commentary*, p. 383.

[79] These documents can be found in English translation in ibid. pp. 503-527.

[80] Ibid., p. 517n34. For the text of the letter, see ibid., pp. 517-522.

The bishop petitioned his monarch to 'take the appropriate measures – sooner rather than later, if possible – and thus benefit these southern regions, which are the solace of the entire *Estado* and Portugal. I hope that Your Majesty will continue to give his undivided attention to these rich and excellent regions'.[81] Bishop Ribeiro Gaio's main grudge against the Dutch is not that they represented a 'locust plague of heretics', 'faithless scoundrels', 'pirates' or 'rebels' as Iberian sources from Asia often labeled them at the time, but that the Dutch were spoiling the spice market for the Portuguese and the Luso-Asian traders. As newcomers or 'greenhorns' in the Southeast Asian world of trade, they were entirely ignorant of local prices, business practices and market conditions. The bishop patiently lectured his monarch not only on the deals struck by the Dutch traders, but importantly also on their likely long-term consequences:

> Of the ten [Dutch] ships that arrived at Bantam,[82] four immediately received cargoes of pepper and spices and sailed home in January 1599, without having done any harm to the Bantamese, let alone the Portuguese,[83] or troubling a single other nation. They bought pepper at thirty ryals-of-eight per *bahar* and mace at eighty and ninety ryals-of-eight per *bahar.*[84] In addition, they purchased cloves, nutmeg and other products of these regions. They were unaware of the local prices fetched by these products, but bought them nonetheless. They ended up spending a lot of money, for they paid the highest price. They were well regarded and highly esteemed by the locals, for they were honest traders who did not resort to any kind of subterfuge, harassment or violence. They became fast friends and allies of the King and Regents of Bantam, and raised great expectations of continuing this trade and friendship on a regular basis, which God forbid.[85]

Ten Haeff and Six Letters of Instruction by the Iberian Monarch

Based on the observations thus so far, it is evident that Grotius's knowledge of the *Estado da Índia* and the Luso-Asian trading regime at the time of beginning his *De iure praedae* was insubstantial. This harsh verdict can only be minimally ameliorated when considering a letter first published by Van Kleffens in the early 1960s and later added to the supplementary volume

[81] Ibid., p. 521.

[82] A port city and Sultanate at the Western tip of Java.

[83] On this claim, see *Commentary*, p. 286.

[84] Ten ryals-of-eight at that point in time amounted to about 76.7 grammes of fine silver. A bahar (composed of three picul) weighs approximately 180.5 kilogrammes.

[85] Ibid., p. 518.

of Grotius's *Briefwisseling* in 2001.[86] As a matter of special interest I point to a letter dated 17 November, 1607, and authored by the Middelburg magistrate Adriaan Hendricksz. ten Haeff who acted as the personal contact between Grotius and the VOC directors.[87] This epistolary testimony shows that Grotius was being 'fed' with yet more information, this time by the company's Zealand Chamber. The immediate context is provided by the on-going truce negotiations between the nascent Dutch Republic and Spain with an eye specifically cast on overseas trade. As Ten Haeff himself confessed, the materials were intended as *poincten van consiterasiën … in de sake van den Oostindischen handel* or 'points of consideration … in the matter concerning trade in the East Indies'. These materials were thus intrinsically meant *tot voltrecken u.E. begonste werck* or 'for the completion of the work that you have begun'. Ten Haeff invited Grotius to cite from these letters wherever he may find them useful.[88]

Within the scope of the present study are the letters that are summarized in Dutch and featured as *brieven van den koninck van Spaengien* or 'letters of the King of Spain'.[89] One recalls that the period under review falls under the Union of the Two Iberian Crowns (1580-1640) when Spain and Portugal were ruled by the same monarch. The majority of the letters highlight reactions of the *Estado da Índia* to the arrival of the Dutch in the waters and marketplaces of the East Indies. Many of the enclosed letters either beseech Asian allies not to admit the Dutch to trade in their ports, or to exhort Asian Princes to expel the Dutch where they are already present. Others issue instructions to beef up security, either in Portuguese-held forts and ports, or around waters plied by Lusitanian-flagged commercial vessels. With reference to the latter, enclosure number 3 merits further elaboration. This is letter written in Madrid on 27 January 1607 instructing the Captain-Major of Malacca and Admiral of the 'Armada of the Southern Seas', André Furtado de Mendonça, to step up security in the Portuguese-held emporium Malacca and to construct 'eenige forten in Sincapura en elders' or 'some fortresses around Singapore and elsewhere'. A second letter, enclosure number 4, bearing the same date was dispatched to the Portuguese Viceroy

[86] E. N. van Kleffens, 'Over zes briefen uit het bezit van Hugo de Groot', *Mededelingen der Koninklijke Nederlandse Akademie van Wetenschappen,* afd. letterkunde, n.r., 23 (1960), 447-491.

[87] See BW, XVII.107A, pp. 37-38.

[88] BW, XVII.107A, p. 37. Generally also Van Ittersum, *Profit and Principle*, pp. 224-225. Van Ittersum recognized a direct link between Ten Haeff's letter, the list of documents, and the commission by the VOC's Zealand Chamber to prepare *Mare liberum* for publication. See ibid., p. 226.

[89] BW, XVII.107A, p. 37-38.

of India, Dom Martin de Castro. In this he is earnestly admonished to construct fortresses 'om tot Achem' that is 'around Aceh' at the Northern tip of Sumatra, as well as 'in de enghten van Sabaon ende Sincapura' or 'around the Straits of Sabam and Singapore'.[90] The latter represented a crucial nodal point in Portuguese intra-Asian trade, and as the VOC would quickly learn, any one who commanded the Strait of Sabam controlled traffic between the Malacca Strait and onward ports in Java, Macassar, Timor and the Moluccas. Anyone who could control the Singapore Straits could also disrupt trade between ports in subcontinental India and Malacca, with ports around the Gulf of Siam, Champa, Cambodia, Borneo, Macassar, Macao, and Japan.[91]

Most unfortunately, these particular items of correspondence between Europe and Portuguese India forwarded to Grotius can no longer be retrieved. From the *Livros das Monções* or 'Letters of the Monsoon' as the official Portuguese correspondence between Europe and the *Estado da Índia* is commonly known, it transpires that security for commercial shipping in the Singapore and Malacca Straits became of paramount concern to Lusitanian officials.[92] This was especially the case after the seizure of the great carrack *Sta. Catarina* in the Singapore Straits in 1603, the capture of

[90] The *Estreito de Sabam* or *Sabão* runs along a north-south axis between the eastern seaboard of the great island of Sumatra, and the present-day islands of Karimun Besar and Kundur in Indonesia's Riau province.

[91] BW, XVII.107A, p. 38., no. 2, 'Een brieff van 28 November anno 1606 wt Lisbona aen don Martin voorzegd, daerin hem gesonden wordt een placcaet, daerbij geordonneert wordt dat men alle vremdelingen als Franchoisen, Italiaenen, Hooghduytsen ende Nederlanders die in Indiën woonen ende wel over Persiën ende Turquijen daer gecomen sijn, sal doen vertrecken.' Ibid., no. 3, 'Een brieff van 27 January 1607 in Madril aen don Andrea Furtado Mendoza, daerbij hem geordonneert wordt aen den vice-roy wel te informeren van 't fortificeren van de stadt van Malacca, het maken van eenige forten in Sincapura en elders.' Ibid., no. 4, 'Een brieff van 27 January 1607 in Madril aen don Martin de Castro, daerin hij ernstigh vermaent wordt om tot Achem ende in de enghten van Sabaon ende Sincapura fortressen te maecken.' Ibid., no. 5, 'Een brieff van 24 November 1606 wt Lisbona aen den capiteyn van de fortresse van Megapatan, daermede incompt van de vremdelingen daer overal te doen vertrecken.' Ibid, no. 6, 'Een brieff van 23 December anno 1606 wt Lisbona aen den coninck van Cananor, daerin hij bedanckt wordt van de rebellen in sijn landt niet geadmitteert te hebben ende daerin voort te willen continueren, enz.' and ibid. no. 10, 'Een brieff van 13 February 1607 wt Lisbona aen don Martin Alfonso de Castro, daerin getracteert wordt van Machau te fortificeren.'

[92] See generally Borschberg, 'Portuguese, Spanish and Dutch Plans to Construct a Fort in the Straits of Singapore, ca. 1584-1625', *Archipel*, 65 (2003), 55-88; 'Remapping the Straits of Singapore. New Insights from Old Sources?' in *Iberians in the Singapore-Melaka Area and Adjacent Regions (16th to 18th Century)* (Wiesbaden: Harrassowitz; Lisbon: Fundação Oriente, 2004), pp. 93-130.

the carrack *Santo António* in the port of Patani (presently in southern Thailand) in 1605,[93] and admiral Cornelis Matelieff de Jonge's unsuccessful sea-borne siege of Malacca in 1606.[94]

Judging by the Dutch summary of the letters, it is clear that these epistolary testimonies represented by far the most credible and probably also the most comprehensive first-hand chunks of information that Grotius received about the *Estado da Índia* and the nature of Portuguese maritime intra-Asian trade. According to Henk Nellen, the editor the *Briefwisseling Supplement,* as well as Van Ittersum the transcripts and/or translations mentioned in the letter of Ten Haeff are no longer extant.[95] Nellen observed:

> In his letter he refers to the enclosed documents that could be of use to Grotius in his defense of Company interests; as a result of the negotiations with Spain for peace or a truce, these interests had come under pressure. Grotius could have incorporated the documents of Ten Haeff in a memorandum which he was preparing at the time and which remain preserved in various drafts among his [personal] papers.[96]

So the 'work that you have begun' as Ten Haeff put it, does not likely refer to *De iure praedae,* but almost certainly to a memorandum Grotius was preparing for the VOC at the time.

VOC Admiral Matelieff de Jonge's *Discours*

Another valuable source dating from about this time is an epistolary report addressed to Grotius by admiral Cornelis Matelieff de Jonge and dated

[93] See Borschberg, 'The Seizure of the Santo António at Patani. VOC Freebooting, the Estado da Índia and Peninsular Politics, 1602-1609', *Journal of the Siam Society*, 90 (2002), 59-72; 'The Seizure of the Sta. Catarina Revisited: The Portuguese Empire in Asia, VOC Politics and the Origins of the Dutch-Johor Alliance (c.1602-1616)', *Journal of Southeast Asian Studies*, 33 (2002), 31-62.

[94] See also Borschberg, 'Luso-Johor-Dutch Relations in the Straits of Malacca and Singapore, ca. 1620-1623', in *Rivalry and Conflict, European Traders and Asian Trading Networks, 16th and 17th century*, ed. by Ernst van Veen and Leonard Blussé (Leiden: Centre for Non-Western Studies (CNWS), 2005; (reprint *Itinerario*)), pp. 188-218.

[95] Van Ittersum, *Profit and Principle*, p. 225n34.

[96] BW, XVII.107A, p. 37n1, 'In zijn brief verwijst hij naar bijgevoegde documenten, die Grotius van nut konden zijn bij zijn verdediging van de belangen van de compagnie; deze belangen waren als gevolg van de onderhandelingen met Spanje over vrede of bestand onder druk komen te staan. Grotius kan de documenten van Ten Haeff verwerkt hebben in een nota die hij in deze tijd in voorbereiding had en die in verscheidene redacties in zijn papieren bewaard is gebleven.' See also Van Ittersum, *Profit and Principle*, pp. 226-227.

Rotterdam, 12 November, 1608. In 1606, Matelieff unsuccessfully besieged the Portuguese stronghold at Malacca and concluded an important alliance with the Kingdom of Johor that, with the benefit of hindsight, became one of the most enduring alliances forged by the VOC with the rulers of the Indonesian Archipelago and the Malay Peninsula. Matelieff's letter shows how the Dutch had quickly learnt the dynamics of power in the East Indies, as well as the intra-Asian trading networks in which the Portuguese also participated.

Entitled *Discours van den stant van Oost Indiën* (Discourse on the State of the East Indies) Matelieff sets out to explore various means by which the war effort can be successfully waged against the Spanish, Portuguese and other competitors, both European and Asian.[97] The admiral formulated two priorities for the VOC in Asia: first, to pluck Malacca from the Portuguese, possibly with the help of Asian allies, such as Siam, Johor or other regional powers like Aceh, Kedah, Perak, Pahang, Patani, and Jambi.[98] And second, to select a *rendez-vous* location as a base for the company's Asian operations where ships could assemble before setting sail for home, or proceeding to other trading emporia in the East Indies.[99] Matelieff emphasized that the location should be accessible all year round, independent of the monsoon winds and recommended Jacatra on Java or Palembang on Sumatra as such ideally situated locations.[100] The new settlements, he continued, should be populated with settlers from Europe, and the best way to attract them to the Indies would be to give them genuine opportunities to make money.[101] The admiral then provided a sweeping synopsis of the balance of power across the region spanning from China, the Indonesian Archipelago, the Malay Peninsula, Siam and locations around the Gulf of Bengal. He recommended tightening security around towns and fortresses including Ambon, the Bandas and Batusawar (Johor). Matelieff encouraged the taking of prizes from the Portuguese enemy in the Strait of Malacca, around Ceylon and in the Bay of Bengal. He underscored that the most damage the VOC could inflict on the Portuguese would be to attack and seize ships outbound from Macao en route to Malacca.[102] He also

[97] See P. J. A. N. van Rietbergen, *De eerste Landvoogd Pieter Both (1568-1615). Gouverneur-Generaal van Nederlandsch Indië (1609-1614)*, 2 vols (Zutphen: Walburg Pers, 1987), I, pp. 134 note 3; II, pp. 196-211. There are two pieces of admiral Cornelis Matelieff de Jonge addressed to Grotius. The first is dated 12 November, 1608, the second dated 16 January 1609.

[98] Ibid., p. 209.

[99] Ibid., p. 197.

[100] Ibid., p. 198.

[101] Ibid., p. 200.

[102] Ibid., p. 208.

alluded to the substantial maritime trade taking place between the South Chinese coastal cities and Manila.

One could claim that Matelieff's *Discours* represented in so many ways the flip-side of the situation addressed in the aforementioned 'packet' of letters forwarded by Ten Haeff and collectively labeled *Brieven van den Koning van Spaingien*. It spelt out priorities for the VOC in the East Indies, yielded a sweeping synopsis of the security situation in East and Southeast Asia, and identified vulnerabilities in the intra-Asian trading networks of the *Estado da Índia*. The *Discours* and the aforementioned *Brieven* taken together probably form the most comprehensive first-hand information on the *Estado da India* and the intra-Asian maritime trading regime that are known to have passed through Grotius's hands.

The question still remains open as to what mentionable impact, if any, these documents might have also come to bear on the argument of *De iure praedae* or even to revisions applied in 1608 and early 1609 to chapter XII *(Mare liberum)*. It is extremely difficult to provide any reliable assessment, especially of the *Brieven* which are no longer extant. Judging from the summaries, the personal names of the Portuguese officials, and the geographic nomenclature provided, however, their impact was marginal at best. None of these topics or names are raised in *De iure praedae* or its published spin-off *Mare liberum*. As for the report of Matelieff, there is no visible evidence that his *Discours* bore any influence on the revision of chapter XII. Unlike the letters from the enemy, from which Grotius was free to quote, the *Discours* of Matelieff may therefore have been considered sensitive or classified information as it set out priorities for the Dutch company's operations in Asia.

Emmanuel van Meteren's Memoriën

Finally I turn to a source that is not specifically mentioned in the *Briefwisseling* but certainly had impacted Grotius's argument in the *pars historica* of *De iure praedae*. This concerns the work of the Dutch historian Emmanuel van Meteren. The Library of the University of Lund in Sweden is in possession of Grotius's personal copy of this work. It was printed in Delft in 1599 and features several underlinings, marginalia and notes by its famous proprietor.[103]

[103] Emmanuel van Meteren, *Memoriën der Belgische Ofte Nederlantsche Historie van onsen tijden* (Delft: Jacob Cornelisz Veenecool, 1599). Printed Source containing the autograph underlinings, marginalia, and comments by Hugo Grotius, Lund: University Library, Bibl. Grotiana 13.

With reference to the *Estado da Índia*, one section stands out in particular. This is found on folio 406 verso where Van Meteren discusses the early voyages of the Dutch to the East Indies. What caught Grotius's eye were three distinct snippets of information that he underlined in the book: the ships had been *gevordert* or 'sponsored' by the States of Holland; they were armed with metal artillery, and the voyages should serve to forge regular trade with Asian peoples in areas where the Portuguese had no *ghebiet,* that is where they had no colonies and exercised no *dominium.* The latter echoes a passage in *Mare liberum.* He concedes in his anonymous spin-off that his arguments are primarily directed at the high seas, and implicitly at access to market places in Asia. The objective is not to discuss places such as 'Goa or Malacca' over which Portugal exerted direct sovereign control.[104]

Refuting Fruin and Alexandrowicz

At the end of this exposé, I return to the two statements of Robert Fruin and Charles H. Alexandrowicz that provided my point of departure. As has been seen, Fruin claimed that the author of *De iure praedae* had conducted research in VOC archival holdings, while Alexandrowicz expanded on this theme to assert that Grotius had conducted extensive first-hand research on documents pertaining to the Asian maritime trading regime. The views of Fruin and Alexandrowicz are by no means isolated, but have entered mainstream Grotius research as almost incontestable truths.

Evidence drawn from Grotius's correspondence and unpublished reading notes, however, lend no support to these or related assertions. The epistolary testimonies evidence that the young Dutch humanist did not seize the initiative

See also: Folke Dovring, 'Une partie de l'héritage littéraire de Grotius retrouvée en Suède', *Mededelingen van de Koninklijke Nederlandsche Akademie van Wetenschappen,* afd. letterkunde, n.r., 12 (1949), 237-250. The copy in Lund University Library is a restored copy of the book that spans up until the year 1598. Grotius's notes are clustered in areas dealing with key topics of historical interest, such as the creation of the Union under Holy Roman Charles V in 1528 and the years of the Dutch Revolt. Concerning the early Dutch voyages to the East Indies, see esp. ibid., fol. 406 verso and 407 recto. On the latter page, the names of Heemskerk, Neck and Warwijk are underlined by Grotius. There are also underlinings or marginalia of interest on fol. 414 recto and in the book's register. Concerning the history of this first edition of van Meteren and the controversy that erupted over it, together with the notes found in Grotius's copy preserved at the Unviersity of Lund, see Cornelia M. Ridderikhoff, 'Een aristocratische geschiedenis van de Opstand: Grotius' Annales et Historiae de rebus Belgicis', *De zeventiende eeuw,* 10 (1994), pp. 278-279.

[104] Borschberg, 'Grotius' Theory of Trans-Oceanic Trade Regulation', p. 41.

to conduct in-depth research on VOC document holdings, but instead relied on selected and biased materials that were steadily 'fed' to him over the years by the VOC directors in Amsterdam and later also Middelburg. It is difficult not to share the verdict of Van Ittersum: 'The "book treating of the cruel, treasonous and hostile procedures of the Portuguese in the East Indies" is conclusive proof that Grotius had never done any independent investigations of his own and simply used the materials put at his disposal by the VOC directors'.[105] As has been seen in this exposé, the lack of 'independent research' certainly extends beyond the affidavits identified and published by Coolhaas in 1965.

Based on the sources Grotius consulted, his knowledge of the *Estado da Índia,* Asian customs and the maritime trading regime of the East Indies was minimal at the time of drafting *De iure praedae* in 1604-1606. In the absence of ready available works pertaining to the *Estado da Índia,* the Dutch humanist relied on a collection of affidavits extolling the harrowing experiences of ship's mates at the hands of the Portuguese. The dearth of reliable information on the legal and commercial ramifications of the *Estado da Índia* was made up for by gleaning principles from the works of the Spanish late scholastics, such as notably Vitoria and to a lesser extent from Covarrubias. These principles were subsequently modified and projected from the Spanish Americas to the Luso-Asian scenario. It is almost inevitable that at best Grotius's reliance on superficial geographic knowledge, affidavits of disgruntled mariners and the transposition of principles from the Americas to Asia would provide nothing but a skewed picture of the *Estado da Índia* and the Luso-Asian trading regime. Grotius's reliance on Vitoria evidences his genuine ignorance of the very legal foundations upon which Portuguese India was established and the mechanisms of administration and trade that sustained it.[106] Grotius did consult Van Meteren's *Historiën,* but there is no evidence in either *De iure praedae,* or indeed, any of his surviving early reading notes to suggest that he had consulted available travel literature, such as the ones contained in Ramusio's *Viaggi* or Linschoten's *Reysgeschrift* and *Itinerario.* He was evidently also not familiar with the text of papal bulls and private treaties between Spain and

---

[105] Van Ittersum, *Profit and Principle*, p. 119.

[106] One of the most authoritative accounts of how the *Estado da Índia* worked can be found in the many treaties signed between the *Estado da Índia* and Asian princes as well as in the exposé of António Vasconcelos de Saldanha, *Iustum Imperium. Dos tratados como fundamento do império dos Portugueses no Oriente* (Macao: Instituto Português do Oriente and Fundação Oriente, 1997). For the collection of Luso-Asian treaties, see Julio Firminio Judice Biker: *Collecção de tratados e concertos de pazes que o Estado da Índia Portugeza fez com os reis e senhores com quem teve relações nas partes da Ásia e Africa Oriente, desde o princípio da conquista até ao fin do século XVIII*, 10 vols (Lisbon: Imprensa Nacional, 1881-1887).

Portugal that formed an integral cornerstone in Portugal's claims to Africa, Asia and the open seas. Grotius's knowledge of East and Southeast Asian geography was sketchy at best, preferring geographic expressions of classical antiquity and Ptolemaic geography to some Asian nomenclature that was already well established in European cartography by the beginning of the seventeenth century.[107]

Finally, there is not a shred of evidence to indicate that he had ever studied Asian customs or legal codes, let alone any accounts that touched upon Portuguese intra-Asian trade. Fruin's confident statement that *De iure praedae* represents 'clean research' that commands 'lasting [academic] value' now seems rather problematic.[108] As for the 'Alexandrowicz thesis' extolling Grotius's supposed familiarity with Asian commercial and maritime practices cannot be sustained by any stretch of the imagination. There is also no evidence to support the view that the young humanist was being 'fed' with such information by or on behalf of the VOC directors. There is no extant information to suggest that such information might have even been important within the ramifications of *De iure praedae's* commission. Certainly, Grotius's own claim to have written something on the 'the universal law of war and booty' must be strictly understood within its Eurocentric context and nothing more.[109]

It is almost inevitable that, at a first glance, Grotius enthusiasts will feel greatly disappointed by such findings. But they will soon find reprieve when they sit back to ponder their fuller consequences. From a helicopter perspective, it is clear that the findings open new opportunities for Grotius research. There remains a lot to be done on the unpublished notes and fragments found scattered in archives in the Netherlands, Europe, and beyond. Rather than just synthesising or rationalising existing commercial trade practices or mechanisms prevalent in the Asian theatre, Grotius arrived at his insights based on far less (diverse) material than anyone has hitherto ventured to surmise. After all, his commission from the Amsterdam directors was to defend the seizure of the *Sta. Catarina* as an act of war against the backdrop of Iberian pretensions of exclusion in the East Indies. Far from knocking the great Dutchman off his humanist pedestal, these insights should nudge modern researchers to seriously rethink the originality of early Grotian thought.

---

[107] Grotius cites for example from the works of Claudius Ptolemy, as well as Pliny and Strabo. He employs the geographic term Taprobana to Sumatra and the 'Golden Chersonese' either to the Malay Peninsula or Japan. See *Commentary*, pp. 264-265, 355.

[108] Fruin, 'Een onuitgegeven werk', p. 372.

[109] See above, note 12.

Evidence from the *Briefwisseling* touching the genesis of *De iure praedae* also raise a number of important questions about the work as a whole: When were the different parts of the treatise actually drafted?[110] Which parts were written first? How important is the *pars historica* really for understanding the *pars dogmatica?* How deeply familiar was Grotius with the diverse sources that he (supposedly) cited from? These are questions that cannot be explored in a short article, chapter or even a book. They pose a challenge that can – and will – only crystallise over time.

---

[110] On this question, see also Van Ittersum, *Profit and Principle*, p. 27: 'It cannot be emphasized enough that the manuscript's *dogmatica de jure Praedae* were written last, not first. The evidence is admittedly circumstantial, but nonetheless convincing.'

Problems of Legal Systematization from *De iure praedae* to *De iure belli ac pacis*

De iure praedae *Chapter II and the* Prolegomena *of* De iure belli ac pacis *Compared*[1]

Laurens Winkel
Professor of legal history, Erasmus University Rotterdam
winkel@frg.eur.nl

Abstract
A comparison between the *Prolegomena* of Chapter II of *De iure praedae* and the *Prolegomena* of *De iure belli ac pacis* leads to the conclusion that the ideas of Grotius on legal systematization have changed considerably between 1604 and 1625. Whereas Grotius starts in *IPC* with general principles with a rather unclear distinction between *leges* and *regulae*, in *IBP* he gives first the philosophical and theological basis of international law, intertwined by a concise set of general legal rules (*IBP*, Prol., 8), mostly derived from Roman law after its reception in Western Europe. The general outlines of legal systematization in the early-modern period are expounded. In the attempts of legal systematization the concept of subjective rights is essential. These subjective rights are not, as is sometimes assumed, a medieval renewal of legal technique, but can be found essentially already in classical Roman law of the first centuries AD.

The institutional system is not yet visible in *De iure praedae*, it might be different for *De iure belli ac pacis*. Significant here are possibly the expressions *ius ad bellum* and *ius in bello*.

Keywords
Grotius, De iure praedae, De iure belli ac pacis, legal systematization, Institutes, subjective rights, *prolegomena*

[1] Elaborated text of a presentation at NIAS in May 2005 and of a guest lecture at a mixed seminar of the Universities of Vienna and Graz held in Graz in June 2007. I am grateful for the comments made on the two occasions and for those made by prof. Robert Feenstra, Tammo Wallinga and Guus van Nifterik. I thank Dr. Paul de Plessis (Edinburgh) for his help with the English style.

Introduction

In the preface of the translation of *De iure praedae* which was published in 1950 we read: 'In spite of the cordial welcome accorded the manuscript of the Commentary by a few scholars, interest in the work has never become widespread. The similarity between the content and that of Grotius's two most famous works naturally gave rise to the question: Since the same doctrines are more thoroughly expounded in other treatises by the same author, long available in many editions and various languages, what is to be gained by further study of the youthful composition which Grotius himself did not trouble to publish?'[2]

All this could have been true if it had been Grotius's own decision not to publish *De iure praedae*, but in fact it was never published for political reasons with the exception of Chapter XII, which was printed anonymously in 1609 under the title *Mare liberum*. Besides, a good reason for studying *De iure praedae* independently from other works is the insight a surviving manuscript of an early work gives us about Grotius's way of writing and thinking. After all, we do not have the manuscript of *De iure belli ac pacis*!

The treatise *De iure praedae* of which the manuscript was discovered as recently as 1864 and which was printed in 1868 is said to have had several purposes: It was written as a defense against the capture of the Santa Catarina with the intention of showing that the practice was in accordance with natural law, first of all defending the capture of the Portuguese vessel Santa Catarina on February 25, 1603 by showing that this practice was in accordance with natural law. A further aim could have been to justify this practice on behalf of the Mennonite shareholders of the VOC who were basically pacifist and opposed to extending hostilities towards Spain (and Portugal) outside Europe and who were about to establish another, more peaceful East India Company in France under the protection of King Henry IV.[3] This question is extensively dealt with in the recent book by Van Ittersum, who stresses the French aspects more than the Mennonite ones.[4]

---

[2] *De iure praedae commentaries. Commentary on the Law of Prize and Booty by Hugo Grotius*, Classics of International Law, tr. by G.L. Williams with the collaboration of Walter H. Zeydel (Oxford: Clarendon, 1950), p. xvii [= *Commentary*].

[3] P. Haggenmacher, *Grotius et la doctrine de la guerre juste* (Paris: Presses Universitaires de France, 1983), p. 54.

[4] Detailed discussion in M.J. van Ittersum, *Profit and Principle. Hugo Grotius, Natural Rights Theories and the Rise of Dutch Power in the East Indies (1595–1615)* (Leiden: Brill, 2006), pp. 110 ff., esp. p. 119n13).

The aim of the following lines is to challenge the quoted statement of 1950 by showing not the similarities, but rather the differences between the approach in *De iure praedae* and in *De iure belli ac pacis.* This article will focus on the systematic approach of legal matters which Grotius uses. After all, systematization is an important topic in the legal science of the sixteenth and seventeenth centuries, not only when it comes to finding leading legal principles, but also when the so-called institutional system is applied in the description of Roman law, as has been done by Donellus,[5] or of legal phenomena such as Dutch private law, as has been done by Grotius in yet another of his main works.[6]

At the same time, this article may be considered as a part of a greater research project aimed at a better understanding of legal humanism as such and at elucidating the differences between French legal humanism in the sixteenth and Dutch legal humanism in the seventeenth century.[7]

Legal Systematization before Grotius

An apparently new systematic approach is announced in Chapter 1 of *De iure praedae*: here, Grotius explicitly invokes the analogy with the reasoning of mathematicians who start their arguments by expounding axioms with which it is easy to agree. This is announcing the new axiomatic *mos geometricus* which gradually came to prevail in legal science of the seventeenth century. Many scholars stress the influence Simon Stevin may have had on Grotius in this respect.[8]

This brings us at first to the structure of arguments in traditional legal discourse as far as it was based on Roman law in the period preceding Grotius,

[5] Hugo Donellus, *Commentarii de iure civili*, first part published Frankfurt/Main, 1589–1590, fully published only after his death: Frankfurt/Main, 1595–1597.

[6] *Inleidinge tot de Hollandsche Rechts-geleerdheid*, written in prison in the years 1619–1621, first published in 1631. Most recent edition ed. by F. Dovring, H.W.F.D. Fischer and E.M. Meijers (Leiden: Universitaire Pers Leiden, 1952).

[7] Mainly in L. Winkel, *Error iuris nocet, Rechtsirrtum als Problem der Rechtsordnung, I: Rechtsirrtum in der griechischen Philosophie und im römischen Recht bis Justinian* (Zutphen: Terra, 1985); 'Die stoische οἰκείωσις-Lehre und Ulpians Definition der Gerechtigkeit', *Zeitschrift der Savigny Stiftung für Rechtsgeschichte*, Rom. Abteilung, 105 (1988), 669-679; *Les origines antiques de l'appetitus societatis de Grotius*, *Tijdschrift voor Rechtsgeschiedenis*, 57 (2000), 393-403.

[8] Haggenmacher, *Grotius et la doctrine de la guerre juste*, p. 69, and n. 73; L. Mok, *Hugo de Groot en Simon Stevin* (Rotterdam: Juridisch Instituut Erasmus Universiteit, 1988); H.J. van Eikema Hommes, 'Hugo de Groot's betekenis voor de rechtsfilosofie', in W. Riphagen et al., *Hugo de Groot 1583–1645*, Symposium gehouden op 18 februari 1983 (Zwolle: Tjeenk Willink, 1983), pp. 32ff.

and secondly to the role of theology in legal arguments. Especially the minor role of general principles and rules must be emphasized here.

Roman law as Grotius knew it has survived mainly in the form of the legislation of the Emperor Justinian (529–534). For the greatest part, it is by no means a systematic treatise of Roman law, only in a small part, the *Institutes of Justinian* (AD 533), an elementary survey of Roman law used for the training of law students, we find a rather elementary systematic survey that was meant for the legal instruction in the law schools. It followed an earlier systematic treatise of the jurist Gaius (± AD 160) which nowadays is to a large extent accessible for modern scholarship, but was not yet known in Grotius's time. Nevertheless, the institutional system was to play an important role in legal scholarship of the early modern period.[9]

The main part of surviving Roman law is to be found in the *Digest*: a compilation of scattered fragments of the Roman legal literature written by jurists from 100 BC – AD 290. It is divided in 50 books, subdivided in titles. The structure of the Digest and its titles is quite complex, but the order of the titles reflects more or less the order of the 'Edictum Perpetuum' of ± AD 138, at the time a kind of codification of the yearly announcements by the magistrate (praetor) of current legal remedies used in the procedure *per formulas.*[10] Although this procedure was substituted by the simpler *cognitio extraordinaria* in the course of the Principate, the order of the 'Edictum Perpetuum' remained important for the simple reason that later classical jurists like Ulpian and Paul wrote lemmatic commentaries on it and the fragments of their works form the major part of the texts in the *Digest.*

A third part of Justinian's legislation is the *Codex Justinianus*, a collection of abridged constitutions of the Roman emperors from Hadrian to Justinian in twelve books (subdivided in titles), twelve books in memory of the Twelve Tables of ± 450 BC, commonly considered as the beginning of Roman law. In every title of the *Codex* a chronological order is preserved. The *Codex* contains predominantly imperial decisions in concrete cases (rescripta), but also younger, more general legislation from the beginning of the fourth century on.

Although the *Codex* starts with some general topics like sources of secular law and ecclesiastical law, the role of general legal principles is very modest,

[9] P. Stein, 'The Fate of the Institutional System', in *Huldigingsbundel Paul van Warmelo*, ed. by J. van der Westhuizen et al. (Pretoria: Universiteit van Suid-Afrika, 1984), pp. 218–227, repr. in Stein, *The Character and Influence of the Roman Civil Law. Historical Essays* (London: Hambledon, 1988), pp. 73-82.

[10] A. Soubie, *Recherches sur les origines des rubriques du Digeste* (Bordeaux: Tarbes, 1960).

whereas the order of the titles reflects, as in the Digest, that of the Edictum Perpetuum'. The *Digest* contains hardly any general provisions either – case law is overwhelmingly present here as well –, although in the first titles of the first book there are some references to legal philosophy and general legal concepts, like the etymology of the word *ius* and the notion of justice. Among the general remarks, mention is made in a fragment of Ulpian (D. 1.1.10) of the very general so-called *praecepta iuris: honeste vivere, alterum non laedere, suum cuique tribuere*, which do not play a direct role in the argumentation of the classical Roman jurists, but in the later history of legal ideas these 'praecepta' became more important[11] and they are indeed so for the structure of Grotius's arguments in *De iure praedae*.[12]

Interesting enough, the *Digest*, not the *Codex*, does end with two titles with a more abstract character: 'De verborum significatione' (D. 50.16) and 'De diversis regulis iuris antiqui' (D. 50.17). These titles were to become important from the end of the Middle Ages on.

In the development of legal science presumed to be the year of the foundation of the oldest European university in Bologna, the teachers of law at that time, the glossators, tried to harmonize at first sight contradictory casuistic texts of Roman law by generalizing some texts to legal rules and by classifying other texts as exceptions to those rules.[13] In this way a process of abstraction has taken place from the casuistic Roman legal texts towards more abstract legal rules in a medieval rather primitive logic of the *distinctio*: an abstract rule with concrete exceptions.

The other branch of medieval law is Canon law, by no means better, indeed even less structured than the Roman legal sources. The *Decretum Gratiani* (± 1140), a private collection of canon rules of very different origin, is built upon *quaestiones* or *causae*, but ends always up with detailed *distinctiones*, just as we find in secular legal literature. Only the last book of the 'Liber Extra'

---

[11] I. Kant, 'Einteilung der Rechtslehre', in: *Metaphysische Anfangsgründe der Rechtslehre*, Akademie-Ausgabe 7 (Berlin: Reimer, 1902), pp. 236–237, K. Vorländer (Hrsg.), *Immanuel Kant, Metaphysik der Sitten* (Hamburg: Meiner, 1966; repr. of 4th edn. 1922), p. 42.

[12] Cfr. The restatement of *alterum non laedere* in *Prolegomena IPC*, Lex 3: ne quis alterum laedat.

[13] On the method of medieval jurisprudence see F. Pringsheim, 'Beryt und Bologna', in *Festschrift für Otto Lenel* (Leipzig: Tauchnitz, 1921) repr. F. Pringsheim, *Gesammelte Abhandlungen*, I (Heidelberg: Winter, 1961), pp. 418–427; E. Genzmer, 'Die Justinianische Kodifikation und die Glossatoren', *Atti del Congresso Internazionale di Diritto Romano* (Bologna e Roma, 17-27 aprile 1933), 2 vols (Pavia: Fusi, 1934-5), I, pp. 345–430, abbreviated repr. in *Das römische Recht im Mittelalter*, ed. by E.J.H. Schrage (Darmstadt: Wissenschaftliche Buchgesellschaft, 1987), pp. 5–53.

(1234), a collection of papal legal decisions (decretales) and of the 'Liber Sextus' (1298) both end with a general part. In analogy with the *Digest* there are two chapters 'De verborum significatione' and 'De regulis iuris'. More or less contemporary theological literature follows the same pattern as the *Decretum Gratiani*: the *Quaestiones* of St Thomas Aquinas do not structurally differ from the *Quaestiones* in Gratian's compilation.

After the twelfth and thirteenth century, the time of the Glossators, legal science gave the impression of a logical stand-still. In one respect this is not entirely true. Due to the fact that 'learned law', especially Roman law, was applied more and more in practice – this is what we normally call the Reception of Roman law – and Roman law had to be applied in such a wide variety of cases, there was more and more attention for the last titles of the Digest and the last titles of the 'Liber Sextus'. There, at least, some leading principles could be found.[14]

Legal methodology changed profoundly as a consequence of a rather remote political event: the conquest of the remains of the Byzantine Empire, Constantinople, by the Ottomans in 1453. The following 'brain drain' of Byzantine intellectuals, especially to Venice and Florence, was the incentive for the renaissance of the study of Greek. For legal scholarship this implied that Greek parts of Justinian's legislation, the *Corpus Iuris Civilis*, became readable again, that contact could be established with independent Greek textual traditions of Roman law (the so-called *Basilica* and its *scholia*), and most important, that Roman law could be studied as part of the civilization of Antiquity. Roman law could e.g. be brought into relation with Greek philosophy.

At first, a historical approach to the text of the *Corpus Iuris Civilis* led to another hierarchy of the manuscripts. For the *Digest*, the version of the oldest manuscript prevails, which leads to textual criticism. In a later stage the historical approach can be found not only on a textual, but also on a conceptual level. The humanist study of legal and other antique sources leads to an approach to Roman law which considers it as an instance of acculturation of Roman intellectual activities in legal practice and adapting it to a predominantly Greek culture. In the sixteenth century we should especially mention here Jacques Cujas (1522–1590) as a champion of the historical approach to Roman law. There is an interesting link between Cujas and Grotius on the methodological level. Both scholars make an extensive use of antique philosophical and literary sources to sustain their arguments.

---

[14] P. Stein, *Regulae iuris* (Edinburgh: University Press, 1966), pp. 150ff, 162ff.

But a need for another approach to law was felt, especially in the universities where the future administrators of growing bureaucracies were trained. As often before and after, there were complaints that the students only came across a minor part of the body of law and did not know how to deal with important practical problems.

This implied a fundamental shift in the approach to Roman law and also drew the attention to the *regulae*, found in the last title of the Digest, and to forms of argumentation where general notions were used. These texts are scattered in numerous other places in the Digest. Examples are references to *aequitas, bona fides* and *boni mores*. There is also a link with renewal of the study of Greek ethics, especially Aristotle's *Ethica Nicomacheia*,[15] from which followed a new approach to equity, in the original – now decisive – context a far more dynamic concept than was perceived in the Middle Ages.

Here we have reached the intellectual climate in which Grotius tried to develop his system to embed some rules of warfare in a legal framework.

The Relation between Private Law and International Law

In *De iure praedae*, Grotius tries – as has been said – to legitimate a concrete case: the capture of the Santa Catarina in 1603 as a legal and justified act. This forms a starting point for more theoretical expatiations on the law of war and especially the law of prize and booty. In *De iure belli ac pacis* Grotius has a different, still more scholarly aim: a systematic approach to the laws of war and peace. In *De iure praedae* the analogy between private law and international law is introduced by a famous quotation of Plato which is at the basis of the analogy.[16]

> *Nam quisque justum bellum gerit, necesse est eatenus judex fiat adversarii, sive, ut Plato dixit, σωφρονιστής, censor atque castigator....*
>
> *For whoever wages a just war must become to that extent the judge of his adversary, or, as Plato (Rep. 471 A)*[17] *has said, censor and chastiser....*

---

[15] See Guido Kisch, *Erasmus und die Jurisprudenz seiner Zeit* (Basel: Helbing & Lichtenhahn, 1960), for medieval jurists: pp. 36ff; for the sixteenth century: pp. 49ff.; N. Horn, *Die aequitas in den Lehren des Baldus* (Köln: Böhlau, 1968), passim; Stein, *Regulae iuris*, for medieval jurists: pp. 131ff; for the sixteenth century: pp. 162ff.

[16] *IPC*, p. 29n2.

[17] The exact reference was added by Hamaker in the printed edition of *IPC* of 1868. In the manuscript there is only a reference to Plato's *Republic*, V.

This quotation of Plato is indeed important. In quoting Plato, Grotius hints at the lack of a legally enforceable procedure between states with conflicting interests. Grotius draws a parallel between litigation between private citizens in a state on the one hand and litigation between states on the other hand. This basically explains the two possible interpretations of Grotius's work on international law as is especially visible in the scholarly literature on *De iure belli ac pacis*. This work can be used for the explanation of the development of the ideas on private law – champion here is our colleague Robert Feenstra, in numerous publications – but evidently also as the historical basis of current international law. International law is construed with as much analogy as possible with private law.[18] In doing so, Grotius is innovative, but as a good humanist he also follows a dogmatic construction of classical Roman law, where *ius gentium*, at that time understood as private law for the relations between Roman citizens and peregrines, is construed in analogy with the *ius civile*, private law for Roman citizens only. In *De iure belli ac pacis* Grotius explains the same ideas in what has become a famous quotation: 'ubi iudicia deficiunt incipit bellum'.[19] Where judicial dispute resolution is not possible, war begins. Anyhow, war is the ultimate way of solving disputes.

Just War

Until the beginning of the seventeenth century, warfare was basically still regulated more in theology than in law. Indeed we can say we owe to Grotius the insight that war was definitely considered as the main problem of a developed system of international law. Using texts by Cicero and Augustine, Thomas Aquinas (1225–1274) systematised warfare in accordance with medieval logical reasoning and therefore developed main rules and exceptions. The main rule was: war is not allowed, unless under certain specific conditions: *iusta causa*, *intentio recta*, *auctoritas principis*. Especially the last requirement caused increasing difficulties in the sixteenth century due to the declining power of both the Emperor and the Pope and the rise of the power of territorial states. This made the requirement of *auctoritas principis* for war increasingly questionable, based as it was on a clear hierarchical and feudal system.

[18] The historical dimension has been largely neglected by H. Lauterpacht, *Private Law Sources and Analogies of International Law* (London: Longmans Green, 1927; repr. Hamden, CN: Archon, 1970), although this work remains very important for a better understanding of the structure of international law.

[19] *IBP* II, 1.2.1.

This might have been one of the reasons for Francisco de Vitoria – who was very important for the development of a legal theory of war before Grotius – to introduce the more lenient concept of 'bellum iustum ex utraque parte', in which there was no longer a distinction between the objective *iusta causa* and the subjective *intentio recta*.[20]

De iure praedae Chapter II

Some attention has to be paid to the name of the second chapter of *De iure praedae: prolegomena*. Here Grotius possibly followed the example of Everardus Bronchorst, leading professor of civil law in Leyden (1587–1621), successor of Hugo Donellus, and a close friend of Grotius's uncle Cornelis de Groot. Bronchorst uses an introductory chapter called *prolegomena* in his very successful survey of the *regulae iuris* of *Digest* 50.17,[21] but the first – unofficial – edition of Bronchorst was only printed and published in 1607, after the manuscript of *De iure praedae* was more or less completed.[22] The possibility cannot be excluded, however, that Bronchorst coined the expression *prolegomena* in his teaching, or that problems of legal systematization were discussed in Leyden in the circles to which both Bronchorst and Grotius belonged. But we do not have direct evidence for this and we have to bear in mind that Grotius was never officially enrolled in the Law Faculty of Leyden University.[23]

In tracing the use of *prolegomena* back in the sixteenth century legal humanism we could think of Donellus, but he does not use the word *prolegomena*, although he is responsible for yet another new systematic approach to

[20] See my 'Francesco de Vitoria on just war and on the legal position of Burgundy', *Tijdschrift voor Rechtsgeschiedenis*, 75 (2007), 355–362.

[21] R. Feenstra, C.J.D. Waal, *Seventeenth Century Leyden Law Professors and Their Influence on the Development of the Civil Law. A Study of Bronchorst, Vinnius and Voet* (Amsterdam: North-Holland, 1975), pp. 47ff. See also R. Feenstra, Review of E. Matthes, *Die juristische Handschriften der Universität Hamburg, I: Foliohandschriften, Tijdschrift voor Rechtsgeschiedenis*, 71 (2003), 232–233: Bronchorst has also used *prolegomena* in his inaugural lecture of 1587. In his turn he could have been influenced by Wesenbecius.

[22] See the article by Martine van Ittersum in this volume. She has shown that after 1610 Grotius made only a few additions to his manuscript.

[23] C. M. Ridderikhoff, 'De universitaire studies van Hugo de Groot', in *De Hollandse jaren van Hugo de Groot (1583–1621)*, ed. by H.J.M. Nellen, J. Trapman (Hilversum: Verloren, 1996), pp. 13–29, esp. pp. 19–20. H.J.M. Nellen, *Hugo de Groot. Een leven in strijd om de vrede 1583–1645* (Amsterdam: Balans, 2007), 40ff.

law in his *Commentaria iuris civilis*, fully published only after his death in 1595.[24] We are able,[25] however, to trace back the expression *prolegomena* in the sixteenth century legal literature to François Baudouin (1520–1573), a French legal humanist who published a commentary on the most systematic Institutes of Justinian, preceded by *prolegomena*.[26]

In chapter II of *De jure praedae* Grotius distinguishes between *regulae* and *leges*, at first sight the *regulae* are more theoretical, the *leges* more practical. This distinction is by no means evident, it does not follow from Roman legal terminology and, more important, seems to have been completely abandoned twenty years later in *De Jure Belli ac Pacis* (1625). The distinction therefore has puzzled modern scholars like Haggenmacher.[27] The *regulae* of Grotius seem at first sight rather theocratic and old-fashioned. Grotius tries to set two pairs of axiomatic rules in order to approach the legal topic of prize and booty. There is no evident reason for distinguishing *regulae* and *leges*, although the former seem to prevail over the latter. It is not the distinction between theology and law, nor is it the distinction between morals and law. More confusion is added by the fact that in the text of the *prolegomena*, the *regulae* and *leges* are completely mixed. Further more, there is at least one case where Grotius seems to have hesitated between the two categories: the actual Regula IX, which indeed is on the legal level only, was first called a *lex*, a word later replaced in the main text by *regula*, which we can see due to the more detailed research of the manuscript.[28]

We have detached the *regulae* and *leges* from the context in which they have been put in chapter II to enable us to have a survey of them, whereas the second number indicates the order in the running text:

---

[24] R. Feenstra, 'Hugues Doneau et les juristes néerlandais du XVIIe siècle: L'influence de son "système" sur l'évolution du droit privé avant le Pandectisme', in *Jacques Godefroy (1587–1652) et l'Humanisme juridique à Genève*, Actes du Colloque Jacques Godefroy, ed. by B. Schmidlin et A. Dufour (Basel: Helbing & Lichtenhahn, 1991), pp. 231–243, reprint as nr 4 in *Legal Scholarship and Doctrines of Private Law, 13th–18th Centuries* (Aldershot: Variorum, 1996), see also the Additions at the end of this volume, pp. 6–7.

[25] Thanks to information kindly made accessible to us by Dr. Douglas Osler (Max Planck Institute, Frankfort/Main).

[26] See A. Wijffels, 'François Baudouin', in *Dictionnaire historique des juristes français*, ed. by P. Arabeyre, J.-L. Halpérin, J. Krynen (Paris: Quadrige/PUF, 2007), pp. 51–52; Michael Erbe, François Bauduin (1520–1573). Biographie eines Humanisten (Gütersloh: Mohn, 1978).

[27] Haggenmacher, *Grotius et la doctrine de la guerre juste*, 60.

[28] Folio 13 of the manuscript which will be made available electronically now under http://textlaboratorium, but in September 2008 only Ch. I and Ch. III are available. We do not have a good explanation for this change in the manuscript, but it may well have been only a simple slip of the pen.

Regulae

1. (1) Quod Deus se velle significarit, id ius est.
   What God has shown to be his will, is law.
2. (4) Quod consensus hominum velle cunctos significaverit, id ius est.
   What the common consent of mankind has shown to be the will of all, is law.
3. (9) Quod se quisque velle significaverit, id in eum ius est.
   What each individual has indicated to be his will, is law with respect to him.
4. (12) Quidquid respublica se velle significavit, id in cives universos ius est.
   Whatever the commonwealth has indicated to be its will, is law in regard to the whole body of citizens.
5. (13) Quidquid respublica se velle significavit, id inter cives singulos ius est.
   Whatever the commonwealth has indicated to be its will, is law for the individual citizens in their mutual relations.
6. (17) Quod se magistratus velle significavit id in cives universos ius est.
   What the magistrate has indicated to be his will, is law in regard to the whole body of citizens.
7. (18) Quod se magistratus velle significavit id in cives singulos ius est.
   What the magistrate has indicated to be his will, is law in regard to the citizens as individuals.
8. (19) Quidquid omnes respublicae significarunt se velle, id in omnes ius est.
   Whatever all states have indicated to be their will, is law in regard to all of them.
9. (21) In iudicando priores sint partes eius reipublicae, unde cuiusve a cive petitur. Quod si huius officium cesset, tum respublica, quae ipsa cuiusve civis petit, eam rem iudicet.

   With regard to judicial procedure, precedence shall be given to the state which is the defendant, or whose citizen is the defendant; but if the said state proves remiss in the discharge of its judicial duty, then that state shall be the judge, which is itself the plaintiff, or whose citizen is the plaintiff.

Leges

1. (2) Vitam tueri et declinare nocitura liceat.
   It shall be permissible to defend one's life and to shun what threatens to be injurious.

2. (3) Adjungere sibi quae ad vivendum sunt utilia eaque retinere liceat. It shall be permissible to acquire for oneself, and to retain those things that are useful for life. (idem)
3. (5) Ne quis alterum laedat. Let no one inflict injury upon his fellow
4. (6) Ne quis occupet alteri occupata
   Let no one take what belongs to another.
5. (7) Maleficia corrigenda
   Evil deeds must be corrected.
6. (8) Beneficia repensanda
   Good deeds must be recompensed.
7. (10) Ut singuli cives caeteros tum universos tum singulos non modo non laederent, verum etiam tuerentur.
   Individual citizens should not only refrain from injuring other citizens, but should furthermore protect them, both collectively and individually.
8. (11) Ut cives non modo alter alteri privatim aut in commune possessa non eriperent, verum etiam singuli tum quae singulis, tum quae universis necessaria conferrent.
   Citizens should not only refrain from seizing one another's possessions, whether these be held privately or in common, but should furthermore contribute individually both that which is necessary to [other] individuals and that which is necessary to the whole.
9. (14) Ne civis adversus civem ius suum nisi iudicio exsequatur.
   No citizen shall seek to enforce his own right against a fellow citizen unless by judicial procedure.
10. (15) Ut magistratus omnia gerat e bono reipublicae.
   The magistrate shall act in all matters for the good of the state.
11. (16) Ut quidquid magistratus gessit respublica ratum habeat.
   The state shall uphold as valid every act of the magistrate.
12. (20) Ne respublica neu civilis in alteram rempublicam alteriusve civem ius suum nisi iudicio exsequatur.
   Neither the state nor any citizen thereof shall seek to enforce his own right against another state or its citizens unless by judicial procedure.
13. (22) Ut ubi simul observari possunt observentur: ubi id fieri non potest, tum potior sit quae est dignior.
   In case where [the laws] can be observed simultaneously, let them all be observed. When this is impossible, [the law] of superior rank shall prevail.
   (translations: *Commentary*, pp. 369–370.)

Grotius is not abandoning theology as we can see in his first and most important *regula*. He must have been fully aware of the epistemological problem how humans can know God's will; therefore there is a close link between the first and the second *regula*.

Regula 8 is very important for the further development of international law: *ius gentium secundarium* – later called *voluntarium* in *De iure belli ac pacis* – paves the way, from the late eighteenth century onwards, for a pure positivist approach towards international law. But this *regula* is also an instance in a very long and complicated discussion about the exact boundaries between *ius naturale* and *ius gentium*. As a starting point we have to go back to classical Roman law. *Ius gentium* and *ius naturale* are defined by Ulpian in two famous fragments of the Digest:

> D. 1.1.1.3–4 *Ius naturale* est quod natura omnia animalia docuit .... 4. *Ius gentium* est quo gentes humanae utuntur. Quod a naturali recedere facile intellegere licet, quia illud omnibus animalibus, hoc solis hominibus inter se commune sit.

The distinction between *ius naturale* and *ius gentium* occupied the mind of generations of ancient,[29] medieval and sixteenth century jurists.[30] Starting point for medieval jurists is here a text by Isidorus of Sevilla,[31] based on an earlier text of Hermogenian, and later taken over by Gratian.[32] Modern scholarship of the twentieth century (Lottin,[33] D'Ors[34] and Van Vlissingen[35]) in turn tried to give a survey of the history of this distinction. In an earlier

---

[29] H. Wagner, *Studien zur allgemeinen Rechtslehre des Gaius. Ius gentium und ius naturale in ihrem Verhältnis zum ius civile* (Zutphen: Terra, 1978), pp. 51ff, 57.

[30] G. Otte, *Das Privatrecht bei Francisco de Vitoria* (Köln: Böhlau, 1964), 24ff.

[31] Isidorus of Sevilla, Etymologiae 5.6: '*Ius gentium* est sedium occupatio, aedificatio, munitio, bella, captivitates, servitutes, postliminia, foedera, paces, induciae, legatorum violandorum religio, connubia inter alienigenas prohibita; et inde *ius gentium*, quod eo iure omnes fere gentes utuntur'. Isidorus must have derived this text from an earlier one of the Roman jurist Hermogenian (± AD 300), surviving in D. 1.1.5: 'Ex hoc iure gentium introducta bella, discretae gentes, regna condita, dominia distincta, agris termini positi, aedificia collocata, commercium, emptiones venditiones, locationes conductiones, obligationes institutae: exceptis quibusdam quae iure civili introductae sunt'.

[32] In his *Decretum*, D. I, 9.

[33] O. Lottin, 'La nature du péché de l'ignorance', *Revue Thomiste*, 37 (1932), 634-652; 723-738 (repr. in Lottin, *Psychologie et Morale aux XIIe et XIIIe Siècles*, III-1 (Gembloux: Duculot, 1949), pp. 11-51); O. Lottin, 'Le problème de l'ignorantia iuris de Gratien à Saint Thomas d'Aquin', *Recherches de Théologie ancienne et médiévale*, 5 (1933), 345-368. (repr. in Lottin, *Psychologie et Morale*, III-1, pp. 53-96).

[34] A. D'Ors, 'En torno a la definición Isidoriana del *ius gentium*', in *Derecho de Gentes y organizacion internacional* (Santiago de Compostella: Seminario de Estudios Internacionales "Alvaro Pelayo" de la Universidad de Santiago de Compostella, 1956-), I, pp. 11-40, esp. pp. 33ff.

[35] P. Clementinus a Vlissingen, *De evolutione definitionis iuris gentium, Studium historico-iuridicum de doctrina iuris gentium apud Auctores Classicos Saec. XVI–XVIII* (Rome: Universitas Gregoriana, 1940), pp. 52ff.

publication (which still calls for further investigation), we have argued that the combined set of definitions of *ius naturale* and *ius gentium* by Ulpian was caused by his syncretism aimed at combining the Stoic concept of οἰκείωσις (community only between rational i.e. human beings) and the Peripatetic corresponding notion (οἰκειώτης exists between all living creatures).[36] As we have shown elsewhere, it is possible to show with a chain of quotations of Gaius, Isidorus of Sevilla and Vitoria how the content of *ius gentium* (not: *ius naturale*) gradually lost its metaphysical connotation and was at last only the law determined by a powerful group of nations.[37] *Ius gentium* for Grotius still refers to metaphysics, but can in another contexts mean plainly international law as well. This applies both to *De iure praedae* and to *De iure belli ac pacis.*

De iure belli ac pacis

In *De iure belli ac pacis* Grotius maintains the structure with *prolegomena*, but now with far more sophistication. The *prolegomena* now serve as a kind of preface, as in the literal sense 'what has to be read at first', in which Grotius mentions the sources which he is going to use and indicates the reasons for writing this book. One of the important passages is where he makes the famous statement commonly known as 'Etiamsi daremus' (§ 11). We have to leave aside here the evolution of Grotius's thoughts about the theological roots of natural law. We can only refer to the extensive literature on this passage. Grotius says that in the *unthinkable* case[38] that there would be no God, there still would be natural law based on common reason.[39] The secularization of

---

[36] L. Winkel, 'Einige Bemerkungen über *ius naturale* und *ius gentium*', in: *"us est ars boni et aequi", Festschrift für Wolfgang Waldstein* (Karlsruhe: Steiner, 1993), pp. 443-449; see already C.O. Brink, 'Οἰκείωσις and οἰκειώτης, Theophrastus and Zeno on Nature in Moral Theory', *Phronesis*, 1 (1956), 123–145; D. Nörr, *Rechtskritik in der römischen Antike* (München: Bayerische Akademie der Wissenschaften, 1974), p. 80, n. 150.

[37] See my article 'The Peace Treaties of Westphalia as an Instance of the Reception of Roman Law' in *Peace Treaties and International Law in European History*, ed. by R. Lesaffer (Cambridge: CUP 2004), pp. 222-237; in a different perspective see my article in the *Studies for Okko Behrends* 'Ist die Bedeutung der gaianischen naturalis ratio von der Zeit abhängig?' (forthcoming).

[38] The phrase 'Etiamsi daremus' is according to Latin grammar an irrealis.

[39] L.F.M. Besselink, 'The impious hypothesis revisited', *Grotiana*, 9 (1988), 3-63; F. Todescan, *Etiamsi daremus, Studi sinfonici sul diritto naturale* (Padova: CEDAM, 2003). See also the article of Mark Somos in this volume and L.C. Winkel, 'Retour à Grotius: lecture critique de la tradition scolastique', *Revue d'éthique et de théologie morale. le supplément*: Degré de modernité des états en Europe, 1er dossier, 226 (2003), 15–26.

natural law by Grotius is sometimes heavily overestimated, for in the later part of the same *Prolegomena* the link with Christian theology remains basically unchallenged.

Another legally very important passage is *Prolegomena*, 8, in which the main rules of *ius naturale* are summarised, in a much shorter and concise way than in *De iure praedae*:

> Haec vero quam rudi modo iam expressimus societatis custodia humano intellectui conveniens, fons est eius iuris[40] quod proprie tali nomine appellatur: quo pertinent alieni abstinentia,[41,42] et si quid alieni habeamus aut lucri inde fecerimus restitution,[43] promissorum implendorum obligatio,[44] damni culpa dati reparation,[45] et poenae inter homines meritum.[46]
>
> This maintenance of the social order, which we have roughly sketched, and which is consonant with human intelligence, is the source of law properly so called. To this sphere of law belong the abstaining from that which is another's, the restoration to another of anything of his which we may have, together with any gain which we may have received from it; the obligation to fulfil promises, the making good of a loss incurred through our fault, and the inflicting of penalties upon men according to their deserts. (translation F.W. Kelsey, Carnegie Endowment)

'Societatis custodia': here, Grotius differs from antique sources, putting forward the social and political order in a wider sense than was done earlier.

'Intellectui conveniens': This expression is a sign that ethical intellectualism, found in Plato, Aristotle and also in Stoic philosophy is part of Grotius's

---

[40] Cfr. Cic. *De legibus*, 1.15.43 (SVF III 344).

[41] Inviolability of property, derived from Roman law, cfr the *formula* of the *reivindicatio*: *aio rem meam esse*.

[42] Porphyrius, *De Abstinentia*, III, 26 '[Greek omitted].....Iustitia in eo sita est ut abstineatur alienis neque noceatur non nocentibus'. Added in the editions *De iure belli ac pacis* 1642, 1646.

[43] From this formula one can deduce the doctrine of unjust enrichment. Historically, this doctrine has its origin in the scholastic philosophy of restitution which in its turn stems from Aristotle's *justitia commutativa* elaborated in Book V of the *Nicomachean Ethics*.

[44] A generalization of a non-Roman principle derived from canon law. Most *pacta* were not enforceable in Roman law. There we found a well-structured system of contracts, and the *pacta* were at first especially relevant for the *actiones bonae fidei*.

[45] A generalization of Aquilian liability for *damnum iniuria datum*. *Iniuria* was already in early Roman law (Quintus Mucius Scaevola) conceived as responsibility for *culpa*. *Reparatio* implies that the aim of the action is no longer a penalty, as it was the case in classical Roman law, but only compensation for damages.

[46] Penalties conceived as retaliation, not as prevention, as we find occasionally in Roman law (*Collatio* 1,11). See A. Wacke, *Unius Poena. Metus Multorum, Abhandlungen zum römischen Strafrecht* (Napels: Jovene, 2008), 21 ff.

thought as well.[47] The reference to Seneca, *De beneficiis*, IV, 13, was added only in the editions of 1642 and 1646 and is another indication of Grotius's gradually growing and maybe even rather late insight in Stoic philosophy. A further indication of this hypothesis is the fact that the most famous 'appetitus societatis' is linked with the Stoic οἰκείωσις only in the editions since 1631,[48] as was already mentioned by Max Pohlenz.[49]

The model of the *Institutes of Justinian* is used with sophistication by Grotius in his *Introduction to Dutch Jurisprudence*.[50] This leads to the supposition that Grotius is using the model of the *Institutes* also in the more or less contemporary *De iure belli ac pacis*, by extending the rather simple, but in reality rather complicated model of it in expounding not only basic principles of Roman private law, but also of international law. In *De iure belli ac pacis* Roman law is presented as a whole in a form derived from the *Institutes of Justinian*. What does this mean in later legal terms after Donellus?

Personae — *Res:* — *Actiones*

- quod nostrum est : ius in re
dominium/iura in re aliena
- quod nobis debetur : ius ad rem
obligationes - ex delicto/quasi ex delicto
- ex contractu/quasi ex contractu

Indeed we could argue that the first book of *De iure belli ac pacis* refers to the actors in international law, in analogy with the law of persons in the institutional system, and that after announcement in *Prolegomena*, 28 book II and III are referring to *ius ad bellum* and *ius in bello* respectively, maybe as an at least terminological echo of *ius ad rem* and *ius in re*, personal rights and real rights in private law.[51] Individual rights are indeed the core of the institutional system. This applies already in Antiquity and continues to do so in the sixteenth and seventeenth centuries.

---

[47] See e.g. Cic. *Tusc. disp.*, 4.12 (SVF III, 438): 'id cum constanter prudenterque fit, eiusmodi adpetitionem Stoici βούλησιν appellant, nos appellamus voluntatem. Eam illi putant in solo esse sapiente, quam sic definiunt: voluntas est, quae quid **cum ratione** desiderat.' This is one of the clearest texts of ethical intellectualism, see A. Dihle. *The Theory of Will in Classical Antiquity* (Berkeley: University of California Press, 1982), p. 133.

[48] Winkel, 'Les origines antiques', 395.

[49] M. Pohlenz, *Die Stoa. Geschichte einer geistigen Bewegung*, 2 vols, 5th edn (Göttingen: Vandenhoeck Ruprecht, 1978), I, p. 471, II, p. 229.

[50] R. Feenstra, 'La systématique du droit dans l'oeuvre de Grotius', in *La sistematica giuridica. Storia, teoria e problemi attuali* (Rome: Istituto della Enciclopedia Italiana, 1991), pp. 333–343, repr. as no. 7 in Feenstra, *Legal Scholarship*; see also the additions: pp. 8–9.

[51] R. Feenstra, *Ius in re* – Het begrip zakelijk recht in historisch perspectief (Zwolle: Tjeenk Willink, 1979), p. 25; further investigation might be useful to find out, whether these terms already occur in *IBP*.

If this is true, it is an important instance in an actual debate between legal historians and historians of political ideas. The latter are following in majority the opinion that the notion of subjective rights originates not in Roman law of Antiquity, but in later medieval jurisprudence and theology, especially since William of Ockam. This opinion goes back to the French legal philosopher Michel Villey, of which Richard Tuck is one of its most influential defenders.[52] However, the *ius utendi fruendi*, occurring in the first 'draft' of the *Institutes* written by Gaius, ± AD 160, which was followed by Justinian, in the explanation of ownership is one of the clearest examples of 'ius' in the subjective sense. We cannot fully enter here into this complicated debate about the discovery of the notion of subjective rights, but we adhere to the decisive arguments given by Donahue,[53] who gives a full list of *Digest* texts in which we find what later would be called *iura in re aliena*, but *iura* are undoubtedly subjective rights. An argument which maybe should be stressed with more emphasis, is the change within the institutional system: actions, as in classical Roman law, do not play a preponderant role anymore after AD 250. Procedural systems *per formulam* with prescribed *actiones* in the 'Edictum Perpetuum' made way for the inquisitory free styled *cognitio extraordinaria*. This seems to us a far more plausible explanation for the earlier dogmatic elaboration of subjective rights than the historical references to amongst others the medieval Franciscan model of poverty and the rise of social contract as has been advocated by Michel Villey[54] and in his footsteps by Richard Tuck.[55]

Conclusions

In chapter II of *De jure praedae*, Grotius is elaborating the Roman concepts of *ius naturale* and *ius gentium* in his *regulae*. In the *leges* we find dispositions of a general nature mostly derived from Roman law. In so far, the distinction between *regulae* and *leges* is between more formal legal rules and more material ones.

---

[52] R. Tuck, *Natural Law Theories. Their Origin and Development* (Cambridge: CUP, 1979), pp. 22ff, quoting several works of Michel Villey.

[53] Ch. Donahue, 'Ius in the subjective sense in Roman law. Reflexions on Villey and Tierny', in *A Ennio Cortese*, I (Rome: Il Cigno, 2001), pp. 506–535. See already G. Pugliese, '"Res corporales", "res incorporales" e il problema del diritto soggettivo', *Rivista Italiana per le Scienze Giuridiche*, 5 (1951), 237–274 (repr. in Pugliese, *Scritti giuridici scelti*, III (Napels: Jovene, 1985), pp. 225–262).

[54] M. Villey, *La formation de la pensée juridique moderne*, 4th edn (Paris: Montchretien, 1975).

[55] Tuck, *Natural Law Theory*, 7ff.

This systematization of *ius gentium* and its difference with *ius naturale* is in fact one of the few systematic attempts made in *De iure praedae*, in other respects *De iure praedae* has remained a mainly historical and legal exposé on an actual political and legal issue. We can conclude that Grotius made an attempt to construct a legal system with the help of general principles (*regulae* and *leges*). A further systematization is not yet visible in *De iure praedae.*

This is different in *De iure belli ac pacis.* Hence the different, more epic structure of the *Prolegomena*: no longer a list of general *regulae* and *leges,* but a philosophical introduction to legal enforcement both in private and international law. In the following books of *De iure belli ac pacis* not only general principles, but also the institutional system is visible, in accordance with general tendencies of humanistic jurisprudence. In this institutional framework individual rights of persons and states are incorporated. These individual rights are by no means a new phenomenon.

Law, War and Method in the *Commentary on the Law of Prize* by Hugo Grotius

Merio Scattola
Professor of History of Political Ideas, Università degli Studi di Padova, Padua, Italy
e-mail: merio.scattola@unipd.it

Abstract
The question whether both enemies in a war could claim the same right, was a fundamental topic in the early modern theory of war and Grotius treated it briefly in his *On Law of Prize and Booty*. The jurisprudence of the seventeenth century developed two explanations: the Scholastic tradition held that only one party could fight with right reason, whereas some authors of the humanistic tradition thought that in some cases it was impossible to solve this question. Grotius took elements from both traditions, applying them to two different levels of his argument. If we namely consider the rulers, we should accept the Scholastic conclusion that only one party can fight with right reason. But the subordinate soldiers do not always have an exhaustive knowledge of the situation and need first of all to acknowledge that their superiors command legitimately. Thus, each level uses a different logical relationship in the Aristotelian square because the enemies follow in the former case the pattern of contrary propositions, but in the latter they obey a pattern of subcontrary propositions.

Keywords
theory of war, right reason, Late Scholastic, legal dialectic, international law, system, method

The Question

The question whether both enemies in a conflict may have an equal right to fight was a central topic in the doctrine of war of early modern times although Grotius treated it in his *Commentary on the Law of Prize and Booty* only within a few pages. Presenting this issue as an appendix to the seventh chapter of his book,[1] he declared that this was a well-known subject, and as a matter of fact, all main authors of the sixteenth century had raised it when treating the

I would like to thank Hans Blom for his friendly help in formulating this article.

[1] Hugo Grotius, *De iure praedae commentarius*. Ex auctoris codice descripsit et vulgavit H. G. Hamaker (The Hague: Nijhoff, 1868), [= *IPC*] VII, Corollarium quaestionis VI, pp. 83–84.

law of war. Peter Haggenmacher has described the main lines of the debate on this topic, which included authors from both theology and civil law such as Francisco de Vitoria, Melchor Cano, Gabriel Vázquez or Raffaele Fulgosio and Andrea Alciato.[2] Nevertheless, the widespread occurrence of this question in scholarly discussion is only one reason for its exceptional meaning, since the same problem is in fact of the greatest importance for the creation of (modern) law of war and of international law in general.

One might say that both – law of war and international law – really began when philosophy and learned jurisprudence accepted the fact that both parties in a war may have an equal right to fight. This is the case with Thomas Hobbes, Samuel Pufendorf or Christian Thomasius. In the natural law theories of the late seventeenth century individuals can have genuine rights and duties because they live under a sovereign, but sovereigns themselves have no mutual obligations since they still live in the same state of nature in which individuals lived before they came together in a society.[3] In such a state of nature, both individuals and commonwealths have all the rights they can enforce. We could say that they all have the same rights over the same things, so that none of them has a particular right to do, to achieve or to possess something special. Since it is impossible (Hobbes) or very difficult (Pufendorf, Thomasius and disciples) to find out exactly the rights of individuals and commonwealths in the state of nature, their claims are equivalent, and they have an equal right to fight one another as enemies. In other words, they cannot measure the rightness of their claims upon an objective measure of justice that can determine, who is right and who is wrong, because both have the same right to judge their quarrel. As an example I would like to quote a brief passage from a book by Nikolaus Hieronymus Gundling, a disciple and a friend of Thomasius.

> Which of the fighting enemies, I ask, should judge whether the one or the other has begun the hostilities with a just reason? The enemy? Well then the other too must have the same faculty of judging in his own case.[4]

---

[2] Peter Haggenmacher, *Grotius et la doctrine de la guerre juste* (Paris: Presses Universitaires de France, 1983), pp. 203–223.

[3] Samuel Pufendorf, *De officio hominis et civis iuxta legem naturalem libri duo* (Cantabrigiae: Impensis Ioannis Creed, 1682; 1st edn Lund: 1673), ed. by Walther Schücking (New York: OUP, 1927), I.1.6, p. 100; I.1.10-11, pp. 102–103.

[4] Nikolaus Hieronymus Gundling, *De efficientia metus tum in promissionibus liberarum gentium tum etiam hominum privatorum auxiliisque contra metum liber singularis [...]* (Halae Magdeburgicae: Prostat in officina Rengeriana, 1711), in Gundling, *Exercitationum academicarum tomus secundus [...]* (Halae: In officina libraria Rengeriana, 1737), II.14, pp. 23–24. Cf. Nikolaus Hieronymus Gundling, *Ius naturae ac gentium connexa ratione novaque methodo elaboratum [...]* (Halae Magdeburgicae: Prostat in officina libraria Rengeriana, 1728; 1st edn 1714), 36.107, p. 464.

Therefore, international justice can only be valid on a voluntarist and positive basis, as a collection of agreements (treaties and customs) between free subjects. The twentieth century version of this doctrine is the theory of anarchy in international relations, as it was stated and repeated by Hans Morgenthau or in Italy by Sergio Pistone.[5]

Positions about the Problem in the Sixteenth Century

If we consider the discussions in the sixteenth century, the opinions in the debate about this topic, as Peter Haggenmacher has pointed out, can be reduced to two main positions. On the one hand, the traditional point of view of lawyers and theologians held to the idea that war is an act of jurisdiction and that therefore only one side can be right according to the legal and moral circumstances of the disputed case.[6] In this sense Francisco de Vitoria assumed that hostilities should be always preceded by a formal judgement of the supreme magistrate. The king should gather together the crown council, hear the opinions of the counsellors and pronounce his verdict against the enemy.[7] He can then justly inflict a punishment upon the guilty enemy by declaring a just war. War is therefore always the consequence of an injustice, as Grotius himself points out in the *Law of Prize* while describing the conditions on which a war is just. He says: 'A just war is execution of justice' (VII, p. 66).[8] Before discussing his own theory, based on the classical four Aristotelian

---

[5] Hans J. Morgenthau and Kenneth W. Thompson, *Politics among Nations. The Struggle for Power and Peace*, 6th edn (New York: Knopf, 1985; 1st edn 1948), especially pp. 31–37; Sergio Pistone, 'Introduzione', in *Politica di potenza e imperialismo. L'analisi dell'imperialismo alla luce della dottrina della ragion di Stato*, ed. by Sergio Pistone (Milan: Angeli, 1973) pp. 7–62; Sergio Pistone, 'Relazioni internazionali', in *Dizionario di politica*, 2nd edn, ed. by Norberto Bobbio, Nicola Matteucci and Gianfranco Pasquino (Turin: Utet, 1990; 1st edn 1983), pp. 949[a]–959[b].

[6] Antoninus Florentinus [Antonio Pierorri de' Forciglioni], *Summae sacrae theologiae, iuris pontificii et Caesarei tertia pars [...]* (Venetiis: Apud Iuntas, 1582), III.4.1.9, fol. 65va; Francisco de Vitoria, *Relectio de iure belli o paz dinamica. Escuela Española de la Paz. Primera generación 1526–1560*, ed. by Luciano Pereña, Vidal Abril, Carlos Baciero, Antonio Garcia and Francisco Maseda (Madrid: Consejo superior de investigaciones científicas, 1981), 4.1.6, p. 138.

[7] Vitoria, *Relectio de iure belli*, 3.4, p. 126: 'Una sola causa iusti belli est, scilicet iniuria accepta'.

[8] Thomas Aquinas, *Summa theologiae* (Albae Pompeiae: Editiones Paulinae, 1962; repr. 1988), IIa IIae, q. 40, a. 1: Utrum bellare semper sit peccatum, ręsp., p. 1266[b]–1267[a]; Gerhard Beestermöller, *Thomas von Aquin und der gerechte Krieg. Friedensethik im theologischen Kontext der* Summa theologiae (Cologne: Bachem, 1990), pp. 92–98; Domingo de Soto, *De iustitia et iure libri decem. De la justicia y del derecho en diez libros [...]*, ed. by Venancio Diego Carro, Span. tr. by Marcelino González Ordóñez (Madrid: Instituto de estudios políticos, 1967–1968; 1st edn Salmanticae: Excudebat Andreas a Portonariis, 1556–1557), V.1. 7, p. 400[b]; Domingo de Soto, *Quaestio 40 de bello*, in Vitoria, *Relectio de iure belli*, 1. 4–6, pp. 304–309.

causes, he classifies briefly all previous attempts and arranges them into seven groups (V, p. 58–59). Nevertheless, all doctrines of the past assume that war is a punishment of an injustice,[9] and that therefore one of the two enemies must be wrong since either he has stolen something or is in debt or has committed some other crime. The other one must consequently be right.

The traditional theory admitted only one case in which there could be some doubts. It was the case that the wrong one was confused by such ignorance that he assumed to be right.[10] In this case, it seems that two parties fight with equal right reasons. But it is only apparently so, because only one of them is justified, whereas the other is thinking to defend justice, but in truth is fighting for a wrong end. Consequently, the enemies are only by chance (*ex accidenti*) combating in this extreme case with equal right.[11]

On the other hand, humanistic jurisprudence, by amplifying the same argument of ignorance, could assume that both parties were justified to wage war. Andrea Alciato, who held to the position of Raffaele Fulgosio, believed that in the most cases the causes that lead to a war are so uncertain and obscure that it is in fact impossible to find out on whose side justice is.[12] This conclusion leads the scholastic argument to its extreme consequences and imagines a situation in which ignorance is so deep on both sides that every decision about justice is impossible.

---

[9] Vitoria, *Relectio de iure belli*, 4.1.6–7, pp. 140–142.

[10] Vitoria, *Relectio de iure belli*, 4.1.8, p. 156: 'Quartum dubium est, an possit esse bellum iustum ex utraque parte. Pro quo sit prima propositio: Seclusa ignorantia manifestum est quod non posse contingere.'

[11] Vitoria, *Relectio de iure belli*, 4.1.9, pp. 156–160; Diego de Covarrubias y Leyva, *Regulae. Peccatum. De regulis iuris, lib. 6. Relectio […] Ex secunda Authoris recognitione aucta et locupletata* (Salmanticae: Excudebat Andreas à Portonariis, 1558 ; 1st edn Salamanca: 1554), 10.6: Bellum an possit esse utrinque iustum, fol. 78^{rb-vb}, Gabriel Vázquez, *Commentariorum ac disputationum in Primam secundae sancti Thomae tomus primus […]* (Lugduni: Sumptibus Iacobi Cardon, 1631; 1st edn Compluti: Ex officina Ioannis Gratiani, apud viduam, 1599), 64.3.15–16, p. 305^{a-b}: 'Tunc autem bellum esset iustum ex utraque parte […], quod videtur absurdum, quia, ut iustum sit bellum ex una parte, ex altera aliquo modo debet esse iniustitia, et culpa re ipsa, aut saltem iure praesumpta […]. Tamen […] nec ullus hactenus ausus fuit concedere hoc iustum bellum ex utraque parte, nisi ex accidenti, nimirum ob ignorantiam invincibilem alterius partis; quia unus ignorat invincibili ignorantia aliquid quod alius certo novit: qualis non censetur ignorantia, quae accidit ex opinionum probabilium contrarietate.'

[12] Andrea Alciato, *Paradoxorum ad pratum libri sex […]* (Lugduni: Iacobus Giunta, 1537), II.21: Bella utrinque licita esse et explicata quaestio doctorum antehac pene irresolubilis Fulgosiique opinio quaedam approbata, pp. 101–105; Raffaele Fulgosio, *In primam Pandectarum partem commentariorum tomus I. et II. […]* (Lugduni: Apud Hugonem et haeredes Aemonis a Porta, 1544), in Digesta, I.1.5 (De iustitia et iure, Ex hoc iure). But in his *Consilia* the same Fulgosio held to the idea that war is execution of justice. Cf. Raffaele Fulgosio, *Consilia excellentissimi domini Rafaelis Fulgosii de Placentia* (Impressa Brixiae: Per Iacobum Britannicum, 1590), cons. 235, fols 228^{r} A–229^{r} A, here fol. 228^{v} A.

Grotius's Solution

Grotius proposes in his *Law of Prize* a complex explanation that seems to take elements from both traditions.[13] In fact he holds to the scholastic doctrine, but he systematizes it into a general frame, in which the humanistic objections appear as particular cases and can be solved without contradiction. Here, he uses method and systematic order as a magnifying glass that clearly shows the pattern of the traditional doctrine and makes it work better.

Grotius intensifies and enlarges the traditional distinction between the chief of an army and his soldiers and he observes that the real difference between enemies is to be found only on the basis of this distinction (VII, 82–83). First of all we have to consider that, if war is waged on the four Aristotelian causes – as he assumes –, three of them can be accomplished by both sides. Both enemies can have a valid instrumentality, a proper way or form of fighting and a correct end, but only one of them will possess the right matter. The matter, the question debated and solved with a war, is justice, and only one party in a quarrel can have it on his side. However, this general principle is valid only for persons who can exercise their whole right and are *sui iuris*. But not all persons living in a commonwealth are equal in this regard, because most of them have transferred their will to the commonwealth and then to the supreme magistrate, with the consequence that only the supreme magistrate (the king, the aristocratic or the democratic council) is still in the plenitude of his rights. In a proper sense, the full use of right pertains only to those human beings who can use their will freely. Subjects, on the other hand, cannot exercise their will freely, but only through the ruler. So they do not possess their legal faculty immediately, but only 'by analogy' or 'by comparison' (VII, 67). It is therefore necessary to distinguish between the position of rulers and the position of subjects, and they will answer the question of the matter in a different way.

The Rulers

The question about justice in a war can be formulated in a strict sense only for rulers. It is therefore only the position, or the opinion of the ruler that shows which side is right. As Grotius explains, justice has the logical form of the relationship between the 'contraries' on the traditional Square of Opposition,[14]

---

13 Haggenmacher, *Grotius et la doctrine de la guerre juste*, pp. 305–311.

14 Aristotle, *On Interpretation*, 17^b 16–26. Cf. Marcello Zanatta, 'Introduzione', in Aristoteles, *Della interpretazione*, introd., tr., ann. by Marcello Zanatta (Milan: Rizzoli, 1992), pp. 34–39.

that is, between two universal propositions of the type *A* and *E*. In his words: 'Here too happens the same that happens between contrary propositions, which can be both false, but not both true' (VII, p. 83). In terms of modern logics, justice has the form of the relation between '$(x)\ \Phi x$' and '$(x)\ {\sim}\Phi x$', which has the same truth table as the relation '${\sim}p \vee {\sim}q$'.[15] When two persons claim an equal right over the same thing, the following three cases are possible: the first person is right and the second wrong, or the second is right and the first wrong, or both of them are wrong. What is impossible is that both of them are right. In some cases it can happen that both kings have a false idea about the reason of the war they fight. Their mistakes may be excusable, and so it could seem that both have a right to wage war. Nevertheless, the fact that their errors are negligible cannot transform them into right causes because the rightness of an action can be measured only upon an objective law. 'As a matter of fact, the actions of those people who act willingly, if they ought to be just, must essentially agree with the law' (VII, p. 83).

So far, Grotius's theory is similar to the opinion of Francisco de Vitoria, who is here explicitly quoted.[16] But neither the one nor the other explains why justice in a war obeys to that particular logical pattern. Gabriel Vázquez gave some more information in discussing Vitoria's opinions about the most difficult case, that is, when both enemies give similar und equally probable reasons for their claims. When both parties have doubtful reasons, the question is easily solved, for none of them may defend its claims by war. The case also is simple when only one party has indubitable reasons to maintain its pretensions, because then one must defend the truth even by waging a war. Difficult is the decision when each party has reasons that seem good enough to declare war, but that cannot clearly prevail over the opposite. In this case Vitoria had assumed that the parties must search for an agreement on the basis of general rules.[17] If this is not possible, one king may uphold the possession of the disputed land even without mutual consent, what nevertheless, as contemporaries noted,[18] would give his opponent sufficient reason for a just war. Martín de Azpilcueta went on and declared that two kings in this situation may

[15] Irving M. Copi, *Introduction to Logic* (New York: MacMillan, 1953), pp. 123–150; Irving M. Copi, *Symbolic Logic* (New York: MacMillan, 1954), pp. 66–75; Julius R. Weinberg, *Introduzione al positivismo logico*, tr. by Ludovico Geymonat (Turin: Einaudi, 1950), p. 92; Ettore Casari, *Introduzione alla logica* (Turin: Utet, 1997), pp. 50–54.

[16] Vitoria, *Relectio de iure belli*, 4.1.9, p. 156.

[17] Vitoria, *Relectio de iure belli*, 4.1.8.4, pp. 150–152.

[18] Vázquez, *Commentariorum ac disputationum in Primam secundae sancti Thomae tomus primus*, 64.3.9–10, p. 304^{a-b}.

fight one another only if in doing so they do not seriously endanger the survival of the Christian community.[19]

Gabriel Vázquez, however, came to the conclusion that this is a false question and that such a conflict cannot exist. The solution of all difficult cases is possible because there is a universal order of justice that rules over all human actions. In this general hierarchy everything has a particular place and it is impossible that two different things occupy the same space at the same time. They could be very similar to each other, but there must be at least one difference, perhaps a very slight one, between them. In the same way two human beings cannot have exactly the same rights, because they then would be the same person. So there must be some kind of difference between them, and this makes a right judgement possible. At the same time there must be a judge able to understand that difference and to give the due judgement.[20] This principle of universal order, that solves the difficult case of a doubtful conflict, also explains why in conflicts between rulers, between genuine right-holders, only one of them can be right. The order of justice does not tolerate that two kings have exactly the same rights, so that one of them of necessity must have something more, whereas the other will have less. Since opposite propositions are in the proper sense universal statements, we should conclude that the order of justice and the claim about it have to a certain extent the attribute of being universal or are similar to universal propositions.

The Subjects

While rulers are thought of in a relationship of contrary statements,[21] subjects in war follow the pattern of 'subcontrary' propositions, that is, the relationship

---

[19] Martín de Azpilcueta, [Martinus Navarrus ab Azpilcueta], *Enchiridion, sive manuale confessariorum et paenitentium [...]* (Venetiis: Apud haeredes Francisci Ziletti, 1589; 1st Spanish edn Coimbra: 1553; 1st Latin edn Salamanca: 1557), I.25: De peccatis diversorum statuum, et primum Regum, num. 4, p. 448^{a}: 'Nono peccat, qui habet cum alio Rege Christiano super aliquo regno, vel dominio aliquam dubiam, et antiquam controversiam, quae de iure non potest extingui, quia non habent superiorem, neque bello, quippe quorum arma adeo creverunt, ut neuter ab altero omnino superari possit, nisi facta per strages copia Turcis invadendi, quod reliquum est Christiani orbis, vel bonam partem eius, et non vult in arbitros suspicione carentes convenire, nec petere, vel accipere conditiones honestas, quibus pax firma fiat.'

[20] Vázquez, *Commentariorum ac disputationum in Primam secundae sancti Thomae tomus primus*, 64.3.18–19, pp. 307^{b}–308^{a}.

[21] Cf. Covarrubias, *Regulae. Peccatum. De regulis iuris, lib. 6. Relectio*, 2.10.6, p. 77va: 'Nam cum hostes contrarii sibi sint, contraria iura necesse esse est habeant: quorum unum iustum sit, alterum vero iniustum. Nec enim ex duobus principibus bello pugnantibus ob aliquam provinciam, quam quilibet eorum sibi propriam esse censet, in veritate potest uterque iustitiam habere

between two particular sentences of the type *I* and *O*, which in modern logical computation appear respectively as '($x) Φx' and '($x) ~Φx', and has the same truth values as '*p* v *q*'.[22] We saw that the statements in a quarrel between rulers or commonwealths have the form of propositions about the same object. Something is said to be owned or owed or have being done by someone. And two such statements cannot be valid at the same time. On the contrary, the statements of subjects are either true propositions about different things or probable propositions about the same thing, cases in which both statements can be valid at the same time. The necessary condition for subjects fighting in a war is that they are truly subjected to their ruler, who decides to make hostilities. Each of them is bound by a statement, perhaps by an oath, which is equally true or valid, but referring to different things, that is, to two different commonwealths and kings. This legal condition institutes a true subject, capable of fighting, and two of these subjects recognise each other as true enemies.

Since soldiers are rightful enemies on both sides, Fulgosio's and Alciato's opinion is true or, better, is not false at all, but it can be accepted only on the particular condition that it refers to subordinate fighters only. In this sense Grotius accepts in his own method or, as he said, in his own 'order' (I, 7) a typical process of the medieval dialectics and of the scholastic tradition.[23] He demonstrates that two diverging opinions are only apparently in opposition, because the one is simply a specification, a limitation or an exception of the other one. The idea that only one enemy is right and the idea that both enemies are right seem to exclude each other, but they can both be true when we displace them to two different levels of the argumentation. The first is valid when we think of the rulers at the top of the argument. But if we look at the bottom of the argument, where the infantry stands, the second one becomes true as well.

Obedience to a supreme magistrate is therefore a necessary reason in order to assume the status of a genuine enemy. Who acts without, outside or against the command of a legitimate superior cannot be regarded and treated in this way.

---

sibi fautricem. Siquidem is iustam habet causam, cuius ea provincia propria sit, ex quo necesse est, quod alter iniustam causam foveat, cum contraria haec duo sint iustum et iniustum. Unde plane illud mihi constat, non posse quo ad veritatem iustum bellum utrinque esse.'

[22] Copi, *Introduction to Logic*, pp. 123–150; Copi, *Symbolic Logic*, pp. 72–73.

[23] On the doctrines of method and order in the political theories of the late sixteenth and the early seventeenth centuries, cf. Merio Scattola, 'Arnisaeus, Zabarella e Piccolomini: la discussione sul metodo della filosofia pratica alle origini della disciplina politica moderna', in *La presenza dell'aristotelismo padovano nella filosofia della prima modernità*, ed. by Gregorio Piaia (Rome: Antenore, 2002), pp. 273–309.

Inside a commonwealth such unlawful enemies are tyrants and rebels, outside it robbers and pirates (VII, p. 84). But we should not think that this condition alone is sufficient, and that whatever subjects obeying to whatever commands are true enemies. In fact, the orders they obey to must be reasonable, not clearly absurd, not inhuman, or, as Grotius says, using the same scholastic terminology as Bartolomé de Medina and Gabriel Vázquez, they must contain a 'probable reason' (VII, p. 84). On the one hand, subjects still remain responsible for their behaviour although they have transferred their will into the will of the supreme magistrate. And this also is the reason why the whole commonwealth must pay for the faults of its king. On the other hand there must be certain limits to the activity of the supreme magistrate, and his subjects should be able to recognise to some extent the content of justice and truth of the commands they receive. They must have, although only partially, access to that universal order of justice in which, as we saw, magistrates are responsible and in which there cannot be two lawful enemies at the same time.

As Grotius himself makes clear, the ideas that there is a double level of responsibility and that only subjects may fight with equal rights on both sides were already defended by authors such as Francisco de Vitoria, Domingo de Soto and Diego de Covarrubias,[24] authors whom Grotius quotes as the *Scholastici* (II, p. 17) and who really make up the very bulk of his sources. Vitoria had admitted the 'invincible ignorance' of one of the enemies, valid both for rulers and for the subordinated.[25] Besides, he had acknowledged that subjects are in a special condition and that they can combat with equal right reasons since obedience to a supreme magistrate is for them a sufficient reason to fight.[26]

Soto paid even more attention to the situation of fighting subjects. He repeated the theory of Vitoria that only one side in a war may be right,[27]

---

[24] Grotius, *IPC,* VII, p. 84, n. 1 quotes Vitoria, *Relectio de iure belli,* 41.9, p. 158; Covarrubias, *Regulae. Peccatum. De regulis iuris, lib. 6. Relectio,* 2.10.6, p. 78^{rb-va}; Soto, *De iustitia et iure libri decem,* V.17, p. 400^{b}; Fernando Vázquez Menchaca, *Controversiarum illustrium aliarumque usu frequentium libri tres,* (Valladolid: Cuesta, 1931; 1st edn Venetiis: 1564), I.9.16, vol. 1, pp. 225–226.

[25] Vitoria, *Relectio de iure belli,* 4.1.4, p. 156: 'Posita ignorantia probabili facti aut iuris, potest esse ex ea parte qua est vera iustitia bellum iustum per se; ex altera autem parte bellum iustum, id est excusatum a peccato bona fide.' Cf. Heinz-Gerhard Justenhoven, *Francisco de Vitoria zu Krieg und Frieden* (Cologne: Bachem, 1991), pp. 121–125.

[26] Vitoria, *Relectio de iure belli,* 4.1.9, p. 158: 'Item ex parte subditorum saepe potest contingere. Dato enim quod princeps qui gerit bellum iniustum sciret iniustitiam belli, tamen (ut dictum est) subditi possunt bona fide sequi principem suum. Et sic ex utraque parte subditi licite pugnant, ut notum est.'

[27] Soto, *De iustitia et iure libri decem,* V.1.7, p. 400^{b}.

recognized the possibility of invincible ignorance, but posed a new question, peculiar to subjects, whether it is possible that two innocents fight each other. So he posed the traditional question of the two rightful enemies, but in the form of a double negation, since an innocent is a person who is not wrong. In a battlefield – he argued – offenders and innocents face each other and they are not able to understand – which might be possible in a duel – who among the enemies is really guilty, and who is not.[28] When a soldier is being assaulted by an enemy, he should ask himself whether the enemy is guilty or innocent, and in the latter case he should persuade himself of being wrong and should not resist. But each enemy for himself has a probable reason to fight, even though he is convinced that the other one is innocent. Moreover, one should defend one's own life even against an innocent and even if, in doing so, one is compelled to hurt or kill the aggressor. It is therefore possible that both enemies are innocent, that is, not wrong, that is, right.[29]

In 1599 Gabriel Vázquez explicitly distinguished the position of the king from the position of the subordinate officers and soldiers, just as Grotius was going to do some years later, and made even more distinctions for instance between the wise and the ignorant. Both Vázquez and Grotius independently came to similar conclusions from the same scholastic premises.[30] Vázquez, like Vitoria and Soto, argued that it is impossible that two rulers involved in a war have exactly the same rights and he held to this idea so firmly that, as we have already seen, he rejected some of the exceptions raised by Vitoria. With regard

[28] Soto, *De iustitia et iure libri decem*, V.1.7, p. 400^{b}: 'Video militem in me irruentem, quem scio innocentem esse, puta qui credit bellum iustum contra me gerere. Videtur ratio suadere quod tunc non possim illum occidere. Nam bellum non potest esse iustum ex utraque parte. Si ergo ille iuste contra me pugnat, non possum ego iuste me defendere.'

[29] Soto, *De iustitia et iure libri decem*, V.1.7, p. 400^{b}: 'Respondetur nihilo minus licere. Primum quia iuste ambo pugnare possumus ex ignorantia, quando uterque putat se iustam defendere causam. Praeterea, licet tunc in conflictu uni militum constaret iustitiam ab alterius parte stare, potest se defendere, quia non tenetur illam pati mortem. Quare non solum tunc ex falsa praesumptione (ut quidam aiunt) nempe quia uterque putat alterutrum esse nocentem, sed etiam si sciat esse innocentem, licite tunc pugnat. Non posset autem alterum occidere nisi in suam defensam. Sed rogas, utrum miles possit alterum aggredi quem scit esse innocentem. Respondetur quod si bona fide credat iustum se gerere bellum, etiam si alium putet esse innocentem, puta quia vel idem ipse credit vel invitus in exercitu retinetur, potest illum aggredi, tum quod aggressus ipse in bello est defensio, tum etiam quod unus princeps ius habet aggrediendi alterum. Qui autem miles crederet bellum se gerere iniustum, aggredi non posset.'

[30] On the similarities between Grotius and Gabriel Vázquez cf. James St. Leger, *The* Etiamsi daremus *of Hugo Grotius. A Study in the Origins of International Law*, (Rome: Gregoriana, 1962), pp. 135–142.

to the subjects, Vázquez resumed a theory of Antonio de Cordoba[31] and developed new arguments in order to give it better foundations. He assumed that subjects must always fight when their ruler has a probable reason, Grotius's *ratio probabilis* (VII, 84), even if the probable reason of the ruler is weaker than their own opinion. In this case subordinates ought to give up their opinion and must adopt the weaker one of their magistrate. Otherwise, if they maintain firmly their (more probable) judgement, they would be compelled to break their obedience, which is a much worse crime. On the one scale we have the more probable opinion of the subjects minus the cost of the disobedience, on the other scale the less probable opinion of the ruler plus the good deriving from obedience. The choice is quite simple, and only a fool would prefer the first option.

An Answer to Two Questions. The Argument of Adrian Florisz

The distinction of Grotius systematises with a peculiar and brilliant sense for deductive order a bundle of problems well known in the scholastic tradition of the sixteenth century. Considering the main concerns of this tradition we can identify the reason why the problem should be divided into two separate sections, one dedicated to the ruler, the other to his subjects. As a matter of fact that distinction was necessary because the argument had to reach two different purposes at the same time: on the one hand it founded a theory of lawful war based on justice and presumed a certain degree of responsibility in subjects, but on the other hand it had to grant obedience and so to limit the capability of subordinates. In this sense, all scholastic authors – Vitoria, Soto, Cano, Covarrubias, Gabriel Vázquez –[32] answered a well-known question raised in its canonical form at the end of the fifteenth century by the humanist Adrian Florisz,[33] who later became pope under the name of Hadrian VI.[34] Florisz stated that nobody might obey a superior when one knows that the command is doubtful, or when one has a better opinion than the superior. In other words, nobody may follow a superior command against the commandment of

[31] Antonio de Córdoba [Antonius Cordubensis], *Tratado de casos de conciencia [...]*, (Toledo: Diego de Ayala, 1578).

[32] Vitoria, *Relectio de iure belli*, 4.18, pp. 152–158.

[33] [Adrian Florisz], *Adriani Sexti ponticis maximi praeclarissimae quaestiones quodlibeticae, accuratius noviter impressae [...]*, (Venetiis: Expensis Luceantoni de Giunta Florentini, 1522; 1st edn Louvain: 1488?).

[34] Rudolf Schüßler, 'Hadrian VI. und das Recht auf Verweigerung zweifelhaft rechtmäßiger Befehle', in *Suche nach Frieden: Politische Ethik in der Frühen Neuzeit I*, ed. by Norbert Brieskorn and Markus Riedenhauer (Stuttgart: Kohlhammer, 2000), pp. 41–62.

one's own conscience.[35] Florisz argued that in such a case there would be two opposite moral statements in the soul of the same human being, the one asserting and the other denying that something must be done. This situation would lead to a contradiction, which would make every moral choice impossible.[36] From this premise we can conclude that a soldier must deny his obedience not only when commands are evidently absurd or inhuman, but also when they are doubtful and he has a better opinion than the superior. This would give room for a continuous uncertainty.

The argument of Gabriel Vázquez and of Grotius and their distinction between the levels of rulers and of subjects reach this purpose and prevent this uncertainty by arguing that only the top level is completely open to the question of justice, whereas on the inferior levels justice plays a role only in extraordinary and particularly dramatic cases, for in normal cases their relation to justice is mediated by the ruler.

By employing a moral voluntarism Grotius attains the same result that Vázquez achieves on the basis of a moral probabilism. The distinction he introduces tries to answer to the same question raised by Vitoria, Soto and Vázquez, but his solution is undoubtedly more systematic than other contemporary solutions. In this respect we can formulate the thesis, that the whole construction of Grotius's system and the particular order of his doctrine are needed in order to solve this question – the question formulated at the beginning, whether both parties in a war may be right – leading to two different conclusions: on the one hand, that a lawful war is possible, and, on the other hand, that soldiers have to obey. The choice of a particular kind of voluntarism is a strategy towards this aim and gives a pattern, in which the upper levels are

[35] [Florisz], *Praeclarissimae quaestiones quodlibeticae*, 2, fol. 9 A: 'Questio cum argumentis est. Utrum tenemur ad mandatum superioris contra propriam sententiam agere: dum scimus propositum apud maiores verti in dubium.'

[36] [Florisz], *Praeclarissimae quaestiones quodlibeticae*, 2. 3: An in probabili dubio doctorum licet obedire contra propriam sententiam seu opinionem, fol. 13 E: 'Ideo pro responsione breviter pono hanc conclusionem. Nulli unquam licet contra propriam sententiam seu opinionem agere: nec iudici contra opinionem pronunciare. Probatur primo per illud exo. 23. [ver. 2] iuxta hebraycam veritatem [...]. Et ibidem [*Ecclesiasticum*, 4, 24] ‹pro anima tua non confunderis dicere verum›. Ratione sic, nullus potest licite agere id de quo non potest iudicare dum agit, quod ipsum licet. Sed impossibile est aliquem iudicare quod sibi licet agere contra suam opinionem vel sententiam de bono vel malo. Ergo et cetera. Minor patet quia sic simul haberet contraria iudicia, verbi gratia iudicaret quod operari *a.* sit malum et quod operari *a.* non sit malum, ex quo ponitur iudicare quod sibi licet. Item si iudex habens opinionem quod de iure pronunciandum est pro *a.* si simul iudicet propter opinionem aliorum pronunciandum esse de iure contra *a.* habet contraria iudicia, puta pronunciandum est de iure pro *a.* et de iure non est pronunciandum pro *a.*'

open to the question of justice and the lower levels are mediated by the will of the superior. The distinction of different levels and the possibility of a just war on both sides are therefore immediately linked with a peculiar structure of the system; they are a consequence of it, perhaps a reason for it.

A New Method

It is true that we can find most arguments adopted by Grotius in other contemporary commentaries of the scholastic tradition.[37] In this sense he rearranges an amount of existing teachings, but his clear and systematic exposition and his choice for a deductive order is something new.[38]

Jurisprudence and political science of the sixteenth century were involved in a fierce debate about the form of practical philosophy, which was a part of a general dispute about the transmission of human knowledge. We can here mention for instance the discussion in Padua between Jacopo Zabarella and Francesco Piccolomini[39] or the debates about the Ramistic method in the German universities.[40] The tendency to explore new possibilities and to adopt new methods was particularly strong among the members of the reformed churches and of heterodox groups, although we cannot formulate a straight relationship between religion denomination and scientific originality. Anyway, Calvinistic jurisprudence and political theory of the late sixteenth century were particularly engaged in founding new (and supposedly better) ways of transmitting practical knowledge. Johann Thomas Freigius (1571), Hermann von Vulte (1590) and Nikolaus Vigel[41] are among the German scholars who arranged the contents of ancient jurisprudence into a new classification.

[37] Franco Todescan, Etiamsi daremus. *Studi sinfonici sul diritto naturale* (Padua: Cedam, 2003), pp. 140–141, with further bibliography.

[38] Haggenmacher, *Grotius et la doctrine de la guerre juste*, pp. 67–69.

[39] Cf. Scattola, 'Arnisaeus, Zabarella e Piccolomini', pp. 278–284.

[40] Cf. Merio Scattola, 'Gelehrte Philologie vs. Theologie: Johannes Caselius im Streit mit den Helmstedter Theologen', in *Die europäische Gelehrtenrepublik im Zeitalter des Konfessionalismus. The European Republic of Letters in the Age of Confessionalism*, ed. by Herbert Jaumann (Wiesbaden: Harrassowitz, 2001), pp. 155–181.

[41] Johann Thomas Freigius, *Partitiones iuris utriusque e Conradi Lagi methodo expressae [...]* (Basileae: Per Sebastianum Henricpetri, 1581; 1st edn Basel: 1571); Hermann von Vulte, *Iurisprudentiae Romanae a Iustiniano compositae libri duo* (Marpurgi: Typis Pauli Egenolphi, 1598; 1st edn 1590); Nikolaus Vigel, *Iuris civilis universi absolutissima methodus [...]* (Basileae: Ioannes Oporinus, 1565; 1st edn Basel: 1561). Cf. Hans Erich Troje, 'Die Literatur des gemeinen Rechts unter dem Einfluß des Humanismus', in *Handbuch der Quellen und Literatur der neueren europäischen Privatrechtsgeschichte. Zweiter Band: Neuere Zeit (1500-1800). Das Zeitalter des*

The young Iohannes Althusius for instance wrote in 1586 a brief handbook[42] in which he systematized the whole of Roman law on the basis of the Ramistic dichotomy of 'persons' and 'rights',[43] and he developed the same pattern thirty years later in his encyclopaedic treatise of the *Dicaeologica* (1617). Althusius applied the same Ramistic approach to his political theory, which is therefore *methodice digesta*, that is, distributed with the proper order, and in the prefaces to the different issues of this book he always made a point of having adopted the right method.[44]

All these efforts had two common features. On the one hand, they treated the idea of 'method' as identical with the idea of 'order', and understood (or misunderstood) the whole question about method as a problem concerning the best disposition of human knowledge. While discussing the quality of their method, these authors did not propose a procedure to achieve new knowledge, but were searching for the best way of transmitting inherited notions. This concern is exemplified in the best way in the work of Theodor Zwinger, a German philosopher, who transformed Aristotle's ethics and politics into a series of diagrams.[45]

On the other hand, all those authors based their arguments and their choice for this or that solution upon the Galenic doctrine of the three types of method

---

gemeinen Rechts. Erster Teilband: Wissenschaft, ed. by Hermann Coing (Munich: Beck, 1977), pp. 615-795 (pp. 741–754); Aldo Mazzacane, 'Methode und System in der deutschen Jurisprudenz des 16. Jahrhunderts', in *Entwicklung der Methodenlehre in Rechtswissenschaft und Philosophie vom 16. bis zum 18. Jahrhundert*, ed. by Jan Schröder (Stuttgart: Steiner, 1998), pp. 127–136.

[42] Iohannes Althusius, *Iuris Romani libri duo, ad leges methodi Rameae confirmati et tabula illustrati* (Basileae: Ad Lecythum Waldkirchianam, 1586). Cf. Merio Scattola, 'Von der *maiestas* zur *symbiosis*. Der Weg des Johannes Althusius zur eigenen politischen Lehre in den drei Auflagen seiner *Politica methodice digesta*', in *Politische Begriffe und historisches Umfeld in der* Politica methodice digesta *des Johannes Althusius*, ed. by Emilio Bonfatti, Giuseppe Duso and Merio Scattola (Wiesbaden: Harrassowitz, 2002), pp. 211–249 (pp. 234–242).

[43] Cf. Michel Villey, *La formation de la pensée juridique moderne. Cours d'histoire de la philosophie du droit. 1961–1966* (Paris: [Monchretien], 1968), pp. 588–594.

[44] Iohannes Althusius, *Politica methodice digesta et exemplis sacris et profanis illustrata [...]* (Herbornae Nassoviorum: Ex officina Christophori Corvini, 1603), Praefatio, fol. (:)2^{r} and fol. (:)3^{r}; Iohannes Althusius, *Politica methodice digesta atque exemplis sacris et profanis illustrata [...]. Editio tertia, duabus prioribus multo auctior* (Herbornae Nassoviorum: [Christophorus Corvinus], 1614; repr. Aalen: Scientia, 1981), Praefatio, fol.):(2^{r-v}. Cf. Scattola, 'Von der *maiestas* zur *symbiosis*', pp. 217–234.

[45] Theodor Zwinger, *Aristotelis Stagiritae de moribus ad Nicomachum libri decem: tabulis perpetuis, quae commentariorum loco esse queant, explicati et illustrati [...]* (Basileae: Per Ioannem Oporinum et Eusebium Episcopium, 1566); Theodor Zwinger, *Argumenta, scholia et tabulae*, in Aristoteles, *Politicorum libri octo ex Dionysii Lambini et Petri Victorii interpretationibus purissimis Graecolatini* (Basileae: Eusebii Episcopii opera ac impensis, 1582).

and order.[46] Followers of Petrus Ramus, such as Iohannes Althusius, applied the so-called 'definitive' order to jurisprudence and political theory, whereas defenders of the Aristotelian orthodoxy used the 'analytical or resolutive' order. Both options were thought to be particularly good for didactic purposes, that is, for the transmission of knowledge. The third method or order, the 'synthetic or compositive' one, was, on the contrary, confined to strictly scientific explanation and was accepted for teaching only partially and on particular conditions.[47]

So far, Grotius's methodical attempt, which he introduces in the first chapter of the *Law of Prize*, is part of a common discussion about the order to be kept in explaining jurisprudence. Nevertheless, his solution shows three particular characteristics. First, Grotius used the compositive order, for he began his deduction by defining the first elements of law, and then combined these basic ideas into greater compounds, until he came to explain the particular and real object of his interest, the prize and its law. Secondly, he paid great attention to the question of the principles of law, and in doing so he shared a main interest of the jurisprudence in the late sixteenth century.[48] Christoph Ehem and Jean de Coras are among those authors who explicitly treated this topic.[49] The Frisian Joachim Hopper was another author who wrote about the problem of principles, with a similar interest. In 1580 he composed the *Elements of Law or Principles of Justice in Four Books* and, with regard to his humanistic education and his high charge at court, he can be considered a kind of Hugo Grotius on the other side of the front, in the Catholic Netherlands.[50] Thirdly, Grotius

---

[46] Jean de Coras, *De iuris arte libellus [...]* (Lugduni: Apud Antonium Vincentium, 1560), I.18–22, pp. 63–78.

[47] Christoph Besold, *Disputatio prima praecognita prudentiae politicae proponens [...]*, in Besold, *Collegii politici classis prima [...]* (Tubingae: Typis Iohannis Alexandri Cellii, 1614), I.47, p. 30; Christian Liebenthal, *De constitutione politices*, in Liebenthal, *Collegium politicum [...]* (Giessae Hessorum: Typis Nicolai Hampelii, 1619), 14, pp. 16–17.

[48] Christoph Ehem, *De principiis iuris libri VII [...]* (Hanoviae: Apud Guilielmum Antonium, 1601; 1st edn Basel: 1556).

[49] Coras, *De iuris arte liber*, I.24-26, pp. 83–94 (p. 83–84): 'Negari certe non potest, quin principia in quavis arte, cognitu valde necessaria semper existant, neque enim ulla est ars, quae commode tradi, aut explicate doceri possit, nisi subiecta disciplinae materies certis principiis distributa, breviter cognoscenda proponatur, de quibus principiis, fuere, qui perquam erudite scripserint, nominatim etiam ea de re aedito tractatu (Christophorus Ehemius Liber de principiis iuris).'

[50] Joachim Hopper, *De iuris arte libri tres*, in Coras and Hopper, *Tractatus de iuris arte duorum clarissimorum iurisconsultorum*, (1st edn Lovanii: 1555), pp. 293–608; Joachim Hopper, *Elementorum iuris, sive de principiis iusti et iniusti, libri IIII*, in Hopper, *In veram iurisprudentiam isagoges ad filium libri octo [...]* (Coloniae: Maternus Cholinus, 1580), pp. 261–503; Joachim Hopper, *Seduardus, sive de vera iurisprudentia ad regem libri XII. Nempe, Νομοθεσίας sive de*

employed Aristotle's doctrine of the four causes (V, 58–59),[51] applying a pattern that was well known in the legal theory of his time, especially in the literature about the first elements of jurisprudence. Christoph Ehem had used it in the middle of the sixteenth century,[52] and Jean de Coras had proposed it again by referring directly to Ehem.[53] Contemporaries of Grotius used the scheme of the four causes in legal and political books.[54] In 1621, the year of Grotius's daring escape from the castle of Loevestein, Theodore van Thulden, published in Louvain *Four Books on the Principles of Jurisprudence* and referred to Coras and Hopper in order to justify the use of the Aristotelian pattern,[55] and even Willem Grotius, Hugo's younger brother, employed it in his *Handbook of the Principles of Natural Law*,[56] which is to a large extent a summary of the *Three Books on the Law of War and Peace.*

For this use of the compositive method there can be an internal reason too, since the scholastic tradition used by Grotius knew a strict hierarchy among the principles of natural law. Thomas Aquinas said – and all his commentators repeated – that the commandments of natural law are obtained in a descending

iuris et legum condendarum scientia, libri IIII. Rerum divinarum et humanarum, sive de iure civili publico, libri IIII. Ad Pandectas, sive de iure civili privato, libri IIII [...]. Adiectus est eiusdem auctoris de institutione principis liber singularis (Antverpiae: In officina Plantiniana, Apud viduam et Ioannem Moretum, 1590).

[51] Aristotle, *Metaphysics*, 1013^{b} 16–28.

[52] Ehem, *De principiis iuris libri VII*, I.1: Ordo librorum, pp. 9–14.

[53] Coras, *De iuris arte liber*, I.1–23, pp. 1–83.

[54] Theophilus Golius, *Epitome doctrinae politicae et oeconomicae [...]* (Francofurti: Iohannes Thimius, 1617; 1st edn Argentorati: 1592), p. 4; Klemens Timpler, *Philosophiae practicae pars tertia et ultima complectens politicam integram libris quinque pertractatam [...]* (Hanoviae: Apud Guilielmum Antonium, 1611), I.2–4, pp. 3–6; Christoph Besold, *Synopsis politicae doctrinae. Editio quinta, prioribus multo auctior* (Amstelodami: Apud Iodocum Ianssonium, 1643; 1st edn Argentinae: 1623), Praecognita, 24–38, pp. 17–24; Christian Matthiae, *Disputationum politicarum secunda. De maiestate et potestate imperatoris [...]*, resp. Daniel Meisnerus (Giessae: Imprimebat Casparus Chemlinus, 1611), in Matthiae, *Collegium politicum secundum iuxta methodum logicam conscriptum [...]* (Giessae: Excudebat Casparus Chemlinus, 1611), pp. 31–64, here th. 2, p. 36: 'In huius [= maiestatis] autem θεωρίᾳ octo membra consideranda veniunt: 1. definitio, 2. notatio, 3. distinctio, 4. causa efficiens, 5. causa conservans, 6. materia, 7. forma, 8. finis'. Cf. Merio Scattola, *Dalla virtù alla scienza. La fondazione e la trasformazione della disciplina politica nell'età moderna* (Milan: Angeli, 2003), pp. 60 and 79.

[55] Theodorus Tuldenus, *De principiis iurisprudentiae libri quatuor [...]* (Lovanii: Typis et sumptibus Aegidii Denique, 1702; 1st edn Louvain: 1621), lib. 1, pp. 3–16 and lib. 2, p. 17–37.

[56] Guilielmus Grotius, *De principiis iuris naturalis enchiridium [...]* (Lugduni Batavorum: Apud Iohannem Arnoldum Langerak, 1719; 1st edn: 1667), III.1–7, pp. 17–23. Cf. Merio Scattola, 'Il principio del diritto nella riflessione di Ugo e Guglielmo Grozio', in *Il diritto naturale della socialità. Tradizioni antiche ed antropologia moderna nel XVII secolo*, ed. by Vanda Fiorillo and Friedrich Vollhardt (Turin: Giappichelli, 2004), pp. 79–101 (pp. 89–93).

order, reflecting the ontological properties of mankind.[57] This series of principles includes the basic rule valid for all beings in general, that they should endure and preserve themselves; then the rule of animated beings, that they should reproduce themselves through their offspring; and finally the rule proper exclusively to human beings, that they should use their reason and gather together into societies. In addition, this tradition knew also the possibility of building a legal system by means of deduction, since Thomas Aquinas and the scholastic commentators admitted two ways of gaining a particular law from a general rule: either by deduction from a principle or by specification of a genus.[58] But the scholastic tradition of the sixteenth century, notwithstanding increasing changes, held to the dialectical and topological pattern of the medieval *quaestio* and therefore did not use the chain of principles as a scheme for arranging the explanation of natural law. It was Grotius who transformed this philosophical idea into a methodological tool, this content into a form. So, the originality of his work is also of methodological nature.[59]

A Voluntarist System

If we think of the famous 'Etiamsi daremus' from the *Prolegomena* of 1625,[60] which is mostly explained as a modern declaration of philosophical realism,[61]

---

[57] Thomas Aquinas, *Summa theologiae*, Ia IIae, q. 91, a. 2, pp. 954[b]–955[b]. Cf. Reginaldo Pizzorni, *Il diritto naturale dalle origini a San Tommaso d'Aquino* (Bologna: Studio Domenicano, 2000), pp. 435–532; Soto, *De iustitia et iure libri decem*, I.4.2, pp. 30[b]–32[b]: 'Praecepta propria naturalis iuris, hoc est prima per se nota principia, sunt plura. Probatur: principia naturalia (ut nomen auribus intonat) sunt illa quae natura nobis impressit; natura autem hominis ex pluribus partialibus constat. Est enim ens, quae utique natura communis illi est cum universis rebus. Mox est cum viventibus vivens, deinde inter animalia animal, ac demum homo, ergo secundum omnes hos naturae gradus peculiaria habet prima principia.'

[58] Thomas Aquinas, *Summa theologiae*, Ia IIae, q. 95, a. 2, p. 960[a]; Soto, *De iustitia et iure libri decem*, I.5.2, p. 41[a]. Cf. Merio Scattola, '*Principium oder principia*? Die Diskussion über den Rechtsgrundsatz im 16. und 17. Jahrhundert', in *Zur Entwicklungsgeschichte moralischer Grundsätze in der Philosophie der Aufklärung. The Development of Moral First Principles in the Philosophy of the Enlightenment*, ed. by B. Sharon Byrd, Joachim Hruschka and Jan C. Joerden (Berlin: Duncker und Humblot, 2004), pp. 3–26 (pp. 24–26) (= *Jahrbuch für Recht und Ethik. Annual Review of Law and Ethics*, 12 (2004), 3-26).

[59] Alfred Dufour, 'L'influence de la méthodologie des sciences physiques et mathématiques sur les Fondateurs de l'Ecole du Droit naturel moderne (Grotius, Hobbes, Pufendorf)', *Grotiana*, 1 (1980), 33–52 (pp. 40–43); Todescan, Etiamsi daremus, pp. 140–143.

[60] Hugo Grotius, *De iure belli ac pacis libri tres. In quibus ius naturae et gentium, item iuris publici praecipua explicantur* (Parisiis: Apud Nicolaum Buon, 1625), Prolegomena, fol. e1[r].

[61] Alessandro Passerin d'Entrèves, *La dottrina del diritto naturale* (Milan: Edizioni di Comunità, 1980; 1st English edn: 1951; 1st Italian edn: 1954), pp. 60–64; Norberto Bobbio,

the foundation of law upon God's will in the *Law of Prize* looks as a striking point. And it is even more striking, for Grotius in this passage quotes Thomas Aquinas as an authority,[62] whereas his own definition reminds more the doctrine of Philipp Melanchthon, who identified in the *Theological Commonplaces* the source of all laws as God's law, that is, God's absolute will.[63]

A major consequence of the voluntarist foundation is that the whole system of law is built upon a series of concentric circles, which are all unified by the first will. The larger the circles, the more general the problems they solve, so that the closer circles might concentrate on more particular questions without touching again the problems of the foundation. Each step towards the centre closes a door behind itself and opens the way to the next source of law. For instance, what God once stated is taken for granted by the supreme magistrate, and the will of the king cannot be investigated by the inferior magistrate, and so on.

Grotius's voluntarism is of a particular kind, for it is consistent with the nature of a thing and with the nature of the world as a whole.[64] So, the sequence of the general rules of natural law corresponds exactly to the chain of principles of the scholastic tradition. As a matter of fact, God's will wants a thing to be what it already is by reason. The first consequence of this premise is that the first law stated directly by the divine will is identical with the first quality of every being and consequently dictates its conservation. From it derive the first general rule and the first two laws. Grotius omits the second scholastic principle, proper of animated beings, which aims at reproduction, but he agrees on the third principle, concerning human beings, whose nature is to pursue reason and society. God's will operates in the general connection that links together all beings through 'eternal accord' and 'universal harmony'

'Il modello giusnaturalistico', in Norberto Bobbio and Michelangelo Bovero, *Società e stato nella filosofia politica moderna* (Milan: Il Saggiatore, 1984; 1st edn: 1979), pp. 14–117 (pp. 15–27); Alfred Dufour, 'Les *Magni Hispani* dans l'œuvre de Grotius', in *Die Ordnung der Praxis. Neue Studien zur Spanischen Spätscholastik*, ed. by Frank Grunert and Kurt Seelmann (Tübingen: Niemeyer, 2001), pp. 351–380 (pp. 358–360).

[62] Thomas Aquinas, *Summa theologiae*, Ia IIae, p. 93, a. 1: Utrum lex aeterna sit summa ratio in Deo existens, p. 949[a–b].

[63] Philipp Melanchthon, *Loci praecipui theologici [...]*, 1559, in Melanchthon, *Opera quae supersunt omnia. Volumen XXI. [...]*, ed. by Karl Gottlieb Bretschneider and Heinrich Ernst Bindseil (Brunswick: Schwetschke, 1854), col. 685. Cf. Merio Scattola, *Das Naturrecht vor dem Naturrecht. Zur Geschichte des* ius naturae *im sechzehnten Jahrhundert* (Tübingen: Niemeyer, 1999), pp. 37–40; Merio Scattola, '*Notitia naturalis de Deo et de morum gubernatione.* Die Naturrechtslehre Philipp Melanchthons und ihre Wirkung im 16. Jahrhundert', in *Melanchthon und die Marburger Professoren (1527–1627)*, ed. by Barbara Bauer (Marburg: Universitätsbibliothek Marburg, 1999), pp. 865–882 (pp. 870–873).

[64] Todescan, Etiamsi daremus, p. 97.

(II, pp. 11 and 12). Human beings partake of this general order by means of their reason, which they can exercise only if they live together. So they universally agree and want the next four laws, which introduce justice, 'mutual actions and passions' and 'social virtue' (II, p. 14). In this deduction, the will appears more as a confirmation of a content of reason than as a foundation of new and independent contents. It is the motion necessary to transform an idea into a valid law, and this teaching resembles the traditional explanation that the will always follows an idea proposed by reason.[65]

In a second sense too, Grotius's doctrine looks particular. The voluntarism of the Lutheran and Calvinistic tradition linked God's will with the doctrine of innate ideas, which are the manifestation or the legal declaration of a divine decree into the human soul: God wants his law and promulgates it by writing it in the hearts of all human beings during the creation.[66] The content of the first innate ideas was then repeated in the Ten Commandments and in the Gospel. Consequently, there have been three positive promulgations of the same original law. The principle that God's will is stated immediately in the human heart is true for Catholic voluntarism too, for instance for Fernando Vázquez de Menchaca,[67] who is assumed as a main source for Grotius's

[65] Thomas Aquinas, *Summa theologiae*, Ia, q. 19, a. 5, p. 105^{a-b}; Ia, q. 82, a. 4, pp. 394^{a}–395^{a}.

[66] Philipp Melanchthon, *Loci praecipui theologici*, 1559, coll. 712–713; Scattola, *Das Naturrecht vor dem Naturrecht*, pp. 42–48; Scattola, '*Notitia naturalis de Deo*', pp. 877–878; Gideon Stiening, '*Deus vult aliquas esse certas noticias*. Philipp Melanchthon, Rudolph Goclenius und das Konzept der *notitiae naturales* in der Psychologie des 16. Jahrhunderts', in *Melanchthon und die Marburger Professoren*, ed. by Bauer, pp. 757–787.

[67] Vázquez Menchaca, *Controversiarum illustrium libri tres*, I.27.11, vol. 2, p. 149: 'Ius enim naturale nihil esse quam rectam rationem ab ipsa nativitate et origine humano generi a Deo innatam supra edocti sumus. Ergo si ipsimet Deus contrariam rationem a nostra origine mentibus nostris imbuerit, id similiter erit ius naturale. Et ut hoc ius naturale, quo utimur, quoque interdum abutimur, bonum est, quia Deus infixum nobis est: ita si contrarium nobis dederit ius, eo ipso quod ipse dederit, bonum erit.' Once a law has been stated, it produces a general order of the good, that cannot be violated without contradiction. Otherwise, the divine will remains always free because it can give another law recreating the world. Cf. Fernando Vázquez Menchaca, *Controversiarum usu frequentium [...] libri tres, alii et omnino diversi ab illustrium controversiarum quaestionibus nunquam adhuc impressi [...]* (Francofurti ad Moenum, Sumptibus Ioannis Theobaldi Schoenwetteri, 1599), I.1. 4–5, pp. 4–5: 'Neque ad rem pertinet quod ordinem iudiciorum possit princeps immutare [...]; [fit] illud verum vel per legem generalem, quae non solum hanc causam, qua de agitur, sed omnes causas comprehendat, ne alias ad laesionem vel aemulationem unius factum videatur [...]; vel id quando fieret ex causa non sine causa, praesertim qui et ipse Deus omnipotens optimus maximus quod malum esse facere non posset. Posse enim peccare vel malum facere non est potentia, sed potius infirmitas et impotentia a malo abstinendi. Unde ille solus recte omnipotens appellatur, qui malum facere non potest; qui autem malum facere posset, is omnipotens nec esset nec recte nominatur [...], quasi plenitudo potestatis in sola dispositione bonitatis, non etiam pravitatis inesse videatur.'

voluntarism.[68] But in the *Law of prize* Grotius seems uninterested in the theory of innate ideas and when he refers to this topic, he does not mention any kind of direct promulgation, but only refers to human understanding as a whole.[69] He repeats that God impressed his own image onto the first man and that some 'seeds of the divine light' remain in our minds despite the original sin (II, pp. 11–12). So, we should assume that God declares his will through the reason of the human being and the internal order of creation, through the natural working of the world. Grotius says: 'The Will of God is revealed, not only through oracles and supernatural portents, but above all in the very design of the Creator' (II, p. 8) and then explains that 'since God fashioned creation and willed its existence, every individual part thereof has received from Him certain natural properties whereby that existence may be preserved and each part may be guided for its own good' (II, p. 9). If we want to understand the law of the world, we have to investigate how the world works. The whole content of the divine will can therefore be understood by means of human reason. It is fully reasonable and it is impossible that it contains an absurd order. We find here at a very abstract level the same pattern we saw in the explanation of the responsibility during a war, and we can see here the premise for that argument. A law is valid only if it is enforced by a will, and the presence of a legislator is a condition for obedience. Nevertheless, a command should not be absurd and must be consistent with the general principles of reason. Modern voluntarism, such as the doctrine of Hobbes, Pufendorf, Thomasius and his disciples, is, on the contrary, originated by a full or partial lack of reason, so that a free will may create law because no reasonable rules are already available.

The Structure of the System

Since a law always implies a will that enforces it, the different kinds of law and the order among them must derive from the differences among the sources of will in the world. Grotius therefore represents the whole system of law as a

---

[68] Ernst Reibstein, *Die Anfänge des neueren Natur- und Völkerrechts. Studien zu den* Controversiae illustres *des Fernandus Vasquius (1559)* (Bern: Haupt, 1949), p. 237; Giovanni Ambrosetti, *I presupposti teologici e speculativi delle concezioni giuridiche di Grozio* (Bologna: Zanichelli, 1955), p. 121; Dufour, 'Les *Magni Hispani* dans l'œvre de Grotius', p. 361.

[69] The same 'dispositional theory' of innate ideas that Jon Miller found in the *Prolegomena* was therefore already present in the *Law of Prize and Booty*. Cf. Jon Miller, 'Innate Ideas and Stoicism in Grotius', *Grotiana*, 22–23 (2001–02), 157–176 (pp. 160–166).

system of sources of will applied to different levels of reason, and organises within this structure the whole knowledge on natural law. Such a hierarchy explains the different types of law and their diverging contents, produces all parts of the legal system, replicates the chain of universal principles, specifies the reasons for their validity and applies to different fields, each with a different extent. In his deduction, Grotius separates nine 'rules' from thirteen 'laws', of which the former indicate the sources of legislative will and the latter the contents of law.

The highest principle is God, the principle itself (II, p. 7), and the first rule states that the divine will is law. But God expresses himself not so much in sudden manifestations as in the regular course of nature. So, the real exposition of divine will is to be found in natural law. In fact this comprehends only that part that was traditionally called *ius naturae primaevum* and embraces the commandments given by God to all animated beings.[70] Some kinds of behaviour are common to human beings and animals and even to inanimate objects (II, pp. 9 and 10); they are performed by instinct. The tradition enumerated into this class self-preservation and reproduction, from which was derived the right to self-defence and the law of family.[71] Grotius accepts explicitly only the first and adds to it the consequent right to use and possess all goods necessary to live a good life. So, he included a right of possession (*possessio*) in the first natural law, although this does not yet create a corresponding obligation (II, pp. 10–11).

The second source of will is human reason. God not only gave all things an instinct to preserve themselves, but also cared for the preservation of the creation as a whole, and pursued this end by linking all beings together in a

[70] Coras, *De iuris arte liber*, 2.5, pp. 109–110: 'Porro autem, ut ius naturale fecerunt interpretes duplex: primarium, instinctu constans et inclinatione naturali, quod non hominibus modo, sed caeteris quoque animantibus commune est, et secundarium, restrictius, quod solis hominibus convenit, cuiusmodi sunt omnia, quae recensuit Ulpianus exempla; ita ius quoque gentium in duas species diduxerunt, primarium appellantes, quod non impetu illo naturali, sed ultroneo vigentis in homine rationis iudicio, eo ipso quo gentes esse coeperunt, hominibus innatum est, et quasi in animo insculptum: ut Deum colere, parentes honorare, patriae magistratibusque obedire, pacta servare, et id genus alia; cuiusmodi gentium ius, primarium, ob id naturale dicitur, quod sola naturae ratione excitetur in homine, gentium vero ideo, quia solae gentes, uti dictum est, non etiam bruta, eo utantur. Quod vero secundarium nominari volunt, non statim ab initio, simul atque rationem Deus insevit animis hominum, ita fuit, sed usu exigente, et ex humani convictus necessitate postea introductum est, natura etiam quodammodo repugnante, ut bella, servitutes, et contractus, naturali siquidem iure, omnia communia erant, et omnes homines aequales, liberique nascebantur.' Cf. Scattola, *Das Naturrecht vor dem Naturrecht*, pp. 178–194.

[71] Cf. Scattola, *Das Naturrecht vor dem Naturrecht*, pp. 190–192.

mutual correspondence, so that one can preserve itself only if it preserves the others. Of this mutual inclination there are a few signs among inanimate beings, many more among animals, but it becomes really clear only in human beings; for it requires the use of reason and is based on it. Of course, human reason was obscured by original sin, but it could not fall so deep that the rational knowledge of good has disappeared completely. Consequently, all human beings will consent about some basic truths that they attain by means of natural reason. Whereas the *ius naturae primaevum* was based on instinct, was shared by all animated beings and was immediately valid, the second type of natural law is based on reason, is proper only to human beings and requires the intervention of understanding. It dictates how a human being should act in general, considering only his humanity, that is, his general qualities as a representative of the human kind. The tradition of the sixteenth century, and Grotius with it (II, p. 12), called this law *ius naturae secundarium*,[72] because it was introduced at a second moment, or *ius gentium primarium*, because it was the first law among human beings[73] The sign for the existence of this law is the presence of consent among all men or among most of them, and so consent can figure as the second source of will and as the origin of this kind of law. As such it figures in the second main rule of Grotius's legal system: 'What all human beings consent to will, that must be law' (II, p. 12). This second type of will is a general one, and its subject is mankind taken as a whole (*cuncti*, II, p. 12), the great society that includes all human beings taken in their mere humanity, that is, in their pure rationality (II, p. 13). Consequently, it is obvious that this law is common to all human beings, but not to other animated beings. It is based on the use of reason, and all reasonable people will consent that they should preserve human society. The preservation of the society implies the respect of justice and its order, which produces obligations of a general kind. From reason, sociability and justice derive the next four laws

[72] Everard van Bronkhorst, 'Εναντιοφανῶν *centuriae sex et conciliationes eorundem [...]* (Lugduni Batavorum: Iacobus Marcus, 1621; 1st edn: 1595), I.3, p. 3: 'Contra hanc iurisconsultorum distinctionem, aliam vulgo interpretes excogitarunt, qua ius naturale, item gentium, aliud primaevum, aliud secundarium appellant. Ius naturale primaevum statuunt, quod omnibus animantibus commune est. Ius naturale secundarium, seu ius gentium primaevum vocant, quod natura homini in prima creatione insevit, ut sunt normae et discrimina honestorum et turpium. Cuius exempla sunt, religio erga Deum, pietas in patriam et parentes, alterum non laedere, neminem locupletari debere cum alterius iactura [...]. Ius gentium secundarium dicunt, quod non a simplici ratione naturali proficiscitur, sed per ratiocinationem, usu et humanis necessitatibus exigentibus, homines communi consensu constituerunt. Cuius iuris sunt bella, servitutes, distinctiones dominiorum, et contractus.' See above note 70.

[73] For the history of the identification of this two branches of natural law cf. Scattola, *Das Naturrecht vor dem Naturrecht*, pp. 178–194.

belonging to *ius gentium primarium*. The third and the fourth law enforce the commandments of *ius naturae*: they state as obligation what the first and second law permitted as right, that we should preserve the body and the property of other human beings. We find here repeated the Roman doctrine, which assigned property, borders, war and slavery to the *ius gentium*.[74] As a consequence, the next two laws (the fifth and the sixth one) introduce punishment and honour.

This law of nations refers to the 'general will' of an abstract human being, but such a general being may, on the contrary, freely determine all its actions that are not submitted to an obligation. Beside the 'general will', we should therefore acknowledge also the existence of a 'particular will', which operates in all cases that are not regulated by general duties towards the other. Here we should think of the great area of actions that are not prohibited by natural law, in which every human being can freely use its will.[75] This is the third source of will, and it is the beginning of a quite long process that ends in civil law. The third rule states that the will of a single man should be law for him. Could a single man be self-sufficient, then his will would create the third level of law, the level of civil law, which depends only on human will. But individuals cannot attain self-sufficiency and they must therefore communicate their right, that is, their will. Moreover, the good life in the great human society is threatened and made uncertain by distance and human wickedness. Human beings must therefore gather together and communicate their mutual will, to which purpose they can make contracts. They create cities and through

[74] *Dig*, 1.1.4 (Ulpianus) and 1.1.5 (Hermogenianus): 'Ex hoc iure gentium introducta bella, discretae gentes, regna condita, dominia distincta, agris termini positi, aedificia collocata, commercium, emptiones venditiones, locationes conductiones, obligationes institutae: exceptis quibusdam quae iure civili introductae sunt.'

[75] Grotius, *IPC*, II, p. 18: 'Fecit Deus hominem αὐτεξούσιον, *liberum suique iuris*, ita ut actiones uniuscuiusque et rerum suarum usus ipsius, non alieno arbitrio subiacerent, idemque gentium omnium consensu approbatur.' Upon this quality Richard Tuck based his interpretation of the *De iure praedae commentarius*, as if individuals were free like states and had no original duties to preserve each other or as if Grotius built up a complete theory of ethical conduct upon the principle of self-preservation interpreted as a fundamental moral right. But this applies only to the first level of the doctrine, to the *ius naturae primaevum*, whereas the second level, the *ius naturae secundarium* or *ius gentium primarium*, introduces the ideas that all things are linked by a mutual consent, that each individual is responsible for the good of the others and that a particular or intermediate kind of justice describes this order from the point of view of mankind (II, 12–13). So, only the first part of the doctrine, a very small one indeed, is based upon the self-preservation. For the remaining and more comprehensive parts other principles are required. Cf. Richard Tuck, *Philosophy and Government 1572–1651* (Cambridge: CUP, 1993), pp. 169–179; Richard Tuck, *The Right of War and Peace. Political Thought and the International Order. From Grotius to Kant* (Oxford: OUP, 1999), pp. 79–89.

a natural 'social covenant' (*civile foedus*, II, pp. 21 and 19–20) oblige themselves to help their community and each single member of it. In this way they identify a common good, which serves as a measure for the actions of each member and of the collective. It is therefore necessary that the society directs the singular actions towards a mutual good, and this is possible because the citizens transfer their particular will to the whole of the community. Every free will can be naturally transmitted to somebody else's will (II, p. 20). A common will that leads common actions is a law, in the proper sense, a civil law. This is the fourth source of will, which is in fact a product or a modification of the third one, for the will of a commonwealth flows from the will of the original human beings (fourth and fifth rule, II, pp. 22–25). Further modification occurs when the society, in order to govern its affairs in a better way, decides to transmit its mutual will to a supreme magistrate (sixth and seventh rule, II, pp. 26–27). The magistrate has the faculty to determine what is right and what is wrong among the subjects, to give law and to administrate justice. His power is also derived, through a long deduction, from that original will of the single human beings.[76]

We know now the reason why subjects must obey to the commands of their supreme magistrate and consequently why subordinates in both armies are to be considered as true enemies, as if justice were on both sides. Individuals, which are free to direct their own actions, have transferred their will to the commonwealth they live in, so that now only the society may decide what is right for its citizens. And the commonwealth then transmitted its will to a supreme magistrate, who can now determine the common and the particular good of each single citizen. The liberty of human beings has been transformed into the command of the supreme magistrate, and each step in the process is like a door that cannot be opened again. After the single man has given his will to the commonwealth, he cannot refer to it from within the civil condition and cannot claim his original will back. In the same sense, the society cannot act freely against its magistrate, once it had given its mutual will to him. There is no way back. So, the best way for the subject to fulfil its original freedom is now to obey to the supreme magistrate.

In this long systematic deduction of the political power we also find the reason why only one of the two fighting magistrates can be right and why, according to this premise, the subject in some extraordinary cases may refuse

---

[76] The traditional scheme of the four levels of law is completed by the 'secondary law of nations', which, as Grotius say, is a mixture between civil law and law of nations, for it contains all those rules that human nations admit by artificial consent and that include international pacts and customs (II, p. 27). Cf. Scattola, *Das Naturrecht vor dem Naturrecht*, pp. 178–194.

obedience. Truly, the deduction of civil law and the foundation of both commonwealth and supreme magistrate, which are like the drawing of smaller and smaller circles, take place within the great circle of law of nations, which prescribes a general order of justice, and in particular the mutual conservation of human beings. This end is the outer limit for the actions of the single human being and, together with the will, is transmitted to the commonwealth, which should search for the common good of its citizens, and then to the magistrate, which should pursuit the good of the commonwealth. There is always a measure for the decisions of supreme magistrates, and they always attain some degree of justice. So, their actions and decisions are to some extent measurable, and it is possible to judge which of them is right and which not.

In the same sense the magistrate is obliged to respect the general order of justice and the common good of a commonwealth, with the consequence that he does not dispose freely of the mutual will. As a matter of fact the contract between the society and the supreme magistrate is a commission (*contractus mandati*), in which he figures as a mandate holder, whereas the commonwealth is the principal (II, pp. 25–26).[77] This obligation to the common good, expressed in the tenth law, makes the commands of the magistrate obligatory for the commonwealth, as Grotius's eleventh law states (II, p. 26), but leaves the possibility of comparing the behaviour of the magistrate with the commandments of reason and justice. To some extent, even the subjects may judge the orders of the magistrate and see if they meet the requirements of the 'sufficient reasons', and, in extreme cases, if they are plainly absurd or inhuman, they may refuse to obey them.

[77] Among the sources of Grotius the *contractus mandati* was defended by Fernando Vázquez and among the contemporaries of Grotius it was one of the characteristic doctrines of Iohannes Althusius. Cf. Vázquez Menchaca, *Controversiarum illustrium libri tres*, I, Praefatio, 105–107, vol. 1, pp. 69–71; I.1.2: Princeps merus et legitimus, vol. 1, pp. 97–98; I.475: Principatus legitimus ex solo populi consensu, vol. 3, pp. 74–75; I.43.5, vol. 3, pp. 20–21; Vázquez Menchaca, *Controversiarum usu frequentium libri tres*, I.1.2: Imperium merum quid, p. 3; num. 3: Imperium non extenditur ad iniuriam, pp. 3–4; Althusius, *Politica methodice digesta*, 1614, 19. 12–18, pp. 331–333; 38. 39, p. 898.

Grotius and Stobaeus

Jon Miller
Professor of Philosophy, Queen's University, Kingston, Ontario, Canada
e-mail: jon.miller@queensu.ca

Abstract
This paper examines Grotius's knowledge of Stobaeus's magnificent anthology of classical literature. After summarizing the contents and significance of that anthology, it shows that Grotius had a life-long interest in and extensive knowledge of the work. Despite this, and even though Grotius made important contributions to the revitalization of Stoicism in the seventeenth century, he never once mentions the material in Chapter Seven of Book II of Stobaeus's work, material which is widely regarded nowadays as a vital source for the ethical views of ancient Stoics. The paper concludes by exploring the implications of this omission for the broader revival of Stoicism in the early modern period.

Keywords
Grotius, Stobaeus, Stoic ethics, neo-Stoicism, early modern ethics

Ioannes Stobaeus's magnificent anthology of classical literature is now widely acknowledged to be one of three key sources for understanding the ethics of the early Stoa.[1] Yet, no one has studied how that material factored into the revival of Stoicism in the early modern period. In this paper, I aim to fill, partially, that problematic gap in the scholarly literature by looking at Grotius's knowledge of Stobaeus.

Why look at Grotius and not doctrinaire neo-Stoics, such as Lipsius or du Vair? For two reasons: because he had both the motivation and the means to use Stobaeus. That is, although Grotius may not have been a doctrinaire neo-Stoic – his thought was too diffuse to belong to any one school – he was still very much attracted to the ideas of ancient Stoicism.[2] This interest gave

[1] The other two are Book III of Cicero's *De finibus* and Book VII of Diogenes Laertius. For an excellent overview of Stobaeus's importance to Stoicism, see Julia Annas' introduction in *Etica stoica: Ario Didimo, Diogene Laerzio*, ed. and tr. by Carlo Natali, intr. by Julia Annas (Rome: Laterza, 1999). More on all of this will be said in section four of my paper.

[2] For more on Grotius and the Stoics, see above all *Grotius and the Stoa*, ed. by Hans Blom and Laurens Winkel (Assen: Van Gorcum, 2004).

him the motivation to consult and exploit any sources about the school he might encounter. Second, because of his intense study of Stobaeus, he possessed a knowledge of the work that would be the envy of many specialists nowadays. This knowledge would have equipped him with the means to use the relevant portions of Stobaeus if he saw their significance. Given that Grotius had both the motivation and the means, he of all people in the seventeenth century should be expected to make frequent use of Stobaeus II.7. As we shall see, however, he didn't do so. That should teach us something important about Grotius as well as the character of Stoicism in the seventeenth century. Or so I shall argue.

To establish those conclusions, I begin with an overview of Stobaeus. Then, I outline what Grotius's general corpus shows about his knowledge of Stobaeus. After that, I look at his usage of Stobaeus, taking the *De iure praedae* (*IPC*) as my case study. Next, I explain what is special about II.7. With this in hand, I end my paper with broader remarks about Grotius, Stoicism and the seventeenth century. By way of an appendix, I strengthen my argument with an overview of Stobaeus in the *De iure belli ac pacis* (*IBP*).

Stobaeus

Since I do not want to presuppose familiarity with Stobaeus, his text or its legacy, I will start with an overview of them.[3] There is not much to be said about the man himself. He apparently lived in the early fifth century A.D. He was not a Christian. And he was immensely learned – indeed, in this respect, Grotius would have been one of his few peers in Western history.

There is a personal connection between the man and his text: it was compiled for the edification of Stobaeus's son Septimius. The so-called gnomological tradition of collecting gnomes or 'pithy sayings's from Greek literature for pedagogical purposes had deep roots in antiquity: traceable to at least the fourth century B.C., it formed a rich genre comprised of numerous volumes.

[3] This overview is derived entirely from other secondary sources. The best recent discussion is David E. Hahm, 'The Ethical Doxography of Arius Didymus', *Aufstieg und Niedergang der Römischen Welt*, Tl I-II, ... vols (Berlin: De Gruyter, 1972 -), Teil II (Principat), vol. 36.4, pp. 2935-3055; I also found Otto Hense, 'Ioannes Stobaios', *Paulys Realencyclopädie der classischen Altertumswissenschaft*, 15 vols (Stuttgart: Metzler, 1894-1978, this vol. 1916), vol. 9.2, cols 2549-86 quite useful. For additional sources, see the bibliography at the end of Hahm, 'The Ethical Doxography', pp 3051-3055. See for the most recent critical edition of Stobaeus: *Ioannis Stobaei Anthologii libri duo priores qui inscribi solent Eclogae physicae et ethicae*, ed. by Curtius Wachsmuth, 2 vols (Berlin: Weidmann, 1884).

Though part of this genre, Stobaeus's work towered above the rest, so much so that it inadvertently contributed to their demise. Not only would it be extremely difficult for any successor to top his achievement but also Stobaeus rendered otiose so many of his predecessors. For why should anyone bother with lesser collections when she could find everything they contain plus so much more in Stobaeus?

In Stobaeus's work – which was originally called *Selections, Sayings and Admonitions* – there is material from more than 500 Greek philosophers, historians, poets, cosmologists and others. The earliest source is Homer; the latest, Themistius (d. 387? AD). Many of his excerpts are culled from other anthologies, though Stobaeus did select a not-insignificant number himself from original sources. The excerpts vary in length from a single line to dozens of pages. Originally, they were placed under some 200 headings across four books; over time, many of the headings came to be chapters. Each book was assigned a distinct topic or set of topics. So, Book One opens with a chapter of selections in praise of philosophy; then, its quotations address the various philosophical schools, mathematics and physics (among other issues). Book Two takes up epistemology, logic, rhetoric and other topics before getting to ethics in the final seventh chapter. Book Three is devoted entirely to ethics, and Four deals with political theory, practice and a number of matters pertaining to day-to-day living (sailing, marriage, burial, farming, etc.). The size of the four books varies greatly, at least as they have been transmitted to us: in the most recent critical edition – that of Wachsmuth – Book Two has only 264 pages while Book Four fills more than 1140.

Because so many of the works which Stobaeus reproduces and saves have been lost,[4] scholars have expended significant effort trying to determine how heavy a hand he exercised as editor.[5] On one level, his impact on the texts is thought to be relatively light. Like others in the gnomological tradition, Stobaeus tended to copy verbatim from his sources. Theoretically, artistic license entered only in the selection of texts and their placement within the work. On another level, though, his impact is considered great. For while he did tend to copy literally, he was not above excising some passages or altering others which were unfavourable to the point being argued. In addition to the damage done by Stobaeus to his sources, significant additional harm was caused during the transmission of his work. Of course there are the ordinary

[4] For example, many crucial fragments from the Greek dramatists – especially Euripides – survived only in Stobaeus.

[5] The most important study of Stobaeus's editorial practises remains S. Luria, 'Entstellungen des Klassikertextes bei Stobaios', *Rheinisches Museum*, vol. 78 (1929), pp. 81-104.

errors which always appear in every manuscript tradition. Besides these, a different kind of influence came to bear: abridgement. Later copyists would paraphrase to save space. Or they would simply omit lines, paragraphs or pages which they deemed superfluous. Whatever their motives, the result was a much-shorter text than what Stobaeus actually compiled. For example, Photius, the great Patriarch of Constantinople (d. 891), recorded 46 chapter headings of Book Two; only 13 have been transmitted to us.

The transmission process also dramatically changed the very structure of the work. As mentioned above, Stobaeus's work originally consisted of four books probably bound together as a single, immense codex. After a few hundred years, it began to appear as two volumes, each likely holding two books. Given that the first two books are topically affiliated and so are the second pair, it was probably inevitable that, once they were printed as two separate volumes, they would begin circulating independently. The first volume, containing Books 1-2, became known as *Selections (Eclogae) of Physical Opinions*; the second, with Books 3-4, was called *Anthology (Florilegium)* or *Sermones*. Fewer manuscripts of the *Eclogae* survived, and they are not as old (the oldest dates to the fourteenth century, compared to the eleventh century for the *Florilegium*). These facts suggest that the *Eclogae* was less popular than the *Florilegium*; it is speculation, but one obvious explanation for the different fates of the two volumes is that the technical and scientific material of the former did not appeal to as many readers as the moral and practical substance of the latter.

During the great swell of scholarship in the Renaissance period, Stobaeus's work finally started to appear in print. Two men, Victor Trincavellius and Konrad Gesner, both produced editions of the *Florilegium* within years of each other.[6] Somewhat later, William Canter oversaw the publication of the *Eclogae*.[7] Thirty years after that, a complete edition of the whole of Stobaeus was published.[8] For a reason noted above, the publication of Stobaeus was a significant event in the history of ideas: because he preserved so many texts which otherwise would have been lost, the wider circulation of his text allowed scholars to

[6] See *Ioannis Stobaei Collectiones Sententiarum*, ed. by Victor Trincavellius (Venice: Bartholomaei Zanetti, 1536) and Konrad Gesner, *Sententiae ex thesauris Graecorum delectae quarum autores circiter ducentos & quinquaginta citat*... (Basil: Ioannis Oporini, 1549); Gesner also published editions of the *Florilegium* in 1543 and 1559.

[7] See W. Canter, *Eclogarum libri duo quorum prior physicas, posterior ethicas complectitur*... (Antwerp: Christoph Plantin, 1575).

[8] See Stobaeus, *Sententiae ex thesauris Græcorum delectæ, Cyri Theodori Dialogus de amicitiæ exilio, opusculum Platoni adscriptum de Iusto, aliud eiusdem an virtus doceri possit. Huic editioni accesserunt eiusdem Ioannis Stobæi Eclogarum physicarum et ethicarum libri duo*... (Geneva: [F. Fabro], 1609); I have not been able to identify the editor of this work.

make important rediscoveries about the classical world. Publication is also significant for our purposes: it meant that Grotius had ready access to Stobaeus. Of course, this is only a statement about the actual text available to him; it reveals nothing about what passages of the text he read. That is the subject of the next section of my paper.

Stobaeus in the Correspondence and the *Dicta Poetarum*

Broadly speaking, Grotius's knowledge and use of Stobaeus can be studied in two different ways: observationally, where one would read his corpus simply to understand the parts of Stobaeus with which he was familiar; and critically, where one would try to determine how he interpreted the parts of Stobaeus that he knew and used. In this paper, I attempt the former: that is, I only want to offer a descriptive account of Grotius's knowledge and use of Stobaeus.[9] In this section, my description concerns Grotius's general knowledge of Stobaeus; in the next, I shall look how he used this knowledge.

The first two points are simply that he had an abiding interest in, and profound grasp of, Stobaeus. The longevity of his interest is amply demonstrated by his correspondence. There, the first reference occurs in a letter to his friend Vossius, sent on July (?) 1619,[10] the last time Stobaeus's name appears is in the letter to Willem de Groot of 8 April, 1645, mere months before Grotius's death. During the nearly twenty-six years in between, Stobaeus is alluded to in literally dozens of other letters. To be sure, the allusions are not evenly distributed. For example, Stobaeus is repeatedly talked about in the early 1620s. By contrast, in the late 1620s and throughout the 1630s, he comes up a bare handful of times. But then, towards the end of Grotius's life, Stobaeus again becomes a regular topic of conversation. Regardless of the distribution, it remains that Grotius was consistently interested in Stobaeus for much of his adult life.[11] This interest has an obvious explanation: with the plethora of material which Stobaeus's text contains, it would have been almost irresistible for someone with Grotius's insatiable appetite for ideas.

[9] A reason for ignoring the interpretive task will emerge from the ensuing discussion: since Grotius never used II.7, it is both unnecessary and impossible to develop views on how he understood that text.

[10] See *Briefwisseling van Hugo Grotius,* ed. by P.C. Molhuysen and others, 17 vols. (The Hague, 1928-2001), vol. II, p. 15.

[11] Indeed, according to his biographer Jean Lévesque de Burigny, Grotius had already formed this interest 'when very young'. See Jean Lévesque de Burigny, *The Life of the truly Eminent and Learned Hugo Grotius*, (London: A. Millar, 1754; orig. in French, tr. unknown), III.4.

The correspondence also reveals the strength of Grotius's grasp of Stobaeus. In several letters sent during the spring of 1622, he is anxious to obtain a copy of the '*librum Eclogarum Physicarum et Ethicarum Stobaei*' (as he puts it in the 11 May, 1622, letter to Vossius). From these letters, it is clear that Grotius knew about the distinction between the *Eclogae* and the *Florilegium*; it is also apparent that he only needed the *Eclogae* to have all of Stobaeus, implying that he already had access to the *Florilegium.*[12] In a later letter, Grotius talks convincingly about Photius's testimony.[13] The year after this, he engaged in a scholarly exchange with the French philologist Claude de Saumaise.[14] Salmasius (the Latinised form of his name) opened with a number of critical comments – emendations, corrections and other changes – concerning a classical text that had recently come into his possession. In the course of making these remarks, Salmasius obliquely refers to a single passage in Stobaeus – a reference which Grotius catches and to which he responds by citing another fairly obscure piece of Stobaeus. It is telling that Salmasius would expect Grotius to catch his reference; just as telling is the way that Grotius delivers. All this shows just how widely respected and thorough Grotius's knowledge of Stobaeus was.

Grotius's expertise is further demonstrated by the edition of Stobaeus that he produced. Called the *Dicta poetarum quae apud Io. Stobaeum exstant*, it was published by Nicolas Buon in 1623.[15] Though the title might suggest otherwise, the *Dicta Poetarum* does not include all the sayings and poetry found in Stobaeus; it draws only on the *Florilegium.* Nor does it include only material drawn from Stobaeus: Grotius supplements it with substantial excerpts from Plutarch and St. Basil. That said, there is a lot of Stobaeus here; by my rough estimate, his material fills three-quarters of the book's nearly 600 pages. Grotius skillfully translates the Greek into Latin. He also proposes a number of emendations and additions for ellipses. I lack the skills to evaluate these changes but I might point out that Ter Meulen and Diermanse cite the laudatory

[12] If de Burigny is to be believed, Grotius eventually obtained access to the complete edition of Stobaeus – mentioned in the previous section – published in the early 1600s. De Burigny writes, 'Fabricius informs us, that in the Library of the College of Leyden there is a copy of the Geneva edition of Stobaeus, in the year 1609, with several notes in Grotius's own hand' (de Burigny, *The Life of… Grotius*, III.4).

[13] See the 6 September, 1630 letter to N.C. Fabry de Peiresc.

[14] See Salmasius's letter to Grotius of 9 April, 1631, and Grotius's reply of 17 April, 1631.

[15] See Hugo Grotius, *Dicta poetarum quae apud Io. Stobæum exstant; emendata et Latino carmine reddita ab Hugone Grotio. Accesserunt Plutarchi et Basilii Magni de usu Græcorum poetarum libelli* (Paris: Buon, 1623) for full details.

words of the great Stobaeus scholar A.H.L Heeren, who credited Grotius with eliminating 'a huge crop of errors by his happy talent [*ingenio*]'.[16]

Rather than extend the discussion any further, let me conclude this synopsis with a bald summary of what I take Grotius's knowledge of Stobaeus to be. I think he knew all of the text: both the *Eclogae* and the *Florilegium*. Admittedly, it is possible and perhaps likely that he knew some passages better than others. To admit this, however, is simply to admit gradations of knowledge and not to allow absolute ignorance of any of Stobaeus. He had a command of the entire text; for much of it, his command was near perfect.

Stobaeus in the *IPC*

If that is what Grotius knew of Stobaeus, what use did he make of his knowledge? To answer that question, I will look specifically at the *IPC*. As with the previous section, my goal is not to interpret or critique but only to develop a full account of the figures discussed and, more importantly, the portions of the text he employed.

Before getting to my summary, I want to make a couple of points. First, some numbers. In the index accompanying the Classics of International Law edition of the *IPC*, there are seventeen references to Stobaeus. In the manuscript itself, Grotius mentions Stobaeus seven times (or less, depending on how one reads certain scribbles in the collotype); the other ten are supplied by the translators in their edition. Second, turning from numbers to content, the seventeen references are to Diogenes, Hierax (twice), Hierocles, Democritus (sextuple), Menander, Nicholas of Damascus, Homer, Polus Lucanus, Antiphanes, an unnamed source about Sparta, and Antisthenes. Since I am not a classicist, I do not know the number of sources which attest these passages. Some are obviously common (e.g., Homer), others presumably less so (Hierax?). The existence of multiple attestations for particular texts is relevant in the cases where Grotius has not provided references himself, for it is possible that the editors have supposed he got them from Stobaeus when he actually used some other authority. When I checked Stobaeus to verify two examples (Antiphanes and one from Democritus), I found that they were there. This audit provides some reason to believe that they are all Stobaean.

[16] See J. ter Meulen and P.J.J. Diermanse, *Bibliographie des écrits imprimés de Hugo Grotius* (The Hague: Nijhoff 1950), 172.

With so much having been said by way of prelude, let me quote and give the exact reference for all seventeen quotations. The location is stated in the left column of Table 1; the full text is in the right, followed by alphabetic bullets indicating (a) what the translator/editor has supplied and (b) what is written in the actual manuscript.[17]

Table 1. Stobaeus in the IPC

Location	Text and Comments
Chap. II (p. 9)	'Thus Socrates (as quoted by Xenophon and Plato) and Diogenes, too, have correctly maintained that justice is a virtue which makes us useful to ourselves as well as to others, so that the just man will in no way inflict injury upon himself or upon any of his members, nor will he bring pain or distress upon himself.' (a) The translator/editor attaches a note to 'Diogenes' which reads: 'Stobaeus, Sermones [in Florilegium], IX [n.49].' (b) The actual marginalia state: 'Stob. sermon.'
Chap. II (p. 17)	'A part of these precepts regarding punishment is so necessary, indeed, that some persons have described justice itself as…, "the exaction of a penalty from those who have previously committed a wrongful act".' (a) The translator/editor attaches a note to 'persons' which reads: 'Hierax in Stobaeus [Florilegium, IX, n.58].' (b) The actual marginalia state: 'Hierax apud Stob.'
Chap. II (p. 21)	'Hierocles says:… "That which is public should not be separated from that which is private […]. For whatever is beneficial for one's country [as a whole] is likewise of common advantage to the various parts thereof." ' (a) The translator/editor attaches a note to 'Hierocles' which reads: '[In Stobaeus, Florilegium, XXXIX, n.35.]' (b) There are no entries in the actual marginalia.

(Continued)

[17] I am using Williams's translation – *De Jure Praedae Commentarius. Commentary on the Law of Prize and Booty. A Translation of the Original Manuscript of 1604,* tr. by G.L. Williams and W.H. Zeydel (Oxford: Clarendon Press, 1950) – as I don't think it is important to cite the original Latin. All page references are to this translation.

Table 1. Stobaeus in the IPC *(Cont.,)*

Location	Text and Comments
Chap. II (p. 23)	'This is the point made by Democritus when he says:… "the laws would not have prohibited that each person should live in accordance with his own free will, had there been no tendency on the part of any man to injure his fellow. For it is ill will that paves the way for civil discord." ' (a) The translator/editor attaches a note to 'Democritus' which reads: '[In Stobaeus, Florilegium, XXXVIII, n. 57]' (b) There are no entries in the actual marginalia.
Chap. III (p. 48)	'On this basis, it has been widely held that wars carry with them a tacit agreement of exchange, so to speak, an agreement to the effect that each belligerent, acquiescing in the turn of the die as the contest proceeds, shall take the other's property or lose his own, thus bearing out Menander's assertion that […] They who desire to snatch a neighbour's wealth, Fall oft from hope to ruinous defeat, Adding their own goods to that alien store.' (a) The translator/editor attaches a note to 'Menander's' which reads: '[In Stobaeus, Florilegium, X, n. 3.]' (b) There are no entries in the actual marginalia.
Chap. VI (p. 60)	'Democritus has said:… "It behoves us to defend with all our might the victims of unjust oppression, and not to leave them neglected; for the former course is just and good, whereas the latter is unjust and wicked." ' (a) The translator/editor attaches a note to 'Democritus' which reads: '[In Stobaeus, Florilegium, XLVI, n. 43]' (b) There are no entries in the actual marginalia.
Chap. VII (p. 71)	In a paragraph which is devoted to explicating the concept of wrong, Grotius says 'The expression "a wrong", when opposed to "a right", has three meanings…' The three wrongs are (1) 'τὸ ἄδικον [wrong in the generic sense, that which is unrighteous or unjust]'; (2) 'ἀδίκημα [intentional wrongdoing] which manifests itself in either of two aspects, ὕβρις καὶ ζημία [wanton violence, and damage]'; and (3) 'ἀδικία [habitual and characteristic wrongdoing, injustice]'. Just after that sentence, Grotius adds that 'Hierax the philosopher, in his book on Justice, draws a neat distinction with regard to these three terms, observing that the first represents

Location	Text and Comments
	ἀποτέλεσμα [completion or result], the second πρᾶξιν [action], and the third ἕξιν [a habit or state of mind]...' (a) The translator/editor attaches a note to 'Hierax' which reads: '[In Stobaeus, Florilegium, IX. 58.]' (b) There are no entries in the actual marginalia.
Chap. VIII (p. 91)	Here the text makes four consecutive references to Stobaeus. They all involve citations of Democritus. 'Democritus, too, in his discussion of natural law, draws an example from the beasts to justify the punishment of the guilty... "As to the question of whether or not animals should be slain, the matter stands as follows: whosoever shall slay animals that are doing harm or desiring to do harm, is free from guilt; indeed, it is even more righteous to have committed such an act of slaughter than to have abstained therefrom." Farther on, the same writer declares: "It is proper in every way and for all persons, that those creatures whose harmfulness exceeds the bounds of law, should be slain." Yet again, he makes the following observation: ... "Furthermore, it would seem that the very acts which we have mentioned in connexion with foxes and harmful serpents are proper in connexion with human beings, also." And to this he adds: ... "That person is innocent who slays a thief and robber in any manner whatsoever, whether by his own hand, by his command, or by his vote of condemnation." ' (a) The translator/editor attaches notes which refer to 'In Stobaeus [Florilegium XLIV. 16, 17, 18, 19]' (b) The actual marginalia state: 'Stob.' Note: the ms. is torn on this page.
Chap. VIII (p. 93)	'Similarly, Nicholas of Damascus informs us that among the Umbrians it was the custom for each individual to avenge himself by his own hand.' (a) The translator/editor attaches a note to 'Damascus' which reads: 'Stobaeus, De Legib. [Florilegium, X. 70]' (b) The actual marginalia state: 'Stob. de Legib.' (??? – it is nearly illegible).
Chap. VIII (p. 103)	'For we seek to do harm to our foes, [...] Whether by fraud or unmasked violence,

(Continued)

Table 1. Stobaeus in the IPC *(Cont.,)*

Location	Text and Comments
	By stealth or openly…' (a) The translator/editor attaches a note to 'violence' which reads: '[Cf. Homer, Odyssey I. 296; Stobaeus, Florilegium, LIV. 46.]' (b) There are no entries in the actual marginalia; however, there is a scratched out mark which may read 'Sto.'
Chap. IX (p. 125)	'War is waged by the virtuous in order that justice may be enjoyed; and justice, as Polus Lucanus so admirably explains, is the very same quality that is called "peace" with reference to the community, whereas with reference to subjects in their relation to rulers it is called "ready obedience".' (a) The translator/editor attaches a note to 'Lucanus' which reads; 'In Stobaeus [Florilegium, IX. 54].' (b) The actual marginalia state: 'Apud Stob. De Iustitia' (??? – the last word is nearly illegible).
Chap. IX (p. 128)	'Antiphanes gives us a rather neat phrase describing the soldier who, […] In quest of a living, forsooth, rushes Forth headlong to death!…' (a) The translator/editor attaches a note to 'Antiphanes' which reads: '[In Stobaeus, Florilegium, LIII. 9.]' (b) There are no entries in the actual marginalia.
Chap. X (p. 157)	'Our inference applies, for example,… to unproven thefts, by Spartan custom, and to loans and deposits, among the East Indians of earlier times.' (a) The translator/editor attaches a note to 'times' which reads: 'Stobaeus [XLIV. 42].' (b) There are no entries in the actual marginalia.
Chap. XV (p. 351)	'As Antisthenes neatly observed long ago: … "We ought to wish that our enemies may have goods and no valour; for in such circumstances the goods become the property, not of the persons who have them [at the moment], but of those who [later] win them." ' (a) The translator/editor attaches a note to 'Antisthenes' which reads: 'In Stobaeus, Florilegium, LII [LIV. 41].' (b) The actual marginalia state: 'Stob. serm. [?] 52.'; note that the second word is nearly unintelligible.

Some observations. First, notice the impressive distribution. While Grotius may not cite Stobaeus for some 200 pages in the middle of the volume, he does draw on him in the crucial 'Prolegomena' and six other chapters. Stobaeus was an important source for Grotius, figuring into his argument at a number of different points. Second, even as the young man he was when writing the *IPC*, Grotius plainly knew Stobaeus well. He cites material from nine different headings scattered across the *Florilegium*. It may be true that his citations are closer to paraphrases than word-for-word quotations but this is more an indication of the fallibility of memory than failure of study. In a way, the very fact that they are paraphrases is proof of his familiarity with the text: he knew it well enough to recount specific passages without citing the original. Third and crucially, though the *Florilegium* is well represented, the *Eclogae* is conspicuous in its total absence. Certainly, it is possible that at this point in his life, Grotius simply hadn't encountered the *Eclogae*. I am inclined, however, to discount the importance of this possibility. As the appendix to my paper demonstrates, although we know for sure that he knew about the *Eclogae* by that time in his life, Grotius make scant use of the *Eclogae* in the *IBP*, too. This makes me think that even if Grotius had known the *Eclogae* when writing the *IPC*, he wouldn't have used it. What we learn from studying the *IPC*, then, is that Grotius didn't take the *Eclogae* to be all that important. This invites the question of my next section.

What's in II.7?

In Section One, I described in general terms the contents of Stobaeus's work. Here I want to move beyond such generalities and concentrate on the final chapter of Book Two and the first one on ethics in the entire volume, Chapter Seven.

This chapter had a forlorn history. Apart from belonging to the largely neglected *Eclogae*, it was also long-misunderstood. For centuries, it was thought to be a pastiche drawn from various sources by Stobaeus himself. It was only in 1859 that August Meineke 'discovered' (his word) that the true author was Arius Didymus.[18] His hypothesis received major support from Herman Diels twenty years later[19] and together the two of them almost

[18] See August Meineke, 'Zu Stobaeus, Sokrates', *Zeitschrift für das Gymnasialwesen*, vol. 13 (1859), p. 564.

[19] See Hermann Diels, *Doxographi Graeci* (Berlin: G. Reimer, 1879), pp. 69-88.

succeeded in closing the question of authorship. *Almost*: there is, predictably, still debate; in 1995, Göransson argued against an attribution to Arius Didymus; his claims were forcefully answered by Inwood that same year.[20] Apart from the desire of scholars to get things right, there is more riding on the correct answer to the question of attribution: if Arius Didymus is indeed the author of II.7, then since he seems to have died shortly after the birth of Christ, the date of composition would be 400 years earlier than if Stobaeus were responsible. Moreover, Arius Didymus seems to have been a philosopher of some repute himself, one whose synthesizing tendencies made him both acquainted with and friendly to Stoicism. So instead of a pastiche by a non-doctrinaire non-philosopher, we would have an authentic text by someone who was sympathetic with, perhaps even a part of, the Stoic tradition.

Let us accept that Arius Didymus was the author and that Stobaeus has presented accurately his work. What does it actually discuss? Apart from an introductory 'ethical prolegomena' (II.7.37-57 – line numbers can be excluded as unnecessary for present purposes), it has two main parts. In the first (II.7.57-116), there is a discussion of Stoic ethics; in the second (II.7.117-152), the subject is Peripatetic ethics. Setting aside the Peripatetics, the section on Stoicism commences with a protracted discussion of Stoic axiology (II.7.57-85). After this, it examines appropriate acts (*kathêkonta* – II.7.85-6), impulse (*hormê* – II.7.86-93) and lives (*bioi* – II.7.93-116). The discussion is often highly technical, which may account for its shoddy treatment through the centuries. Faced with a choice between the elegances of Cicero or the fervour of Seneca and the dry analyticity of Stobaeus, most readers would unhesitatingly go for the former.

Most. Not all. Here we come to the real import of II.7. Without impugning the value of many other fragments and shorter texts, there can be no doubt but that three most important sources for Stoic ethics are Diogenes Laertius (D.L.) VII.84-131, Cicero's *De finibus* III.16-76 and Stobaeus *Ecl.* II.7.57-116. That is, modern scholarship has agreed that Arius Didymus's testimony in II.7 is one of three seminal texts for reconstructing and understanding Stoic ethics.[21] Of course, the fact that II.7 is one of three might not seem

[20] See T. Göransson, *Albinus, Alcinous, Arius Didymus* (Göteborg: Ekblad, 1995) and Brad Inwood, 'Review of Göransson, *Albinus*', *Bryn Mawr Classical Review*, 95.12.8 (1995). For more assessment, see Jaap Mansfeld and David T. Runia, *Aëtiana the method and intellectual context of a doxographer* (Leiden: Brill, 1997).

[21] Reflecting its importance, several new translations have been published in recent years. See *Hellenistic Philosophy: Introductory Readings*, 2nd edn, ed. and tr. by Brad Inwood and Lloyd Gerson (Indianapolis: Hackett, 1997); *Etica stoica*, ed. by Natali; and *Arius Didymus: Epitome of Stoic Ethics*, ed. and tr. by Arthur J. Pomeroy (Atlanta: Society of Biblical Literature, 1999).

so important. For one might wonder what the value is of consulting a third source when one already has two others at one's disposal. And indeed, there is significant overlap between Diogenes, Cicero and Arius. But rather than be discouraged by such overlap, it is wiser to find encouragement in it, for the congruence of ideas and arguments helps to reassure us that these testimonies – and they are all testimonies, even Arius, for even he is prized especially because he leads us back to the founding Stoic scholarchs (Zeno, Cleanthes and Chrysippus) – these testimonies are more-or-less accurate and valid representations of early Stoicism.

However, despite the congruence among the three, they are not exactly the same. This is no surprise: for they were written by vastly different authors with vastly different abilities and access to at least somewhat different resources. In their differences lies the final and enormous value of Arius: he provides different and/or more robust evidence of various Stoic themes, without which our knowledge of Stoicism would be greatly diminished. What exactly does Arius provide that Cicero and/or Diogenes do not? It would be too much to answer this question fully, so instead let me just cite four prime examples, two of which are substantive and two, methodological.[22] First, while D.L.'s discussion of indifferents (VII.104-7) resembles Arius's in both order and content, Arius's is much more extensive and it does clash with D.L. on specific points. Second, Arius's account of the traditional moral virtues is painstakingly detailed. When coupled with his discussion of numerous other 'good' qualities and skills, it completely overwhelms its counterpart in D.L. (VII.89-101). Turning to the methodological examples, Arius does not start with impulse as the primary ethical concept; instead, his starting point is value. This is different from both Cicero and Diogenes, and so constitutes different evidence for the foundations of Stoic ethics. Also, Arius tends not to go into the arguments for the doctrines he is discussing or reporting. Instead, his goal is generally to classify concepts systematically, through the identification of distinctions and the defining of relations among the entities which have been posited. To sum up this and other differences, I can do no better than quote A.A. Long: 'the distinctive features of Arius's exposition appear to be: (1) his opening division into goods, evils and indifferents; (2) his lack of interest in 'impulse' as a primary ethical concept; (3) the amplitude, coherence and exhaustive nature of his mapping of ethical concepts'.[23]

[22] For more, see Annas, 'Introduzione', in *Etica stoica*, ed. by Natali and especially A.A. Long, 'Arius Didymus and the Exposition of Stoic Ethics', in *On Stoic and Peripatetic Ethics: the Work of Arius Didymus*, ed. by W.W. Fortenbaugh (New Brunswick, N.J.: Rutgers University Studies in Classical Humanities, 1983), pp. 44-51.

[23] Long, 'Arius Didymus', p. 51.

Could one develop a plausible reconstruction of Stoic ethics without II.7? Absolutely. But would it be incomplete? For sure. And would it be different from our best-guess today about the nature of Stoic thought? Without a doubt.

Conclusion: Grotius and Seventeenth Century Stoicism

Just now, I said that nowadays scholars take D.L. VII, *De finibus* III and Stobaeus II.7 to be the main texts on ethics of the early Stoa. Let us grant that earlier generations would have recognized at least those texts available to them as central in the same way. So if someone such as Grotius did not have Stobaeus but did have *De finibus* or D.L., he would have given them pride of place in his analysis. Now, Grotius did have *De finibus*: of the three texts, *De finibus* alone is used in *IPC*. Assuming as we are that Grotius would have appreciated the importance of *De finibus* for understanding Stoic ethics, what effect would it have on his interpretation?

The issue is complicated, not least because it would be a serious mistake to infer that the mere presence of a text has necessary implications for how one will read it. Allowing for such underdetermination, however, it is still the case that strong themes will show up in one's readings. Now, Cicero's discussion of *oikeiosis* is relatively more prominent than D.L. and Stobaeus. As §6 of the 'Prolegomena' to the *IBP* shows, *oikeiosis* is also central to Grotius's response to and embrace of Stoicism. It certainly cannot be *deduced* that Grotius elevated *oikeiosis* because of his familiarity with *De finibus* and ignorance of Stobaeus. But it does constitute inductive evidence in support of that conclusion. It also illustrates a larger and more important point.

What is that point? I can put it quite simply: because he relied on different texts from us, Grotius's understanding of Stoicism will be different from ours. Furthermore, because he didn't use Stobaeus II.7 at all, the differences between his Stoicism and ours are concretely specifiable. Perhaps not easily specifiable; nor are they necessary. But they are (in my opinion) extremely likely and extremely important.

The reasons for their likelihood have already been given, so instead and by way of conclusion, I shall concentrate on the reasons for their importance. They are not hard to state. Grotius was one of the seventeenth century's most careful and thorough readers of ancient literature. Despite all his research, he never used II.7. Because Grotius of all seventeenth century intellectuals was the most likely to know and use about II.7 and he didn't, it can be inferred with some confidence that it was not widely used at the time. This is almost certainly the case in philosophical circles: Descartes, Spinoza, Malebranche,

Arnauld, Locke – to my knowledge, none of them ever discusses Stobaeus at all, much less II.7. With a knowledge of the history of ideas which matches (if not exceeds) Grotius, Leibniz is aware of Stobaeus, but even he does not speak about II.7. The absence of II.7 in these philosophers' *oeuvres* strengthens the conclusion that it was not associated with Stoicism in their time.

Another, broader and to me ultimately more interesting conclusion follows from this plus another premise. Because Grotius's Stoicism was formulated without II.7, and because seventeenth century intellectuals didn't use the text themselves, the wider seventeenth century understanding of Stoicism would have been different from ours. It is beyond the scope of the present paper to explain how it would be different. Indeed, the point I am urging now is much more modest than explaining *how* it would be different; all I am urging is *that* and *why* it would be different.

To rehearse my argument, then: Grotius knew about both *Florilegium* and the *Eclogae*. Since he knew both portions of the text, he also likely knew II.7. That chapter contains the analytical exposition of Stoic ethics formulated by Arius Didymus. Although Grotius likely knew about it, he didn't use that exposition. Since he didn't use that exposition, his understanding of Stoicism would have been different from ours in fairly predictable and quantifiable respects. Further, Grotius was not alone in not using II.7; his near-contemporaries didn't, either. Because they didn't, their understanding of Stoicism would also have been different. Since Grotius was an important vector for Stoicism into the early modern era, those who received their understanding of Stoicism from him would also have it affected in fairly predictable, indeed quantifiable respects. The contention that seventeenth-century interpretations of Stoicism are different from our own may not be entirely novel or unexpected. What has been unsaid, however, is that the differences may be at least partly due to a difference in source-texts. What we learn from Grotius is which of those texts is missing. And this provides us with a key to unlock the mystery of the status of Stoicism in the early modern era.

Appendix – Stobaeus in the *De Iure Belli ac Pacis*

As noted in my introduction, I am appending a table on Stobaeus in the *IBP* to my paper, so as to strengthen the conclusions I have reached in its main body. The left column indicates the location of each citation; the right gives the quotation itself. Alphabetic bullets are added to the right column supplying more information.

Table 2. Stobaeus in the IBP

Location	Text (Trans. by Kelsey)
Prol. §12	Note four states: 'Hierocles, in his commentary on the Golden Verse [rather *How parents should be treated*, quoted by Stobaeus, *Anthology*, tit. lxxix. 53] calls parents "gods upon earth…" ' (a) The bracketed insertion is the translator/editor's.
Prol. §23	'If no association of men can be maintained without law, as Aristotle showed by his remarkable illustration drawn from brigands…' (a) The translator/editor adds a note which reads: '[Stobaeus, x. 50.]'
I.4.4.4	'The words of Iamblichus bear upon the same subject: "The private interest is not dissociated from the public interest; rather, the good of the individual is comprised in the general good. In states, as in the case of animals and the rest of nature, the welfare of the parts is dependent upon the welfare of the whole." ' (a) The translator/editor adds a note which reads: '[In Stobaeus, xlvi. 74.]'
I.5.2.2	'In the words of Menander: "If we our strength should all together join, Viewing each other's welfare as our own, If we should each exact full punishment From evil-doers for the wrongs they do, The shameless violence of wicked men Against the innocent would not prevail; Guarded on every hand, and forced to pay The penalties which their misdeeds deserve, They soon would cease to be, or few become." ' (a) The translator/editor adds a note to 'Menander' which reads: '[In Stobaeus, xliii.30.]'
I.5.2.2	'Similar is this saying of Democritus: "Those who are oppressed by wrong-doing must be defended to the limit of our strength, and not neglected; for that is a work of justice and goodness." ' (a) The translator/editor adds a note to 'Democritus' which reads: '[In Stobaeus, xlvi.43.]'

Location	Text (Trans. by Kelsey)
I.5.3	'Says Democritus, "Use slaves just as parts of the body, one for one purpose, another for another." ' (a) The translator/editor adds a note to 'Democritus' which reads: '[In Stobaeus, lxii.45.]'
II.5, p. 241	'Hippodamus the Pythagorean speaks of "unrestrained and unnatural desires, made impulses, abominable pleasures." ' (a) The translator/editor adds a note which reads: '[Hipparchus, *De Animi Tranquilitate*, cited by Stobaeus, cviii.81.]'
II.5, p. 255	'The same writer of comedy [Eubulus] elsewhere said: "To his own manger many a slave returns, Who once had run away and lived as free." ' (a) The translator/editor adds a marginal note which reads: 'Stobaeus, lxii. 32.]'
II.7, p. 270	'Also in the tragedy Dictys the same Euripides says that "there is one law for all, which is common to men both among themselves and along with other animals." ' (a) The translator/editor adds a marginal note which reads: '[Stobaeus, lxxxiii.17 = 702.]'
II.7, p. 273	'Elsewhere Menander says: "The mother loves her children more than does the sire; The mother knows they are hers, the father thinks they are" ' (a) The translator/editor adds a marginal note which reads: '[In Stobaeus, lxxvi.7.]'
II.11, p. 332	'What is done without deliberate intent does not, as we also believe, attain to the force of an obligation, a fact which Theophrastus noted in his book on *Laws*' (a) The translator/editor adds a marginal note which reads: '[Stobaeus, xliv. 22.]'
II.12, p. 353	'... the seller should have the profit of the commodity, as well as the risk, as Theophrastus noted in a passage found in Stobaeus; in the same passage you may find also many other rules concerning the formalities of sale, of payment to bind the bargain, and of retraction, all very different from the Roman law.' (a) Grotius inserts a footnote, supplemented by the translator/editor, after 'Stobaeus's which reads: 'On Laws [XLIV. xxii].'
II.13, p. 362	'For as Sophocles says in the *Hippodamia*: The mind is wont by oath to be aroused With earnest care to shun these evils twain, That friends should blame, and gods should take offence.' (a) The translator/editor adds a marginal note which reads: 'In Stobaeus, *Sermones*, xxvii.6.]'

(Continued)

Table 2. Stobaeus in the IBP *(Cont.,)*

Location	Text (Trans. by Kelsey)
II.13, p. 372	'Therefore the person who takes an oath is bound in two ways: first, that his words should agree with his intent, which Chrysippus calls "to swear truly"; and secondly, that his action should be consistent with his words, which the same writer calls "swearing faithfully." ' (a) The translator/editor adds a marginal note which reads: '[In Stobaeus, Florilegium, xxviii.15.]'
II.13, p. 379	'Alexis the comic actor says: My nod is just as valid as an oath.' (a) The translator/editor adds a marginal note which reads: '[Stobaeus, *Sermones*, xxvii.3.]'
II.18, p. 449	'Also Charondas established the rule, that one who had taken a promise in place of payment should not have the right to prosecute.' (a) Grotius adds a marginal note, supplemented by the translator/editor, which reads: 'Stobaeus, *On Laws* [xliv.40].'
II.18, p. 452	'Moschion thinks that the occasion [i.e., the advent of the custom of burying the dead] was given by the savagery of the giants in devouring men, and that burial marked its abandonment. He, in fact, speaks as follows: By laws then 'twas ordained to give to earth The bodies of the dead, or sprinkle with the dust Those not yet buried, lest the dreadful signs Of former feastings should be left to view.' (a) The translator/editor adds a marginal note which reads: '[Stobaeus, *Eclogues*, I.viii.38.]'
II.19, p. 455	'Euripides in the *Antigone* gives this reason: Death is for mortal man the end of strifes; Then what else greater can to death be added?' (a) The translator/editor adds a marginal note which reads: '[Stobaeus, *Florilegium*, cxxv.6.]'
II.19, p. 458	'It is no objection to this custom that Homer, Aeschylus, Sophocles, Moschion, and others say that the dead are without feeling; in consequence they are not affected by injury or shame.' (a) Grotius adds a marginal note, supplemented by the translator/editor, which reads: 'Stobaeus, cxxvi [cxxv.14].'
II.20, p. 462	'Hierax, furthermore, from this most noble viewpoint defined justice as "the exacting of punishment from those who have first done wrong"…' (a) The translator/editor adds a marginal note which reads: '[Stobaeus, ix.55.]'

Location	Text (Trans. by Kelsey)
II.20, p. 465	'This view has been advanced by certain theologians. Says Democritus: "It is in harmony with nature that the better should rule."' (a) Grotius adds a marginal note, supplemented by the translator/editor, which reads: 'Thomas, II.ii.64.x, and Cajetan thereon [Stobaeus, xlvii. 19.]'
II.20, p. 468	'Musonius says: "To meditate how one may bite the one who bit him and harm the one who has done harm is the mark of a beast and not of a man."' (a) The translator/editor adds a marginal note which reads: '[In Stobaeus, xix.16.]'
II.20, p. 475	'This is true to-day among the Moschians, when a certain time has elapsed after the appeal to a judge.' (a) Grotius adds a marginal note, supplemented by the translator/editor, which reads: 'In Stobaeus, On Laws [X. lxx=frag. 7, p. 146, edit. Dindorf]'
II.20, p. 476	'Concerning this law of nature Democritus, whose words I shall quote because they are important, speaks as follows: First, the question of the right to kill wild beasts presents itself to him in this way: "In the matter of killing or not killing animals the situation is this: whoever has killed animals which actually do or desire to do harm is innocent, so much so indeed that to have done this is more justifiable than to have failed to do it." And shortly after: "It is absolutely necessary to kill all those things which unjustly do us harm." And surely it is not improbable that good men lived in this fashion prior to the flood, before God revealed His will to adapt to human nourishment other sorts of animals. Again he says: "What we have written concerning foxes and poisonous reptiles, the same it seems should be done in the case of men also." Then he continues: "One is innocent who kills a robber or a thief in any way at all, either by his hand, or by his order, or by his vote."' (a) The translator/editor adds a marginal note which reads: '[Stobaeus, xliv.16-17.]'
II.20, p. 477	'So Democritus: "The laws would not have prevented each man from living according to his own judgement, had not one been wont to abuse another. For envy marks the beginning of civil strife."' (a) The translator/editor adds a marginal note which reads: '[In Stobaeus, xxxviii.57.]'

(Continued)

Table 2. Stobaeus in the IBP *(Cont.,)*

Location	Text (Trans. by Kelsey)
II.20, p. 483	'This Eusebius the philosopher had expressed thus: "Since they can do so in no other way, let them then set themselves free in this manner from the present bondage of evil and procure for themselves a means of escape."' (a) The translator/editor adds a marginal note which reads: '[In Stobaeus, xlvi.41.]'
II.20, p. 488	'Therefore, the belief that it is natural for man to sin has been expressed by the philosophers Sopater, Hierocles, Seneca, and Philo among Jewish writers, the historian Thucydides, and very many Christian writers.' (a) The translator/editor adds a marginal note which reads: '[Stobaeus, xlvi.59.]'
II.20, p. 490	'The Stoics deny that [it is permissible to pardon or forgive], as one may see in a fragment of Stobaeus under the title *On Magistracy*...' (a) The translator/editor adds a marginal note which reads: '[Stobaeus, xlvi.50.]'
II.20, p. 491	'The remark of Sopater is to the point here: The corrective element of justice in the matter of contracts altogether spurns the family of the Graces. But the element that is concerned with punishments does not shun their mild and kindly countenance.' (a) The translator/editor adds a marginal note which reads: '[Stobaeus, xlvi.60.]'
II.20, p. 498	'With this agree the words of Antiphanes: He who when rich yet does act wickedly, What think you he would fail to do, were he but poor,' (a) The translator/editor adds a marginal note which reads: '[Stobaeus, ii.3.]'
II.20, p. 501	'Isaeus the orator also said that it was necessary that the laws be drawn up with severity, but that punishments milder than the laws should be exacted.' (a) The translator/editor adds a marginal note which reads: '[Stobaeus, xlviii.25.]'
II.21, p. 532	'On the other hand, you find that this is said of an evil-doer in the same tragedy [Children of Hercules]: Who conscious of his crimes, and trusting not in laws, A suppliant, falls at altars of the gods, I scruple not to drag before the court; For always should he suffer ills who evil does.' (a) The translator/editor adds a marginal note which reads: '[Euripides, fragm. 1036, in Stobaeus, xlvi. 3.]'

Location	Text (Trans. by Kelsey)
II.21, p. 538	'Thus he who has promised something because of another's debt suffers loss, according to the ancient proverb, 'Go surety, and expect loss'; but the immediate cause of the obligation is the promise itself.' (a) The translator/editor adds a marginal note which reads: '[Stobaeus, iii.79.]'
III.1, p. 605	'The question is often raised, however, whether one may resort to ruses also. Homer, at any rate, said that one must harm his foe – By ruse or violence, by open ways or hidden.' (a) The translator/editor adds a marginal note which reads: '[Cf. Homer, *Odyssey*, I.296; Stobaeus, liv.46.]'
III.1.6.1	'Sophocles says: What is foreign to truth it is never fitting to utter. Yet, if the telling of truth will bring sure doom to another, Pardon to him must be granted who does that which is not fitting.' (a) The translator/editor adds a marginal note which reads: '[Fr. of *Creusa*, in Stobaeus, xii.4.]'
III.1.9.1	'Cleobulus has this line: Falsehood is hateful to him who in his heart is wise.' (a) The translator/editor adds a marginal note which reads: '[Menander, in Stobaeus, xii.16a.]'
III.1.9.4	'Says Diphilus: The falsehood told for safety's sake, If I may judge, can cause no detriment.' (a) The translator/editor adds a marginal note which reads: '[Stobaeus, xii.12.]'
III.1.14.2	'Democritus says: "We must speak the truth, wherever that is the better course."' (a) The translator/editor adds a marginal note which reads: '[Stobaeus, xii.13.]'
III.4.2.2	'Musonius rebukes those kings "who are in the habit of saying, 'This is permissible for me,' not 'This is right for me.' "' (a) The translator/editor adds a marginal note which reads: '[Stobaeus, xlviii.14.]'
III.14.2.3	'This saying of Philemon is to the same effect: He, Master, who is born a man, though he may serve In slavery, still ceases not to be a human being.' (a) The translator/editor adds a marginal note which reads: '[Stobaeus, lxii.28.]'

(Continued)

Table 2. Stobaeus in the IBP *(Cont.,)*

Location	Text (Trans. by Kelsey)
III.15.8	'This very thing is indicated in a comedy by Heniochus, a writer of those days, in the following manner: Then drew near to them two women, Who turned all things to dire confusion; The one called Aristocracy, Democracy the other Through whose solicitation the cities were driven to madness.' (a) The translator/editor adds a marginal note which reads: '[Stobaeus, xliii.27.]'
III.15.9	' "Kings subject to the Romans" is the phrase in the *Commentaries* of Musonius;…' (a) The translator/editor adds a marginal note which reads: '[Stobaeus, xlviii.67.]'
III.20.42.1	'There follows a much disputed question concerning combats which are agreed upon with definite numbers, for the sake of ending a war; such combats, for example,… with thirty on each side as that between the Lacedaemonians and the Argives.' (a) The translator/editor adds a marginal note which reads: '[Stobaeus, Florilegium, vii.67.]'

The Patristic Context in Early Grotius

Silke-Petra Bergjan
Professor of Church History, Ancient and Medieval Christianity
Department of Theology, University of Zurich
e-mail: bergjan@access.uzh.ch

Abstract
The use of patristic texts was tightly bound up with the needs of the contemporary discussion which provided Grotius with sources for his patristic citations. His use of ancient texts especially in *Ordinum Hollandiae ac Westfrisiae pietas* proved to be highly controversial.

Grotius's advocacy of tolerance with respect to various forms of Christianity determines his use of patristic texts as well. He looks for examples of moderation in the Early Church and by this accomplishes a significant shift of perspective. He points out the diversity of expressions in the Early Church and therefore replaces questions of dogmatic definition with the question of how to handle orthodoxy and heresy in society. In doing so, he implies requirements for the proper reading of patristic texts in his own times. Grotius's notion of Christian liberty is connected to awareness of context and intrinsically linked to a historical understanding. In his writings, contextualisation involves both religious-historical comparison and the integration of general sources from antiquity. With regard to early Christian sources, this means that Grotius understands them as deeply rooted in the broader ancient context. This approach to early Christian literature is already visible in *De Iure Praedae*. His sensibility for cultural variation, his comparative method and historical interest in ancient institutions are outstanding, and Grotius has these characteristics in common with legal humanists like François Baudouin.

Keywords
Grotius, patristics, historical method, development of doctrine, tolerance, legal humanism, De iure praedae, Ordinum pietas, De imperio

At first glance the handling of patristic sources by Grotius in his Dutch period seems hardly to differ from what can be found in the writings of theologians who wrote in the second half of the sixteenth century, as for example Bullinger – Grotius calls him 'one of the more recent commentators'[1] – or on the other hand Brentz or Chemnitz. As they do, Grotius draws on Augustine, Ambrose,

[1] *Hugo Grotius, De imperio summarum potestatum circa sacra. Critical edition with introduction, English translation and commentary*, ed. by Harm-Jan van Dam, Studies in the History of Christian Thought 102 (Leiden: Brill, 2001), 11,6 (p. 534.20). *De imperio* will be cited from this edition, by section (and page and line number).

Cyprian, Lactantius, somewhat less often on Athanasius, Justin, and the historians Eusebius, Socrates and Theodoret, and occasionally on Chrysostom. After 1613, Grotius cites Greek authors more extensively. Unlike Bullinger, Grotius refers to the Greek editions that had been printed in the meantime. But other than this, did nothing change in the fifty years separating Bullinger and Grotius regarding the reading of patristic texts?

In his Dutch period Grotius uses patristic sources most extensively in two writings, *Ordinum Hollandiae ac Westfrisiae pietas*[2] of 1613 and *De imperio summarum potestatum circa sacra*, finished in 1617.[3] The citations in these works serve to display academic erudition, and Grotius meets thereby the scholarly expectations of his time. But one man's meat is another man's poison. His direct opponent, Sibrandus Lubbertus, speaks of *arrogantia*[4] in describing *Ordinum pietas*, and Lubbertus' own writings appear rather plain in comparison to Grotius'.[5] As the reactions to *Ordinum pietas* quickly demonstrated, Grotius's efforts to show intellectual mastery did lasting damage to the reception of the book and to his reputation. However, Grotius had reason to do as he did, and he continued to use all the intellectual and rhetorical means at his disposal in *De imperio*, though more carefully.[6] His competence, as a *jurisconsult*, to consider religious matters was sharply disputed, reflecting the broader conflict between State and Church. Showing familiarity with the tools of scholarly discourse was an attempt to demonstrate his qualifications in religious affairs.

The ongoing debate shaped its canon of quotations. A quotation supports argumentation only insofar as there is agreement on the value and importance of its author. The use of patristic texts was therefore tightly bound up with the needs of the contemporary discussion. This is evident as long as patristic references served merely to support partisan positions within a normative

---

[2] *Hugo Grotius, Ordinum Hollandiae ac Westfriesiae pietas (1613). Critical edition with English translation and commentary*, ed. by Edwin Rabbie, Studies in the History of Christian Thought 66, (Leiden: Brill, 1995). *Ordinum pietas* will be cited from this edition, by section (and page and line number).

[3] van Dam, *De imperio*, introduction, p. 19. *De Imperio* was published only in 1647.

[4] Sibrandus Lubbertus, *Responsio Ad Pietatem Hugonis Grotii* (Franeker: Rombertus Droyema, 1614), dedication letter, cf. p. 110.

[5] Lubbertus' principal writings show clearly the limitation of his knowledge, being based mainly on a collection of the acts of councils and a number of quotations of Augustine, and using Stephanus' Thesaurus for broader ancient material; cf. Sibrandus Lubbertus, *De conciliis libri quinque, Scholastice & Theologice collati cum disputationibus Roberti Bellarmini* (Geneva: Petrus Rouerianus, 1601).

[6] On the background and context of *Ordinum pietas* and *De Imperio*, see Edwin Rabbie, 'L'Eglise et l'Etat dans la pensée de Hugo Grotius', *Grotiana*, 16/17 (1995/96), 97-117.

discourse. However, this also holds for a debate in flux, a debate that became cognizant of other texts that were relevant from a new point of view and no longer followed exclusively the pattern of the already known. It has already been recognized that Grotius depended heavily on the writings of his contemporaries as a source for his patristic citations. In their editions, Rabbie and van Dam have identified numerous examples of patristic quotations present in Grotius that can also be found in the contemporary literature.[7] It may be concluded that these quotations do not indicate Grotius's own reading of ancient texts but rather originated in the books of his contemporaries.

More interesting, however, is the way in which the quotations in Grotius are embedded in the contemporary debate. For example, Grotius cites Gregory of Nazianzus, ep. 130,[8] as follows: 'Gregory of Nazianzus spoke rather harshly of synods, for he said that he "avoided any assembly of bishops" since he had seen no meeting that did not cause rather "an increase than a solution of trouble, for contentiousness and lust of power are stronger than reason"'.[9] At the time of Grotius's writing, the authority of the State in matters of religion was being challenged, and the call for a synod on the predestination controversy was in the air. Grotius supports his reservations concerning a synod by quoting Gregory of Nazianzus. The context shows clearly that Grotius[10] was relying on William Whitaker.[11] However, the quotation is found not only in Whitaker's book[12] but also in the first chapter of the treatise *De conciliis* by Sibrandus Lubbertus, Grotius's opponent.[13]

---

[7] Rabbie ('L'Eglise et l'Etat', p. 113) mentions in particular three books that Grotius may have purchased in London: William Whitaker, *Praelectiones de conciliis*; Thomas Bilson, *De perpetua ecclesiae Christi gubernatione*; Lancelot Andrewes, *Tortura Torti*.

[8] Gregory of Nazianzus, ep. 130,1-2 *ad Procopium* (GCS, 53, p. 95.20-23, Haelewyck).

[9] *Ordinum pietas*, 74. Here and in the following, Rabbie's (cf. fn. 1) translation is cited.

[10] Grotius continues by citing Hilary of Poitiers, *ad Const.* 2,5, (CSEL, 65, p. 200.9-13, Feder), as does Whitaker. But Grotius quotes a longer passage.

[11] William Whitaker, *Praelectiones, in quibus tractatur controversia de concilijs contra Pontificios inprimis Robertum Bellarminum* (Cambridge: James Allenson, 1600).

[12] Johannes Bogerman, *Ad Scripti Magnifici & Clarißimi viri H. Hugonis Grotii, Partes priores duas, In quibus tractat causam Vorstii & Remonstrantium, sive Pastorum illorum qui sequuntur sententiam Arminii, Annotationes* (Leeuwarden: Abraham Radaeus, 1614), praef. Here Bogerman comments upon this citation from Whitaker using Whitaker's own words: 'Whitakerus *contra Campianum pag. 83. edit. Lich. 1601.* Neque ego Conciliorum dignitatem verbis conabor extenuare & Nazianzenum miror (epist. 42. ad Procop.) de Conciliis tam inique judicasse, & acerbe scripsisse. Secum enim deliberasse ac plane constituisse ait, ut omnem Episcoporum congressionem fugeret, quandoquidem nullius unquam synodi foelicem exitum vididisset. Id etsi de multis verum fuit, quae propter quorundam ambitionem ac πολυπραγμοσύνην non veteres controversias sustulerunt, sed novarum potius controversiarum semina sparserunt: tamen nonnulla concilia ipse exitus longe optatissimus comprobavit. Quare quod provocas ad concilia, in multis quidem & maximis judiciis sequimur: in omnibus enim nec ipsi necessarium esse judicatis'.

[13] Sibrandus Lubbertus, *De Conciliis*, p. 2. ep. 130 ad Procopium.

Grotius was not one to introduce new texts into the debate, but all the same, his use of ancient texts in *Ordinum pietas* proved to be highly controversial. Lubbertus called Grotius's choice of texts 'unfortunate'.[14] Johannes Bogerman, who wrote a rebuttal to *Ordinum pietas* in the form of annotations, addressed Grotius's use of patristic texts as well. In Bogerman's critique can be read the reproach that in his readers' best interest, Grotius should have indicated his sources more precisely,[15] a point in a debate *de usu patrum* that was hardly justified by Grotius's actual handling of citations or by his dependence on Whitaker. Rather, the criticisms levied by Lubbertus and Bogerman show that the controversy had affected the reading of patristic sources.

The task presents itself to describe transitions in the debate in the beginning of the seventeenth century and their effect on the reading of patristic sources. Grotius's own observations concerning the use of patristic sources in *Ordinum pietas* and *De imperio* shall serve as a starting point. Even though in Grotius clusters of proofs can be found that draw on the normative discourse, attention will be given to passages that reflect a certain contextualization of patristic texts within antiquity. In the second part of the essay, this line will be traced back to Grotius's earlier work, *De iure praedae.*

I. Examples of *modestia* in History

Patristic References in Ordinum Pietas *(1613) and* De Imperio *(1616)*

In *Ordinum pietas* and *De imperio* there are a few passages where Grotius reflects on the use of patristic texts. Without using the technical term, Grotius situates himself in the *consensus patrum*.[16] Confronting his addressees and opponents, he points to the very quantity of citation: 'How many examples of this does Antiquity provide!';[17] 'What are you going to reply to this mass of examples – Sibrandus?'[18] What is meant are references to the Early Church. Continuity with the Old Faith, and legitimation through the same, remain

[14] Sibrandus Lubbertus, *Responsio Ad Pietatem Hugonis Grotii*, p. 110.

[15] Bogerman, *Annotationes*, p. 61.

[16] For example, in *Ordinum pietas* 64 (p. 152). The argument of *consensus patrum* was very common and was even adapted to the Protestant context in the form of a consensus of the Reformed Churches. Sibrandus Lubbertus writes: *Huc accedit omnes reformatas Ecclesias hanc opinionem improbare. Vnanimi enim consensus docent ..., Responsio Ad Pietatem Hugonis Grotii*, p. 5, cf. pp. 109, 132, 159.

[17] *Ordinum pietas*, 85 (p. 166.3f.).

[18] *Ordinum pietas*, 151 (p. 208.31f.).

the undisputed basis of the debate. The claim to be in agreement with the ancient Church was made over and over again on all sides, and Grotius is no exception in this respect. Nevertheless, he differs in his approach from, for example, his opponent Sibrandus Lubbertus. Various parties could claim the authority of the Early Church only because contradictory things were said by ancient writers. But how should one deal with this diversity? Or how should it be interpreted? In contrast to Sibrandus Lubbertus, these questions are important to Grotius. Consider a statement like the following: 'Do not Calvin and others when they loudly protest against the freedom of will often repeat, in this respect the Fathers should not be listened to?'[19] Grotius disagrees with both content and method, but his alternative is not simply to follow the Early Church in every respect. On the contrary, he recognizes the variety of expression in the Early Church. This is the point of departure for developing a picture of Grotius's conception of the Early Church.

Grotius's advocacy of moderation and tolerance with respect to various forms of Christianity is a major purpose in *Ordinum pietas* and *De imperio* and determines his use of patristic texts as well. It was precisely this *modestia* or moderation that Grotius insisted upon and that he found to be lacking in his opponents' treatment of the Vorstius affair.[20] For his opponents, it was merely a matter of proscribing certain forms of public speech. Yet at the same time they held themselves to be tolerant in religious affairs.[21] Grotius was familiar with the distinction being made here and quotes the unique relevant sentence from the Theodosian Code 16,5 *De haereticis* in *De Imperio:*[22]'He shall have the right to know such noxious doctrines only for himself but shall not reveal them to others to their hurt'.[23] Grotius, however, employs this quotation from the Theodosian Code primarily as a reference to the freedom of opinion

[19] *Ordinum pietas*, 52 (p. 142.17f.).

[20] Cf. Jonathan I. Israel, *The Dutch Republic. Its Rise, Greatness, and Fall 1477-1806*, (Oxford: OUP, 1998), pp. 421-432; Henk J.M. Nellen, *Hugo de Groot (1583-1645)* (Weesp: Heureka, 1985), pp. 24-33, now Idem, *Hugo de Groot. Een leven in strijd om de vrede, 1583-1645* (Amsterdam: Bakker, 2007), see also Nellen in this volume.

[21] Lubbertus, *Responsio Ad Pietatem Hugonis Grotii*, p. 109.

[22] *De Imperio* 3,9 (p. 218.1, v.D.). Here and in the following, van Dam's translation (cf. fn. 1) is cited.

[23] CTh, 16, 5.5.4f (p. 856, Mommsen/ Meyer). In *De imperio*, 8.3 (p. 378.19-25) Grotius gives a summary of the laws against heretics in CTh, 16, 5 and Augustine's response: 'In the same way the Christian emperors forbade assemblies of heretics and schismatics; they ordered them to give up their basilicas to the Catholic Church, they prevented heretics and schismatics from gaining access to high offices; they even took away the right to acquire anything by testament. All these things are defended extensively by Augustine against the Donatists. For the ancient Church did not disapprove of the kind of punishment that left time for repentance to those who

granted to heretics by this edict. Grotius refers to Lactantius and Cassiodor to confirm the principle that belief is not a matter of command.[24] This brings to the fore the tension between the freedom of opinion implicit in CTh 16,5,5 and the imposition of Nicene orthodoxy in CTh 16,1,2.[25] This tension is relevant for Grotius's own times. In *Ordinum pietas* Grotius points out critically that Anabaptists in Friesland could be tolerated, whereas Vorstius could not be suffered in their own ranks.[26] In support of his position Grotius turns to the Early Church.

According to Grotius, the experience of the Early Church already showed that mistakes in the handling of heterodoxy, such as possibly happened in the case of the Dutch states against Vorstius, do not discredit those that erred in their assessment. Grotius undergirds this with a quotation from Eusebius, which accordingly carries some weight. Grotius takes Firmilian of Caesarea's wait-and-see attitude at a synod that was to judge Paul of Samosata, mentioned in Eusebius,[27] as an example that demonstrates that a false favourable estimation of somebody later deemed to be heretic did not necessarily merit condemnation.[28] Prior to Grotius this quotation from Eusebius was only rarely cited. It nevertheless found print in the diatribes against Vorstius and was thus available to Grotius.[29]

Grotius replaces questions of dogmatic definition with the question of how to handle orthodoxy and heresy in society. Grotius looks for examples of moderation in the Early Church and in this way accomplishes a significant shift of perspective. Issues of procedure rather than content come to the fore,

sinned inexcusably in religious matters.' See Caroline Humfress, 'Roman law, forensic argument and the formation of Christian orthodoxy (III-VI centuries)', in *Orthodoxie, christianisme, histoire – Orthodoxy, Christianity, History*, ed. by S. Elm, É. Rebillard, and A. Romano, Collection de l'École Française de Rome 270 (Rome: École Française de Rome, 2000), pp. 125-147; Klaus Schreiner, "Duldsamkeit" (tolerantia) oder "Schrecken" (terror). Reaktionsformen auf Abweichungen von der religiösen Norm, untersucht und dargestellt am Beispiel des augustinischen Toleranz- und Gewaltkonzepts und dessen Rezeption im Mittelalter und in der frühen Neuzeit', in *Religiöse Devianz*, ed. by D. Simon, Studien zur Europäischen Rechtsgeschichte 48, (Frankfurt: Vittorio Klostermann, 1990), pp. 159-210.

[24] This principle was put forward by the Donatists against Augustine, Augustine, ep. 185,22 (CSEL, 57, p. 21.9f, Goldbacher), cf. ep. 173, 1-3.

[25] CTh, 15, 1.2 (p. 833, Mommsen/ Meyer).

[26] *Ordinum pietas*, 31-33 (pp. 128-130).

[27] Eusebius of Caesarea, h.e. 7.30.4-5 (GCS, Eusebius II/2, p. 706.17-708.3, Winkelmann).

[28] *Ordinum pietas*, 33 (p. 130.1-3): 'For Firmilian and other bishops did not cease to be orthodox even though, for a very long time, they tolerated Paul of Samosata'.

[29] *Wt-Legghinghe, Coenradi Vorstii, Over sommighe Schrifuer-plaetsen, vergheleken. Met de verklaringhe der Socinianen: Mits-gaders De kettersche Practijcken Pauli Samosateni ende Arij. Wt de kerckelijcke Historien* (Vrieslant, 1611).

which is of course closely connected to Grotius's own role in the controversy. He states most clearly: 'But the opposite method: "He disagrees with me on predestination, I cannot tolerate him. He is heterodox, he is a heretic, he is a Pelagian. He is a Socinian" should be given up as quickly as possible'.[30] This way of going about things – the sharp drawing of lines, the habit of separation – Grotius identifies as 'the spirit of Donatus'.[31] By identifying his opponents with the 'heretic' opponents of Augustine, he skewers them on their own weapons.

Moderation was not merely a much visited topos and a general call for good sense; moderation, peace and tolerance – '*concept van de moderatie, vrede ende dulding*' – were the subject of a burning debate in the Netherlands, as can be seen in the writings of Jacobus Trigland, 1615[32] but also in the reactions to Grotius's *Ordinum pietas*.[33] For Trigland, as much as for Lubbertus, tolerance in matters of doctrine is inadmissible. Characterizing the situation by the question '*Of twee strijdighe Leeringen in een Kercke geduldet/ ende de Leeraers vande selve/ voor Leeraers der Waerheyt/ ende getrouwe Herders vande Kudde Christi/ erkent moghen worden*',[34] Trigland explained to his readers the concept of *moderatie* as he understood it. Lubbertus also wanted to hold on to the notion of tolerance. It is not the act of tolerating itself that is in question, writes Lubbertus in response to Grotius: '*Non enim in quaestionem venit, An tolerandus sit, qui diversum credit?*'[35] This was doubly true; for one, because a person cannot be forced to believe against his own convictions, and for another, because there are times and circumstances that make tolerance a matter of practical necessity.[36]

---

[30] *Ordinum pietas*, 91 (p. 170.17-19).

[31] *Ordinum pietas*, 92 (p. 170.30).

[32] See the introduction in Jacobus Triglandius, *Den Recht-gematigden Christen: Ofte vande waere Moderatie* (Amsterdam: Paulus van Ravesteyn, 1615) repr in *Het Eerste Deel/ Vervatende die Boeken ende Schriften Jacobi Triglandii, de welcke handelen vande vijf Artyckelen Ende vande Moderatie* (Amsterdam: M.J. Brandt, 1639), pp. 25-67; see also Jacobus Triglandius, *Advys Over een Concept van moderatie* (Amsterdam: M.J. Brandt, 1615; Kn. 2192), repr. in *Het Eerste Deel*, pp. 3-24.

[33] See J. ter Meulen and P.J.J. Diermanse, *Bibliographie des écrits sur Hugo Grotius imprimés au XVIIe siècle* (The Hague: Martinus Nijhoff, 1961).

[34] The question is 'whether two conflicting doctrines can be tolerated in one Church, and whether the teachers of these doctrines can be acknowledged as teachers of truth and faithful shepherds of the flock of Christ' (Trigland, *Den Recht-gematigden Christen*, p. 29).

[35] Lubbertus, *Responsio*, p. 109.

[36] See Cornelis Augustijn, 'Die Ketzerverfolgung in den Niederlanden von 1520 bis 1545', in *Ketzerverfolgung im 16. und frühen 17. Jahrhundert*, ed. by H.G. Guggisberg, B. Moeller and S. Seidel Menchi, Wolfenbütteler Forschungen 51 (Wiesbaden: Otto Harrassowitz, 1920), pp. 49-63.

However, toleration, according to Lubbertus, was only the *libertas credendi*,[37] which did not include the freedom to make thoughts public. The public sermon leaves no room for heterodoxy. One cannot be a heretic with heretics and at the same time be recognized by the orthodox as orthodox.[38] Thus Lubbertus introduces the element of deceit, relevant in part because Vorstius was blamed for interpolating heretical texts and then recommending them under his own authorship to unsuspecting readers.[39]

The motto 'deceit' gave Lubbertus the opportunity to refer to the passage from Eusebius' Church history that Grotius had cited, one of the very few patristic references in *Ordinum pietas* that caught his attention.[40] For Lubbertus, as for Grotius, the postponed trial of Paul of Samosata corresponds to the case of Vorstius, but it does so in a fundamentally different way. For Lubbertus, Firmilian does not exemplify moderate and careful judgement; rather, it was the deceit in the two cases that serves as the point of comparison. In taking this position Lubbertus was correcting Grotius by invoking the interpretation given in Eusebius, who emphasized repeatedly that it was Paul of Samosata's trickery that explains Firmilian's hesitation in judgement. In Grotius's paraphrase of Eusebius, the element of deceit still appears, but Grotius's point of reference is different. Grotius distinguishes historical facts and their interpretation. Thus he tries to extract a historical example from Eusebius while leaving behind its interpretation.

For Grotius Firmilian's example stakes out a space for moderation, as Firmilian's postponement of the condemnation of somebody later seen as a heretic did not result in his own orthodoxy being questioned. The moderation exhibited here entails a self-limitation that affects doctrinal condemnations but also the stringency of doctrine itself: 'Since when has it been a heresy to say less?'[41] But Grotius could have found examples in the history of the fourth century, where to say less was indeed not enough and further clarification proved to be necessary, and Bogerman refers to this very point in his critique.[42] In the texts of the fourth century, however, Grotius finds two threads that he takes up here, namely, the conviction that matters of religion are fundamentally simple, and the requirement not to be too curious in matters

[37] Lubbertus, *Responsio*, p. 108.

[38] Ibid., p. 101.

[39] Ibid., p. 100.

[40] Ibid., p. 104.

[41] *Ordinum pietas*, 43 (p. 136.31f.).

[42] Johannes Bogerman, *Annotationes*, p. 116: '*Plane incogitanter hoc quaeris: An nescis Samosatenum et Arrium damnatis eße haereseos, eo quod* minus *dicerent de Christo? Annon Pelagius damnatus est, quod* minus *diceret de gratia?*'.

of religion, not to raise too many questions. Both values are often referred to in the Early Church. The prohibition of curiosity in religious matters was specifically aimed at the Eunomians, a rather intellectual, speculative group to whom a particularly high degree of curiosity was attributed.[43] Grotius knows of these themes through a small number of quotations of Gregory of Nazianzus, who reappears significantly in this connection.

It is tempting to ask whether Grotius's notion of ancient moderation was influenced by his interest in this particular figure of the Early Church, Gregory of Nazianzus, who challenged Julian's notion of hellenism and formulated philosophical requirements for Christian leadership.[44] However, the quotations in *De imperio* do not lead to the conclusion that Grotius had studied Gregory on his own. It is clear that many of them could be found in secondary sources that Grotius had at his disposal.[45]

To deepen his argument Grotius returns to the Theodosian and Justinian Codes. For example, he refers to the prohibition of public discussion of the Christian faith imposed by Marcian after the Synod of Chalcedon.[46] Grotius adds further evidence, such as the law of Leo and Anthemius, which he paraphrases as forbidding those who leave their monasteries from discussing faith and doctrine. What is meant here is that monks who have business outside the monastery are forbidden to walk about through Antiochia and other cities arguing matters of doctrine.[47] By referring to the Theodosian and Justinian Codes, Grotius introduces historical information. This leads to a second aspect, Grotius's historical approach to patristic sources.

Grotius uses concepts from the fourth century to discuss the handling of orthodoxy in ancient times. In doing so, he puts to practice requirements for

---

[43] See Richard Lim, *Public Disputation, Power, and Social Order in Late Antiquity*, The Transformation of the Classical Heritage 23 (Berkeley: University of California Press, 1995), pp. 109-148.

[44] Susanna Elm, 'Orthodoxy and the True Philosophical Life: Julian and Gregory of Nazianzus', *Studia Patristica*, 37 (2001), pp. 69-85. This question arises especially against the background of the poetic works of both Gregory and Grotius, in view of the fact that in his 1608 work, *Tragoedia Christus Patiens*, Grotius was inspired by Gregory's text, as is clear from Grotius's foreword. A work of Gregory's had been published under that same title in Rome in 1542. Its authenticity was disputed among Grotius's contemporaries. like 1588 Baronius, 1593 Possevin, 1594 Lipsius, 1613 Bellarmin, 1614 Casaubon, 1647 Vossius. Cf. *Grégoire de Nazianze. La Passion du Christ Tragédie*, ed. by André Tuilier, Sources Chrétiennes 149 (Paris: Les Éditions du Cerf, 1969), Introduction, p. 11-18.

[45] Grotius cites some phrases of Gregory's speeches in Greek, others in Latin. It remains unclear whether he knew the Greek edition by Johannes Herwegen of Basel published in 1550.

[46] CJ, I.1.4 (p. 6, Krüger).

[47] CJ, I.3.29 (p. 22, Krüger).

the proper reading of patristic texts in his own times. In *Ordinum pietas* as well as in *De imperio,* Grotius identifies self-restriction, or the liberty to say less, with Augustine's admonition to the Christian rhetorician spelled out in *De Doctrina Christiana,*[48] that it is not appropriate to say everything everywhere, but rather it is necessary to adapt oneself to the context of the listeners and their possibly limited understanding, as well as to consider the customs of the land. Grotius's notion of moderation or Christian liberty is connected to awareness of context and thereby intrinsically linked to a historical understanding. Grotius still explains Firmilian's false estimation of Paul of Samosata by pointing out that Paul spoke in riddles and thereby led Firmilian astray. But underlying this is the idea that doctrine and orthodoxy undergo a process of development, which implies the requirement to assess historical circumstances and personalities according to the conditions of their time. Anything else leads to the *arrogantia* of false standards: 'Was Chrysostom a Socinian, was Ambrose, were so many other ancient Fathers? If they lived now, would they not be acceptable in our Church? These questions I would like to see answered. If someone says they are not to be tolerated, his arrogance will be intolerable to all pious people; if he thinks that they should be tolerated, let him not be a respecter of persons; let there be equity, which requires equal treatment in equal cases'.[49] Grotius's argument points out the anachronism that would arise if Justin, Chrysostom and Ambrose were to be judged under the Augustinian paradigm. Using these and similar formulations, he shows that orthodoxy exists in time and is therefore subject to development. As a result, anti-Nicene ideas became an object of interest in their own context, but above all, the era of orthodoxy came to be understood as an historical era.

It is this aspect of Grotius's use of patristic sources that was most controversial and that Bogerman took pains to argue against in his response. Bogerman's argumentation shows that Grotius did not develop his arguments against opponents entirely lacking in historical insight. Certainly Bogerman would have agreed that orthodoxy exists in time. However, this does not lead Bogerman to conclude that orthodoxy is one thing at one time and something else at another time. History provides examples of manifold and even contradictory ideas. Bogerman knows that Augustine condemned many things in Pelagius that can also be found in the writings of Origen and Tertullian, but also Clement, Justin, Irenaeus and Epiphanius. According to Bogerman, however, historical variation comes into being only through mistakes, which

[48] *Ordinum pietas*, 43 (pp. 136.34-138.2); cf. *De Imperio*, 6.11 (p. 314.23-25) = Augustine, ep. 54.2 (CSEL, 34, p. 160.13-15, Goldbacher).

[49] *Ordinum pietas*, 49 (p. 140.23-29).

in the course of time are corrected through progress and learning. Bogerman therefore concludes that there are many instances of error in history, but these do not result in a continuity of error. If an error happens to occur, that does not mean that the mistake persists or is to be tolerated. According to Bogerman there is no equation between Justin, Ambrose, Chrysostom and Augustine. If Chrysostom had lived only a few decades later, he would have followed the example of Augustine. Orthodoxy puts an end to the history of error, and the history of error does not support a call for tolerance.[50] Bogerman sees progress and change in history as the mechanism by which orthodoxy comes into being, but this does not entail that orthodoxy itself is subject to development. Precisely that, however, would be the precondition for finding exemplary models of tolerance in history.

Bogerman's concept of orthodoxy implies distance from the historical Chrysostom. The Chrysostom for whom there would be a place in Bogerman's Church would be a different one from the real-life bishop of Constantinople, with his problems with the empress and the aristocracy. Grotius's work also exhibits historical distance, but in his case the distance comes from his interest not only in the history of ideas and their context but also in historical events and circumstances.

There are many examples, particularly in *De imperio*, where Grotius switches to a descriptive, historical language and develops historical argumentation. In line with his own point of view, he describes the emperors of the fourth to sixth centuries as being involved in matters of religion: 'It was not the Church of Alexandria that sent Dioscur to the Synod of Chalcedon, but the Emperors Theodosius and Valentinianus themselves who ordered him to attend'.[51] Here Grotius is clearly shifting to a descriptive perspective. He singles out significant events that he finds in the writings of the historians, particularly in Socrates and Theodoret, in the acts of the councils, and finally in ancient legal sources. By referring to the decree that forbade monks to leave their monasteries and stir up unrest by provoking doctrinal debates and to the decree forbidding the clergy to play dice or attend the theatre,[52] Grotius illustrates his points with historical vividness. The question of jurisdiction over sacred matters, particularly episcopal jurisdiction,[53] leads him to quote from the

[50] Bogerman, *Annotationes*, esp. praef. and pp. 122-127.

[51] *Ordinum pietas*, 105 (p. 180.7-9), cf. ACO, II.1.1, (p. 68.18-24, Schwartz).

[52] *De Imperio*, 8.7 (p. 382.22f.); CJC, Nov. 123, 10.1 (pp. 602f., Schoell/ Kroll).

[53] Cf. Peter E. Pieler, 'Gerichtsbarkeit' (XV Die kirchliche Gerichtsbarkeit), *Reallexikon für Antike und Christentum*, 10 (1978), pp. 466-492; W. Waldstein, 'Zur Stellung der episcopalis audentia im spätrömischen Prozess', in *Festschrift für Max Kaser*, ed. by D. Medicus and H.H. Seiler (Munich: Beck, 1976), pp. 532-56.

pertinent texts in the *Codex Theodosianus* and the *Leges novellae.* Grotius sets the quotations in a historical framework and invokes them as evidence for his theses: 'It was only after the emperors had embraced Christianity that a part of jurisdiction was given to the pastors'.[54] In another passage Grotius differentiates between two concepts, found in the *Codex Theodosianus,* namely, the ἀρχισυνάγωγοι and the *patres synagogarum,* identifying the latter with elders or seniors. And again, his conclusions are interesting: first, that there was a hierarchy in which the ἀρχισυνάγωγοι were subordinate to the elders, and second, that these 'remarks serve *ad illustrandam episcoporum originem*'.[55]

Raising the question of the roots of the office of bishop is a shift from description to explanation. For Grotius, explanation means, first of all, that he places historical matters in context. He relates the office of bishop to the offices of the synagogue; he places Christian institutions in relation to pagan Roman customs. After distinguishing various forms and extents of episcopal jurisdiction involved, Grotius turns to regulations concerning jurisdiction within the ancient Jewish community. Laws concerning Jewish privileges serve as an explanatory background.[56] Grotius has even more material at his disposal: he brings in remarks by Caesar concerning Druids in *The Gallic War* and by Plutarch concerning the Athenians, and he takes this line even further into the Old Testament, pursuing the notion of ancient usage, *vetustissima consuetudo.* Grotius relates the ancient Christian practice of publicly proclaiming the name of the man to be elected as bishop to analogous practices concerning imperial offices.[57] In his writings, contextualisation involves both religious-historical comparison and the integration of general sources from antiquity. This juxtaposition of sources, typical for Grotius, always reflects a historical

---

[54] *De Imperio,* 9.12 (p. 412.8f.). Here and in the following van Dam's (cf. fn. 1) translation is cited.

[55] *De Imperio,* 11.8 (pp. 544.16-25; 546.2), CJC, Nov. 146 (p. 716,22/23, Schoell/Kroll).

[56] *De Imperio,* 9.16 (p. 418.12-14): 'We must not be surprised by the fact that this right was granted to Christian pastors by the Christian emperors, since the same emperors gave the Jews permission not to receive anyone into their sect or help him to be reconciled with it as long as their own primates were against it'.

[57] Grotius cites a chapter from Lampridius, *Life of Alexander Severus* 18,45,6-7 (SHA, 1, 287.18-26, Hohl) in *De Imperio,* 10.8 (p. 466.19-24): 'Whenever Alexander (Severus) desired to name any man governor of a province, or to make him an officer in the army, he always announced his name publicly and charged the people, in case anyone wished to bring an accusation against him, to prove it by irrefutable evidence, and he used to say it was unjust that, when Christians and Jews observed this custom in announcing the names of those who were to be ordained priests, it should not be similarly observed in the case of governors of provinces.' The quotation was used by Bilson, but its inclusion shows Grotius's interest in the comparison of ancient secular and early Christian references.

dimension for him. With regard to early Christian sources, this means that Grotius understands them as deeply rooted in the broader ancient context.

Grotius's drawing of connections between Christianity and other ancient traditions does not only serve to search for the old, fundamental truths or to find in the concord between Christianity, Judaism and Antiquity an indication of 'right reason', common to humankind, or existing before the corruption of the old faith.[58] Much more to the point, there is a historical aspect to the juxtaposition of these religious sources, and, as when Grotius speculates on a relationship between the *patres synagogarum* and the origin of the office of bishop, it can create a historical context.

The historical context serves as an explanation, and this implies that Grotius was aware of historical problems and participated in raising historical questions. This becomes clear from the following example. Grotius discusses the formal procedures of the synods of the Early Church, and, in this context, their convocation by the emperor. This last point leads to the question of synods during the time of pagan emperors. Grotius concludes that 'no permission was needed where no imperial edicts stood against it'.[59] To prove this, Grotius refers to attestations of the existence of religious associations, *collegia,* which he finds in the *Digests*[60] and of associations in general, *hetaeria*, in Asia Minor, which he deduces from the letters of Pliny to Trajan.[61] To apply this historical information to the legal situation of Christians at the end of the first century, he uses material on the Jews given by Philo. In this passage Grotius presents a historical argument of several steps, a part of which is his reading of the Pliny letters.[62]

A further element that bespeaks a historical approach is Grotius's notion of change. Although Grotius is only concerned to show that a certain way of electing pastors cannot be taken as the general practice in the time of the Early Church (a very common mode of argumentation), it is remarkable that Grotius emphasized that change affected even apostolic institutions, that requirements of canon law were not always followed, and that the rules laid

---

[58] Cf. *De Imperio*, 1.9 (p. 170.1-5).

[59] *De Imperio*, 7.3 (p. 330.13-15).

[60] D 47.22.1.1 (840, Mommsen/Krueger).

[61] Pliny, ep. X, 93, 96 (336.21-337.4, 338.1-340.2, Mynors).

[62] The information about the Christians in Asia Minor to be found in Pliny, was common knowledge at the time of Grotius. Cf. G. Vossius, *In Epistolam Plinii de Christianis et Edicta Caesarum Romanorum adversus Christianos, Commentarius* (Amsterdam: Valckenier, 1656).; François Baudouin, *Ad Edicta Veterum Principum Romanorum de Christianis* (Basel: Joannes Oporinus, 1557).

down by Justinian differed from earlier custom. Grotius concludes: 'For whether we look at ancient or more modern times, we find enormous variation in the method of election; not only across centuries and provinces, but also over years and individual cities'.[63] These few remarks show that the idea of change is an integral part of Grotius's picture of the Early Church; the last quotation makes it particularly clear that he was aware of context.

Ordinum pietas and *De imperio* show elements of a historical approach that has much in common with the French method of teaching law, the *mos gallicus*. A sense for cultural variation, the notion of change, the question of origins, but above all the comparative method and a historical interest in offices and institutions have characterized legal humanism since Guillaume Budé. It is evident that methods of humanist jurisprudence appear in Grotius's writings on ecclesiastic and religious matters. The interest of philologists in Roman law from a historical perspective led to the French convergence of legal and historical studies and to the historicization of the studies of Roman law. Budé insisted that not only lawyers but also philologists be admitted to legal studies.[64] Grotius took this route by studying the Early Church as a lawyer and philologist. His comparative method brought together diverse sources to explain historical circumstances. He uses Roman legal texts as a historical source in the context of Church history. This corresponds to the practise of François Baudouin in his *Constantine* of 1556,[65] which Grotius later mentions having read.[66] Baudouin was the one who most clearly spelled out the need to study history alongside law and who gave shape to the historicization of law.[67] Even more significant for reading Grotius, however, is Baudouin's insistence on not separating civil history and Church history.[68] This position was part of

---

[63] *De Imperio*, 10.31 (p. 516.27-30).

[64] Donald R. Kelley, *Foundations of Modern Historical Scholarship. Language, Law, and History in the French Renaissance* (New York: Columbia University Press, 1970), esp. pp. 53-85.

[65] Fran. Balduinus, *Constantinus magnus, sive De Constantini Imp. Legibus Ecclesiasticis atque Ciuilibus Commentariorum Libri duo* (Basel: Joannes Oporinus, 1556), cf. idem, *De Institutione Historiae Universae, & eius cum Iurisprudentia Coniunctione*, in *Artis Historicae Penus* (Basel: Petrus Perna, 1579), pp. 599-742 (pp. 679-682).

[66] Ep. 2134, June 5th, 1635 (BW, VI, p. 10).

[67] *De Institutione Historiae Universae*, p. 641, esp. liber II, pp. 667ff, cf. Donald R. Kelley, 'Historia Integra: François Baudouin and his Conception of History', *Journal of the History of Ideas*, 25 (1964), 35-57.

[68] *Ad Edicta Veterum Principum Romanorum de Christianis*, praef. p. 6. This was a line of thought that became important in his correspondence with Flacius, cf. Gregory B. Lyon, 'Baudouin, Flacius, and the Plan for the Magdeburg Centuries', *Journal of the History of Ideas*, 64 (2003), 253-272.

his concept of a universal history, one that encompasses civil, religious and military spheres.[69] This integrative approach to history is founded on the observation of concrete particulars and circumstances.

Grotius's comparative approach assumes a similar connection between civil history and Church history and requires a corresponding breadth of scope. This breadth is illustrated by a list given by Gerardus Vossius in his *Ars Historica* of 1623, consisting of elements such as regions, cities, customs, institutions, philosophical teachings, military exploits and the public and private life of individuals. Grotius acquired many books on ancient times from Vossius,[70] and they conducted an intensive exchange while Grotius was working to justify his position by writing *De imperio*. The comparison with Vossius's *Ars historica,* which can serve to illustrate the state of reflection on method in Grotius's immediate circle, underlines the impact of legal humanism on Grotius. Vossius's *Ars historica* is still in the rhetorical tradition that describes the *ars* and *techne* of historical craft and seeks a balance between a history that risks degenerating to a *nuda narratio,* and a history in the sense of *notitia* or *cognitio* of what is useful to remember for the sake of a good and happy life. Vossius can define the goal of history thus: *ut ex singularibus universale praeceptum observetur.*[71] Keckermann had a similar formulation: 'History, therefore, is the explanation and knowledge of particular or individual things, undertaken in order that through them we may understand universal truths more clearly and find them confirmed'.[72] In contrast to Vossius and Keckermann however, Grotius's interest in historic institutions and details was not subservient to his allegiance to universal truths; rather, his sources provide historical evidence of the practice and customs in question.

---

[69] *De Institutione Historiae Universae*, esp. pp. 618, 626.

[70] Cf. Cornelis S.M. Rademaker, *Life and work of Gerardus Joannes Vossius (1577-1649)*, Respublica Literaria Neerlandica 5 (Assen: van Gorcum, 1981); idem, 'Books and Grotius at Loevestein', *Quaerendo*, 2 (1972), 2-29; Edwin Rabbie, 'The History and Reconstruction of Hugo Grotius' Library. A Survey of the Results of Former Studies with an Indication of New Lines of Approach', in *Bibliothecae selectae da Cusano e Leopardi*, ed. by E. Canone, Lessico Intellettuale Europeo 58 (Firenze: Olschki, 1993), pp. 119-137.

[71] Vossius, *Ars historica, sive de historiae et historices natura, historiaeque scribendae praeceptis* (Leiden: Marie, 1623), p. 25.

[72] Keckermann, *De natura et proprietatibus historiae commentarius* (Hanoviae: G. Antonius, 1610), 'Historia ergo est explicatio & notitia rerum singularium, sive individuorum, eo fine suscepta, ut universalia ex iis evidentius a nobis intelligi & confirmari possint.' The quotation is used by Nicholas Wickenden, *G.J. Vossius and the Humanist Conception of History* (Assen: Van Gorcum, 1993; diss. 1967), p. 69.

II. Comparative Method and Patristic Texts in *De Iure Praedae*

Reading through *De iure praedae* (*IPC*),[73] the juxtaposition of patristic and other classical sources again catches the attention. This contextualization of Christian texts, which later largely characterized Grotius's reading of early Christian literature, is already visible in *IPC*.[74] His approach to early Christian literature had therefore already been formed before he came into contact with Vossius in 1613 and before the debate required him to engage himself with patristic sources. This may be illustrated through examples, beginning with chapter four of *IPC*. There, Grotius shifts to his main topic, the question of prize and booty. After Grotius has deduced from legal principles that the institution of prize and booty must be considered as part and parcel of warfare, and that it is in accordance with the law of nature, as well as the law of nations, he must address Christian objections. Grotius seeks to persuade the reader through examples, and the interpretation of Scripture plays a role here. The copious material concerning warfare in the Old Testament (OT) clearly exhibits the taking of booty as a practice of the Israelites. But the pertinent passages in the OT, for example Deut. 20.14, seem to be contradicted by John the Baptist's dictum in Luke 3.14, 'And the soldiers likewise demanded of him, saying, And what shall we do? And he said unto them, Do violence to no man, neither accuse any falsely; and be content with your wages'. Grotius gives a historical explanation of the verse that is interesting, above all, against the background of western exegesis.

Grotius understands the verse as a potential objection and in response states that the situation assumed in Luke 3.14 was fundamentally different from the situation of the taking of booty, as John the Baptist's addressees were not soldiers at war but instead occupation troops stationed in Judaea, and their potential victims were provincials, tenants and farmers. John called upon the soldiers to spare them and not to rob innocent peasants. According to Grotius, John says nothing more than what was already anchored in law. Grotius echoes thereby a broad consensus, but it turns out that the consensus is limited to the understanding that the verse is not to be taken as an admonition to give up soldiery. In fact, Luke 3.14 was generally interpreted against the background

[73] Hugo Grotius, *De Iure Praedae Commentarius*, ed. by H.G. Hamaker (The Hague: Martin Nijhoff 1868); Translation: Hugo Grotius, *De Iure Praedae Commentarius. Commentary on the Law of Prize and Booty*, tr. by G.L. Williams, Classics of International Law 22 (Oxford: Clarendon Press 1950).

[74] Cf. David J. Bederman, 'Reception of the Classical Tradition in International Law: Grotius' *De Jure Belli ac Pacis*', *Grotiana*, 16/17 (1995/96), 3-34.

of a strong tradition epitomized by the often quoted words *Militare non est delictum*, found in a homely that was printed in the sixteenth-century editions among the works of Augustine.[75] But who is intended in Luke 3.14 under *miles*? The answer often given is: whoever receives wages (*stipendia*), and this includes the cleric, so that the lemma is often found in connection with ecclesiastical offices and simony.[76] The tradition reaches from Ps.-Augustine to Ivo of Chartres and Gratian. In the East as well, Luke 3.14 finds application, being integrated into general ethical instructions. These instructions do concern soldiers, but they are far from the real soldiers of Grotius in the winter station in Judaea. Grotius's historical reasons for stating that the verse is not concerned with *res hostium* are clearly distinct from the Augustinian tradition of exegesis. In his interpretation, Grotius merges different lines of thought. As Grotius indicates in the margin, he was led to mention the Judaean peasants by Cajetan, who still wrote in the tradition of ethical instructions. Later, in the *Annotationes ad Lucam*, Grotius collected extensive material concerning soldiers in Judaea, particularly from Josephus.[77] In *IPC* these historical explanations bring Grotius to the conclusion that in Luke 3.14 nothing is required that is different from what is in Roman law.

Grotius comes to the same conclusion when he turns to the example of Abraham. Abraham's conduct in war appears to coincide with Roman legal principles. Genesis 14, which recounts Abraham's campaign to free Lot and to recover his possessions from the Sodomites, serves as a classical reference for questions of waging war. Indeed, Abraham relinquished his share of the booty, but according to Grotius, he does thereby nothing other than what Plutarch ascribes to Pericles,[78] Fabius,[79] Fabricius,[80] Valerius Publicola and Marcus

[75] The spurious character of the attribution to Augustine was already recognized in the sixteenth-century editions. It was printed as part of a collection of homelies *De verbis Domini in Evangelio secundum Matthaeum in Tomus Decimus Operum D. Aurelii Augustini* (Basel: Froben, 1529, 59B; Basel: Froben, 1543, 88D; Venice, 1550, 20rE). An editorial note casts doubt on the attribution of this collection. In an appendix it was printed in *Tomus Decimus Operum D. Aurelii Augustini* (Antwerp: Chr. Plantinus, 1576, 642C).The quotation *Militare non est delictum* actually comes from Maximus of Tyre, 'De id quod scriptum est: Reddite quae Dei sunt Deo, et De militantibus' 1 (CChr, 23, 101.9-10, Mutzenbecher), and is found in *Decretum Gratiani*, II.23. qu.1.c.5 (Corpus Iuris Canonici I, 893, Friedberg).

[76] Abbo Floriacensis, Hugo Francorum, Robertus Francorum Canones, PL, 139, 506D.507A.508A.

[77] Annotationes ad Lucam, in *Opera Omnia Theologica* II/I (Amsterdam: Joannis Blaev, 1679), pp. 359-362.

[78] Plutarch, *Vitae*: Pericles 16.

[79] Plutarch, *Vitae*: Fabius Maximus 4.

[80] Plutarch, *Vitae*: Pyrrhus 17-18.

Cato.[81] This pattern of comparison occurs repeatedly. Three examples will illustrate the point. According to Grotius, Abraham's expedition described in Gen. 14 falls under the category of *bellum privatum*, which, however, did not make Abraham hesitate to take away spoils, as it also did not prevent Caesar from taking booty from the pirates that he captured.[82] Grotius finds the Caesar episode again in Plutarch, as he notes in the margin. Abraham 'instructs his allies in regard to the justice of his cause': a similar accounting was required by Achilles. As source, Grotius refers to Statius.[83] The justification given in the campaign of the Israelites against the men of Gibeah bore comparison to that given to Minos in his expedition of revenge against the Athenians, according to Diodor of Sicily.[84]

Abraham and Pericles, Abraham and Caesar, Achilles or Minos are placed alongside each other. Most of these examples from Plutarch Grotius is still citing in his *Annotationes ad Genesin*.[85] Plutarch, Dionysios Halicarnassos and Diodor of Sicily appear on the exegetical horizon of the OT. This means nothing more than that Grotius uses his own resources to interpret Gen. 14, namely classical literature, as he cannot draw on the patristic or scholastic tradition of exegesis. Accounts in the OT become plausible in the context of classical antiquity; they become comparable to non-biblical sources. Here the 'juxtaposition of sources' later elaborated by Grotius is already present, without Grotius actually developing a historical argument. However, he gives a certain emphasis to the historical parts of the OT. He returns to Deut. 20.14 and especially to Gen. 14 in various chapters in *IPC*. He draws a certain historical thread through the text. But what about the patristic texts? How does he bring them into play?

This question is particularly pressing because Grotius cannot draw on the strongly allegorical patristic or scholastic tradition of interpretation of the texts mentioned above (Luke 3.14, Deut. 20 and Gen. 14), as represented by Hrabanus Maurus or Bede, for example. When one considers that the five kings against whom Abraham fights in Gen. 14 represent for Bede the five senses, or that for Ambrose, the *virtus* and faith of Abraham bring about the victory, the distance to Grotius becomes clear. Yet still Grotius tries to integrate patristic sources into *IPC* when he depicts Abraham not only

[81] Plutarch, *Vitae*: Marcus Cato 10, cf. Dionysius of Harlicarnassos, Exc. 19,16,4.
[82] *IPC*, X (p. 134.5-11, H.).
[83] *IPC*, VII (p. 70.25-27, H.).
[84] *IPC*, VIII (p. 97.13-15, H.).
[85] Annotationes ad Genesin, in *Opera Omnia Theologica* I (Amsterdam: Joannis Blaev, 1679), p. 12.

alongside Caesar but also next to Constantine.[86] The manuscript shows that Grotius later inserted the example of Theodosius, then a quotation of Ambrose on justice, followed by Seneca, which then led him back to Cicero and to his original text.

Patristic texts, and there are only a few examples in *IPC,* are also brought into the exegetical argument. Here the names of Ambrose and Augustine come up through two short excerpts, one from Ambrose's work on Abraham[87] and another from Augustine's *Quaestiones in Heptateuchum*; both are cited in *Decretum Gratiani.*[88] From Ambrose's work, only the first book is cited and not the second, far more allegorical book. But the first book also pursues a theological aim in its exegesis of Gen. 14, where Ambrose treats the question raised by Abraham's refusal of the spoils. Why did Abraham choose to forgo the spoils? According to Ambrose, Abraham was aware that he owed the victory not to his own efforts but to God. Ambrose then uses the principle that reckons wage labour as a form of slavery, so that the choice arises, either to lower oneself to the level of a mercenary or to preserve one's honour. This line of thought, which connects the taking of spoils with wage dependence, did not interest Grotius.

For Grotius, the Abraham story establishes the right to take spoils, for Abraham could not in good conscience have given to his men something to which he himself had no claim. Grotius mentions a tradition according to which Abraham had taken a vow before the campaign to forgo all booty. What is meant here is Ambrose's explanation, which Grotius paraphrases as involving a vow. Such a self-imposed disclaimer necessarily entails there being something to which one is entitled. But do the spoils really belong to Abraham? Ambrose, who depicts Abraham as an example of virtue, encounters a further problem when he raises the question of why the King of Sodom offers part of the spoils to Abraham. This question leads Ambrose to point out the duty to share the spoils among allies, and Grotius concludes that this principle was in force up to the time of the Maccabees.[89]

Ambrose's last-mentioned explanation is the only text that Grotius actually quotes later, which he does in connection with the Roman customs depicted by Livy and Dionysius of Halicarnassus. Grotius singles out details from the Ambrose text and arranges them in such a way that they are relatable to

[86] *IPC,* IX (p. 124.24-27, H.)

[87] Ambrose, *De Abraham,* I.3.16-17 (CSEL, 32, p. 514, C. Schenkl).

[88] *Decretum Gratiani,* II.23.qu.2.c.3 (Corpus Iuris Canonici I, 895, Friedberg); II.23. qu.5.c.25 (Corpus Iuris Canonici I, 938, Friedberg) .

[89] *IPC,* X (p. 153.25-154.7, H.).

Plutarch, Livy and Dionysius of Halicarnassus, and as mentioned he can move from the *virtus* of Abraham as described by Ambrose to the motives of Pericles and Marcus Cato. The same bridging can be seen in Grotius's quoting of Augustine's comment on the war of the Israelites against the Amorites in *Quaestiones in Heptateuchum*.[90] Grotius explains the right of transit with the words of Augustine as a 'law of human fellowship'. As such, the denial of this right was seen as a just reason for war by Augustine, referring to the war of the Israelites against the Amorites, and by others, as illustrated by further examples that Grotius found in Sophocles, Tacitus and again in the Crusades.

These two examples – the dictum of John the Baptist and the figure of Abraham – may suffice, first, to illustrate a certain continuity in Grotius's approach to ancient texts through the juxtaposition of Christian and other ancient sources in *IPC*, second, to draw attention to hints that reveal Grotius's development of a historical approach, and third, to show his contextualization of patristic texts within the framework of antiquity.

[90] Augustine, *Quaestiones in Heptateuchum*, IV.44 (CSEL, 28, 2, p. 353.2-5, Zycha), *IPC*, XII (p. 207.5-9, H.).

Secularization in *De Iure Praedae*: From Bible Criticism to International Law[1]

Mark Somos
Department of Government, Harvard University
e-mail: msomos@gmail.com

Abstract

This article shows that the conspicuous and consistent idiosyncrasy of Grotius's Biblical interpretation is an important part of his revolutionary effort to secularize natural law. In *De iure praedae* and related works, Grotius systematically deployed a range of exegetical techniques in order to demonstrate that the Bible, like all texts, is open to multiple interpretations and susceptible to hijacking by rival agendas. This strategy aimed to render the Bible inadmissible as evidence in legal disputes and political legitimacy claims. The consistent instrumentality of Grotius's use of the Bible in *IPC* cannot be dismissed as mere legalistic opportunism or described as an atheistic move. Rather, Grotius's exegetical strategy was motivated by pacifism and a desire to protect religion from politicization. The article positions this secularization strategy in the intellectual environment of the Leiden Circle, and shows how competing Catholic, Calvinist, and Mennonite political readings of the same key biblical passages during the Dutch-Iberian conflict provided the immediate occasion for writing *IPC*. In order to construct a natural law theory that was independent from, and therefore acceptable to, all religious sides, it was necessary to ensure that the Bible have no final word in law or politics, lest its invocation link disagreements to belief and thereby render them impossible to resolve.

Keywords

Grotius, De iure praedae, secularization, international relations, natural law

---

[1] I owe debts of gratitude to Ioannis Evrigenis, Dániel Margócsy and Isaac Nakhimovsky, who untiringly read and commented on every draft of this paper. The paper could not have been written without the generous support and hospitality of Hans Blom. He invited me to the *IPC* Conference, provided an outstanding working environment in Rotterdam, and kindly discussed several full drafts with me. The paper benefited greatly from extensive comments by Jan Bloemendal, Michael Edwards, Lasse Gerrits, Stanley Hoffmann, István Hont, Joe Kochanek, J. Russell Muirhead, Henk Nellen, Koen Stapelbroek, Anna Stilz and Jan Waszink. József Kömüves developed and maintained an invaluable database of all biblical references, cross-references, editions and sources encountered while researching *IPC*. For their prompt and instructive replies to specific inquiries I thank Peter Borschberg, Mark Greengrass and Norman Housley; I assert the right to all remaining errors.

'Secularization' has ill-defined and contradictory meanings today. To avoid them, the French *laicisation* and the triad of detheologization, dechristianization and decatholicization were

Introduction

The realization that Grotius had undermined the Bible in legal thought with uncommon efficacy is not new, only forgotten. In *An Abridgement of All Sea-Laws* (1613), the Scottish jurist William Welwod (1578-1622) accused Grotius of advocating free-for-all fishing rights in *Mare liberum* (*ML*), published in 1609 and originally chapter twelve of *De iure praedae* (*IPC*), which was written in 1604/5. Welwod's first and most sustained criticism targeted the Dutchman's use of the Bible, in particular his hierarchy of sources and authorities – not an inconsiderable point in a legal debate.

> Now remembering the first ground whereby the author would make Mare Liberum to be a position fortified by the opinions and sayings of some old poets, orators, philosophers, and (wrested) jurisconsults - that land and sea, by the first condition of nature, hath been and should be common to all, and proper to none - against this I mind to use no other reason but a simple and orderly reciting of the words of the Holy Spirit.
>
> And thus far have we learned concerning the community and propriety of land and sea by him who is the great Creator and author of all, and therefore of greater authority and understanding than all the Grecian and Roman writers, poets, orators, philosophers, and jurisconsults, whosoever famous, whom the author of Mare Liberum protests he may use and lean to without offence.[2]

Welwod continues in much the same vein: Grotius is wrong to argue that natural features make the best borders, because 'God, who is both the distributer and first author of the division and distinction of both land and sea, hath given an understanding heart to man' exactly so that he can measure nature and construct artificial boundaries for states. Grotius's reasoning that the waters move, therefore borders cannot be established upon them, is again countered by Welwod with the argument that it is God's purposeful design that makes the body of seas stay constantly in the same place (pp. 71, 72).

experimented with, but in the end they raised more problems than they solved. In this article I shall use 'secularization' in the broad, intuitive sense, not with reference to the Victorian decline in church attendance, the 1905 French Law of Separation, or to the Dutch sociological phenomenon that began in the 1960s. Fortunately, the common-sensical meaning I use here can still be found in recent writings in several languages, including A.P. d'Entrèves, *Natural Law: An Introduction to Legal Philosophy*, rev. edn (Edison NY: Transaction, 1994), pp. 50ff., F. Todescan, *Le Radici Theologiche del Giusnaturalismo Laico* (Milan: Guiffrè, 1983), esp. ch. 3; the fine but now rarely read A. Klempt, *Die Säkularisierung der universalhistorischen Auffassung* (Göttingen: Musterschmidt, 1960), and ch. 4 of E.G. Léonard, *Histoire Générale du Protestantisme*, 3 vols (Paris: Presses Universitaires de France, 1961), I.

[2] *ML* (Indianapolis: Liberty Fund, 2004), p. 66, 67.

Welwod exploited with great relish and consistency what he considered to be Grotius's principal vulnerability, namely the radical exclusion of Christianity from his argumentation.

Why would Welwod regard this as Grotius's biggest vulnerability? After reading almost any European political treatise written between the seventh and the seventeenth century, the answer becomes obvious. In a very real and tangible sense, the Bible was the law of the land. Christianity permeated all aspects of medieval thought, from natural sciences to politics. Since religion is about the highest good, its ideologues cannot take prisoners. Institutional religion is almost never patient or kind, but envious and quick to take offense. Orthodoxy mixed with politics leads to zero-sum games. Divine legitimacy is an indivisible resource; claims to it lock the participants in murderous struggles. The Reformation exploded the entire European conceptual edifice, and this is why the Reformation, not for example the Investiture Controversy or the Avignon Papacy, led to the Wars of Religion, the greatest trauma in European history. The solution to the Wars of Religion had to be built on new, more stable intellectual foundations. A great number of attempts were made, but with hindsight we can say that secularization, the radical disconnection of religion and politics, was the only solution that could have worked. A reaffirmation of the old orthodoxy, the victory of a new, or the co-existence of several exclusivist religious-political ideologies were not practical options.[3]

What Welwod and other contemporaries could not have known is the historical significance of Grotius's move in *ML* and the whole *IPC*. Successful solutions to political problems in the aftermath of the Reformation often involved the neutralization of controversial articles of faith, without necessarily wishing to eradicate religion. On the contrary, some of them hoped to save religion by disjoining it from politics, while others did have an anti-religious

---

[3] See Eijnatten in this volume. Norman Housley, *Religious Warfare in Europe, 1400-1536* (Oxford: OUP, 2002) and his chapter 'Pro Deo et patria mori: sanctified patriotism in Europe, 1400-1600', in *War and Competition between States*, ed. by Philippe Contamine (New York: OUP, 2000), compellingly traces the continuity of holy and just war traditions from Augustine to the seventeenth century. Housley shows how religious claims were used by kings, noblemen, the national clergy, the papacy, and all other political actors. He also points out that the explosive combination of religion and politics was pervasive not only in the countries that heavily participated in the Crusades. The continuity from medieval to early modern religious justifications is important, but a crusading past is neither sufficient nor necessary for early modern theological politics. In all early modern states, some form of religious politics was integral to the centralization and the construction of nation-states. Tomaž Mastnak's *Crusading Peace: Christendom, the Muslim World, and Western Political Order* (Berkeley: California University Press, 2002), is an excellent treatment of European just war theory and practice in the Middle Ages, and also identifies several problems and characteristics that remained acute in early modern Europe.

and/or a radically skeptical agenda. As long as they meant to solve post-Reformation violence by disentangling religion and politics, this whole range of theories can rightly be called 'secularizing', though not always 'secular'.[4] Secularizing solutions, from institutionalized toleration to natural laws that would apply even 'if there is no God', added up to a conceptual toolkit that gradually made it impossible to continue or revive religious politics. After the Reformation blew up the foundations under Europe's entire conceptual edifice, this trial-and-error process of reconstruction eventually led to the secular state, modern international law and historiography, and 'new science'.[5] It was not a straightforward process by any means, but Grotius was responsible for much of the winning strategy and the eventual shape of the new world order that International Relations specialists now tend to epitomize as 'the Westphalian system'.[6] One distinguishing feature of Westphalian states and the

[4] 'Secularization' is a useful term, but its very width that enables us to look at the wide historical context also imposes stringent limitations on doing justice to the complexity of events. Analytical rigour is salvaged if we bear in mind several contexts for *IPC*, including the Wars of Religion, the Leiden environment and the particular circumstances of writing *IPC*. For example, Pufendorf's adaptation of Suarez's permissive/prescriptive distinction to Grotius's theory of property is less secularizing than Grotius's own theory, because it does not close the door entirely to claims of divinely legitimated earthly power. Suarez did not, of course, want anything stronger; see István Hont, *Jealousy of Trade: International Competition and the Nation-State in Historical Perspective* (Cambridge: Belknap Press, 2005), pp. 426-30. It is the same pattern of using Grotius to counter a divine legitimator that we find later in the Filmer-Locke exchange.

[5] This turning-point in intellectual history is described exactly the way this article requires in Michael Walzer, 'Exodus 32 and the Theory of Holy War: The History of a Citation', *Harvard Theological Review*, 61:1 (1968), 1-14. See also Anthony Grafton, 'The footnote in history', in *Proof and persuasion in history*, ed. by Anthony Grafton and Suzanne L. Marchand, theme issue of *History and Theory*, 33 (1994), 53-76. Peter van Rooden, 'Contesting the Protestant nation: Calvinists and Catholics in the Netherlands', *Etnofoor*, 8 (1995), 15-30, esp. Section 1. Norman Housley, *Religious Warfare in Europe* gives as good a rendering of the situation as one can wish for.

[6] The literature on Grotius's role in the Westphalian system is massive. Today Western leaders and many scholars justify various acts, including embargoes and armed intervention, based on notions of rationality and self-interest that all men share, and they categorically avoid religious justifications. The claim is that this is the Westphalian system, and Grotius is its father. I need not take positions on current affairs or on Grotius's impact to note that this claim, and the mere size of scholarly literature on the subject, shows the importance and urgency of clarifying the importance of secularization in Grotius's work.

A recent example of relating the Grotius-Westphalia nexus to current affairs is Mehdi Mozafarri, 'Just War Against an "Outlaw" Region', in *A Matter of Principle: Humanitarian Arguments for War in Iraq*, ed. by Thomas Cushman (Berkeley: California University Press, 2005), ch. 6 (esp. p. 122).

rules for their interaction is that they are strictly secular. Again: this does not mean that they set out to disprove Christianity, but to disconnect it from politics.

The story of Westphalian secularization lends further significance to what otherwise would still be a valid curio in the history of political thought, namely Grotius's use of the Bible in *IPC*, identified correctly by Welwod from the *ML* alone as its most striking feature. The overwhelming majority of Grotius's biblical references not only ignored the original context of the verses but flagrantly contradicted their *prima facie*, common-sensical meaning. Grotius usually disagreed with, and often directly reversed, the interpretation that most of his contemporaries, whether Catholic or Protestant, attributed to the same passages. In addition to explicitly denying the applicability of the Bible in a legal dispute, we will see how he rebutted anyone who mixed religion with politics, including Catholics such as the Iberian legal theorists, those who attributed the Spanish and Portuguese conquests to divine ordainment, papal apologists, but also Protestants like the Mennonite pacifists, the Calvinist resistance theories in contemporary Dutch writings and in the *Vindiciae,* and chosen nation theorists of all countries and denominations. His peculiar use of the Fathers also seems to be in keeping with the rest of his secularizing strategy.[7]

This article aims to present a few of Grotius's unusual Bible-interpretations, and suggests that their oddity is best explained in two contexts: Leiden secularization as Grotius's intellectual background, and the Dutch-Iberian

---

Notable milestones in this literature are Hedley Bull, *The Anarchical Society: a Study of Order in World Politics* (London: Macmillan, 1977), and 'The importance of Grotius', in *Hugo Grotius and International Relations*, ed. by Hedley Bull, Benedict Kingsbury and Adam Roberts (Oxford: Clarendon, 1990), pp. 95-131. Edward Keene, 'The reception of Hugo Grotius in international relations theory', *Grotiana*, 20/21 (1999/2000), 135-158. Overviews of this literature are provided by A. Claire Cutler, 'The Grotian tradition', *Review of International Studies*, 17 (1991), 41. Richard Tuck, *Natural Rights Theories* (Cambridge: CUP, 1979), p. 175. Hont, *Jealousy*, pp. 13-5, 164-6, 419. Fine critical surveys of this literature are given in Randall Lesaffer, 'The Westphalia Peace Treaties and the Development of the Tradition of Great European Peace Settlements prior to 1648', *Grotiana*, 18 (1997), 71-95; by Peter Haggenmacher in *Grotius et la doctrine de la guerre juste* (Paris: Presses Universitaires de France, 1983), and by Roelofsen in 'Grotius and the Development of International Relations Theory. The "Long Seventeenth Century" and the Elaboration of a European States System', *Grotiana*, 18 (1997), 97-120 (pp. 99-104). Benno Teschke, *The Myth of 1648* (London: Verso, 2003), is refreshingly skeptical, although for our present purpose it makes little difference whether the Treaty of Westphalia was the beginning of a new model or the end of the old one (Ibid., 'Conclusion', p. 245).

[7] Vid. Bergjan in this volume. Most of the pro and contra positions around Christian pacifism are as old as Christianity itself. Compare the Mennonites, for example, to Walter Map's criticism of the crusades, *De Nugis Curialium*, ed. by M.R. James, C.N.L. Brooke and R.A.B. Mynors (Oxford: OUP, 1983), Section I.20.

conflict as the occasion for writing *IPC*. These contexts indicate that the main thrust of *IPC*'s argument is that the Bible must not be used in legal and political arguments, especially not in international legal disputes.

The question of Grotius's authorial intention presented itself readily, given the consistent pattern of his idiosyncratic readings and his many explicit statements about the Bible's inadmissibility as a legal source. To figure out Grotius's exegetical strategy, the study adopted the simple method of widening sweeps of source-checking. First, all biblical references in *IPC* were catalogued and checked against Bible editions that may have shaped Grotius's interpretation;[8] almost all of Grotius's readings turned out to be extremely peculiar. Is the peculiarity his own, or did he borrow his readings from one or several sources? The study next turned to Jacques-Paul Migne's *Patrologiae cursus completus Latina* (221 volumes) and the Nicean-AnteNicean series of Church Fathers (38 vols, ed. by A. Roberts-J. Donaldson and P. Schaff-H. Wace), but found no similar readings. The next sweep took in the *Digital Library of Classic Protestant Texts* (which had 708 works at the time), the *Digital Library of the Catholic Reformation* (83), and some basic texts not included in these collections, like the *Complete Works* of Aquinas, Calvin's *Institutes* and Luther's *Sermons*. No similar readings were found. Third, Grotius's readings were placed side by side with the interpretations advanced by other authors he referred to in *IPC*, including Vitoria, Cajetan, Vazquez, and also de Soto, Ayala, Gentili and Suarez. Fourthly, the study looked at some of the authors Grotius cited in other early works, notably *De republica emendanda, Commentarius in theses XI, De antiquitate, Ordinum pietas, Tractatus de iure magistratuum circa ecclesiastica, De imperio,* and *De satisfactione*. Of course, the Bible interpretations in *IPC* were also compared with Grotius's use of the same passages in these early works. Finally, I checked the use of Bible passages in probable sources, like Marnix's Bible-ridden but satirical *Beehive*, Beza's *De iure magistratuum*, the *Dissertation sur l'église visible* by du-Plessis Mornay and the *Vindiciae contra tyrannos*. I looked at how these authors used each of the biblical passages that occur in *IPC*, as well as their war-related discussions featuring Abraham, Melchisedec, Joshua, David, John the Baptist, Christ, and other figures who play a role in Grotius's discussion of war in *IPC*.

There are very few readings in these thousand-odd books, or even in Grotius's later works, that are similar to the ones he advanced in *IPC*. To underscore this exceptionality, the on-line Appendix II gives the exegeses that come closest to

[8] Including the Douay-Rheims, the Tremellius, the Geneva, and the Erasmus-Stephanus 'Regia'.

Grotius's. Appendix II gives some other authors' readings that come closest to Grotius's. Finally, I picked out representative cases. The two criteria of selection were the illustrative power of a case, and that the presentation of the cases here should be economical, involving the smallest possible total number of biblical references. This allows for more detailed treatment of individual cases, and hopefully enables the reader to appreciate the variety of Grotius's techniques for bending the Bible to his own intentions. To add breadth to depth, to show that the instances of a unique reading strategy given here are the norm and not the exception, other *IPC* cases will be given in the footnotes.

Three possible objections to this method, namely an unidentified source, Grotius's carelessness and the lawyer's cavalier and instrumental approach to texts, are easy to dismiss. Even if such a source existed, the significance of Grotius's odd usage would remain. Identifying his source(s) would have only helped us better explain his reasons and perhaps refine our understanding of his working method. The fact that he studiously avoided the exegesis of all the authors examined is already interesting. Secondly, the consistent instrumentality of his own exegesis and his explicit statements on the Bible's inadmissibility show that carelessness is an insufficient explanation. Finally, I fully appreciate that Grotius was happy to wrench and cite any passage out of context, as long as it helped him make a case.[9] However, the Bible references in *IPC* oftentimes do not help, but contradict his arguments, whether about prize-taking, collective responsibility, or the treatment of non-combatants. The Bible passages are not only taken out of their context, but are carefully placed in new contexts and consistently put to uses that flagrantly discredit them. Many of the references that Grotius puts to an odd use are then *not* invoked when he is making a point that would have been much better supported by the same reference. His humanist and rhetorical skills were indeed put to excellent use, if the purpose behind the biblical references in *IPC* was to show in action the serious danger of ignoring his warnings about the Bible's inadmissibility as evidence:

> *IPC*, 6: Considerably better and more dependable is the method chosen by those who prefer to have such questions decided on the basis of Holy Writ, except that the persons employing this method frequently cite simple historical accounts or the civil law of the Hebrews in the place of divine law. For the materials collected indiscriminately from the annals of all nations, while they are extremely valuable

[9] See e.g. Carleton's letter from 1618, the parts cited in van Dam's edition of *De imperio*, p. 21.

in elucidating the question, have little or no value in providing a solution, since as a general rule the wrong course is the one more often followed [in the instances recorded in those annals].[10]

ML, Prolegomena, 8: But that which we here propound hath nothing common with these; it needeth no man's curious search; it dependeth not on the exposition of the Bible (whereof many understand not many things), not on the decrees of one people whereof the rest may justly be ignorant.

The arguments advanced throughout *IPC*, except for the last that ends in prayer, work well 'even if there is no God'.[11] Grotius's contribution to secularization in turn draws attention to the intellectual background that enabled him to write like this. To recreate this context, it is helpful to postulate a 'Leiden project' or circle of thinkers, who substantially influenced each other's secularizing work. Within two decades before and after 1600 Leiden saw Scaliger's (1540-1609) secularization of chronology and of the status of the Hebrew language, Lipsius's (1547-1606) Tacitist 'realism', the theological philology of Drusius (1550-1616), the confederative theology of Arminius (1560-1609), Episcopius (1583-1643), Voetius and Cocceius (1603-69), in which voluntary contracts imposed mutually binding obligations, whether between God and the people, or between the Sovereign and his subjects; the ancient constitutionalism of Scriverius (1576-1660) and Janus Dousa the Elder (1545-1604), the groundbreaking works of Gerhardus Vossius (1577-1649) on deism, history and pedagogy, and of Daniel Heinsius (1580-1655) on secular drama and history, Cunaeus's (1586-1638) work on the Jewish Republic, which made it impossible to use the biblical model as a source of religious legitimacy claims, and Grotius's secularized international law. Erpenius, Louis

[10] 'Melius aliquanto illi et certius, qui ex sacris litteris ista malunt disceptari, nisi quod nudas plerunque historias, aut jus civile Hebraeorum pro jure divino obtendunt. Nam quae passim ex omnium gentium Annalibus alii collegerunt, ut ad rem illustrandam plurimum, ita ad dijudicandum aut nihil aut parum valent, cum fere idem saepius fiat, quod male fit'.

I used the Carnegie translation and the Latin edition of H. C. Hamaker, 1868, The Hague, in the Boston: Elibron facsimile edn, 2003, and the new transcript being prepared by Messrs. Blom, Nellen and Waszink, generously shared by Dr. Hans Blom.

[11] 'Et haec quidem quae iam diximus, locum aliquem haberent etiamsi daremus, quod sine summo scelere dari nequit, non esse Deum, aut non curari ab eo negotia humana', *IBP*, Prolegomena, 11, ed. Molhuysen, 1919, p. 7. The literature on *etiamsi daremus* is gargantuan; here I only present the original for the sake of its nuances. More relevant here than the *etiamsi daremus* literature is H. J. de Jonge 'Joseph Scaliger's Historical Criticism of the New Testament', *Novum Testamentum,* 38 (1996), 176-193. Idem, 'Grotius as an interpreter of the Bible, particularly the New Testament', in *Hugo Grotius, a great European*, ed. by Nellen et al. (Delft: Meinema, 1983), pp. 59-66, and *Hugo Grotius, Theologian*, ed. by H.J.M. Nellen and Edwin Rabbie (Leiden: Brill, 1994).

de Dieu (1590-1642), the great Constantijn l'Empereur (1591-1648), Gronovius (1611-71), Sylvius (1614-72) and Levinus Warner (1619-65) were not simply Orientalists; their work was part and parcel of the Leiden project. One gets a sense of a division of labour, which may be no more than the normal process of Leiden scholars piquing each other's interest and continuing their teachers' works along parallel but not overlapping paths.[12]

The immediate context of *IPC* is of course the situation in the East Indies and the capture of the Catharina. The two larger contexts, post-Reformation reconstruction and Leiden scholarship, explain the why and how of Grotius's use of the Bible in *IPC*. By 1604 Grotius had the insight and the required conceptual tools to be able to eliminate religious reasonings about trade, war and conquest from his legal justification of the Dutch position. The neutralization of the religious components of this conflict would have made it much easier to come to a viable arrangement in the East Indies, and even to ally with the Spanish or the Portuguese against the other.[13] This is not the place to give a history of early modern colonial conflict, but let me draw attention to two events that may help to explain the pattern of Bible misuse in *IPC*, and may not be discussed at length in other contributions in this volume. The first is the 1604 Treaty of London between James and Philip, whereby Spain made peace with England, the traditional ally and comrade-at-sea of the Dutch in the Indies. This peace lasted officially until 1654; the Dutch would have been right to worry about the Treaty and the preceding negotiations (the Somerset House Conference) just around the time of *IPC*'s composition.

[12] Although outstanding books have been written on the early modern Leiden University and the lives of and interaction between some of its members, there is still no thoughtful monograph on the Leiden Circle's collective work and its significance for the history of political thought. *Leiden University in the seventeenth century: an exchange of learning*, ed. by G.H.M. Posthumus Meyjes, Th. H. Lunsingh Scheurleer, with the assistance of A.G.H. Bachrach, H.J. de Jonge, G.I. Lieftinck, A.M. Luyendijk-Elshout, J.J. Woltjer (Leiden: Brill, 1975); John Platt, *Reformed thought and Scholasticism: the arguments for the existence of God in Dutch theology, 1575-1650* (Leiden: Brill, 1982), ch. 6; H.J. de Jonge in *Grotius, a great European*, ed. by Nellen et al. On federative theology, Hans Joachim Hillerbrand, 'Covenant' in *Historical dictionary of the Reformation and Counter-Reformation* (Lanham, MD: Scarecrow Press, 2000), Charles S. McCoy, *Fountainhead of federalism: Heinrich Bullinger and the covenantal tradition* (Louisville KY: Knox Press, 1991), David A. Weir, *The origins of the federal theology in sixteenth-century Reformation thought* (Oxford: OUP, 1990), W.J. van Asselt, *The federal theology of Johannes Cocceius* (Leiden: Brill, 2001), A. M. Yoffie, 'Cocceius and the Jewish Commentators', *Journal of the History of Ideas*, 65:3 (2004), fn 7, 8, 17.

[13] Jonathan I. Israel, *The Dutch Republic and the Hispanic world, 1606-1661* (Oxford: Clarendon, 1982); Introduction in Israel, *The Dutch Republic: its rise, greatness and fall, 1477-1806* (Oxford: Clarendon, 1995); Housley, 'Pro Deo', pp. 243-6 on the themes of chosen nation, covenant, and 'Messianic nationalism' in Spanish imperial ideologies.

It probably redoubled Grotius's motivation to try to split the Iberian front and to construct a Christian-looking, but in effect secular argument that not only the Dutch and the Iberians, but also James would find acceptable.

With the new motivation came a new opportunity. Philip II (1527-1598) promised Portugal that she would retain substantial autonomy under the union of crowns; the Duke of Lerma (1553-1625) under Philip III (1578-1621) reversed that policy. The Duke gave Grotius a great chance to split the Portuguese from the Spanish; and James gave him an excellent reason to do this as quickly and forcefully as possible. Failing that, the justifications for war and prize-taking, and the set of international laws proposed in *IPC*, were still secular(ized) enough to serve as the foundation of a good peace or at least a sensible *modus vivendi* between the Europeans engaged in commercial and colonial expansion.

In any case, neither the justification of Dutch actions nor the Iberian split was likely to happen without a conclusive demonstration that the standard religious justifications for the Spanish and Portuguese possessions, from the Treaty of Tordesillas to Christian theories of conquest, were in fact untenable.[14] The most direct and decisive way of doing this would have been to establish that the Bible was totally inapplicable to such cases. However, stressing this too often would have cost Grotius his and his arguments' credibility; hence the perfectly consistent, often witty and ingenious exposition of the Bible in *IPC*.[15] These two contexts not only help us uncover the

---

[14] On the status of papal bulls, see Benjamin Straumann, ' "Ancient Caesarian Lawyers" in a State of Nature. Roman Tradition and Natural Rights in Hugo Grotius's *De iure praedae*', Political Theory, 34 (2006), 328-350.

[15] Leo Strauss, *Persecution and the Art of Writing* (Glencoe IL: Free Press, 1952). However, in 1604-5, more than a decade before the Synod of Dordt, Grotius may have been tempted to write a text that worked on these two levels (embedded, but wholly unusable biblical support) not so much because of his fears of persecution, but rather due to the disastrous failures of all French experiments with toleration without Erastianism that took place under Catherine Medici and Henry IV, each of which led to a corresponding series of international debâcles (Coligny's and the Guizes' pressure on Catherine and Charles IX through the threat of international alliances, which made the elimination of one party or the other inevitable, in spite of any number of declarations of toleration). All of these experiments and their failures concerned the United Provinces closely, and may have inspired Grotius's more subtle method. *IPC* is written such that if it ever became an element in Dutch-Iberian negotiations, it would have helped the parties to come to terms without public announcements and pledges of religious toleration, and avoid the rage of domestic and international religious factions. If Grotius's set of secular laws of nations, with its entirely unusable biblical references, were formally accepted by both sides, it would have put all contracting parties into an early modern version of the Mutually Assured Destruction dilemma.

Walzer, 'Exod. 32', conclusion, p. 14 'Only when the Bible had ceased to be an authoritative text could men free themselves from the need to debate its precise meaning and to describe their own positions as consistent with that meaning. Then the way was open for the historical critics,

intention behind Grotius's Bible-reading techniques, they also spare us the embarrassment of imputing unlikely intentions to him. To appreciate *IPC*'s place in the story of secularization there is no need to imagine, for example, that Grotius was a crypto-atheist or -Catholic.

A little hindsight is a dangerous thing. Grotius was clearly no atheist, and I doubt that he set out to write *IPC*, and later *IBP*, to construct a secular theory of international relations. However, constricting the Bible to the role of just another historical source does appear, with hindsight, to have been the only masterstroke that could cut the Gordian knot made from the three threads of Dutch vs. Iberians (within which there was now hope to split the Spanish and the Portuguese), Mennonites vs. belligerents, and sacred nation theorists vs. laicisers (including those who knew that biblical support can only cause further dissent among and within the Provinces, as well as minimalists and ecumenists, who still hoped for the eventual reunification of Christendom).[16]

---

and open also for a kind of judgment which could never have been uttered by Augustine, Aquinas, or Calvin.' Housley, 'Pro Deo et Patria Mori', p. 225 and passim, shows how the biblical story of the Maccabees was used and abused in these conflicts. J.P. Somerville, 'Hobbes, Selden, Erastianism, and the history of the Jews', in *Hobbes and History*, ed. by G.A.J. Rogers and Tom Sorell (London: Routledge, 2000), pp. 159-187. shows various political uses of Matthew 16 and 18, pp. 168, 175, and fn18. To these we can add a few examples of similar uses of both Exod. 32 and the Maccabees in religious politics: in May 1590 the Legate Caetani blessed the 1300 monks who swore to defend Paris against Henry of Bourbon as the 'new Macchabees'; while *La Satire Ménippée*, the outstanding political lampoon that did much to turn Parisian public opinion in favour of Henry in 1594, described the scenery of the abortive Estates-General of 1593, at which the League proposed that the next king of France should be the Duc de Guise: 'The first peece of tapistrie nigh to the cloath or chaire of estate, was the historie of the golden calfe, as it is described in the 32. chap. of Exodus, where Moses and Aaron were there represented by King Henry the 3. lately dead, and Monsieur late Cardinall of Bourbon: but the golden calfe was the figure of the late Duke of Guise, lifted up on high and adored by the people', as it reads on p. 19 of the 1595 English translation under the title *A pleasant satyre or poesie*. The integral unity of events in France and both Netherlands around the turn of the seventeenth century is all too often ignored these days. Temple and Motley knew it, and H.-J. van Dam is right to say '*De imperio* is the mature fruit of Grotius's political thought on church and state, sovereignty and law, written in the spirit of French sixteenth-century legal and historical thinking', *De imperio*, p. 3. *The Cambridge History of Medieval Political Thought*, ed. by J.H. Burns (Cambridge: CUP, 1988), effectively surveys many more, from the two swords in Luke 22.38 to Peter's keys, Caesar's money, stadial histories built upon Daniel, and so on.

16 'Biblical references also took a special importance in Grotius's work [the *IPC*], not least because of the role he attributed to theology in working out a law of nations. A pacification of nations (though also at a domestic level, as Grotius himself had experienced during the last years of his political career in Holland) required a new theological consensus among Christians, and his reception of (inter alia, Spanish) sixteenth-century theological writings in his own works on international law should therefore not be viewed too exclusively in a polemical context'. Alain Wijffels, 'Early Modern Literature on International Law and the Usus Modernus',

Discussion: Cases

This is my tentatively proposed explanation. Still, if I only managed to show that Grotius systematically used the biblical citations in *IPC* for a radically new purpose, I would regard this article a success. Let us examine a few representative cases.

1) If it Does not Break, Bend it a Few Times: Deut. 20 and the Inversion of Universal and Positive Laws of Spoil

A three-page section from ch. 4, in which Grotius sets out one of his early justifications for taking spoils, illustrate several of his Bible-twisting methods. First, he rejects the argument that despoliation among Christians is an act of civil war:

> As for the argument derived by our opponents from civil war, it is doubly absurd. For, in the first place, who will acquiesce in their assumption that the wars of Christians are civil wars, as if to say, forsooth, that the whole of Christendom constitutes a single state? (*IPC* 51)[17]

This must be one of the pithiest dismissals of centuries of *Corpus Christianorum* and *Respublica Christiana* in theories of international relations. For twelve hundred years, the opposite of Grotius's position was the matter-of-fact, unquestioned starting point for every papal bull and decree, and all too often

Grotiana 16-17 (1995-6), p. 49. The same technique is identified by Borschberg in Grotius's justification of the Dutch revolt, see his *Hugo Grotius 'Commentarius in theses XI'*, p. 109: 'it appears that Grotius sought to assuage Iberian sensitivities by steering clear of polemical issues. For example, religion and religiously inspired actions which assume a key role in many Protestant accounts of the Dutch Revolt, are almost completely neglected in the *Commentarius*'.

Please note that in this article I do not even touch on the conventional humanist or Protestant techniques of *critice* applied to the Bible, which ranged from questioning the Vulgate's and the Pentateuch's authority on the grounds of, respectively, Greek and Hebrew philological examination and hermeneutical analysis of their originals, to raising the problem of what is and what is not apocrypha, or who wrote all those books of the Bible that report and continue beyond the death of their alleged author. All these criticisms are taken as given in *IPC*; as noted earlier, here I present only the Bible uses that were unique to Grotius. For a good summary of the history of Bible editions, which is in many ways the quickest introduction to the hermeneutical debates, see B.M. Metzger and B.D. Ehrman, *The text of the New Testament*, 4th edn (Oxford: OUP, 2005).

17 'Nos ex principiis ante positis rem tam perspicuam putamus, ut longiore disputatione non egeat: quin et hoc animadverti posse, diversae sententiae auctores ne hoc quidem ipsum, quid esset praeda, satis intellexisse. Quod autem a civili bello sumunt argumentum dupliciter absurdum est: primo enim quis illis concedat, bella Christianorum esse civilia, quasi vero totus orbis Christianus una sit respublica?'

the pretext to attack any other state that has exchanged ambassadors or so much as traded with an infidel.[18]

Grotius continues: 'Surely, since the despoliation of enemies is accepted under the law of nations, it must necessarily be sanctioned by civil law, too' (pp. 51-2). To support this, he cites Roman law, canon law, Scripture, and ancient history. As biblical references he gives Deut. 20.14, Num. 31, Joshua 8.2 and 22.8 and ISam. 30.26. There are two secularizing techniques at work here: the demotion of God's commands to the Jews to the status of the civil law of any pagan state, and the demonstration of the Bible's inapplicability through the selection of stunningly inappropriate biblical passages in support of the point that Grotius is seemingly making. Let us look them in turn.

1. a) Israel, Model No More

Christ had no secular power, but the God of the Old Testament was active in both local and regional politics. He directly intervened in battles, promised and delivered land to the chosen nation, ruled them directly for a while, and

---

[18] Some cases are given and explained in James A. Brundage, *The crusades, holy war, and canon law* (Aldershot: Variorum, 1991); J.N. Figgis, 'Respublicana Christiana ["The Concession Theory" of the Church within the State and the challenge to it]', *Transactions of Royal Historical Society*, Third Series, 5 (1911), pp. 63-85; F.H. Russell, *The just war in the Middle Ages* (Cambridge: CUP, 1975); Michael Walzer, *Just and unjust wars: a moral argument with historical illustrations*, 2nd edn (New York: Basic Books, 1992); David Nicol, 'The Crusades and the Unity of Christendom', in *The meeting of two worlds: cultural exchange between East and West during the period of the Crusades*, ed. by V.P. Goss and C.V. Bornstein (Kalamazoo, MI: Medieval Institute Publications, Western Michigan University, 1986), pp. 169-80; Glenn Bowman 'Christian ideology and the image of the holy land', in *Contesting the Sacred: the Anthropology of Christian pilgrimage*, ed. by John Eade and Michael J. Sallnow (London: Routledge, 1991), pp. 98-121. The numerous calls from all Christian sects for joint European efforts against the Ottoman threat unfailingly invoked these notions. For a discussion more focused on this period, see Roland H. Bainton's classic *Christian Attitudes Toward War and Peace* (New York: Abingdon Press, 1979); Eijnatten in this volume; and Richard Tuck, *The rights of war and peace. Political thought and the international order from Grotius to Kant* (Oxford: OUP, 1999) on Sepulveda and Vitoria; Tuck in *The Cambridge History of Political Thought, 1450-1700*, ed. by J.H. Burns and Mark Goldie (Cambridge: CUP, 1991), pp. 504-9. Several chapters in *Peace Treaties and International Law in European History*, ed. by Randall Lesaffer (Cambridge: CUP, 2004). For the wider importance of the relegation of these concepts see Carl Schmitt, *The Nomos of the Earth in the International Law of the Jus Publicum Europaeum*, tr. G.L. Ulmen (New York: Telos Press, 2003), pp. 58-9. Even in the passage cited, Grotius retains *totus orbis Christianus* as a meaningful entity, only denies that it is one state. But this is a long cry from the Corpus Christianorum in Fulcher of Chartres, Ekkehard of Aurach (both in *Recueil des Historiens des Croisades/Historiens Occidentaux*), Bernard of Clairvaux, and the others cited by Brundage, Holmes, Housley and others. For more on Grotius's use of related terms see Haggenmacher, *Grotius et la doctrine*, pp. 132-3 and 229ff.

regularly interfered in the appointment and removal of kings and prophets.[19] No wonder that so many of the medieval and early modern political theories claimed to be proven right by one Old Testament scene or another. There could be no better proof of a system than showing that God approved of it. This of course made for terribly volatile politics, since (whether as cause or effect of such theories) all biblical scenes and passages were constantly debated. It was impossible to ground a political theory in Scripture in such a way that all would accept it; and religious politics is a zero-sum game, it does not allow for nuance or compromise.

The 'Jewish Commonwealth' theme gives a good example of this dynamic. There had been many theories of state that used the Old Testament description of the time when Jahveh actually reigned over Israel, elected by the people, confirmed by the covenant and represented by Moses and the High Priests. Nobody doubted that the best form of state was what God Himself instituted; the disagreements arose about what this actually was. Was it a theocracy, a monarchy (absolute or limited, depending on the emphasis put on the election or the covenant), or an aristocracy, given the importance of the elders or the Sanhedrin in negotiations with God and in the execution of religious and political duties? Or was it perhaps a federation of tribes and territories, where councils were the main legislative and judicial power? Or a republic, even a democracy, since the approval of all Jews was required to make God the political sovereign in the first place, just as *vox populi* replaced God with Saul? All possible and several impossibly utopian forms of government were derived from the Bible, and each gave rise to competing legal claims by medieval and early modern ultramontanists, papal apologists, royal absolutists, monarchomachi, conciliarists, aristocratic parliamentarians and a thousand sects of republicans.[20]

---

[19] See F.M. Cross, *Canaanite myth and Hebrew epic* (Cambridge MA: Harvard University Press, 1973), for elements of the Bible's politics (e.g. limited monarchy) that the European tradition of political thought picked up on.

[20] We cannot of course cite even a representative cross-section of these. Some of the most extreme cases are Philip Augustus, Louis IX and Philip IV of France, especially the latter's legal justification for attacking Boniface VIII and holding the next pope captive at Avignon, setting up the Gallican Church, sanctifying the French monarchy, and so on. For texts that justify absolutism by claiming descent from OT Israel, see the bull *Rex glorie*, Plaisians's defence of Philip's seizure of church assets, and the convocation of the Estates in 1308, cited in E.A.R. Brown, 'Taxation and Morality in the Thirteenth and Fourteenth Centuries: Conscience and Political Power and the Kings of France', *Studia monastica*, 8 (1973), 1-28; Idem, *The monarchy of Capetian France and royal ceremonial* (Aldershot: Variorum, 1991); J.R. Strayer, *The reign of Philip the Fair* (Princeton: Princeton University Press, 1980); Pethő Sándor, *Démosz vagy Deus?* (Budapest: Osiris, 2001); *Philip the Fair and Boniface VIII: State vs. Papacy*, ed. by C. T. Wood

The historicisation of the Hebrew commonwealth was the Leiden Circle's *coup de grâce* to religious politics. In *De Republica Hebraeorum* (1617) Cunaeus showed that nobody's hand is strengthened in the theologico-political debate

---

(Huntington, NY: Krieger, 1971). Similar texts can be cited from the reigns of Otto II of Germany, Edward I and III of England and others, and from practically any of the medieval Popes, who also claimed supreme legitimacy on the same grounds. For Renaissance and early modern examples of the same before *IPC*'s composition, see also Savonarola and Jan of Leiden at Munster. Such concerns could still not be ignored when Grotius came to write *IPC*. In the early 1530s Amsterdam almost became another Munster or Florence due to the rhetoricians' popularization of the the apocalyptic vision of the Anabaptist heresiarch Melchior Hoffmann. See K. Deppermann, *Melchior Hoffman*, tr. M. Wren (Edinburgh: Clark, 1987; orig. German publ. Göttingen: Vandenhoeck and Ruprecht, 1979). On the rederijkers see Gary K. Waite, *Reformers on Stage* (Toronto: Toronto University Press, 2000), and 'On the stage and in the streets', in *Conformisten en rebellen: Rederijkcultuur in de Nederlanden*, 1400-1650, ed. by Bart Ramakers (Amsterdam: Amsterdam University Press, 2003), pp. 163-73, one of the arrested rhetoricians came from Leiden, fn16. Further examples and literature in J.C. Breen, 'Gereformeerde populaire historiographie in de 17e eeuw', *Tijdschrift voor Geschiedenis*, 37 (1922), esp. pp. 254-73 and 372-82; G. Groenhuis, *De predikanten* (Groningen: Wolters-Noordhoff, 1977), ch. 3; Simon Schama, *The Embarrassment of Riches* (Berkeley: California University Press, 1988), esp. ch. 2. The best examples from across the Channel would be James Harrington, esp. Book II of *The Art of Law-giving*, and John Toland's *Reasons for naturalizing the Jews* (1714). Further references in William L. Lamont: *Godly rule: politics and religion 1603-60* (London: Macmillan, 1969). For an excellent reconstruction of various seventeenth-century English political groups' use of the OT to argue their case, see J.P. Somerville, 'Hobbes, Selden, Erastianism', pp. 159-187.

As the meme rapidly spread, mutations and variations appeared: many groups claimed descent from Adam but not Noah, Noah but not Abraham, Abraham not Moses, the Essenes, the Karaites (J. van den Berg, 'Proto-Protestants? The image of the Karaites as a mirror of the Catholic-Protestant controversy in the seventeenth century', in *Jewish-Christian relations in the 17th century*, ed. by J. van den Berg and E.G.E. van der Wall (Dordrecht: Kluwer, 1988), pp. 31-49), the lost tribes, the First Temple but not the Second, the Maccabees, or other biblical groups that could be shown to have been the one and only approved by God. Claims of legitimacy through descent from, or at least precise analogy with, the OT commonwealth(s) were the norm, not the exception. Even Furly, Penn, and famously John Winthrop were no less exclusivist in their legitimacy claims. The exception was the Leiden Circle's attack on the foundations of all such discourse. The Synod of Dordt drove Leiden innovations underground (see e.g. Yoffie, 'Cocceius and the Jewish Commentators'), and the torch they received from the similarly suppressed French lawyer-historians was passed on to England. Nicholas Tyacke, *Anti-Calvinists: the rise of English Arminianism* (Oxford: OUP, 1987). Gerard Reedy, S.J. *The Bible and reason: Anglicans and Scripture in late seventeenth-century England* (Pennsylvania: Pennsylvania University Press, 1985); *Protestantism crossing the seas: a short-title catalogue of English books printed before 1801*, compiled by Michel L.H.M. Le Cat (Houten: HES, 2000). For the next chapter of this story, see G.R. Cragg, *From Puritanism to the Age of Reason* (Cambridge: CUP, 1950); Peter Harrison, *'Religion' and the religions of the English Enlightenment* (Cambridge: CUP 1990). Thomas M. Lennon, 'Bayle, Locke, and the metaphysics of toleration', in *Studies in seventeenth-century European philosophy*, ed. by M.A. Stewart (Oxford: Clarendon 1997). John Marshall, *John Locke: resistance, religion and responsibility* (Cambridge: CUP, 1994).

by any reference to the OT Commonwealth, because the only divine polity ceased without a legal successor, and even its form and institutions were designed by God to fit the circumstances, therefore these should not be borrowed or imitated with any less precaution than those of Athens, Sparta, Rome or Venice.[21] To do this, Cunaeus described literally dozens of times and ways in which the legal succession from God had been broken.

Grotius and Cunaeus were close in the early 1600s,[22] and Grotius's emphasis on the historicized nature of the Hebrew state in *IPC* strongly suggests that they discussed the desirability of countering chosen nation theories, even those of fellow Dutch patriots.[23] In the *IPC* passage cited above (from p. 6), and in several other early works Grotius performs the same neutralization-by-historization that Cunaeus laid out in a detailed and systematic fashion.

> The first [sort of men who failed to lay down ground-rules for argument], correctly perceiving that the judgment of our own natural reason is utterly weak and unreliable, inferred that the true rules of inquiry were to be sought from the Holy Writ. However, they made the mistake of failing to distinguish adequately the law of God, that is, the civil law peculiar to the Hebrew people, from the law which

[21] For more comparativism, see also Eco O.G. Haitsma Mulier, *The myth of Venice and Dutch republican thought* (Assen: Van Gorcum, 1980). Tuck, *Philosophy and Government*, pp. 164-6. Since Cunaeus usually argued against both Bertram and Sigonio in *DRH*, perhaps a more pertinent precedent for this book was Franciscus Junius, *De politiae Mosis observatione* (Leiden: Plantijn, 1593). The simplified and hugely popular English version of Cunaeus's argument is *Moses and Aaron* by Thomas Godwin (1625, 12th edition in 1685; see Somerville, 'Hobbes, Selden, Erastianism', p. 178), while the higher-order recognition of the need to neutralize the OT commonwealth is picked up by Selden, Basnage, and many others.

[22] Eyffinger's Introduction to *De republica emendanda*, in *Grotiana*, 5 (1984), 5-56. G.H.M. Posthumus Meyjes's Introduction to *Meletius* (Leiden: Brill, 1988), pp. 15, 45, 59. Also see their early correspondence in Peter Burmann, *Petri Cunaei, elonquentiæ & Juris Romani quandam in Academia Batava Professoris, & doctorum virorum ad eumdem epistolæ. Quibus accedit Oratio in ubitum Bonaventuræ Vulcanii* (Leiden: Petrus van der Aa, 1725).

[23] Borstius and Wittewrongel, humanist playwright Coornhert's *Comedy of Israel*; Hooft, Vondel, Valerius's *Neder-Lantsche Gedenck-Clanck* (1626), in which he thanks God for bringing the Dutch to this land and enriching them through trade and commerce: compare the end of *IPC*. Abraham de Koning's dramas *Esther* (1618) and *Samson* (1619). See Groenhuis, *Predikanten*, pp. 77-102. Smitskamp, 'Calvinistisch nationaal besef', and Schama, *Embarrassment of riches*, give references aplenty, esp. pp. 93-125 on Borstius, Wittewrongel, Coornhert, Valerius, de Koning, etc. See also Perlove, S. 'An irenic vision of Utopia – Rembrandt's "Triumph of Mordecai" and the New-Jerusalem', *Kunstgeschichte*, 56:1 (1993), 38-60. In popular culture the chosen nation topos was equally pervasive; e.g. *De Machabeen, Abrahams offerhande*, both in 1590 alone. These used the chosen nation idea for close to make topical political comments: B. Ramakers, 'Voor stad en stadgenoten. Rederijkers, kamers en toneel in Haarlem in de tweede helft van de zestiende eeuw', in Ramakers, *Conformisten en rebellen*, pp. 109-24, esp. pp. 114-8. For a medieval version of this discourse, see Sophie Menache, 'Les Hébreux du XIVe siècle', *Ethno-Psychologie*, 35 (1980), 55-66.

> is common to all mankind. Similarly, they did not distinguish the things permitted under divine law from those things ordained by it, nor the things prescribed under particular circumstances, from those things which are necessarily binding for all time. Often, indeed, they took the events narrated in the Holy Scriptures to be commandments or patterns for [future] behaviour, when they might have seen that these same actions were done either incorrectly, or if performed correctly, then in accordance to a specific commandment of God.[24]
>
> These are the points of agreement with the Hebrew form, which are so many and so striking that you may rightly wonder why we should not reasonably hope that, given such a similar model, we can simply adapt the remaining few points of difference, the more so since we do not intend to change all the points in which we differ forthwith. Every nation has its own morals and a nature of its own, and particular institutions corresponding to them. Once you start trying to transfer these to another structure, the outcome will as likely as not be a completely dissimilar duplicate.[25]

Then Grotius begins to list the differences between the Dutch and the Hebrew polities. His conclusion is that the Dutch should use the *lessons* learnt from the Bible, as from all other histories. There is a Copernican revolution in politics, right here: it is religion that revolves around the safety of the republic.[26]

---

[24] *Commentarius in theses XI*, ed. by P. Borschberg (Bern: Lang, 1994), Preface, §4, pp. 208-9: 'Primi cum illud recte intellegerent, naturalis nostræ rationis iudicium esse admodum imbecille atque incertum, ideoque veras regulas ex sacris oraculis petendas, tamen in eo errarunt, quod legem Dei quæ Judæorum erat civilis et propria ab ea quæ humano generi communis esse debet non satis distinguerent. Neque item ea quæ sunt iuris divini permittentis ab iis quæ sunt eiusdem iuris imperantis quæque ex certis circumstantiis dicuntur ab his quæ perpetuo sunt necessaria. Sæpe etiam narrata pro iussis aut exemplis sequendis acciperent, cum tamen possent ea ipsa aut non recte facta esse, aut si recte, ex Dei mandato speciali'.

[25] *Rep. em.*, 49, pp. 109-11: 'Videmus communia; quae sane tam multa esse tamque insignia non immerito mireris; quo minus etiam desperandum est posse caetera, quae non admodum multa sunt, ad tam propinquum exemplar emendari. Neque enim omnia quae distant mutata continuo volumus: sunt sui populis mores, sua ingenia; quibus propria instituta respondent, quae si in alio velis imitari saepe rem efficias in simili dissimillimam'. For similar passages of frustration with his contemporaries who require biblical precedents for their politics, see also H.-J. van Dam's introduction to the *Tractatus de iure magistratuum circa ecclesiastica* (finished late August 1614), in *Grotiana*, 20-21 (1999-2000), 13-27, and his remarks in *De imperio*, pp. 33, 886-7. Both in the Epistle to the Reader of *Adamus Exul* (1601) and in his autobiography of 1613 Grotius refers to his *Illustratio in historiae Mosaicae ex scriptis Ethnicorum*, now sadly lost. In the *Parallelon Rerumpublicarum*, written in 1601-02 and of which only the third book survives, he compared the Athenian, Roman and Batavian peoples. Franciscus Junius may be again more of an inspiration here than Bertram or Sigonius.

[26] Interestingly, compare Welwod: *Iuris diuini iudaeorum. Ac iuris ciuilis romanorum parallela; siue utriusque e suis undequaque sedibus ad verbum transcripti Ocularis collatio*. (Leiden: Plantijn, 1594).

Somerville makes the same point about Selden's *History of tithes* (1618) and *De synedriis* (finished in 1638, but continuously revised until his death): 'He de-mythologized the Scriptures,

> And is it not clear that the state of the Hebrews, that was instituted by God, that is, before the people asked for a king, was governed by a council of the best? … However, when praising this form of government, I do not want to detract from those who use another. For it must be acknowledged that there is not one form which fits all people, and that there are many peoples who should rather be entrusted to the power of a king than left to their own freedom.[27]

This is the approach that we also find in the *IPC* passage on Deut. 20. Grotius takes God's commands to be a set of historical civil laws, perfectly comparable with Greek and Roman laws. He does not attribute higher authority to the Bible. Later we will see him use the same technique of historicizing the Old Testament that we find in Scaliger and Cunaeus to develop further cases in *IPC*, including his two responses to the Mennonites and his re-evaluation of the role of Melchisedec in political thought. The historicization of the OT commonwealth may also be the linchpin for all other cases of historicization in *IPC*, where Grotius treats the whole Bible as he does any other source of history, subject to the same rules of criticism, with the evidence gleaned from the critical reading accorded no more compelling power or applicability.

1. b) The Inappropriateness of the Bible Verses Cited

Another one of Grotius's techniques for discrediting the Bible in legal arguments was to invert the order of natural and positive divine laws. There was tremendous disagreement about the divine precepts given in the Old and New Testaments, whether the new law replaced or perfected the old, and how much of which applied to the 'new Jews'. Many doubted even that all Ten Commandments were universally binding. As we saw above, a great number of early modern political actors claimed to be the new Jews, to whom a particular set of biblical laws may or may not apply, depending on whether their observance was enjoined upon the Jews or upon whomsoever happened

---

treating them simply as ancient texts which can be understood adequately only if they are seen in their historical and linguistic contexts. There was relatively little new about his overall theoretical stance, however, and he recognized his own debt to earlier writings including Grotius, whom he praised.' Selden drew from the MSS of Grotius's *De imperio summarum potestatum circa sacra* (finished in 1617, first published in 1647).

[27] *On the Antiquity of the Batavian Republic*, ch. 7, 18-19, pp. 112-5. 'Quid quod Hebraeorum quoque rempublicam, qualis a Deo fuit instituta, antequam regnum populus deposceret, optimatium consilio administratam satis apparet? … Neque tamen hanc cum laudamus reipublicae formam, illis quicquam detractum volumus, qui alia utuntur. Fatendum enim est, non eadem omnibus convenire; multosque esse populos, qui rectius potestati regiae, quam libertati suae committantur'. The rest of Section 19, the penultimate chapter of *IPC*, gives further reasons why laws cannot simply be copied, not even from the Bible.

to be the chosen nation.[28] What better way to demonstrate the futility of such debates than by the extreme measure of reading the cruelest atrocities in the OT as universal laws, and the reasonable ones as positive laws given to the Jews alone?

Deuteronomy 20.10-17 gives one such command that has long troubled canon lawyers. Here God tells the Israelites to kill all males in far-away cities, but take the women and children alive; in nearby places they wish to keep, they must kill everybody (Appendix I.1). This incitement to slaughter was hard to accept as a straightforward divine law. Vitoria joined a long list of thinkers when he argued that this was a special command given under special circumstances. This was not very hard to show, since the commands begin with dedicating new houses, eating grapes and sleeping with new wives in case any man dies in battle, and build up from there to smiting everybody in the towns captured. Unless women and grapes were to be obligatory before all wars, it was easy to show that the indiscriminate murder in Deut. 20 was an exception. Vitoria had no difficulty concluding that what God wanted understood as a universal rule was that all civilians and non-combatants are protected from every fighting party, and the maximum degree of reasonable mercy must be shown at all times (Appendix II.1).

In contrast, Grotius takes Deut. 20, one of the most discussed Bible passages in the theory of war, and reads it as a straightforward law of nations![29] He does

---

[28] A curious corollary is that one could attack one's enemies by arguing that they deviated from the Bible, or because they stuck too close to it. The latter usually took the form of accusations of 'Judaising'. This is a frequent theme in early modern polemics, including Locke's last book, *A paraphrase and notes on the Epistles of St. Paul*, ed. by A.W. Wainwright (Oxford: Clarendon, 1987; first publ. 1707). See e.g. his 1 Cor. Synopsis G, his notes on 1 Cor. 2.6*, 3.1†(b), 1 Cor. 3.4,* and 17, 1 Cor. 4.6(a), 1 Cor. 14.2*, 2 Cor. 7.12ff, 2 Cor. 1.14*, 2 Cor. 12†, 2 Cor. 5.16*, 7.11, 10.1, 10.12†, 11.22, 11.23, Rom. 1.32‡, 2.7*, 8*, Expl. Notes for Romans Section 2, 3.6* 'to stop the mouths of the blasphemous Jews', 7* 'to Stop the Jews mouth', 8* 'Tis past doubt that these were the Jews', 9†, Romans Section 6. Contents (j). While Locke also takes the Epistle to the Galatians to be a condemnation of 'Judaising seducers' (p. 120), Grotius in the *Annotationes* reads the same to refer to philosophers. On 'Judaiser' readings known to but not used by Grotius see Yoffie, 'Cocceius and the Jewish Commentators', fn12. Instead, Grotius relied on the equally well-established but secular principle of non-transferability. Aristotle's geographical effects, irreproducibility of history, spirit of nations, ancient constitutionalism, whatever version; but not the biblical chosen nation discourse or the 'Judaiser' criticism.

[29] This contrast reminds us of the one between Augustine's, Aquinas's and Calvin's reading of Exod. 32. Walzer, 'Exod. 32', esp. pp. 9-11, where he shows that a similar subversion of Augustine's reading by Aquinas 'in effect denied the value of the citation altogether'. Walzer also argues that Grotius extended Aquinas's trick into 'a modernist parody of the medieval argument about the Old Law'. Note that Walzer's account of Calvin's reading of Exod. 32 is also perfect

exactly the same with Num. 31, the second in the sequence on spoils (pp. 51-3), which posed a similar embarrassment for later interpreters (Appendix II.1.3). So did Joshua 8.2, in which God delivers the city of Ai to the Israelites, who then 'had utterly destroyed all the inhabitants'. The only new element here is that unlike Deut. 20 and Num. 31, Joshua 8 is not even about spoils, which is a very ancillary part of this particularly grisly tale (Appendix II.1.4).

Joshua 22.8 describes a fairly complex and unmistakably particular, not universal, deal between the tribes, whereby Joshua shares out the spoils among the Reubenites, the Gadites and the second half of Manasseh's tribe, which also receives land at last, along with some spoils. At least Deut. reported God's word; Joshua 22.8 leaves no doubt that there was no divine command, let alone a universalizable one, in the story.[30] Like the others, it is exactly the wrong verse for Grotius to invoke in support of his argument (Appendix II.4).

1 Sam. 30 is about David and the Amalekites, another stock theme in reasonings about state and war. Grotius's reading is, again, unique (Appendix I.2). The Amalekites capture Ziklag, one of David's cities, and take the women and children captive; 'they slew not any either great or small'. David consults God with the ephod and leaves in hot pursuit. Two hundred of his men cannot keep up with the host and fall behind. David catches the Amalekites, and 'smote them from the twilight even unto the evening of the next day', with no intention of sparing anyone. He recovers everything the Amalekites had taken. A dispute ensues whether the 200 should receive their share of spoils, some of which may have originally been their own property. David makes a new law: from now on, those who stay behind to guard the baggage train will receive the same share as those who fight. When he returns to Ziklag, he also sends a share of the spoils to the elders of Judah and to his friends.

for showing both the issues and the methods on which Grotius clashed with the Dutch Calvinists in *IPC*.

Compare *IBP*, I.2.2. Note however the danger of overrating comparisons of Grotius's use of the same biblical reference in his various works, including the *Annotationes*. To do so would mean ignoring the specificities of the works' context. See Walzer's warning to this effect in the case of Calvin, 'Exod. 32', fn22.

[30] Calvin even read the same passage as an expression of Joshua's liberality beyond and *in contradiction* to the strict law of sharing! 1st publ. 1562, *Ioannis Calvini, magni theologi, commentarii in librum Iosuae. Cum indice rerum ac verborum*, in *Ioannis Calvini Noviodunensis opera omnia; in novem tomos digesta* (Amsterdam: Schipper, 1671), pp. 56-7. The Carnegie *IPC* edition's alternate reading is Joshua 22.11, an equally odd verse to cite and one that had an equally extensive tradition of commentaries, as well as political tracts like Beza's *Concerning the rights of rulers over their subjects*, in Question 7, transl. H-L. Gonin, H.A.U.M., 1956, p. 73, that Grotius could react against. On the original biblical politics of these verses see Carolyn Pressler, *Joshua, Judges, and Ruth* (Louisville, KY, Westminster/John Knox, 2002).

Several elements of this story were used in later arguments. David consulting the ephod was often said to show papal supremacy, and his new law about giving a stake in the battle to the camp guards was seen as a sensible piece of strategy.[31] The contrast between the ruthless slaying of Amalekites and their aversion to bloodshed posed much the same problem as Deut. 20. Grotius simply glossed over the problem of divinely sanctioned slaughter, and to corroborate that spoil-taking is just by the law of nations, he cited David's message to Judah:

> "Behold a present for you of the spoil of the enemies of the Lord". Sufficient proof [of the justness of taking spoils] was afforded, however, in the sole fact that it was God's will that the Israelites, a nation formed by God Himself, should defend their rights in this fashion; or again, in the fact that He prescribed limits for the seizure of spoils'. (pp. 52-3)[32]

The scene of David creating a new law on the spot comes in the immediately preceding verse: 'And it was so from that day forward, that he made it a statute and an ordinance for Israel unto this day.' This is one of those evergreen law-giver stories we often find in ancient literature, the story of how a great king – not God – handled a tricky situation by issuing a new law, one so good that it worked perfectly ever after. The emphasis is on David and the law's novelty, not, as Grotius would have it, on God and the law's universality. Even if Grotius's reading is taken at face value, we still run into the problem that if the act of taking spoils is justified by God's institution of it, must we not also observe the 'prescribed limits for the seizure of spoils'? One does not even need to know the passage Grotius cited in order to recognise his inversion of particulars and universals.

2) Deut. 20 Re-Inverted: Israel's Naturally Conscientious Objection to God's Command

Another good thing about Deut. 20 is that Grotius used it many times in *IPC*, so it offers us a chance to uncover more than one of his strategies. In ch. 8 of *IPC* Grotius set out to show that there was no need for a formal declaration of war in the Dutch-Iberian conflict, since the other side was already behaving like an enemy. He chose Deut. 20.10 in support:

---

[31] Grotius vs. the Pope: *IPC* 64, pp. 222-3, 245, 258, 300. On the ephod, see e.g. Benedictus Aretius, *S.S. Theologiae problemata hoc est: loci communes Christianae religionis, methodice explicate* (Geneva: s.n., 1617; 1st edn. Bern 1573), p. 353.

[32] 'Accipite benedictionem de praeda hostium Domini. Sed vel hoc solum sufficere poterat, quod Deus Israelitas, formatum a se populum, ea ratione jus suum tutari voluit: aut etiam quod modum praedae circumscripsit et quomodo dividi deberet ostendit'.

> A notable example is found in the history of the Israelites, who had been commanded by God to refrain from making an armed attack against any people without first inviting that people, by formal notification, to establish peaceful relations; for the Israelites thought that this prohibition was inapplicable to many of the Canaanite tribes, inasmuch as they themselves had previously been attacked in war by the Canaanites. (p. 102)[33]

Grotius's point here is that it is indeed right and seemly to attack in some cases, including the capture of the Catharina, without a prior declaration of war. In other words, he finds *for* the Israelites in the case cited. Instead of the usual process of deriving a universal law of nations from a positive command given by God to the Israelites, Grotius takes the Israelites' side in their disobedience to God's direct command, which he said was given in contradiction to a law of nations!

Grotius deliberately set out to subvert the status of the Bible in contemporary legal arguments. He made specific commands out of universal ones, and vice versa, in order to demonstrate that the Bible should not be used in law, and also to overturn centuries of Bible-based patterns of legal argumentation. The inherently debatable nature of biblical interpretation, therefore the Bible's undesirability in such matters, is shown through these inversions of the universal and the particular in the conventional readings.[34]

3) Deut. 20 Thirdly Bent: The Law of Mercy

We saw Grotius use Deut. 20 to justify despoliation (p. 53), and to show up its absurdity by insisting that it be taken literally. Then we saw the same passage support the point about attacking enemies without a formal declaration of war (p. 102), only this time Grotius upheld the Israelites' disobedience to God as in accordance with the law of nations, and the right thing to have done. A few pages later (p. 109) we come to another highly irregular, subverted use of this passage, this time in favour of unlimited rights of butchery against an enemy nation, with no regard for innocents.

---

[33] 'Nobile est exemplum in Israelitis, qui cum praeceptum haberent a Deo ne quam gentem armis aggrederentur, nisi quam denuntiando prius ad pacem invitassent, hoc ipsum tamen adversus gentes Chananaeorum plerasque observandum non putarunt, cum essent ab illis priores bello lacessiti'.

[34] On this technique of inversion see Jonathan Swift, *The mechanical operation of the spirit, affixed to A Tale of a Tub* (1703/05), and *The Battle of the Books* (1704). Swift wrote both while still secretary to William Temple.

> In so far as bodily attack is concerned, it is permissible – in accordance with the laws of the first order, which do not take into account the intent of one's adversary – to make an attack upon all enemy subjects who resist, whether knowingly or in ignorance, the execution of our rights. For such subjects, without exception, are 'bringing about' an injury, even though that injury may not be 'voluntary'. This assertion is expressly confirmed by divine law, which decrees the slaughter of the whole adult population of certain cities taken by storm, although many of the adults in question must be innocent.[35]

For this, he sets up the following sequence: Tacitus ('the innocent and the guilty fall side by side'), Deut. 20.13, Joshua 6, and 1 Sam. 15. The three biblical passages show, according to Grotius, that an army does have the right to murder all enemy subjects who resist it, 'whether knowingly or in ignorance' of the army's justness of cause (Appendix II.5).

Grotius declines to follow any of the conventional interpretations of these embarrassingly brutal biblical passages. The online Appendix II for Deut. 20 gives Vitoria's discussion of the same matter of innocents in wartime with reference to an identical sequence: Deut. 20, Joshua, and 1 Sam. 15. Vitoria defended the unusual cruelty in these verses as *speciali mandato Dei*. Grotius did the opposite: with horrifying implications, he argued for their universality. Again, he flipped conventional exegesis on its head to show that it could be done, and therefore these core biblical passages were open to endless debate and invited fanatical opinion; and so they had no place in clarifying the law of nations.

Deut. 20 has been sufficiently discussed, but note how Grotius used it here for a different purpose. Joshua 6 is about the capture of Jericho, a glorious story that was usually seen even within biblical history as coming under rather special and unrepeatable circumstances.[36] For a start, God does not intervene quite so directly in all biblical battles. By giving it general cognizance, Grotius denies the uniqueness of the event. This remains true if we accept the conjecture of the editors of the Carnegie *IPC* that Grotius's specific reference is to Joshua 6.25, in which Rahab, the harlot who saved the lives of Joshua's spies,

---

[35] 'Et num recte Tacito dictum: in pace causas et merita spectari, ubi bellum ingruat innocentes ac noxios juxta cadere. Ex hac enim similitudine jus praedae apertius fiet. Ad corpus quod attinet, offendi ex legibus primi ordinis, quae animum adversarii non respiciunt, subditi hostium omnes possunt, qui juris nostri exsecutioni resistunt, scientes sive ignorantes: faciunt enim injuriam quamquam non injuria. Hoc divina lege expresse confirmatur, quae in expugnatione urbis puberes omnes interfici jubet, quorum multi non possunt non esse innocentes'.

[36] Typically, William Allen, *De Sacramentis*, (Antwerpen: Foulerus, 1576), ch. 41, p. 685 and passim cites Josh. 6 and Jericho to prove the absolute uniqueness of Christianity.

is rescued from Jericho before the siege. This would be in keeping both with Grotius's universalization of obviously specific cases (here the treatment of the 'innocent' Rahab in war), as well as with the sense of humour we saw in the other cases (Appendix II.6).

1 Samuel 15 is similar to the Deuteronomy passage: God expressly commands the Jews to kill *all* the Amalekites (Appendix I.3). What is different here is that Grotius blithely fails to mention that Saul, who has just replaced God as Israel's new king, actually disobeyed God's order to slaughter. When Saul spares the Kenites and returns with live captives and animals, Samuel accuses him of rebellion against the Lord. Saul at first denies this outright, then he tries to defend himself by saying that he only kept slaves and goods in order to sacrifice to God. This does not sit well with Samuel. v22 'Hath the Lord as great delight in burnt offerings and sacrifices, as in obeying the voice of the Lord? Behold, to obey is better than sacrifice, and to hearken than the fat of rams'. Saul then blames the people for keeping the spoils, but Samuel remains adamant: Saul disobeyed God, therefore God dethrones Saul. They make up in the end, and in a touching act of reconciliation Samuel hacks the Amalekite king into pieces. But in his heart he mourns for Saul, and God agrees that it was a mistake to make Saul king. Apart from the Fall and 1 Sam. 8, the people's deposition of God in favour of Saul, this was probably the most cited OT passage in the political literature (Appendix II.7).

If we assume that Grotius knew any of this literature, or had simply read the passage he cites, then ironies abound. Instead of siding with the people who followed the law of nations in defiance of God's positive command, this time Grotius accepts and universalizes God's undeniably positive command to his chosen nation in a very specific historical situation, and against the sparing of innocents, including even the Kenites, who knew well the justness of the attackers' cause, and therefore qualified for mercy even by Grotius's own admission: 'Nevertheless, if there are some individuals who can be separated from the whole body of the enemy and who do not impede the execution of our rights, such individuals should of course be spared altogether from attack upon their persons'.

Let us pause and count the oddities so far: after refuting the conventional reading *and* his own earlier reading of Deut. 20, Grotius takes 1 Sam. 15 to show the justness of killing all innocents who impede the pursuit of the attackers' just cause of action. In 1 Sam. 15 God gives a positive command in a highly particular situation, which Saul disobeys in three ways: he spares the Kenites, who did nothing wrong; he spares the Amalekite king, and he keeps some of the livestock as prize. If all three kinds of mercy were wrong, and this is indeed a universalizable law, as Grotius asserts, then not only is indiscriminate cruelty justified, but Grotius directly contradicts himself on both the justness of spoils and on sparing unresisting innocents. In spite of *IPC*'s consistent pattern of such Bible misuse and the explicit statements on the Bible's inadmissibility, this must still be one of the most idiosyncratic uses to which this passage has ever been put.[37]

Having taken the brutal biblical passages at face value, Grotius then begins to argue for mercy, but using only pagan history, Plato, Cicero and Roman law. It is from Cicero that – a relief to his readers – he now comes to the same conclusion that Vitoria drew from the same biblical sequence alone. Some people can be separated from the totality of the nation, and should be spared, at the very least those who surrendered and are patently innocent. In fact, natural law dictates that you spare as many as possible.

In this last case we saw three biblical passages, beginning with the third use of Deut. 20, used in several ways to guide the reader by example to agree with Grotius's opening statement in *Mare liberum*: his thesis really 'dependeth not on the exposition of the Bible'.

---

[37] The only seventeenth-century usage in the same league is the 1st edn of Pierre Bayle's *Historical and Critical Dictionary* in 1697, 'David', Remarks D, G and H (ed. by R.H. Popkin and C. Brush (Indianapolis: Hackett, 1991; 1st edn Indianapolis: Bobbs-Merrill, 1965), pp. 53-9). After the Huguenot church in Rotterdam indicted him for this entry, he removed much of it from the 1702 edition, including the Remarks in question. In D, Bayle criticized David for indiscriminate slaughter, whether or not it was authorized by God, and irrespective of David's inferior knowledge of just war to ours. In G, Section VII, Bayle presented exquisitely the dilemma of faith or reason, which become incompatible as one ponders the OT scenes of violence. He ended up condemning David's cruelty, and cited 2 Sam. 12.31 as one of the damning references. Grotius used 2 Sam. 12.30 in *IPC*, p. 163, to discuss how captured public property becomes the public property of the victor. He gives a great number of historical and contemporary laws and events, only one of which is biblical: David taking Rabbah's land and crown in 2 Sam. 12.30. The next verse shows David maiming, torturing and horribly killing 'the children of Ammon'. Yet again, Grotius picked the most controversial biblical reference possible, one that had more than a millennium of embarrassed exegesis written about it. He could not just come out and say that the God of the Old Testament, Abraham, David and other sacred figures of Christianity were guilty by his own standards of just war – even a hundred years later Bayle was publicly tried and humiliated for reading 2 Sam. 12.31 literally, as a statement of historical fact, and thereby condemning David for his cruelty in war. Not even Voltaire could raise this point in his entry on David in the *Philosophical Dictionary* (1764-72) without inciting enormous controversy. What would have happened to Grotius if *IPC* was published in his lifetime? As we said at the beginning, the same kind of case can be built up, with the same result, for almost every single Bible reference in *IPC*.

4) The Bible Disqualified: Contradictory Interpretations are Equally Tenable, and Pagan Sources are Superior. Deut. 20 for the Fourth Time[38]

As supporting evidence for the natural law of mercy that he deduced from pagan sources, Grotius then recycles Deut. 20.14 for the fourth time (p. 110), now taking out of context *the other half* of God's command, the one that says women and children should be spared:

> Yet again, just as the precepts of equity and those of divine law [Deut. 20.14 and Plato, *Republic* 471a, b], that infallible guide of equity, direct us to spare all persons in a surrendered city, so also they direct that in the case of a city taken by

---

[38] The other elements as well as the sequence we started with (Deut. 20, Num. 31, Josh. 6 and 22) undergo several drastically different interpretations in *IPC*. For example, in arguing that the right over spoils is not in the individual but in the state (pp. 145ff), Grotius deploys several secularizing techniques. We have the deprioritization of Scripture: his hierarchy of sources is 1 logic, 2 consensus of all nations and the tradition of all ages, 3 historical examples, 4 Homer, 5 the OT. This complements the technique of historicization. The passages used here: Num. 31.27, 31, 47, Josh. 6.27, 22.7-8, and 1 Sam. 30.22. He gives very unusual readings for each (the fourth technique). He vividly illustrates their inadmissability by constructing interpretations that contradict his earlier, equally convincing ones (the fifth technique). Yet another use of the sequence discussed in Case 1 above is at the end of ch. 4, where Grotius promises to marshall 'examples set by holy men' to prove the justness of taking spoils. He begins with Abraham (p. 54), in the peculiar fashion discussed in Section 6 later. That is all. We get no more holy men; instead, Grotius relates the actions of six ancient Romans as corroborating examples. When he finally remembers his promise to bring scriptural examples to bear (p. 56), and cites Moses, Joshua and David, specifically Num. 31, Josh. 8. and 22, and 1 Sam. 30 – the very same sequence that he similarly misuses elsewhere, as we saw in Section 1! He continues in much the same vein: another Christian element that proves the legitimacy of spoils is history. Christian princes have always taken spoils, and slaves, too, although they do not do that any more. Christian customs are not, in other words, any more binding for the present than biblical history. Next Grotius knocks out either the Bible or Christian historical precedents (both of which, he claims, support his point) by showing that the Bible actually forbade the kind of spoil-taking that Christian princes were doing. All throughout we see the same terrible choice of passages; the only thing they are really good for is to demonstrate why the Bible should be disregarded in such matters.

These were examples of further Bible misuse in *IPC*, related to the Deut. 20 case in hand. The same techniques are applied to other passages and sequences. Another good case unravels from *IPC*, pp. 41 ff.: Just wars were waged by various OT figures, and if we have the same faith (as the OT figures!), then we can follow suit. However, not all just wars are ordained by God: a war can be just as in just under natural law, declared by a sovereign, fought for a just cause and in a just manner. Here again Grotius leads us to the realization, step by step, that the Bible should not be allowed to feature in international relations, because it can destroy any negotiation but has nothing to add to them.

> assault, all those whose lives do not impede the execution of our rights shall be spared in so far as is possible.[39]

Let us recapitulate. Vitoria pointed out the specificity of Deut. 20. Grotius first agrees with this, but only to side with the Jews who disobeyed God's specific command, just as he does with 1 Samuel 15. A few pages later he emphatically disagrees, and reads Deut. 20 as a universal principle of brutality and cold-heartedness – which he then modifies with a universal law of mercy derived from pagan history and philosophy, not – as a Christian might be expected to, all else failing – with Christ's message of love and compassion. Finally, Grotius cites another chopped-up half-sentence from the same verse to corroborate the universal principle of mercy that he found in Cicero and other Ancients. This is the usage of sources that Welwod strongly objected to in *ML*, and we can only speculate what reception the whole of *IPC* would have had.

5) Choosing Flamboyantly Unsuitable Passages in Support: Collective Guilt in Gen. 20

Still in ch. 8, Grotius has another argument for which he enlists downright strange biblical support.[40] What he wants to illustrate is that all Iberian citizens, including the owners and crew of the Catharina, are culpable for offenses against the Dutch. They all conferred authority on a ruler, and did nothing against his wicked deeds. To find proof of this, Grotius cites Genesis 20.4 and 9, where, he says, God punished people for the sins of their princes (pp. 105-6) (Appendix I.4).

The original Gen. 20 borders on a comedy of errors. It narrates a would-be love triangle, thwarted by God. Abraham goes to Abimelech and pretends that his wife Sarah is his sister. Abimelech marries Sarah, but then God steps in and tells him the truth. Abimelech is terrified: he protests his innocence to God. His intentions were pure, and nothing actually happened. God agrees: integrity of heart and 'innocency' decide the case. Abimelech nonetheless reprimands Abraham for the deception, which could have condemned the

[39] 'Sicut autem in dedita urbe omnibus, ita in ea quae expugnatur quantum fieri potest illis parci, quorum corpora exsecutioni nostrae non obstant, aequitas praecipit et lex divina certissima aequitatis magistra'.

[40] See also pp. 295-6: the legal standing of States General and VOC established by parallel between Rome and the States General on the one hand, and between Christ and the VOC, on the other.

whole nation. If ever there was an odd biblical passage to cite in support of collective responsibility, this is it (Appendix II.8).

6) Historicization

Historicization is another technique that Grotius used to undermine the Bible's authority in legal debates.[41] He often took biblical passages conventionally read as expressing a universal law, and put them into a historical context to show that they expressed a particular command, not to be applied elsewhere. Our first example is his controversy with the Mennonites. Grotius addresses them directly (pp. 51-4). To evaluate their anti-war stance, he cites their favourite passage, John the Baptist's *Do violence to no man* (Luke 3.14). Grotius readily concedes that John could not have contradicted divine law, but maintains that general violence can be justified, and is in fact often necessary and divinely ordained.[42] How is this possible? According to Grotius, the Bible, a rather foundational text in European thought, recorded in this instance nothing more than John's perfunctory words to some soldiers who happened to be harassing peasants. Grotius probably knew Augustine's and

[41] More good cases: ancient Hebrews and meaning of 'state' (p. 63); one can attack when the call for satisfaction is unheeded, and the Israelite instances given in the Bible are not superior to Minos vs. Athens; same on arbitration (pp. 98ff). See C. L. Heesakkers, 'Grotius as a historiographer', in *Grotius, a great European*, ed. by Nellen et al., pp. 79-84. On historicization as a technique in post-Reformation reconstruction, see George Huppert, *The Idea of Perfect History* (Chicago: Illinois University Press, 1970). Historicization was a principal technique of secularization in French New History. See Huppert on Pasquier against divine intervention in history (p. 55), his criticism of Sleidan (p. 62), 'Bodin's *Method* was, to the best of my knowledge, the first book published to advance a theory of universal history based on a purely secular study of the growth of civilization. Such a view of history was by no means uncommon among the humanists and jurists who dominated the intellectual world of Paris in Bodin's time. Still, Bodin published his book first'. (p. 104) With the publication of Le Roy's *Vicissitudes* in 1575 '[t]he break with theological history was complete'. (p. 117) Anything by Kelley is well worth reading on the subject. Grafton also captured perfectly the essence and post-Reformation significance of these works in 'The footnote in history', pp. 53-76. 'Bodin presented readers terrified by the European religious wars of the mid- and late sixteenth century and crushed by the rapid expansion of European scholarly writing with a massive program of social reconstruction through discriminating scholarship'. (p. 66) 'Like Bodin, de Thou had watched the French polity fall apart in the Wars of Religion. Unlike Bodin, he contin-ued to believe that Catholic France bore as much of the blame as the Protestants, or per-haps more. An honest, impartial narrative, he decided, would serve as a foundation for social and political peace'. (p. 67) On the forces at work for and against these projects, see pp. 68-70.

[42] For a different solution to the same problem, see *IBP*, II.7.3, ed. by Richard Tuck (Indianapolis: Liberty Fund, 2005), pp. 200-201.

Calvin's famous attacks on, respectively, the Manichean and Anabaptist pacifist readings of this passage. Either of these responses would have given Grotius a perfect reply to the Mennonites, but both used other, equally debated Bible passages in their exposition of Luke 3.14. Grotius relinquished the authority of these two authors in favour of the very Leidenian, fully historicized and secularizing interpretation (Appendix II.9).

A more sophisticated historicization comes right next. In Genesis 14 Abraham turned down his share of booty, and the Mennonites took this to mean that all war and booty were illegal (p. 54) (Appendix I.5). Grotius counters this from the same verse: Abraham gave the spoils to the priests, and this was not a one-off event but an institution. The *institution* of paying tithes from war booty in turn proves the legitimacy of wars and spoils in the first place![43] Having replaced the literal with the historical reading, Grotius turned the passage's meaning around. He then adjoined the examples of Pericles, Fabius, Cato and others, who also turned down their share of spoils in order to avoid the suspicion of pursuing their self-interest in war. Grotius has the pacifists coming and going; he ends the passage with the aside that Marcus Cato's reasoning for refusing his share was almost identical to Abraham's - only Cato put it a bit more elegantly (Appendix II.10).

7) Omission

Omission is yet another technique for separating religion and politics through creative Bible (dis)use. This involves taking a well-known, much-debated problem, like the state's authority over tithes, and marshalling all the usual sources and evidence – except for the Bible. Of all the rhetorical techniques

---

[43] In a very similar argument in ch. 10, using a different biblical passage to the same secularizing effect, Grotius adds the rider that while tithes may be an institution, they fall under secular jurisdiction; the church has no independent claim. The consensus of nations, not theology, is the authoritative source on tithes, and this consensus says that tithes are awarded by the secular government. David's transfer of spoils to his priests was a gift. Grotius does not cite the exact passage, but if he has 1 Sam. 30.26 in mind, then in addition to this being another case of historicization, it is also an instance of Grotius ascribing several wildly different meanings to yet another passage in *IPC* (p. 156).

Compare Grotius's move on Gen. 14 with Scaliger's attack on the Franciscan Feuardent, who tried to lend new life to the argument that the Septuagint's divine inspiration was proven by the Jews' commemoration of the event. Scaliger, in a withering attack on Feuardent in *Thesaurus Temporum* (1606), showed that the fast on the Tenth of Tevet was *instituted* as an annual re-enactment of chagrin, regret and remonstrance against Ptolemy's forced translation. A. Grafton, *Joseph Scaliger*, 2 vols (Oxford: OUP, 1993), II, pp. 646-7. Scaliger and Grotius made their case by emphasizing the historical origin and character of the institution.

used in *IPC*, omission yields perhaps the funniest, most straightforward and most ostentatiously pagan instances of secularization.

In the Prolegomena Grotius sets out to show that God is the King and supreme ruler of the world. Had he used the Bible for this, he would have gotten himself into the immense theological debates that surrounded every chapter and verse. His intended audience consisted of Catholic Iberians and the United Provinces. The latter was formed in 1581 by the seven mainly Protestant provinces of the originally 17-province Netherlands after they entered the Union of Utrecht in 1579, in reaction to the other ten, mostly Catholic provinces' Union of Atrecht. Religious tension ran high at home and abroad, between regions and groups, and the threats of military defeat and further secession were never far away in the early 1600s. This may be why in a space of 6 pages Grotius uses Cicero, Seneca, Homer, Hesiod, and a host of other pagans, but not the Bible or any theologian, to argue that God is the supreme ruler of the world, that He divided mankind into states, and He is the author and guarantor of the arrangement between prince or the magistrate, and the people (pp. 20-6).[44]

Near the end of the book, Grotius accuses the Portuguese of slandering the Dutch by spreading rumours of their atheism, thereby scaring off the natives from trading with the Dutch.

> But every charge that can brought is exceeded by the abominable wickedness ascribed to those men who acknowledge no god and no religion; for such an attitude is so abhorrent to human nature that one may truthfully deny the existence of any nation that does not cherish some innate conception of divinity and practise some form of divine worship. Yet all of these charges have been heaped upon the Hollanders by the Portuguese... (p. 266)[45]

And to support this point about human nature and the horrors of atheism, he promptly cites Cicero – and Cicero alone.

---

[44] Although doubts about the peaceful reunification of the seventeen provinces may have been prominent by 1605, all hope was not lost. Understandably, military conquest of the Spanish Netherlands was always on the cards; viz. the 1599-1600 campaign of Maurice. For the enduring significance of the terms of the two Unions in the first two decades of the seventeenth century, see e.g. van Dam's introduction to *De imperio*, pp. 10-1. On fears of further secession, see e.g. G.H.M. Posthumus Meyjes's introduction to *Meletius*, pp. 14-5, and J.L. Motley, *History of the United Netherlands from the Death of William the Silent to the Twelve Year's Truce*, 4 vols (The Hague: Nijhoff, 1860-67) IV, chs 38-40.

[45] 'sed supra omne quod dici potest illorum est nefas, qui Deum et religionem non agnoscunt, cum id eousque ab humana natura abhorreat, ut vere dictum sit nullum esse populum, cui non appareat aliquam inesse notitiam et cultum divinitatis'.

8) *More Striking Omissions: Melchisedec*

Of course, the most striking secularizing omission of all is that Grotius in *IPC* constructed a comprehensive theory of man, society, state, stadial theory of development and mankind that worked quite well without God.[46] We cannot go through all of these 'omissions' here. The few that are presented are chosen as typical of only Grotius's neutralization of the Bible.

In one of these he invokes the same Genesis 14 we saw earlier:

> This same principle – namely, that allies and subjects should have a share in the spoils – was in force among God's chosen people at all times, that is to say, from the age of Abraham to the period covered in the Books of Maccabees.[f]
>
> f: Genesis, xiv, at end; 2 Macc. 8.28, 30.[47]

He then cites the Greek custom, and its Roman imitation, of promising a tenth to the gods in case of victory, to be paid strictly in the name of the state, not the general. It is an interesting passage to choose. Earlier he used it to show the legitimacy of spoils. Here he uses it to clarify the division of spoils. Gen. 14 ends with Abraham giving his share to Melchisedec, the high priest (or king) of Salem (which may or may not be Jerusalem), who offers him bread

---

[46] E.g. Grotius promises to use divine authority to confirm that self-love is due to natural reason, but never does (p. 7); natural reason comes from God, point proven from pagan sources alone (p. 12); (pp. 34-6); the state must punish its own citizens for crimes against foreigners, otherwise it becomes liable: Grotius does not use the well-worn example of Jews falling out of divine favour for crucifying Jesus (p. 106); 153; 'It is generally agreed that lands captured from the enemy are not a part of the private spoils but become, instead, public property', without reference to the most famous example, Canaan (p. 161); at first no private property, only communal, then private property in moveables, then extended to land (pp. 227-30), all proofs from thoroughly pagan sources, myths, Cicero, Seneca, absolutely nothing from Scripture; commerce and states (p. 230), a similar stadial theory in his *Defense of ML* (Liberty ed., pp. 85-7); some things are common to all and can never become private property, argued from Cicero and others, even Plautus' plays, but no Christian source (p. 232); power not with the prince but with the people, proved from pagan history (pp. 284-7); to disprove Welwod's accusation of impiety, Grotius sets out to show God's role in his theory, but then bluntly replaces Him with nature: 'The sea is open, that is, it is free, therefore it does not permit a servitude. It is open to all, therefore no one is to be excluded. It is open by nature to all, therefore there is no one who can make a decree against anyone else, since nature is no less potent against princes and peoples than against private individuals.' (p. 95), oaths bind, see Euripides, Alcibiades, Augustus, Roman history, but no biblical covenant (pp. 295-6). One could list more; the point is that Grotius's claim is true, all his arguments work without the Bible – and all, save the very last one in *IPC*, work also without God. *IPC* is the dress rehearsal before the published *IBP* in more ways than one.

[47] 'Et hoc ipsum in Dei populo perpetuo obtinuit, ab Abrahamo scilicet ad Maccabaica usque tempora, ut socii subditique praedae participes fierent'.

and wine (p. 158).[48] Together with the Melchisedec reference in Psalm 110, and their NT counterpart, Paul's *Letter to the Hebrews*, these verses were heavily debated by European theorists of all political and religious colours.[49]

Paul relates the same story as Genesis, but endows Melchisedec with much more authority. So much so that he, rather than the patriarch Abraham, is said to be the forerunner, the image of Christ. Not surprisingly, Melchisedec was used in a vast number of debates over many issues, ranging from biblical hermeneutics, sacrosanct monarchy, papal authority within the church and over secular arms and money, to the nature of Christ and the Eucharist (Appendix II.11). Melchisedec was everywhere; a notable but typical example is the Colloquy of Poissy in 1561. It was when Beza brought up Melchisedec and the Eucharist that the Colloquy broke down and the French Wars of Religion began;[50] but divisions lurking among the Protestants were also serious enough by this time to prevent them from presenting a unified front at this initially very promising attempt to stem the tide of violence. The doctrinal debates over the Melchisedec passages became the principal manifestation not only of the Catholic-Protestant, but also of the intra-Protestant divisions. The most relevant instance is the Belgic Confession, which was presented at Poissy. Though mostly copied from the French Confession of 1559, it inserted several

---

[48] The Maccabees references Grotius adds to this are also specious: they are not about sharing spoils with allies but with orphans and widows. Which would have struck readers especially because Grotius's next point is the distinction between allies and subjects (p. 159). The idea that the Maccabees were still God's chosen people, and therefore the biblical passages about them also apply to the Dutch as God's new chosen nation, is the basis of the rhetorician Pieter Aelbertsz's play *De Machabeen* (MS Verzameling Trou Moet Blijcken, 1590). Instances of predikanten's use of Macc.-Dutch parallel as chosen nation, in Groenhuis, *Predikanten*, pp. 80-1. Note that most Protestants considered all four books of Maccabees to be apocryphal, and that 2 Macc. in particular had a huge history in many political arguments (Housley). See also fn 15 above.

[49] And of course even before European politics. Claudio Gianotto, *Melchisedek e la sua tipologia* (Brescia: Paideia, 1984). Although Gianotto's account takes us only to the third century AD, it is extremely useful for understanding early modern views on Christ and Melchisedec, since he traces this debate in Jewish-Christian polemics, Josephus, and the early Fathers. David Elgavish, 'The encounter of Abram and Melchizedek', in *Studies in the book of Genesis*, ed. by A. Wénin (Leuven: Leuven University Press, 2001), pp. 495-508. Bruce Harbert, 'The quest for Melchisedek', *New Blackfriars*, 68:810 (1987), 529-39. Yumi Dohi: Melchisedec in late medieval religious drama, *Early Drama, Art, and Music Review*, 16:2 (1994), 77-95; Van Dam, *De imperio*, pp. 911-2, fn6.

[50] J.R. de Melin, 'Rome et Poissy (1560-1561)', *Mélanges d'archéologie et d'histoire*, 39 (1921-2), 47-151. Claude d'Espence (?), *Journal*, ed. by Alphonse de Ruble, *Mémoires de la société de l'histoire de Paris et de l'Isle de France*, 16 (1889), 1-56. Outram Evenett, 'Claude d'Espence et son "Discours du colloque de Poissy"', *Revue historique*, 164 (1930), pp. 40-78.

references to Melchisedec (from Gen. 14 and Heb. 7). One of these came in Article 18 in order to 'confess, against the heresy of the Anabaptists', that Christ wholly assumed flesh. Cunaeus' *De Republica Hebraeorum* raised huge furore by undercutting every legitimacy claim derived from Melchisedec.[51] This may be a specific instance of Leiden co-operation. At any rate, we can safely assume that Grotius knew about these debates, at the very least about those surrounding the Belgic Confession; consequently in his discussion of church and state he made a very loud point with the silent half of his exegesis on the explosive story of Abraham and Melchisedec. He *would* talk about Abraham at war, guided by the same rationale as Pericles or Cato in their relationship with their troops (who would follow more loyally if their chiefs were not self-aggrandizing); but he would *not* contemplate Abraham facing the same problem as a king or a general commissioned by the state to wage war, and having to demonstrate the continued authority of the state over the general in the process of rewarding the troops and thanking the deities. By refusing to enter this debate, by conspicuously ignoring one of the key biblical precedents in state-church relations - especially after he just used the same reference several times in support of other points - Grotius deliberately broke with the legal and exegetical tradition that became increasingly unsuited to the challenge of his times.

9) Selective Citation, Pagan Superiority: Judges of Genesis

Let us take another example of this humanist lawyer reading the Bible inventively for rhetorical advantage. On pp. 89-90 Grotius shows that vengeance is just according to natural law. Lucretius, Cicero and other Ancients said so, and they have not been condemned for *this* by the most eminent theologians; therefore they must be correct.[52] This is already tongue-in-cheek. The principle that vengeance can be just is taken from the Ancients; its validity is confirmed by the theologians' silence (and Grotius pokes fun at the good Doctors many

[51] Peter Heylyn, *The history of the Sabbath In two bookes* (London: Henry Seile, 1636), p. 287, respectfully disagrees with Cunaeus's position on Melchisedec. Peter Tanner, *Primordia, or, The rise and growth of the first church of God* (London: Chiswell, 1683), pp. 97-8, disagrees with Cunaeus in no uncertain terms. He is also critical of the lack of Christian faith in Cunaeus' historical method: pp. 130, 136. John Edwards, *Polpoikilos sophia* (London: Daniel Brown, 1699), attacks Cunaeus very strongly for this, pp. 288-9.

[52] *Defense*, p. 86: eminent theologians believe there was no property in Paradise. What can make their speculations somewhat more probable is not more theology but historical and anthropological facts (in the form of Essenes and Americans). Grotius is even more dismissive of theologians in *IPC*, e.g. pp. 56ff.

times in *IPC*), and finally by instances from Scriptural history. To add insult to injury, he cites the aftermath of the Flood, when all survivors were members of the same household, but did not belong to any commonwealth. Yet the right to punish existed, which shows that it is a *natural* law, preceding and superior to *civil* law. Noah's Ark was one of the most often used images of chosen nation theorists, whether monarchists or republicans, Calvinists, Catholics, Anabaptists, visionary theocrats or Holy Roman Emperors, and especially for the water-bound and ship-happy Lowland Protestants, a sea-faring nation living largely on reclaimed land.[53] These all hinged on the premise that Noah's family did constitute a divine polity. Grotius wittily undercuts all Noahide legitimacy claims with this one move, and in agreement with Cunaeus he puts the biblical story to better use as a historical evidence of pre-state punishment.[54]

The actual reference is Gen. 9.6, which Grotius cites as: 'Whoso sheddeth man's blood, by man shall his blood be shed.' He leaves out the final clause: 'for in the image of God made he man.' I looked at the structure of chapter 8 to try to figure out the reason for this striking omission.[55]

Ch. 8 is tightly and rigorously constructed. Its starting point is justice in private war. Private war is unacceptable within the state, but private vengeance is more acceptable than the preceding, first injury. This gradation of justice, the continued presence of natural law under the surface of the civil, is already telling (p. 86). Grotius then refers back to his earlier contention that private wars can be just outside the state. 'Necessity based upon a superior law' can therefore render his Ninth and Twelfth Laws dormant, 'and it is understood that this necessity arises when judicial means for the attainment of our rights are defective' (p. 87). There are degrees at work here, too; a little delay in the court trial of a debt does not authorize the creditor to break into the debtor's house and seize his assets, or to enslave him. But what happens when judicial means are continuously defective, through 'defect in law or a defect in fact'? This case is analogous to

[53] Everhard van Reyd, for example, in *Historie der Nederlandtscher oorlogen* (Leeuwarden: Gysdert Sybes, 1650; he died in 1602) grounds Dutch legitimacy on both Noah and the Maccabees; Georg Horn, *Arca Noae: sive historia imperiorum et regnorum a condito orbe ad nostra tempora*, (Leiden: Hackius, 1666); further examples in Groenhuis, *Predikanten*, pp. 80-1, and in Schama, *Embarrassment.*

[54] Interestingly, Selden used the idea that the whole surface of the Earth was owned collectively by Noah's sons to counter the argument Grotius made this chapter of *IPC*, which became ML: Tuck, *Philosophy*, p. 117.

[55] Consider, for example, the sheer size of the secondary literature on Hobbes's mis-citation of the phrase "The fool hath said in his heart…" *IPC* is a veritable catalogue of these.

> what it was before states and courts of justice were established. But in those days human beings were governed in their mutual relations solely by the six laws which we laid down first of all. Those six precepts were the source of all law, and also of the principle that each individual was the executor of his own right, a principle consonant with the natural order, as we have already remarked, and as is indicated by the conduct of other living creatures.[56]

Throughout the ensuing discussion Grotius writes about natural laws and self-interest that apply to all living creatures, explicitly including animals.[57] The very first Scripture reference we get in this discussion is Samson's attack on the Philistines, who carried off his wife (Judges 15.1-8). Grotius cites the story as a case of defending a loved one. This, as Cicero and Tacitus rightly point out, is justified by natural law. But what Grotius cites is in fact one in a string of episodes in which Samson's wife is used by her own family to play tricks on Samson. In this instance her father sends her away with the Philistines, and tries to convince Samson to sleep with her younger sister instead. A very strange passage to choose, but we have seen this trick before. The selective citation of Gen. 9.6 in the next paragraph exemplifies a different technique, also used throughout *IPC*. After evaluating Samson's justice, Grotius writes:

> Accordingly, that precept of law which demands the punishment of evildoers is older than civil society and civil law, since it is derived from the law of nature, or law of nations. This assertion would seem to be supported by the Sacred Scriptures. For I find in them no reference to the existence of any civil state in the period following the Flood, during which the survivors of the human race were included in a single household, yet I do find reference to a law of that period which commands that evil deeds be punished: 'Whoso sheddeth man's blood, by man shall his blood be shed'. (Gen. 9.6; Appendix I.6)[58]

---

[56] 'His casibus eo fere devenitur, quo in loco res erant, antequam respublica et judicia instituerentur, ut recte dicit Castrensis. Tunc autem secundum sex duntaxat leges, quas initio posuimus, inter homines agebatur: hinc omne jus et juris quisque sui exsecutor: quod naturaliter contingere diximus et animantia caetera nos docent'.

[57] The *IPC* assertion that natural law and self-interest is shared by all creatures is perfectly compatible with the claim that all creatures have natural sociability, too, and they voluntarily constrain the exercise of their natural rights in order to help their offspring or the species. Grotius's main example in *IBP* of a complex case of natural sociability is the stork: Prolegomena 6, 7, p.8, edn B.J.A. de Kanter-van Hettinga Tromp, 1939 (Scientia Verlag reprint, 1993). Compare the wildly popular and widely influential Andrea Alciato, *Emblematum liber* (Augsburg: s.n., 1531 1st but unauthorized edn), Emblema XXX about the stork that nurtures the chicks, and who in their turn take care of their mother in her old age. Emblem V in the 1534 Paris edition shows not only the stork nurturing its chicks, but also a grown chick carrying its parent on its back and feeding it with fish.

[58] 'Lex igitur illa quae maleficos punire jubet, cum ex jure naturae sive gentium descendat, civili societate et lege est antiquior. Quod a divina scriptura non videtur alienum, in qua post orbem submersum, cum in una domo reliquiae essent generis humani, civitatem non video,

As we saw, he left out the clause 'for in the image of God made he man'. In the context it means that God's authority, not man's, is the underlying cause of this right. When it comes to pre-political *ius*, Grotius accepts the argument that God's law precedes and remains superior to civil law. What he seems to reject with this tailored citation and through the superiority ascribed to pagan sources is the Christian version of this argument, which says that man is special, and owes God for having natural rights that other creatures lack.

One is tempted to chalk this up to Grotius being in a hurry, often not bothering to check his references. But in the next sentence he states that this law is subordinate to another, also laid down in Gen. 9, which 'delivers beasts into man's service.' Then he begins to discuss the idea that wicked men are 'stripped, as it were, of all likeness to God or humanity' – Grotius practically cites the other half of the biblical verse in a context that gives it the opposite meaning. He attributes this idea of wicked men as beasts to both 'the theologians' (Aquinas is the only one he cites) and the philosophers: Democritus, Seneca and Aristotle are quoted at length, and finally we come to pre-state human society (p. 92). But all I hope to show here is that Grotius misquoted Gen. 9.6 for a pointedly secularizing purpose.[59] If he included the image clause, man's natural right would rest on God's gift and not on necessity, and Grotius's argument would become open to every theological debate over the respective status and relative cognizance of every kind of divine law.[60] Necessity and self-interest were more promising cornerstones for a new law of nations that Catholics and Protestants could accept and live by.

10) Steering Clear from all Religions: The IPC and the Vindiciae

It is important to realize that Grotius's Bible-reading techniques in *IPC* do not simply undermine Catholic interpretations, they truly secularize. We already saw his counterargument to the Mennonites, and illustrated his rejection of all Dutch sacred nation theories. Let me suggest that ch. 4 of the *Vindiciae contra Tyrannos* may have been a source for *IPC*, and that it is significant that Grotius

legem video, quae maleficia puniri jubet: Qui sanguinem hominis effudit, per hominem sanguis ejus effunditor.'

[59] One finds an equally deliberate omission from Num. 35 on p. 107.

[60] J.T. Johnson, 'Grotius's use of history and charity', *Grotiana*, 4 (1983), p. 28 on how Grotius restricted parts of *IBP* to Roman examples because of the wars of religion. Gen. 9.5-6 is traditionally understood as explaining why vengeance is *not* just, and blood may be shed only as the very last resort: for example John Chrysostom, *Homily* 74.

refused to adopt those arguments from this 'handbook of international Calvinist resistance' and foreign intervention that mixed politics with religion.[61]

On p. 126 Grotius starts to explain that one can instigate a just war for the sake of one's allies' rights. He gives three examples:

> So it was that Abraham undertook to wage war in behalf of Lot and the citizens of Sodom. Constantius did likewise in behalf of the Romans against Maxentius, as did Theodosius for the cause of the Christians against Chosroes the Persian. (p. 127)

The first thing we notice – by this point hopefully without much surprise – is that Grotius treats Abraham as any other historical figure. The OT has no claim to preferential treatment.[62] But which Abraham-Lot passage is he talking about? Presumably not the one in which Abraham confronts the Lord over Lot, Sodom, and Gomorrah, for surely Grotius would not go so far as to call this 'a just war'. The other possibility is Genesis 14, which he used at least six times in *IPC* so far, in six different contexts, in six different ways. Interestingly, Vitoria uses the same sequence of references in *De Indis* to discuss the same issue, though his conclusion was one that Grotius could not accept:

> For there is no doubt, as Cajetan also asserts (Secunda Secundae, qu. 40, art. 1), that the cause of allies and friends is a just cause of war, a State being quite properly able, as against foreign wrongdoers, to summon foreigners to punish its enemies. And this is confirmed by the fact that this was a method very much in vogue among the Romans for the extension of their Empire; that is, they brought aid to their allies and friends and so making a just war came, by right of war, into possession of fresh provinces. Yet the Roman Empire is approved by St. Augustine (De civitate Dei, bk. 5 [bk3]) and by St. Thomas (Opusculum 21) as a lawful one. And Sylvester reckoned Constantine the Great as Emperor, as St. Ambrose did Theodosius. Now, there does not seem to be any other juridic title whereby the Romans came into possession of the world, save in right of war, and the most especial cause of their wars was the defense and protection of their friends [*Non videtur autem quo alio iuridicio titulo venerint Romani in possessionem orbis nisi iure*

[61] On this chapter see Robert M. Kingdon, 'Calvinism and resistance theory, 1550-1580,' in *Cambridge History of Political Thought*, ed. by Burns and Goldie, p. 214. Borschberg dates the *Theses* as cotemporaneous with *IPC* (p. 197), and establishes Grotius's familiarity with the *Vindiciae* and the *Du droit des magistrats* (pp. 75-81); it is probably not a stretch then to say that they also had an effect on *IPC*, traceable in the text.

[62] 'Historical sources, in particular drawn from biblical and classical ancient history, also play an important part [in *IPC*], but not, as Grotius points out, as illustrations or for the sake of providing anecdotes, but precisely as a source which reveals the *ratio naturalis*, the fundamental authority on which the principles governing the relations between nations are based'. Wijffels, 'Early Modern Literature on International Law and the Usus Modernus', p. 49. This approach leads to the same secular result.

> *belli, cuius maximae occasiones fuerunt defensio et vindicatio sociorum.*]. In just the same way Abraham championed the cause of the King of Salem and of other kings who had struck a treaty with him, and he fought against four kings of that region, though they had done him personally no wrong (Genesis, ch. 14). This is the seventh and the last title whereby the Indians and their lands could have come or might come into the possession and lordship of Spain. Vitoria, *De Indis*, III.17 (pp. 112, 114 in edn of Walter Schätzel, Tübingen, 1952)

Is this Grotius's source? If so, he is getting the story all wrong. Constantine's famous victory over Maxentius at the Pons Milvius in 312 was celebrated as the victory of Christianity over the pagan world. Nevertheless, it would be hard to argue that Constantine won this battle as a formal ally of the Roman people, or of Christianity for that matter. Neither has any Theodosius ever encountered any of the Persian Chosroes (or Khusrow) kings.[63] There was, however, another famous Christian triumph, celebrated as much as Constantine's victory and conversion. Chosroes II sacked Jerusalem in 614, killed or enslaved a huge number of Christians, and carried off the True Cross. It took 13 years for Byzantium to recapture it, her army led by Emperor Heraclius.[64] As you can see in Appendix II.1, Abraham, Constantine and Theodosius were connected in Vitoria's discussion on allies; yet the last thing Grotius wanted to do was subscribe to Vitoria's conclusion that the Spanish dominion over the Indies had divine approval. In transforming Vitoria's argument, he also added Chosroes to the picture, joined with Theodosius. Where did these references come from?

The last chapter of the *Vindiciae contra Tyrannos* deals with the question: 'Whether neighbour princes may, or are bound by law to, aid the subjects of other princes, persecuted for true religion, or oppressed by manifest tyranny'. This is the same subject for which Vitoria and Grotius employed the same sequence of references. The *Vindiciae* chapter includes the following passage:

---

[63] Theodosius I (The Great), 346-95, reigned from 379. Theodosius II lived 401-450. Theodosius III, originally a tax collector, was emperor 715-7, and IV and V both lived in the thirteenth century. Chosroes/Khosrow I lived 531-79. One of the last Sassanian kings, Chosroes II lived 590-628. In short, no Theodosius could have fought a Chosroes. But when the Byzantine Emperor Maurice, his friend and ally, was assassinated in 602, Chosroes II embarked on a protracted campaign of revenge against the Romans. In 614 he invaded and sacked Jerusalem, and carried off the remains of the Holy Cross to Ctesiphon. Heraclius recaptured lost territories from the Persians and returned the Cross to Jerusalem in 627.

[64] A few works may be mentioned to indicate the popularity and significance of these themes. Raphael and Romano painted frescoes in the Vatican about Constantine's victory over Maxentius, and Piero della Francesca painted one at Arezzo in 1458, during attempts to retake Constantinople from the Turks, about Heraclius' recapture of the Cross.

> Constans favoured the orthodox Christians, Constantus, being the elder, leaned to the Arrians, and for that cause banished the learned Athanasius from Alexandria; the greatest professed adversary of the Arrians. Certainly, if any consideration in matter of confines be absolutely requisite, it must needs be amongst brethren; and notwithstanding, Constans threatened to war on his brother if he restore not Athanasius, and had without doubt performed it, if the other had long deferred the accomplishment of his desire. And if he proceeded so far for the restitution of one bishop, had it not been much more likely and reasonable for him to have assisted a good part of the people, if they implored his aid against the tyranny of those who refused them the exercise of their religion, under the authority of their magistrates and governors? So at the persuasion of Atticus the bishop, Theodosius made war on Chosroes, King of Persia, to deliver the Christians of his kingdom from persecution, although they were but particular and private persons; which certainly those most just princes, who instituted so many worthy laws, and had so great and special care of justice, would not have done, if by that fact they had supposed anything were usurped on another man's right, or the law of nations violated.

Although this text does not feature Abraham, it makes a nice connection between the brotherly love of Constans and Constantus on the one hand (neither of them Constantine the Great, but close in time and spelling, and easier to confuse) and the liberation of true believers from tyranny on the other – in other words, religious justification for armed intervention. It is also the only other text I found that makes the exact same mistake of confusing Theodosius with Heraclius. Perhaps events went something like this: Grotius reread Vitoria's *De Indis* as he was preparing *IPC*. One of the most authoritative Calvinist responses to Catholic international law was the *Vindiciae*. Most of these texts used essentially the same references, but put a different spin on them. Grotius took Vitoria's sequence of Abraham, Constantine and Theodosius, and he looked through the *Vindiciae* in an effort to invalidate Vitoria's point about the Spanish right to the Indies. He found a good counterargument to the Catholic position – but he was not prepared to adopt the Calvinist one instead.[65]

[65] He gets the references right in *IBP*: pp. 38-40 and 247. Note that the salient dividing line is not between regicides and populists; the *Vindiciae* allowed the murder of a tyrant, but in the same decade Juan Mariana, S.J., also approved the assassination of Henry III in *De rege et regis institutione* (Toledo: Petrus Rodericus, 1599). Catholic Paris, left without a ruler, maintained the claim to be the nation's capital by setting up a representative Council of Twelve. The 'grand design' that Sully claimed in his *Mémoires* to have proposed to Henry IV and James I/VI around the time Grotius wrote *IPC*, whereby France, England, Scotland, Protestant Germany, the United Provinces, Denmark, Sweden, Venice and Switzerland were to ally and together defeat the Habsburgs, seize America from Spain, free Germany from the Emperor, drive out Spain from the Netherlands, and set up a united Christian federation of 15 European states (not including Turkey, Russia, Italy and Spain) with free trade and foreign policy under a supreme federal

This would be all the more remarkable, given the occasion for writing *IPC*. It would have been extremely easy for Grotius to adopt the justification for attacking Portugal and Spain, non-Calvinist states that repressed 'true believers'. Instead, he lifted the anti-Catholic part of the argument, and eschewed all religion-based legal justifications for a Dutch attack on the Iberians. The justifications he did develop were all secular – this is the only thing that made sense, if he wanted to split the Spanish-Portuguese front or to avoid religious disagreements within the Provinces, within Holland, and among the VOC subscribers. His brief note at the end of this passage, in which he says that tyrannicides are acceptable, but are all too often staged by self-serving warriors ready to imperil the entire state, may even be a veiled criticism of Calvinist and other Dutch resistance theorists' rhetoric, and a gesture of peace toward the Iberians.[66] Attention to the sensibilities of his Dutch readership would also dictate that this gesture be made through a neutralization of the Bible, not through any particular discussion of the political problem in hand.

11) New Genies in Old Bottles: Grotius's Defense

After Welwod called him to account over his exegesis in *IPC*, Grotius published a *Defense of Mare Liberum against Welwod*. He would not apologise or retract. Instead, he again denied that the Bible has relevance in law, and played wonderful extended jokes at Welwod's and the Bible's expense. These jokes are even more noticeable and shocking than those in *IPC*, as if Grotius wanted to use his retort to Welwod to draw more attention to his explicitly stated and abundantly demonstrated view on the Bible's inadmissability in legal arguments. Perhaps it is fitting to look at a few, in closing.

Grotius says that Welwod should not have used the Bible in his criticism, because the Bible is the source of many contentions, and it is by and large irrelevant to nation-to-nation problems (*ML*, p. 105ff). Moreover, God did not legislate for everything explicitly.

> For example, in the marriage of persons who are joined by proximate ties of blood or affinity, even if we did not have the written law of God, nevertheless it would

council, is just one of many great counter-examples to the simplistic accounts of Protestant proto-democracy and Catholic absolutism that are sometimes given as the historical context for Grotius's work.

[66] See Heinrich Bullinger: *Sermonum decades quinque* (London: Radulph Newberry, [1587]; 1st ed. 1552), p. 272.

> by no means be licit to ignore that such a union is illicit, since the Roman jurists say that any such is incest by the law of nations and the Apostle Paul says that such a crime "was not even mentioned among the gentiles". [1 Cor. 5.1] Now if anyone wishes to give a reason for this precept, he will not easily find one to which no objection can be made, or equally certain and evident as is the precept itself. And surely what need to scrutinize causes, when these are to be referred "to the judgement of God." [Rom 1: 32] For in these also "the nations disclose the work of the law written in their hearts, their conscience bearing witness to them". [Rom 2:15]

The point that jumps out first is that 'the Roman jurists' seem to enjoy a higher authority than the 'written law of God'.[67] But the devil is in the references. Contrary to Grotius's presentation, in every one of them the Jews did something *in violation* of God's explicit law, while it was the Godless, natural law of the Gentiles that worked in compliance with justice (Appendix I.7).

All three passages show Saint Paul railing against the Jews who, in spite of the added advantage of directly revealed divine laws, broke them. '[K]nowing the judgment of God' may have been a cause that needed no scrutiny, but it failed, all the same. Yet again, Grotius argues that doctrinaire usage of the Bible in a legal debate is inappropriate, and he does this by saying it outright on the one hand, and on the other by supporting his statement with twisted and subverted citations from the Bible. Rejection and subversion, in harmony of form and substance – we could not ask for better proof.

But the *Defense* continues: 'Rightly therefore in the *Institutes* are the natural laws, among which are also to be included certain precepts of the law of nations, said to have been established by a certain divine providence'.

Again, we see divine authority validated by Roman law. In further support Grotius brings in Sophocles, Isocrates and other Ancients – but not a single Christian. He really is playing here. The paragraph concludes: 'Therefore this very fact, that God has insinuated such precepts in the minds of men, is sufficient to induce obligation even if no reason is apparent.' Even by early modern standards this is a most unusual and radical argument. Like in the *IPC*, in the *Defense* Grotius also used both content and form to make the same point: no agreement can be reached if any of the parties invoked any part of the Bible to justify their politics. To drive the point home, we saw him deploy omission, historicization, flamboyant subversion, straightforward denial of the Bible's applicability, and combinations of these.

---

[67] This is a separate technique we find often in *IPC*, pp. 35-6, 158: logic comes first; at its best, Scripture confirms it.

12) *From Fox to Hedgehog*[68]

There is only one thing in *IPC* that Grotius attributes to direct divine intervention: the Dutch track record in impressing the superiority of true Christianity upon the Indian peoples. In addition to the straightforward, earthly rewards of Dutch *virtù*, this success, according to Grotius, is a sign of divinely ordained expansion of trade and missionary activities. It is in this sense that the war against the Spaniards and the Portuguese in the Indies is divinely – but never biblically! – justified:

> In fact, there is nothing that serves the cause of the true religion better than such acts of kindness [i.e. defending the natives against the Spanish]. Care must be taken to keep men safe, lest the hope of converting them (as the Church Fathers were formerly wont to say) should perish with their bodies. The Indian peoples must be shown what it means to be a Christian, in order that they may not believe all Christians to be as the Spaniards are. Let those peoples look upon religion stripped of false symbols, commerce devoid of fraud, arms unattended by injuries. Let them marvel at the faith which forbids that even infidels should be neglected. In achieving these ends, we shall be preparing men for God. (p. 316)[69]

Commerce is God's instrument for spreading the true faith, though not (of course) through the Spanish and the Portuguese; for these false believers only use commercial opportunities to oppress the natives and acquire luxuries for themselves.[70] With an audacious twist Grotius describes the contents of the recently seized Catharina to illustrate that the Portuguese have all the wrong intentions behind their commercial enterprises.[71] The Dutch must persevere

[68] After Isaiah Berlin on Tolstoy and his road to eventual conversion. *The hedgehog and the fox* (London: Simon and Schuster, 1953).

[69] 'Nec sane quidquam magis interest verae religionis, quam istud fieri. Servandi sunt homines, ne cum ipsis (ut Patres quondam loquebantur) spes exstinguatur conversionis. Ostendi Indis debet, quid sit esse Christianum, ne putent Christianos omnes hoc esse quod Hispanos. Videant religionem sine simulacris, mercaturam sine fraudibus, arma sine injuriis. Admirentur fidem, quae negligi vetet etiam infideles. Hoc erit homines Deo praeparare'.

[70] Catholicism certainly lost some credibility at this time through its association with commercial imperialism. The Protestants were not without unease, either: Schama, *Embarrassment.*

[71] Much the same argument, including blaming Portuguese moral shortcomings for the failure of missionary attempts, had been already made at least equally amusingly by an extraordinary Portuguese writer and adventurer, Fernão Mendes Pinto (1510?-1583), in his immensely popular *Peregrinaçao*, modern ed. Rebecca D. Catz, 4th edn (Lisbon: Afrodite, 1989; 1st edn 1971). For thought-provoking parallels with Grotius's concept of man, see Joan-Pau Rubies, 'The Oriental Voices of Mendes Pinto, or the Traveller as Ethnologist in Portuguese India', *Portuguese Studies* 10 (1994), 24-43. Camões's *Disparates da India*, written while in jail in Goa, also come to mind. Portuguese corruption in the Indies was well known to the Dutch audience before *IPC*

in the Indies, and go on to establish a 'substantial presence' in China. He goes so far as to argue that God guided the Estates' hand when they helped create the VOC (pp. 339-43). The very end of *IPC* is a prayer with as fervent a belief in interventionism as any medieval saint's: God *chose the Dutch* to convert the heathen in the newly discovered worlds (pp. 365-6). How much of this was in earnest and how much formulaic is not relevant to our present thesis; but this concluding section of *IPC* may prefigure the *Truth of Christianity*, perhaps the most extraordinary book in its genre because of its real minimization of revelation in favour of more reason, and quickly translated into Arabic, Persian and Chinese by Edward Pococke for missionary work.[72] The point is that Grotius does not ground the idea of a Dutch commercial mission in prophecy, or derive a chosen nation theory from the Bible. His main concern is to come up with a legal framework that all parties, irrespective of religious convictions, could agree on. For this the Bible had to be neutralized, and Grotius rose to the task with skill, aplomb, verve and ingenuity.

Still, these closing pages of *IPC* seem to go against the rest of the work, in which he parried all legal attacks, but also carefully avoided religious arguments in favour of the Dutch position. The claim of religious orthodoxy and the other party's heterodoxy inevitably leads to a zero-sum game, in which no agreement can be reached without one party's total defeat, or the revision of the starting claims. Whether Grotius's final prayer was due to a reluctance to give up a customary gladiator's weapon in the arena of early seventeenth-century international relations, or it expressed Grotius's genuine belief and fervour, it serves as a reminder to avoid historical determinism or the imposition of any over-abstracted explanation of such works, however definitive these works may later turn out to be. Gomarus, chief ideologue of the Counter-Remonstrants, also taught at Leiden. Many people other than the Leideners attempted to develop a secular or a minimalist Christian historiography acceptable to all the warring factions: Lorenzo Valla, Isaac Casaubon, Fra Sarpi, De Thou, La Popilinière, the Bollandists and Mabillon come to mind, and we saw a glance at the English debate in Dorman.[73]

---

was written, for example from the *Navigatio ac itinerarium* by Johan Huighens van Lynschotten (1583). C.L. Heesakkers et al., *Jan Huygen van Linschoten and the Moral Map of Asia* (London: s.n., 1999), pp. 187-265.

[72] J. Brugman, 'Arabic Scholarship', in *Leiden University in the Seventeenth Century*, ed. by Lunsingh Scheurleer and Posthumus Meyjes, pp. 203-15, (p. 210). G.H.M. Posthumus Meyjes, 'Grotius as a theologian', in *Grotius, a great European*, ed. by Nellen et al., pp. 51-8.

[73] Tuck on Grotius and secularization: *Cambridge History of Political Thought*, ed. by Burns and Goldie, pp. 516-7.

Even after due respect to the contingency of historical events we can still say that the *causes* of the events are clear. Once the Reformation successfully broke the monopoly of the papacy over the interpretation of the Bible, and the humanistically educated European nobility recognized the possibilities offered by a wholesale rearrangement of religious and the secular powers, bloodshed became inevitable. This bloodshed allowed for no other solution than a re-construction of the power structure on the basis of a new kind of sovereignty, and a legal framework that was entirely secular. Leiden is a synecdoche of this story, and in *IPC* we see Grotius make good use of what he learnt from his Leiden colleagues about strategies of secularization.[74]

In conclusion, let me restate once more that I do not argue that Grotius did not believe in God or that he set out in *IPC* to undermine the Bible. Instead, he presented an unbroken string of forced interpretations that had shocking implications for just war theory, and he did so in order to show that the Bible should not be used in international law at all, because using it would only perpetuate the situation in which all debates about legitimacy and international relations were open-ended and impossible to settle, anchored as they were in rival traditions of biblical exegesis, including the debates concerning the legitimacy of having seized the Catharina. At the beginning of *IPC*, of *De republica emendanda*, of the *Commentarius*, of *De imperio*, and at the end of *De antiquitate*, in the passages cited above, Grotius declares that one major cause of continued disagreement and conflict is the category mistake made by those who try to derive universal and divine laws from all and/or any part of the Bible. His arguments, in contrast, are no less compelling without Scripture, or even in the absence of God. What we see unfolding in *IPC* is simply him making good on his promise: sometimes he used the Bible as a source of mere historical incidents, carefully sandwiched between non-biblical historical events in order to show that the Bible had no claim to special privileges; at other times he used it in an absurd fashion to underscore and illustrate the dangers of its application in international law. It would not be hard or far-fetched to argue that one of the reasons why Grotius removed the Bible from politics was his genuine faith in the Good Book. The fact remains that his use of biblical references in *IPC* indicate that he was already thinking in terms of the essentially secular, new system of laws that we find in *De iure belli ac pacis*.

---

[74] Note that here we only looked at how *IPC* combated Bible-based exclusivism; plenty of other options were available. Language, a non-Christian chosen nation theory (lost tribes, sole inheritance of Egyptian and/or Cabalistic wisdom, most direct descent from a non-Christian hero), ancient constitutionalism, racism, Europe-centrism, natural masterhood and such like also could, and were, turned into organizing principles of exclusivism. 'Secularization' is only one of the grand discourses of early modernity, in which Bible-neutralization is a mere rivulet.

Appendices

The Appendices referred to in this article are too long – some 60 pages altogether – for insertion into the journal; they are accessible at the website of Grotiana (www.brill.nl/grot/appendices). Below you find a summary description of the two Appendices.

Appendix I: Biblical Texts

I.1 Deut. 20.
I.2 1 Sam. 30
I.3 1 Sam. 15
I.4 Genesis 20
I.5 Gen. 14
    Heb. 6.19-7.22
I.6 Judges and Genesis 9.6
    Judges 15
    Genesis 9
I.7 Pauline letters cited in the *Defensio*
    1 Cor. 5. 1
    Romans 1.32
    Romans 2

Appendix II: Excerpts from the Exegetical Tradition

II.1 Texts for Deut. 20: Vitoria, Clement of Alexandria, Turnbull, Gibbens, Aretius, Gentili
II.2 Texts for Num. 31 in *IPC*: Ambrose, John Chrysostom, Musculus, Aretius
II.3 Texts for Joshua 8: St. Thomas Aquinas
II.4 Texts for Joshua 22: Rudolf Gwalther
II.5 Texts for 1 Sam. 15 in *IPC*: Beza, Peter Ramus, Wolfgang Musculus
II.6 Rahab in Joshua: St Cyril, Augustine
II.7 Texts for 1 Sam. 15 in *IPC*: Augustine, Dorman, Edgeworth, Gregory of Nyssa, Parsons, Arias, Arminius, Canisius, John Chrysostom, John Cassian
II.8 Texts for Genesis 20: Clementine, Richard Parsons
II.9 Texts for Luke 3.14: Augustine, Chrysostom, Calvin, Aretius, Socinus
II.10 Texts for Gen. 14: Cassian, Chrysostom
II.11 Texts on Melchisedec: Theophilus, Eusebius, Clement of Alexandria, Jerome, Ambrose, Augustine, Vitoria, Luther, Confessio Belgica

War, Piracy and Religion: Godfried Udemans' *Spiritual Helm* (1638)

Joris van Eijnatten
Professor of Cultural History, VU University Amsterdam
E-mail: j.van.eijnatten@let.vu.nl

Abstract
The Calvinist minister Godfried Udemans (1581/2–1649) is generally considered to be one of the more important seventeenth-century theologians from the province of Zeeland. He specialized in writings for a broader public, including, in particular, publications on ethical and religious codes in trade and seafaring. Of his various writings on moral theology, *'t Geestelyck roer van 't coopmans schip*, first published in 1638, is the most important.
The *Spiritual helm* appeared in print some thirty years after Grotius occupied himself with *De jure praedae* (the manuscript dates from 1604), but Udemans had already begun articulating his thoughts in 1608. It is instructive to examine the ethical writings of a contemporary of Grotius. It has been claimed that in the early modern period, Calvinism, especially in its English Puritan variety, did much to propagate the medieval traditions of holy war that to all appearances had been laid to rest by Spanish theoreticians during the sixteenth-century Renaissance. In this article, I examine the extent to which Udemans draws upon religion as a means of legitimizing violence on behalf of secular political authorities such as the prince (or, as in the case of the Dutch Republic, the States or States General), and, more in particular, the Dutch East India Company (VOC) and West India Company (WIC). If Udemans is representative of the religious tradition to which he reckoned himself, holy war thought did not figure prominently in Dutch Calvinism.

Keywords
Godfridus Udemans; holy war; moral theology; piracy; ethics; Dutch Republic

Introduction: Godfried Udemans

Having read theology at the university of Leiden, Godfried or Godefridus Udemans (1581/2–1649) followed a career as a clergyman in the province of Zeeland. He worked as a minister in Haamstede for several years and then in 1604 became a pastor in Zierikzee, where he remained until his death. Udemans is generally considered to be one of the more important seventeenth-century theologians from Zeeland. He specialized in writings for a broader public, including, in particular, publications on ethical and religious codes in trade and seafaring. He published a *Spiritual compass* in 1617 and a *Merchant's yacht* in 1637.[1] Of his various writings on moral theology, *'t Geestelyck roer van 't coopmans schip*, first published in 1638, is the most important.[2] The book covers aspects of morality and ethics on which Udemans had been writing since 1608. It was dedicated to the directors of the East and West India Companies.

The title, *'t Geestelyck roer van 't coopmaans schip*, is best translated as *The spiritual helm of the merchant's vessel*. The book's subtitle explains Udemans' choice of metaphor:

> that is: a faithful account of how a merchant and seafaring trader should conduct himself in his actions, in times of peace and war, with respect to both God and people, on water and on land, and especially among the heathens in the East and West Indies: for the glory of God, the foundation of His congregations, and the salvation of His souls: and also for the temporal well-being of the fatherland and his family.

A motto on the title page further clarifies his preference for the *gubernaculum spiritualis* as metaphor. It is a passage from the New Testament: 'Behold also the ships, which though they be so great, and are driven of fierce winds, yet are they turned about with a very small helm, whithersoever the governor listeth' (Jas 3.4).[3]

---

[1] *Geestelick compas, dat is nut en nootwendich bericht voor alle zee-varende ende reysende luyden (met name de visscherye)* (1617); *Coop-mans-jacht brenghende goede tydinghe uyt het landt Canaan, voor alle vroome koop-luyden om te verkrijgen ende te behouden eenen gewenschten segen over hare negotie* (Dordrecht: Boels en Van Esch, 1637). On the latter book, see A. Vergunst, 'Godefridus Cornelisz. Udemans en zijn Coopmansiacht', in *Wegen en gestalten in het gereformeerd protestantisme*, ed. by W. Balke, C. Graafland, and H. Harkema, (Amsterdam: Bolland, 1976), pp. 123-140. A.Th. Boone, '"Om een woesten hoop te brengen tot de kerck". Een onderzoek naar zendingsgedachten in piëtistische zeemansvademcums', in A.Th. Boone en J. van Ekeris, *Zending tussen woord en daad. Twee hoofdstukken uit de geschiedenis van gereformeerd piëtisme en zending* (Kampen: De Groot Goudriaan, 1991), pp. 12-46. Practically all biographical information on Udemans is in Dutch; see e.g. the article on Udemans in *Biografisch lexicon voor de geschiedenis van het Nederlandse protestantisme*, 6 vols (Kampen: Kok, 1978-2006) I, pp. 385-386.

[2] Godefridus Udemans, *'t Geestelyck roer van 't coopmans schip, dat is: trouwbericht hoe dat een coopman en coopvaerder hem selven dragen moet in syne handelinge in pays, ende in oorloge, voor God ende menschen, te water ende te lande, insonderheydt onder de heydenen in Oost ende West-Indien: ter eeren Gods, stichtinge syner gemeyten, ende saligheyt sijner zielen: mitgaders tot het tijtlick welvaren van het vaderlandt, ende sijne familie*, 2nd edn (Dordrecht: Boels, 1640; facsimile repr. Dordrecht: van der Tol, 1965).

[3] All quotations are from the Authorized (King James) Version of the Bible, which most resembles the Dutch translations available at the time.

During his professional course through life in regions abounding with dangers and temptations, a merchant required moral guidance. Udemans' *Spiritual helm* offers such counselling. It is an ethical compass comprising more than 1,000 pages, divided into six books, which respectively treat:[4]

I. the origin, utility and necessity of trade;
II. the profession of merchant;
III. the profession of sailor in the merchant navy;
IV. trade with the East and West Indies;
V. trade with Constantinople and other Turkish lands; and
VI. naval warfare, in particular regarding the conduct of sailors on war vessels.

Udemans puts forward his views on war mainly in Book VI. This book contains four sections, each dealing with a particular problem concerning naval warfare:

(a) whether an enemy may be resisted by using force;
(b) the discipline that should be maintained on board ship;
(c) the vocation of a navy officer; and
(d) several cases of conscience concerning naval warfare.

Section (a),[5] on the question of the use of violence in resisting an enemy, is mainly a refutation of Mennonite pacifism. The question was an important one, according to Udemans, since some powerful merchants were Mennonites who hesitated to provision with cannon ships bound for the Indies. Christians, they believed, had to turn the left cheek, rather than fight back.[6] Like all mainstream Calvinists, Udemans strongly disapproved of this view, and his arguments reflect the standard anti-pacifist repertoire of the time. Section (b) discusses the various articles on religion in the naval code issued by the States General, treating such issues as worship, prayer and swearing, and the general maintenance of religious discipline.[7] Udemans elaborates on this in Section (c), in which he points out the responsibilities of officers in enabling the navy and its personnel to perform their tasks properly.

---

[4] Note that the pagination in the edition I have used is not uniform. The volume is paginated as follows: regular pagination: 1-176; pagination on every other page, i.e. with the same page number for recto (r) and verso (v): fol. 89r-fol. 184v; regular pagination: 369-546; pagination on every other page: fols 273r-370r. The sections relevant to this article are on pp. 471-483 (Book 6, section 1) and fols 316v-332r (Book 6, section 4).

[5] Udemans, *Geestelyck roer*, pp. 471-483.

[6] Udemans, *Geestelyck roer*, pp. 472.

[7] Udemans, *Geestelyck roer*, pp. 484-530.

Officers in his view were required to ensure the quality of the physical and spiritual life of their subordinates.[8]

The part most relevant to this article is section (d), the content of which I will attempt to set out and subsequently relate to contemporary ideas on just war and piracy, including those of Hugo Grotius. The *Spiritual helm* appeared in print some thirty years after Grotius occupied himself with *De jure praedae* (the manuscript dates from 1604), but we saw that Udemans had already begun articulating his thoughts in 1608. It is instructive to examine the ethical writings of a contemporary of Grotius. As a scholar of law, the latter examined the legality of the activities of trading companies acting on behalf of the Dutch Republic as a state at war. As a clergyman, Udemans discussed moral rather than legal issues. His topic was the cases of conscience that weighed upon the minds of company employees in the practice of war – at least, those employees who had any regard at all for their own souls. Grotius, furthermore, sympathized with the Remonstrant / Arminian party in the Reformed church, while Udemans sided unilaterally with the Counter-Remonstrant / Calvinist faction. The Remonstrant tradition, at the root of which stood thinkers like Grotius, Uijtenbogaert and Episcopius, has traditionally been associated (not least by its own adherents) with the practice and theory of toleration and peaceful co-existence, and, in the nineteenth and twentieth centuries, with libertarianism and ecumenism.[9] Calvinism, on the other hand, has often been, and still is, associated with fearless heroism, bellicose assertiveness and ruthless violence, attributes that manifested themselves in religiously inspired actions ranging from the so-called Iconoclastic Storm of 1566 to the Dutch resistance to German occupation during World War II. More to the point, it has been claimed that in the early modern period, Calvinism, especially in its English Puritan variety, did much to propagate the medieval traditions of holy war that to all appearances had been laid to rest by Spanish theoreticians during the sixteenth-century Renaissance.

James Turner Johnson has made the claim that Puritanism (or, more precisely, certain influential Puritans) justified aggression on religious grounds.[10]

---

[8] Udemans, *Geestelyck roer*, p. 530–fol. 317v.

[9] See Joris van Eijnatten, *Liberty and Concord in the United Provinces. Religious Toleration and the Public in the Eighteenth-Century Netherlands*, Brill's Studies in Intellectual History 111 (Leiden: Brill, 2003).

[10] James T. Johnson, *Ideology, Reason, and the Limitation of War: Religious and Secular Concepts 1200-1740* (Princeton: Princeton UP, 1975); James T. Johnson, *Just War Tradition and the Restraint of War: A Moral and Historical Inquiry* (Princeton: Princeton UP, 1981); David Little, '"Holy War" Appeals and Western Christianity: A Reconsideration of Bainton's Approach', in *Just war and jihad. Historical and theoretical perspectives on war and peace in Western and Islamic traditions*, ed. by John Kelsay and James Turner Johnson (New York: Greenwood, 1991).

He argues that 'classic' just war doctrine, containing statements on *ius ad bellum* (the right to make war) as well as *ius in bello* (that which is allowable in the course of war), originated around the end of the Middle Ages. The sixteenth century witnessed the rise of two traditions of just war thought. The naturalist tradition, which grounded the *ius ad bellum* in natural law, excluded religion as a motive for just war. By contrast, the theological tradition was concerned to justify religion as a cause for war; a 'holy war' would thus be validated as a just war. Johnson accords to Calvinism a crucial role in the revival of holy war thought. For example, he sees the *Sermonum decades quinque de potissimis christianae religionis capitibus* (1552) by the Swiss reformer Heinrich Bullinger (1504-1575) as an important milestone. Bullinger's fifty sermons deeply influenced the thought of English Puritans, and they were translated into German, French, English and Dutch.

In an earlier examination of Puritan thought, Roland H. Bainton suggested that a holy war essentially has four features:[11]

1. There is a holy cause.
2. Violence takes place under God's direction and with his help.
3. There is a distinction between godly crusaders and ungodly enemies.
4. Enemies are not spared.

Elaborating on and refining Bainton's characterization, Johnson defines the concept of holy war as it occurs in Bullinger and several sixteenth and seventeenth-century Puritan authors. He refers to six 'positions':

1. There is a religious purpose ('holy cause').
2. A defensive war for the sake (or in defence of) religion is a just war.
3. An offensive war for the sake of religion is a just war (for example a war expressly 'commanded' by God).
4. Soldiers must be personally godly.
5. A just war is a *justified* war (rather than a *justifiable* war, as in classic just war thought), which suggests that both the cause and its champions are righteous.
6. A holy war must be fought without restraint.

There is no need here to dispute Johnson's excellent analysis, although one could question the significance or representativeness of the Puritan authors whose books he examined. The point is that he offers a useful conceptual instrument with which to test seventeenth-century writings on moral theology

[11] Roland H. Bainton, *Christian attitudes toward war and peace. A historical survey and critical re-evaluation* (New York: Albingdon, 1960), 148.

concerning their proclivity towards holy war. Applying Johnson's findings to the Dutch Republic is all the more germane because he sees Puritans as the main exponents of Christian *jihad*. Clergymen like Udemans are often reckoned to the so-called 'Further Reformation' movement, which as a whole was under the spell of English Puritanism. Emphasizing heartfelt piety and strict morality, the Further Reformation aimed at bringing the 'magisterial' Protestant Reformation to completion. Its adherents often took Puritan authors as their role models.[12] One might assume that the latter's aggressive rhetoric spilled over into the 'Public' (Calvinist) Church of the Dutch Republic.

Udemans achieved some notoriety in modern times because of a passage on slavery in his *Spiritual helm* in which he insisted that Christians were allowed to enslave 'Heathens and Turks' on condition that they had been captured during a 'just war' or bought from their parents at a fair price.[13] The argument could well have been taken from Grotius, who also defended slavery as an outcome of war.[14] But where Grotius drew on the principles of natural law, Udemans quoted the Bible (Lev. 25.44-46) as well as a theology professor at Leuven, the Catholic Johannes Molanus (c. 1505-1585).[15] In other words, he used religious arguments to defend the enforced slavery of fellow humans. One might hypothesize that religion similarly offered him arguments in support of other forms of inter-human violence, such as war.

This article, then, examines the extent to which Udemans draws upon religion as a means of legitimizing violence on behalf of secular political authorities such as the prince (or, as in the case of the Dutch Republic, the States or States General), and, more in particular, the Dutch East India Company (VOC) and West India Company (WIC). In the next section, I shall first provide a summary of the various cases of conscience concerning naval warfare and piracy treated by Udemans.

---

[12] Willem Jan op 't Hof, *Engelse piëtistische geschriften in het Nederlands, 1598-1622* (Rotterdam: Lindenberg, 1987).

[13] Udemans, *Geestelyck roer*, fol. 182r.

[14] Grotius, *IBP*, III.7.1; for the text of *IBP*, I have used Hugo Grotius, *De iure belli ac pacis libri tres*, ed. by B.J.A. de Kanter-van Hettinga Tromp (Leiden: Brill, 1939; repr. Aalen: Scientia 1993) which is based on the *editio princeps* of 1625. On the context of both Grotius and Udemans, see Gerald Francis De Jong, 'The Dutch Reformed Church and Negro Slavery in Colonial America', *Church History*, 40 (1971), 423-436; James Q. Whitman, 'The Moral Menace of Roman Law and the Making of Commerce: Some Dutch Evidence', *The Yale Law Journal*, 105 (1996), 1841-1889. On Grotius: Gustaaf van Nifterik, 'Hugo Grotius on "Slavery"', in *Grotius and the Stoa*, ed. by Hans W. Blom and Laurens C. Winkel (Assen: van Gorcum, 2004), pp. 233-243.

[15] The reference is to Johannes Molanus, *De canonicis libri tres* (Louvain: Amplius, 1587), III.37.

Casuistry for Christians under Arms

This section provides a synopsis of section (d) of Book 6 of the *Spiritual helm*.[16] Udemans begins by explaining that it is necessary to provide advice both for the benefit of the pious Christian soldier whose conscience is troubled by sins he believes he may commit, or has committed, under arms, and for the godless soldier whose sinful behaviour had already imperilled his own soul. He then discusses twelve cases of conscience.

Case I

The first issue, 'Is it permissible to wage war against a common enemy at the behest of the civil authorities?', is an easy one to resolve, since Udemans had already offered an answer earlier in Book VI. His response is, yes, Christians may wage war on condition that they do so according to God's Word, in faith and with due respect for justice.[17]

Case II

Case II addresses the problem of the conditions a war needs to meet in order for it to be waged lawfully and in good conscience. In dealing with this ethical issue, Udemans draws on classical just war thought. In this tradition, usually three criteria by which to determine the justness of a war were mentioned: right authority (a sovereign ruler), just cause (defending oneself, retaking something wrongly taken, punishing evil) and right intention (proper motivation). First, argues Udemans, a war is justly waged if its cause is just, serious and necessary, and if we are able to account for it before God and any impartial person, to whom we can also demonstrate that we have beforehand tried all friendly and non-violent means to resolve the dispute.[18] The war against Spain is such a war, Udemans insists, referring to his own explanation of the Calvinist Heidelberg Catechism, called *Practice, or real exercise of the chief Christian virtues of faith, hope and charity* (1612).[19] Second, because war

---

[16] Udemans, *Geestelyck roer*, fols 316v-332r.

[17] Udemans, *Geestelyck roer*, fol. 316v. He refers the reader to William Ames, *De conscientia, et ejus jure, vel casibus, libri quinque* (Amsterdam: Jansonius, 1630; reissued in 1631, 1634, and 1635), V.30 ('De bello'); as well as his own *Noodighe verbeteringhe dat is Schriftmatige aenmerckinghen op seker boecxken van Francoys de Knuyt* (Zierikzee: Doll, 1620).

[18] Udemans, *Geestelyck roer*, fol. 316v. Udemans again cites Ames: Ames, *De conscientia*, V.30.

[19] Udemans, *Practycke, dat is Werckelijcke oeffeninghe vande christelicke hooft-deuchden, gheloove, hope, ende liefde* (Middelburg: Schilders, 1612). Udemans refers to his explanation of the Fifth Commandment.

is a form of justice, only a lawful government may begin a war. This, too, was a standard argument in the sixteenth-century, 'classic' just war tradition.[20] Third, a war must be waged in a just manner, according to divine and human laws. Fourth, the prince must ask God's approval before beginning a war, in the manner of Old Testament leaders. This means that the prince should seek God's advice through prayer, by reading the Bible, and by asking the advice of prophets, i.e. the ministers of the church. Fifth, the aim of war must be a proper one. A prince must not wage war out of pride, greed or revenge, but only for the glory of God and out of love for justice, to protect the good and punish the bad. The ultimate aim of war is peace.[21] Finally, a prince should wage war in faith, and trust in God rather than human force. Wars fought in faith are not called *bella Jehovae* for nothing (Num. 21.14; 1 Sam. 18.17).[22]

Case III

Are soldiers always obliged to inquire closely into the justness and legitimacy of the wars in which they participate? In his response to this third issue, Udemans advises his readers to make two distinctions, one between officers and soldiers, and the other between the home government and a foreign prince. All those who take part in the council of war (the officers) must have a clear conscience regarding the war's legitimacy. Common soldiers, on the other hand, may rely on the judgement of their superiors. However, they should refrain from fighting when they are personally convinced that the war is an unjust one.[23] It follows that no soldier may fight against his fellow believers, or otherwise provide help in destroying the true religion, since wars with this objective are unjust. English mercenaries who aid the Spanish in suppressing their Dutch fellow believers sin against God, faith, charity, the communion of saints, good conscience, and nature itself.[24] Consequently, to serve a foreign, unbelieving prince for the sake of money is out of the question. Soldiers should enter into the service of a foreign prince only after having made certain that the war for which they fight is a just one, and that the ruler into whose service they have entered is a pious prince who acts for

[20] See e.g. Johnson, *Ideology, Reason, and the Limitation of War*, p. 158 (on Franciscus de Vitoria).

[21] Udemans cites Augustine, *De civitate Dei*, XIX.12.

[22] Udemans, *Geestelyck roer*, fol. 317v.

[23] Udemans quotes Ames, *De conscientia*, V.30, thesis 18.

[24] Udemans, *Geestelyck roer*, fols 318r-318v. Udemans discusses this latter point at greater length in *Spiritual helm*, pp. 383-389 (on contacts with the Turks), to which he refers the reader.

the glory of God and the well-being of his church. Apart from English soldiers, the Swiss and even the Dutch are prone to neglecting this rule. This includes such seamen who defect to the enemy because of the plunder they can obtain. The Dunkirk pirates are a case in point. But the contrary is true also. It is commendable to help one's fellow believers, as the English and Scots did who helped the Dutch in their war against Spain. Peter Martyr[25] offers some additional reasons for not participating in warfare for the sake of money. Mercenaries, he wrote,

* put themselves into jeopardy;
* act not from obedience or love of *patria*, but recklessness, pride, greed, laziness, and so on;
* foster warfare as such;
* cause damage to their own country's reputation;
* cause damage to their own country since they will not be available to it in times of need;
* cause damage to people (foreigners) who have done no harm;
* damage themselves unnecessarily through bodily injuries sustained in war, or through spiritual injuries resulting from contact with foreign peoples (since the latter hold different beliefs and have different customs).

A soldier may only enter into the service of another country in certain cases.[26] Some may object that many men will not be able to earn a living if they cannot fight. Even if this is the case, Udemans points out, a good conscience is always preferable to a full stomach.[27]

Case IV

Case IV is related to the previous one. Is a Christian government justified in seeking aid from unbelieving princes, or (vice versa) in giving aid to an unbeliever, assuming that the war is just? A Christian government, says Udemans, may not conclude a treaty that guarantees mutual aid under all circumstances. The government must ensure that such a covenant with an unbelieving prince does not contradict the covenant with God, since a government must above all foster the glory of God.[28]

[25] The reference is to Petrus Martyrus Vermigli, *In duos libros Samuelis prophetae qui vulgo priores libri Regum appellantur* (Zurich: Froschouer, 1564).

[26] As Ames points out in *De conscientia*, 5.30, thesis 12.

[27] Udemans, *Geestelyck roer*, fols 319r-321r.

[28] Udemans, *Geestelyck roer*, fol. 321r.

Case V

Is a just war, waged with evil intent, in effect an unjust war? The answer to this question depends on whose intent we are discussing. The position of the sovereign power who declares war is not the same as that of the officers and soldiers who do the fighting. As far as the sovereign power is concerned, we should take care to distinguish between secret and public intent. Secret intent is known only to God, while the latter may be examined to see if it meets the conditions of a just war. As for officers and soldiers, Udemans again points out that they should always wage war in faith. However, a just war cannot become unjust only because some soldiers fight with evil intent, or because some soldiers make regrettable mistakes. The legitimacy of the war as such ought to be judged, not the individual trespasses that occur in the course of that war.[29] The Jesuits, and especially the ones oriented towards Spain, condemn the Dutch Revolt on these grounds. They claim that we did not begin war for the sake of religion or the land's freedoms and privileges, or because of the introduction of new bishops, or Alva's taxation policy, or the imposition of foreign governors, advisors and officers, or the establishment of the council of blood, and so on. Instead, they insist that the Dutch nobility was jealous of the Spanish; William of Orange in particular is supposed to have sought honour and glory (*eergiericheyt*).[30] However, the Spanish apologists do not dispute the principle itself. All individuals in government must examine their consciences before God to determine whether their actions in the affairs of war agree with their own public manifests, publications, contracts and treaties.[31]

Case VI

In his response to the sixth problem, Udemans again addresses the issue of the *ius in bello*. He poses two questions. Who may be harmed in war, and to which degree? Regarding the first question, it is important to keep in mind (against the Mennonites) that a just and legitimate war is in fact a species of justice, and that the purpose of justice is to protect the good and punish evil.[32]

[29] Udemans, *Geestelyck roer*, fols 321r-321v; he insists here that the objections of the Mennonites concerning this issue do not obtain.

[30] Udemans cites Famiano Strada's *De bello Belgico* ([Rome: Corbelletti] 1632), which makes the point that the nobility fought to defend its own interests; he also points out that the *Apologie* (1581) by William of Orange and the *Plakkaat van verlatinge* (1581) form adequate antidotes to Strada.

[31] Udemans, *Geestelyck roer*, fol. 322r-323v.

[32] Udemans refers to Ames, *Conscientia*, V.30.1; Grotius, *IBP*, I.2.

A legitimate war is waged directly against a guilty party, i.e. against those who have perpetrated a crime against a prince or republic. A war is either defensive or offensive. A defensive war is a war waged against those who without just cause seek to oppress us and taken away from us that which God and nature have given us. This in effect is the cause of the Dutch Revolt, which is in origin a defensive war.[33] The King of Spain trespassed on Dutch privileges and would not be swayed by peaceful means. Hence the States declared on 26 July 1581 (in the so-called *Plakkaat van verlatinge*) that he had forfeited his rights *ipso jure*. The right of defence as such is a reasonable principle based on nature, as Grotius, among others, makes clear.[34] An offensive war often follows from a defensive one, since we may well be obliged to take back from the enemy the things he took from us.[35] The Dutch war is, in fact, partially offensive, partially defensive. It began as, and still is, a defensive war; but it is also an offensive one, since Spain not only caused a lot of damage but also tore away ten provinces.[36]

At any rate, even during an offensive war we should take care to treat those who live within the territory of the enemy, and who have done us no harm, with mercy and moderation, especially the elderly, youths and women. True, the Lord God sometimes ordered Israel to annihilate complete peoples. However, these are extraordinary examples, since they refer to cursed nations which God wanted specifically to obliterate. We should refrain, furthermore, from treating harshly our friends, allies and fellow believers, as well as our enemy's peaceful neighbours. The same applies to farmers, fishermen, merchants, craftsmen and artisans, in so far as they do not serve the enemy. Learned people should be spared especially, since they concern themselves only with religion, law or medicine.[37] In brief, we should avoid hurting anyone who does not carry arms. Witness the examples set by Nebuchadnezzar, Alexander the Great and Camillus.[38] Christian generals should not hand towns over to plunder and burning, as the Spanish so often do: in 1572 Alva, Bossu and Don Frederico respectively devastated Mechelen, Rotterdam and Naarden. Such atrocities are in conflict with Scripture, justice, equity,

---

[33] Udemans refers to William of Orange's *Apologie*.

[34] Grotius, *IBP*, I.2; Udemans refers also to Cicero, *Pro milone* and Josephus, *De bello judaico*.

[35] Udemans, *Geestelyck roer*, fols 323v-324v. See Cic. *off.* I.34-39.

[36] Udemans, *Geestelyck roer*, fol. 325r. Udemans takes pains to point out that the government made this clear in several manifests (dating from 1579, 1602 and 1632).

[37] See Grotius, *IBP*, III.2.9-12.

[38] For Nebucadnezzar, see Jer. 39.11-14; Jer. 40.1-7; Alexander the Great treated mildly the gymnosophists he encountered in India; on the dictator Camillus, see Livius, *Ab urbe condita*, V.

goodness, mercifulness, reasonableness (*redelijckheyt*) and human nature itself. The Spanish acted worse than did such heathens as Camillus or Gryphus, king of Sicily, both of whom spared the women. Pious Christian generals should forbid the destruction of towns on pain of corporal punishment.[39]

To which extent, then, may soldiers or armies cause bodily harm (the second question posed in Case VI)? A just war is an instrument of justice – the protection of the good and the punishment of evil – and so it follows that damage to property and body will necessarily occur. However, military leaders should mete out punishment mercifully, as all pious generals do. In this manner, the eleven tribes of Israel treated the tribe of Benjamin with mercy, sparing the youth and elderly, for God had not ordered them to destroy the Benjamites. Undue destruction contradicts nature, Scripture and international law (*recht der volckeren*) when God has not given an explicit order to do otherwise. There are many examples of leaders who went beyond all bounds: Pekah massacred the people of Judah (2 Chr. 28), and the emperor Theodosius those of Thessalonica (in 390). For this reason, one should never take up a sword in anger, as pagan authors have pointed out.[40] The rape of women should be forbidden on pain of corporal punishment, since this is not a form of justice, but an expression of barbaric cruelty. Furthermore, victorious soldiers should be prevented from unnecessarily destroying orchards, houses, villages, churches, convents, towers, homes for the elderly, and orphanages.[41]

There are three exceptions to the rule that moderation and reticence are mandatory. First, all 'instruments of idolatry' may be destroyed, i.e. objects that serve the purpose of idolatrous worship, such as altars, images and tabernacles (*Sacraments-huysen*), for God has ordered expressly to destroy them.[42] Second, wholesale carnage is permissible if God has given a public order to this effect, as in the case of Jericho or Ai.[43] Third, in some extreme cases there may be a military need to destroy. Thus, an army may raze part of a town when it refuses to surrender, both for its own protection and to hurt the enemy.[44]

In general, however, the innocent must be spared. How, then, to judge the wars of Spain and Austria, waged for more than 300 years in Asia, Africa, Europe and America? The Habsburgs have a history of tyranny that goes back to Albert Duke of Austria, who deposed Adolph of Nassau-Weilburg in 1298.

---

39 Udemans, *Geestelyck roer*, fols 325v-326v.

40 Udemans mentions the philosophers Architas Tarentinus and Athenodoros.

41 Udemans, *Geestelyck roer*, fols 327r-328v.

42 See Ex. 34.13, Num. 33.52, Deut. 7.5.

43 See Jud. 6.17, Jos. 8.28.

44 Udemans, *Geestelyck roer*, fol. 328v. (cf. Deut 20-21).

Around 1500 the Spanish tyrannized 'poor Heathens' in America and the West Indies. Then there was the capture of Navarre by the King of Aragon; the annexation of Portugal by the Duke of Alva; the wars of Emperor Ferdinand II in Bohemia, Silesia, Moravia and Germany; and, finally, the Dutch Revolt, during which the Spanish committed many barbarous atrocities.[45] Udemans regrets and condemns all excesses, including those committed on the Dutch side, but it is clear to him that Spain in particular favours tyranny. If one thing is clear, the King of Spain is the root cause of all the cruelties that have occurred and will occur in this war.[46]

Cases VII-IX

Case VII concerns the use of stratagems during wars, i.e. the use of what we would variously call 'guerrilla' tactics or state-sponsored 'terrorism'. Is this lawful? Udemans thinks it is, as long as using stratagems does not contradict the word of God. Stratagems should not contradict the ninth commandment (Thou shalt not bear false witness against thy neighbour).[47] Case VIII (is it lawful to hold duels?), to which Udemans offers a negative response, need not be discussed here.[48] In his response to Case IX, he observes that suicide is not permissible when a sailor is attacked by the enemy but has the opportunity to blow up the ship, together with both the enemy and himself.[49]

Case X

Udemans then comes to the issue of piracy. He asks, Are soldiers permitted to share in the spoils of war? The issue is of eminent importance, observes Udemans, so that he will treat it in the same way he did the question concerning slavery, i.e. by listing and discussing various theses. He mentions twelve theses, which may be summarized as follows:

1. Many pious believers believe that Scripture forbids plunder, so that it is wise to examine this issue seriously.[50]

---

[45] Udemans here provides a number of excerpts from William of Orange's *Apologie*, as a justification of the war against Spain.

[46] Udemans, *Geestelyck roer*, fols 328v-330v.

[47] Udemans, *Geestelyck roer*, fols 330v-331r.

[48] Udemans, *Geestelyck roer*, fols 331v- 332r.

[49] Udemans, *Geestelyck roer*, fols 332r- 333r. Interestingly, Udemans does not agree with Ames, who allows for this course of action, in case it obstructed the enemy.

[50] Udemans, *Geestelyck roer*, fols 333r-333v.

2. Not all plunder is absolutely forbidden. If a war is just and legal, so too are its spoils. Pious princes have not opposed booty in the past.[51]
3. There are exceptions to the rule that the justness of a war legitimizes plunder. In some just wars, God commanded all enemy property to be either destroyed or consecrated. The treatment of the Amalekites in 1 Sam. 15.3 is one obvious example, to which Udemans adds the case of Jericho:

   > But all the silver, and gold, and vessels of brass and iron, are consecrated unto the LORD: they shall come into the treasury of the LORD. (Josh. 6.19)

   Similarly, Theodosius melted all the gold and silver he found in heathen shrines and gave it to the church; Constantine did the same in the case of the heathen temples outside Jerusalem. Indeed, it is proper that soldiers do not take this kind of plunder; instead, they should give it to the church or the poor.[52]
4. To justify plunder, the means used in a war need to be just. The mere fact that the war of the Dutch against Spain is just does not mean that all plunder is justly taken. Extremely violent acts should be avoided; spoils are justified only when war is waged in moderation.[53]
5. Plunder is righteous when taken from a public enemy (see Case VI above). This means that spoils may not be taken from allies, neutrals, innocents, and so on.[54] The Dutch government has tried to uphold this policy with regard to women, as well as fishermen sailing from Dunkirk, Nieuwpoort and Grevelingen. The Spanish by contrast perpetrate heinous crimes against Dutch fishermen, for instance in 1627.[55]
6. Plunder must not be the objective in taking up arms. A war must be conducted with the same dispassionate attitude one assumes when exercising justice. Soldier should not even be motivated by pay, but solely by justice.[56]
7. No one should make plunder his occupation in life, since piracy is not a proper calling. Piracy is forbidden, because (a) piracy is permitted only by order of the government; (b) pirates do not commit their acts out of the proper attitude, i.e. as dispassionate judges; (c) pirates aim to further their

---

[51] Udemans, *Geestelyck roer*, fol. 334r. The examples include Moses (Num. 31.26-31) and pious princes such as Joshua, Gideon, David, Asa and Josaphat (cf. Josh. 8.2).

[52] Udemans, *Geestelyck roer*, fol. 334v.

[53] Udemans, *Geestelyck roer*, fol. 335r. cf. Grotius, *IBP*, III.11-14, chapters on *temperamentum* or moderation in treating the conquered enemy.

[54] See Grotius *DIBP*, III.9.9-12.

[55] Udemans, *Geestelyck roer*, fols 335v-336r.

[56] Udemans, *Geestelyck roer*, fols 336r-336v.

own private good; (d) after robbing the enemy, pirates rob each other; (e) pious and simple people reject all pirated merchandise.[57]

8. There are some commonly used arguments that need to be qualified. (a) For example, some claim that the laws of war permit piracy. This is true, responds Udemans, but he points out that law scholars, too, maintain that mercy and moderation need to be exercised during a war. (b) Furthermore, it is said that the government issues privileges that legalize the practice of piracy. Again, this is true, but it does not mean that we can commit acts of piracy with a peaceful conscience. The 'tribunal of conscience' (*vierschaar van het geweten*) is something quite different from worldly law. (c) Some people point out that if the tribunal of conscience prohibits piracy, then it logically proscribes trade with the East and West Indies as well, since trade depends on piracy. This is untrue, observes Udemans:

   > For concerning the commerce of the two Companies mentioned, their aim is in fact not to commit piracy, but to trade peacefully: to cut off the nerve of war, that is, the treasures in the East and West Indies, from our public enemy, the Spaniard and his adherents: to secure for our state new alliances, towns and forts in those wealthy lands: to expand the borders of the Kingdom of Christ through the conversion of those poor, blind heathens: to deliver the same poor Indians from the Spaniard's tyranny etc.[58]

   Any spoils gained in this commercial, political and military project are either legitimately taken from the Spanish enemy, or accidental in nature, that is, a form of collateral damage. (d) Then there are those who argue that piracy has damaged the enemy and served the Republic well. Concerning this issue, we should distinguish carefully between the public enemy and innocent victims. Plunder captured from the enemy is justly taken. (e) If piracy is not permitted, then soldiers should not be allowed to undertake preventive action against the enemy when the situation so requires, that is, on the spur of the moment. Udemans (who uses the term *op hazard lopen*) remarks that soldiers certainly may do so at the behest of their commander, when the enemy is being provided with victuals or ammunition, when the enemy is threatening the borders, or when individuals are suspected of aiding the enemy. (f) Finally, some insist that the tribunal of conscience forbids all piracy. On the contrary, responds Udemans, acts of piracy are praiseworthy when they are committed by

---

[57] Udemans, *Geestelyck roer*, fols 336v-337v.

[58] Udemans, *Geestelyck roer*, fols 338r-338v; the quotation is on fol. 338v (I have left out italics and capital letters).

pious patriots at the behest of the high authorities and with a righteous aim, that is, with the intention of preserving the freedom of our trading routes, in conformity with the demands of a truly defensive war.[59]

9. No one will profit from unjustly gotten gains. What applies, say, to usury, applies also to pirated goods.
10. Justly obtained pirated goods should be justly divided according to the Word of God. One part should go to God (the Church), another to the prince and the country, a third part to the men who left their homes, a fourth to those who stayed at home to defend the frontiers, and a fifth to the poor.[60]
11. Nothing is acceptable in a war unless it is done in faith and with a righteous conscience. This is why we should spurn soldiers who have no regard for the Word of God.[61]
12. The plunder committed by the Spaniards, Dunkirkers, Imperial troops, Croatians and other groups is nothing but public robbery. The war they wage is unjust, and not in agreement with either Scripture or the law of nature.[62]

Case XI

This case concerns the orientation on religion of the soldier's conscience. How should a soldier prepare himself for death, especially before battle? Udemans sums up his obligations. He must (a) live in the Lord;[63] (b) refrain from evil, for example by ignoring temptations and looking for friends in whom to confide;[64] (c) possess a proper knowledge of the true faith; (d) fulfil his duties well;[65] (e) and humbly confess his sins, reconcile himself with God through Jesus Christ, thank God, inquire into his own soul to find out whether God has shown him signs of His favour, reconcile himself with his neighbours, speak with a pious minister if his conscience displays any misgivings, take care of his earthly property, and fearlessly confront the enemy.[66] Concerning the last point, Udemans notes that a soldier will be able to master his fear if

[59] Udemans, *Geestelyck roer*, fols 338v-339v.
[60] Udemans, *Geestelyck roer*, fols 340r-340v.
[61] Udemans, *Geestelyck roer*, fol. 340v.
[62] Udemans, *Geestelyck roer*, fol. 340v.
[63] Udemans, *Geestelyck roer*, fols 341r-342r.
[64] Udemans, *Geestelyck roer*, fols 342r-345r.
[65] Udemans, *Geestelyck roer*, fols 345r -345v.
[66] Udemans, *Geestelyck roer*, fols 345v-350v.

he realizes that he fights for a good cause, that is, for God's people and God's towns. He will know that God is on his side, but his conviction is conditional on his having prepared himself properly before setting out on a risky undertaking.[67]

Case XII

Finally, Case XII addresses the obligations of army preachers with respect to soldiers, and vice versa. Udemans' comments on the subject would fit in well with a preacher's manual; I shall not comment on the topic here.[68]

Holy War, Holy Plunder

Before moving on to a discussion on the relations between war and religion in the *Spiritual helm*, a brief note on Udemans' sources is in order. As a Protestant theologian, he was, of course, bound to quote the Bible, and he did so amply throughout his manual; I have provided only a few pertinent examples, but there are many, many more. One important non-biblical source is the religious casuistics of William Ames (1576-1633), a professor at the university of Franeker in the province of Frisia (Friesland). Between 1611 and 1619, Ames had been employed as a minister by the Englishman Horace Vere (1565-1635), who for many years served as a commanding officer in the armies of the Dutch Republic. Vere had distinct Puritan sympathies and patronized religious non-conformists such as Ames, who had been dismissed as a fellow of Christ's College in Cambridge for a militant sermon against gambling. Ames's *De conscientia eiusque iure vel casibus* (1630), a treatise on moral theology translated as *Conscience with the power and cases thereof* (1639), was famed in Puritan circles. Given the combative environment in which Ames worked, one might perhaps suspect him of holding belligerent views on holy war. Interestingly, however, Johnson puts Ames fair and square in the classical just war tradition.

It is probably from Ames that Udemans drew a substantial part of his just war argument. Compared to the 800 odd pages of the *Spiritual helm*, however, Ames's chapter on warfare in *Conscience with the power and cases thereof* is very brief: it comprises less than 9 pages, in which the issue of war is treated in 39

---

[67] Udemans, *Geestelyck roer*, fol. 349r.
[68] Udemans, *Geestelyck roer*, fols 350v-357r.

theses.[69] The topics broached by Udemans correspond closely to those treated by Ames. The latter poses the following questions (between brackets is the related case discussed by Udemans):

Question I:	'Whether or no Warre bee lawful for Christians' (Case I)
Question II:	'What conditions are requisite to make a War lawfull?' (Case II)
Question III:	'It is here a Question about the first condition [just cause], how farre those that wage Warre are to bee acquainted with the Iustice of their cause.' (Case III)
Question IV:	'In the second condition [just authority], it is a Question whether it bee lawfull for a Christian Prince in a just Warre to accept the aid of Infidels, or to give them aid in such a Warre.' (Case IV)
Question V:	'In the third condition [right intention], it is a Question what what [sic] kind of sinne is the intention of him, that makes Warre, as for hatred, envy, desire of honour, or riches?' (Case V)
Question VI:	'It is a Question in the fourth condition [just manner of waging war]. First, What persons are they that wee may lawfully damage by Warre, and how farre may wee damage them.' (Case VI)
Question VII:	'In what things may wee damnifie Enemies?' (Case X)
Question VIII:	'Whether or no it bee Lawfull to use deceits and stratagems in a just Warre.' (Case VII)

Ames discusses duels and suicide (Udemans's Cases VIII and IX) elsewhere in his book. The additional subjects raised the *Spiritual helm* (the religious duties of soldiers and ministers: Cases XI and XII) characterize Udemans as an adherent of the Puritan 'Further Reformation' movement. The main difference between Ames and Udemans is that the former's concise discussion of warfare hardly refers to religion, whereas the latter, in fleshing out the cases of conscience, brings religion explicitly into the equation.

Several other sources may be mentioned. One is Grotius himself; Udemans quite frequently quotes *De iure belli ac pacis*. Another source is the Italian reformer Peter Martyr Vermigli (1499-1562). Udemans consulted his *In duos*

---

[69] William Ames, *Conscience with the power and cases thereof* ([Leiden: Christiaens; London: E. Griffin, J. Dawson], 1639; facsimile edition Amsterdam: Theatrum Orbis Terrarum, 1975), pp. 184-192.

libros Samuelis prophetae qui vulgo priores libri Regum appellantur (1564), a commentary on the Old Testament books of Samuel.[70] Also, Cicero's *De officiis* is quoted often enough to be conspicuous.

Does Udemans draw upon religion as a means of legitimizing violence, and if so, to which extent does he do so? Given that Udemans is a clergyman, and that his subject is moral theology, it stands to reason that religion figures prominently in his argumentation. The proposition underlying his essay is that 'Christians may wage war on condition that they do so according to God's Word, in faith and with due respect for justice' (Case I). This is tantamount to saying that Christians must act as Christians, which of course applies to warfare as much as it applies to anything else. A better way to look at the relations between religion and violence in the *Spiritual helm* is to apply to it each of the 'positions' listed by Johnson in his account of holy war thought.

Position 1: Religious Purpose or 'Holy Cause'

Theorists of just war thought usually mentioned right intention, or proper motivation, as a criterion by which to determine the justness of a war: This excludes, for example, ambition and glory as reasons for starting a war. By contrast, holy war thought admits religious purpose – sacred ambition, or the glory of God – as a laudable motivation. For Udemans, warfare is by definition religiously motivated, given that anything Christians do must be done for religion's sake. Isolated from its context, such a claim seems boil down to an appallingly familiar justification of death and destruction in the name of religion. My point here is that no early modern clergyman (or, indeed, no Christian) would have argued otherwise. Everything a Christian does in life, from eating his food to killing his enemy, should be performed with God on his mind. We may find the argument unappealing, but it should be clear that it is not in itself specifically Calvinist.

In his response to Case III, Udemans states that no soldier may commit acts of war against the true religion. He points out that wars bringing harm to fellow believers are by definition unjust. Soldiers should only enter into the service of a pious prince who stands for the glory of God and the well being of his church. In this sense, too, all Christian warfare is religiously motivated. We should interpret this in the context of Udemans's response to Case III.

[70] For Vermigli's ideas on just war, see Robert M. Kingdon, *The political thought of Peter Martyr Vermigli. Selected texts and commentary.* (Geneva: Droz, 1980)

If ordinary soldiers are in conscience convinced that the war in which they participate is unjust because it subverts the true religion, they should refrain from fighting. Likewise, according to Case IV, a Christian government may not conclude a treaty with an unbelieving prince, unconditionally guaranteeing mutual aid. A Christian government must always ensure that such a treaty does not contradict God's commandments. In the *Spiritual helm*, then, religious purpose is not a motive by and of itself, but one consideration among others. At most, it serves as a negative test for the criterion of right intention: a war conducted for any reason whatsoever against adherents of the true religion is never a just war.

Position 2: Defensive War with the Aim of Securing Religion

Udemans supports this second position, but not categorically. He regards the Dutch Revolt against the might of Habsburg Spain as a war that in origin was fought *religionis causa*, for the sake of religion. However, even for the theologian Udemans religion is not an autonomous objective, but connected with the preservation of liberty (*libertatis causa*). One of the examples of Spanish aggression he mentions is the introduction of new bishops in 1559. It is as easy to construe this historical fact as an infringement of legally binding privileges as an attack on the 'true religion'.

Position 3: Offensive War for the Sake of Religion

Udemans mentions offensive 'holy' wars only in the context of the *ius in bello*, so that I shall defer my discussion of this topic to Position 6 (see below).

Position 4: Personal Godliness

Like all other clergymen, Udemans repeatedly insists that soldiers and officers should engage in war with a clear conscience, which means that they ought to fight as believers. In Udemans' response to Case XI, he stresses that soldiers must demonstrate personal piety and prepare themselves accordingly before battle. This position obviously figures prominently in a manual intended to lend advice to individuals professionally involved in war situations. On the other hand, Udemans's argumentation in itself does not preclude the possibility that godliness degenerates into uninhibited aggressiveness for the sake of religion. He makes the point that a good conscience will result in a fearless attitude, since a soldier who has tried seriously to achieve personal godliness will know that God is on his side. 'For the LORD your God is he that goeth with you, to fight for you against your enemies, to save you' (Deut. 20.1). This provides the spiritual basis for Position 6.

Position 5: A Just War is a Justified War

Wherever Udemans justifies the Dutch Revolt as both defensive and offensive, a war against the Spanish overlord fought *religionis et libertatis causa*. He sees this as a justifiable war. In other words, Udemans, like Ames, essentially argues from within the classic just war tradition.

Position 6: War Fought without Restraint

In discussing Question II, regarding the conditions under which war must be waged if it can in conscience be called a just war, Udemans in conformity with classic just war thought broaches the *ius in bello*. A war, he states, ought to be waged in a just manner, according to divine and human laws. For knowledge of the divine laws, Udemans refers his Christian soldier to Deut. 20.1 to 23.9. This notorious pericope includes passages that justify unrestrained warfare on religious grounds. The following is one of them:

> And if it will make no peace with thee, but will make war against thee, then thou shalt besiege it: And when the LORD thy God hath delivered it into thine hands, thou shalt smite every male thereof with the edge of the sword: But the women, and the little ones, and the cattle, and all that is in the city, even all the spoil thereof, shalt thou take unto thyself; and thou shalt eat the spoil of thine enemies, which the LORD thy God hath given thee. Thus shalt thou do unto all the cities which are very far off from thee, which are not of the cities of these nations. But of the cities of these people, which the LORD thy God doth give thee for an inheritance, thou shalt save alive nothing that breatheth: But thou shalt utterly destroy them (...). (Deut 20.12-17)

At the very least, this passage legalizes the unrestrained killing of males and the unreserved taking of spoils, including women, children and cattle. At the very most, it permits the wholesale obliteration, women, children and cattle included, of specific peoples (namely, Hittites, Amorites, Canaanites, Perizzites, Hivites and Jebusites) who happen to reside in territory given by God 'for an inheritance' to the Israelites. Udemans provides no specific interpretation of the divine legislation in Deut. 20-23. For example, he does not say explicitly that divine commands to obliterate male populations and plunder complete cities are restricted to the Old Testament, to a time when God still led his chosen people directly. On the other hand, citing such Stoic celebrities as Cicero and Lipsius,[71] he goes on to point out that there also are human laws regarding the *ius in bello*.

In his discussion of Case VI (who may be harmed in war, and to which degree), Udemans returns to the *ius in bello*. He emphasizes that pious Christian officers must exercise mercy and moderation, and that generals should forbid the destruction of towns on pain of corporal punishment. He again observes that God sometimes ordered Israel to annihilate a whole people, such as the Amalekites. 'Now go and smite Amalek, and utterly destroy all that they have, and spare them not; but slay both man and woman, infant and suckling, ox and sheep, camel and ass' (1 Sam. 15.3).[72] He points out that these are cursed nations which God wanted specifically to obliterate; again, he does not say that these commands no longer occur under the New Testament. In fact, at this point Udemans makes three exceptions to the rule that moderation is at all times obligatory:

(a) He supports the destruction of objects that serve idolatrous worship, such as altars, images and tabernacles. These may be (or are to be) destroyed on God's express commandment, such as in Ex. 34.13, 'But ye shall destroy their altars, break their images, and cut down their groves'.
(b) He again allows for the devastation of cities as long as God has given a public order to this effect. Examples are Jericho and Ai, as in Jos. 8.28, 'And Joshua burnt Ai, and made it an heap for ever, even a desolation unto this day'.
(c) In some extreme cases, there may be a military need to destroy part of a town.

Similar arguments turn up in the discussion of piracy (Case X). In some just wars (waged under the Old Testament), God commanded all enemy property either to be destroyed or consecrated. The dispossession of Catholic churches by Protestant forces, and their conversion to Protestant places of worship, is justifiable (or justified) on this account. Another interesting point Udemans makes here is that soldiers should not be motivated by pay, but solely by their sense of justice, since war is an instrument of justice. Such a statement supports ideologically motivated warfare: if soldiers consider themselves instruments of God's justice, then the appropriate term for the war they are waging is holy war.

---

[71] Udemans refers to Cicero, *De officiis* and Lipsius, *Politicorum sive civilis doctrinae libri sex*.
[72] See also Josh. 6.17 and 8.25; Ps. 137.9; Ezek. 9.6.

Conclusion

Godfried Udemans did not propagate holy warfare in his manual for seafaring Christians. He subscribed to, and elaborated on, the classic just war position sketchily advocated by Ames. This is not to say, however, that he rejected wars *religionis causa*. He did not formally exclude religious considerations from his argument (but he did qualify them: I shall put these qualifications in brackets). The glory of God is the chief aim of Christian warfare (at the very least, warfare undertaken by Christians must not harm the Christian religion). The defence of religion is a just cause of war (although it is difficult, in the early modern context, to distinguish secular from religious arguments, if only because there was no separation of church and state). Soldiers must be personally godly (but so should everyone else). In some cases, soldiers may be under divine command to destroy cities and even people (although these instances are in practice restricted to the Old Testament). The destruction of cultural (i.e. religious) artefacts is permissible or even praiseworthy if such objects detract from the glory or proper worship of God. This latter consideration is the only one that Udemans does not qualify.

If we take for granted that Udemans's thought is representative of mainstream clerical Calvinism in the Dutch Republic – and we can safely say that he is[73] – then we must conclude that holy war thought did not figure prominently in the Dutch version of early modern Puritanism. On the other hand, Udemans did not fully exclude religious considerations either. The extent to which such considerations are introduced largely determines the nature of the Christian society Udemans envisaged. His ethics allows both a minimal interpretation (which includes the destruction of 'idolatrous' artefacts by the victorious party) and a full interpretation (which condones in certain specific cases the destruction of cities and the killing of non-military). Only the latter, theoretical position can be qualified as 'holy war'. It is clear that Calvinist moral theology, for all its resemblance to the classic just war tradition, is not an ethics that we should care to revive in the modern world. From the point of view of just war thought, including that of Grotius, Udemans's theological ethics is sloppy; in the end, it contains too many excuses to start a holy war.

[73] For an account of mainstream Dutch Calvinist thought on this issue, see Joris van Eijnatten, 'Religionis Causa. Moral Theology and the Concept of Holy War', *Journal of Religious Ethics*, 34 (2006), 609-635.

Using the Work. Remarks on the Text of *De iure praedae*[1]

Jan Waszink
Post-doctoral Researcher, Department of Classics, Radboud University Nijmegen
e-mail: jan.waszink@let.uu.nl

Abstract
This paper aims at showing that all scholars writing on *De iure praedae* should refer to the extant manuscript of the work, or to the new electronic edition when it becomes available, to check the passages they use in their arguments. The printed text as edited by Hamaker, though generally reliable as a nineteenth-century edition, must now be considered outdated because of its suppression of all previous stages of the text, as well as its replacement of the original punctuation with a new one, which more than once does affect the meaning of the text. Moreover, Hamaker's edition gives no authentic image of the sources of Grotius's thought. Secondly, signalling a need for more detailed textual research on *IPC*, the present paper calls attention to Grotius's extensive changes in chapter 10, and to the contribution which philological approaches might make to answering questions such as that regarding *IPC*'s intended audience.

Keywords
Grotius, *De iure praedae*, textual criticism, sources, Hamaker, ms. UBL BPL 917, history of philology

At the core of the Grotius activities at the NIAS in 2004-5 was the project to produce a new, critical and complete edition of Grotius's *De iure praedae*. During the year at NIAS the present author worked on a new transcription of the text from the well-known Leiden manuscript. This very detailed work also produced some insights which seem worthwhile to consider for all readers of *De iure praedae* (further: *IPC*). The aim of this paper therefore is to present some preliminary conclusions about the usefulness of Hamaker's edition and

[1] I thank Martine van Ittersum, André Lardinois and Victor Enthoven for their comments to this paper, and I thank Peter Borschberg and Martine van Ittersum for freely providing me with the results of their research during the NIAS year (which they will publish separately) to supplement and compare the ideas in this paper; see also their papers in this collection.

about Grotius's revisions of the text, his use of sources, and the nature and the intended audience of *IPC* that I hope will be useful to all students of the work (in its various available versions). First, however, a bit more about the need for a new edition.

A New Edition of *De iure praedae*

A new edition is needed because the existing one by H.G. Hamaker of 1868, though highly praiseworthy in its time, has now become outdated. Hamaker edited the final stage of the text as indicated by the author in the original manuscript (Leiden UL, *Bibliotheca Publica Latina* 917; further: BPL 917) i.e. without recording any deletions, insertions or corrections. His edition formed the basis of the other editions and translations of *IPC* that exist at the moment, apart of course from the well-known Collotype Reproduction of 1950 of the original manuscript. Hamaker's book commands respect for the enormous effort of extracting the last revision of *IPC* from the manuscript it represents, and for the precision by which this task has been accomplished. Apart from the length of the text, Grotius's hand is often difficult to read, and the task of correctly assembling all additions and deletions scribbled between lines, in margins or on additional pieces of paper is huge and complicated indeed. Though the 1868 edition contains occasional errors, it would not be easy to do a better job, and the present editors gratefully benefit from Hamaker's work, not just because a computer scan of this edition (freed from computer reading errors) serves as the basis of the present edition project, but also because Hamaker clarifies many difficult places in the manuscript.

However, BPL 917 is full of longer and shorter additions, deletions and replacements in the text, which are invisible or unrecognisable as such in Hamaker's edition. The edition gives only the final stage of the text, without offering the reader any insight into its previous stages, nor does it provide any indications of where revisions were carried out. Deleted passages have become invisible altogether. Modern research practice and interests require an edition which does provide this information. Until this exists, critical readers should remind themselves that *IPC* is not a finished and 'closed' treatise or argument, but work-in-progress, an open-ended text that its author never explicitly finished and send to a printer. When they quote a passage to support their own argument, scholars of *IPC* should check what other forms that passage might have had.

They should also be aware that this means that the work was never authorised, for this fact imposes at least some limitations on the possibilities for us to identify views held in *IPC* with the person of Hugo Grotius. It is not certain that the author would have been happy to know that today printed editions of *IPC* undistinguishable in form from his 'ordinary' published works, exist. Though Grotius did use both general ideas and specific material from *IPC* in other works such as *De iure belli ac pacis* and the polemics on *Mare Clausum*, this does not necessarily imply that he wanted the world to read *IPC* as a whole and as it is, and as a work by him. He kept the manuscript with him, and even *if* he kept considering publication, he might still have wanted to change or delete any particular bit of it (specific statements or connections in the text, the type of philosophical and/or legal reasoning, the arrangement and organisation, or whatever else).[2] On the other hand, the text exists as a witness to Grotius's work and thought, and the many changes in the text do allow us to get an idea of the development of Grotius's thought over the years on the subjects in question and his way of reasoning with respect to them, and for that purpose *IPC* can be properly used.

Finally, Hamaker's edition has become outdated as it follows nineteenth-century editorial conventions which are no longer acceptable (including an entirely new spelling and punctuation, of which we shall discuss a few examples below), and it has a very limited apparatus of sources. The ambitious aim of the new edition project is to provide an edition, if possible both on paper and in electronic form, which gives access to all stages of the text and to all the various sources used by Grotius, and includes quick access to translations, background articles and other relevant information. Thus we hope to provide all students of Grotius's life and works, and those of natural law, history, philosophy and political thought of the seventeenth century with a complete and reliable edition of this important text.

In the now following parts of this paper, I shall first examine some characteristics of Hamaker's edition that its users should be aware of and that illustrate the need for a new edition. I shall then turn to the manuscript and discuss a few questions that came up during the above philological work on the text, i.e. questions regarding the nature, dating, purpose and intended audience of the work. Finally, we shall look at one of Grotius's larger changes in the text, in order to illustrate the open and unfinished character of the work, and in order to suggest ways in which such changes might be connected with the larger questions regarding the interpretation of the work.

---

[2] For authorisation, see M. Mathijsen, *Naar de Letter: Handboek editiewetenschap*, 2nd edn. (The Hague: Huygens Instituut, 1997), pp. 123-148.

Hamaker's Edition as Research Text of *De iure praedae*

At present, Hamaker's edition of *IPC* is the text used by almost all students of *IPC*, either directly, or indirectly through the available translations of *IPC*. The statements above prompt the question whether it is still acceptable for a modern student of *IPC* to use Hamaker's edition. By comparing a few pages from Hamaker with the original manuscript, I hope to show that yes, it is OK to *read* Hamaker, but not to *quote* him. Until a modern and complete edition of *IPC* is available, scholars publishing on *IPC* should check all their quotes from *IPC* with the manuscript, which is available in the collotype facsimile edition of 1950, though of course this is no easier to use than the original manuscript.[3] In fact, it is sometimes more difficult to use than the original: note for example that the 1995 re-edition of the collotype reproduction has omitted the empty pages, so that recto and verso are often not on the right- and left-hand pages respectively. This is confusing among other things when one tries to reconstruct what happened when a section was inserted, and which deleted passages were once connected; the example of fols 63-67 discussed below is a clear case in point. However, when one quotes a passage from *IPC*, earlier stages of that passage should be taken into consideration, and the correctness of Hamaker's rendering of the text should be checked as well.

One Quotation

For an example of the differences between Hamaker and the manuscript, see ill. 1, which shows pages 12-13 from Hamaker, and ill. 2 and 3, which show fol. 6v and 7r in the manuscript. In ill. 2 the beginnings of the insertions have been marked.[4] The original text from the top of p. 13 went from *tradiderunt*: directly to *de qua praeclare Hesiodus*: τόνδε γὰρ ἀνθρώποισι ... *cessit;* and then from *cessit* directly to *Ex regula* ... etc., leaving out the entire paragraph in between. This added paragraph consists of three separate insertions, probably dating from three different moments in time (in reverse order:

[3] *De Iure Praedae Commentarius by Hugo Grotius, vol. II. The Collotype reproduction of the original manuscript of 1604 in the handwriting of Grotius*, The Classics of International Law (Oxford: Clarendon Press, 1950; reprint Buffalo: Hein, 1995); the reprint has reproductions of poorer quality.

[4] Based on Hamaker's page 12; see ms. fol. 7; for a translation, see Hugo Grotius, *Commentary on the Law of Prize and Booty*, tr. Gwladys L. Williams, ed. by Martine Julia van Ittersum, Natural Law and Enlightenment Classics (Indianapolis, Liberty Fund, 2006), p. 26 (further referred to as: Grotius/Williams/Ittersum, *Commentary*, 2006).

cunctos significaverit, id jus est. Maxime autem in eo consentitur, aliena nobis commoda curanda esse, quia id fere homini proprium est: unde Senecae [6] sapientia *bonum* dicitur *et suum et alienum.* Hinc illa justitia proprie dicta incipit, quam Aristoteles [7] aliique *circa bonum alienum versari* tradi-

[1] [ap. Clem. Alex. Strom. l. 6. p. 719.] [2] Arist. de mor. ad Nicom. l 2. c. 5. [p. 1106. 2. vs. 29.] et l. 9. c. 4. [p. 1166. 1. vs. 13.] et c. 6. [p. 1167.

DE JURE PRAEDAE. CAP. II. 13

derunt, Cicero [1] et Apuleius [2] *foras spectare* dicunt: de qua praeclare Hesiodus [3]:

> τόνδε γὰρ ἀνθρώποισι νόμον διέταξε Κρονίων,
> ἰχθύσι μὲν καὶ θηρσὶ καὶ οἰωνοῖς πετεηνοῖς
> ἐσθέμεν ἀλλήλους, ἐπεὶ οὐ δίκη ἐστὶ μετ' αὐτῶν,
> ἀνθρώποισι δ' ἔδωκε δίκην, ἣ πολλὸν ἀρίστη.
> *Humano generi nam lex datur ab Jove summo.*
> *Quippe ferae, pisces, avium genus altivolantum*
> *Mutua se vertunt in pabula, juris egentes:*
> *Justitia at nobis, quae res est optima, cessit.*

Seneca [4]: *ut omnia inter se membra consentiunt, quia singula servari totius interest, ita homines singulis parcent, quia ad coetum geniti sumus. Salva autem esse societas, nisi amore et custodia partium non potest.* Idem [5] alibi: *Securitas securitate mutua paciscenda est.* Haec est illa hominum inter se cognatio, illa mundi civitas, quam tot tantisque praeconiis veteres philosophi nobis commendant, praesertim Stoici, quorum sententiam etiam Cicero [6] exsequitur. ex qua et illud est Florentini [7]: *cum cognationem quandam inter nos natura constituerit, consequens esse ut hominem homini insidiari nefas sit;* quod ille [8] optime ad jus gentium refert. Unde apparet quam non recte magistri ignorantiae Academici contra justitiam disputaverint, eam quae natura est ad utilitatem duntaxat suam ducere, civilem vero non ex natura esse, sed ex opinione. Hanc enim mediam justitiam, quae humano generi propria est, omittebant [9].

Ex regula igitur prima et secunda leges duae procedunt de bono alieno, quae prioribus de bono suo respondent, easque justo limite circumscribunt [10]. Una: *Ne quis alterum laedat;* *Lex III.*

[1] de rep. l. 2. [ap. Nonium in v. Projectum.] [2] de philos. Plat. [vol. 2. Oudendorpii. p. 229.] [3] Op. et D. [vs. 276. sqq.] [4] de ira l. 2. c. 31. [5] de clem. l. 1. c. 19. [6] Cic. de leg. l. 1. [c. 7. § 23.] [7] l. ut vim. ff. de just. et jure. [D. 1. 1. 3.] [8] Cic. de rep. l. 3. [c. 19. et 20.] Lact. Instit. div. l. 5.

Illustration 1: *Hugonis Grotii De jure praedae: commentarius*, ex auctoris codice descripsit et vulgavit H.G. Hamaker (The Hague: Nijhoff, 1868), fragments of pp. 12 and 13

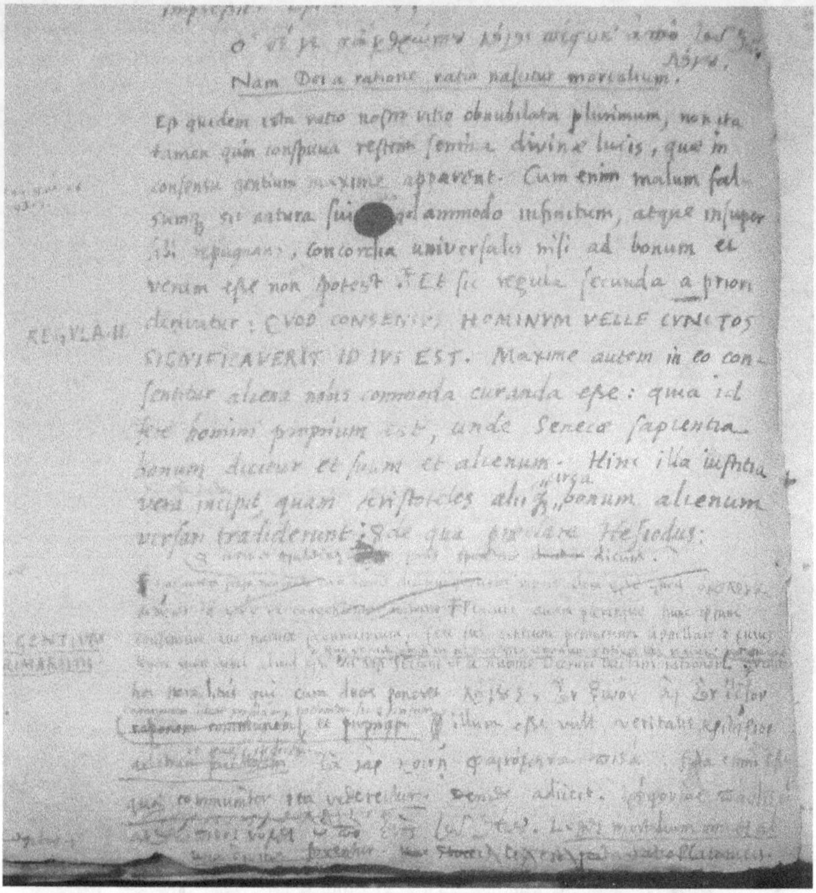

Illustration 2: Leiden, University Library, ms. BPL 917, fol. 6v

ex qua et illud ... omittebant was inserted first, then *Haec...exsequitur*, then *Seneca...paciscenda est*, as can be seen in the manuscript (fol. 7: one can see Grotius's insertion mark 'X' move up with each new addition, nearer to the top of the page).[5] The 1868 edition provides no indication that these changes were made, while a critical reader would want to be aware at least of the fact that Grotius re-considered and re-wrote his argument here so extensively.

[5] See the following passages in Grotius/Williams/Ittersum, *Commentary*, 2006: first insertion: 'This view is also the basis of the statement made by Florentinus ... aspect of justice which is characteristic of humankind' (p. 27); 2nd insertion: 'Herein lies that brotherhood of man ...Stoics, whose view Cicero adopts' (p. 27); 3rd insertion: 'Seneca has said ...security in exchange' (p. 26-27).

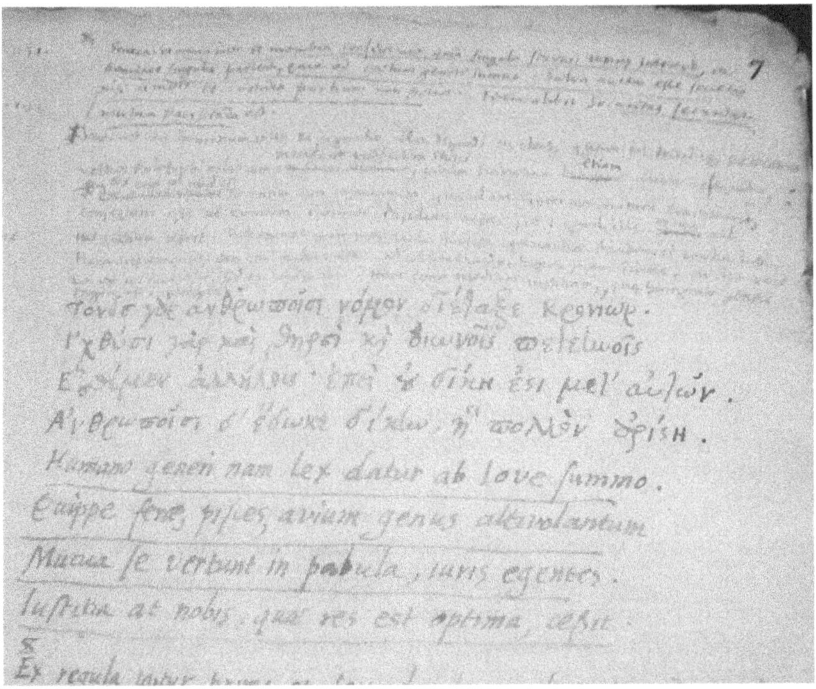

Illustration 3: Leiden, University Library, ms. BPL 917, fol. 7r

The Greek quotation from Hesiod can serve as a further example of an outdated editorial practice that obscures Grotius's real sources from sight. Grotius quotes Hesiod, *Works and Days* 276-279 (modern numbering) to illustrate the divine origins of justice. In BPL 917 the lines appear in this form:

> τόνδε γὰρ ἀνθρωποῖσι νόμον διέταξε Κρονίων·
> Ἰχθύσι γὰρ καὶ θηρσὶ καὶ οἰωνοῖς πετεεινοῖς
> Ἐσθέμεν ἀλλήλους· ἐπεὶ οὐ δίκη ἔστι μετ' αὐτῶν.
> Ἀνθρωποῖσι δ' ἔδωκε δίκην, ἣ πολλὸν ἀρίστη.
>
> Because this law Zeus set for mankind:
> For fishes, wild animals and the winged birds,
> to devour each other: since justice is nowhere among them.
> But to humans he gave Justice, the best thing of all by far.

This powerful and imaginative passage made a great impact on readers in Antiquity; it is cited in eleven other extant ancient texts.[6]

---

[6] Plutarchus, *De sollertia animalium*, ed. Stephanus, p. 964B, line 8; Sextus Empiricus, *Adversus mathematicos*, 2.32.5; Aelianus, *De natura animalium*, 6.50.19; Aristonicus, *De signis*

In Hamaker's edition of *IPC*, the quotation is presented thus:

> τόνδε γὰρ ἀνθρώποισι νόμον διέταξε Κρονίων,
> ἰχθύσι **μὲν** καὶ θηρσὶ καὶ ὀιωνοῖς πετε**η**νοῖς
> ἐσθέμεν ἀλλήλους, ἐπεὶ οὐ δίκη **ἐστὶ** μετ' αὐτῶν,
> ἀνθρώποισι δ' ἔδωκε δίκην, ἣ πολλὸν ἀρίστη.

Hamaker's substitution of μὲν for γὰρ and -εη- for -εει- in πετεεινοῖς in the second line, and the correction of the accent on ἐστὶ might suggest that he quoted the lines as they are printed in the Hesiod- editions of his own time (which have μὲν and -εη-), but this appears not to be the case. In the edition by Van Lennep of 1847, the lines appear thus:[7]

> τόνδε γὰρ ἀνθρώποισι νόμον διέταξε Κρονίων,
> ἰχθύσι **μὲν** καὶ θηρσὶ καὶ ὀιωνοῖς πετεηνοῖς
> ἔσθ**ειν** ἀλλήλους, ἐπεὶ οὐ δίκη ἐστὶν **ἐν αὐτοῖς·**
> ἀνθρώποισι δ' ἔδωκε δίκην, ἣ πολλὸν ἀρίστη
> γίνεται· (...)

If we look up the quote in Hesiod-editions from Grotius's own time, it appears that the differences between the generally accepted text of the seventeenth and that of the nineteenth-century are not very great. The Hesiod-edition by Grotius's friend and scholarly colleague Daniel Heinsius, printed in 1603 and 1613 has:

> τόν δε γὰρ ἀνθρώποισι νόμον διέταξε Κρονίων
> Ἰχθύσι **μὲν** καὶ θηρσὶ καὶ ὀιωνοῖς πετε<u>ει</u>νοῖς
> Ἔσθ**ειν** ἀλλήλους, ἐπεὶ οὐ δίκη ἐστὶν **<u>ἐπ</u>΄ αὐτοῖς·**
> Ἀνθρώποισι δ' ἔδωκε δίκην, ἣ πολλὸν <u>ἀ</u>ρίστη
> γίνεται· (...)

Odysseae, ad Od. 9.106; Porphyrius, *De abstinentia*, 1.5.15; Porphyrius, *Quaestionum Homericarum ad Odysseam pertinentium reliquiae*, ad Od. 9.106 sqq; Stobaeus, *Anthologium*, 1.3.1.4; Orion, *Anthologion*, 6.10.4; *Scholia in Hesiodum*, Prolegomena, (p. 274ter, line 5); *Scholia in Homerum*, ad Od. 9.106; Clemens Alex., *Stromateis* 1.29. Note that three of these places are notes to Homer, *Odyssey* 9.106, where the wild Cyclopes are called ἀθεμίστοι, 'ignorant of Justice'. Grotius does not bring this place into his discussion here (or anywhere else that I have met).

[7] *Hesiodi Opera et Dies, librorum mss. et veterum editionum lectionibus commentarioque instruxit David Iacobus van Lennep* (Amsterdam: Mueller, 1847).

An earlier, anonymous, edition printed by Plantin in 1581 has:[8]

> Τόνδε γὰρ ἀνθρώποισι νόμον διέταξε Κρονίων,
> Ἰχθύσι **μὲν** καὶ θηρσὶ καὶ οἰωνοῖς πετε<u>ει</u>νοῖς
> Ἔσθειν ἀλλήλους. ἐπεὶ οὐ δίκη ἐστὶν **<u>ἐπ</u>′ αὐτοῖς·**
> Ἀνθρώποισι δ' ἔδωκε δίκην, ἣ πολλὸν ἀρίστη
> γίνεται· (...)

Note that Grotius put a full stop after ἀρίστη, whereas in the original text the sentence continues with just one word.

By comparing the quotations in the ancient texts mentioned above, it appears that Grotius's actual source must have been the *Stromateis* ('Miscellanies') by Clement of Alexandria, book 1 cap. 29,[9] which has the fragment in almost identical form to that presented by Grotius (the only difference being the two commas in line 2 and the accent on ἐστὶ in line 3, which could be an oversight on Grotius's part):

> τόνδε γὰρ ἀνθρώποισι νόμον διέταξε Κρονίων·
> Ἰχθύσι **γὰρ** καὶ θηρσὶ, καὶ οἰωνοῖς πετεεινοῖς,
> Ἐσ**θέμεν** ἀλλήλους· ἐπεὶ οὐ δίκη ἐστὶ **μετ' αὐτῶν**.
> Ἀνθρωποῖσι δ' ἔδωκε δίκην, ἣ πολλὸν ἀρίστη.[10]

The *Stromateis* by Clement of Alexandria (2nd-3rd century AD) is a text on the good Christian life from partly Gnostic inspiration. Clement's aim is to lead his readers (both pagans and Christians) towards this life by means of knowledge, and to show that the Christian religion is not hostile to wide learning. He acknowledges that the pagan poets and philosophers have

---

[8] ΗΣΙΟΔΟΥ ΤΟΥ ΑΣΚΡΑΙΟΥ ΕΡΓΑ ΚΑΙ ΗΜΕΡΑΙ. ΧΡΥΣΑ ΕΠΗ ΠΥΘΑΓΟΡΟΥ. *Hesiodi Ascrei Opera et Dies. Aurea Carmina Pythagorae* (Antwerp: Christoffel Plantijn, 1581). The same reading in the Paris editions of Hesiod of 1556 (Morelius) and 1581 (Morellus).

[9] In the edition by Friedrich Sylburg (1536-1596), ΚΛΗΜΕΝΤΟΣ ΑΛΕΞΑΝΔΡΕΩΣ ΤΑ ΕΥΡΙΣΚΟΜΕΝΑ. *Clementis Alexandrini opera quae exstant*, ([Heidelberg]: In officina Sanctandreana, 1592). The Hesiod-citation is printed like the surrounding prose, but with recognisable line divisions that mark it as poetry. Sylburg's edition was available in Leiden's university library in Grotius's time, as appears from the contemporary printed catalogue (Bertius, *Nomenclator*, repr. Leiden 1995, B4r). Daniel Heinsius, already mentioned, published an edition of Clement (also based on Sylburg's) in 1616, which again has the Hesiod-citation in the same form (p. 154); Heinsius' copy of Sylburg's edition is preserved in Leiden UL, 754 A18 (see the inscription ἐκ τῶν τοῦ Ἑινσίου on the title page). Note that Heinsius did not adapt the reading of the fragment to that in his own edition of Hesiod.

[10] Of the 11 quotations referred to above, only two can have been Grotius's source: Stobaeus, *Anthologium* 1.3.1.4 and the place in Clement of Alexandria, for these are the only ones which quote all four lines present in DIP, and end with ἀρίστη. However, Stobaeus has ἔσθειν and ἐν αὐτοῖς· in line 2, unlike Grotius. Thus Clement remains as the only likely source.

perceived part of the truth, and that their writings are useful to read for the Christian looking for truth.[11] He discusses at length a whole series of topics, and quotes abundantly from the pagan writers. Thus the *Stromateis* can also be used as a source of quotable *sententiae*, and it preserves more than a few passages from classical texts that have not otherwise survived; this no doubt made the *Stromateis* an attractive text for humanists and philologists.

Contrary to what students of the Delft scholarly miracle seem to have believed in the past, it is unlikely that Grotius was actually deeply familiar with each and every text that he quotes or refers to. Close study of his quotations and the relationships between them shows that he regularly took over groups of quotations from intermediate sources, located relevant quotes by means of indexes, or just inserted additional citations at relevant places later on, when he happened upon them. In BPL 917 this last procedure can often be recognised in the handwriting.[12] What we need first therefore, if we want to understand the influence of his sources on Grotius's thought, is not a full discussion of the backgrounds in all quoted texts, but a reasoned and realistic assessment of which texts really made a difference, and a closer consideration of those.

The conclusion that Clement's *Stromateis* is Grotius's source for the Hesiod-quote is further supported by the fact that the verse line by the comic poet Epicharmus quoted one page earlier in *IPC* must have been taken from the *Stromateis* as well.[13] Interestingly, in 1626 Grotius published an edition of surviving fragments (in other ancient texts) from Greek tragic and comic poets,[14] which also contains this fragment with a large number of emendations

---

[11] See a.o. L. Früchtel in *Reallexikon für Antike und Christentum*, vol. III (Stuttgart: Hiersemann, 1957), s.v. Clemens Alexandrinus.

[12] This has been noted several times before, e.g. Peter Borschberg, 'Hugo Grotius' Theory of Trans-Oceanic Trade Regulation. Revisiting Mare Liberum (1609)', *IILJ Working Papers, History and Theory of International Law*, August 2006, p. 8; see also Borschberg in the paper in this collection (n. 75). Richard Tuck, *Philosophy and Government* (Cambridge: CUP, 1993), p. 171 also noted that most references to the Spanish scholastics were added later.

[13] ὁ δέ γε τἀνθρώπου λόγος πέφυκ' ἀπὸ τοῦ θείου λόγου, 'Human reason sprang from divine reason'. This is the last line of a fragment of 9 lines from Epicharmus' *Politeia*, which has only survived through Clement, *Stromateis* 5.118 (Eusebius quotes it too, but taken from Clement, though with a small variance; the γε proves that Grotius took the line from Clement). Hamaker renders the fragment correctly as it is in BPL 917 and points at Clement (there is no source-ref. in the ms.), but to the wrong place (bk. 6); see ms. fol. 6v and Hamaker p. 12.

[14] *Excerpta ex tragoediis et comoediis Graecis tum quae exstant, tum quae perierunt*, (Paris: Nicolas Buon, 1626) (TMD 468). Grotius had worked on the book for several years (see e.g. see *Briefwisseling*, II, no. 590 of July 1619; no. 845 of 29 July 1623); he prepared the edition right after he had finished *De iure belli ac pacis* for the press: see no. 930 of 8 Nov. 1624.

in the text (two of which still stand in modern editions).[15] This is important to note because it suggests that for Grotius the *Stromateis* was not just a handy reservoir of quotations, but a text he spent more than a little time upon–not surprisingly given the strong philological aspect of Grotius's training in Leiden. And, no less importantly, Clement's undogmatic, tolerant and intellectual approach to the faith certainly appealed to Grotius's own religious preferences. Especially with respect to the relationships between human ordered society and the divine world, the *Stromateis* might well be an influence on Grotius's thought on natural law to take seriously. The fact that Heinsius published an edition of Clement in 1616 can serve as a further indication of his popularity in Grotius's circle of acquaintances. Whether he studied the *Stromateis* in great depth or not, Grotius may have had the quotation ready in a collection of commonplaces into which he had once put it from Clement's text.[16]

The context in *Stromateis* 1.29 from which the Hesiod-quote is taken, shows further similarities with the context in *IPC*. Clement's topic is reliable knowledge, and after having discussed myth, he remarks that reliable knowledge and guidance are also provided by a good commandment, and in this way passes on to law and its ultimate author, God. Having quoted Hesiod, he refers to the distinction between natural law and positive law, and points at the etymology of the word God (θεός) from the verb 'to pose' (τίθημι), in a way very similar to the way Grotius connects *ius* with Jove, and *iura* with *iussa* at the opening of *IPC* chapter 2.[17]

---

[15] See *Poetae Comici Graeci* [= PCG], ed. by R. Kassel and C. Austin, (Berlin: De Gruyter, 2001), I, p. 139; Epicharmus fr. 240. Grotius's emendations are not in the line quoted here.

[16] For the use of commonplace books by early-modern scholars, see A. Moss, *Printed Commonplace-books and the Structuring of Renaissance Thought* (Oxford: Clarendon Press, 1996), and J. Waszink, 'Introduction' in J. Lipsius. *Politica. Six books of Politics or Political Instruction*, Bibliotheca Latinitatis Novae, ed. by J. Waszink (Assen: Van Gorcum, 2004), pp. 49-55.

[17] 'Similarly, also, demonstrations from the resources of erudition, strengthen, confirm, and establish demonstrative reasonings, in so far as men's minds are in a wavering state like young people's. "The good commandment," then, according to the Scripture, "is a lamp, and the law is a light to the path; for instruction corrects the ways of life". "*Law is monarch of all, both of mortals and of immortals*," says Pindar. I understand, however, by these words, Him who enacted law. And I regard, as spoken of the God of all, the following utterance of Hesiod, though spoken by the poet at random and not with comprehension: "*For the Saturnian framed for men this law: fishes, and beasts, and winged birds may eat each other, since no rule of right is theirs; but right (by far the best) to men he gave.*" Whether, then, it be the law which is connate and natural, or that given afterwards, which is meant, it is certainly of God; and both the law of nature and that of instruction are one. Thus also Plato, in *The Statesman*, says that the lawgiver is one; and in *The Laws*, that he who shall understand music is one; teaching by these words that the Word is one, and God is one. And Moses manifestly calls the Lord a covenant: "*Behold I am my Covenant with thee*," having previously told him not to seek the covenant in writing. For it is a covenant which

A Latin translation, if it is there, might help to further corroborate or refute our hypotheses in cases like the present one, and indeed in this case it seems to point in the same direction, though less unambiguously. Among the Latin translations of the above Hesiod-passage available in Grotius's time, I found two 'lineages' (but there may be more). The translations in the contemporary bilingual editions of Hesiod follow this form:

Namque hanc hominibus legem disposuit Saturnius,
Piscibus quidem et feris et avibus volucribus,
Se mutuo ut devorent, quandoquidem iustitia carent.
Hominibus autem dedit iustitiam, quae multo optima
Est.[18]

A wholly different strain of translations of this passage can be found in the Latin translations of Clement. They follow this pattern (from G. Hervet's Latin edition of Clement of 1555):[19]

Humano generi lex namque est a Iove lata,
Pisces atque ferae volucresque per aera nantes
Sese edunt cum illis ulla haud sit notio iuris.
Ast hominum generi iustum, est res quae optima cessit.

Heinsius in his 1616 edition of Clement includes an alternative that improves the scansion of the third and fourth lines:

Humano generi lex namque est a Iove lata
Pisces atque ferae volucresque per aera nantes
Sese ut consumant, nam ius nescire putantur.
Ast hominum generi ius, res pulcherrima, cessit.

Grotius too seems to have made his own (and very effective) translation based on that printed in Hervet's book, as the similarities in the wording suggest:

God, the Author of all, makes (τίθεται). For God (θεός) is called from θέσις (placing), and order or arrangement.' (tr. from *The writings of Clement of Alexandria*, tr. W. Wilson, 2 vols (Edinburgh: s.n., 1869-71). See also H.U. Meyboom, *Clemens Alexandrinus V, Vlechtwerken I*, Oud-Christelijke Geschriften in Nederlandsche Vertaling 12 (Leiden: Sijthoff, 1914).

[18] In: ΗΣΙΟΔΟΥ ΑΣΚΡΑΙΟΥ ΤΑ ΕΥΡΙΣΚΟΜΕΝΑ. *Hesiodi Ascraei opera quae exstant ...*, ([Heidelberg]: 1591), and ΗΣΙΟΔΟΥ ΤΟΥ ΑΣΚΡΑΙΟΥ ΕΡΓΑ ΚΑΙ ΗΜΕΡΑΙ, etc., *I. Spondanus Rupellanae provinciae Praefectus recensuit...*, Rupellae (La Rochelle: apud Hieronymum Haultinum, 1592). The edition *Poemata Hesiodi Ascraei* ... with annotations by Melanchton and the Wittenberg professor M.E. Schmidt (Wittenberg: 1601) has an even less transparent alternative for the third line: *Namque hanc hominibus legem disposuit Saturnius,/Piscibus quidem et feris et avibus volucribus,/Se mutuo ut devorent, quoniam non est ultio pro illis./Hominibus autem dedit iustitiam, quae multo optima/Est. ...*

[19] *Clementis Alexandrini viri longe doctissimi, ... Gentiano Herveto Aureliano interprete* (Basle: [Michael Isengrin], 1555).

Humano generi nam lex datur ab Iove summo.
Quippe ferae, pisces, avium genus altivolantum
Mutua se vertunt in pabula, juris egentes:
Justitia at nobis, quae res est optima, cessit.

Two conclusions can be drawn from all this. The first is that Grotius did not quote the Hesiod-lines from an edition of Hesiod, but from an intermediate source, *viz.* Clement of Alexandria's *Stromateis*. Detailed research of Grotius's quotations in *IPC* shows that this is true for more than a few of them. Studies of *IPC*'s intellectual and philosophical background will have to take this use of intermediate sources, indexes etc. serious as an influence on Grotius thought, not just as a mere complication in the identification of the right source-references.

The second conclusion is that Hamaker's rendering of Grotius's text presents neither Grotius's 'original' *nor* a version printed by the editors of Hesiod, but a mixture of both. Hamaker follows Grotius in line 3 ἐσθέμεν and μετ' αὐτῶν, but the Hesiod-editions in μὲν, and moreover follows nineteenth-century practice in the spelling -εη-, his capitalisation and punctuation.

In this case the differences between the versions have little effect on the content of the citation,[20] or its effects within Grotius's argument, but precisely because of that they can be used to identify Grotius's actual source (for there was no reason for the author to look for another version). The connection between the intermediate source (Clement) and *IPC*, as well as the relevance of Clement's *Stromateis* among the intellectual background to *IPC* deserve further scrutiny (but may well be significant). However, we can only begin to ask such questions when we know Grotius's actual source for the quote. It is obvious that Hamaker's edition is useless in this respect, for it leads us only to the Hesiod-passage in general, not to Grotius's actual source for it.

Punctuation

For another example of the differences between the manuscript of *IPC* and the edition by Hamaker, we shall now look at Hamaker's page 76-77, (ills 4 and 5) and manuscript fol. 33r (ill. 6). The noteworthy differences are in the punctuation. The manuscript reads (above middle of fol. 30): *ut apud Ciceronem est. Omne autem...*, not with semicolon after *est* as Hamaker prints it. The difference is small, but not to be overlooked: in Grotius's version *Omne autem...* explains the entire preceding paragraph, not just the sentence *sunt enim servi*

[20] Note that δίκη μετ' αὐτῶν means 'justice among them', while δίκη ἐπ' αὐτοῖς means 'revenge taken for them'.

legum, as it does in Hamaker's text. This obviously affects the structure of the argument in this place.

Similarly, Grotius has a full stop after *excusari* (Ham. p. 77, ms. bottom of fol. 33r in the insert marked 'x'), and *Nam* explains the entire preceding thought, not just the preceding clause, as it does in Hamaker. Also, there is another reading error in *imperatum* for *Imperatorem*. In defense of Hamaker, it should be added immediately that the number of reading errors in this selection is unrepresentatively high, and that genuine, let alone important, reading errors in Hamaker's edition are actually rare. As to the punctuation, the 1868 edition reflects the editorial practices of its time. Early-modern punctuation can be confusing to modern readers, and therefore it was customary in the nineteenth and twentieth centuries for editors to supply a wholly new punctuation. However, changes in punctuation change the structure of paragraphs and the connections between the elements of an argument, and will inevitably exclude or introduce shades of meaning present or absent in the

ἥμισυ τῆς ἀρέτῆς ἀποαιρεῖ δούλιον ἦμαρ.
Dimidia virtute caret servire coactus.

Quod autem in servo idem in subditis aliis obtinet, ut in filio. Nam, ut inquit ille, virtus pueri *οὐκ αὐτοῦ πρὸς αὐτόν ἐστιν, ἀλλὰ πρὸς τὸν τέλειον καὶ ἡγούμενον*, *non ipsius ad ipsum, sed ad eum qui ut perfectior illi praeest.* Et universalis haec differentia est *τοῦ ἄρχοντος καὶ ἀρχομένου*, *eius nimirum quod imperat et eius quod paret:* in quo ordine sunt et cives sigillatim considerati. Sunt enim servi legum, ut apud Ciceronem [1] est; omne autem quod imperat est ei quod paret causa virtutis, [2] ut Aristoteles explicat. Quo respicit Tacitus [3]: *Principi summum rerum judicium Dii dederunt, subditis obsequii gloria relicta est.* In his igitur verum est, quod Carneades et Academici perperam ad omnes transtulerunt, justitiam in opinione consistere: *οὐ φύσει ἀλλὰ νόμῳ*, *non natura sed lege.* Esse enim obtemperationem institutis populorum. Eamdem justitiam Peripatetici modo legalem vocant, modo generalem, quia ratione eadem esse potest cum omnibus virtutibus, quatenus in praeceptionem cadunt. Addunt scholastici, sicut eam

[1] pro Cluent. [c. 53. §. 146.] [2] V. Paul. Col. 3. 20. et 22. ad Tit. 3. 1. Eph. 3. 1. Rom. 13. 1. [3] Annal. l. 4.

† [Locus Homeri est in Od. l. 17. vs. 322. sq. sed verba discrepant; nam hodie editur:

ἥμισυ γάρ τ'ἀρετῆς ἀποαίνυται εὐρύοπα Ζεὺς
ἀνέρος, εὖτ'ἄν μιν κατὰ δούλιον ἦμαρ ἕλησιν.

Illustration 4: *Hugonis Grotii De jure praedae,* ed. by Hamaker, p. 76

leges oriuntur. Tritum illud, satius Deo parere quam hominibus [4], quod ad nostram disputationem ita adaptat cum exemplo Ambrosius [5]: *Julianus Imperator quamvis esset apostata habuit tamen sub se Christianos milites: quibus cum dicebat: Producite aciem pro defensione reipublicae, obediebant ei: cum autem diceret eis: Producite arma in Christianos, tunc agnoscebant imperatum coeli.* Quin et jurisconsulti [6] omnes non esse obediendum dicunt Principi, a quo manifestum sit id quod injustum est imperari. Et in maleficiis neminem mandato excusari [7], nam et domino piraticam facienti aut simile quid injustum natura, non sine poena servum dicto audientem esse [8]. Et Seneca [9]: *Non enim aut nos omnia jubere possumus, aut in omnia servi parere coguntur. Contra rempublicam imperata non facient, nulli sceleri manus commodabunt.* Supra [10] autem ostenderat, quae servi est in dominum, eam esse militis in ducem et in

Illustration 5: *Hugonis Grotii De jure praedae,* ed. by Hamaker, p. 77

original. On the scale of an entire work, the sum of many such small adaptations as shown above can make a difference to the content of the work.[21] Thus, in accordance with current practice, we have chosen to remove the nineteenth-century punctuation and capitalisation, as if they were a layer of discoloured veneer on an old painting, and restore their original form.

Of minor importance, but still in need of correction are spelling matters such as i/j (Hamaker introduced the j into the text, which is neither used by Grotius nor in modern practice) and m/n in for example *tanquam*/*tamquam*, *plerunque*/*plerumque*, etc.

It appears from all this that Hamaker adapted punctuation and spelling in ways that affect the content of the text. Thus we can add to the conclusions already drawn above, the conclusion that if we quote from *IPC*, the exact wording and punctuation of the citation(s) must be checked with the original manuscript, the collotype reproduction or the new edition when it appears. The 1868 edition is no longer sufficient to be quoted from directly.

[21] See also F. Simmler, 'Prinzipien der Edition von Texten der Frühen Neuzeit aus sprachwissenschaftlicher Sicht' in *Probleme der Edition von Texten der Frühen Neuzeit,* Beihefte zu *Editio,* vol. 3, ed. by L. Mundt et al. (Tübingen: Niemeyer, 1992), pp. 49-56.

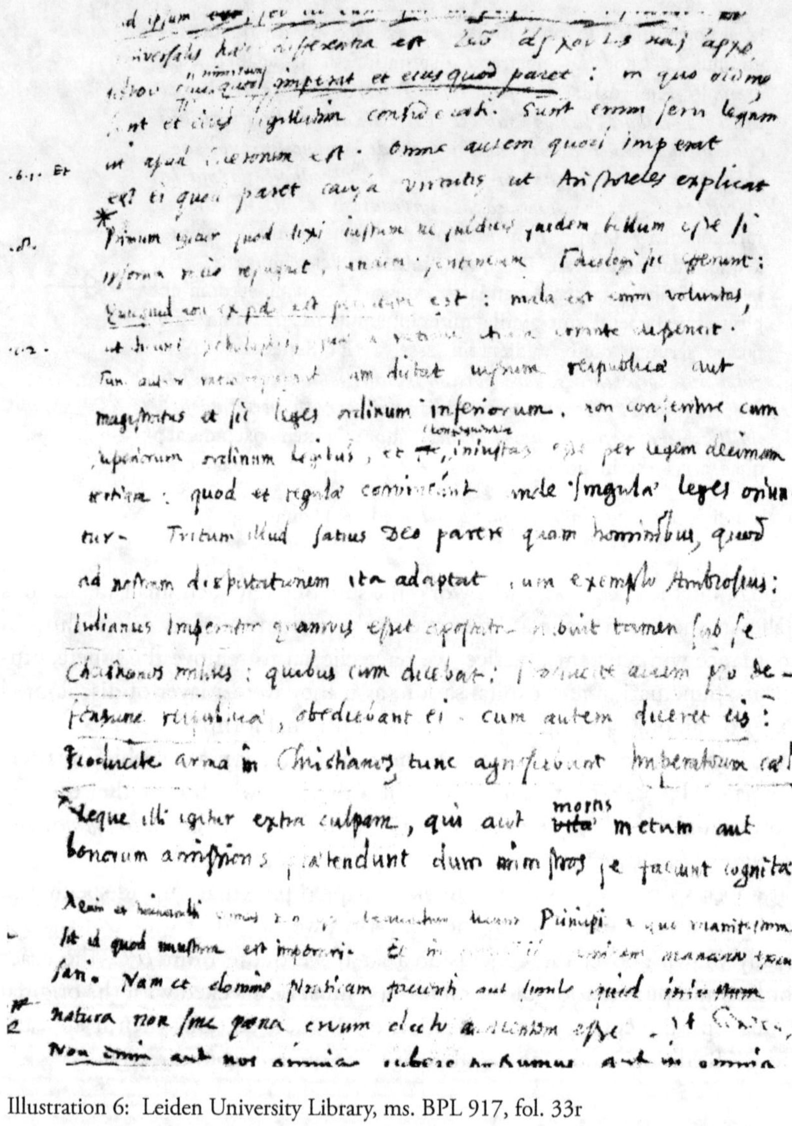

[illegible] Tritum illud satius Deo parere quam hominibus, quod ad nostram disputationem ita adaptat cum exemplo Ambrosius: Iulianus Imperator quamvis esset apostata habuit tamen sub se Christianos milites: quibus cum dicebat: [illegible] aciem pro defensione reipublicae, obediebant ei. cum autem diceret eis: Producite arma in Christianos, tunc agnoscebant Imperatorem caeli. Neque illi igitur extra culpam, qui aut mortis metum aut bonorum amissionem praetendunt [illegible]

Illustration 6: Leiden University Library, ms. BPL 917, fol. 33r

The Purpose, Nature and Intended Audience of *IPC*, and the Dating of BPL 917[22]

Although *IPC*, as precursor to the famous *De iure belli ac pacis*, has received a great deal of attention from scholars, some basic questions regarding the work are still open to debate. These concern for example the actual manuscript BPL 917 and its dating, as well as the nature and purposes of *IPC* and the organisation of the work. Moreover, these questions do involve matters crucial to its philosophical and historical interpretation. Answering them requires an integrated approach which combines historical, philosophical, philological and physical insights into *IPC* and the manuscript BPL 917. It is imperative therefore that Grotius scholars with backgrounds in these fields cooperate and inform themselves about each other's results.

The argument in *IPC* starts from the most basic principles of natural law to build up an argument about rights, self-interest and just war, which defines the rightful beginnings and conduct of private and public wars, including the issue of war booty and whom it belongs to. *IPC* then moves on to a historical part, which first demonstrates the legitimacy of the revolt of the Provinces against their Habsburg lord, in order to show that Portugal and the Dutch republic were formally at war with each other (Portugal being united with the Spanish Habsburg realm in the person of their shared overlord), and that this was a just war on the part of the Dutch. This is followed by a discussion of past and present atrocities by the Portuguese against Dutch sailors in the East. *IPC* then defends the right to free navigation and commerce (the later *Mare Liberum*), and the impossibility for the Vatican to forbid the (heathen) peoples overseas and the Dutch to trade with each other. Finally, *IPC* claims that it is both honourable and profitable for the Dutch to take prizes like the *Santa Catharina*.

The Manuscript

The text of *IPC* is known to us from one single source, the manuscript BPL 917, in which at least two stages of the text are preserved together (but probably several more). The manuscript has been kept in Leiden UL ever since it was bought at an auction in The Hague in 1864, not long after its rediscovery.

[22] Detailed research into the physical characteristics of BPL 917 (watermarks, page-numberings, binding) was performed by Martine van Ittersum and Peter Borschberg in Leiden UL during the NIAS-year 2004-05. I thank Martine van Ittersum for providing me with a draft of her article on the results of this research, which will be published in the future.

There is no doubt that the text in this manuscript is written in Grotius's hand, but in what sense it can be called the original manuscript requires further scrutiny and definition.

In all likelihood Grotius made BPL 917 originally as a fair copy of the text (meant to be sent to the printer or to be circulated among friends and acquaintances),[23] in which Grotius subsequently, over the years, added new changes: additions, deletions and revisions of varying length (between a single word and several pages). What state the work was in when Grotius started making this fair copy is unknown, and anything between two extremes is possible: the one being that Grotius copied the text from a set of draft sheets with the entire work in a finished, but perhaps cluttered state, the other extreme that he wrote BPL 917 down straight away (in which case there was no earlier draft version). The last scenario must be considered unlikely, given the fact that the first, original stage of the text in BPL 917 contains very few changes of mind (though there are indeed a few, to which we shall return below). This leads us to assume that BPL 917 was made from one or more draft documents (of parts or the whole of the work), which would have constituted the earliest version of the work. However, as far as we know, no such draft copies of *IPC* or parts of it are extant.

The difference between BPL 917 and its hypothetical precursors is relevant because it is tempting to connect physical data about BPL 917 (which contains clues to the relative dating of the various parts of the manuscript) with the formulation of Grotius's ideas in *IPC*. Such hypotheses are obviously much less interesting if BPL 917 is only a 'later' copy. At present it is unclear precisely how much time passed between the writing of the (hypothetical) lost draft(s) and the preparation of BPL 917, though it cannot have been more than two years.

Dating the Manuscript

Most specialists now assume that *IPC* was written between September/October 1604 and November 1606. The *terminus post quem* date is clear (see below); the *ante quem* date however is a much more complex issue.

An absolute *ante quem* date for BPL 917 is available in the fact that Grotius published chapter 12 of *IPC* separately as *Mare Liberum*, and made the revisions for this publication on the very pages of BPL 917. From the correspondence we know that he worked on this revision from November 1608 to

[23] From his correspondence it appears that Grotius did so with several of his works before publication.

February 1609. The conclusion of *De Mari Libero* on fol 117-118 is younger than one of the folio numberings that cover the whole of BPL 917.[24]

This dating can be further refined. Grotius wrote on 1 November 1606 to Georg Lingelsheim that he had finished his 'little work on the Indian affairs':

De rebus Indicis opusculum perfectum est: sed nescio, an ita ut scriptum est prodire debeat, an ea duntaxat quae ad universum ius belli et praedae pertinent; multi quidem veterum et recentum id argumentum tractarunt. Sed puto, posse aliquid novae lucis accedere ex certo docendi ordine, iurisque divini et humani cum philosophiae dictatis commodo temperamento.

> The little work on the Indian affairs is finished: but I do not know whether it should be published as it is, or only those parts which concern the universal law of war and booty. Many authors indeed, both ancient and modern, have dealt with this subject; however, I believe that new light can be thrown on the matter by a fixed order of teaching and by a right proportion of human and divine law mixed with the precepts of philosophy.[25]

Most scholars now regard this letter as written at the moment Grotius finished *IPC*. Closer study of the physical evidence in the manuscript, as performed by Borschberg and Van Ittersum, may allow for a further refining of this dating, but also produces a new set of questions. When published, their results may allow for a more sophisticated dating of the manuscript and its parts. However, at present it does not seem that these results will fundamentally change the above-mentioned view of the relationship between the content of *IPC* and the fair copy BPL 917 -i.e. the idea that there must have been a draft stage prior to BPL 917.

However, that the composition of the content of *IPC* and the preparation of the fair copy now BPL 917 were not completely separate things, appears from small-scale changes of mind effectuated while Grotius was making the fair copy. The pattern in these cases is different from the usual pattern. Usually, a bit of text is added to the existing text (in a margin, above the line, or on a separate piece of paper), or a finished bit of text is deleted or replaced by a different bit of text–see the various illustrations from the manuscript in this volume. In the cases meant here however, an (apparently) unfinished bit of text is replaced by a different bit of text, while the 'new' version is part of the *original* text in the manuscript (not added above a line or in a margin).

---

[24] See Martine van Ittersum's article in this collection.

[25] *Briefwisseling van Hugo Grotius*, ed. P.C. Molhuysen, B.L. Meulenbroek and H.J.M. Nellen, 17 vols. (The Hague, 1928-2001), I, ep. 86; translation mine.

These cases are rare, and they do not affect the idea that BPL 917 was made as a fair copy, but they do occur. A clear example can be seen in ill. 7, ms. fol 27r, at the beginning of chapter 6 (Hamaker p. 60). After ... *idem recte alteri praestabimus.* Grotius originally wrote a sentence not visible in Hamaker's edition, *Homines enim hominibus non sunt alieni ob communionem scilicet naturae quae efficit ut mala aliis illata nos etiam tangant* ('Humans are not entirely extraneous to each other, since obviously they have human nature in common, so that ills inflicted upon others affect us too).[26] Before he had finished writing out the rest of the page, he had crossed that sentence out and composed a new version, which appears about half-way down the page (8 lines down): *Quodsi etiam caetera desint vincula tamen totius humani generis societatis, haec origo naturaeque communio hoc efficit, ut mala aliis illata nos etiam tangant.*[27] This shows that in his mind Grotius was still working on the final text when he prepared the fair copy. This implies that, even if there was a draft copy prior to BPL 917, information on the dating of BPL 917 can still of be of some importance to the dating of the content of *IPC*.

In any case, after the completion of the fair copy Grotius continued to make changes in the text (such as most notably the changes in chapter 8 and the long insertion in chapter 10). He also revised chapter 12 for separate publication in 1608-9, and seems to have continued making little changes in the text and additions to the source-references at least into the 1620s, when he was working on *De iure belli ac pacis*. *IPC* has often been interpreted as a forerunner in Grotius's thought of *De iure belli ac pacis*, which he published in 1625 when he lived in Paris.

The Nature of IPC

The topic of *IPC* is the legal and moral rightfulness of the capture of a Portuguese carrack, the *Santa Catharina*, by the Dutch commander Johan van Heemskerck in the straits of Singapore on 25-26 February 1603, as well as the advantage it will bring to the Dutch cause. Van Heemskerck carried a commission from the Republic's supreme military commander, Prince

---

[26] In Grotius/Williams/Ittersum, *Commentary*, 2006, see p. 92-3: the original line was after '...when we ourselves are in distress', end of p. 92.

[27] *haec origo* was deleted at a later time. In Williams's translation: 'For that matter, even if other bonds are lacking, the universal fellowship of mankind and the communion established by nature, will still cause us to be affected in our turn by ills inflicted upon others', p. 93. Grotius's *communio naturae* seems better rendered by something like 'the fact that they have human nature in common' than by 'the communion established by nature'.

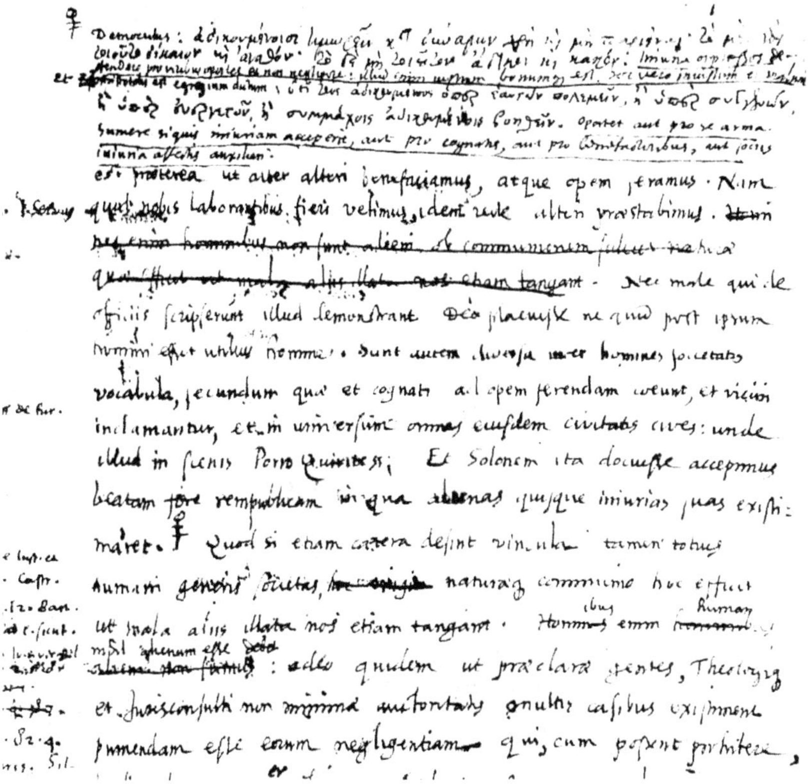

Illustration 7: Leiden University Library, ms. BPL 917, fol. 27r

Maurice, which authorised him to use arms, but in self-defence only. *IPC* includes a defence of this taking, which might be interpreted as an act of piracy. Ship and cargo yielded over 3 million guilders when sold at two auctions in Amsterdam in August and September 1604.[28]

A court case on the *Santa Catharina* served before the Amsterdam prize court in 1604. The claimants were Van Heemskerck himself, the Dutch East India Company (VOC) on behalf of the United Amsterdam Company (one of the legal precursors of the VOC), and *ex officio* the advocate-fiscal of the

[28] See also R. Fruin, 'Een onuitgegeven werk van Hugo de Groot' in Idem, *Verspreide Geschriften*, ed. by P.J. Blok, P.L. Muller, S. Muller, 11 vols (The Hague: Nijhoff, 1900-1905), III, pp. 367-445 (English: 'An Unpublished Work of Hugo Grotius', in: *Bibliotheca Visseriana Dissertationum ius internationale illustrantium*, tomus 5, X, (Leiden: Rijksuniversiteit, 1925), pp. 1-100).

province of Holland,[29] who claimed ownership of the vessel and its contents against other parties which might claim ownership. As no such parties appeared, verdict was passed in favour of the claimants, who were granted ownership of ship and cargo. This verdict is dated 9 September 1604.[30]

Grotius wrote *IPC* in response to a request by the VOC, which must have reached him somewhere in September 1604 through his friend Jan ten Grootenhuys, whose brother, Arent, was a director in the Amsterdam chamber of the VOC. The VOC also provided Grotius with relevant information, in the form of reports, journals and documents. There can be little doubt that the verdict of the Admiralty Board occasioned the VOC's request to Grotius; however, the precise connection, needed also to clarify the purpose of the argument(s) in *IPC* and its intended audience, must be reconstructed from other documents and is thus subject to discussion.[31]

From *IPC* itself it does not become unambiguously clear what its precise purpose is, whether it must be read as a treatise or as a plea,[32] whether it is a justification of the capture itself of the ship or also of the Admiralty Board's verdict, what its intended audience is, or in what setting(s) Grotius envisaged it to convince. The connection with the Amsterdam court case is puzzling, for the work on *IPC* was only begun when the Admiralty Board were reaching their verdict, or even after the verdict, so that *IPC* cannot have been written with a view to functioning in that lawsuit. These difficulties are increased by the fact that *IPC* in fact contains several arguments in unclear relationships to each other. The discussion regarding the purpose and intended audience of the work as a whole is still going on. There is a good possibility that such a unifying purpose does not exist, and that this figures among the reasons why Grotius never published the work.

The fact that the VOC directors requested Grotius to write the work at the time mentioned above makes it attractive to assume that they expected legal attacks on the verdict or its validity (as had happened in the case of the captured vessel *St Jago* in the same years) against which they wanted to have a

---

[29] This office would be held by Grotius from 1607 onwards.

[30] Two letters from Jan ten Grootenhuys to Grotius are preserved dated 15 and 20 October 1604, which accompanied the materials Grotius needed for his work. For the letters and archival documents mentioned in this chapter see Appendix II of Grotius/Williams/Ittersum, *Commentary*, 2006; see also Van Ittersum, *Profit and Principle*, p. 24-25.

[31] See e.g. 'Introduction' and appendix 1 and 2 in Grotius/Williams/Ittersum, *Commentary*, 2006.

[32] According to Richard Tuck the form of the work is that of an essay (*Philosophy and Government*, Cambridge 1993, p. 171). Fruin conjectured that Grotius actually conducted the lawsuit for the Company (and thus presented the argument to the Admiralty Board, see 'Unpublished Work', p. 39).

defence ready.[33] However, no such attacks are known to actually have come forward in the case of the *Santa Catharina*. As we shall see below, in the year 1605 there were only lawsuits concerning the parts of the booty which Van Heemskerck had handed out to his sailors on the way home. In *IPC* chapter 10 Grotius extensively re-wrote a passage on the ownership of war booty and the question of who has the right to distribute it. We shall examine these changes in more detail in the final section of this article.

Intended Audience

Whom did Grotius direct the argument(s) in *IPC* to? The question is obviously relevant for the interpretation of its content, and several answers have been proposed in the scholarship. Answering it involves the question why *IPC* was written in Latin, and requires an hypothesis about the *purpose* of *IPC*-another question without a final answer. For the sake of the present argument, I shall here assume that *IPC*, given the connection with the Amsterdam court case, is primarily a plea (though one never actually delivered), and with many characteristics of a treatise. This is similar to what Grotius would do in *De antiquitate Reipublicae Batavicae* of 1610, which is a plea dressed up as a historical account.[34] In his recent biography on Grotius, Henk Nellen writes that Grotius's aim in writing *IPC* was 'to encourage the leadership, shareholders and employees of the VOC'.[35]

Grotius's own utterances on the matter are somewhat vague, and can be found in two places in chapter 1. First he writes, right at the beginning of *IPC*:

> Thus we find that a considerable number of Hollanders (...) are apparently ashamed to lay claim to the spoils of war, being moved forsooth, by compassion for those who in their own relations with the Dutch have failed to observe even the legal right of enemies!

Further on in chapter 1, when he announces the arrangement of the work, Grotius refers to the people who dispute his views, and classifies them into three groups:

---

[33] As Van Ittersum points out (*Profit and Principle* p. 190), 'Inchoate notions of freedom of trade and navigation already informed Dutch privateering in the East Indies before Grotius sat down to write DIP. (...) Yet the judges' references to natural rights, *ius gentium* and the law of war were haphazard at best, which Grotius sought to correct in DIP.'

[34] See 'Introduction' p. 19-23 in: Grotius, *The Antiquity of the Batavian Republic, with the notes by Petrus Scriverius*, Bibliotheca Latinitatis Novae, ed. by Jan Waszink et al. (Assen: Van Gorcum, 2000).

[35] H.Nellen, *Hugo de Groot. Een leven in strijd om de vrede* (Amsterdam 2007), p. 84.

- those who consider the prize as 'wrongfully acquired and illegitimate';
- those who feel they 'bring a stain upon their reputations by approving it'; and
- those who do not fear that it endangers their good name, but fear that it 'may in the end result in some loss or harm'.[36]

The first of the above statements indicates quite clearly that the moral dimension of seizures of this type was subject of debate in the Netherlands. Unfortunately, Grotius does not make it clear who precisely these people are. Fruin assumed that they were Mennonite and Anabaptist shareholders in the VOC, but this hypothesis has now been dismissed.[37]

As to the second statement, in which Grotius subdivides those whom he sets out to convince into three groups, Van Ittersum remarks perceptively that the purpose of this subdivision is primarily to structure Grotius's own argument,[38] and that it does not necessarily refer to existing groups in the real world. In combination with the first statement however, it seems hard to deny the reality of a debate in the Netherlands on the legitimacy of prize taking.

Van Ittersum concludes that the States-General were *IPC*'s intended audience,[39] in order to remind them that they had more or less instructed the VOC to defend Dutch interests in the East, and should compensate the company for the costs involved in this task accordingly.[40] Given her view that the chapters 2-10 of *IPC* are a later insertion, this view of *IPC*'s intended audience must apply primarily to a *IPC* consisting of chapters 1 + 11-15, i.e. the historical section with introduction and conclusions. In my view, however, it is also applicable to the chapters 2-10, though on a different level. In her discussion of the purpose of *IPC*, Van Ittersum points at the case of the *St. Jago*, another ship captured by the Dutch, a case partly parallel to that of

---

[36] Grotius/Williams/Ittersum, *Commentary*, 2006, p. 9 and 15; Van Ittersum, *Profit and Principle*, 121.

[37] R. Fruin, 'Onuitgegeven werk' and Van Ittersum, *Profit and Principle*, ch. 3.

[38] Discussions at the NIAS seminar, spring 2005.

[39] *Profit and Principle*, ch. 3, pp.105-188. In 'Hugo Grotius in Context: Van Heemskerck's Capture of the *Santa Catharina* and its Justification in *De Jure Praedae* (1604-1606)', *Asian Journal of Social Science*, 31.3 (2003), p. 524, she describes the VOC's purpose as winning support with potential allies such as the French and English kings and the other Dutch provinces.

[40] In March 1606, the VOC submitted a petition to the States-General (written by Grotius) to ask for financial material assistance. They referred to the importance of their efforts in the Indies for the war in the Low Countries, the taxed levied by the Generality on booty captured, and the high costs incurred by the Company; they propose to bring all goods captured in the East together in a military fund, from which further military exploits in the East can be financed. See Van Ittersum, *Profit and Principle*, p. 177-186.

the *Santa Catharina*. The case served before the Admiralty Court in Middelburg, Zeeland, in 1602-1605. The *St. Jago* was a ship owned by a neutral party, the Italian Francisco Carletti, who had good contacts at the Medici court and the French court. Through these channels Carletti put enormous pressure on the Zeeland chamber of the VOC, the Middelburg Admiralty Board, the States of Holland and the States-General to have his goods returned to him. His royal French and Italian patrons suggested to the Dutch that the case might have repercussions for Dutch merchants in French and Italian harbours if the goods were not returned, and the States of Holland and the States-General yielded to this pressure. They in turn put pressure on the Zeeland chambers of the VOC to return the goods, but these tenaciously refused to do so, claiming that their legal argumentation to keep the goods was watertight. After a lengthy diplomatic and legal struggle, an out-of-court settlement was reached by which Carletti received some compensation for his losses.

Given this context, the argumentation in *IPC* 2-10 could also be read as directed at the States-General (and the States of Holland), not so much in order to remind them of their obligations to the VOC, but as a renewed confirmation of the VOC's right to prizes like the *St Jago* and *Santa Catharina*, since the States of Holland and the States-General had effectively sided with Carletti in the *St Jago* affair. The Carletti context however also widens the intended audience of *IPC*. It shows that other European governments had to be addressed as well, and that legal proceedings challenging an Admiralty Court's verdict were a real possibility. Thus Grotius's legal colleagues defending the interests of ship owners, as well as those in law courts where future cases might serve, had to be convinced of the legitimacy and beneficial nature (to the Republic) of the capture, and are to be included among our vision of the intended audience of *IPC*. And for such audiences (the international audience and that in the legal profession) the choice of Latin was the right one; for a work directed at the Dutch States-General alone it would not have been the obvious choice. The fact that no new lawsuits regarding the ownership of the Santa Catharina were actually started, might then help explain the fact that Grotius left most of the work unpublished.

Thus it seems that the intended audience of *IPC* consisted of three main groups:

- The Dutch States-General (for two purposes, as above) and the States of Holland;
- European governments whose subjects might start lawsuits against the VOC;
- lawyers and judges involved in this and/or similar case(s) in the future.

As we shall see in the next chapter, the modification in *IPC* chapter 10 might have been made in response to a an impending lawsuit regarding the distribution of parts of the spoils of the *Santa Catharina*.

The *St. Jago* affair shows furthermore that the three classes of objections referred to by Grotius did indeed figure in the various debates on the rightfulness of prize-taking by the VOC,[41] but it remains unclear to what extent Grotius actually wanted to speak to merchants or shareholders in the VOC who entertained such doubts - a long argument like *IPC*, in Latin moreover, does not seem to be the most effective way to reach such an audience.

The Deletion and Insertion in *IPC* Chapter 10

The original text and revisions preserved in BPL 917 reflect the development of Grotius's thought on just war, booty and natural rights between 1604 and 1609 (but possibly up to the mid-1620s). Thus they figure among the most important sources for the history of political thought (and that of natural law in particular). The revisions in BPL 917 occupy a special place first because of the clues they give to the development of Grotius's thought, and secondly because revision always adds emphasis, as second thoughts carry more weight than first ones, from the perspective of the author as well as that of the reader. The price itself so to speak of the extra trouble invested attaches itself to a passage, and makes it more valuable to the interpreter than an unchanged one. It is no coincidence that the most heavily reworked chapter in *IPC* (ch. 2) is also philosophically the most important and most challenging chapter.

For that reason alone, an edition which points out which parts of a text were reconsidered and changed, and in what way, is an indispensable tool for its full understanding (provided of course that such information has survived). The revisions in a text constitute an added layer of meaning, which more often than not contains crucial clues to its interpretation. The 1868 edition of *IPC* keeps this additional layer of meaning invisible: it only gives the final and most developed stage, without clues to the process from which the text resulted.

---

[41] Fruin, 'Unpublished work', p. 11 refers to the capture of the St. Jago near St. Helena in March 1602 in which naval captains from Holland and Zeeland had conflicting opinions on the legitimacy of an attack on a Portuguese ship. The captain of a vessel from Amsterdam refused to assist a vessel from Zeeland when it planned to capture a Portuguese galleon, since he felt his instructions did not permit such an action; see also Van Ittersum, *Profit and Principle*, pp. 124-129.

To show an example of the changes to be found in the text of *IPC* we shall now look at the long insertion-and-deletion in chapter 10. This modification is as such invisible in Hamaker's edition, for that edition prints only the final version. The translation by G.L. Williams is a rendering of the version printed in Hamaker and mentions the deletion in the notes. However, the reassuring assertion that 'The material stricken out by Grotius at this point reappears on other pages of the collotype' obscures Grotius's modification of the content rather than highlights it.[42] In the manuscript, the folios 63v and 67r are crossed out, and a few sheets (64r-66v) have been inserted.[43] The insertion itself has subsequently been adorned with new deletions and additions, two of which again on separately inserted pieces of paper (64va and 65a). By means of this deletion and insertion, Grotius changed his argument as to whom, in Roman times, war booty belonged, and to whom the decision what to do with it: to the state and the senate, the soldiers, their commander (or perhaps the Emperor?). Such questions also came up in several lawsuits in ancient Rome, and these are Grotius's point of reference.

In the original version visible in BPL 917 (not included in Hamaker and the translations), Grotius's argument can be paraphrased as follows. 'War booty is property of the state, not of an individual nor even the commander of the army in question. It had to be handed in to the Quaestor in Rome. He who breaks this rule is guilty of peculation (*peculatio*–Dutch: *verduistering*). In Antiquity there were strict rules for soldiers regarding both the kind and the value of goods they were allowed to take with them from an area in which they were stationed or on campaign. Soldiers had to bring all goods beyond a well-defined limit (one silver coin a day) to their commander within three days, or return them to their original owner. The accusation of peculation is also brought against high-placed persons (e.g. Verres), and even the Emperors were bound by these rules. Coriolanus was accused of not having distributed booty

[42] Note also that Williams made a mistake at the beginning of the insertion (the place marked [64], p. 147 (Williams, 1950) or 215 (Grotius/Williams/Ittersum, 2006): the words 'According to Dionysus' are not in the ms. or in Hamaker.

[43] The end of fol. 63v was originally followed by the beginning of 67r (*FURES ... PUBLICI in auro atque purpura...*, a quotation from Cato's speeches, quoted by Gellius, *Noctes Atticae*, XI.18.18); similarly the end of fol. 66r connects with the beginning of 67v (*Cum igitur apud... omnes nationes*); 66v is empty: the unused last page of the insertion. The folio numbers quoted here are those of the numbering in the upper outer corners of the pages (the manuscript contains several folio-numberings). This numbering is obviously younger than the insertion, for it includes the folio-numbers of the insertion (Williams points out that there is another folio numbering just below, in which 63v and 67r are 56v and 57r respectively, but ignores the complication that 64r *also* carries the number 57 in what seems to be the same series).

according to the traditional rules, and Cato complains about lack of punishment for peculation in a famous phrase (*Fures publici in auro atque purpura* - 'Thieves of public property going dressed in gold and purple'). When the Empire expanded, and campaigns moved out of the direct control of the Senate, the *Imperatores* (commanders) were given more freedom to decide and settle such matters, just as they were allowed a greater freedom to make peace. Not all commanders used this freedom in the same way: some put booty into the Treasury, others divided it among their soldiers, prudent commanders asked the Senate what it wanted them to do. Others again divided it among the troops, not according to who caught what, but according to rank and merit, so that also the men not directly involved in obtaining the booty could get a share in it. The Justinian Code gives rules for such divisions. Since, then, all nations consider booty as public, not private property, this rule must be accepted as a binding precept, even if it had not been demonstrated from natural law'.

In the adapted version written out in the inserted section, the argument is longer and markedly different. It amounts to a claim that, yes, war booty is public property, BUT the right to share it out belongs to the *imperator*.[44]

The content of this change is more or less clear, but not its purpose. Is Van Heemskerck the commander Grotius is thinking of, or is the *imperator* the

---

[44] In paraphrase: 'War booty is public not private property' [begin inserted new version:] '-which is what the accusers of Coriolanus bring in against him, and this is not untrue, but can easily be taken too literally. Though booty belongs to the state, in Roman law the decision what to do with it belongs to the *imperator*. Some imperatores delegated this task to others, such as the Senate, in order to avoid all appearances of a conflict of interests, others performed it themselves, each in their own way. Those who wanted to avoid all blemish sent the value of the booty to the Quaestor or had it auctioned *sub hasta,* the results (called *manubiae* according to some) being put into the Treasury; others sold it themselves and then put the results into the Treasury. However, although the records of Roman history are full of lists of booty put into the treasury by military commanders, it pays off to have a closer look at this. For the same history shows that these commanders were under no formal obligation to do so, in spite of what some accusers say. Sometimes booty was offered to the gods, sometimes to the soldiers involved, sometimes to others [follows a digression with examples and various different systems for division among soldiers], and whichever system was adopted, the *imperator* could take a special portion called ἐξαίρετον, of what size he liked (and others says that this *imperator*'s portion is the thing called *manubiae*). When they refrained from taking or took only little for themselves, the *imperatores* were praised. The rights of the *imperatores* with respect to this are put down in the Justinian Code. This type of division of the spoils has always been criticised, not because its lawfulness was in doubt, but because imperatores were suspected of promoting their own interests too much (e.g. Servilius, Coriolanus, Camillus). Sometimes the soldiers were allowed to divide the spoils themselves [examples], which practice was not approved of by all, because it works to the disadvantage of the slower men. If parts of the booty were given to non-soldiers, these were usually people who supported the campaign financially, and had their money returned to them in this way. All this varied with every war, just as the system adopted for the division, e.g. by a given

supreme military commander, i.e. Maurice, or is he perhaps the Roman Emperor, that is, the head-of-state (i.e. in the Dutch case the provincial States, or even the States-General (viewed as the supreme authority in the United Provinces)? Grotius's terminology may be found unclear; he writes *Imperatores* (plural, but with capital -note that Hamaker prints *imperatores*). Most of Grotius's discussion refers to republican times, and indeed when contrasting *milites* and *imperatores* he must be speaking about soldiers and (their) commander(s), not an Emperor. Thus *Imperator* must refer to a military commander, but which one? In the Dutch case of the *Santa Catharina* lawsuits, there would be Maurice as supreme commander of the armed forces, and Van Heemskerck as the commander of the campaign. In the place of the Roman Senate, one would first think of the States-General, as the sovereign body responsible for the war, but in fact the States of Holland had at one point also considered claiming the booty of the *Santa Catharina*, until Van Oldenbarnevelt passed a resolution that this and all future war booty would belong to the federal government of the Dutch Republic (in 1604).[45] Moreover, even the king of Johore might be interpreted as a party involved, for Van Heemskerck acted in his defence, as Grotius himself argues at the end of *IPC* chapter 13.[46]

Furthermore, it must be noted that at the end of the insertion the argument reconnects with the unchanged existing environment in *IPC*. Thus, after elaborately constructing a qualification to the respublica's ownership of war booty (namely the commander's right to decide about the distribution),

---

ratio or by type of booty [examples]. This overview shows that by Roman law, booty is public property, but that the distribution is left to the *imperatores*, with this condition that they are brought to trial if they are caught committing fraud [examples -Cato complains about lack of punishment for peculation, *Fures publici* etc.] Verres too was accused of peculation. However, since false accusations arose, an oath was instituted whereby all swore not to hand out parts of any booty. This in turn might be connected with the legal formula recorded in Gellius, by which soldiers are instructed not to take anything above the value of one silver coin away from the camp, or to take it to the consul, or to return it within three days. This is why Modestinus says that whoever takes booty from the enemy, is guilty of peculation. This is the place our own professors of law should have adduced to show that booty falls under public ownership, for there can only exist peculation with respect to public or religious property. With this respect, Roman, Greek and other practices are perfectly congruous. Since, then, [end insertion] all nations consider booty as public, not private property, this rule must be accepted as a binding precept, even if it had not been demonstrated from natural law'.

[45] Van Ittersum, *Profit and Principle*, p. 116-117. The Dutch text of the decree by which they renounced their claims is published in Grotius, *Commentary The Law of Prize and Booty*, tr. Williams, 1950 p. 379-80; an English translation in Grotius/Williams/Ittersum, *Commentary*, 2006, p. 515-516.

[46] See also Van Ittersum 'Hugo Grotius in context', p. 535.

Grotius surprisingly re-affirms the unqualified ownership of booty by the *respublica*. It goes beyond the purposes of this paper to propose an explanation and interpretation of this; I just want to make two further notes that might be helpful to such an interpretation.

The fact that this revision was made after the original fair copy of chapter 10 had been finished suggests that it was made at a relatively late stage, possibly after November 1606. The watermarks in the paper of this insertion (a crest and Basle crosier or bishop's staff) can also be found in the paper of letters sent by Grotius in January 1607 and January and October 1609, while the watermarks in the surrounding original sheets in chapter 10 are different.[47] On the basis of this link in the watermarks, the insertion in chapter 10 would perhaps be datable from January 1607 onwards, but further research remains necessary.

If we look for controversies regarding the distribution of war booty connected with the *Santa Catharina* case, two things appear. In March 1605, the States-General took a decision regarding the division of the booty from the *Santa Catharina* between the VOC and Heemskerck and his crew. The crew were accorded 4% of the booty, considerably less than the 6,3% (1/16) normally received by the crews of warships. Van Heemskerck and his men immediately filed a formal protest with the States-General, who revised their decision. The crew's portion was subsequently enlarged further by the VOC itself. The Generality received 23% (instead of the normal 20) of the booty; there seems to be no mention of a portion for Prince Maurice, as one would expect.[48]

In the same period, the VOC directors started legal procedures against Van Heemskerck and his crew regarding the parts of the spoils from the *Santa Catharina* handed out by Van Heemskerck to his crew on his way home (once at Bantam, once on St. Helena). After their return in Holland, the VOC directors accused Van Heemskerck of embezzlement. According to a notarised statement filed by them, 3000 guilders worth of booty had been found in Van Heemskerck's possession.[49] However, this happened in May 1605, when it seems unlikely that the fair copy now BPL 917 had already been made, let alone particular *changes* in any of the chapters. Dutch ships however continued to catch foreign ships and bring back booty to the Netherlands. As Enthoven points out, in 1604, at the time of the settlement of the *Santa Catharina*-case, the rules governing the distribution of these prizes had not yet

[47] I thank Martine van Ittersum for this information.

[48] V. Enthoven, *Zeeland en de opkomst van de Republiek. Handel en strijd in de Scheldedelta* c. 1550-1621. Leiden, 1996, p. 207-210.

[49] See Van Itterum, *Profit & Principle* ch.1, p. 37 n. 39 and 'Hugo Grotius in context' p. 545 (app. III).

fully developed. By 1606, there was greater clarity, and Grotius's changes in chapter 10 might be a response to more definitive arrangements from that year (e.g. as occasioned by the settlement of the proceeds from the captured vessels *St. Francisco* and *St. Antonio* in 1606-7). This arrangement allowed the VOC to sell booty obtained in Asia in Asia itself, if proper accounts were kept of the proceeds.[50] Hopefully further research will shed more light on the backgrounds of the change in chapter 10 in the future.

Conclusion

Grotius's *De iure praedae* is an unfinished and unauthorised text, which will continue to inspire and inform the study of Grotius's thought on natural rights and its development. Its unfinished state creates both possibilities and imposes limitations. The text as presented by Hamaker cannot be taken for granted, as the manuscript contains a wealth of information not visible in that edition. Though the edition can be used as a reading text of *IPC*, scholarly quotes from *IPC* should always be checked with the manuscript or the future critical edition. Scholars should be aware that for any passage they are studying, the manuscript might preserve an older version worth taking into account. Revisions, i.e. deleted, revised or added sentences or even paragraphs can provide important clues to the meaning or intention of any particular statement, to the connections in the author's thought, the development of that thought, or the interpretation of the text in its philosophical or historical context. Also Grotius's sources must be accessed through his own actual citations and references in the manuscript, as appears from the details of Grotius's citation from Hesiod studied in this paper. These references can lead to his actual sources, as Hamaker's edition or the translations do not. The new edition that is currently being prepared should facilitate this research for a wider group of scholars, for *De iure praedae* needs to be studied by scholars of philosophy, history, law and philology in cooperation.

---

[50] With thanks to Victor Enthoven for this suggestion. For references to sources, see Enthoven, Zeeland en de opkomst van de Republiek and Enthoven, 'Van steunpilaar tot blok aan het been. De Verenigde Oost-Indische Compagnie en de Unie', in *De Verenigde Oost-Indische Compagnie tussen oorlog en diplomatie*, ed. by G. Knaap and G. Teitler (Leiden: KITLV, 2002), pp. 45ff; P. van Dam, *Beschryvinge van de Oostindische Compagnie*, ed. by F. Stapel, RGP 63, vol. 1 (The Hague: Nijhoff, 1927), p. 44 & n. 1; and The Hague, Nationaal Archief, VOC 13389, *Repartitie van de veroverde goederen...*, 1606 (quoted from Enthoven, 'Steunpilaar').

Preparing *Mare liberum* for the Press: Hugo Grotius' Rewriting of Chapter 12 of *De iure praedae* in November-December 1608*

Martine Julia van Ittersum
Lecturer in European History, University of Dundee, Scotland (UK)
E-mail: m.j.vanittersum@dundee.ac.uk

Abstract
This article reconstructs the printing history of Hugo Grotius's *Mare liberum* (*The Free Sea*, 1609). It examines the political circumstances which prompted the pamphlet's publication, but then seemed to conspire against it, and relates these to Grotius's revision of chapter 12 of Ms. BPL 917 in Leiden University Library, the one surviving copy of *De iure praedae* (*The Commentary on the Law of Prize and Booty*, 1604-1608). While preparing chapter 12 for the press, he made a serious effort to tone down its bellicose rhetoric, erasing, for example, all references to the Spanish claims to the Americas. His aim was to placate the French envoy Pierre Jeannin and his own political patron Johan van Oldenbarnevelt, the driving forces behind the negotiations for the Twelve Years' Truce (1609-1621). In the context of these negotiations, Grotius was at pains to downplay his radical rights theories. The subjective right of punishment only received a mention in the conclusion of *Mare liberum*, for example. Yet a discarded outline for the pamphlet's preface shows that the argument of *De iure praedae* remained uppermost in his mind, witness the outline's denunciation of the 'poisonings, perfidy and crimes of the Portuguese'. Both *De iure praedae* and *Mare liberum* had been commissioned by the Dutch East India Company (VOC) for the express purpose of influencing political developments in its favour. Yet neither treatise had the impact originally intended by Grotius and the VOC directors. Ironically, these occasional writings became classics of international law instead.

Keywords
Hugo Grotius, Mare liberum, De iure praedae, Twelve Years' Truce, Dutch East India Company, Dutch imperialism

* The research for this article was made possible by a grant from the Carnegie Trust for the Universities of Scotland and a sabbatical leave at the Netherlands Institute for Advanced Study, Feb.-June 2005. The librarians at the Peace Palace in The Hague kindly provided a photocopy of the first edition of *Mare liberum*. The generous help and assistance of four specialists on Neo-Latin literature – Dr. Jeanine Delandtsheer (University of Leuven), Dr. Henk Nellen (Constantijn Huygens Institute), Dr. Arnoud Visser (University of St. Andrews) and Dr. Jan Waszink (Radboud University of Nijmegen) – proved indispensable in deciphering and decoding the changes which Grotius made in chapter 12 of *De iure praedae*. Dr. Nellen commented

Introduction

Hugo Grotius's first publication on natural rights and natural law theory, *Mare liberum* (*The Free Sea,* 1609), has been the object of renewed scholarly attention in recent years. Legal historians and historians of political thought have sought to reconstruct the pamphlet's historical context and draw out its implications for international politics.[1] Grotius's wholehearted support for the United Dutch East India Company or VOC, founded in 1602, has been highlighted in the publications of David Armitage, Peter Borschberg, Edward Keene, Benjamin Straumann, Richard Tuck, Eric Wilson, and the present author. The enormous growth of Dutch trade and navigation in the first half of the seventeenth century was perceived in the Iberian Peninsula and British Isles as, on the one hand, undermining the integrity of the Portuguese empire in Asia, and, on the other hand, as a threat to the Scottish herring fisheries in the North Sea, the commercial viability of the English East India Company, and the claims of the Stuart monarchs to 'own' and control the waters surrounding the British Isles. Little wonder, then, that *Mare liberum* ignited a Europe-wide debate on the dominion of the seas, which has been

---

extensively on a first draft of this article. I am greatly indebted to all these colleagues for their constructive criticism and moral support.

[1] Richard Tuck, *The Rights of War and Peace: Political Thought and the International Order from Grotius to Kant* (Oxford: Oxford University Press, 1999); Edward Keene, *Beyond the Anarchical Society: Grotius, Colonialism and Order in World Politics* (Cambridge: Cambridge University Press, 2002); Monica Brito Vieira, 'Mare Liberum versus Mare Clausum: Grotius, Freitas, and Selden's Debate on Dominion over the Seas', *Journal of the History of Ideas,* 63 (2003), 361-77; Hugo Grotius, *The Free Sea,* tr. by Richard Hakluyt, ed. by David Armitage (Indianapolis: Liberty Fund, 2004); Helen Thornton, 'Hugo Grotius and the Freedom of the Seas', *International Journal of Maritime History,* 16 (2004), 17-38; Peter Borschberg, 'Hugo Grotius' Theory of Trans-Oceanic Trade Regulation: Revisiting Mare Liberum (1609)', *Itinerario,* 29 (2005), 31-53; Hugo Grotius, *The Rights of War and Peace,* ed. Richard Tuck, 3 vols. (Indianapolis: Liberty Fund, 2005); Eric Wilson, 'Erasing the Corporate Sovereign: Inter-Textuality and an Alternative Explanation for the Publication of Hugo Grotius' Mare Liberum (1609)', *Itinerario,* 30 (2006), 78-103; Martine J. van Ittersum, 'Mare Liberum versus The Propriety of the Seas? The Debate between Hugo Grotius (1583-1645) and William Welwood (1552-1624) and Its Impact on Anglo-Scotto-Dutch Fishery Disputes in the Second Decade of the Seventeenth Century', *Edinburgh Law Review,* 10, no. 2 (May 2006), 239-76; Helen Thornton, 'John Selden's Response to Hugo Grotius: The Argument for Closed Seas', *International Journal of Maritime History,* 18 (2006), 105-27; Martine Julia van Ittersum, *Profit and Principle: Hugo Grotius, Natural Rights Theories and the Rise of Dutch Power in the East Indies, 1595-1615* (Leiden: Brill, 2006); Grotius, *Commentary on the Law of Prize and Booty,* tr. Gwladys L. Williams and ed. by Martine Julia van Ittersum (Indianapolis: Liberty Fund, 2006); Benjamin Straumann, *Hugo Grotius und die Antike: Römischen Rech und römische Ethik im frühneuzeitlichen Naturrecht,* Studien zur Geschichte des Völkerrechts 14 (Baden-Baden: Nomos, 2007).

reconstructed by David Armitage, Helen Thornton, Richard Tuck, Monica Brito Vieira, and me. The question whether, and to what extent, Grotius's defence of Western imperialism and colonialism informs modern international relations has been examined by Edward Keene, Richard Tuck and Eric Wilson. The plethora of new studies has increased our knowledge of the nature and scope of Grotius's argument in *Mare liberum*. Yet the historiography has so far failed to take account of one important piece of evidence: Ms. BPL 917 in Leiden University Library, the pamphlet's extant manuscript. This article examines the various alterations made in the text when Grotius prepared *Mare liberum* for the press in November and December 1608. I argue that Grotius diluted his original argument at the behest of his patron, Johan van Oldenbarnevelt (1547-1619), the political leader of the United Provinces. The latter made it very clear that he could not condone a pamphlet which might upset the negotiations between the States General and Philip III of Spain and Portugal (r. 1598-1621). At his insistence, its publication was postponed until the Twelve Years' Truce had been signed at Antwerp on 9 April 1609.

For a proper understanding of Grotius's revisions, it is necessary to know something about the origins of the text and, more broadly, about the author's intellectual development in the 1600s, which was closely tied to his political aspirations. I will first provide a brief biography of Grotius, focusing on his meteoric rise in Dutch politics prior to 1618. I will then discuss the origin and nature of manuscript BPL 917 in Leiden University Library, the one remaining autograph manuscript of *De iure praedae* (*On the Law of Prize and Booty*, 1604-1608), which forms the basis of *Mare liberum*. Turning to the pamphlet proper, I will take a closer look at the political exigencies that prompted its appearance in print, and Grotius's dealings with Elzevier Publishers in Leiden, which can be reconstructed on the basis of his correspondence. Grotius submitted the text to the printer in late December 1608 or early January 1609. The slim quarto volume did not become available in Dutch bookshops until three or four months later. For a variety of reasons, the printing process had slowed to a crawl even before Oldenbarnevelt's direct interference in early March 1609. Finally, I will analyze Grotius' reworking of the text in order to prepare it for publication. Grotius deleted the second half of chapter 12 of *De iure praedae* and substantially revised the first half, omitting, for example, three explicit references to the Spanish empire in the Americas. Manuscript BPL 917 also contains the new conclusion that he wrote for *Mare liberum*, a preliminary list of chapter titles, which differs at points from the pamphlet's table of contents and chapter divisions, and a first outline for his introduction to *Mare liberum*, subsequently discarded, which bears little relation to what eventually appeared in print.

The Life and Times of Hugo Grotius

Hugo Grotius was born in the town of Delft in the province of Holland in 1583. Only two years earlier, the States General had abjured Philip II of Spain and Portugal as the ruler of the Low Countries. Grotius was a Delft patrician, or regent, by birth: his ancestors had played an important role in local government since the thirteenth century. His father, Jan de Groot, was a trustee of Leiden University, founded in 1575, and a personal friend of Johan van Oldenbarnevelt. The son inherited these important political connections. At age eleven, he went to Leiden University, where he studied the liberal arts under the aegis of Joseph Justus Scaliger, the foremost humanist scholar of the age. In 1598, Grotius joined a Dutch diplomatic mission to France and purchased a doctorate in law from the University of Orléans. This was a perfectly normal thing to do for a seventeenth-century gentleman on the *grand tour.* At his return home, Grotius set up shop as a solicitor in The Hague, and argued civil cases before the Court of Holland (*Hof van Holland*). He did not forsake his liberal arts education, however. So much is clear from his correspondence with Daniel Heinsius, Professor of Poetics (1601) and Greek (1605) at Leiden University, who assisted Grotius with literary publications of various kinds. In 1601, Grotius was given the opportunity to harness his humanist training to the defence of Dutch national interests. At Oldenbarnevelt's suggestion, the States of Holland commissioned him to write a history of the Dutch Revolt against Spain. Following the spectacular capture of the Portuguese merchantman *Santa Catarina* in Singapore Straits in February 1603, the Amsterdam directors of the VOC asked him to write an apology for their privateering campaign in monsoon Asia. The resulting treatise, *De iure praedae* (*On the Law of Prize and Booty*), marked the start of Grotius's long and fruitful career as a political theorist and legal scholar. It remained in manuscript until the nineteenth century, however, with the exception of its twelfth chapter, which was published as *Mare liberum* in April 1609.[2]

Meanwhile Grotius's political career went from strength to strength. At Oldenbarnevelt's behest, he was offered the job of solicitor general (*advocaat-fiscaal*) of Holland in November 1607. This appointment enabled him to

[2] Henk Nellen, *Hugo de Groot: Een leven in strijd om vrede, 1583-1645* (Amsterdam: Balans Publishers, 2007), pp. 25-64; C.M. Ridderikhoff, 'De Universitaire Studies van Hugo de Groot', Florike Egmond, 'Hugo de Groot en de Hoge Raad: Over Connecties Tussen Geleerden, Kunstenaars, Juristen en Politici' and Harm-Jan van Dam, 'Filoloog en dichter in Leiden', in *De Hollandse jaren van Hugo de Groot (1583-1621)*, ed. H.J.M. Nellen and J. Trapman (Hilversum: Verloren Publishers, 1996), pp. 13-44, resp. pp. 67-86.

marry Maria van Reigersbergh, daughter of the burgomaster of the port of Veere, nine months later. By all accounts, he was a devoted husband. He and his wife had eight children, only four of whom survived into adulthood. The marriage also brought Grotius important political connections in Zeeland. In 1613, he succeeded Oldenbarnevelt's elder brother as pensionary (legal adviser) of the town of Rotterdam, which deputed him to the States of Holland. Just four years later, he took his seat in the States General as a representative of his home province. The religious troubles that convulsed the United Provinces during the Twelve Years' Truce (1609-21) cut short Grotius's dazzling rise in Dutch politics. Maurice of Nassau, commander in chief of the Dutch army and navy, committed a coup d'état in the summer of 1618. The Stadtholder sided with the orthodox Calvinists against the so-called 'Remonstrants', followers of the Leiden theologian Arminius, who had emphasized the freedom of the will. According to Arminius, the elect could reject the salvation freely offered them by God. Although his followers were a minority in the Dutch Reformed Church, they enjoyed the support of the States of Holland, and, in particular, Oldenbarnevelt and Grotius. Arrested at Maurice's orders in August 1618, they were convicted of treason by the States General. Following Oldenbarnevelt's execution, Grotius was banished for life to the Dutch castle of Loevestein. Once he regained access to his books and papers, Grotius put his enforced leisure to good use. He prepared his *Introduction to Dutch Jurisprudence (Inleiding tot de Hollandsche rechts-geleertheyd)* and initiated his most famous work of legal scholarship, *On the Law of War and Peace* (*De iure belli ac pacis*), which appeared in Paris in 1625. His detention came to a dramatic end on 22 March 1621, when he escaped from Loevestein Castle in a book trunk. He spent most of the remainder of his life as an exile in Paris.[3]

Manuscript BPL 917 in Leiden University Library

Mare liberum was Grotius's first publication on natural law and natural rights theory, but it was by no means his only, or even his earliest, work on the subject. The extant manuscript of *Mare liberum* constitutes just one chapter of a much larger work, currently known as *De iure praedae (On the Law of Prize and Booty)*. It is designated in Grotius' correspondence as the treatise on Indian

[3] Nellen, *Hugo de Groot*, pp. 82-262; J.G. Smit, 'De Rotterdamse jaren van Hugo de Groot', A. Th. van Deursen, 'Oldenbarnevelt en Maurits', and H.J.M. Nellen, 'Een tweespan voor de arminiaanse wagen: Grotius and Wtenbogaert', in *De Hollandse jaren van Hugo de Groot*, ed. Nellen and Trapman, pp. 125-43, resp. pp. 155-77.

affairs, '*de rebus Indicis*' and '*indicas mea*'.[4] In addition, his working papers contain a number of spin-offs such as *Theses XI* and *Theses LVI*, which seek to justify the Dutch Revolt against Spain on the basis of just war and social contract theories. Leiden University acquired both sets of papers at an auction of Grotiana in November 1864, following the death of the jurist's last male descendant in the direct line. Four years later, Ms. BPL 917 was published as *De iure praedae*, the title which it still bears today. An English translation appeared in 1950 and was reprinted in 2006.[5]

The publication of *De iure praedae* in 1868 was accompanied by a seminal article by the Dutch historian Robert Fruin, who argued that *De iure praedae* was essentially a defense of Dutch privateering in the East Indies, particularly Jacob van Heemskerck's capture of the *Santa Catarina* in Singapore Straits in February 1603. Fruin surmised, correctly as it turned out, that it had been commissioned by the Amsterdam VOC directors. The publication of the *Briefwisseling*, the modern edition of Grotius's correspondence, confirmed that he had been in regular contact with VOC directors in Amsterdam, Rotterdam, and Middelburg (the capital of the province of Zeeland) and

---

[4] Grotius, *De Jure Praedae Commentarius*, ed. H.G. Hamaker (The Hague: Martinus Nijhoff, 1868) [= *IPC*]; Grotius, *Commentary on the Law of Prize and Booty*, 2 volumes, The Classics of International Law, no. 22 (Oxford: Clarendon Press, 1950) Vol. I: *A Translation of the Original Manuscript of 1604 by Gwladys L. Williams* and vol. II: *The Collotype Reproduction*, Grotius, *Commentary on the Law of Prize and Booty*, trans. by Gwladys L. Williams, ed. by Martine Julia van Ittersum (Indianapolis: Liberty Fund, 2006) [= *Commentary*]; Grotius, *Briefwisseling van Hugo Grotius*, ed. P.C. Molhuysen, B.L. Meulenbroek and H.J.M. Nellen, 17 vols. (The Hague, 1928-2001) [= BW], 1.72 and 7.583.
The construction '*indicas mea*' is grammatically incorrect. It should be '*indica mea*' or '*indicas meas* [*historias*]'. However, the words '*indicas mea*' are to be found on p. 864 of Hugo Grotius, *Epistolae quotquot reperiri potuerunt* ed.Hugo and Jan de Groot (Amsterdam, P & I Blaeu, 1687). Grotius's letter to Willem de Groot of 14 December 1636 is no longer extant. The modern edition of Grotius's correspondence reproduces this letter on the basis of the text of *Epistolae quotquot.*

[5] Peter Borschberg, *Grotius' "Commentarius in Theses XI": An Early Treatise on Sovereignty, the Just War, and the Legitimacy of the Dutch Revolt* (Berne: Peter Lang, 1994); idem, '*De Pace:* Ein unveröffentlichtes Fragment von Hugo Grotius über Krieg und Frieden', *Zeitschrift der Savigny-Stiftung für Rechtsgeschichte, Romanistische Abteilung*, 115 (1996), 268-92; idem, '*De Societate Publica cum Infidelibus*: Ein Frühwerk von Hugo Grotius', *Zeitschrift der Savigny-Stiftung für Rechtsgeschichte, Romanistische Abteilung*, 115 (1998), 355-93; idem, 'Grotius, the Social Contract and Political Resistance: A Study of the Unpublished Theses LVI', IILJ Working Paper 2006/7, History and Theory of International Law Series (www.iilj.org); *Catalogue de Manuscrits Autographes de Hugo Grotius*, 2nd ed., annot. by W.J.M van Eysinga and L.J. Noordhoff (The Hague: Martinus Nijhoff, 1952), p. 25; L.J. Noordhoff, *Beschrijving van het zich in Nederland bevindende en nog onbeschreven gedeelte der papieren afkomstig van Huig de Groot welke in 1864 te 's-Gravenhage zijn geveild* (Groningen: Noordhoff Publishers, 1953), pp. 7-19.

suggested that *De iure praedae* had been written between September 1604 and November 1606. A series of archival discoveries in the twentieth century revealed the true extent of his advocacy of Dutch expansion overseas. Grotius served as VOC spokesman during negotiations with the English East India Company in 1613 and 1615, for instance. On these and other occasions, he did not just defend the Company's existing policies; he also helped the directors develop new ones. For example, Grotius advised them in January 1608 on the forthcoming peace negotiations between the States General and Philip III of Spain and Portugal. It was in the directors' own interest to keep him abreast of developments in the East Indies, where they sought to gain control of the Spice Islands and disrupt Portuguese trade and shipping.[6]

De iure praedae exemplifies the close collaboration between Grotius and the Amsterdam VOC directors. Chapter 11 is an account of the early Dutch voyages to Southeast Asia, based almost entirely on the materials the directors put at his disposal. In October 1604, they sent Grotius a 'book treating of the cruel, treasonous and hostile procedures of the Portuguese in the East Indies': fifteen notarized attestations of Dutch merchants and mariners, drawn up at the Company's behest. Grotius could not have written chapter 11 of *De iure praedae* without it. Other parts of his argument relied in equal measure on information obtained from the directors of the Amsterdam Chamber of the VOC.[7] A similar level of cooperation between Grotius and their counterparts in Middelburg facilitated the publication of *Mare liberum* five years later.

It is important to know something about the structure of Grotius' argument in *De iure praedae* in order to understand why chapter 12 was selected for publication, and the changes made in the text in November and December 1608. *De iure praedae* consists of three parts of unequal length, an arrangement that owes much to Grotius' liberal arts education. It is an attempt, albeit a flawed one, to adhere to Ciceronian guidelines for forensic oratory, which

---

[6] Robert Fruin, 'Een onuitgegeven werk van Hugo de Groot', in *Robert Fruin's Verspreide Geschriften,* ed. by P.J. Blok, P.L. Muller, and S. Muller, 8 vols. (The Hague: Martinus Nijhoff, 1901), III, pp. 367-445, translated into English as 'An Unpublished Work of Hugo Grotius', *Bibliotheca Visseriana,* 5 (1925), 3-71; BW, 1.44-45, 72, and 17.37, 63-66; P.C. Molhuysen, 'Over Grotius' '*De Jure Praedae Commentarius*', *Bijdragen voor Vaderlandsche Geschiedenis en Oudheidkunde,* 6th ser., 4 (1926), 275-82; W.J.M. van Eysinga, 'Quelques observations au sujet du Mare Liberum et du De Iure Praedae de Grotius', *Grotiana* 1st ser., 9 (1941-42), 61-75, especially 72-75; Van Ittersum, 'Hugo Grotius in Context: Van Heemskerck's Capture of the *Santa Catarina* and Its Justification in *De Jure Praedae* (1604-1606)', *Asian Journal of Social Science* 31 (2003), 511-48, Van Ittersum, *Profit and Principle,* 1-104, 217-45, and 359-96.

[7] W. Ph. Coolhaas, 'Een bron van het historische gedeelte van Hugo de Groot's *De Jure Praedae*', *Bijdragen en Mededelingen van het Historisch Genootschap,* 79 (1965), 415-540; *Commentary,* pp. xiii-xxi, 497-556.

requires an examination of the legal principles involved, followed by a narrative account of relevant 'facts', and, finally, a concluding analysis that applies theory to practice. The so-called '*dogmatica de jure praedae*' ('the dogmas relating to the law of prize and booty') are discussed in chapters 2 through 10. The right of self-defence forms the basis of a complex set of legal and philosophical principles, the purpose of which is to distinguish between just and unjust wars. Chapter 11 comprises the second strand of Grotius's argument, which presents the 'facts' of the case, or rather, his selection thereof. Significantly, he wrote '*sequitur historica*' ('here follows the historical account') above the chapter number. It details the hostility that the Portuguese showed to Dutch merchants and their Asian trading partners in the period 1595-1602. In the third part of *De iure praedae*, chapters 12 to 15, these 'facts' are examined with reference to the legal principles expounded in chapters 2 through 10. Grotius jotted down the words '*sequuntur examen*' ('here follows an analytical discussion') at the top of the first folio of chapter 12.[8]

A further subdivision was made at this point: chapters 12 to 15 of *De iure praedae* constituted a tripartite argument, along the lines of Cicero's *On Duties (De Officiis)*. In order to meet Cicero's criteria for moral action, Grotius intended to prove that the capture of the *Santa Catarina* had been just, honourable and beneficial. It was his contention in chapters 12 and 13 that the capture of the *Santa Catarina* had been an act of justice. The hostilities in the East Indies were conceptualized as a private war, in chapter 12, and a public war, in chapter 13. Since the Portuguese denied them freedom of trade and navigation, his compatriots had every right, so Grotius argued in chapter 12, to exact collective punishment for this flagrant transgression of natural law. Jacob van Heemskerck did not need authorization from anybody to take the *Santa Catarina*: natural law allowed him to conduct a private war, acting as judge and executioner in his own cause. As it happened, all VOC commanders were granted commissions by Prince Maurice, Lord High-Admiral of the United Provinces, making them agents of the Dutch state. Grotius claimed in chapter 13 that, by virtue of these commissions, they could legitimately seize Portuguese merchantmen as an act of public war. In support of this he cited the States General's decree of April 1599, which imposed an embargo on all trade with the enemy and explicitly endorsed indiscriminate attacks on Iberian shipping. The United Provinces was, after all, fighting a war of independence against the King of Spain and Portugal. Finally, Grotius emphasized in chapters

[8] Leiden University Library, Ms. BPL 917, fol. 5r, 72r, 96r; *Commentary*, pp. 18, 243, 300, 499-500; Van Ittersum, 'Hugo Grotius in Context', p. 512.

14 and 15 that Dutch privateering in the East Indies was both honourable and beneficial. Maritime victories over the Spanish and Portuguese redounded to the honour of the Dutch Republic and increased its standing in international politics. Rich prizes like the *Santa Catarina*, worth three million Dutch guilders (£300,000), were not just a windfall for the VOC, but also benefited the war effort of the fledgling state. All booty landed in Dutch harbours was subject to a 20 percent levy, collected by the Dutch Admiralty Board, which used these and other tax revenues to fund the naval war against Philip III of Spain and Portugal. According to Grotius, Dutch privateering in the East Indies was a win-win situation all around. In his peroration, he called on Dutch merchants and magistrates to work together for the common good, namely the independence and security of the United Provinces.[9]

The Political Context of *Mare liberum*

De iure praedae was never published during Grotius's own lifetime because its justification of naval warfare in the East Indies held no attractions for the political elite of the Dutch Republic in the context of the peace and truce negotiations of 1608-1609. Grotius informed George Lingelsheim in November 1606 that he had completed the work. Five months later, the States General agreed to an armistice in Europe. Although *De iure praedae* had been superseded by political events, the VOC directors did not dispense with Grotius's services as political lobbyist and legal adviser. In January 1608, he supplied them with an important policy document that outlined the possible consequences of the peace negotiations for the VOC. His analysis of the situation suggested that it would be very difficult, if not impossible, for the States General to sacrifice the VOC for the sake of peace. In his view, a peace treaty should either guarantee freedom of trade and navigation in the East Indies or otherwise be strictly limited to Europe, allowing the war to continue elsewhere. The directors submitted his recommendations to the States General, which took them to heart. Throughout the month of March, the representatives of Philip III were lectured on freedom of trade and navigation and they finally agreed to a compromise on the Indies trade, which postponed a final settlement for ten years and effectively granted the VOC a free hand in

[9] *Commentary*, pp. 300-497; Van Ittersum, 'Hugo Grotius in Context', pp. 535-41; Tuck, *The Rights of War and Peace,* 78-94; Borschberg, *Grotius' "Commentarius in Theses XI"*, pp. 268-283; Victor Enthoven, *Zeeland en de opkomst van de Republiek: Handel en Strijd in de Scheldedelta, ca. 1550-1621* (Leiden: 1996), pp. 173-213.

monsoon Asia. The Spanish monarch rejected this compromise as soon as it reached him in June 1608 and the peace talks collapsed two months later.[10]

There was no return to outright war, however. Both parties lacked the financial means to continue fighting. Pierre Jeannin, the envoy of Henry IV of France, took it upon him to arrange a 'truce of many years' instead. He was supported in his efforts by Oldenbarnevelt. Yet realizing that a truce treaty would reduce the size of the armed forces, his most important source of power and patronage, Prince Maurice objected to any kind of negotiations with the enemy and wanted to resume hostilities as soon as possible. His opposition caused great political upheavals in Holland and Zeeland in the autumn of 1608. Indeed, he had so much influence in the States of Zeeland – he controlled three of the seven votes – that it continued to drag its feet until January 1609, when it finally bowed to the arguments of Oldenbarnevelt and Jeannin. In the midst of these difficult deliberations, the Zeeland VOC directors (many of whom were also members of the provincial assembly) decided to contact Grotius about the publication of what became *Mare liberum*. The course of events can be reconstructed on the basis of Grotius' correspondence, primarily the letters which he exchanged with his close friends Daniel Heinsius and Johan Boreel, a lawyer in the Zeeland town of Middelburg and eldest son of VOC director Jacob Boreel.[11]

The Zeeland VOC directors commissioned Grotius to publish *Mare liberum* in their letter of 4 November 1608. It was imperative, so they wrote, that 'the right of navigation – which is competent to the Dutch nation over the whole wide world – [be] thoroughly examined and adduced with rational as well as legal arguments'. They were pleased to learn from Johan Boreel that Grotius had already 'prepared all the material on this topic'. A strong sense of urgency pervaded their letter. The pamphlet's publication was not just opportune, but absolutely necessary 'because of the peace and truce negotiations'. The King of Spain desired a treaty for no other reason than to undo the Company's trade, along with its 'conquests and alliances'. The directors counted on Grotius to 'persuade both our government and neighbouring princes to staunchly defend our, as well as the nation's, rights'. He should literally rush into print, in order that the Company might 'enjoy the benefit during the negotiations'.[12] The would-be pamphleteer needed little persuasion.

---

[10] BW, 1.72; Commentary, p. 552; Van Ittersum, *Profit and Principle*, pp. 105-282.

[11] Idem, pp. 283-342.

[12] BW, 1.128-29 (Zeeland VOC directors to Grotius, 4 Nov. 1608 and Grotius to G.M. Lingelsheim, 4 Dec. 1608), and 17.41-42 (Johan Boreel to Grotius, 6 Nov. and 13 Dec. 1608).

Oldenbarnevelt had different priorities, however. As the truce negotiations entered their final stage, he told his protégé in no uncertain terms to postpone the pamphlet's appearance in print. Grotius immediately wrote to Heinsius, who had undertaken to oversee *Mare liberum*'s publication. Although disappointed, he admitted in his letter of 7 March 1609 that he could see why Oldenbarnevelt did not want to take any risks. The truce negotiations had reached a critical juncture, when 'all such things must be avoided which may offend the minds of the parties'. Yet he assured Heinsius that their labours had not been in vain. Presentation copies were still needed for immediate distribution among 'men endowed with judgment and well affected to the fatherland', meaning Jeannin and other foreign envoys in The Hague, who represented the allies of the Dutch Republic. The pamphlet could also be sent to the Frankfurt Book Fair (*Frankfurter Messe*), 'lest the printer complains loudly of his loss'. The spring catalogue of 1609 does indeed contain an entry for *Mare liberum,* listed, significantly, under 'historical, political and geographical books'. Yet its publication in the Low Countries had to await the Twelve Years' Truce, signed at Antwerp on 9 April. *Mare liberum* appeared one or two weeks later. Even so, the publisher took the precaution of issuing it without the author's name on the cover.[13]

The Printing History of *Mare liberum*

Grotius's correspondence with Heinsius is fundamental to our knowledge of the printing history of *Mare liberum.* The author informed Heinsius on 23 November 1608 that, in accordance with the wishes of the Zeeland VOC

---

[13] *Mare Liberum Sive De Iure Quod Batavis Competit ad Indicana Commercia Dissertatio* (s.n., Leiden: Elzevier Publishers, 1609); BW, 1.141, 144-45 (Grotius to Heinsius, 7 Mar. 1609 and Apr. 1609); *Catalogus Universalis Pro Nundinis Francofurtensibus Vernalisbus,* De Anno MDCIX (Frankfurt: 1609), fol. C3v; Bibliographie des écrits imprimés de Hugo Grotius, ed. by Jacob ter Meulen and P.J.J. Diermanse (The Hague: Martinus Nijhoff, 1950, reprinted Zutphen: Matthys de Jongh, 1995) [= TMD], p. 211; Nellen, *Hugo de Groot,* pp. 94-97; Van Ittersum, *Profit and Principle,* pp. 283-358.

Mare liberum found itself in good company at the Frankfurt Book Fair of spring 1609. The titles listed right above and underneath it in the catalogue include John Selden's *Analecton Anglobrittanicon* (1607) and a contemporary history by Jacques Auguste de Thou ('Jacobi Augusti Thuani historiarum sui temporis libri 125. Lutetiae apud Hier. Drovart in 12').

Of all contemporary historians, De Thou was the one whom Grotius admired most and sought to emulate in his capacity as 'historiographer of Holland'. See Jan Waszink, 'Tacitisme in Holland: de Annales et Historiae de rebus Belgicis van Hugo de Groot', *De Zeventiende Eeuw,* 20 (2004), 240-63.

directors, he worked tirelessly for a 'quick publication'. A new introduction and conclusion were required for chapter 12 of *De iure praedae*, not to mention the fact that the text had to be revised in significant ways. Meanwhile, it took Heinsius quite a while to find a publisher for the pamphlet in Leiden. Although Elzevier finally agreed to do it, the actual printing was subcontracted to another Leiden stationer, J. Balduinus. In his letter of 18 December, Grotius complained loudly about the 'neglect and idleness of the printer', who refused to fix a date for the first printing or even to guarantee a publication before February. There was little Grotius could do about it: 'sudden business' prevented the ever-busy solicitor general from visiting Leiden in early December, while the illness of his young wife demanded his presence in Zeeland later that month. He had to wait until the New Year until he could examine the first page-proofs. On 11 January 1609, he informed Heinsius that he was pleased with the typeface and the 'format of the little book', although he objected to the 'ugly paper'. Further delays in the printing process, which he blamed on 'these gain-seekers' (that is, Elzeviers and Balduinus), remained a sore point for him. Yet the would-be pamphleteer was just as guilty of procrastination himself. It was not until 18 February that he finally got round to sending Heinsius the preface and appendix of *Mare liberum*. Two weeks later, the printing was put on hold at Oldenbarnevelt's behest.[14]

The printing history of *Mare liberum* left many traces in manuscript BPL 917, which have received little attention in the scholarly literature. For example, Grotius's line-count on fols 96v-116r, 117v-118v suggests that a scribal copy was prepared for the publishers, which must have been thrown away once the printing process was complete, a standard procedure in the seventeenth century. Normally, an author did not retain a manuscript copy either: the printed book was seen as effectively replacing whatever came before. The autograph of *Mare liberum* has survived for the simple reason that it is not a self-contained piece of writing, but forms part of a much larger manuscript that, crucially, remained unpublished in Grotius' own lifetime.

Grotius's line-count on fols 96v-116r, 117v-118v of manuscript BPL 917 and his calculations on fol. 121v testify to the fact that he sought to ensure a 'quick publication'. The revised text of chapter 12 of *De iure praedae* was copied out at least once. Although Grotius could have done this himself,[15] it is

---

[14] BW, 1.129-34, 139 (Grotius to Heinsius, 23 & 27 Nov. 1608, 5, 11 & 26 Dec. 1608, 5 & 11 Jan. 1609, 18 Feb. 1609); Nellen, *Hugo de Groot*, pp. 94-97; *TMD*, p. 211.

[15] As Jan Waszink argues elsewhere in this conference volume, Ms. BPL 917 was at one point a fair copy, written out by Grotius himself. In most cases, Grotius left it to others to prepare scribal copies of his treatises. Compare Hugo Grotius, *Meletius sive De iis quae inter Christianos*

far more likely that he assigned this task to one of the clerks whom he employed in his capacity as solicitor general. The scribal copy would have enabled two compositors to work on *Mare liberum* simultaneously, one setting up the type for the first half of the text, the other doing the same for the second half. In order to facilitate such a procedure, Grotius had to determine the middle point of the text beforehand. This was the purpose of his line-count on fols 96v-116r, 117v-118v and his calculations on fol. 121v. Grotius counted the number of lines of text that would make up *Mare liberum* and included in his calculations the new conclusion on fol. 117r-118v, an inserted bifolium.[16] With the exception of fol. 116v, he put numbers in the bottom left corners on fols 96v-118v, which more or less correspond with the number of text-lines on each folio-page. Grotius sought to add them up by arranging them in three columns at the top of fol. 121v, which he treated as a piece of scrap paper. (He had previously crossed out fols 119r-122r, thus indicating to the copyist that this part of the text should be omitted from *Mare liberum*.) The calculations on fol. 121v, which do not inspire much confidence in his numerical abilities, are reproduced in appendix 1. The middle point of the text was allegedly on fol. 107v, between lines three and four from the top. Grotius put a horizontal line in the margin and repeated three words from the text – '*nisi ivissent eo*' – in the bottom left corner of fol. 107v.[17] It is entirely conceivable, however, that the printer redid the calculations when he received the scribal copy. Although chapters 1 to 13 of *Mare liberum* cover sixty-six pages in the pamphlet's first edition, the words '*nisi ivissent eo*' are found on page 34, eleven lines from the bottom, not on page 33, the real midpoint of the text.[18]

---

conveniunt Epistola, ed. and tr. by G.H.M. Posthumus Meyjes (Leiden: Brill, 1988), pp. 7-8; Grotius, *Ordinum Hollandiae ac Westfrisiae Pietas (1613), Critical Edition,* tr. and ed. by Edwin Rabbie (Leiden: Brill, 1995), pp. 46-52; Grotius, *De Imperio Summarum Potestatum Circa Sacra,* ed. and tr. by Harm-Jan van Dam, 2 vols (Leiden: Brill, 2001), I, 46-50, 55-58; Jan Waszink, 'Hugo Grotius' *Annales et Historiae de Rebus Belgicis* from the Evidence In His Correspondence, 1604-1644', *LIAS* 31 (2004), 249-67 (pp. 253-54).

[16] A folio is a sheet folded once, which gives you four sides (17r, 17v, 18r, 18v).

[17] Philip Gaskell, *A New Introduction to Bibliography* (Oxford: Oxford University Press, 1972), 40-56; BPL 917 fol. 96v-116r and 117r-118v, 121v; see also appendix 1.

On fol. 107v, Grotius also put a horizontal line in the margin next to lines 3-4 from the top. The author of *Mare liberum* erred by a wide margin in his efforts to determine the midpoint of the text. So much is clear from his calculations on fol. 121v. The modern editor of Grotius's correspondence, Dr Henk Nellen, confirms that the author of *Mare liberum* was numerically challenged. It was Dr. Nellen, in fact, who suggested to me that the numbers in the left bottom corner of fols 96v-116r and 117r-118v represented line-numbers, not folio-numbers.

[18] *ML*, p. 34; appendix 1 below.

Revising Chapter 12 of *De iure praedae* for Publication (1)

Although chapter 12 of *De iure praedae* formed the basis of *Mare liberum*, it could not be published as it stood. In the context of the truce negotiations, it made no sense to retain those parts that specifically referred to Van Heemskerck's capture of the *Santa Catarina* or, more generally, to the VOC's sustained attempts to dislodge the Portuguese from the East Indies. Grotius also decided to play down a key tenet of *De iure praedae*, namely that of an individual's right to punish transgressions of the natural law. In his view, a company of private merchants like the VOC could exact damages for injuries sustained from every subject of Philip III, whether merchant or soldier. Crucially, Grotius's notion of what constituted an injury was very expansive. Besides the loss of life and possessions, it included the violation of natural rights, such as freedom of trade and navigation. The seriousness of this 'crime' required a hard-hitting Dutch privateering campaign in the East Indies, if only to collect adequate reparations. In the latter half of chapter 12 of *De iure praedae*, the capture of the *Santa Catarina* is justified in the following manner:

> it is just that an amount should have been taken from the Portuguese, sufficient to provide an additional reserve fund for future warfare, since the injury has not been wiped out, the peril has not ceased and the struggle increases in severity. Thus we find, not only that the warlike act in question did not pass beyond the limits of the right contested, but that it even stopped far short of those limits.[19]

This kind of brazen warmongering is absent from *Mare liberum*. Grotius sensibly omitted the second half of chapter 12 of *De iure praedae*, a total of 9½ folios. He literally had no choice. The Zeeland VOC directors had commissioned *Mare liberum* in order to influence the truce negotiations in the Company's favour and to obtain more guarantees for peaceful trade, either from Philip III or the States General. Any suggestion that it was business-as-usual for the VOC would defeat the purpose. No wonder, then, that Grotius only hinted at his just war theories in the conclusion of *Mare liberum*, which he wrote in December 1608:

> a good man judging it would adjudge liberty of merchandise unto the Hollanders and would forbid the Portugals and others who hinder that liberty to do any violence, and would command them to restore their losses. But that which should be obtained in judgment, where justice could not be had by just war should be revenged.... Wherefore he that shall stop the passage and hinder the carrying out

[19] Leiden University Library, Ms. BPL 917, fol. 124v; *Commentary*, pp. 381-82.

> of merchandise may be resisted by way of fact, as they say, even without expecting any public authority.[20]

The warlike implications of Grotius's plea for freedom of trade and navigation were toned down in other ways as well. He realized that in the context of the truce negotiations he could not get away with contesting Spanish claims to the New World, or even so much as mention the Americas. 'For example, an inserted text block which, citing the papal bull *Inter Caetera* of 4 May 1493, explicitly recognized the Spanish discovery of the sea-route to the Caribbean was deleted at the bottom of f. 106v'.[21] Other references to the New World were removed from the running text as well. In order to undermine the Portuguese claim to the East Indies, Grotius contested their title of discovery on fol. 98r. He pointed out that Europe's trading contacts with the Orient dated to Classical Antiquity. So how could the Portuguese claim to 'have discovered India'? 'For what applies to the Americas, does not apply to India'. (*alia enim Indiae, alia Americae ratio est*). This eye-catching juxtaposition of the Old World and the New is not to be found in *Mare liberum*. Its author also changed his mind about an explicit allusion which he had made to the theological disputes in sixteenth-century Spain about the status of the Amerindians. He had maintained on fol. 100r that, far from being subjects of the Portuguese, the natives peoples of Asia remained 'free and in their own power' (*sui juris*) according to the 'very Spanish doctors themselves when they discuss the American Indians' (*cum de Americanis disputent*). Those last four words, still visible on fol. 100r, were omitted from *Mare liberum*. Grotius inserted a new chapter break instead.[22]

---

[20] *The Free Sea,* pp. 59-60.

[21] *The Free Sea*, 35; *Commentary*, pp. 334-35; *ML*, p. 32; Leiden University Library, Ms. BPL 917, fol. 106v. The deleted insertion at the bottom of fol. 106v reads as follows:

> [in margin: Dato 4 Non. [crossed out: Cal.] Maii 1493] *atque adeo ut plerisque aliis ita & hac ratione multo est speciosior Castellanorum causa, qui Americam petiverunt, quantum sciri potest nunquam antea* [crossed out: *cognito*] *tentato itinere. Unde et in ipso pontificis diplomate diserte exprimitur DE MARI NUNQUAM NAVIGATO ET INSULIS INCOGNITIS* [crossed out: *unde colligit*] *additque Pontifex nemini se ius quaesitum auferre, quod hic dici non potest.*

Dr. Nellen and Dr. Visser were kind enough to correct my transcription.

[22] Leiden University Library, Ms. BPL 917, fol. 98r (I owe this reference to David Armitage) and 100r; *Commentary*, pp. 306-307, 314; *The Free Sea*, 14, 20; *ML*, pp. 6, 13.

The argument of *Mare liberum* was certainly strengthened by Grotius's decision to omit a direct comparison between the Spanish discovery of the New World and Europe's longstanding trading contacts with monsoon Asia. By obfuscating a real difference between the West and East Indies, Grotius could argue – as he did in the case of the ship *Swimming Lion* ('*Zwemmende*

Grotius's rights theories were not given much prominence in *Mare liberum* either. He had contended on fol. 116v of *De iure praedae* that the violation of natural rights was a sufficient cause for war. According to the fourteenth-century jurist Baldus de Ubaldis, 'it is proper for me to attack the person who prohibits me from exercising my right'. Yet in November/December 1608 he deleted not just this sentence but the entire bottom half of fol. 116v. In consequence, the close connection between his rights theories and his plea for freedom of trade and navigation was lost to the readers of *Mare liberum*.[23]

Not every textual revision in chapter 12 of *De iure praedae* was made with the high drama of the truce negotiations in mind. The first half of the chapter comprises many small corrections, Grotius putting in a few words here and there. On fol. 104v, he replaced *in quo haud* in the running text with *nec forte*, for instance. He similarly substituted *competit* for *fuit* in the running text of fol. 105r. Minor changes like these may not be crucial for our understanding of *Mare liberum*, but they do provide important information about the writing and rewriting of *De iure praedae*.[24]

Dating Textual Revisions in *De iure praedae*

Grotius's revisions in the first half of chapter 12 can be dated quite precisely on the basis of ink-colour, in combination with evidence from his correspondence. For example, Grotius dipped his quill in a pale grey-brown ink in order to add text lines at the top of fols 96v, 101v-102r, and 114v.[25] With the same

Leeuw') – that freedom of trade and navigation applied everywhere. See the previous footnote and my 'Mare Liberum in the West Indies? Hugo Grotius and the Case of the Swimming Lion, a Dutch Pirate in the Caribbean at the Turn of the Seventeenth Century', *Itinerario*, 31 (2007), 59-94.

It is suggestive that Grotius drew a line, indicating a chapter break, right after the deleted words '*cum de Americanis disputent*' on fol. 100r of Ms. BPL 917 (lines 1-2 from the bottom). He must have deleted textual references to the Americas at the same time that he inserted new chapter divisions.

[23] Leiden University Library, Ms. BPL 917, fol. 116v; *Commentary*, p. 363; Straumann, *Hugo Grotius und die Antike*, 60, footnote 191; Van Ittersum, *Profit and Principle*, 387-88.

[24] Leiden University Library, Ms. BPL 917, 104v, 105r.

[25] The pale grey-brown ink is clearly visible at the top of fol. 114v of Ms. BPL 917 in the Leiden University Library:

> —'*Unde navium exercitionem ad summam rempublicam pertinere dicit Ulpianus: institorum non eundem esse usum. Quia illa omnino…*'. (*ML*, p. 54; compare *The Free Sea*, 51: 'Whereupon Ulpian saith that taking of money for freight of shipping appertaineth to the highest and greatest commonwealth'.)

ink, he made small corrections, mostly in the running text, on fols 104r-105v, 110v, and 113r-v.[26] There is reason to assume that all these corrections stem from the period November-December 1608. For the new chapter divisions on fols 97v, 98v, 99r, 100r-v, 108r-v, 113v, and 115r, and the conclusion of *Mare liberum* on fols 117v-118v were also written with pale grey-brown ink. As noted earlier, the Zeeland VOC directors commissioned the pamphlet in their letter of 4 November 1608. Since Grotius received page-proofs at the beginning of January, he must have provided the printer with a scribal copy of the revised text in middle or late December. The fact that the pale grey-brown ink is found only in the first half of chapter 12, and nowhere else in the manuscript, confirms that Grotius used this particular ink in November/December 1608 to prepare the text for publication.

The insert at the top of fol. 107r is written in a garish orange-yellowish ink, which appears in other parts of the manuscripts. Grotius used this ink for minor corrections and additions on fols 3r, 5v, 39v, 40v, 53a, 61r, 139v and 140r, for example.[27] With the same ink, he reformulated the laws of

—'*Seneca: quae emeris, vendere gentium jus est*'. (*ML*, p. 54; compare *The Free Sea*, 51: 'Seneca saith, "the law of nations warranteth thee to sell that which thou has bought"'.)

Grotius used the same ink to add text at the top of 96v (compare *The Free Sea*, 10: 'Our purpose is shortly ... God himself speaketh this in nature') and fol.101v-102r (compare *The Free Sea*, 23-24: 'and the philosopher, "All things pertaining to the Horsemen belonged to the gentlemen of Rome, yet amongst them is my proper place which I possessed"', and 'Seneca saith, "we call those the bounds of the Athenians or Campanians which afterward the borderers divide among themselves by private bounds"'). The pale grey-brown ink is also found in the left margins of fol. 100v and 116v (compare *The Free Sea*, 56: 'Ambrose inveigheth against ... enhanceth the price of victuals').

I will publish a separate article on the Seneca quotations inserted in Ms. BPL 917. See my '"The Wise Man is never merely a Private Citizen": The Roman Stoa in Hugo Grotius' *De Jure Praedae* (1604-1608)', proceedings of the international conference on 'Cosmopolitan Politics: On the History and Future of a Controversial Ideal', held at the Johann Wolfgang Goethe University in Frankfurt-am-Main, Germany, 6-8 December 2006, forthcoming.

[26] Leiden University Library, Ms. BPL 917, fols 104r ('*eruditiores*' and '*proprie*'), fol. 104v ('*forte*') and 105r ('*competit*'), 105v ('*de*' and '*perit*'), 110v ('*explicata est*' and '*supra*'), 113r-v ('*ne omnes*', '*sit*', '*Lusitani*', '*negotiatione suppleri id quod natura deest quo*' and '*id ita intelligi potest*').

[27] Leiden University Library, Ms. BPL 917, fols 3r, 5v, 39v, 40v, 53a, 61r, 107r, 139v and 140r. The garish orange-yellowish ink of the insertion at the top of fol. 107r is also found on 3r (correction of insert at the top, viz. '*quatenus ius fasque est*'), 5a-r ('*oleo*'), 5v (insert completely at bottom, starting with the words '*Et quem modo*' + correction of insert at top, starting with the words '*Ac incrito primi principii*'), 39v (insert at top of page, starting with the words '*Quin et in sacra historia*'), 40v ('*videtur*', correction in the first line of the running text), 53a ('*unde apparet dominium bis esse translatum*'), 61r (Livy insert at bottom '*Indicat hoc Scipio*'), 139v ('*machinarum*'), 140r ('*cui rubio*').

self-defence and self-preservation on fol. 6r. The passage in question is reproduced here. Deletions are indicated by bold type, while square brackets are used for insertions:

> *Prior VITAM TUE***NDAM***[RI] ET DECLINA* **NDA***[RE]* **QUAE** *NOCITURA LICEAT. Altera: ADIUNGE***NDA** *[RE] SIBI QUAE AD VIVENDUM SUNT* **NECESSARIA; concessum enim est, ut inquit Tullius** *[UTILIA EAQUE RETINE***NDA***RE LICEAT: quod quidem cum Tullio ita interpretabimur]*[28]

It should be noted that Grotius revised the law of self-preservation twice. He first added '*utilia eaque retinenda*', and then changed it, using orange-yellowish ink, into '*retinere liceat; quod quidem cum Tullio ita interpretabimur.*' He then proceeded to delete the Sophocles quotation right underneath it.

It is possible to date Grotius's use of this orange-yellowish ink. Since the insert at the top of fol. 107r was included in *Mare liberum*, it must predate January 1609. The *post quem* date is less clear-cut. The insert at the top of fol. 107r was carefully written around a folio number which had previously been put in, and then amended, by Grotius himself ('98', a correction for '88'). The number is part of Grotius's initial foliation of the entire manuscript, which can be dated to January 1607 (at the latest) on the basis of watermark evidence. This suggests that Grotius used the orange-yellowish ink to reformulate parts of his argument sometime between January 1607 and January 1609. Can the revisions in orange-yellowish ink be dated even more precisely? Assuming that a supply of ink lasted for several weeks at most, the revisions in orange-yellowish ink may well stem from November/December 1608, when Grotius took up the manuscript again in order to revise chapter 12 for publication. At that point, he could easily have made changes in others parts of the text as well.[29]

The garish orange-yellowish ink found on fol. 5a-r, fol. 39v, 40v, and 53a can be used to date these inserted pieces of paper. Although not originally part of the manuscript, it suggests that Grotius added them *before* Nov.-Dec. 1608. After all, he could not revise what was not there in the first place.

[28] Leiden University Library, Ms. BPL 917 fol. 6r; *Commentary*, p. 23:

Accordingly, for this combination of concepts, two precepts of the law of nature emerge: first, that *It shall be permissible to defend one's own life and to shun that which threatens to prove injurious*; secondly, that *It shall be permissible to acquire for oneself, and to retain, those things which are useful for life.*

[29] Leiden University Library, Ms. BPL 917, fol. 107r.

Grotius's initial foliation of Ms. BPL 917 includes fol. 64, an inserted folio-page. The watermark of fol. 64 consists of a crest and Basle crozier. The same watermark occurs in Grotius's correspondence with Daniel Heinsius in January 1607 (Leiden University Library, Ms. BPG 77, letter 30). See also Theo and Frans Laurentius, *Watermarks 1600-1650, found in the Zeeland Archives* ('t Goy-Houten, The Netherlands: HES & GRAAF Publishers, 2007) 22, 135 (watermarks no. 296 and 297).

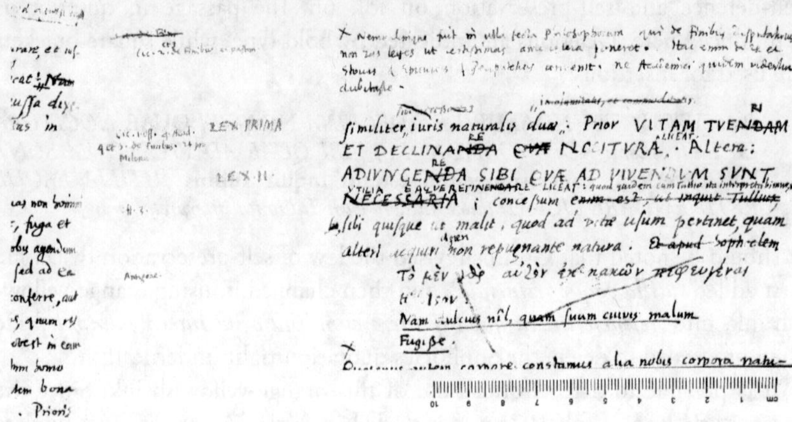

Illustration 1. Leiden, University Library, ms. BPL 917, fol. 6r. This and the other reproductions in this volume from the ms. of *De iure praedae* are printed with permission of Leiden University Library.

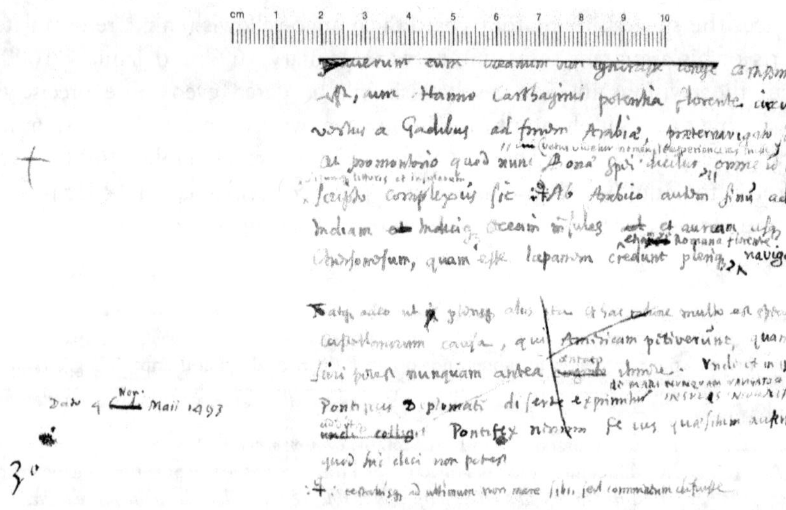

Illustration 2. Leiden, University Library, ms. BPL 917, fol. 106v.

I am preparing a study of Grotius's writing and rewriting of *De iure praedae* in the period 1604-1608, based on the watermarks, quire divisions and different sets of foliation found in manuscript BPL 917.

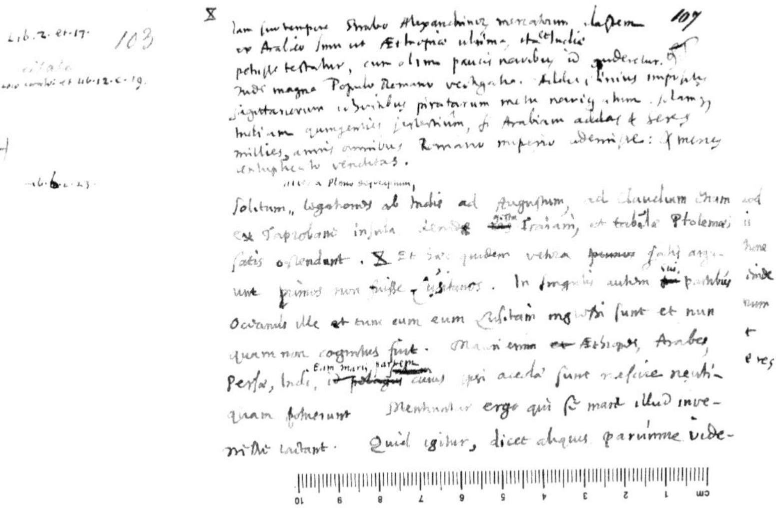

Illustration 3. Leiden, University Library, ms. BPL 917, fol. 107r.

Neither legal historians nor historians of political thought have considered the possibility that Grotius tinkered with the laws of self-defence and self-preservation at such a late stage in the game. Almost four years after first formulating them, Grotius may still have been concerned about 'getting it right'. Both laws formed the corner stones of his theory of the just war, after all. What is equally striking, however, is the rarity of any substantial changes in manuscript BPL 917 that can be dated as late as November/December 1608. By that point, Grotius had largely ceased to develop the argument of *De iure praedae*.[30]

[30] Straumann, *Hugo Grotius und die Antike*, 34-39; Tuck, *The Rights of War and Peace*, 79-94; Grotius, *The Rights of War and Peace,* 1.xix-xx; see also my '"The Wise Man is never merely a Private Citizen"', forthcoming.

A few scholars have remarked on differences in ink color as one notable characteristic of Grotius's marginal references in Ms. BPL 917. It suggests that the references were added in multiple sessions.

Compare Robert Fruin, 'An Unpublished Work of Hugo Grotius', *Bibliotheca Visseriana* 5 (1925), 40; J. Kosters, 'Het jus gentium van Hugo de Groot en diens voorgangers', *Mededeelingen der Nederlandsche Akademie van Wetenschappen, Afd. Letterkunde* 58B, no. 4 (1924), 87; Peter Haggenmacher, 'Genese et signification du concept de "ius gentium" chez Grotius', *Grotiana*, n.s., 2 (1981), 44-91; Tuck, *Philosophy and Government, 1572-1651* (Cambridge: Cambridge University Press, 1993), 171; Borschberg, 'Grotius, the Social Contract and Political Resistance: A Study of the Unpublished Theses LVI', 18-19 (see also Borschberg's contribution elsewhere in this conference volume).

Revising Chapter 12 of *De iure praedae* for Publication (2)

The autograph notes on fol. 117-118 of Ms. BPL 917 suggest that Grotius sought to make bigger changes in the first half of chapter 12 than eventually materialized. Fols 117-118, an inserted sheet of paper, do not just contain the conclusion of *Mare liberum*, written out by Grotius himself, but also an outline for the pamphlet's preface and a provisional table of contents. Arguably, the table of contents on fol. 118r predates Grotius' writing of the conclusion. When it had served its purpose, he crossed it out and drew a big line underneath it, which allowed him to write (part of) his conclusion underneath it. Appendix 2 reproduces the provisional table of contents, along with some of the notes which Grotius jotted down besides it. The footnotes of appendix 2 correlate the provisional table of contents with the chapter titles on fol. 96v-116v and in the pamphlet's first edition.[31]

It is instructive to compare the draft chapter titles of *Mare liberum* with the final version. Grotius was still concerned with softening the tone of chapter 12 of *De iure praedae* and adapting its argument to the realities of the truce negotiations. For example, the table of contents on fol. 118r suggests that he had the following title in mind for the second chapter of *Mare liberum*:

> [t]he Portuguese are not the overlords of the Indians to whom the Dutch sail; nor does any just title of ownership against the Dutch belong to the Portuguese[32]

In other words, the Portuguese had no dominion in the East Indies and therefore could not claim a monopoly of trade and navigation. Crucially, Grotius intended to disprove the Portuguese title of discovery under a separate heading – '*c. 2 Nec inventionis*'. When we turn to fol. 97v, we see that he did indeed write the word '*INVENIRE*', 'to discover', in capital letters halfway down the left margin of fol. 97v, and put a corresponding division mark in the running text. Yet he subsequently concluded that both Portuguese claims – to the title of lordship and the title of discovery – really added up to one and the same thing, and should be discussed together. He inserted a new chapter title at the top of fol. 97v, which was retained in the printed edition:

> [t]hat the Portugals have no right of dominion over those Indians to whom the Hollanders sail by title of invention[33]

[31] Leiden University Library, Ms. BPL 917, fols 96v-116v, 117-118; appendix 2.

[32] Leiden University Library Ms. BPL 917, fol. 118r; see also appendix 2.

[33] Leiden University Library Ms. BPL 917, fols 118r, 97v; *The Free Sea*, 13; see also appendix 2.

The title of chapter 8 of *Mare liberum* was also subject to an elaborate process of revision. The table of contents on fol. 118r seems to indicate that Grotius started with the idea that '[t]he right to trade with the Indians has not become the property of the Portuguese by virtue of occupation.' Although an important strand in his argument, the VOC lobbyist quickly realized that it was in the Company's interest to formulate this differently, turning a negative statement into a positive one. He crossed out what he had written on fol. 118r and replaced it with a more appealing chapter title: 'Likewise, the Dutch are free to trade with the Indians by virtue of the law of nations'. This did not mark the end of his thought process. For the sake of the truce negotiations, he continued to 'massage' the chapter title. What he inserted in the left margin of fol. 113v was different still: '[t]hat trading is free by the law of nations among all or between any'.[34] The parties involved in the truce negotiations would have found it hard to object to this seemingly innocuous statement of principle. It was retained as a chapter title in *Mare liberum*.

Grotius struggled hard to adapt his rhetorical style and conceptual apparatus to the new political situation. He did not always succeed on his first try. This much is clear from a discarded outline for the preface of *Mare liberum* found on fol. 117r. As noted earlier, Grotius wrote out the pamphlet's conclusion on fols 117v-118v. This left fol. 117r as an empty page. At some point, he decided to put it to good use by doing a bit of brainstorming. The discarded outline reveals that he had great difficulty 'letting go' of *De iure praedae*:

> Understand what the law conveys
>
> In the introduction something about the poisonings, perfidy and crimes of the Portuguese
>
> [Something] about the utility of commerce
>
> [Something] about the respectability and public dignity of distinguished persons
>
> [Something] about the favour of kings; about the military support given by states
>
> [Something] about the leagues with Indians; about maritime fortune; about the French and English[35]

---

[34] Leiden University Library Ms. BPL 917, fols 118r, 113v, see also appendix 2; *The Free Sea*, 49.

[35] Leiden University Library, Ms. BPL 917, fol. 117r:

> *Quid conferat, ius intellige*
> *In prefatione aliquid de veneficiis, perfidia*
> *& sceleribus Lusitanorum*
> *De utilitate commercij*

These points perfectly mimic the argument of *De iure praedae*, its second half in particular. Grotius must have had chapter 11 in mind when he jotted down the words 'something about the poisonings, perfidy and crimes of the Portuguese'. His musings about 'the utility of commerce' and 'the leagues with Indians' were a clear throw-back to chapters 14 and 15. In Grotius' view, Dutch trade and privateering in the East Indies fulfilled the Ciceronian criteria for moral action because it was just (chapters 12 and 13), honourable (chapter 14), and beneficial (chapter 15). On the last two counts, he contended that the war effort of the United Provinces was crucially dependent on VOC successes in trade and privateering, and that alliances with native rulers did not just confirm the country's de facto independence from Spain, but also increased its standing in international politics.[36] These concerns were still uppermost in his mind when he mulled over the preface of *Mare liberum* in January or February 1609.

There are also striking similarities between the discarded outline and Grotius's memorandum of January 1608 advising the VOC directors on the imminent peace negotiations between Philip III and the States General. Grotius admitted in his memorandum that, as long as shareholders were properly compensated, the States General could, in principle, sacrifice the VOC for the sake of peace. Yet he was confident that the federal authorities would not go down this route for two reasons. First, a revocation of the Company charter would entail the loss of an important strategic reserve of warships and battle-hardened crews paid for by private merchants. Should Philip III unexpectedly break the peace, how could the Dutch Republic defend itself against his naval forces without VOC assistance? It was a pertinent question to ask in January 1608, when, as any VOC director could have told Grotius, the Dutch Admiralty Board was on the verge of bankruptcy. Grotius also noted in his memorandum that a VOC withdrawal from monsoon Asia would leave its indigenous allies at the mercy of Iberian colonial officials. Without the VOC present, these officials should have no difficulty browbeating the natives into submission. This would not reflect well on the United Provinces. The Company had treated with the natives on behalf of the States General, and, in exchange

---

De honestate & decore publico praecipuorum
De favore regum: auxiliis publicis:
foederibus Indorum: fortuna maritima
[de?] Gallis & Anglis

Dr. Nellen and Dr. Visser kindly corrected my transcription. Dr. Visser helped me with the English translation as well.

36 Idem; Leiden University Library, Ms. BPL 917, fols 72r-163r; *Commentary*, pp. 243-497, 548-52; Van Ittersum, *Profit and Principle*, pp. 177-86, 224-44.

for trade concessions, had promised Asian rulers military and naval support against all enemies. If the federal authorities reneged on such promises for the sake of peace in Europe, Dutch merchants would find it impossible to return to the East Indies and resume trading there at a later point in time. They would not just face a resurgence of Habsburg power, but also the open hostility of native peoples, who would be unwilling to trust them again. Judging from the outline's references to 'the utility of commerce' and 'the leagues with Indians', the issues raised in Grotius' memorandum had lost none of their urgency a year later.[37]

The discarded outline is also proof that Grotius conceived of *Mare liberum* as a direct appeal to the States General and, abroad, Henry IV of France and James I of England. This should not be cause for surprise. When the Zeeland VOC directors commissioned the pamphlet, they expected Grotius to 'persuade both our government and neighbouring princes to staunchly defend our, as well as the nation's, rights'. These concerns are evident in the discarded outline. Grotius first intended to say something about the 'respectability and public dignity of distinguished persons', that is the regents who made up the States General, and then discuss 'the favour of kings', in particular 'the French and English [monarchs]'. The enthusiastic cooperation of the States General, while necessary, was not sufficient to obtain solid guarantees for the Company's trade and navigation. Grotius realized that he also had to win over Pierre Jeannin and Ralph Winwood, the French and English envoys, respectively, who jointly presided over the truce negotiations. Did he contemplate expressing the country's gratitude for 'the military support given by [neighbouring] states'? Henry IV of France and James I of England were the most important allies of the United Provinces. Without their support, the Dutch rebels could not hope to win the war against Philip III or outmanoeuvre him in the truce negotiations. Conversely, Grotius must have realized – as did other VOC pamphleteers – that their friendship involved a quid pro quo. Surely, it was the strategic reserve of VOC warships and battle-hardened crews which made the United Provinces a valuable ally for the French and English monarchs. Both rulers had an interest in safeguarding the Company's future. And so it turned out to be. The representatives of the Archdukes, who governed the Southern Netherlands on behalf of Philip III, were persuaded to sign a secret amendment that promised the VOC full access to Asian markets. In addition, the Treaties of Guarantee signed

[37] Dutch National Archives, Grotius Papers, Supplement I, fols 295-299 (first draft of Grotius's memorandum of January 1608) and fols 405-413 (second draft); Van Ittersum, *Profit and Principle*, pp. 224-44, 289-331.

by Jeannin and Winwood on 17 June 1609 stated explicitly that Henry IV of France and James I of England would regard any infringement of Dutch trade in the East Indies as a breach of the Twelve Years' Truce. They also recognized that the VOC had the right to continue the war in Asia, in case the treaty was not implemented there.[38] Ironically, the envoys needed no public encouragement from Grotius to do the Company's bidding. Nearly all references to the 'special relationship' between the States General and the French and English monarchs had been removed from the preface of *Mare liberum* by the time it reached Heinsius.

This was probably for the best. Had Grotius followed the outline on fol. 117r, *Mare liberum* might well have backfired on him and the VOC. The outline's sabre-rattling made it appear as if the Company could not accept the outcome of the truce negotiations. The VOC directors did not want to create this impression in the winter and spring 1609, when they tried to obtain as many guarantees for the Indies trade as they could. Nor would a pamphlet which needlessly antagonized Philip III have amused the French and English monarchs, who had made their own peace with Spain in 1598 and 1604, respectively, and who had invested a lot of political capital in the high-level talks in The Hague. Any mention of 'the poisonings, perfidy and crimes of the Portuguese' would not have endeared its author to Oldenbarnevelt either, who did his utmost to bring about a treaty. Even before a decision was taken to postpone *Mare liberum*'s publication, Grotius must have realized that a healthy dose of self-censorship was in order.

The preface which Grotius ended up writing for *Mare liberum* was tame and conventional by comparison. Few contemporaries would have taken umbrage at the fact that he equated natural law with right reason, 'engrafted in the minds of all'. This definition was taken straight from the teaching of the Stoics, as incorporated in Cicero's philosophical works. Grotius explicitly denied in the preface that natural law could be derived from 'the exposition of the Bible', an assertion which proved more problematical. William Welwood, professor of civil law at the University St. Andrews, criticized him for it in the *Abridgement*

---

[38] See footnote 32; *Commentary*, pp. 555-56; Van Ittersum, *Profit and Principle*, pp. 295-358, 360, 478-79; *Les Negotiations de monsieur le President Jeannin,* 4 vols. (Amsterdam: 1695), pp. 4.6-9, 11 (Jeannin's address to the States General, 18 Mar. 1609), p. 66 (articles 4 and 5 of the Twelve Years' Truce), p. 76 (secret addendum, signed by Spinola, Richardot, Mancicidor, Verreyken and Neyen, along with representatives of the States General), p. 161 (the Treaty of Guarantee's clause on Dutch trade in the East Indies, 17 June 1609).

Grotius was on good terms with Jeannin, to whom he dedicated his play *Christus Patiens* in March 1608. He frequently mentioned the French envoy in his correspondence. Compare BW, 1.97, 98-100, 103, 108, 110, 112, 117, 126, 128-130, 132, 135, 137, 142, 149.

of All Sea-Lawes (1615).[39] The right of punishment, which had been so prominent in *De iure praedae*, was carefully circumscribed in the preface of *Mare liberum*. The author made it appear as if the right of punishment belonged to sovereign rulers alone: 'the king of all the world [God] hath commanded you [sovereign rulers] to take notice and punish all other men's faults'.[40] He called upon the 'Princes and Free States of the Christian World' to decide the question in dispute between the Dutch and the Spanish:

> whether the huge and vast sea be the addition of one kingdom (and that not the greatest); whether it be lawful for any people to forbid people that are willing neither to sell, buy nor change nor yet to come together; and whether any man could ever give that which was never his or find that which was another's before, or whether the manifest injury of long time give any right.[41]

As if forty years of warfare in the Low Countries had been about nothing else but freedom of trade and navigation. Grotius cleverly suggested that he would argue his case on the basis of 'hostile evidence', citing 'those who among the Spaniards are the principal doctors of the divine and humane law'.[42]

---

[39] *The Free Sea*, pp. 8, 66-67; Straumann, *Hugo Grotius und die Antike*, p. 27; on the uses of Stoicism in *De iure praedae*, see also my '"The Wise Man is never merely a Private Citizen"', forthcoming; on the Grotius-Welwood debate, see my 'Mare Liberum versus The Propriety of the Seas?'.

[40] *The Free Sea*, p. 7.

[41] Ibid.

[42] Ibid.

Mare liberum is filled with references to sixteenth-century Spanish scholastics , particularly Francisco de Vitoria, Fernando Vázquez de Menchaca, and Diego de Covarruvias y Leyva. Various scholars have pointed out that Vitoria is the author most often cited in *De iure praedae* and *De iure belli ac pacis*, the total number of references being 123. The runners-up are Vázquez, quoted 103 times, and Covarrubias, cited 87 times. The Grotius Papers in Leiden University Library contain a sheet with Grotius's reading notes on the *Relectiones Theologicae XII*. Peter Borschberg considers these 'the most extensive excerpts of Vitoria that have survived'.

Both Richard Tuck and Benjamin Straumann contend that the Spanish scholastics were utterly unimportant for the development of Grotius's natural law and natural rights theories. Allegedly, Grotius could have written *De iure praedae* and *De iure belli ac pacis* on the basis of his knowledge of the classics alone. Neither of them seems to have given a moment's thought to the working practices of early modern scholars. Rhetorical conventions demanded that an author support his argument with references to the 'authorities', even if these were taken out of context and/or used for illustrative purposes only. Clusters of references were frequently copied from one book to the next, in fact. The *Relectiones* of Vitoria were an important source for marginal references for Grotius when he wrote *De iure praedae*. In order to uncover Grotius's intellectual sources, more research needs to be done on autograph annotations in the surviving books once owned by him. For example, the University of Lund possesses Grotius's edition of Thomas Aquinas's *Summa Theologiae,* 4 vols. (Lyon: 1581). It is quite clear from Grotius's underlining that he was more interested in Cajetan's commentary on Aquinas than in the *Summa Theologiae* itself.

Should these proofs be insufficient, then the Dutch would abide by the verdict of Henry IV of France and James I of England – at least, that was what Grotius wanted them to believe:

> If we demand any unjust thing, ye know of what account your authority and *theirs who amongst you are nearer unto us* [emphasis added] hath always been with us: advise us, and we will obey.[43]

What happened if the Spanish were found guilty of denying freedom of trade and navigation to everyone else? Grotius was confident that the French and English monarchs would side with the underdogs, his compatriots. Since the Dutch had accepted arbitration, they must be protected against sudden attack. Should the King of Spain of Portugal assault them regardless, then it was imperative to repulse his forces 'by the common aid, not as enemies of one, but of all'. This was as far as Grotius would go in the preface of *Mare liberum*. He refused to say what his compatriots would do if the French and English

---

Compare Straumann, *Hugo Grotius und die Antike*, 123 (particularly footnote 161); Borschberg, 'Grotius, the Social Contract and Political Resistance', 18-19, and 'Hugo Grotius' Theory of Trans-Oceanic Trade Regulation', 36-40; Ann Blair, 'Reading Strategies for Coping with Information Overload, ca. 1550-1700', *Journal of Intellectual History*, 64 (2003), 11-28; Annabel S. Brett, 'Natural Right and Civil Community: The Civil Philosophy of Hugo Grotius', *The Historical Journal*, 45 (2002), 31-51; Tuck, *The Rights of War and Peace*, p. 81; Brett, *Liberty, Right and Nature: Individual Rights in Later Scholastic Thought* (Cambridge: Cambridge University Press, 1997), pp. 165-204; Borschberg, *Hugo Grotius' 'Commentarius in Theses XI'*, pp. 48-52, 92-93; Antonio Truyol y Serra, 'Francisco de Vitoria Y Hugo Grocio', *Ciencia Tomista*, 111 (1984), 17-27; Robert Feenstra, 'Ius commune et droit comparé chez Grotius. Nouvelles remarques sur les sources citées dans ses ouvrages juridiques, à propos d'une réimpression du *De Iure Belli ac Pacis*', *Rivista internazionale di diritto commune*, 3 (1992), 7-36, reprinted in Feenstra, *Legal Scholarship and Doctrines of Private Law, 13th-18th Centuries* (Aldershot: 1996); idem, 'Quelques remarques sur les sources utilisées par Grotius dans ses travaux de droit naturel', in *The World of Hugo Grotius (1583-1645), Proceedings of the International Colloquium Organized by the Grotius Committee of the Royal Netherlands Academy of Arts and Sciences, Rotterdam, 6-9 April 1983* (Amsterdam: 1984), pp. 65-81; idem, 'Hugo de Groot's eerste beschouwingen over *dominium* en over de oorsprong van de private eigendom: *Mare Liberum* en zijn bronnen', *Acta Juridica* (= Essays in Honour of Ben Beinart, vol. 1) (1976), 269-75, published in French as 'Les origines du dominium d'après Grotius et notamment dans son Mare Liberum' in: *Homenaje al profesor Alfonso García-Gallo*, 5 vols. (Madrid: Universidad Complutense, 1996) I, 179-190, reprinted in Feenstra, *Histoire du droit savant, 13e-18e siècle* (Aldershot: Variorum, 2005); idem, 'L'Influence de la scolastique Espagnole sur Grotius en droit privé: quelques experiences dans des questions de fondet de forme, concernant notamment les doctrines de l'erreur et de l'enrichissement sans cause', in Feenstra, *Fata Iuris Romani: Etudes d'Histoire du Droit* (Leiden: Leiden University Press, 1974), pp. 338-63; Folke Dovring, *Une Partie de l'Héritage Littéraire de Grotius Retrouvée en Suède*, Mededelingen der Koninklijke Nederlandsche Akademie van Wetenschappen, Afdeling Letterkunde, n.s. 12, no. 3 (Amsterdam: 1949), pp. 237-49; Dovring, *Nouvelles Recherches sur la Bibliothèque de Grotius en Suède et en Italie*, Mededelingen der Koninklijke Nederlandsche Akademie van Wetenschappen, Afdeling Letterkunde, n.s., 14, no. 10 (Amsterdam: 1949), 331-38.

43 *The Free Sea*, 8.

monarchs refused to come to the rescue. Presumably, they would still have the right to defend themselves against attack. Yet Grotius never said this out loud. Instead, he expressed the pious hope that, 'things being well weighed', the readers of *Mare liberum* would recognize that the Dutch were no more to blame for 'the delays of peace' than for 'the causes of war'.[44]

As we know, the Twelve Years' Truce was signed at Antwerp on 9 April 1609 and ratified, rather reluctantly, by Philip III two months later. The Low Countries were spared the horrors of war until 1621. Yet the truce failed to take hold in the East Indies. The VOC continued to strengthen its position in the Spice Islands, at the expense of the Spanish and Portuguese and, later, the English. *Mare liberum* proved a perfect justification for this war-by-proxy, fought thousands of miles from Europe, nominally by a company of private merchants, in reality with substantial support from the States General.[45]

Conclusion

This article has reconstructed the printing history of *Mare liberum*, the political circumstances which first prompted its publication and then seemed to conspire against it, and the changes that Grotius made in chapter 12 of *De iure praedae* in order to accommodate Jeannin and Oldenbarnevelt, the driving forces behind the truce negotiations with Spain. When the Zeeland VOC directors commissioned *Mare liberum* in November 1608, the States of Zeeland were still unwilling to assent to a truce with Philip III, due largely to the recalcitrance of Prince Maurice, who controlled three of the seven votes in the assembly. As a protégé of Oldenbarnevelt, the author of *Mare liberum* had no intention of being bracketed together with Prince Maurice and the war party. He made a serious effort to tone down the bellicose rhetoric of chapter 12 of *De iure praedae*, erasing all references to Spanish claims to the Americas, for example. Time was of the essence, of course. As soon as Grotius had decided what he wanted to include in *Mare liberum*, he counted the number of text lines in order to determine the middle point of the treatise, and arranged for a scribal copy to be prepared for the printer. In consequence, two compositors could set up type simultaneously, thus expediting the printing process. The first page proofs reached Grotius at the beginning of January 1609. Yet *Mare liberum* appeared too late to influence the truce negotiations. In early

[44] Ibid., 9.
[45] Van Ittersum, *Profit and Principle*, pp. 283-483.

March, Oldenbarnevelt told Grotius in no uncertain terms to postpone its publication – 'all such things must be avoided which may offend the minds of the parties [involved in the talks]'. The VOC directors had no reason for complaint, however. Dutch colonial interests in Asia received official recognition in a secret amendment of the Twelve Years' Truce, signed by representatives of the Archdukes in April 1609, and in the Treaties of Guarantee, signed by the English and French ambassadors in June 1609.

While preparing chapter 12 for the press, Grotius revised his argument in other parts of *De iure praedae* as well, including the laws of self-defence and self-preservation in chapter 2. As noted by Richard Tuck, these two laws are crucial to Grotius's understanding of natural law and natural rights. When he reformulated the law of self-preservation in November/December 1608, he substituted the word '*utilia*' for the word '*necessaria*' on fol. 6r of Ms. BPL 917. Did he intend to bring legal theory into line with what was actually happening in the East Indies at that time? The spices which the VOC imported from the Moluccas, Ambon and the Banda Islands were not exactly 'necessities' of life. The Company's concerted campaign to acquire a monopoly of trade in the Spice Islands, which Grotius would valiantly defend at the Anglo-Dutch colonial conferences of 1613 and 1615, was in keeping with the revised law of self-preservation, however: 'it shall be permissible to acquire for oneself, and to retain, those things which are *useful* for life' (emphasis added).[46]

In the context of the truce negotiations, Grotius was at pains to downplay his radical rights theories. He had argued in *De iure praedae* that, in the absence of an independent judge, private persons (including a company of merchants) could avenge transgressions of the natural law. Yet the subjective right of punishment received no mention in the first twelve chapters of *Mare liberum*. Its author did not want to create the impression that the VOC would continue to play judge and executioner in its own cause, regardless of the Twelve Years' Truce. Grotius hedged his bets in the preface as well. The Dutch promised to abide by the verdict of the 'Princes and Free States of Christendom'. The latter would surely find fault with the Spanish for denying freedom of trade and navigation to everybody else, and punish them accordingly. The gloves only came off on the pamphlet's last page. In the conclusion (written in November/December 1608, that is *before* the introduction), Grotius darkly hinted that transgressors of the natural law could be resisted 'by way of fact … without expecting any public authority'. Yet this opaque reference to the subjective

[46] Leiden University Library, Ms. BPL 917 fol. 6r; *Commentary*, pp. 23, 500; Van Ittersum, *Profit and Principle*, pp. 359-483.

right of punishment must have seemed an afterthought to the readers of *Mare liberum*, assuming, of course, that they got as far as the conclusion.[47]

Folio 117r of Ms. BPL 917[48] contains a discarded outline for the preface of *Mare liberum*, which shows that the argument of *De iure praedae* remained uppermost in Grotius's mind. So much is clear from the outline's references to 'the poisonings, perfidy and crimes of the Portuguese', 'the utility of commerce' and 'the leagues with Indians', which echo chapters 11, 14 and 15 of *De iure praedae*. Originally, Grotius sought to address both the States General and the French and English monarchs in his preface. According to the outline, he wanted to say something 'about the respectability and public dignity of distinguished persons' and 'about the favour of kings'. The VOC could not hope to obtain solid guarantees for its trade and navigation without the cooperation of the States General and Henry IV of France and James I of England. Yet Grotius realized that 'the military support given by states' was not a one-way street. The strategic reserve of VOC warships and battle-hardened crews went a long way to explain why the French and English monarchs valued their alliance with the United Provinces. For all his outspokenness in the outline, Grotius was a lot less specific in the preface that eventually appeared in print. Did Oldenbarnevelt's criticism prompt him to discard the first outline, just as it forced him to postpone the pamphlet's publication? There is a certain irony here. Both *De iure praedae* and *Mare liberum* had been commissioned for the express purpose of influencing political developments in the VOC's favour. Yet neither treatise had the impact originally intended by Grotius and the VOC directors. Instead, these occasional writings became classics of international law.

---

[47] *The Free Sea*, 60; *ML*, p. 42.

[48] Leiden University Library, Ms. BPL 917 fol. 117r.

Appendix 1
Preparing *Mare liberum* for the Press: Grotius's Calculations on fol. 121v of Manuscript BPL 917 (Leiden University Library)

In order to speed up typesetting, it was customary to give one half of a manuscript to one compositor, and the other half to a second compositor. For this purpose, Grotius determined the midpoint of the text. He counted lines on each of the folio-pages of Ms. BPL 917 that he wanted to include in *Mare liberum*.

The numbers which Grotius arranged in three columns in the top left corner of fol. 121v are reproduced here. Round brackets are used for the corresponding folio-pages (which, obviously, are not found on fol. 121v). Grotius's line-count and his additions on fol. 121v are corrected in the footnotes.

Left Column	Middle Column	Right Column
	7[49]	100[50]
30 (fol. 96v)	32 (fol. 101v)[51]	30 (fol. 108r)
28 (fol. 97r)[52]	35 (fol. 102r)[53]	30 (fol. 108v)
26 (fol. 97v)	36 (fol. 102v)[54]	28 (fol. 109r)
30 (fol. 98r)[55]	30 (fol. 103r)	30 (fol. 109v)
31 (fol. 98v)	41 (fol. 103v)[56]	40 (fol. 110r)[57]
27 (fol. 99r)[58]	38 (fol. 104r)[59]	31 (fol. 110v)

(Continued)

[49] This may refer to fol. 116v, which lacks a number in the bottom left hand corner. Grotius crossed out half the page when he revised chapter 12 for publication as *Mare liberum.*

[50] This may refer to the number of lines on fols. 117v and 118r, the conclusion of *Mare liberum.* Grotius counted 50 lines on each folio-page.

[51] In fact, 33. Grotius put this number in the bottom left corner of fol. 101v.

[52] In fact, 27.

[53] In fact, 33. The line-count includes the insertion at the top of fol. 102v, which was perhaps counted twice.

[54] In fact, 34. The line-count includes the inserts at the top and bottom of fol. 102v. Grotius may have counted the insert at the top twice.

[55] The deleted text at the top of fol. 98r is omitted from the line-count, which does include, however, the inserted text at the bottom of 98r ('*Recte igitur dicit Victoria*...').

[56] The insertions at the top and bottom of 103v are included in the line-count.

[57] In fact, 38. The insertions at the bottom of 110r are included in the line-count.

[58] The deleted insert at the bottom of the folio-page is omitted from the line-count.

[59] The insertions at the top and bottom of fol. 104r are included in the line-count.

(Cont.,)

Left Column	Middle Column	Right Column
27 (fol. 99v)	32 (fol. 104v)	30 (fol. 111r)
32 (fol. 100r)[60]	34 (fol. 105r)	27 (fol. 111v)
31 (fol. 100v)	29 (fol. 105v)	28 (fol. 112r)
29 (fol. 101r)[61]	29 (fol. 106r)[62]	36 (fol. 112v)[63]
	30 (fol. 106v)[64]	37 (fol. 113r)[65]
	37 (fol. 107r)[66]	40 (fol. 113v)[67]
	28 (fol. 107v)[68]	32 (fol. 114r)[69]
	Media[70]	40 (fol. 114v)[71]
		33 (fol. 115r)
		31 (fol. 115v)
		41 (fol. 116r)[72]
276[73]	**440**[74]	**664**[75]

[60] In fact, 30.

[61] In fact, 32.

[62] The deleted insert at the bottom of the folio-page is omitted from the line-count.

[63] This should be 26, the number that Grotius wrote in the left bottom corner of fol. 112v.

[64] The line-count includes the inserted line completely at the bottom of the folio-page, but excludes the deleted insert right above it.

[65] In fact, 35. The insertion at the bottom of 113r is included in the line-count.

[66] In fact, 35. Grotius included in his calculations the inserted text at the top of 107r.

[67] In fact, 38. The inserted text at the bottom of fol. 113v is included in the line-count.

[68] Grotius put this number twice at the bottom of fol. 107v and wrote above it: '*nisi ivissent eo*'. These words are found in lines 3-4 from the top. It is the midpoint of the text of *Mare liberum*. Grotius indicated it by inserting a horizontal line in the left margin of fol. 107v, right next to lines 3-4 from the top.

[69] In fact, 34.

[70] Midpoint of the text of *Mare liberum*; see footnote 20.

[71] In fact, 38. The line-count includes the inserted text at the top of 114r.

[72] Should be 26, the number that Grotius wrote down in the left bottom corner of fol. 116r.

[73] In fact, 291 (if you add up the numbers in the left column).

[74] In fact, 438 (if you add up the numbers in the middle column).

[75] Grotius correctly added up the numbers in the right column. He then put together 664 and 440, which equal 1104. Finally, he added 276, which, in his opinion, made 1480 lines. (The sum total was 1380, however).

Appendix 2
The Flowchart for *Mare liberum*, Including Provisional Chapter Titles

Leiden University Library, BPL 917, fol. 118r[76]

Cap. 1 Batavis ad Indos jure gentium liberam esse navigationem[77]
in praefatione aliquid dicitur de argumentis
[crossed out: et] ex literatura sumtis

Vide [inserted: c.] 2: Lusitanos non esse dominos Indorum ad quos Batavi †navigant†[78]; neque Lusitanis ullum justum dominii titulum adversos eos competere 88 verso line[a] 2[79]
c. 2 Nec inventionis 88 verso fin 16[80]
nec quatenus Indi dici possunt
infideles nec quatenus barbari

---

[76] Dr. Jan Waszink and Dr. Jeanine Delandtsheer were so kind as to correct my transcription. They compared it directly with the text of Ms. BPL 917 on 14 July 2005. In September 2008, Prof. Robert Feenstra compared my transcription with the collotype reproduction of Ms. BPL 917. I am grateful for his suggestions for improvement.

Grotius's flowchart for *Mare liberum* is found on *the left side* of folio 118r. It is reproduced in normal type here. The provisional chapter titles are followed by a) folio-numbers, which correspond exactly with Grotius's right-hand numbering in Ms. BPL 917, and b) line-numbers, which Grotius counted from the top of any given folio.

Grotius also jotted down some thoughts on *the right side* of folio 118r. These notes are reproduced here in bold. (Regrettably, not all of them: Grotius's handwriting is notoriously hard to read.) I have put the notes directly underneath the chapter title to which they seem to be related. It should be emphasized, however, that Grotius himself did not make these connections explicit on fol. 118r.

[77] Grotius inserted a different chapter title at the top of fol. 96v: '*Caput 1 Iure Gentium Quibusvis ad Quosvis Liberam Esse Navigationem*'. This is the chapter title found on p. 1 of the first edition of *Mare Liberum*.

[78] Conjeci pro: †naviga..i†

[79] Refers to the chapter division on fol. 97v, where Grotius drew a horizontal line, stretching into the left margin, between lines 1 and 2 from the top. He inserted a slightly different chapter title in the left margin of fol. 97v: '*Cap. II Lusitanos nullum habere ius dominii in eos Indos ad quos Batavi navigant titulo inventionis*'. This chapter title is found on p. 4 of the first edition of *Mare liberum*, where chapter 2 starts with the words '*non esse autem*', just as Grotius indicated on fol. 97v of Ms. BPL 917.

[80] Reference to fol. 97v, where the word *INVENIRE* is inserted in capital letters in the left margin, halfway down the page. There is a division sign in the running text, between the words '*sententia*' and '*primum*' in line 16 from the top. The division sign was subsequently crossed out by Grotius. The actual chapter division is between lines 1 and 2 from the top. See also footnote 33.

c. 3 Nec donationis pontificiae 89verso[81]
c. 4 Nec iuris bellici 90 lin. 8[82]
[inserted: 3] 5 Mare aut jus in eo navigandi [inserted: ad Indos] non esse proprium Lusitanorum titulo occupationis[83]
6 Nec donationis pontificiae 99 lin. 20[84]
7 Nec praescriptione aut consuetudine 99 verso. lin. 24[85]
[inserted: Etiam mercatur†am†[86] Batavis iure gentium in Indis †liberam†[87] esse]
8 [crossed out: Jus mercandi cum Indis proprium non esse factum Lusitanorum occupatione 104 lin 19][88]

---

[81] Reference to the chapter division on 98v, where Grotius drew a line separating '*impius censetur*' from '*secundo si*' in line 5 from the top. He wrote out the full chapter title in the left margin of fol. 98v: '*Cap. III Lusitanos in Indos non habere ius dominii titulo donationis Pontificiae*'. The same chapter title is found on p. 7 of the first edition of *Mare liberum*, where chapter 3 starts with the words '*secundo si*', just as Grotius indicated on fol. 98v of Ms. BPL 917.

[82] Reference to the chapter division on 99r, where Grotius drew a line separating '*unquam spoliatos*' from '*his igitur*' in line 8 from the top. He wrote out the full chapter title in the left margin of fol. 99r: '*Cap. IV Lusitanos in Indos non habere ius dominii titulo bello*'. The same chapter title is found on p. 9 of the first edition of *Mare liberum*, where chapter 4 starts with the words '*his igitur*', just as Grotius indicated on fol. 99r of Ms. BPL 917.

[83] Reference to the chapter division on 100r, where Grotius drew a line separating '*Hispani non dubitant*' from '*si ergo*' in lines 1-2 from the bottom. Yet he inserted a slightly different chapter title in the left margin of fol. 100r: '*Cap. V Mare ad Indos au ius eo navigandi non esse proprium Lusitanorum titulo occupationis*'. This chapter title is found on p. 13 of the first edition of *Mare liberum*, where chapter 5 starts with the words '*si ergo*', just as Grotius indicated on fol. 100r of Ms. BPL 917. While Grotius inserted the chapter division on fol. 100r, he crossed out the words '*cum de americanis disputent*', which followed '*doctores Hispani non dubitant*'.

[84] Reference to the chapter division on fol. 108r, where Grotius drew a line separating '*expressum est*' from '[*d*]*onatio Pontificis Alexandri*' in lines 18-19 from the top. He wrote out the full chapter title in the left margin of fol. 108r: '*Cap VI Mare aut ius navigandi proprium non esse Lusitanorum titulo donationis Pontificiae*'. This chapter title is found on p. 36 of the first edition of *Mare liberum*, where chapter 6 starts with the words '*donatio Pontificis Alexandri*', just as Grotius indicated on fol. 108r of Ms. BPL 917.

[85] Reference to the chapter division on fol. 108v, where Grotius drew a line separating '*nihil diminutum*' from '*ultimum iniquitatis*' in lines 23-24 from the top. He wrote out the full chapter title in the left margin of fol. 108v: '*Mare aut ius navigandi proprium non esse Lusitanorum titulo praescriptionis aut consuetudinis*'. This chapter title is found on p. 38 of the first edition of *Mare liberum*, where chapter 7 starts with the words '*ultimum iniquitatis*', just like Grotius indicated on fol. 108v of Ms. BPL 917.

[86] Conjeci pro: †mercatur..†

[87] Conjeci pro: †liber..†

[88] Reference to the chapter division on fol. 113v, where Grotius drew horizontal and vertical lines, stretching into the left margin, in order to separate '*ad Indos prohibeant*' from '[*q*]*uod si dicant*' in line 19 from the top. Yet he inserted a different chapter title in the left margin of fol. 113v: '*Cap. VIII Iure gentium inter quosvis liberam esse mercaturam*'. This chapter title is found on p. 52 of the first edition of *Mare liberum*, where chapter 8 starts with the words '*quod si dicant*', just as Grotius indicated on fol. 113v of Ms. BPL 917.

9 Mercaturam cum Indis non esse factam propr†iam†[89] †Lusitanorum†[90] occupatione 105 lin. 7[91]

10 Nec donationis pontificiae ibid. lin. 17[92]

11 Nec praescriptione aut consuetudine 106 lin 7[93]

12 Nec aequitatem quidem ullam esse pro Lusitanis 106 lin 4 [crossed out: 0][94]

de monopoliis ex Naziazeno [= Gregory of Nazianzum]
... aliquid huc transferendum[95]...

13 Conclusio [crossed out: et] [inserted: seu] pace [crossed out: et] [inserted: seu] [crossed out: bello] et induciis retinendam libertatem commerciorum.[96]

de pace et induciis aliqua
Vide ex c. 9 de manutio [= Paulus Manutius, 1512-74] et lipsio [= Justus Lipsius, 1547-1606] et alijs de pace
Item inducijs

---

[89] Conjeci pro: †proprus in†

[90] Conjeci pro: †Lusi.†

[91] Reference to the chapter division on fol. 114v, where Grotius drew horizontal and vertical lines, stretching into the left margin, in order to separate '*juste empediat*' from '[*p*]*rimum inventio*' in lines 7-8 from the top. He wrote out the full chapter title in the left margin of fol. 114v: '*Cap IX Mercaturam cum Indis propriam non esse Lusitanorum titulo occupationis*'. This chapter title is found on p. 55 of the first edition of *Mare liberum*, where chapter 9 starts with the words '[*p*]*rimum inventio*', just as Grotius indicated on fol. 114v of Ms. BPL 917.

[92] Reference to the chapter division on fol. 114v, where Grotius drew horizontal and vertical lines, stretching into the left margin, in order to separate '*aliter potest*' from '[*c*]*oncessit nemo*' in line 17 from the top. He wrote out the full chapter title in the left margin of fol. 114v: '*Cap X Mercaturam cum Indis propriam non esse Lusitanorum titulo donationis Pontificiae*'. This chapter title is found on p. 55 of the first edition of *Mare liberum*, where chapter 10 starts with the words '[*c*]*oncessit nemo*', just as Grotius indicated on fol. 114v of Ms. BPL 917.

[93] Reference to the chapter division on fol. 115r, where Grotius drew horizontal and vertical lines, stretching into the left margin, in order to separate '*Pontificis auctoritatem*' from '[*r*]*estat praescriptio*' in line 7 from the top. He wrote out the full chapter title in the left margin of fol. 114v: '*Cap XI Mercaturam cum Indis non esse Lusitanorum propriam iure praescriptionis aut consuetudinis*'. This chapter title is found on p. 57 of the first edition of *Mare Liberum*, where chapter 11 starts with the words '[*r*]*estat praescriptio*', just as Grotius indicated on fol. 115r of Ms. BPL 917.

[94] Reference to the chapter division on fol. 115v, where Grotius drew horizontal and vertical lines stretching into the left margin, in order to separate '*ista usurpatio*' from '[*e*]*x his quae dicta*' in line 17 from the top. Yet he inserted a slightly different title in the left margin of fol. 115v: '*Cap XII Nulla aequitate niti Lusitanos in prohibendo commercio*'. This chapter title is found on p. 59 of the first edition of *Mare Liberum*, where chapter 12 starts with the words '[*e*]*x his quae dicta*', just as Grotius indicated on fol. 115v of Ms. BPL 917.

[95] Reference to insert in left margin of fol. 116v, included on p. 61 of the first edition of *Mare Liberum*.

[96] There is a chapter division on fol. 116v, eleven lines from the top. A chapter title is lacking, however. The title of the concluding chapter is slightly different on p. 62 of the first edition of *Mare Liberum*: '*Caput XIII Batavis ius commercii Indicani qua pace, qua induciis, qua bello retinendum*'.

'Sequuntur Dogmatica De Iure Praedae' Law and Theology in Grotius's Use of Sources in *De Iure Praedae*

Franco Todescan
Professor of Philosophy of Law, Università degli studi di Padova
e-mail: franco.todescan@unipd.it

Abstract
This contribution aims at reconstructing the system of legal sources as it can be recognised in all its clarity in the *De iure praedae*. After pointing out that Grotius applied in this work the mathematical method, it is observed that the law has a clear voluntaristic character: 'voluntas universorum ad universos directa lex dicitur'. Even the 'first notion', quoted in *Regula I*, that is the *lex aeterna*, has this specific character: 'Quod Deus se velle significarit, id ius est'. Interesting is also the way in which the issue of the *ius naturae* is developed. Actually, natural law is consistent with *Regula I* precisely because it is bound to God as a manifestation of his will: 'Dei voluntas non oraculis tantum et extraordinariis significationibus, sed vel maxime ex creantis intentione apparet'. Thus, the creation of the *ius gentium primarium* and *ius gentium secundarium* follows the same pattern: it is always a *voluntas* that splits into a cascade like a 'baroque fountain'. At the end of the same argument we find finally the *ius civile*: 'Quidquid respublica se velle significavit', as *Regula V* states. In conclusion, the system of legal sources in *De iure praedae* is based on premises that differ in many respects from the legal sources of *De iure belli ac pacis*.

Keywords
legal sources, method, legal voluntarism, law, natural law, ius gentium

Introduction

In this contribution I present a synthetic overview of the 'system of sources' that is at the basis of Grotius's *De iure praedae*, with special attention to theology. This system of sources is to be found in chapter 2 of Grotius's text, where it presents itself, so to say, in miniscule detail. I will use for an ideal-type comparison the similar system in the *Summa theologiae* of Aquinas,[1] an author

[1] I^a-II^{ae}, pp. 90-108. See for the extensive bibliography on Aquinas: *Tommaso d'Aquino*, ed. by O. De Bertolis and F. Todescan (Padua: CEDAM, 2003).

whom Grotius knew and cited regularly. The Thomistic system, moreover, has been neatly reproduced in the most important treatises of the Late Scholastics,[2] written at the same time as *De iure praedae*. The latter would certainly also allow a better comparison with the system underlying *De iure belli ac pacis* that I have attempted to reconstruct[3] in one of my previous publications, aiming to discover the roots of the famous 'etiamsi daremus' of *Prolegomena* 11.

Hence in this essay I will not discuss the contribution Grotius gave in *De iure praedae* to the substance of modern international law. Instead, I concentrate on the intricacies of the normative structure that Hugo Grotius developed, precisely given the still underdeveloped status of the field and the ensuing necessity for it to be reigned in by a solid framework of general principles. One only has to think of the enormous scope of colonial traffic that in the sixteenth and seventeenth centuries had opened a world of trans-Atlantic connections to the seafaring countries of Europe, in particular to 'the sea carriers' from Holland. In this youthful work that *De iure praedae* was, Grotius had already started to construct the new discipline of international law, bringing to fruition his vast theological and humanist scholarship,[4] by way of a deductive skeleton that is developed from a set of *regulae* and *leges* and adequately set out at the start.[5]

---

[2] See on the legal thought of Late Scholastics, also on issues *de jure belli,* the following recent works: I. Trujillo Pérez, *Francisco de Vitoria. Il diritto alla comunicazione e i confini della socialità umana* (Turin: Giappichelli, 1997); J. Belda Plans, *La Escuela de Salamanca y la renovación de la teología en el siglo XVI* (Madrid: Biblioteca de Autores Cristianos, 2000); F. Grunert and K. Seelmann, ed., *Die Ordnung der Praxis. Neue Studien zur spanischen Spätscholastik* (Tübingen: Niemeyer, 2001); G. Tosi, 'La teoria della schiavitù naturale nel dibattito sul Nuovo Mondo (1510-1573): "Veri domini" o "servi a natura"?', *Divus Thomas*, 33 (2002), pp. 15-258, with an updated bibliography.

[3] *Le radici teologiche del giusnaturalismo laico*, I: *Il problema della secolarizzazione nel pensiero giuridico di Ugo Grozio* (Milan: Giuffré, 1983), pp. 79-115.

[4] The connection between humanistic and theological thought has been recently discussed in F. Mühlegger, *Hugo Grotius: ein christlicher Humanist in politischer Verantwortung* (Berlin: de Gruyter, 2007).

[5] Cfr. A. Cavanna, *Storia del diritto moderno in Europa*, I: *Le fonti e il pensiero giuridico* (Milan: Giuffré, 1982), p. 326. Here follows the listing of *Regulae* and *Leges* of *De iure praedae*, divided according to their respective sources: [LEX AETERNA] *Regula I*: Quod Deus se velle significarit, id jus est. [JUS NATURAE] *Lex I*: Vitam tueri et declinare nocitura liceat; *Lex II*: Adjungere sibi quae ad vivendum sunt utilia eaque retinere liceat. [JUS GENTIUM PRIMARIUM] *Regula II*: Quod consensus hominum velle cunctos significaverit, id jus est; *Lex III*: Ne quis alterum laedat; *Lex IV*: Ne quis occupet alteri occupata; *Lex V*: Malefacta corrigenda; *Lex VI*: Benefacta repensanda. *Regula III :* Quod se quisque velle significaverit, id in eum jus est; *Lex VII*: Ut singuli cives caeteros tum universos, tum singulos non modo non laederent, verum etiam tuerentur; *Lex VIII*: Ut cives non modo alter alteri privatim aut in commune possessa non eriperent, verum etiam singuli tum quae singulis, tum quae universis necessaria conferrent. *Regula IV*: Quidquid

As I said, I will here consider in particular the theological sources. In *De iure praedae*, as later in *De iure belli ac pacis*, we find numerous references to the Church Fathers as well as to Scholastic theologians,[6] above all to Aquinas,[7] while authors like Luther and Calvin are not quoted, as being hostile to the theory of natural law. The works of these Catholic theologians were being taught at the protestant universities of the Dutch Republic, in Leiden in

respublica se velle significavit, id in cives universos jus est. [JUS CIVILE] *Regula V*: Quidquid respublica se velle significavit, id inter cives singulos jus est; *Lex IX*: Ne civis adversus civem jus suum nisi judicio exsequatur; *Lex X*: Ut magistratus omnia gerat e bono reipublicae; *Lex XI*: Ut quidquid magistratus gessit respublica ratum habeat. *Regula VI*: Quod se magistratus velle significavit, id in cives universos jus est. *Regula VII*: Quod se magistratus velle significavit, id in cives singulos jus est. [JUS GENTIUM SECUNDARIUM] *Regula VIII*: Quidquid omnes respublicae significarunt se velle, id in omnes jus est; *Lex XII*: Ne respublica neu civis in alteram rempublicam alteriusve civem jus suum nisi judicio exsequatur; *Regula IX*: In judicando priores sint partes ejus reipublicae, unde cujusve a cive petitur. Quod si hujus officium cesset, tum respublica, quae ipsa cujusve civis petit, eam rem judicet; *Lex XIII*: Ut ubi simul observari possunt observentur: ubi id fieri non potest, tum potior sit quae est dignior.

6 Here an overview of the main references to theologians in *De iure praedae*; *Churchfathers*: Clemens of Alexandria, 1; Tertullianus, 1; Ciprianus, 1; Lactantius, 5; Gregory of Nazianzus, 1; Ambrosius, 17; Augustine, 43; Jerome, 3; Isidore of Seville, 1; *Scholastics*: Thomas Aquinas, 56; Duns Scotus, 6; Juan de Torquemada, 3; Gabriel Biel, 3; *Late Scholastics*: Silvestro Mazzolini de Prierias, 91; Tommaso de Vio (Cajetan), 31; Francisco de Vitoria, 69; Domingo de Soto, 7; Alfonso de Castro, 3; Roberto Bellarmino, 2; *Jurists* (with strong theological leanings): Fernando Vázquez de Menchaca, 52; Diego de Covarruvias y Leyva, 31. In *De iure praedae* we miss however other, later representatives of the Late Scholastics, who are nonetheless quoted in *De jure belli ac pacis:* Domingo Báñez, 4; Luis de Molina, 21; Juan de Mariana, 68; Gregory of Valencia, 3; Gabriel Vázquez, 3; Francisco Suárez, 4; Leonardus Lessius, 34.

7 'Tommaso d'Aquino è l'unico autore di età non classica la cui autorità venga addotta da Grotius nelle argomentazioni in cui espone la fondazione del diritto. L'Aquinate è autore molto citato dal filosofo olandese, sia nel *De iure praedae*, dove abbiamo contato cinquantasei rimandi, sia nel *De iure belli ac pacis,* dove ne abbiamo contati quaranta. Sappiamo che una copia della *Summa theologiae* faceva parte della biblioteca personale che Grotius possedeva quando risiedeva in Olanda. Grotius raccomanda come fondamentale la lettura della *Summa theologiae*, in una lettera del 13 maggio 1615, a un amico, B. Aubery du Maurier, il quale vuole introdursi agli studi di filosofia [...] In una lunga e importante lettera a G. V. Vossius del 10 febbraio 1616, la quale costituisce una sorta di trattatello sulla predestinazione, in aspra polemica con Lutero e Calvino, e sulle competenze del re in materia religiosa, l'Autore richiama in due differenti contesti l'opera di Tommaso *De regimine principis*, per sostenere la tesi secondo cui la cura della religione spetta direttamente al re. E' da rimarcare infine che il modo di citazione di Tommaso è affiancabile solamente a quello con cui Grotius tratta Agostino di Ippona (autore molto amato, di cui abbiamo quarantatré rimandi nel *De iure praedae* e ben centosettantasei nel *De iure belli ac pacis*): i rimandi all'Aquinate sono sparsi con una certa regolarità nel corso delle opere, per scandire le più diverse materie esposte, comprese quelle attinenti direttamente il concetto stesso di diritto, a differenza delle citazioni di altri teologi scolastici, le quali perlopiù si addensano in riferimento a temi specifici': P. Negro, 'Intorno alle fonti scolastiche in Hugo Grotius', in *Dalla prima alla seconda Scolastica. Paradigmi e percorsi storiografici*, ed. by A. Ghisalberti (Bologna: Studio domenicano, 2000), pp. 213-214.

particular where Grotius was a student from 1694 to 1598. Their confessional denomination helped to proof the existence the *communis consensus* that Grotius, in the midst of all disagreements, so tenaciously wanted to be our guide to that one single truth and fundament of the essential unity of Christianity of which he was so imperturbably convinced:

> I testi sia del *De iure praedae* che del *De iure belli ac pacis* sono cosparsi di una galassia di citazioni, stampate dagli editori in corsivo; prevalentemente di autori classici, di testi biblici, di Agostino di Ippona; mentre l'esposizione è affiancata da rimandi a margine ad autori classici, medievali e moderni, di cui viene indicato l'opera e il luogo di riferimento. La maggioranza delle citazioni e dei rimandi a margine sono consentanei al pensiero dell'Autore, mentre sono rare le discussioni critiche con tesi divergenti. Tale lussureggiare di riferimenti colti non è solo uno sfoggio di erudizione, la quale comunque denota l'amplissima cultura umanistica di Grotius e la sua grande familiarità con la cultura alta del suo tempo; familiarità che ci viene confermata dalle numerosissime lettere, dove frequentemente si sofferma a commentare con i suoi interlocutori opere di giuristi, teologi, filosofi moderni. Si tratta di un appoggiarsi ad *auctoritates* per perseguire [...] un *consensus gentium* il più vasto possibile, che metta l'Autore al riparo dalle critiche dei contemporanei, inserendo il suo pensiero in una tradizione universalmente umana.[8]

Different from what I did previously for *De iure belli ac pacis*, I will proceed in a 'descending' way in this exposition—from sources that are axiologically more elevated to those less elevated, i.e. from eternal to human laws. Such an approach seems as a matter of fact more in accordance with the letter and spirit of this early work of Grotius.

The Mathematising Method

First a few remarks on Grotius's method. The innovation of modern science has in fact required new modes of investigation in order to bring the scientist – also in the field of law – into closer contact with reality. Of this requirement the sixteenth century only had a vague idea, while the seventeenth century is explicitely aware of a need for more refined methods, informed by the actual progress of mathematics and experimental science. This method will subsequently present itself at times as a rigorous inductivism that rejects any apriorism and wants to draw, *a posteriori* and critically, from the phenomena our knowledge of the essential, immanent structures of the world (the Baconian method of the *Novum Organum*), at other occasions as a deductive process

[8] Negro, Fonti scolastiche, pp. 213-4.

that disregards the experimental mode and wants to reconstruct *a priori* the general order of the world (the mathematical method of Descartes' *Discours*).[9]

As Grotius says in the first chapter of *De iure praedae*:

> Sed quemadmodum mathematici, priusquam ipsas demonstrationes aggrediantur, communes quasdam solent notiones, de quibus inter omnes facile constat praescribere, ut fixum aliquid sit, in quo retro desinat sequentium probatio, ita nos quo fundamentum positum habeamus, cui tuto superstruantur caetera, *regulas* quasdam et *leges* maxime generales indicabimus, velut anticipationes, quas non tam discere aliquis, quam reminisci debeat. Eam ad rem novitatis mihi, forte etiam prolixitatis venia oranda est.[10]

Hugo Grotius has a clear insight in the novelty he is about to introduce, and appears determined to follow the road of mathematics. As Basdevant has put it:

> Grotius déclare qu'il va suivre une méthode analogue à celle des mathématiciens et consistant à poser d'abord des *règles et lois admises généralement sur lesquelles seront édifiées les solutions*. Ce procédé ne doit point surprendre dans un ouvrage où – ne l'oublions pas, car ce trait domine toute l'oeuvre – il s'agissait de calmer les scrupules qui s'élevaient dans la conscience des actionnaires hollandais. Il convenait donc de présenter de la capture et des attributions de parts de prise qu'elle avait amenées une justification complète, se suffisant à elle-même, pour cela de remonter aux principes premiers du droit afin d'en déduire ensuite toutes les conséquences favorables à la thèse présentée. C'est ce que fit Grotius: après avoir rappelé, dans le chapitre II, les fondements du droit et les règles essentielles des rapports humains, il en tire, par une série de déductions, les solutions doctrinales dont il aura à faire état pour trancher le problème qu'il agite.[11]

An analogous methodological perspective seems to be found twenty years later, in the *Prolegomena* to the opus magnum, *De iure belli ac pacis*. Once again modelling his methodology on that of mathematics, Grotius wants to underline the specifically theoretical character of the system he was erecting:

> Injuriam mihi faciet si quis me ad ullas nostri saeculi controversias, aut natas aut quae nasciturae praevideri possunt, respexisse arbitratur. Vere enim profiteor, sicut

---

[9] Cfr. G. Faggin, *Storia della Filosofia*, II: *Dal Rinascimento a Immanuel Kant* (Milan: Giuffré, 1964), pp. 40 e 65.

[10] Ed. by H. G. Hamaker (The Hague: Nijhoff, 1868), p. 7 (emphasis added).

[11] J. Basdevant, 'Hugo Grotius', in *Les Fondateurs du Droit international*, ed. by A. Pillet (Paris: Giard et Brière, 1904), p. 157; quoted in: A. Dufour, 'L'influence de la méthodologie des sciences physiques et mathématiques sur les Fondateurs de l'Ecole du Droit naturel moderne (Grotius, Hobbes, Pufendorf)', *Grotiana*, 1 (1980), 33-52 (p. 43). Dufour's article is one of the most important studies of Grotius's methodology. See also B. Vermeulen, 'Simon Stevin and the geometrical method in *De jure praedae*', *Grotiana*, 4 (1983), 63-66.

mathematici figuras a corporibus semotas considerant, ita me in jure tractando ab omni singulari facto abduxisse animum.[12]

Thus, in both works Grotius sketches a parallelism of mathematical and juridical method. In *De iure praedae* he draws attention to his deductive proceeding, and not by chance he does so at the beginning of the text. For the Dutch author this way of proceeding should also be applied to the juridical science and it is interesting that a jurist of the seventeenth century draws such a parallel. Aquinas had in a way given a start in *Summa theologiae* for the *ratio speculativa* and *ratio practica*, yet noting that in the *ratio practica* passions frequently intervene, and human sentiments, jeopardizing the coherence of the discourse.[13] Moreover the first principle of the ratio practica of Thomism, 'bonum faciendum, malum vitandum' is a principle that can hardly stop at a purely formal interpretation, because it appears necessary to give a precise content to bonum, while in mathematics it does not create any difficulty that the principle is formal, because all the mathematical discourse is formal. While on the other hand in moral and juridical discourse a formal principle is insufficient, because such a discourse cannot be *solely* formal as it is necessary to know what is good and what is bad, what is just and what is unjust.[14]

In *De iure belli ac pacis*, however, we see Grotius prefer geometric arguments abstracting from the concrete (which is a typical geometrical procedure). We find it at the end of the *Prolegomena*; i.e. after having examined all single cases, Grotius wants to analyse exclusively formal characteristics of these cases. So we see here that the parallel does not mean a perfect correspondence. In *De iure praedae* the prevailing model of reference is mathematics, in *De iure belli ac pacis* geometry. In the first case, the emphasis is on the deductive procedure of the argumentation, in the second on the symbolic function performed by the geometric forms with respect to 'real' forms. At any rate remaining faithful to the programmatic intentions, it would seem to be a triumph of mathematical logic, yet it cannot be overlooked that not in so much in *De iure praedae* but in *De iure belli ac pacis* the lawyer from Delft did not always know how to carry out his own ambitious project, given that too often the overlapping

[12] *De jure belli ac pacis*, ed. by B. J. A. de Kanter-van Hettinga Tromp (Leiden: Brill, 1939; repr. Aalen: Scientia, 1993), Proleg. 58, p. 27.

[13] *Summa theologiae*, I^{a}-II^{ae}, q. 94, a. 4.

[14] An attempt of a formalist interpretation of natural law in Aquinas can be found in S. Cotta, *Il concetto di legge nella Summa theologiae di San Tommaso d'Aquino* (Turin: University, 1955); see also A. M. Quintas, 'Una tesi sul carattere formalistico della legge in S. Tommaso', *Rivista Internazionale di Filosofia del Diritto*, 36 (1959), 86-95.

of historical proofs rhetorically quoted to support his argument, ends up suffocating the deductive rigour of the argumentation.[15] The mathematical purity of the *Prolegomena*, finally, will be blurred in *De iure belli ac pacis*, and loose its transparency in a syncretic methodology of natural law: in order to fix the principles of natural law, according to Hugo Grotius, apart from the *a priori* methods, one could make reference to the *a posteriori* method, which draws from what is considered to be just 'apud omnes gentes'.[16] It is true that Grotius will establish a sort of hierarchic scaffold: he considered the second method *popularior*, and the first *subtilior*. Hence, according to the mathematical approach, the *a priori* method represented the authentic method, while the *a posteriori* one appeared to some extent faulty, since it provides conclusions that are not certain but only probable. Nonetheless the preference for one method means the rejection of the other: in this sense, in *De iure belli ac pacis*, the two main methods are occasionally used, with some hesitation or overlooked inconsistence. This in the end makes Grotius, as Solari[17] already noticed, more a lawyer, reluctant to detach from historical reality than a philosopher exclusively oriented towards logically indubitable solutions.

The Definition of Laws (Lex Proprie Dicta)

For Grotius as the author of *De iure praedae*, law in essence – the lex proprie dicta – has a clearly voluntarist character.

> Voluntas universorum ad universos directa *lex* dicitur: quae a Deo procedit, unde εὕρημα καὶ δῶρον θεοῦ, *inventum ac munus Dei*, nuncupatur [...] constat denique singulorum conventione atque placito, quo respectu κοινὴ πόλεως συνθήκη i.e. *communis pactio civitatis* Demostheni et Platoni interdum appellatur.

---

[15] Cfr. M. Villey, *La formazione del pensiero giuridico moderno*, Italian tr. (Milan: Jaca Book, 1986), p. 532 ss.

[16] *De jure belli ac pacis*, I.1.12.1: 'Esse autem aliquid juris naturalis probari solet tum ab eo quod prius est, tum ab eo quod posterius. <quarum probandi rationum illa subtilior est, haec popularior.> A priori, si ostendatur rei alicuius convenientia aut disconvenientia necessaria cum natura rationali ac sociali: a posteriori vero, si non certissima fide, certe probabiliter admodum, juris naturalis esse colligitur id quod apud omnes gentes, aut moratiores omnes tale esse creditur. Nam universalis effectus universalem requirit causam: talis autem existimationis causa vix ulla videtur esse posse praeter sensum ipsum communis qui dicitur' (p. 38).

[17] G. Solari, *Filosofia del diritto privato*, I: *Individualismo e diritto privato*, 2nd edn. (Turin: Giappichelli, 1959), p. 13; see my 'Dalla "persona ficta" alla "persona moralis". Individualismo e matematismo nelle teorie della persona giuridica del sec. XVII (1982-83)', in Todescan, *Etiamsi daremus. Studi sinfonici sul diritto naturale* (Padua CEDAM, 2003), pp. 142-144.

Ex prioribus igitur regulis et ista descendit [Regula IV]: Quidquid respublica se velle significavit, id in cives universos jus est.[18]

This conception of law, already *in limine* distinguishes itself from the Thomistic position of the famous definition of *Quaestio 90* of the *Summa*, in which Aquinas forcefully stresses the role of reason in law: 'rationis ordinatio ad bonum commune, ab eo qui curam communitatis habet, promulgata'.[19]

Per san Tommaso "la legge è una regola e misura delle azioni secondo la quale si è indotti ad agire oppure ci si astiene dall'agire" [...] Regola e misura delle azioni umane è la ragione, perché appartiene alla ragione l'ordinare ad un fine (e l'ordinare ad un fine, aveva insegnato Aristotele, è il principio primo in ciò che riguarda l'azione, ossia nella morale); perciò la legge è "qualcosa di attinente alla ragione (*aliquid pertinens ad rationem*)". Più precisamente, essa "è il dettame della ragione pratica nel sovrano che governa una comunità perfetta" [...] La legge ha per suo fine il bene comune, al quale è sempre ordinata; e la sua più precisa definizione è quindi "un'ordinazione della ragione al bene comune, promulgata da chi ha il governo di una comunità". Queste definizioni – le quali, si osservi, precisano l'essenza della legge nella razionalità – valgono per la legge in generale, a qualunque specie di essa ci si riferisca. San Tommaso infatti distingue varie specie di legge, di cui tre strettamente connesse tra loro, perché la seconda è parte della prima, e la terza deriva dalla seconda: *lex aeterna, lex naturalis, lex humana*. Oltre e al di sopra di queste vi è poi la *lex divina* (da non confondersi con la *lex aeterna*), legge rivelata da Dio.[20]

We can notice, nonetheless, that the topic of the absence of law is not to be found at the beginning, like in Aquinas, instead it is to be found inbetween paragraphs dedicated to respectively respublica and jus civile, and that there is no reference to Scholastic sources. It should not be forgotten, in fact, that in

---

[18] *De iure praedae*, II, pp. 22-23 (emphasis added); the main references are to the Digest, Aristotle and Fernando Vázquez de Menchaca.

[19] *Summa theologiae*, I^{a}-II^{ae}, q. 90, a. 4.

[20] G. Fassò, *Storia della filosofia del diritto*, I: *Antichità e medioevo*, rev. ed. by C. Faralli (Rome-Bari: Laterza, 2001), pp. 208-209: 'For St. Thomas "the law is a rule and measure of actions according to which one is induced to act, or to abstain from acting" [...] The rule and measure of human actions is reason, because it belongs to reason to ordinate towards an end (and to ordinate towards an end, as was taught by Aristotle, is the first principle of action, i.e. of morality); therefore the law is "something that pertains to reason (*aliquid pertinens ad rationem*)". More precisely, the law is "the prescription of the practical reason of the sovereign who rules a perfect commonwealth"[...] The law has as its aim the common good, to which it is always directed; and its most precise formulation is therefore "an ordinance of reason for the common good, promulgated by who has the rule of a community". These definitions – that detail the essence of the law, as one easily sees, in their rationality – are equally applicable to law in general, of whatever sort it may be. St. Thomas in fact distinguished several kinds of laws: *lex aeterna, lex naturalis, lex humana*. Next to that and above these there is also the *lex divina* (not to be confused with the *lex aeterna*), as it is revealed by God'.

the Grotian system aside from the impact of theological and Scholastic culture, various elements merge: old and new, sacred and profane, abundant and arid, in most of the cases inherited from the medieval juridical culture. Here they flow together in reciprocal interconnections giving rise to the problem of the sources in Grotius. Rather a problem of history than of logic: since a great historical problem is hidden behind the *dogmata* with which the jurist from Delft who was educated in the logical categories of Roman and Dutch law, had occupied himself first as a student and then as *advocatus fisci*. It was not so much a problem connected to the potential tension between natural law and positive law, but to an opposition of a more radical nature: the eternal conflict of the old and the new, of the medieval and the modern.[21]

Eternal Law (Regula I)

On the basis of this insight and the mentioned parallelism with the mathematical method, Grotius prepares the ground to establish the common points of departure. The first and foremost insight that Grotius presents in *Regula I* is that of the *lex aeterna*. In the Scholastic conception, more in particular in Thomism, the eternal law is the law that governs the whole universe, as the expression of God's reason (*ratio Dei*), and from which the natural law obtains its being by participation. In the Spanish Scholastics of the sixteenth century it was still present, both in the intellectualist version of Gabriel Vázquez, as 'ratio in mente Dei rerum faciendarum',[22] and in the voluntaristic version of Francisco Suárez, as 'decretum liberum voluntatis Dei, statuensis ordinem servandum'.[23] This law was called *fons et origo* of all law, which from the former drew obligatory nature. It was the law *per essentiam*, while the others were *per participationem*.[24]

Grotius puts it this way:

> Unde nobis principium, nisi ab ipso principio? Prima igitur esto regula, supra quam nihil: *Quod Deus se velle significarit, id jus est.* Haec sententia ipsam juris

[21] See on this more or less universal issue: F. Calasso, *Medio evo del diritto*, I: *Le fonti* (Milan: Giuffrè, 1954), pp. 387-388.

[22] *Commentaria ac disputationes in Primam Secundae sancti Thomae*, q. 91, a. 1, expl. 5 (in the Venice ed., 1609, t. II, fo. 13 b); cfr. H. von Garssen, *Die Naturrechtslehre des Gabriel Vázquez* (Göttingen: s.n., 1951), pp. 41ff.

[23] *Tractatus de legibus ac Deo legislatore* (Conimbricae: 1612; reprint Madrid: 1967-68), 1.2.3.6 (fol. 109 a); see also J.-F. Courtine, *Nature et empire de la loi. Etudes suaréziennes* (Paris: Vrin, 1999), p. 102 ff.

[24] See my *Le radici teologiche*, I, pp. 111-112.

> causam indicat ac merito primi principii loco ponitur videturque jus a Jove dictum, unde et jurare et jusjurandum, Jovisjurandum: aut quia veteres quae nos jura dicimus, *jusa*, hoc est jussa dixerunt. Jubere autem potestatis est.[25]

One sees immediately the presence of this philosophically very dense term: 'principium'. Hugo Grotius looks for the beginning and gives the first rule, the first of the common notions, one might almost say the most common one. And he expresses it in the fact that what God indicated to be his will is law. In the seventeenth century the fact that God exists was taken almost for granted, presupposed; hence it was not necessary on Grotius's part to address the issue. Moreover, he will face it later, in *De veritate religionis Christianae*.[26] Yet even more remarkable is the voluntaristic twist given to this first rule and hence to the eternal law. From amongst the various meanings of law (whether eternal, divine, natural or human) Thomas Aquinas chose that of a rule dictated by (divine or human) reason; identifying law with positive law (in particular that revealed by God) had been on the contrary characteristic of Franciscan voluntaristic thought, particularly and forcefully present in the fourteenth century, bringing to the fore one of the two aspects present in the thought of Augustine, who had defined *lex aeterna* both as divine will and as divine reason (*ratio divina vel voluntas Dei*).[27]

According to Duns Scotus the first and absolute cause is the will of God that is its own cause, determined or regulated by nothing else, and thence neither by reason. The will is above the intellect. God wants what he wants without any other motive than that he wants it. The moral laws are as they are because wanted by God: no law is just unless received by the divine will (see *Opus Oxoniense*, I, d. 44, q. unica, 2). Similarly man directs himself to the good, not because it is revealed to his understanding as being good, but because his will conforms freely to God's will. Aquinas called the commands of the Decalogue

---

[25] *De iure praedae*, II, pp. 7-8 (emphasis added).

[26] This apologetic work was originally published in Dutch, in 1622 with the title: *Bewijs van den waren godsdienst* (cfr. J. ter Meulen-P. J. J. Diermanse, *Bibliographie des écrits imprimés de Hugo Grotius* (The Hague: Nijhoff, 1950) pp. 57-59 [n. 143]), printed again, in Latin, in Leiden in 1627; it is considered one of his most important books. Here he develops a quest for universalism that surfaces in the systematic completeness of his project, and in the abundant use of philological-juridical arguments that bring the bear on biblical exegesis the most refined techniques of classical scholarship. See A. H. Haentjens, *Hugo de Groot als godsdienstig denker* (Amsterdam: Ploegsma, 1946); Ugo Grozio, *Della vera religione cristiana*, ed. and intr. by F. Pintacuda de Michelis (Rome-Bari: Laterza, 1973), pp. V-XXXIX.

[27] Augustine, *Contra Faustum manichaeum*, 22.27: 'ratio divina vel voluntas Dei, ordinem naturalem conservari jubens, perturbari vetans'; cfr. Fassò, *Storia della filosofia del diritto*, I, pp. 158, 232.

good, not because commanded by God, but commanded by God because good in themselves. To him Duns Scotus objects that 'if we say that the will of God's Creatures must necessarily conform itself to these precepts in order to be just, nevertheless the will of God does not have to want in conformity with such truth: rather for the very fact that God wants in conformity with these truth they do exist'.[28]

The opening, basic claim of *De iure praedae* is a very far cry from that of twenty years later, in the *Prolegomena* 11 of *De iure belli ac pacis*.[29] The central element of law in the former is the will of God. In chapter 1 still much stress was put on natural reason,[30] but within the space of a few lines there seems to be a change. We should therefore try to understand what for Grotius is the relation, if any, between *voluntas Dei* and *ratio naturae*. These lines in fact seem to proceed in a voluntaristic way. We find here philological considerations, as

[28] *Opus Oxoniense*, III, d. 37, q. unica, 4; see Fassò, *Storia della filosofia del diritto*, I, p. 234: 'For Duns Scotus the first and absolute cause is the will of God, which is a cause in itself and not determined or regulated by anything else. Hence not even by reason. The will is above the intellect; God wants that which he wants, without any other motive besides that wants it. Moral laws are such because they are wanted by God: "no law is just unless conforming to God's will" (*Opus Oxoniense*, I. d.44. q. unica, 2). Even man tends towards the good not because it is perceived by his intellect as good, but rather because man's will spontaneously conforms itself to God's will.'

[29] 'Et haec quidem quae jam diximus locum <aliquem> haberent etiamsi daremus, quod sine summo scelere dari nequit, non esse Deum, aut non curari ab eo negotia humana' (p. 10). On the topic of the Grotian *etiamsi daremus*, already shortly discussed by O. Gierke, *Johannes Althusius und die Entwicklung der naturrechtlichen Staatstheorien*, 4th edn (Breslau: Marcus, 1929; 1st edn Breslau: Koebner, 1880), p. 74n45, the following are particularly relevant two articles from 1950: G. Fassò, 'Ugo Grozio tra medioevo ed età moderna', repr. in Idem, *Scritti di filosofia del diritto*, 3 vols (Milan: Giuffré, 1982), I, pp. 99ff.; G. Del Vecchio, 'Note groziane', now reprinted as 'Per l'interpretazione del pensiero di Grozio', in Idem, *Contributi alla storia del pensiero giuridico e filosofico* (Milan: Giuffré, 1963), pp. 69ff.; A. Grumelli, 'Prospettive moderne nel pensiero di Ugo Grozio', *Studia Patavina*, 4 (1957), 143ff; J. St. Leger, *The "etiamsi daremus" of Hugo Grotius. A Study in the Origins of International Law* (Rome: [Herder], 1962); M. B. Crowe, 'The "Impious Hypothesis": a Paradox in Hugo Grotius?', in *Tijdsschrift voor Filosofie*, 38 (1976), 379ff; J. Hervada, 'The Old and the New in the Hypothesis "Etiamsi daremus" of Grotius', in *Grotiana*, 4 (1983), 3ff; L. Besselink, 'The impious Hypothesis revisited', in *Grotiana*, 9 (1988), 3ff; P. Negro, 'Un "topos" in Hugo Grotius: "etiamsi daremus non esse Deum"', in *Studi Filosofici*, 18 (1995), 57ff.

[30] *De iure praedae*, I, pp. 5-6: 'Prima igitur juris erit quaestio, quae caeterarum quodammodo praejudicialis est. Ad hanc autem illa *naturae*, quam dixi, *ratio* vel maxime pertinet. Nam illi quidem operam mihi ludere videntur, qui res non inter cives sed populos diversos gestas, idque non pace sed bello, ex scriptis duntaxat legibus dijudicant [...] Quos auctores si illi non legunt, at Baldum suum audire debuerant, qui sapienter docuit inter eos, qui supremam imperii potestatem sibi vindicant, si quid inciderit contentionis, non alium dari judicem, quam *naturalem rationem*, bonorum atque malorum arbitram [...] Nec longe abit vulgatum illud, intellectus penuria eum laborare, qui legem quaerat ubi *naturalis* suppetat *ratio*' (italics added).

where he derives jus from Jupiter by way of the term and the concept of oath, *jusjurandum*. This would explain why the Romans would use the term *jusa* (closer to *jussa* then to *jura*). Even while it might look like a play of words, these lines still remind us of the medieval controversy between the Domenican concepts of law and justice (*jus quia justum*) and that of the Franciscans (*jus quia jussum*). When Grotius critically engaged himself with the issue of the foundation of law, it became necessary for him as much as for the major exponents of the Second Scholastics,[31] to encounter an old polemic that through centuries of the declining Middle Ages preluded the birth of a modern age. The First Scholastics, in its most mature phase articulated itself in two great systems, i.e. the Thomistic on the one hand, and the Scotist and nominalistic on the other. Herein the antinomic tension between intellect and will inherent in the dynamics of human experience arose with an exceptional clarity, moreover transformed itself by virtue of an internal dialectics into an open conflict between a mainly intellectualistic and a mainly voluntaristic concept of ethics.[32] Grotius does not quote the two formulas, but it is evident that he follows the second road, *jus quia jussum*. It does not come as a surprise because he is still and at any rate a Calvinist of the pre-arminian kind, and Calvinism after all is close to voluntarism.[33]

In any case, as it has been acutely observed,[34] in the margin of *Regula I*, Grotius made reference to the place in *Summa theologiae*, where Aquinas talks about *lex aeterna*. Such a reference to Thomistic writing seems effectively to play down the role of *voluntas* attributed by Grotius to God, whom Grotius extols as Creator, rather than as Supreme Legislator.

> Respondeo dicendum quod, sicut in quolibet artifice praeexistit ratio eorum quae constituuntur per artem, ita etiam in quolibet gubernante oportet quod praeexistat ratio ordinis eorum quae agenda sunt per eos qui gubernationi subduntur. Et sicut ratio rerum fiendarum per artem vocatur ars vel exemplar rerum artificiatarum, ita etiam ratio gubernantis actus subditorum, rationem legis obtinet servatis aliis quae supra (q. 90) esse diximus de legis ratione. Deus autem per suam sapientiam conditor est universarum rerum, ad quas comparatur sicut artifex ad artificiata, ut in Primo habitum est. Est etiam gubernator omnium actuum et motionum quae inveniuntur in singulis creaturis, ut etiam in Primo

---

[31] See my *Lex, natura, beatitudo. Il problema della legge nella Scolastica spagnola del sec. XVI* (Padua: CEDAM, 1973), pp. 83ff.

[32] Cfr. E. Piergiovanni, *La metamorfosi dell'etica medioevale* (Bologna: Patron, 1967), pp. 21ff.; see for the complex historical, ideological and institutional developments in the early Middle Ages the classical work by R. and A. Carlyle, *Il pensiero politico medievale*, Italian tr. (Bari: Laterza, 1968), with an excellent bibliography by L. Firpo.

[33] Cfr. Villey, *La formazione*, pp. 267ff.

[34] Negro, Fonti scolastiche, pp. 210.

> habitum est. Unde sicut ratio divinae sapientiae inquantum per eam cuncta sunt creata, rationem habet artis vel exemplaris vel ideae; ita ratio divinae sapientiae moventis omnia ad debitum finem, obtinet rationem legis. Et secundum hoc, lex aeterna nihil aliud est quam ratio divinae sapientiae, secundum quod est directiva omnium actuum et motionum.[35]

We indeed might ask why Grotius quotes exactly that passage from Aquinas where the problem appears whether the eternal law is *summa ratio*, while he himself sustains a voluntaristic claim. Supposedly, Grotius does not quote Aquinas in order to contradict himself. So why is he quoting him? In the *Prolegomena* to the *De iure belli ac pacis* Grotius does not talk any longer about eternal law,[36] as already Leibniz noticed: 'Meo judicio recte Grotius doctrinam Scholasticorum de lege Dei aeterna cum principio socialitatis conjunxit'.[37] In *De iure praedae*, instead, he referred to the eternal law, but apparently in a contradictory way: he talked about it but relying on a passage from an author who surely is not voluntaristic. Why didn't he quote Duns Scotus, as he did on other occasions in the same chapter 2?[38] There are two possible explanations. Either it is a marginal note made in a hasty and unprecise way, or – which is more probable – there exists a hidden relation, which emerges only later in the sequel of the argument. In the *Summa theologiae* Aquinas presents a prototypical approach in which 'the eternal law is nothing but the plan of divine knowledge of every action and movement'. God has with all things of which he is the Creator 'a relationship similar to that between the artisan and his manufacture', having of all the things a prototype at hand. We find in this conception even a volitional element, because God wants that the prototype be realised. Grotius highlights the volitional element, which nonetheless is not the most important in the quotation.

Grotius's referring to where Aquinas defines the eternal law as 'ratio divinae sapientiae secundum quod est directiva omnium actuum et motionum' at any rate puts – as Paola Negro observes – the Grotian argument within a

---

35 *Summa theologiae*, I^{a}-II^{ae}, q. 93, a. 1: *Utrum lex aeterna sit summa ratio in Deo existens.*

36 See the lexicographical study of P. Negro, *Index verborum dei 'Prolegomena' al 'De jure belli ac pacis' di Hugo Grotius* (Florence: Olschki, 1996); also published as *Lessico Intellettuale Europeo*, ed. by A. Lamarra, special issue of *Lexicon Philosophicum. Quaderni di terminologia filosofica e storia delle idee*, 8-9 (1996), 139-288, p. 178.

37 *Epistolae mutuae G. G. Leibnitii et F. G. Bierlingii*, Responsio Leibnitii ad Epistolam V, § XXII (in Leibniz, *Opera omnia*, ed. L. Dutens (Geneva: Tournes, 1768), V, p. 371); see also the recent observations of Besselink, The impious Hypothesis revisited, pp. 16-22.

38 As to the antinomies in Lex XIII: Ut ubi simul observari possunt observentur: ubi id fieri non potest, tum potior sit quae est dignior (*De iure praedae*, p. 29), the reference is to Duns Scotus, *Quaestiones in Librum IV Sententiarum* [*Opus Oxoniense*], d. XXI, q. 2, ad sextum 24 (where he maintains that if the precepts support contrary claims, the one of a higher order obligates more and therefore will be maintained with more determination).

theological and cultural perspective that is not subject to the freedom of the absolute will, rather one in which the search for the first cause of law points us to the common notion which has the consent of all: that God is the cause of everything. Such argumentation provides Grotius with the support which he needs in order to deduct with logical decisiveness from the first rule all other rules concerning *jus naturae*, *jus gentium*, and *jus civile*. Grotius's train of thought, rather than articulating the concepts of nature and divine will, seems to privilege the linear structure of the argumentative system in which there is no place any longer for the differentiation of *lex aeterna*, *lex naturalis*, and *lex divina*, on which the *Doctor Angelicus* had still pondered.

In the end a peculiar note. In order to touch upon the issue whether a thing is commanded because it is good, or whether it is good because it is commanded, Grotius refers us to a philosopher nowadays completely forgotten: Anaxarchus of Abdera.

> ... recte Anaxarchus colligebat non tam ob id Deum aliquid velle, quia justum est, quam justum esse, quia Deus vult: etsi ille eo dicto abutebatur.[39]

Why doesn't he quote here (and the same will occur again in the *De iure belli ac pacis*)[40] the much better know and earlier passage from Plato's *Eutyphro*,[41] or the great controversy between the Domenicans and the Franciscans that dominated the high Middle Ages?

Natural Law (Jus Naturae)

Of similar interest is the development of the topic of natural law in *De iure praedae*:

---

[39] *De iure praedae*, II, p. 8. This is a quotation from Plutarch, *Alexandros*, 52: '"Do not you know," said he, "that Jupiter is represented to have Justice and Law on each hand of him, to signify that all the actions of a conqueror are lawful and just?"', in the translation of John Dryden; cfr. *I Presocratici. Testimonianze e frammenti*, ed. by G. Giannantoni, t. II, 6th edn (Rome-Bari: Laterza, 1999), p. 841 (= DK 72 A 3).

[40] *De jure belli ac pacis*, I, I, XV, 1: 'In hoc jure [jus voluntarium divinum] locum habere potest, quod nimium indistincte dicebat Anaxarchus, non ideo id Deum velle quia justum est, sed justum esse, id est jure debitum, quia Deus voluit' (p. 41).

[41] Plato, *Eutyphro*, 10 a, in the translation of Jowett: 'The point which I should first wish to understand is whether the pious or holy is beloved by the gods because it is holy, or holy because it is beloved of the gods.' This is the more remarkable not only because Anaxarchos lived after Plato ('Anaxarchus ... flourished about the hundred and tenth Olympiad' [340-37 a. C.], in the translation of Yonge, according to Diogenes Laertius, IX, 58-60 [= DK 72 A 1; *I Presocratici*, II, p. 839]), but Plato himself is quoted by Grotius (referring to the dialogue of *The laws*)

> Dei voluntas non oraculis tantum et extraordinariis significationibus, sed vel maxime ex creantis intentione apparet. Inde enim *jus naturae* est [...] Cum igitur res conditas Deus esse fecerit et esse voluerit, proprietates quasdam naturales singulis indidit, quibus ipsum illud esse conservaretur et quibus ad bonum suum unumquodque, velut ex prima originis lege, duceretur. Unde principium totius naturalis ordinis recte poëtae et philosophi veteres *amorem* statuerunt, cujus prima vis primaque actio reciproca est in se ipsum [...] Omnis enim natura, ut plurimis locis Cicero inculcat, diligens est sui seque salvam ac *beatam* vult, idque non in hominibus solis videre est sed in bestiis etiam, imo et in rebus inanimis. Hic enim est ille verus et divinus sui amor, omni ex parte laudabilis. Quae enim in vitiis ponitur φιλαυτία, hoc est *nimium sui studium*, istius amoris excessus est [...] Quippe hominem justum nullo modo sibi ipsi suarumve partium ulli facturum injuriam, causamve sibi futurum doloris aut incommodi [...] Alii qui nomina subtilius distinguunt, non tam justitiae hoc opus esse volunt, quam caritatis, ad quam nos natura astringat, illud interim fatentes, in rebus humanis primam esse hominis adversus se ipsum officii rationem. Officium autem omne est, ut philosophi loquuntur, περὶ τά πως ἔχοντα πρός ἡμᾶς, hoc est, *quae certo modo ad nos referuntur*. Sunt autem haec duplicia, alia enim boni, alia mali ad nos rationem habent: quod et affectiones indicant duae, quas non homini soli sed animantibus cunctis natura indidit, fuga et *appetitus*.[42]

Also in this case the pride of place is given to a quotation of the *Summa theologiae* of Aquinas:

> Respondeo dicendum quod, sicut supra dictum est, propria et per se causa peccati accipienda est ex parte conversionis ad commutabile bonum; ex qua quidem parte omnis actus peccati procedit ex aliquo inordinato appetitu alicujus temporalis boni. Quod autem aliquis appetat inordinate aliquod temporale bonum, procedit ex hoc quod inordinate amat seipsum: hoc enim est amare aliquem, velle ei bonum. Unde manifestum est quod inordinatus amor sui est causa omnis peccati. Ad primum ergo dicendum quod amor sui ordinatus est debitus et naturalis, ita scilicet quod velit sibi bonum quod congruit. Sed amor sui inordinatus, qui perducit ad contemptum Dei, ponitur causa peccati secundum Augustinum.[43]

This quote that speaks of the uncontrolled self-love as the root of sin is used by Aquinas and Grotius to demonstrate with an argument *a contrario* that the ordinate love imposes instead to love oneself doing the *true* good to oneself.[44]

---

in the same note that mentions the passage of Plutarch. But maybe Plato was not quoted because the answer in Eutyphro was less congenial to Grotius than the one by Anaxarchos.

[42] *De iure praedae*, II, pp. 8-10; emphasis added.

[43] *Summa theologiae*, I^{a}-II^{ae}, q. 77, a. 4: *Utrum amor sui sit principium omnis peccati*; but maybe it had been even more appropriate to quote II^{a}-II^{ae}, q. 25, a.4: *Utrum homo debeat seipsum ex caritate diligere*.

[44] Well-ordered self-love belongs to *jus naturae* and is expressed in the first two laws: Lex I: Vitam tueri et declinare nocitura liceat; Lex II: Adjungere sibi quae ad vivendum sunt utilia eaque retinere liceat.

Yet another topic, equally important, that of *beatitudo* and *appetitus beatitudinis*, appears only in passing in the paragraph that Grotius dedicated to *jus naturale*, while in Aquinas it played a central role.

The basic principle of moral and legal philosophy in Aquinas pivoted on 'desire' which stimulates every creature to aspire beatitude, in other words he based it on a profound inclination that drives the internal dynamics of every human act. All actions obtain their axiological meaning as far as they comply with the drive of unfathomable impulse. This topic on which the grandiose construction of the *Summa theologiae* relies had its immediate predecessor, and to some extent it's most accomplished expression, in the clear exposition of the third book of the *Summa contra Gentiles*, written just before. All Thomist doctrine about love and knowledge, epistemology as much as ethics, follows as a undeniable consequence from the universal desire of happiness. Within his rigorous theological conception that 'omne agens agit propter finem',[45] Aquinas starts out by stressing that every created being, in all of its desires, desires God more profoundly than any of the specific things that it has in view: animals, plants, inanimate beings, 'omnia appetunt divinam similitudinem quasi ultimum finem'. All beings, animate or inanimate, operate with the sublime end in view, and the way in which they tend to the divine *similitudo*, as well as the extent to which they are capable of attaining it, certainly depend also on their nature, but it is that nature that is questioned.[46]

For Aquinas man is not and can absolutely not be just a rational animal, *homo physicus*, in whom there is an ideal symmetrical correspondence of active and passive potential, instead man remains always a paradoxical being, fundamentally needful, animated by the desire of the absolute, which only the Absolute can satiate. Aquinas certainly does not present this latter conflict within man with the same *pathos* of Augustin: his language remains always peaceful as befits a scholastic philosopher. Yet he never stops underlining the radical ontological difference of human nature as opposed to other natural beings. Human nature is never self-reliant, concerned only with itself and this world, because there is a irresistible desire in man that prompts man to be continuously aware of the fact that it is not simply about realising nature, but about overcoming it.[47]

In Grotius's phrasing we may certainly notice before all the coherence with *Regula I*, because here the natural law is related to the will of God. Grotius talks in fact about the manifestation of this will. Yet he does not want

---

[45] *Contra Gentiles*, I.3.2.

[46] See my 'Presupposti antropologici della filosofia morale e giuridica di S. Tommaso' (1978), reprinted in my *Etiamsi daremus*, cit. p. 46-47.

[47] Todescan, *Etiamsi daremus*, p. 51.

mainly to refer to the moment of promulgation, the moment in which the will normally appears, but rather to something more profound, something that must be discovered by way of excavation: the challenge is to discover the intention of the Creator in his Creation, to go beyond the phenomenal data, beyond the appearances. This observation allows us to notice something of major relevance in the above citation of Aquinas that we examined when talking about the *lex aeterna*: Grotius in fact seems to be interested here in the model-prototype according to which God wanted to create the world.[48] The idea of God as an artificer is still very present.

Grotius then introduces the element of the end. It was the second constitutive element of law in Aquinas, for whom the end consisted in *bonum commune*, which Aquinas identified with *beatitudo*.[49] Also in *De iure praedae* there is a reference to the good, yet for Grotius the end is self-preservation. 'The *rational* and *social nature* of man', as Fassò notices,[50] 'is for Grotius the source of the law in the strict sense which precisely is the *natural* law, because it derives from the essential and specific characteristics of human nature, and towards the realisation and conservation of which it tends. His fundamental principles are the respect for the property of others, the restitution of property of others and the profits bygone, the obligation to keep promises and penal responsibility'. Still, in continuation of this argument it may seem that 'good' was something of a later stage as opposed to the end of self-preservation: the latter is only 'entailed' in the good, which itself is a broader concept. Later on Grotius talks in connection to the *end*, as in a kind of *climax*, about salvation and beatitude. But Grotius did not thematise beatitude, although he mentioned it. Indeed, he talks about the 'bonum suum' pertaining to all beings, hence also to man. He hints that every being has its own peculiar good. Yet he does not seem to analyse in full detail the disparity between man and his end, nor that between man and the other created beings. This was something that Augustine had underlined, although it had been missing in Greek culture, e.g. in the Aristotelian anthropology and cosmology of *De caelo*.[51] In this sense the words of *De iure praedae* prepare for *Prolegomena* 6 of *De iure belli ac pacis*, in

---

[48] See on this B. P. Vermeulen and G. A. van der Wal, 'Grotius, Aquinas and Hobbes. Grotian natural law between "lex aeterna" and natural rights', in *Grotiana*, 16-17 (1995-96), 69-78.

[49] *Summa theologiae*, I^{a}-II^{ae}, q. 90, a. 2: 'Primum autem principium in operativis, quorum est ratio practica, est finis ultimus. Est autem ultimus finis humanae vitae felicitas vel beatitudo, ut supra habitum est'.

[50] G. Fassò, *Storia della filosofia del diritto*, II: *L'età moderna*, rev. ed. C. Faralli (Rome-Bari: Laterza, 2001), pp. 76-77.

[51] As we find in the 'new' doctrine of *potentia oboedientialis* of Cajetan; see on the latter the fundamental study of J. Alfaro, *Lo Natural y lo Sobrenatural. Estudio histórico desde santo Tomás hasta Cayetano (1274-1534)* (Madrid: CSIC, 1952).

which the *appetitus societatis* tends to substitute the *appetitus beatitudinis* of the Augustinian-Thomist tradition.

This suppression of the Augustinian-Thomist theme of natural desire for extra-natural beatitudo, which was already visible in the Second Scholastic, seems to gain emphasis in fact in the anthropological conception underlying *De iure belli ac pacis*. In *Prolegomena* 6, Grotius claimed that the constitutive element of human nature is neediness or the situation of neediness, to which is connected a 'appetitus societatis, id est communitatis', and for that reason – Grotius adds – man is meant for a life 'non qualiscunque, sed tranquilla, et pro sui intellectus modo ordinata'.[52] We must make a comparative reference to this article of the *Prolegomena*, because it is implied in it that *tranquillitas societatis* is a *telos* of human nature, a regulative idea to which the aspirations of every individual are subordinated, whether he knows it or not. Grotius does not contemplate the society as a mere agglomeration of individuals, brought together for utilitarian ends; society is based on *appetitus societatis*, i.e. on an irresistible instinct of human nature. The individual feels the need to live next to its neighbours, in a community of regulated life, just as his wits suggest. He can only survive through a reciprocal exchange because everyone needs the others. From the duty to conserve the social network and in order to guarantee peace between its various members, ensues the need to observe certain fundamental rules, under which only a meaningful life can be lived. The *custodia societatis*, the proximate end of social life, in this way becomes the source of these rules, i.e. of natural law.[53]

Grotius has therefore kept *appetitus* societatis as the driving force of his anthropology, but it is no longer appetitus beatitudinis of Augustine or Aquinas, in the end it is not even the *appetitus* of a *finis ultimus naturalis*, of which Suárez and Lessius spoke,[54] but it is the desire of social life articulated in a more horizontal way. For Augustine and Aquinas the individual discovers

[52] *De jure belli ac pacis*, Proleg. 6: 'Verum quod hic dicit Philosophus [Carneades] ... admitti omnino non debet. nam homo animans quidem est, sed eximium animans, multoque longius distans a caeteris omnibus quam caeterorum genera inter se distant: cui rei testimonium perhibent multae actiones humani generis propriae. Inter haec autem quae homini sunt propria, est appetitus societatis, id est communitatis, non qualiscunque, sed tranquillae et pro sui intellectus modo ordinatae cum his qui sunt sui generis: <quam οικείωσιν Stoici appellabant>' (p. 7); cfr. R. Tuck, 'Grotius, Carneades and Hobbes', *Grotiana*, 4 (1983), 43-62; and for the relation to Stoicism: H. Blom and L. Winkel, 'Grotius and the Stoa: introduction', *Grotiana*, 22-23 (2001-2002), 7ff.

[53] Todescan *Radici teologiche*, I, pp. 48-49; see also F. Palladini, '"Appetitus societatis" in Grozio e "socialitas" in Pufendorf', *Filosofia Politica*, 10 (1996), 63ff.

[54] Cfr. H. de Lubac, *Agostinismo e teologia moderna*, Italian tr. (Milan: Jaca Book, 1978), p. 205 ff.

his social dimension by way of the critical operation itself, as a consequence of which he gains consciousness of his own *desiderium beatitudinis*. In the consciousness of his inexhaustible thirst for the Absolute, man's *ratio* found the certitude of being rooted in the indestructible relationship with all other persons, in equal need of the Absolute.[55] For Grotius, *societas* is a not a concept belonging theological anthropology, instead it is autonomous and isolated in a Stoic sense, reconnected to the human being, taken in itself and for itself, determined and guided by his *ratio*.[56]

Jus Gentium Primarium

As has been rightly observed by one of the greatest scholars of *De iure praedae*, Peter Haggenmacher,[57] also in the case of *jus gentium primarium* Grotius refers us to the system of the sources contained in the second chapter of *De iure praedae*, that I am trying here to reconstruct. Grotius defines a series of juridical sources, each of which is subjected to a *regula* that defines its creative role and scope of validity. The process of creation is always the same and consists in each case of a *voluntas*; and it would seem that it can be ultimately reduced to one and the same will, which is ramified and combined 'comme les cascades d'une fontaine baroque'. The primary source is the divine will from which *jus naturae*, i.e. the universal law common to all created beings, draws its origin. Through the mediation of the collective will of men, taken as rational creatures, derives from the jus naturae the *jus naturale secundarium* (or *jus gentium primarium*), which is hierarchically followed by a category of hybrid norms belonging at the same time to *jus civile*, *jus gentium*, *jus gentium secundarium*, springing from the will of all the states scattered upon earth. As the last come about, born from the individual will, in this hierarchical order (which is different from the order of presentation) contracts and in particular the social contract that founds civil society and the state,[58] the creator of *jus civile* by means of the instituted magistrate.

[55] Cfr. F. Cavalla, '*Scientia*', '*sapientia*' *ed esperienza sociale*, II: *Le due città di S. Agostino: società, diritto e giustizia* (Padua CEDAM, 1974), p. 5 ss.

[56] Cfr. *Le radici teologiche*, I, cit, pp. 53-54.

[57] Peter Haggenmacher, *Grotius et la doctrine de la guerre juste* (Paris: Presses Universitaires de France, 1983), p. 312.

[58] *De iure praedae*, II, pp. 19-20: 'His ita constitutis, cum accideret ut multi, quae hominum quorumdam ex corrupto ingenio malitia est, aut obligationibus non satisfacerent aut etiam fortunas alienas ipsamque vitam impeterent, idque plurimum impune ferrent, quia parati improvidos aut multi singulos adoriebantur, novo remedio opus fuit, ne humanae societatis leges invalidae destituerentur, excrescente praesertim in eam multitudinem hominum numero, ut

> Placuit autem plerisque hunc ipsum consensum jus naturae secundarium, seu jus gentium primarium appellare: cujus legem Cicero nihil aliud esse ait, nisi *rectam et a numine Deorum tractam rationem*, qui et alibi: *omni in re consensio omnium gentium lex naturae putanda est* [...] Maxime autem in eo consentitur, aliena nobis commoda curanda esse, quia id fere homini proprium est.[59]

This is related to Regula II:

> Et sic regula secunda a priori derivatur: Quod consensus hominum velle cunctos significaverit, id jus est.[60]

Grotius is not the inventor of this terminology. Here again all he does is to collect the harvest of a secular ripening. Nowhere he is a more masterful re-user, perhaps nothing else qualifies him more for the title of the 'Father of the modern science of international law',[61] as in presenting his conception of *jus gentium*. No doubt, the distinction between *jus gentium primarium* and *jus gentium secundarium* dates back to antiquity, and no doubt the distinction could crystallize on the basis of two collations of texts (building on Roman law and canonical law) that had been realised since the 12th century. In addition the Scholastic reflection on these texts that was at the origins of the debate has conditioned the writings of Grotius.[62]

It is noticeable that *jus gentium primarium* is also called *jus naturale secundarium*. Seen under the latter title, *jus gentium* evidently has to do with

---

longissimis discreti spatiis benefaciendi inter se occasiones amitterent. Minores igitur societates unum in locum homines colligere coeperunt, non quo illam, quae cunctis hominibus intercedit, tollerent, sed ut eam certiori praesidio immunirent: simul etiam, ut multa, quae humanae vitae usus postulat, distincta multorum opera commodius conferrentur [...] Et in hac re, ut in aliis omnibus, humana industria naturam imitata est, quae universi conservationem foedere quodam rerum omnium confirmavit. Haec igitur minor societas consensu quodam contracta boni communis gratia, i. e. ad se tuendum mutua ope et acquirenda pariter ea, quae ad vivendum necessaria sunt sufficiens multitudo, *respublica* dicitur et singuli in ea *cives*'.

[59] *De iure praedae*, II, p. 12 (emphasis added); the reference is to M. Tullius Cicero, *Orationes Philippicae*, 11.12.28; and *Tusculanae disputationes*, 1.13.30.

[60] *De iure praedae*, II. To *jus gentium primarium* also belong, in addition to Regula 1, the following laws supporting liberty and property: *Lex III*: Ne quis alterum laedat; *Lex IV*: Ne quis occupet alteri occupata; *Lex V*: Malefacta corrigenda; *Lex VI*: Benefacta repensanda; supporting contracts, including the social contract that is the foundation of the respublica, there is *Regula III :* Quod se quisque velle significaverit, id in eum jus est; with *Lex VII*: Ut singuli cives caeteros tum universos, tum singulos non modo non laederent, verum etiam tuerentur; and *Lex VIII*: Ut cives non modo alter alteri privatim aut in commune possessa non eriperent, verum etiam singuli tum quae singulis, tum quae universis necessaria conferrent; and as bridge to jus civile: *Regula IV*: Quidquid respublica se velle significavit, id in cives universos jus est.

[61] H. Vreeland jr., *Hugo Grotius the Father of the Modern Science of International Law* (New York: Oxford University Press, 1917).

[62] Cfr. Haggenmacher. *Grotius et la doctrine*, pp. 312-313.

natural law. Aquinas, while talking about human law, said that it could be connected to natural law in two ways: *per modum conclusionis* and *per modum determinationis*. For the *Doctor Angelicus* the first stood for *jus gentium*: in this way one should say that *jus gentium* is all natural law, because the syllogism does not add anything to the assumptions. *Jus gentium* has been all subsumed under *jus naturale*.[63] What is the relationship between the two according to Grotius? Concerning *jus gentium* he does not refer to any theologian, but to a jurist and philosopher like Cicero. And quoting Cicero it might seem that *jus gentium* is extracted by means of *ratio* (*recta ratio*). It therefore seems founded more on ratio than on voluntas. Hence for Grotius *jus gentium primarium* is a part of natural law. For Grotius *jus gentium* is also related to consent: and consent in its turn is related to *ratio* as well as to *voluntas*. Consent is not possible only because it is wanted, but it is also agreement on what is recognised as good, true, and rational. One may therefore conclude that *jus gentium*, at least the primary one, can be characterised in its elaboration if not as more 'rationalistic', at least as less 'voluntaristic', in its being related to *jus naturae*.

Jus Gentium Secundarium

From the systematic point of view, *jus gentium primarium* is followed by *jus gentium secundarium*. Let us consider for a moment the passage in which Grotius defines it: we find it towards the end of chapter 2, where he concludes and completes the system of sources. We are confronted here, says Grotius, with a mixed type:

> Annectendum nunc illud est, esse quoddam jus mixtum ex jure gentium et civili, sive jus gentium quod recte ac proprie *secundarium* dicitur. Ut enim commune bonum privatorum ea induxit, quae jam recitavimus, ita cum sit aliquod commune rerumpublicarum inter se bonum, eas inter gentes quae respublicas sibi constituerant de hoc etiam convenit.[64]

This set of norms aims at assuring the common good of a society of states, after the model of civil law which guarantees this common good to the

---

[63] *Summa theologiae*, I^{a}-II^{ae}, q. 95, a. 4: 'Et secundum hoc dividitur jus positivum in jus gentium et jus civile, secundum duos modos quibus aliquid derivatur a lege naturae [...] Nam ad jus gentium pertinent ea quae derivantur ex lege naturae sicut conclusiones ex principiis: ut justae emptiones, venditiones, et alia hujusmodi, sine quibus homines ad invicem convivere non possent; quod est de lege naturae, quia homo est naturaliter animal sociale, ut probatur in I *Polit.* Quae vero derivantur a lege naturae per modum particularis determinationis, pertinent ad jus civile, secundum quod quaelibet civitas aliquid sibi accommodum determinat'.

[64] *De iure praedae*, II, p. 26 (emphasis added).

citizens of a single state: Regula VIII derives its meaning from this reasoning, and this Regula VIII also is made after the preceding regulae, stating: Quidquid omnes respublicae significarunt se velle, id in omnes jus est.[65] By way of example, Grotius quotes the inviolability of ambassadors and the obligation to bury the dead. These norms are considered valid because being posed by a lawgiver, yet what Grotius says on this point does not allow us to see precisely how he conceives of the positeveness. Yet the uncertainty disappears thanks to the famous *Nova declaratio*, inserted in the manuscript on a separate sheet. Here Grotius distinguished neatly from *jus gentium* in the strict sense that which only has its appearance.[66]

> [Nova declaratio] Sunt autem haec duorum generum. Alia enim pacti vim habent inter respublicas, ut quae modo diximus: alia non habent, quae receptae potius consuetudinis nomine, quam juris appellaverim. Sed tamen et haec juris gentium frequenter dicuntur, ut quae de servitute, de certis contractuum generibus et successionum ordine populi omnes aut plerique, cum seorsim singulis ita expediret, in eamdem formam imitatione aut fortuito statuerunt. Quare ab his institutis licet singulis recedere, quia nec communiter sed sigillatim introducta sunt. Nam et simili ratione non quidquid in republica plerisque usitatum est statim jus faciet, sed id demum quod civium inter se communicationem respicit [...] Sed inter leges caeteras ejus gentium juris, quod velut ex contractu populos ligat, praecipua est quae primae legi civili assimilatur: [Lex XII] Ne respublica neu civis in alteram rempublicam alteriusve civem jus suum nisi judicio exsequatur.[67]

It is very important that Grotius makes a direct reference to the Spanish jurist Fernando Vázquez de Menchaca. Even though this atypical author does not belong to the Second Scholastic (frequently mistaken for the homonymous Jesuit Gabriel) he should be taken into consideration, despite a certain meagerness of his philosophical thought, because it represents in its wavering a true witness of a spiritual climate in which the new natural law thought was germinating.[68] One must recognise the contribution of Menchaca to the

---

[65] To *jus gentium secundarium* belong, apart from *Regula VIII*, with *Lex XII*: Ne respublica neu civis in alteram rempublicam alteriusve civem jus suum nisi judicio exsequatur; also *Regula IX*: In judicando priores sint partes ejus reipublicae, unde cujusve a cive petitur. Quod si hujus officium cesset, tum respublica, quae ipsa cujusve civis petit, eam rem judicet; with *Lex XIII*: Ut ubi simul observari possunt observentur: ubi id fieri non potest, tum potior sit quae est dignior.

[66] Cfr. Haggenmacher. *Grotius et la doctrine*, p. 359.

[67] *De iure praedae*, II, p. 27 (emphasis added). The reference is to Lex IX (relevant to *jus civile*): Ne civis adversus civem jus suum nisi judicio exsequatur. It is followed by yet another 'Nova declaratio' (pp. 27-30).

[68] See on this author: E. Reibstein, *Die Anfänge des neueren Natur- und Völkerrechts. Studien zu den 'Controversiae illustres' des Fernandus Vasquius (1559)* (Bern: Haupt, 1949); F. Carpintero Benítez, *Del derecho natural medieval al derecho natural moderno: Fernando Vázquez de Menchaca*

doctrine of natural law by way of an elaboration of and addition to the juridical system of a complex problematic of *jus gentium*. In this situation that was historically and doctrinally uncertain and confused, F. Vázquez tried to sketch, even if not always successfully, a sufficiently organic outline. Albeit foreign to the theological disputes on the idea of nature, he basically reflected the Roman tradition, according to which the natural law extends itself on the whole world, while *jus gentium* is only a peculiar moment therof and is the subject matter of the science of law.[69]

> *Naturale jus* dicitur, quod omnibus animantibus tam brutis quam ratione utentibus commune est; *jus* vero *gentium naturale vel primaevum* dicitur, quod solis hominibus, non etiam reliquis brutis animantibus competit [...] Hoc jus gentium naturale vel primaevum a jure naturali simpliciter prolato differt ut genus, a sua specie.
>
> *Jus* autem *gentium secundarium* est, quod non simul cum ipso genere humano proditum fuit, sed labentibus temporibus a plerisque earum gentium, quae moribus ac legibus reguntur, nec ritu aut more ferarum sylvestrem vitam agunt, receptum reperitur.[70]

By natural law in a broad sense one therefore has to understand, in the writings of Vazquez, both that which God has instilled in irrational beings, as well as what He has given to man; but natural law in the strict sense relates to man and man only, it is the law of human nature because it was, like the Roman jurists would put it, born together with humanity.[71] This *jus gentium naturale* (or *primaevum*) was given to man already in the original state, and it reflects the permanent and indefectible structural data of man. *Jus gentium secundarium* stands in front of man, but does not participate in the indefectibility and

(Salamanca: Universidad, 1977); G. P. van Nifterik, *Vorst tussen volk en wet. Over volkssoevereiniteit en rechtsstatelijkheid in het werk van Fernando Vázquez de Menchaca (1512-1569)* (Rotterdam: Sanders Instituut, 1999).

[69] See my *Lex, natura, beatitudo*, pp. 174-175; also C. Barcia Trelles, 'Fernando Vázquez de Menchaca (1512-1569). L'école espagnole de Droit International du XVIe siècle', *Recueil des cours de l'Académie de Droit International de La Haye*, 1 (1939), 433ff.

[70] Vázquez de Menchaca, *Controversiarum illustrium aliarumque usu frequentium libri tres*, 1.2.89. 24-25 (1st edn Barcelona, 1563; ed. by F. Rodríguez Alcalde, with Spanish tr., *Controversias fundamentales y otras de más frecuente uso*, 4 vols (Valladolid: Cuesta, 1931-34), IV, pp. 423-424); the Spanish jurist adds: 'id jus gentium secundarium non tam naturale, quam positivum dicituresse'.

[71] See also C. Barcia Trelles, *Fernando Vázquez de Menchaca*, p. 482: 'Ici se revèle la formation romaniste de Vázquez de Menchaca, en contraste manifeste avec la pensée de Vitoria, car l'immortel professeur de théologie Prima, de l'Université de Salamanque, avec une vision géniale, nous dit que le droit des gens régit, non pas les relations juridiques auxquelles les individus sont soumis, mais celles en vertu desquelles agissent les gens, les nations ou les Etats'.

unrenounceability of the *primaevum*, because it was not born with humanity, instead it was produced by it, it develops in time in line with the cultural development of single nations. In its origin it is positive law, jus civile of single communities, but it keeps its character of logical and historical independence, because it has met general approval and agreement, drawing its validity from a joint awareness of juridical consciousness. From his many examples it follows clearly that F. Vazquez meant to refer here not to the universal principles of law – which belong, to the extent to which they correspond to *recta ratio*, to *jus gentium primaevum* – but to single, concrete juridical institutions (property, war, trade) whose wide dispersion was easily observed. This is why the degree of inflexibility is much lower than of *jus gentium primaevum*, it is subject to prerequisites and changes which may take place as human relationships develop, by way of special agreements or even as a consequence of transformations (more or less fast, more or less radical) of entire juridical ideologies.[72]

As to Grotius (who in his comments on the following Regula IX does not fail to refer to other representatives of late/Scholastical thought, like Cajetan or Vitoria)[73] he dissociates from jus gentium in the strict sense that which only has the appearance thereof, because a vast category of rules and institutions would in fact be narrowed down to being only *jus civile* common to many states. Whether this is an accidental coincidence or produced on purpose, these rules would still depend from *jus civile* in such a way that the state would be free to respect them, modify them, or suppress them, at its leisure, without any responsibility to the other states (Grotius gives the example of contracts and successions). From this common civil law, qualified as customs rather than law ('potius consuetudinis nomine, quam juris appellaverim'), is to be distinguished the authentic *jus gentium secundarium* which obliges the states as if it were a pact. ('quod velut ex contractu populos ligat'); the pact of which

[72] Todescan, *Lex, natura, beatitudo*, pp. 175-176; Reibstein, *Anfänge*, p. 67ff.

[73] The reference to Cajetan concerns his comment on *Summa theologiae*, II^{a}-II^{ae}, q. 40, a. 1, where he sustains that the state takes care of itself and its members, not only to restrain violence by moderation, but also to punish offences, of their own citizens, but also of foreigners; the reference to Vitoria concerns the *Relectio de Indis posterior seu de jure belli*, § 17 (Tertia propositio: *Licet occupare ex bonis hostium impensam belli et omnia damna ab hostibus injuste illata*); § 19 (Quinta propositio: *Nec tantum hoc licet, sed etiam parta victoria et recuperatis rebus et pace etiam et securitate habita, licet vindicare injuriam ab hostibus acceptam et animadvertere in hostes et punire illos pro injuriis illatis*), § 46 (Secunda propositio: *Parta victoria et rebus jam extra periculum positis, licet interficere nocentes*) e § 56 (Septima propositio: *Etiam pro injuria illata et nomine poenae, hoc est in vindictam, licet pro qualitate injuriae acceptae mulctare hostes parte agri, aut etiam hac ratione occupare arcem aut oppidum*); in *Obras de Francisco de Vitoria. Relecciones teológicas*, ed. by T. Urdánoz (Madrid: Editorial Catolica, 1960), pp. 827-828; 848; 854-855.

Grotius does not specify the properties, but which the states would not be free to modify according to their leisure, or to disregard. This is therefore the true *jus gentium secundarium*, international and positive in virtue of a tacit consent of the states.[74]

So we may ask ourselves at this point, is there a different logic implied in *jus gentium secundarium* as compared to *jus gentium primarium*? From the text it appears that the secondary law of nations does not refer anymore to *jus naturae*, but to *jus gentium primarium*, and to jus civile, as much as *jus gentium primarium* refers to *jus naturae*. So therefore for Grotius between *jus naturale* and *jus civile* we find *jus gentium*, which in turn is double-headed, has two faces, one turned to *jus naturae* (*jus gentium primarium*), the other to *jus civile* (*jus gentium secundarium*). Here Grotius reconnects to Vázquez de Menchaca: but the two-headed character of *jus gentium* can be read as an indication of the impossibility to separate by rationalistic means natural law from civil law. Finally it should be observed that

> les deux types de *ius gentium* surgissent en des endroits presque opposés du système: alors que le droit des gens primaire est proche de sa source initiale, le droit des gens secondaire ne s'obtient qu'au bout de plusieurs médiations. La différence de leur portée se trouve à peine voilée par la consonance de leurs désignations; celle-ci est due à leur champ d'application commun, coextensif dans les deux cas avec l'humanité; mais comme on envisage cette dernière sous deux aspects différents – ici en tant que communauté d'humains, là comme société d'Etats – les deux espèces de *ius gentium* visent en fait des destinataires distincts.[75]

Human Law (Jus Civile)

Finally we come to examine the last normative source: *jus civile*. It should be considered in all its peculiarity in dialectic relation both with *jus naturae* and with *jus gentium* representing the insightful expression of the existence of one *jus commune*.

> Hinc oritur jus illud quod [...] juris auctores civile vocant: quod non est jus per se, sed ex alio. Quemadmodum si bos cum ove permutetur, non sunt quidem

---

[74] Cfr. Haggenmacher. *Grotius et la doctrine*, p. 359; Haggenmacher proposes to interprete the expression 'velut ex contractu' in an imaginary sense. See on *fictio* in modern legal thought my publications: *Diritto e realtà. Storia e teoria della 'fictio iuris'* (Padua: CEDAM, 1979); '"Socialitas" e stato di natura in Pufendorf', in: *Il diritto naturale della socialità. Tradizioni antiche ed antropologia moderna nel XVII secolo*, ed. by V. Fiorillo and F. Vollhardt (Turin: Giappichelli, 2004), pp. 139-157.

[75] Haggenmacher. *Grotius et la doctrine*, p. 312.

> haec per se aequalia, sed quia contrahentibus ita placuit. Nihil ergo mirum est, quod alioquin illicitum non foret hac ratione illicitum fieri, aut cum jura naturalia, ut quae causam habeant perpetuam, ipsa etiam perpetuo durent, ista jura mutari cum sua causa, hoc est cum hominum voluntate, aut alia alibi esse, quia scilicet bona rerum publicarum sunt diversa.[76]

The idea of one *jus commune* derives from Roman law, and was during the Middle Ages scholarly elaborated by the Glossators and Commentators (Cynus, Bartolus, Baldus).[77] Strictly speaking in the Roman vocabulary the expression *jus commune* did not have a well-, defined technical meaning, but instead designated a norm valid for all, as opposed to a norm valid only for some. It had a rather vast and flexible designation. A definition of *jus commune* did not even exist in Roman sources, notwithstanding quite vivid and neat conceptual oppositions of *jus commune*; when e.g. Roman jurists put *the totality* of humanity against *individual* nations. Here we have the dichotomy – as we find in Grotius – of *jus gentium* on the one hand and *jus civile* on the other, the first representing the law 'quod naturalis ratio inter omnes homines constituit' and which 'apud omnes peraeque custoditur', the latter the law 'quod quisque populus ipse sibi constituit'. The first was therefore *jus commune omnium hominum*, the latter *jus proprium civitatis*.[78]

Also this passage of Grotius contains an important reference to the *Summa* of Aquinas:

> Respondeo dicendum quod, sicut dictum est, jus, sive justum, est aliquod opus adaequatum alteri secundum aliquem aequalitatis modum. Dupliciter autem potest alicui homini aliquid esse adaequatum. Uno quidem modo, ex ipsa natura rei: puta cum aliquis tantum dat ut tantundem recipiat. Et hoc vocatur jus naturale. Alio modo aliquid est adaequatum vel commensuratum alteri ex condicto,

---

[76] *De iure praedae*, cap. II, p. 23. To *jus civile* belong: *Regula V:* Quidquid respublica se velle significavit, id inter cives singulos jus est; together with (and as foundation and support of the judicial power and that of the various magistrates) *Lex IX*: Ne civis adversus civem jus suum nisi judicio exsequatur; *Lex X*: Ut magistratus omnia gerat e bono reipublicae; and *Lex XI*: Ut quidquid magistratus gessit respublica ratum habeat; *Regula VI* Quod se magistratus velle significavit, id in cives universos jus est; *Regula VII* Quod se magistratus velle significavit, id in cives singulos jus est.

[77] See for an introduction to the writings of the Glossators and Commentators: E. H. Kantorowicz, *Studies in the Glossators of the Roman Law* (Cambridge: Cambridge University Press, 1938); P. Weimar, 'Die legistische Literatur und die Methode des Rechtsunterrichts der Glossatorenzeit', *Ius Commune*, 2 (1969), 43-83; N. Horn, 'Die juristische Literatur der Kommentatorenzeit', *Ius Commune*, 2 (1969), 84-129; Cavanna, *Storia del diritto moderno*, I, pp. 105-145.

[78] Cfr. Calasso, *Medio evo del diritto*, I, pp. 378-379.

> sive ex communi placito: quando scilicet aliquis reputat se contentum si tantum accipiat. Quod quidem potest fieri dupliciter. Uno modo, per aliquod privatum condictum: sicut quod firmatur aliquo pacto inter privatas personas. Alio modo, ex condicto publico: puta cum totus populus consentit quod aliquid habeatur quasi adaequatum et commensuratum alteri; vel cum hoc ordinat princeps, qui curam populi habet et ejus personam gerit. Et hoc dicitur jus positivum.[79]

The reference to Anaxarchos (which we quoted while speaking about *lex aeterna*), again noticed by Paola Negro,[80] is not the only symmetry between *De iure praedae* and *De iure belli ac pacis*. There is also symmetry in the reference to the *Summa theologiae* in which the *Doctor Angelicus* uses the same *topos*:

> Jus divinum dicitur quod divinitus promulgatur. Et hoc quidem partim est de his quae sunt naturaliter justa, sed tamen eorum justitia homines latet: partim autem est de his quae fiunt justa institutione divina. Unde etiam jus divinum per haec duo distingui potest, sicut et jus humanum. Sunt enim in lege divina quaedam praecepta quia bona, et prohibita quia mala; quaedam vero bona quia praecepta, et mala quia prohibita.[81]

Nonetheless, in *De iure praedae* reference is made to the definition of *jus civile* which 'non est jus per se, sed ex alio': the only law which at the time of the writing of this work, Grotius considered completely positive. The reference to the lucid Thomistic formula shows that already in 1605 Grotius was aware of the philosophical implications underlying the relationship between positive law and non-positive law, founded *per se*. In the *De iure belli ac pacis* he deals with natural law, defined in the style of Suárez as 'dictatum rectae rationis',[82] in this text Grotius literally returns to Thomistic argumentation. The reference to Aquinas is accompanied by a reference to Duns Scotus,[83] remarking with reference to both texts: 'Nec spernenda'. Such references

[79] *Summa theologiae*, II^{a}-II^{ae}, q. 57, a. 2: *Utrum ius convenienter dividatur in ius naturale et ius positivum*.

[80] Negro, Fonti scolastiche, p. 211.

[81] *Summa theologiae*, II^{a}-II^{ae}, q. 57, a. 2, ad 3.

[82] *De jure belli ac pacis*, I, I, X, 1-2: 'Jus naturale est dictatum rectae rationis indicans, actui alicui, ex ejus convenientia aut disconvenientia cum ipsa natura rationali, inesse moralem turpitudinem aut necessitatem moralem, ac consequenter ab auctore naturae Deo talem actum aut vetari aut praecipi. Actus de quibus tale extat dictatum, debiti sunt aut illiciti per se, atque ideo a Deo necessario praecepti aut vetiti intelliguntur: qua nota distat hoc jus non ab humano tantum jure, sed et a divino voluntario, quod non ea praecipit aut vetat quae per se ac suapte natura aut debita sunt aut illicita, sed vetando illicita, praecipiendo debita facit' (pp. 34-35).

[83] *Quaestiones in Librum III Sententiarum*, dist. XXXVII.

appear in the edition of 1642 (and also in the edition of 1646) of *De iure belli ac pacis*, that is about twenty years after its publication and forty years since the *De iure praedae*.

> Il filosofo olandese rintraccia nella formulazione tomistica un *topos* filosofico che egli può usare nelle due opere in situazioni argomentative di senso opposto. Anche nel testo di Duns Scoto troviamo un accenno a tale *topos* filosofico. Scoto sta criticando Tommaso d'Aquino per il quale (*Summa theologiae*, I-II, q. 100, aa. 1-8) tutti i precetti del decalogo sono anche di diritto naturale; per sostenere la diversità tra alcuni dei precetti del decalogo e la legge di natura, argomenta che Dio ha *di fatto* dispensato alcuni uomini dalle leggi del decalogo, mentre Dio non potrebbe dispensare gli uomini dalla legge di natura, la quale possiede una verità necessaria che Dio non può rendere falsa. Tra le spiegazioni del perché Dio possa dispensare dall'obbedienza al decalogo, viene addotta l'argomentazione secondo cui "si dicatur voluntatem creatam necessario debere conformare se istis [le verità del decalogo] ad hoc, quod sit recta, non tamen voluntatem divinam oportet conformiter velle istis veris, sed quia conformiter vult, ideo sunt vera".[84]

So the reference to Aquinas served to delimit the scope of *jus naturale*; the reference to Duns Scotus served to specify the sense of *jus voluntarium divinum*, referring to the precepts of the Decalogue, to be distinguished from *jus naturale*. Precisely because he was referring to different concepts, Grotius could quote in the same note two theologians as far apart one from the other as *Doctor Angelicus* and *Doctor Subtilis*.

> Tale rimando parallelo a Scoto e a Tommaso – ricorrente quest'ultimo in due opere, in un senso totalmente diverso – esemplifica il metodo di citazione di Grotius, con cui egli si appropria degli altrui testi, spesso decontestualizzando frammenti che egli piega alle sue esigenze, le quali non sono tanto quelle di dialogare criticamente con i suoi predecessori, ma piuttosto di mostrare la consentaneità alle sue tesi di autori spesso lontani tra loro. Tale modalità di riferimenti testuali, che Grotius peraltro mutuava dalla cultura della sua epoca, per un filosofo giusnaturalista non è mero espediente retorico, ma corrisponde a un'esigenza filosofica forte: dimostrare che le proprie teorie godono di un *consensus gentium*, il quale è tanto più marcato, quanto più le opere degli autori menzionati hanno un impianto divergente.[85]

In conclusion, the 'system of sources' of Grotius's *De iure praedae*, even while it is sometimes an expression of ideas still in the process of ripening, had a particular importance because it would be developed in an accomplished

---

[84] Negro, Fonti scolastiche, pp. 211-212.
[85] Negro, Fonti scolastiche, p. 212.

way with innovative outcomes in *De iure belli ac pacis*, and later on by succeeding representatives of modern natural law, such as Pufendorf, Thomasius, Wolff. With respect to the latter, Grotius put forward most of all assumptions that were partly voluntaristic, partly individualistic.[86] In this sense the *De iure praedae* is already a work which clearly forestalls modernity.

[86] See Cavanna, *Storia del diritto moderno*, I, p. 328; in particular M. Villey, 'Les fondateurs de l'école du droit naturel moderne au XVIIe siècle (Notes de lecture)', *Archives de Philosophie du Droit*, 6 (1961), 73ff.

The VOC, Corporate Sovereignty and the Republican Sub-Text of *De iure praedae*

Eric Wilson
Senior Lecturer, International Law, Monash University, Melbourne, Australia
e-mail: eric.wilson@law.monash.edu.au

Abstract
This essay discusses some of the ways in which *De iure praedae* may be understood to constitute a republican text. It is my argument that the 'Commentary on the Law of Prize and Booty' should be firmly located within the over-arching republican discourse of the juvenilia, although the text's republican content is not immediately apparent. On close examination, a republican sub-text is detectible through the author's treatment of the discursive object of the text, the Dutch East India Company (the VOC), a corporate body. By attempting to legitimate the VOC's natural right to wage just war, Grotius invests a private entity with a public mark of sovereignty. This investiture of a non-state actor with public international legal personality forces a careful reappraisal of two central characteristics of seventeenth-century republican thought: (i) the divisibility of sovereignty, and (ii) the fluid demarcation between the 'public' and the 'private' spheres. I conclude that the VOC may be accurately denoted a 'corporate sovereign', an entity whose legal personality is derived from the corporatist principles that underlined early republican and federalist theory.

Keywords
republicanism, corporatism, divisible sovereignty, Jean Bodin, Johannes Althusius, corporate sovereignty, *occupatio duplex*, *dominium*, *imperium*, Modern World-System, Capitalist World-Economy, Giovanni Arrighi

To an international lawyer, it is something of a surprise to discover that there is so little Law in Hugo Grotius's *De iure praedae*. Indeed, the text far more closely resembles a political treatise rather than the legal brief it is so widely taken to be.[1] Even when read under the somewhat restrictive title of the 'Commentary on the Law of Prize and Booty', it proves a jurisprudential

[1] If so, then *De iure praedae* is historically positioned within 'the pamphlet war' waged in the Netherlands from 1606-9 concerning the activities of the VOC and the concurrent peace negotiations with Spain. J. Israel, *The Dutch Republic and the Hispanic World 1606-1661* (Oxford: Oxford University Press, 1982), pp. 30-32.

disappointment; although prize-taking constituted a central part of early modern maritime law, there is nothing of the specialist expertise or terminological exactitude demonstrated by the classic sources of the field, such as the Rhodian Sea-Law, the *Roles d'Oleron*, or the Black Book of the English Admiralty.[2] What we encounter instead is a political pamphlet formally masquerading as a juridical treatise,[3] one that transverses the conventional boundaries between the legal and the political through its treatment of a private trading company as an international actor commensurate to that of a state. *De iure praedae* is conventionally divided into two asymmetrical parts: (i) the *Historica*, primarily Chapter XI, which provides the historical discussion of the background to the seizure of the *Santa Catarina*, and (ii) the *Dogmatica*, all of the other chapters, dealing with the substantive legal issues concerned with the Dutch struggle against Portugal as an instance of just war and the lawful classification of the carrack as a maritime prize. When examined in detail, the *Historica* is revealed to display a sophisticated understanding of the early development of the modern world-system, in which Dutch-Portuguese relations were governed by irrepressible conflict: 'a just cause of war exists when the freedom of trade is being defended against those who would obstruct it'.[4] As Neils Steensgaard has demonstrated, it is precisely within 'the question of sovereign rights on the open sea that the pre-capitalist nature of the Portuguese Empire is most clearly reflected, and where the discontinuity in relation to the North-West European Companies is most marked'.[5] This interstate conflict is juridically reconfigured by Grotius in terms of the latent incompatibility of two rival taxonomic categories of property rights, *dominium* and *occupatio* (or, *occupatio duplex*); in this sense, the two contending states, Holland and Portugal, do little more than serve as discursive signifiers of antithetical proprietary regimes.

What links the two on a deeper meta-narrative level, is the question of 'universal monarchy'. For the Iberians, this meant the global legitimation of a territorialist world-empire, while for the Papacy it signified the reactionary

---

[2] J.H.W. Verzijl, *International Law in Historical Perspective. Part IX-C: The Law of the Maritime Prize* (Leyden: A.W. Sijthoff, 1992), pp.10-119, (*passim*).

[3] A point implicitly underscored by Richard Tuck when referring to *De iure praedae* as the locus of 'the first modern political theory'. Richard Tuck, *The Rights of War and Peace: Political Thought and International Order from Grotius to Kant* (Oxford: Oxford University Press, 1999), p. 232.

[4] Hugo Grotius, *[De iure praedae] De Iure Praedae Commentarius. Commentary on the Law of Prize and Booty*, trans. Gwladys L. Williams and Walter H. Zeydel (London: Wildy & Sons, 1964), p. 202.

[5] Neils Steensgaard, *Carracks, Caravans and Companies: The Structural Crisis in the European-Asian Trade in the Early 17th Century* (Denmark: Studentlitteratur, 1973), p. 86.

triumph of a theocratic model of international public order. *De iure praedae* serves as both an anti-Portuguese and anti-Papal text, striving to discursively de-legitimate both variants of universal monarchy. As I have shown at great length in my recent book, *The Savage Republic: De Indis of Hugo Grotius, Republicanism, and Dutch Hegemony in the Early Modern World System (c. 1600-1619)*[6] the anti-Iberian stratagem of *De iure praedae* is mediated by the rhetoric and discourse of early Dutch republicanism. Both in my longer work and in this essay I very much understand *De iure praedae* to constitute a republican text, albeit one that was not written as such in a wholly systematic or 'self-conscious' manner. I agree with Martine van Ittersum's recent work that the VOC is the central discursive object of the Grotian text;[7] however, I feel that the author rhetorically appropriated and actively re-formulated the Dutch East India Company (the VOC) as the bearer, or 'sign', of republican principles and values, even while engaged in the comparatively pedestrian task of explicating its 'interests'. I feel that it is possible for us to detect the presence of a 'double discourse' within *De iure praedae*: the VOC is simultaneously a 'corporation' in its own right and a metaphor for the 'republic'. The text, therefore, constitutes a singe instance of Grotius's wider and continuous project of developing an early theory of Dutch republicanism.

1. Republicanism and Divisible Sovereignty

The entirety of *De iure praedae* is devoted to a dual agenda: (i) to invest a 'private' trading company with a 'public' international legal personality, and; (ii) effectively collapse the distinction between private and public warfare. It is my belief that Grotius deliberately represented the VOC as a 'double' of the early Dutch Republic; by so doing, the VOC is rhetorically deployed as a 'signifier' of both Dutch republicanism and Dutch nationalism; this rhetorical innovation, in turn, allows us to situate *De iure praedae* quite neatly within the broader discursive continuity of the other texts of the early Grotian period, the 'juvenilia'. In 1601 Grotius was appointed Historiographer of Holland; in other words, he was historically situated as the self-conscious producer of republican and patriotic texts. Whatever the nature of his relationship with the VOC, the Author was clearly within the immediate political orbit of

[6] Martinus Nijhoff, 2008.

[7] Martine van Ittersum, *Profit and Principle: Hugo Grotius, Natural Rights Theories and the Rise of Dutch Power in the East Indies, 1595-1615* (Leiden: Brill, 2006).

Holland's Advocate (*lands-advocaat*), Johan van Oldenbarnevelt.[8] This would strongly indicate that Grotius's textual 'production' would have operated within the parameters of an emergent political discourse, that of republicanism.[9] The juvenile works of Grotius – which include such texts as *De republica emendanda* (c. 1600), *Annales et historiae de rebus Belgicis* (1601-12), *Commentarius in theses* XI (1603-8), *Mare liberum* (1609), and *De antiquitate Republicae Batavicae* (c.1610) – constitute a singular and unified discursive formation premised upon the twin political imperatives of early Dutch sovereignty and republicanism. The composition of the 'Commentary' from 1603 to 1608 – or, possibly, as late as 1613[10] – transverses the entirety of Grotius's republican phase as an apologist and propagandist for the newly emergent Dutch Republic. I argue that the deeper, and more subversive, meaning of *De iure praedae* goes far beyond the rather pedestrian task of legally justifying the privateering activities of the VOC,which, as pointed out above, receive next to no formal legal consideration.Rather, it lies within the structural tensions within early modern, or 'primitive', international public order engendered by the emergence of a republican model of both inter-state and intra-state relations as a rival model to territorial Univeralism. The central discursive stratagem at the heart of the text lies within the Grotian signature of conflating private agency with public legal rights. In large part this reflects the precarious nature of the Dutch penetration of the East Indies at the time of the production of the text. Composition of the text predated the beginning of Dutch colonization and the forcible incorporation of the Indies into the Dutch colonial network; the Dutch Republic is 'present' in the region almost solely

[8] The chief administrator, or 'clerk', of the Province of Holland, whose subjective political power was largely extra-constitutional, comprising a form of *governance*. As Sir Thomas Rodley put it, 'all here [in the Netherlands] is directed by Holland and Holland is carried away by Barnevelt.' Geoffrey Parker, *The Dutch Revolt*, rev. edn (London: Penguin, 1985), p. 248. Evidence of Oldenbarnevelt's continuous patronage is demonstrated by Grotius's meteoric rise within the Dutch Republic: Solicitor General of the Province of Holland, 1607–13; Pensionary of Rotterdam, 1613-18; Member of the Estates of Holland and Member of the Dutch Estates-General, 1617. Not for nothing did Oldenbarnevelt refer to the Author as 'my Grotius'. Jan den Tex, *Oldenbarnevelt*, 2 vols (Cambridge: Cambridge University Press, 1973), II, p. 683.

[9] See below, Chapter One.

[10] The recent pioneering, albeit contentious, work by Borschberg and van Ittersum on the watermarks of the pages in the original manuscript provide evidence that Grotius may have been working on the Text as late as 1613. Peter Borschberg and Martina Julia van Ittersum, 'Profit and Principle? Hugo Grotius, the VOC, and the Estado da India: the Historical Context of *De Jure Praedae*', conference paper, 'Piracy, Property, and Punishment: Hugo Grotius and *De iure praedae*', Netherlands Institute for Advanced Study in the Humanities and Social Sciences, Conference June 9–11, 2005, Wassenaar.

through the privateering operations of the VOC.The fundamental legal dilemma that the Company posed to the Author was the legitimation of extra-territorial actions performed both by the private corporation as well as by its individual agents, the merchant-captains of the VOC fleet, such as the infamous Jacob Heemskerck. Eschewing any argument derived from prescription, Grotius was compelled to settle on a highly expansive notion of both *ius naturale* and *bellum iustum*.

> Freedom of trade [*liberum commercium*]... springs from the primary law of nations [*ius gentium secondarium*], which has a natural and permanent cause [*ius gentium primarium*], so that it cannot be abrogated. Moreover, even if its abrogation were possible, such a result could be achieved only with the consent of all nations. Accordingly, it is not remotely conceivable that one nation may justly impose any hindrance whatsoever upon two other nations that wish to enter into a contract with each other... Therefore, if the Portuguese do not possess any right that gives them an exclusive privilege of trade with the East Indians, that right must have arisen, after he fashion of other servitudes, from an express grant, or from a tacit concession (that is to say, from prescription); for under no other circumstance could it exist. But no one made such an express grant, unless perchance the Pope did so; and he was not properly empowered to act thus.[11]

Technically, Grotius does not invest the VOC with formal legal personality; however, his text is riddled with rhetorical friction on precisely this point: it was the VOC that provided the conditions for the merchant-captains to be physically present in the Indies and waging a privateering campaign against the Iberians. In *The Savage Republic* I argue at great length that Grotius is rhetorically forced, even if only as a manoeuvre sub rosa, to at least tacitly invest the VOC with the degree of legal personality requisite to the investment of its governance-like form of empowerment, not just of the right (ius) of self-defense but of punishment and compensation as well. Even if only unconsciously, the VOC as the discursive object of the text, is re-formulated as a cognisable international legal person bearing enforceable rights and obligations.[12]

For Richard Tuck, this is, in fact, the basis for his strong claim for *De iure praedae* as a major work of seventeenth-century political theory. The text is the site of a remarkable re-working of the fundamental categories of early modern property law as a means of legitimising the ability of trading companies to enforce international legal rights, including the freedoms of trade and

[11] Grotius, *De iure praedae*, p. 257.

[12] I owe the development of this section to discussions with Professor Hans W. Blom. For further discussion of tis point, see below, Conclusion.

navigation; 'In executing his ideological aim, Grotius... brings about a major simplification of the concept of property. Property is now confined to private property, in the sense of an exclusive right, and it presupposes actual possession'.[13] The text's strategy of alteration between public and private notions of both property and personality is fully consistent with the author's over-arching purpose, essentially republican in nature, of discursively reconfiguring the VOC as both a public and a private actor; 'Nations in their relation to the whole of mankind occupy the position of private individuals... Public property [is] the property of a given nation'.[14]

This point is critical to the argument of *The Savage Republic*; the Luso-Dutch struggle has to be understood as a form of interstate rivalry particular to the contours of an emergent capitalist world-economy. The two warring parties were not merely rival nations, but fundamentally incompatible forms of political economies, each relying upon incommensurable modes of proprietary regimes: *imperium* as against *dominium*. As J.G.A. Pocock reminds us, 'property was a judicial term before it was an economic one',[15] an insight replete with Grotian significance. *De iure praedae* formally classifies *imperium* as *iurisdictio et protectio*,[16] and *dominium* as *proprietas*.[17] 'Dominium is property and imperium is sovereignty... limited to protection and jurisdiction, to be exerted... for the sake of safety for all'.[18] This binary classification scheme is derived from Gentili's seminal work *De Iure Belli*: 'Things which are common to all so far as their use is concerned are the property of no one; their

[13] Richard Tuck, *Natural Rights Theories: Their Origin and Development* (Cambridge: Cambridge University Press, 1979), p. 70. 'Actual possession' here means *occupatio duplex*. Edward Keene has rightly argued'The law of nations was not, in Grotius's scheme, exclusively a law for nations; for it included rights and duties, albeit limited ones, for individuals and private corporations. While he conceptualised the rights of public authorities in terms of their possession of marks of sovereignty, the main vehicle that Grotius used to think about the rights of private individuals and bodies was the concept of property ownership.' Edward Keene, *Beyond the Anarchical Society: Grotius, Colonialism and Order in World Politics* (Cambridge: Cambridge University Press, 2002), p. 52.

[14] Grotius, *De iure praedae*, pp. 237 and 236.

[15] J.G.A. Pocock, *Virtue, Commerce and History: Essays on Political Thought and History, Chiefly in the Eighteenth Century* (Cambridge: Cambridge University Press, 1985), p. 56.

[16] Grotius, *De iure praedae*, pp. 237 and 245.

[17] Ibid., pp. 220, 226–7 and 228.

[18] J.K. Oudendijk, Status and Extent of Adjacent Waters: A Historical Orientation (Leyden: A.W. Sijthoff, 1970), p. 27. See Masahara Yanagihara, '*Dominium* and *Imperium*', in *A Normative Approach to War: Peace, War, and Justice in Hugo Grotius*, ed. by Yasuaki Onuma (Oxford: Clarendon Press, 1993), pp. 148 and 154. Also, Frans De Pauw, *Grotius and the Law of the Sea* (Brussels: Institut de Sociologie, Universite de Bruxelles, 1965), pp. 147-73 at 32.

jurisdiction and protection belong to the sovereign'.[19] The investment of certain proprietary forms of *ius* with the status of Natural Law in itself establishes the demarcation of lawful sovereignty; *imperium* prevails precisely wherein it may be exercised with legitimacy. Thus, a 'war will be called natural, if it is undertaken because of some privilege of nature which is denied us by man. For example, if a right of way is refused us, or if we are excluded from harbours, or kept from provisions, commerce, or trade'.[20] If 'real' property is now private, then any holder of private property, even if only a private person, is able to exert an inalienable set of legal rights commensurable with those of the public state, which is now revealed to be a metaphorical 'private individual'. The importance of this proprietorial innovation for *De iure praedae* can hardly be over-estimated, for it is precisely by this means, the private property owner as bearer of enforceable international right (*ius*), that the VOC can be re-constituted by Grotius as possessing a form of sovereignty.[21] More precisely, the corporate body, operating in parallel manner to the state, is shown to both possess and to successfully enforce virtually all of the critical marks of the sovereign; these include the policing of trade monopolies, the administration of colonial territories, the construction and manning of fortifications, the possession and maintenance of 'private' military forces, the formation of treaties, and, perhaps most important, the declaration of lawful warfare – just war.[22] As Tuck quite rightly argues, both the logical and the political implications of this radical innovation linking private property with sovereignty are profound. As I endeavour at great length to show in *The Savage Republic*, not the least of these is the possibility of dividing the monist state into sub-statist sovereign entities. The Grotian theory of property makes conceivable the constitutional theory of the divisibility of sovereignty, *which is replete with republican significance*.[23]

---

[19] Alberico Gentili, *De Iure Belli Libri Tres*, ed. with intr. by Coleman Phillipson (New York: Oceana Publications, 1964), p. 92.

[20] Ibid., p.86.

[21] See F.W. Maitland, 'Translator's Introduction', in Otto von Gierke, *Political Theories of the Middle Ages* (Cambridge: Cambridge University Press, 1900), pp. vii-xlv *(passim)*.

[22] Marjolein't Hart, *The Making of the Bourgeois State: War, Politics and Finance During the Dutch Revolt* (Manchester: Manchester University Press, 1993), p. 23; C.H. Boxer, *The Dutch Seaborne Empire 1600–1800* (Harmondsworth: Penguin Books, 1965), pp. 20, 24 and 26. 'The distinction between the company as a private body of enterprise and as a public authority enjoying more or less sovereign power was actually somewhat lost'. P.W. Klein, 'The Origins of Trading Companies', in *Companies and Trade*, ed. by Leonard Blussé and Femme S. Gaastra (Leiden: Leiden University Press, 1981), pp. 17-28 at 23.

[23] For a good overview of the Grotian meaning of this term, see Peter Borschberg, 'Critical Intr'., in Hugo Grotius, *Commentarius in Theses XI. An Early Treatise on Sovereignty, the Just War,*

What is at stake here is the wider issue of how the binary opposition between competing forms of sovereignty, both divisible and non-divisible, was itself the product of the evolution of International Relations in the early seventeenth century. For Edward Keene

> It has always been hard for orthodox [International Relations] theorists to appreciate the international dimensions of relationships in the extra-European world, largely because they make the misguided assumption that their unitary conception of sovereignty has always defined the discipline of international politics and international law. They argue that international relations are relations between mutually independent states, because that is the only conception they possess as a way of thinking about the modern world; they lack the more flexible vocabulary of Grotius, and are thus at a loss to know how to describe, say, relations between the British paramount power and the 'semi-sovereign' Native States of India. What they typically do, then, is simply ignore this way of organizing international relations, perhaps giving it a breezy acknowledgement but hastily moving on to the familiar business of international politics in the European states-system. The inadequacy of their conceptual apparatus and the narrowness of their historical vision are faults of the orthodox theory that continually reinforce each other.[24]

Keene's commentary is useful because it reminds us of the radically heterogeneous nature of the juridico-political landscape that *De iure praedae* was embedded within, an embryonic world-system that the text strove, however imperfectly and unconsciously, to invest with formal juridical expression. Both the composition of *De iure praedae* and the later significance awarded it as a landmark of international legal discourse are inextricable from the contemporaneous dual transformation of the modern world-system: the shift of the European core zone from Lombardy/Mediterranean to the northwest/Atlantic, and the self-aggrandizing transition of a regionally bounded sub-system to a globally encompassing Capitalist World Economy.[25] However, 'new' intra- and interstate systems were wholly derivative from an earlier heteronomous system of sovereign and quasi-sovereign personalities. The

and the Legitimacy of the Dutch Revolt, ed. Peter Borschberg (New York: Peter Lang, 1994), pp. 15-199 at 115–35, (*passim*).

[24] Keene, *Beyond the Anarchical Society*, p. 95.

[25] On the spatial demarcations of world economies and world systems, see Fernand Braudel, *The Perspective of the World* (vol. iii of *Civilization and Capitalism 15th – 18th Century*) (New York: Harper & Row, Publishers, 1984), pp. 21–45.'We may deduce that a world-economy is a sum of individualized areas, economic and non-economic, which it brings together; that it generally represents a very large surface area (in theory the largest coherent zone at a given period, in a given part of the globe); and that it usually goes beyond the boundaries of other great historical divisions'. Ibid. 24.

political landscape inhabited by *De iure praedae* is a profoundly alien one by contemporary state-centric standards, with its exhaustive identification of legal personality with sovereign agency. By 1500, Europe consisted of a *multiversum* of competing sovereign forms: the Papacy,[26] the City- Leagues (the Hansa),[27] the Italian communes/city-states,[28] the Imperial Free-City States,[29] the Holy Roman Empire,[30] feudal principalities (for example, the Duchy of Burgundy), and the 'international' regulatory and joint-stock trading companies, none of which are readily cognisable in terms of the essentializing 'statism' of the Westphalian System with which Grotius's name is so frequently attached. Contrary to expectations, *De iure praedae* is an early modern text, constitututing a highly faithful reproduction of contemporary international relations:[31] the 'main "source" of the Grotian system is to be found in the author's experience of international relations and his extensive knowledge of contemporary diplomatic history'.[32] Grotius's framing of the VOC as the discursive object of the text highlights the facile nature of the belief in statism as the central tenet of either the Westphalian System or the Grotian Heritage; the young Grotius expressly repudiates any rigid demarcation between the 'public' and the 'private' spheres. This should come as a surprise to no one except the contemporary international lawyer; for all of its affiliations with contemporary 'deconstructive' International Relations theory, divisible sovereignty is, in fact, an extremely well established doctrinal innovation, lasting well into the 19th century. As late as 1864, Henry Sumner Maine wrote

> Sovereignty is a term which, in international law, indicates a well-ascertained assemblage of separate powers and privileges … there is not, nor has there ever been, anything in international law to prevent some of those rights being lodged with one possessor and some with another. Sovereignty has always been regarded as divisible.[33]

---

[26] Hendrik Spruyt, *The Sovereign State and its Competitors: An Analysis of Systems Change* (Princeton: Princeton University Press, 1994), pp. 34–57.

[27] Ibid., pp. 109–29.

[28] Ibid., pp. 130–50.

[29] Ibid., pp. 118–20 and 172–78.

[30] Ibid., pp. 114–17.

[31] C. G. Roelofsen, 'Grotius and State Practice of His Day', *Grotiana*, 10 (1989), pp. 3–46 at 16 and 44–6.

[32] Roelofsen, 'Some Remarks on the "Sources" of the Grotian System of International Law', 79.

[33] Cited in Keene, *Beyond the Anarchical Society*, p. 77. See also, Richard K. Ashley, 'Untying the Sovereign State: A Double Reading of the Anarchy Problematique', *Millenium*, 17 (1988), pp. 227–62, *(passim)*.

What is far more contentious, and which forms a central argument of The Savage Republic, is that the Grotian adoption of divisibility theory carries with it a specifically republican connotation.

The discursive convergence among republicanism, private property and divisible sovereignty may be better appreciated by illuminating in greater detail the juridico-political space that *De iure praedae* inhabits. The necessary, even if only sub-textual, correlation between the divisibility of sovereignty and the republican polity is made clear from even the most cursory reading of Grotius's near-contemporary Jean Bodin (1529/30–1596), the progenitor of absolutist political theory.[34] The entirety of Bodin's later thought is that the essentialist indivisibility of sovereignty guarantees the logical necessity of a strictly hierarchical polity.[35] The key element of Bodin's discursive stratagem is the fusion of Civic Humanist scholarship with a thoroughgoing Aristotelian essentialism; 'But it is clear that to have true definitions and resolution in any subject matter, one must not fix on accidents, which are innumerable, but on essential differences of form. Otherwise, one could fall into an infinite labyrinth which does not admit of scientific knowledge'.[36] For Bodin, 'Sovereignty is the absolute and perpetual power of a commonwealth which the Latins

[34] Jens Bartelson, *A Genealogy of Sovereignty* (Cambridge: Cambridge University Press, 1995), p. 28: 'Since [Jean] Bodin, indivisibility has been integral to the concept of sovereignty itself. In international political theory, this means that whenever sovereignty is used in a theoretical context to confer unity upon the state as an acting subject, all that it conveys is that this entity is an individual by virtue of its indivisibility, which is tautological indeed. What follows from this search for the locus of sovereignty in international political theory, however necessary to its empirical testability, is thus nothing more than a logical sideshow; the essential step towards unity is already taken whenever sovereignty figures in the definition of political order. Whether thought to be upheld by an individual or a collective, or embodied in the state as a whole, sovereignty entails self-presence and self-sufficiency; that which is sovereign is immediately given to itself, conscious of itself, and thus acting for itself. That is, as it figures in international political theory, sovereignty is not an attribute of something whose existence is prior to or independent of sovereignty; rather, it is the concept of sovereignty itself which supplies this indivisibility and unity'.

[35] 'The system of political power and authority put forward in *Six Livres* [1576] through the use of the word 'sovereignty' is... essentially interested in the hierarchical structure of governance in society'. Stephane Beaulac, *The Power of Language in the Making of International Law: The Word Sovereignty in Bodin and Vattel and the Myth of Westphalia* (Leiden: Brill, 2004), p. 117. See Julian H. Franklin, 'Sovereignty and the Mixed Constitution', *The Cambridge History of Political Thought 1450–1700*, ed. by J.H. Burns and Mark Goldie (Cambridge: Cambridge University Press, 2001), pp. 298–328, *(passim)*.

[36] Jean Bodin, *On Sovereignty: Four Chapters from the Six Books of the Commonwealth*, tr. and ed. by Julian H. Franklin (Cambridge: Cambridge University Press, 1992), p. 89. On Bodin's Aristotelianism, see Kenneth D. McRae, 'Ramist Tendencies in the Thought of Jean Bodin', *Journal of the History of Ideas*, 16/3 (1955), pp. 306–23, *(passim)*.

call *maiestas*'.[37] From this definition flow two logically necessary propositions. Firstly, that sovereignty, as it actually exists, both conceptually and factually, must necessarily remain indivisible in nature.

> If it were otherwise, and the absolute power conceded to a lieutenant of the prince were called sovereign, he would be able to use it against his prince, who would then command his lord, and the servant his master, which would be absurd. The person of the sovereign, according to the law, is always excepted no matter how much power and authority he grants to someone else; and he never gives so much that he does not hold back even more. He is never prevented from commanding, or from assuming cognisance – by substitution, concurrence, removal, or any way he pleases – of any cause that he left to the jurisdiction of a subject.[38]

Accordingly, sovereignty is inalienable and cannot be irrevocably delegated or conveyed to either a subordinate or to a rival sovereign.[39] For just as God, 'the greatest Sovereign, cannot make a God equal to Himself because He is infinite and by logical necessity two infinities cannot exist, so we can say that the prince whom we have taken as the image of God, cannot make a subject equal to himself without annihilation of his power'.[40]

Secondly, that the resultant sovereignty assumes the form of an exclusive supremacy, serving as the basis of an absolutist conception of the political order.[41]

> A subject who is excepted from the force of the laws always remains in subjection and obedience to those who have the sovereignty. But persons who are sovereign must not be subject in any way to the commands of someone else and must be able to give law to subjects, and to suppress or repeal disadvantageous law and replace them with others – which cannot be done by someone who is subject to the laws or to persons having power of command over him.[42]

---

[37] Bodin, *On Sovereignty*, p. 1.

[38] Ibid., p. 2.

[39] Ibid., pp. 6–7.

[40] Ibid., p. 50. 'On Bodin's principles, no delegation of sovereign authority could have any element of permanence'. Julian H. Franklin, *Jean Bodin and the Rise of Absolutist Theory* (Cambridge: Cambridge University Press, 1973), p. 103. Not surprisingly, Bodin was notorious for his unconditional rejection of that favourite categorical construction of early-modern republicanism, the 'mixed constitution'. Ibid., pp. 27–9.

[41] 'Sovereignty, for Bodin, merely consisted in the highest and most general, the ultimate and final power of command. Bodin continually stressed the idea of absolutism conceived as hierarchical superiority, as distinct from absolutism conceived as the simple exercise of arbitrary control'. Preston T. King, *The Ideology of Order: A Comparative Analysis of Jean Bodin and Thomas Hobbes* (London: Allen and Unwin, 1974), pp. 129–30.

[42] Bodin, *On Sovereignty*, p. 11; also see ibid., pp. 12–15. On this basis Bodin erects an entire sign-system for the purpose of recognizing the objective 'marks' of the 'true' sovereign. 'To be able to recognize such a person – that is, a sovereign – we have to know his attributes, which are

It is abundantly clear that Bodin formulated his views on the indivisibility of sovereignty in response to the sectarian conflicts and civil wars that were threatening France in the latter part of the sixteenth century.[43] Yet his emphasis upon hierarchy and the political monism of the state effectively doubled as a juridical and ideological legitimation of territorialist world-empire. My own account of Dutch republicanism as presented in *The Savage Republic* is very much based upon the world-system analysis developed by Immanuel Wallerstein and Giovanni Arrighi. For me, the paradoxical intrastitial position of the Dutch Republic as lawful rebel waging just war against the Iberian world-empire on the one hand and as legitimate hegemon globally enforcing natural justice on the other highlighted the discursive correlation between a war of national liberation and Dutch leadership within the early modern world-system. The Grotian text, therefore, had to perform the somewhat difficult task of providing an internally coherent rhetorical stratagem that would symbolically validate latently contradictory agendas: the creation of a heterogenous inter-state system of formally equally states within the core zone of Europe – generically de-noted as 'the Westphalian system'– and the legitimation of the mercantile penetration, and ultimate incorporation, of the non-European periphery by these same states.

The main discursive differences between Bodin's *Six Livres* and Grotius's *De iure praedae* may, therefore, be attributable to the different roles played by their respective countries (France; Holland) within the core zone of the modern world-system. France, as a non-hegemon but a 'strong' state, or 'major power', within the core zone, led Bodin to concentrate on the requirements of robust intra-state formation, yielding a textually constructed reification of political unity founded upon an ontological monism. As I discuss at greater length in *The Savage Republic*, there exists a very clear and precise correlation between the Civic Humanism and the unitary *civitas* of Alberico Gentili with

properties not shared by subjects. For if they were shared, there would be no sovereign prince… For the prerogatives of sovereignty have to be of such a sort that they apply only to a sovereign prince. If, on the contrary, they can be shared with subjects, one cannot say that they are marks of sovereignty. For just as a crown no longer has that name if it is breached, or if its rosettes are torn away, so sovereign majesty loses its greatness if someone makes a breach in it and encroaches on a part of its domain'. Ibid., pp. 46 and 49. The 'marks' of sovereignty identified by Bodin include the promulgation of law; binding declarations of war and peace; the appointment of senior magistrates; serving as the court of last instance; receiving all acts of fealty and homage; the printing of currency; and confiscation of estates for the crime of treason. Ibid., pp. 46–88.

[43] Franklin, *Jean Bodin and the Rise of Absolutist Theory*, pp. 41–53. Bodin's 'theoretical goal was the suspension of conflict through the elimination of all plural sources of power and authority'. Thomas O. Hueglin, *Early Modern Concepts for a Late Modern World: Althusius on Community and Federalism* (Waterloo: Wilfrid Laurier University Press, 1999), p. 170.

a strict monist ontology that expressly privileges a positivist construction of law. Holland, in contrast, as the nascent hegemon (versus Portugal) within the still crystallizing modern world-system lay at the vital nexus between intra- and interstate crosscurrents. As a result, Grotius moved towards a discursive strategy of formulating the hegemonic requirements of maritime supremacy and world-market penetration within an international schema that permitted a plurality of political actors. Here we encounter a widely under-appreciated phenomenon: the vital interconnection between intra-state constiutional theory and inter-state relations. As I argue in *The Savage Republic*,[44] it was the very indeterminate nature of the Dutch constitutional model that proved optimally suited for legitimising Dutch leadership within the decentralized and heterogenous early modern world-system.[45] The intra-state political realities of the Dutch Republic simply cannot be understood in isolation from the emergent state's position within the inter-state system; the 'paradox' of the Dutch hegemonic cycle was that the leader, the United Provinces, was a constitutionally weak State. Therefore, it is 'no exaggeration to say that in the seventeenth century, it was [sic?] the more speculatively metaphysical system-builders [Bodin] who believed in the indivisibility of sovereignty, while the more pragmatic and constitutionally-minded experts on the law of nations [Grotius] were the ones who upheld the empirically verifiable doctrine that sovereignty was divisible'.[46] By contrast, the Grotian theory of divisible sovereignty

> Recalls the complex hierarchies of overlapping jurisdictions that... were symptomatic of medieval Christendom, and precisely the opposite of the modern world where political authority is believed to come in neat territorial packages labelled 'sovereignty'... The imperial constitution, the territorial sovereignty of the states and the reserved right of the emperor made it hard for lawyers to ignore the fact that, whatever the attractions of the Bodinian theory in principle, sovereignty was divided in practice.[47]

More appropriate to Holland's position within the World-System was the radical theory of popular sovereignty pioneered by Johannes Althusius (1557–1638), in his *Politica Methodice Digesta* (first edition 1603), a text virtually contemporaneous with *De iure praedae*. There is no direct evidence that

---

[44] See *The Savage Republic*, chapters four and five.

[45] Bouwsma has made this point explicit. 'The mixed constitution thus occupied much the same place in the structure of internal politics as the balance of power in international affairs; its principle of operation is identical'. William J. Bouwsma, *Venice and the Defence of Republican Liberty: Renaissance Values in the Age of the Counter Reformation* (Berkeley: University of California Press, 1968), p. 17.

[46] Keene, *Beyond the Anarchical Society*, p. 105.

[47] Ibid.

Grotius utilized the *Politica* when composing his own work. However, Grotius is frequently less than honest in his acknowledgements, and there remains a distinct possibility that Althusius was known to Grotius's mentor Jan Oldenbarnevelt; in his capacity as syndic (legal counsellor) to the city of Emden, Althusius formed part of the legations regularly dispatched by that city to The Hague.[48] More direct proof of a 'Dutch Connection' is provided by Althusius himself in the Dedication to the third edition of the *Politica* (1614), where he devotes the text 'to the illustrious leaders of the estates of Frisia between the Zuider Zee and the North Sea most worthy lords'.[49] Althusius goes so far as to intentionally situate the Eighty-Years War within the contours of the early Modern World-System, clearly identifying the United Provinces as the global protector of popular sovereignty.

> For the success of your admirable deeds and those of your allies, is so abundant that it overflows into neighbouring countries, indeed, into all of Germany and France. It is even experienced by the nations of the Indies and many other realms plagued by Spanish arms that have been sustained and defended by you and the other provinces united with you.[50]

In the *Politica*, Althusius, who operated within the moderate tradition of the German Monarchomachi,[51] formulated a similar notion of the delegated 'inferior magistrate', the 'Ephors', who are responsible for keeping the civil power of the executive, or the 'supreme magistrate',[52] in check during periods of political crisis. Like 'Stephen Junius Brutus', Althusius follows a descending line of argument, predicating the Ephors upon *lex divina*.

> God has formed in all peoples by the natural law itself the free power of constituting princes, kings, and magistrates for themselves. This means that in the measure in which any commonwealth that is divinely instructed by the light of nature has civil power, it can transfer this power to another or others who, under the titles of kings, princes, consuls, or other magistrates, assume the direction of its common life.[53]

---

[48] Carl Friedrich Joachim, 'Intr.', in Johannes Althusius, *Politica Methodice Digesta of Johannes Althusius (Althaus)* (Cambridge: Harvard University Press, 1932), pp. xiii-xcix at xxxviii.

[49] Johannes Althusius, *The Politics of Johannes Althusius*, trans. with intr. by Frederick S. Carney (Boston: Beacon Press, 1964), p. 8.

[50] Ibid., p. 11.

[51] Van Gelderen, 'Aristotelians, Monarchomachs and Republicans: Sovereignty and *respublica mixta* in Dutch and German Political Thought, 1580-1650', in *Republicanism and Constitutionalism in Early Modern Europe*, 2 vols, ed. By Martin van Gelderen and Quentin Skinner (Cambridge: Cambridge University Press, 2002), I [*Republicanism: a Shared European Heritage*], pp. 195-217 at 205–6.

[52] Althusius, *The Politics of Johannes Althusius*, pp. 115–29.

[53] Ibid., p. 91.

Closely following the *Vindiciae contra tyrannos*, the *Politica* simultaneously affirms both a descending and an ascending argumentation, the two rhetorics converging at the site of the national level of delegated authority.

> Ephors are the representatives of the commonwealth or universal association to whom, by the consent of the people associated in a political body, the supreme responsibility has been entrusted for employing its power and right in constituting the supreme magistrate and in assisting him with aid and counsel in the activities of the associated body. They also employ its power and right in restraining and impeding his freedom in undertakings that are wicked and ruinous to the commonwealth, in containing him within the limits of his office, and finally in fully providing and caring for the commonwealth that it not suffer anything detrimental by the supreme magistrate's private attachments, hatreds, deeds, negligence, or inactivity… For this purpose the ephors have the power of helping the general and supreme magistrate by counsel and aid, and of admonishing and correcting him when he violates the Decalogue of divine law, or the sovereign rights and laws of the realm. Therefore, they have received the right of the sword (*ius gladii*) for the sake of discharging the required responsibility.[54]

We should not be terribly surprised, therefore, that Althusius holds up the United Provinces as an outstanding example of the ephors at work; for 'the universal association entrusted to its ephors the care and defence of these rights against all violators, disturbers, and plunderers, even against the supreme magistrate himself. The Dutch Wars of Independence offer examples of this care and defence by ephors during forty years of exploits against the King of Spain'.[55]

In deliberate opposition to Bodin, Althusius develops the first modern theory of federalism, premised upon the subsidiarity, or partial divisibility, of an inalienable sovereignty that resides within *respublica*.[56] Althusius deliberately utilises the United Provinces and The Eighty-Years War as his primary contemporary exemplar for the nature and operation of radical republican sovereignty.

> To demonstrate this point [of the inalienability of popular sovereignty] I am able to produce the excellent example of your [i.e. the Frisian's] own and the other

---

[54] Ibid., pp. 94 and 99.

[55] Ibid., p. 101.

[56] Thomas O. Hueglin, 'Federalism, Subsidiarity and the European Tradition: Some Clarifications', *Telos*, 100 (1994), pp. 37–55 at 46: 'Althusius' *Politica*… was the first modern theory of federalism. The first modern conceptualisation of the principle of subsidiarity can be traced to his attempt to balance the allocation of powers between commercial self-determination and the universal requirements of Statehood… The entire polity is a federally constructed edifice of multiple layers of association'. See also, Hueglin, *Early Modern Concepts for a Late Modern World*, pp. 52–68.

> provinces confederated with you. For in the war you undertook against the very powerful king of Spain you did not consider that the rights of sovereignty adhered so inseparably to him that they did not exist apart from him. Rather, when you took away the use and exercise of them from those who abused them, and recovered what was your own, you declared that these rights belong to the associated multitude and to the people of the individual provinces. You did this with such a courageous spirit, with such wisdom, fidelity and constancy, that I cannot find other peoples to compare with your example. And this among other reasons leads me to dedicate these political meditations to you.[57]

Within the *Politica*, the United Provinces serve as an exemplar in two different ways. Firstly, the intra-state arrangements of the Dutch Republic provide Althusius with his leading example of (con-) federated constitutional praxis: 'It even leads me to refer very often in [the *Politica*] when illustrations of political precepts are to be used, to examples chosen from your cities, constitutions, customs and deeds, and from other confederated Belgic provinces'.[58] Secondly, the Republic serves as the perfect foil to Habsburg universal monarchy, personified by Philip II, who is textually re-presented as the archetypal instance of the first type of anti-republican tyranny, 'the overthrow and destruction of the fundamental laws of the earth'. This form of tyranny occurs 'when the supreme magistrate violates, changes or overthrows the fundamental laws of the realm, especially those that concern true religion. Such.... was Philip, king of Spain, who established an administration in Belgium by force and arms against the fundamental laws and hereditary ways of the Commonwealth'.[59] Accordingly, legal historians of corporatism, such as Otto von Gierke, are able to historically identify a Reformationist theologico-political jurisprudence as the discursive template directly reflective of newly emergent forms of republican intra-state arrangements; in 'the question of the centralizing or federalistic construction of the State, everything depended on whether and how far, within the unitary State, the exclusive sovereignty of the whole, which is thereby characterized as a State, was compatible with a separate and independent communal life of the partial societies'.[60] Althusian federalism, therefore, constituted the deliberate and self-conscious repudiation of the indivisibility of sovereignty in strict accordance with the associational

---

57 Althusius, *The Politics of Johannes Althusius*, pp. 10–11.

58 Ibid., p. 11.

59 Ibid., pp. 186, 188 and 185–94, *(passim)*, C. XXXVIII on the 'Removal of Tyrants'.

60 Otto von Gierke, *The Development of Political Theory*, tr. Bernard Freyd (New York: Fertig, 1966), p. 263.

doctrine of popular sovereignty and the 'negation of the World-State' of anti-republican and monistic absolutism.[61]

The republican *Politica*, therefore, is an almost inverse re-presentation of the absolutist *Six Livres*. The unifying principle of the republican text is the heterogenous concept of consociation, the pre-political community that gives rise to all formal modes of constitutional expression.[62]

> Politics is the art of associating (*consociandi*) men for the purpose of establishing, cultivating, and conserving social life among them. Whence it is called 'symbiotics'. The subject matter of politics is therefore association (*consociatio*), in which the symbiotes ['those who live together'] pledge themselves each to the other, by explicit or tacit agreement, to mutual communication of whatever is useful and necessary for the harmonious exercise of social life.[63]

Consociation, in turn, permits subsidiarity, the potential for the sub-division of the unitary sovereignty of the people into an over-arching integrated federalist polity.

> But the owner and usufructary of sovereignty is none other than the total people associated in one symbiotic body from many smaller associations. These rights of sovereignty are so proper to this association... that even if it wishes to remove them, to transfer them to another, and to alienate them, it would by no means be able to do so, any more than a man is able to give the life he has to another.[64]

The signature innovation of Althusian federalism is that the heterogenous republic 'is not seen as a political institution which governs and controls a completely separate sphere of social and political activities, but is itself the symbiotic coordination of these activities'.[65] Althusius thereby eradicates any self-grounding demarcation between the public or private spheres of the polity; the resultant re-conceptualisation of both the public and the civil

---

[61] Ibid., p. 264.

[62] Thomas Hueglin, 'Johannes Althusius: Medieval Constitutionalist or Modern Federalist?', *Publius*, 9/4 (1979), pp. 9–41 at 38: 'In the last analysis, the political system of Althusius presents itself as the attempt to reconciliate the medieval plurality of rule with the modern concept of sovereignty. Thus it aims at the coordination of corporate particularism and central authority. What Althusius arrives at, is neither a unitary state however administratively decentralized, nor a 'balkanisation' of a socio-political unity, which ought to jointly master its common heritage. It is, in other words, a proposal for a political system maintained by a strong sense of community but constitutionally held together by a kind of reduced or co-sovereignty'. See also Hueglin, *Early Modern Concepts for a Late Modern World*, pp. 85–106, (*passim*).

[63] Althusius, *The Politics of Johannes Althusius*, p. 12.

[64] Ibid., p. 10.

[65] Hueglin, 'Johannes Althusius: Medieval Constitutionalist or Modern Federalist?', p. 22.

domains in terms of associative corporate ('symbiotic') structures yields an intensely heterogenous form of 'societal federalism'.[66]

> Now this axiom stands firm and fixed: all symbiotic association and life is, essentially, authentically, and generically political. But not every symbiotic association is public. There are certain associations that are private, such as conjugal and kinship families, and collegia. And these are the seedbeds of the public association. Whence it follows that the private association is rightly attributed to politics.[67]

Thus, the heterogenous federated *respublica* is, at all times, the antithesis of the absolutist nation-state, whose master-sign is political centralisation.[68] It is within this very precise space of juridico-political contest that the discursive apparatus of *De iure praedae* must be situated.

2. Grotius as Republican

It is one of the central tenets of *The Savage Republic* that a commitment to an early form of republican theory provides the entirety of the early Grotian corpus, the 'juvenilia', with a unifying thematic; this includes the very first works, such as *De republica emandanda* (c. 1600). Numerous scholars have had serious reservations in attributing *De republica* to Grotius as its highly centralised federalism is at such fundamental variance with his otherwise staunch con-federalist support of the rights of the provinces.[69] However, as Cornelis Roelofsen reminds us, experimental constitutional reform programs 'like those sketched by Grotius were... not unusual at the time. Indeed, even

---

[66] Hueglin, *Early Modern Concepts for a Late Modern World*, pp. 109–35, (*passim*).

[67] Althusius, *The Politics of Johannes Althusius*, p. 27. 'Thus, on any level of association, the higher units are always composed of lower ones, which, as such collective bodies constituting the higher unit, retain self-determination in their sphere as singuli... [Althusius] does not present his political system in terms pyramidal construction logically progressing from the bottom to the top level, but rather as a matrix-construction, which contains various organizational patterns within various arenas or cells of smaller and larger associational units. It is a network of political and social relations which on the whole reflects the plurality of late medieval society, but which appears to be transformed into a coherent constitutional system'. Hueglin, 'Johannes Althusius: Medieval Constitutionalist or Modern Federalist?', p. 28.

[68] Hueglin, *Early Modern Concepts for a Late Modern World*, pp. 42–55 (*passim*).

[69] 'The criticism in his manuscript *De Republica emendanda* directed against the preponderant position of the Provincial States and favouring a stronger federal government, makes rather odd reading if one considers Grotius' later impassioned defence of provincial sovereignty'. C.G. Roelofsen, 'Grotius and the International Politics of the Seventeenth Century', in *Hugo Grotius and International Relations*, ed. by Hedley Bull, Benedict Kingsbury and Adam Roberts (Oxford: Clarendon Press, 1990), pp. 95-131 at 103.

Oldenbarnevelt seems to have toyed with similar ideas'.[70] We know that Oldenbarnevelt convened 'two secret deliberations' concerning the constitution in 1602 and 1603; also discussed at these clandestine sessions were the imminent incorporation of the disparate *voorcompagnieën* into the centrally integrated VOC.[71] It appears a plausible inference that contemporary dissatisfaction among the Dutch political elites with the progress of the war of national liberation expressed itself in the demand for a constitutional shift away from con-federalism and towards a more politically centralised – and, therefore, a more militarily efficient – federal State. It is also by no means impossible that the Grotian proposal, premised upon the constitutional bolstering of the executive power of the thinly disguised Land Advocate of Holland, was intended to provide a more orthodox republican alternative to the quasi-monarchical option represented by the Orangist Stadholder of Holland, Zeeland and Utrecht Prince Maurits of Nassau (1567–1625).[72] By attempting to establish the covenantal basis for the centralised republican state Grotius could simultaneously neutralise the political ambitions of the Orange dynasty while undercutting the corporatist political demands presented by the synodal organisation of the Low churches. It follows from Grotius's critique that, contrary to general perceptions, the United Provinces in their current form do not constitute a 'true' *respublica* but, instead, a mere 'confederation'.

> I believe that many people who are not well acquainted with our political status imagine that what we call the United Provinces, forms a single and true republic, just as the twelve tribes of Israel constitute one republic: but things are in fact quite different. For they do not form a republic, but only a confederacy, an alliance and a unity in the event of war contained in certain paragraphs which

[70] Ibid.

[71] Jan den Tex, *Oldenbarnevelt*, 2 vols (Cambridge: Cambridge University Press, 1973), II , p. 413.

[72] Velema has persuasively argued that political resistance to Orangist dynastic ambitions, coupled with perennial uncertainty over the precise constitutional powers and privileges of the Stadholder, accounts for the systemic 'anti-monarchism' of Dutch republicanism. Wyger R.E. Velema, '"That a Republic is Better than a Monarchy": Anti-Monarchism in Early Modern Dutch Political Thought', in *Republicanism*, ed. by van Gelderen and Skinner, I, pp. 9-25 (pp.10–11). 'Despite or because of the opaque nature of their position, the Stadholders, elected by each province separately, succeeded in accumulating a considerable amount of symbolic and real power on both the national and the provincial level. Particularly important in this respect was the fact that their function combined substantial political power and the supreme military command in one and the same person'. Ibid., p. 11. For a general discussion of the intractable problem of constitutional uncertainty, see Herbert Rowen, 'The Dutch Republic and the Idea of Freedom', in *Republicanism, Liberty and Commercial Society, 1649-1776*, ed. by David Wootton (Stanford: Stanford University Press, 1994), pp. 310-40, *(passim).*

> themselves are not duly observed either [*Sed aliter se res habet: neque enim republica est, sed fedus tantum et belli societas atque communio, certis capitibus conmprehensa – quae nec ipsa satis observantur*].[73]

It is as though the heterogenous political pluralism of the United Provinces categorically belies the unitary monism of *civitas*.

I argue in *The Savage Republic* that Grotius's overriding need is to formulate a juridico-political discourse commensurate with a republican State that is incorporated along essentially con-federal principles; therefore, the issue of whether the United Provinces constituted a federal – or, in Grotius's terms, a 'true' – republic is one of central importance to an overall interpretation of the Grotian corpus. As Blom has candidly admitted, it 'seems inadequate to label the Republic a federal state, if only because it possessed no detailed regulation of the respective rights and duties of its different parts'.[74] Blom is not alone in his dilemma; in the Preface to the third edition of his *Politica*, Althusius clearly refers to the United Provinces as a confederacy.[75] Insofar as it is subject to historical 'retrieval', the Dutch Republic appears to have been subject to a kind of 'informal governance',[76] based upon the extra-constitutional convergences among the class interests of the regionally dispersed political and mercantile elites – who were, in most instances, virtually one and the same[77] – centred upon the entrepot of Amsterdam.

> While the principle of equal representation in the States General for every province regardless of wealth or the size of its financial contribution [to the war effort] remained inviolable, the principle of provincial autonomy could be used not only to protect Holland from being outvoted and subjected to the will of the smaller

[73] Hugo Grotius, *De Republica emendanda; a juvenile tract by Hugo Grotius on the emendation of the Dutch polity*, ed. by Arthur Eyffinger, et al., *Grotiana*, 5 (1984), pp. 3-134 at 113.

[74] Hans W. Blom, 'The Republican Mirror: The Dutch Idea of Europe', in *The Idea of Europe: From Antiquity to the European Union*, ed. by Anthony Pagden (Cambridge: Cambridge University Press, 2002), pp. 91-115 at 97.

[75] 'To demonstrate this point [of republican sovereignty] I am able to produce the excellent example of your own and the other provinces confederated with you.' Althusius, *The Politics of Johannes Althusius*, p. 10.

[76] See Hans W. Blom, 'Patriots, Contracts and Other Patterns of Trust in a Plyarchic Society: the Dutch 17*th* Century', in *'Patria' und 'Patrioten' vor dem Patriotismus. Pflichten, Rechte, Glauben und die Rekonfiguration europeischer Gemeinwesen im. 17. Jahrhundert*, ed. by Robert von Friedeburg (Wiesbaden: Harrassowitz Verlag 2005), pp. 193-213, *(passim)*.

[77] Olaf Moerke, 'The Political Culture of Germany and the Dutch Republic', in *A Miracle Mirrored: The Dutch Republic in European Perspective*, ed. by Karel Davids and Jan Lucassen (Cambridge: Cambridge University Pres, 1995), pp. 135-72 at 151: 'Local elites, mainly those of the bigger cities, remained the focus of political decision-making. Starting from the local level, decision-making continued in the provincial Estates and in the States General. It is of primary

> provinces, but in practice to impose Holland's will on the rest. In brief, provincial independence gave the lesser provinces protection from their powerful allies and at the same time allowed Holland to mould the policies of the new state in accordance with its own wishes and needs.[78]

J.L. Price has mischievously labelled this extra-judicial combination of informal with formal techniques of political control as 'typically Dutch'[79] and identified it as the centrepiece of the Land Advocate of Holland's strategy of governance; 'If there was one principle that underlay the whole of Oldenbarnevelt's internal policy, it was provincial autonomy which enabled Holland to dominate the political life of the Republic'.[80] This 'typically Dutch' mode of governance seemed to have remained constant throughout the period of Dutch hegemony (1609-c.1740).[81] What I would like to suggest is that it was precisely the two-fold dimension of the United Provinces within the modern world-economy – the status of Amsterdam as the premier entrepot of the capitalist world-economy and the convergence site of all vital economic and political interests of the Dutch urban patriciate – that not only maintained the 'typically Dutch' practice of obviating constitutional reform but also guaranteed that any political system would be grounded upon con-federal principles and practices. The question now becomes: in what ways may Grotius's treatment of the VOC, in *De jure praedae*, be viewed as reflecting a republican agenda? The answer lies with the text's investiture of the VOC with what I call 'corporate sovereignty'.

---

importance that at all those levels one and the same group, the urban or noble *regenten*, held the decisive influence. The process of political decision-making went step by step from the basic local level to the level of the Union. The oligarchy, ruling the bigger cities, ruled the country. Anyone who wanted to influence the Republic's politics had to strengthen his influence within the basic elite formations'.

[78] J.L. Price, *Holland and the Dutch Republic in the Seventeenth Century: the Politics of Particularism* (Oxford: Oxford University Press, 1994), p. 239. Compare this with Moerke; 'In the Dutch Republic the lasting dominance of Holland also determined the effectiveness of the States General. That dominance could not be questioned by the other provinces. Holland functioned as the political centre for the Republic, not against it!' Moerke, 'The Political Culture of Germany and the Dutch Republic', p. 150.

[79] Price, *Holland and the Dutch Republic in the Seventeenth Century: the Politics of Particularism*, p. 255.

[80] Ibid., p. 272.

[81] Oldenbarnevelt's 'spiritual successor' the Grand Pensionary Johan de Witt (1625–72)'maintained regular contacts with supporters and clients throughout the voting towns, the nature of which are at least partly revealed in his correspondence, though the short distances between most towns and the Hague meant that this is probably only the tip of the iceberg, as face-to-face contacts are likely to have been far more important than letters'. Ibid., pp. 167–8.

3. The VOC and Corporate Sovereignty

My treatment of the VOC as a corporate sovereign in *The Savage Republic* closely follows Giovanni Arrighi's work on 'systemic cycles of accumulation'; these are the sequential sequences of contending national hegemonies that serve as the historical divisions of the modern world-system.[82] In Arrighi's view, one that I greatly enlarge upon, the second, or 'Dutch" cycle (1609-c. 1740), more closely resembles the fourth 'American' cycle (1945 onwards) than it does the other more territorialist cycles of Iberia and the United Kingdom. The vital structural convergence between the Dutch and American hegemonies is the effective subordination of the capitalist world-economy to the governance mechanisms and practices of trans-national corporations. In both cycles, private corporations, acting trans-nationally, are able to exert political and economic governance globally through their ability to successfully exercise a requisite degree of control throughout political space ordinarily understood to be 'public'. As a result, a defining characteristic of the second and fourth cycles is the semi-institutionalisation of a privatised quasi-sovereignty that I de-note as 'corporate sovereignty'.

From the perspective of the contemporary international lawyer, the primary interest of *De iure praedae* lies within Grotius's seemingly uncanny ability to give coherent legal form to a seventeenth-century juridico-political landscape that in many ways closely corresponds to that of the early-twenty-first century. Although one must guard against the intellectual sin of projection, I take it as self-evident that it is the text's exploration of a private form of trans-national authority that constitutes the relevance of the Commentary to today's legal readership. The great irony for the international legal scholar, of course, is that it is none other than Hugo Grotius, the postulated seminal founder of the state-centric – and, therefore, 'modern' – Westphalian system who succeeds in conveying a model of international public order far more commensurate with pre-modern notions of private authority than with 'modern' notions of the statist monopolization of international legal personality.[83] Here, the problem,

---

[82] Giovanni Arrighi, *The Long Twentieth Century* (London: Verso, 1994) and Giovanni Arrighi and Beverly J. Silver (eds.), *Chaos and Governance in the Modern World System* (Minneapolis: University of Minnesota Press, 1999).

[83] The non-statist and pre-modern nature of the Westphalian system has been exhaustively discussed in Benno Teschke, *The Myth of 1648:Class, Geopolitics and the Making of Modern International Relations* (London: Verso, 2003). Teschke's central argument is that a truly 'modern' form of international public order did not emerge until the early-nineteenth century, with the historical supersession of the patrimonial model of the Nation-State; in other words, the unconditional repudiation of the polity as a mode of private property.

in part, is terminological: it is very difficult to convey with total precision the fluid categories of early modern republican thought, especially in regard to the foundational problem of the public versus the private interest. There is an undeniably 'dialectical' aspect to republican theory that renders any strictly binary taxonomy between 'the public' and 'the private' spheres – so central to contemporary constitutional theory – utterly impossible to uphold within the terms of seventeenth-century discourse.[84]

Nonetheless, if we were to employ current political and legal language with the relevant historical factors in mind, we may hypothesize that corporate sovereignty possesses two aspects, *de iure* and *de facto*. As of law, every private authority is fully subject to the terms of legal incorporation by the State and is territorially grounded in the exercise of its conveyed governance capacities. As of fact, however, private actors are able to exert decisive power over national political and economic decision-making, a trend that has been greatly exacerbated by recent developments in neo-liberal 'privatisation'; the State is vacating traditional areas of concern, creating pockets of 'empty' juridico-political space that are increasingly coming to be occupied by corporations or other forms of 'private actors.[85] The practical outcome is an unstable convergence between public and private functions, both domains perpetually interfering in the 'internal operations' of the other, resulting in a net increase of private power at the expense of public authority.[86] It is on the basis of these similitudes between the Dutch and the American cycles that I was able to formulate the central premise of *The Savage Republic*: that there is a close and complex correlation between the Grotian version of divisible corporation theory and the text's appropriation of the VOC as a sign of an early but robust republicanism. In terms of corporate sovereignty, contemporary trans-national corporations display a remarkable similarity to seventeenth-century joint-stock companies.[87] In my opinion, the 'pre-modern' mercantile trading company exemplifies the

---

[84] I owe this insight to Professor Hans W. Blom.

[85] For a recent, and comprehensive, account of the contemporary 'de-territorialization' of the internal juridical space of the State, see Saskia Sassen, *Territory/Authority/Rights: From Medieval to Global Assemblages* (Princeton: Princeton University Press, 2006), especially chapters four, five and seven (*passim*). I deliberately omit consideration of the thorny problem bequeathed us by J.A. Hobson as to whether a 'ruling class', particularly one such as the Dutch oligarchy, undertakes a colonizing enterprise out of the 'national interest' or 'private interest'.

[86] For an excellent general discussion, see Stephen J. Kobrin, 'Economic Governance in an Electronically Networked Global Economy', in *The Emergence of Private Authority in Global Governance*, ed. by Rodney Bruce Hall and Thomas J. Biersteker (Cambridge: Cambridge University Press, 2002), pp. 43-75, *(passim)*.

[87] Arrighi, *The Long Twentieth Century*, pp. 72–4, 80–4 and 318–19.

political and logical reversibility operating between the corporation, traditionally defined as an 'imperatively co-ordinated corporate group' and the nation-state, a specifically 'political' variant of the broader 'corporate group'.[88] Within the Grotian text, this defining characteristic of the Dutch cycle is discursively formulated through an implicit, or sub-textual, linkage between corporatism and republicanism, both of which are unified through the VOC's status as an early, or primitive, corporate sovereign.

The critical factor at work here is the historical nexus between the textual production of *De iure praedae* and the concomitant incorporation of the VOC. *Jan Compagnie* was itself an 'assemblage' of earlier and smaller trading and privateering 'firms', the *voorcompagnies*.[89]

> In 1602 the precompanies were joined together... by a charter issued by the Estates General. The charter was the result of long deliberations and hard bargaining. Both the habits of the Dutch merchants and provincial separatism spoke against a centralized monopoly company. But the Netherlands was at war, and a united company was a potential threat against Spain and Portugal; it might divert part of the Iberian war effort to overseas regions and thus lessen the pressure on Europe, and it undoubtedly would become a new means of economic warfare.[90]

Lacking any of the cognisable features of either the earlier guild or the regulatory company, the VOC focused exclusively on capital allocation, at the expense of share holding based on social estimations of status or professional expertise, unlike its contemporary the English East India Company. The early modern trading company was from its inception a 'quasi-public institution',[91]

[88] Max Weber, *The Theory of Economic and Social Organization*, ed. with Intr. by Talcott Parsons (New York: The Free Press, 1947), p. 154.

[89] Steensgaard, *Carracks, Caravans and Companies*, p. 126.

[90] Ibid., 240–41. The self-sustaining financing of the VOC through the internalisation of protection costs appears to have always formed part of Oldenbarnevelt's original plan. 'The permanent maintenance of a strong fleet in the East would be far too expensive for the States General, unless it could be paid for by spoils and profits.' Den Tex, *Oldenbarnevelt*, I, p. 301; see pp. 299–313, *(passim)*. See also Jonathan I. Israel, *The Dutch Primacy in World Trade* (Oxford: Oxford University Press, 1982), pp. 67–73.

[91] Karl Burch, *'Property' and the Making of the International System* (London: Lynne Reiner Publishers, 1998), p. 118. 'In every instance European ventures on the oceans were sustained by a combination of public, quasi-public, and relentlessly private enterprise'. William H. McNeill, *The Pursuit of Power: Technology, Armed Force, and Society Since A.D. 1000* (Chicago: University of Chicago Press, 1982), p. 103. See M.N. Pearson, 'Merchants and States', in *The Political Economy of Merchant Empires*, ed. by James D. Tracy (Cambridge: Cambridge University Press, 1991), pp. 41-116 at 77–100, (*passim*); Holden Furber, *Rival Empires of Trade in the Orient 1600–1800* (Minneapolis: University of Minnesota Press, 1976), pp.185–229 (*passim*). The 'correct' mixture of public and private elements appears to have been a critical variable to the long-term economic and political success of the Corporation. See Pearson, 'Merchants and States', *(passim)*.

generating reciprocal benefits for both the private and public domains.[92] Joint-Stock companies like the VOC constituted a 'unique form of cooperation between merchant entrepreneurs and government interests. It became historically important, because it did not lead to the total subjection of mercantile interests to the whims of government, but rather to a balanced co-operation, in which the market forces repeatedly proved to be the strongest'.[93] The state enjoyed a dramatic increase in the national supply of available credit,[94] the corresponding expansion of national production capacity, and the sustainable private subsidization (re. cost-efficiency) of critical 'state-building enterprises', such as exploration, long-distance trade, and colonization. In exchange, companies exploited the legalization – that is, the legitimation – of new forms of mobile property rights (credit, interest, financial assets), and the establishment of new 'institutional-legal' regimes of commercial and economic *ius*.[95] In order to service the newly emergent 'coercion-intensive colonial trade' in the most economically efficient manner, the VOC undertook four significant innovations in both structure and policy. First, *Die Heeren XVII* focussed on the control of stock (spices; bullion) as a guarantee against radical fluctuations in supply and demand, rather than in maximising short-terms profits. Second, there was a correlative shift from short-term to medium- and long-term

[92] Burch, *'Property' and the Making of the International System*, p. 119. 'The mechanisms by which the Dutch merchant elite and political oligarchy together regulated internal competition within the Dutch entrepot, in the interests of the entrepot as a whole, and at the same time thwarted the successive challenges of the rivals of the Dutch in the quest for hegemony over world trade, were various and complex. But the common thread... was a unique and characteristically Dutch blend of political intervention and business efficiency. What it all amounted to was a harnessing of the Dutch entrepot to the machinery of the Dutch state. The Dutch business world of the seventeenth century was fundamentally shaped by an assortment of companies, national and local, consortia with political links, cartels and combinations'. Israel, *The Dutch Primacy in World Trade*, p. 16.

[93] Neils Steensgaard, 'The Companies as a Specific Institution in the History of European Expansion', in *Companies and Trade*, ed. by Blussé and Gaastra, pp. 245-64 at 263. 'The rise of the joint-stock companies offers a historic microcosm of many neo-realist concerns with international relations and international political economy, including collective goods, regimes, hegemonic stability, and burgeoning norms'. Burch, *'Property' and the Making of the International System*, 133. 'It was the singular character of the VOC as a joint-stock company with its operational parameters of capital input and financial profit, and as an institution with authorities comparable to that of a state that made it use its powers more prudently and economically than any sovereign state in Europe'. Peter Kirsch, 'VOC – Trade Without Ethics?', in *Maritime Asia: Profit Maximisation, Ethics and Trade Structure c. 1300–1800*, ed by. Karl Anton Sprengard, and Roderich Ptak (Wiesbaden: Harrassowitz Verlag, 1994), pp. 189-202 at 202.

[94] Kobrin, 'Economic Governance in an Electronically Networked Global Economy', pp. 48–9, 50, 58 and 63.

[95] Burch, *'Property' and the Making of the International System*, pp. 111–13 and 132.

considerations; 'for the European investor it was very difficult to give up the purely bilateral model, which also dominated the trade of the Portuguese crown'. Third, the Company prioritised market penetration – especially throughout the intra-Asian 'country' trade – but, critically, expressly refrained from an Iberian-type practice of territorialism, yielding a vastly superior 'information network' that further enhanced long-term capitalistic planning.[96] Fourth, the Company's resultant trade and communications network permitted the creation of permanent reserves of vast quantities of disposable capital. [97]

From the very moment of its amalgamation, therefore, the VOC possessed an inherently geo-strategic dimension, in accordance with the authorial intent of Oldenbarnevelt. Years afterwards, he referred to 'the great East India company, with four years of hard work, *public and private*, I have helped establish in order to inflict damage on the Spaniards and the Portuguese'.[98] Incorporated under an early capitalist republic, the VOC deliberately eschewed the territorialist model of the 'universal' Iberian monarchies. In addition to ideological legitimacy, this also proved enormously cost effective.

> As no new technique, unknown to the Portuguese, was at the disposal of the companies, it is a reasonable hypothesis that the companies, by virtue of their institutional structure, were able to do things outside of the reach of the Portuguese, or to do the same, but with more economical use of their resources; i.e., that they were institutional innovations. The VOC integrated the functions of a sovereign power with the functions of a business partnership. Political decisions and business decisions were made within the same hierarchy of company managers and officials, and failure or success was always in the last instance measured in terms of profit. By this means, the company as a business venture was able to internalise protection costs, and protection costs were added to the overheads that might be calculated rationally.[99]

[96] Ibid., 238–9:'Planned operations in time and space were made possible by an efficient communications network, established already in the second decade of the seventeenth century. Batavia was at the centre of the network; it was there that the information from the Netherlands and from all Asian factories was gathered and co-ordinated, and from there the resources were allocated and the ships, goods, men and money were distributed and redirected according to the information received… in the seventeenth century the system hardly had its equal'.

[97] Ibid. This may be seen in 'the relations between the company centre in Batavia and the company centre in the Netherlands. To the principals in the Netherlands, the balance remaining in Batavia originally meant stock ready to be returned to Europe or stock [bullion] ready to be exchanged for commodities that might be returned with short notice. To the company merchants in Batavia, it came to mean something different, namely the capital remaining and circulating in Asia in order to make a profit with which to finance the company overheads in Asia and the shipments to Europe'. Idem.

[98] Ibid., p. 128. Emphasis added.

[99] Ibid., p. 237.

Institutional innovations cannot, however, be reduced to pure expediency; in Grotius's hands they operated fully within the parameters of a deliberate discursive stratagem. Not only does *De iure praedae* strive to negate the legitimacy of the Papal Donation of *imperium*, or exclusive prescriptive title, conveyed by the Treaty of Tordesillas, it also positively affirms the natural right (*ius*) of the VOCto trade and to navigate.

As I readily acknowledge, it would be wholly anachronistic of me to attribute to Grotius a fully developed theory of international corporate personality; the notion of international legal personality was first developed by Gottfried Wilhelm Leibniz (1646–1716).[100] Nevertheless, the praxis of the early seventeenth-century joint-stock company within trans-national space is highly indicative of a sovereign personality. To the extent that Grotius displayed a notion of corporate personality within *De iure praedae*, it would seem to correspond to an early, or 'primitive', formulation of Althusian 'corporate realism', in which the corporate body

> originates from its real existence and is not created by the process of incorporation. A corporate body does not owe its personality to state recognition. This legal personality is in no sense artificial or fictitious, but is as real and natural as the personality of a human being; its will is the will of the group. As a consequence, all entities with real personality would have legal personality.[101]

It is precisely the text's conveyance of fundamental property and political rights from state to company that provides the basis for that discursive alteration between 'private' and 'public' that is so central to the purpose of *De iure praedae*: the legitimate conveyance of all of the necessary signs of sovereignty to a private legal personality, now able to operate as a 'quasi-government'.[102] I argue that it is this very convergence between what we would de-note today as 'the public' and 'the private' that provides the nexus for Grotius's appropriation of the corporatist VOC as a discursive signifier of republicanism; the jurisdictional and governance functions exercised by the joint-stock company render it taxonomically identical with generic political association. As I have shown above, the threat that republican corporatism posed for the constitutional division of sovereignty provoked diametrically opposed responses from

---

[100] Janne Elisabeth Nijman, *The Concept of International Legal Personality: An Inquiry into the History and Theory of International Law* (The Hague: T.M.C. Asser Press, 2004), pp. 29–84 (*passim*).

[101] Daniel Zimmer, 'Legal Personality', in *VOC 1602–2002: 400 Years of Company Law*, Ella Gepken-Jager, Gerard van Solinge and Levinus Timmerman (GA Deventer: Kluwer Legal Publishers, 2005), pp. 265-80 at 268.

[102] Burch, *'Property' and the Making of the International System*, p. 129.

the most prominent political theorists of the period. The absolutist Bodin ruthlessly subordinated the existence of all corporate bodies to the positive law of the absolutist state.[103] The republican Althusius, in deliberate contrast to Bodin, places a divisible corporate sovereignty that is derived from a providential Natural Law at the centre of his federalist constitutionalism,[104] *communicatio* the highest expression of a specifically Christian notion of love grounded in Divine Being.[105] It is on these Althusian grounds that Gierke was able to identify the ultra-capitalistic joint-stock company as a form of 'fellowship'.[106] 'The capitalist nature of the whole is always in evidence; and, insofar as the entire organization refers back to the collectivity of the shareholders as its ultimate representative, the association is in fact manifested solely as organised capital'. However, it is 'the organization of the joint-stock company which, above all, makes it a fellowship'.[107]

> Thus the very *existence* of a joint-stock company is by no means determined by the original capital sums alone, but in addition by a personal *collective will*. Collective will brings the corporation into existence by a constitutive act... and in the *articles*. Collective will gives [the company] its constitution, its law of existence; and, within the bounds of this constitution, it is a collective will [that] in the first instance controls any changes in, and the final dissolution of, the organism. Creative collective will manifests itself as the collective will of the *plurality*, and finds expression in civil autonomy; on the other hand, the collective will acting according to a constitution is the collective will of a *single* entity and sets *corporate* autonomy in motion; both, however, are capable of autonomous decision-making, creating objective right.[108]

From Gierke's viewpoint, the joint-stock company is morphologically identical with the republican polity: 'The joint-stock company has in every respect the legal status of a fellowship personality, possessing within the life-sphere prescribed for it constitutionally and limited by law, an independent capacity to do justice, to will and to act'.[109] Operating with similar corporatist principles,

[103] Ibid., pp. 129–31. In one of his most controversial moves, Bodin asserts that the Estates-General of France possess no independent legislative or judicial authority. Bodin, *On Sovereignty*, pp. 19 and 23–4.

[104] Antony Black, *Guilds and Civil Society in European Political Thought from the Twelfth Century to the Present* (New York: Metheun, 1984), pp. 131–42.

[105] For Black, it was in Althusius that 'Germanic Christianity achieved its truest and finest philosophical expression in social and political thought'. Ibid., p. 141.

[106] Otto von Gierke, *Community in Historical Perspective: a Translation of Selections from Das deutsche Genossenschaftsrecht (The German Law of Fellowship)* ed. by Antony Black, trans. Mary Fisher (Cambridge: Cambridge University Press, 1990), pp. 196–204.

[107] Ibid., p. 199.

[108] Ibid., pp. 198–9.

[109] Ibid., p. 201.

Grotius accomplishes the same republican feat. The investment of the joint-stock company with *ius* effects a parallel substitution of *dominium*, a proprietary regime, by a quasi-*imperium*, the 'privatised' exercise of public sovereignty as a legitimate exercise of 'natural' or just war. *De iure praedae* taxonomically re-classifies the basic categories of naturalist jurisprudence as a means of legitimating the private authority and governance of the VOC within trans-national juro-political space, a 'primitive' form of corporate sovereignty, discursively legitimated by the republican difference between the proprietorial *dominium* of a centralized world-empire and the jurisdictional *imperium* of the de-centralized world-system.[110]

4. Conclusion: the Republican Sub-Text of *De Iure Praedae*

Perhaps the most commonly under-appreciated fact of the Grotian era is that the Eighty Year's War, the Dutch war of national liberation, was a revolutionary event. Not only were the 'Batavians' fighting a bitter war of national independence against their Iberian overlords, they were simultaneously re-formulating the entirety of the constitutional basis of their longed-for sovereignty. Within this dual struggle, both internal and external, the very nature of the emergent Dutch Republic was under constant threat, the site of interminable political contestation. It must never be forgotten that the political elites who lived through the Dutch Revolt, thoroughly educated and trained in the tradition of Humanism, understood their own times in terms of the radical dangers and uncertainties of the revolutionary cycle classically described by Polybius.[111] What provides the most vital link between Polybius and an oligarchic writer such as Grotius is that the political revolutions that both describe are populist uprisings that are driven 'from below'. In the case of the Lowlands, these are centred upon the middle-class *populares* organised

---

[110] Intriguingly, English Merchant Companies also attempted a *sub rosa* conflation of *dominium* with *imperium*. David Armitage, *The Ideological Origins of the British Empire* (Cambridge: Cambridge University Press, 1995), pp. 92–4. 'The problem of uniting *dominium* with *imperium* would persist… as the fundamental and ultimately combustible dilemma at the core of British imperial ideology'. Ibid., p. 94. The crucial difference with the Dutch, however, was that English publicists framed the problem in terms of Crown title, reflecting the gradual drift towards Stuart absolutism. Ibid., 104–5. The resolutely republican nature of the United Provinces and its doppelganger the VOC served to restrict Grotian discourse within the confines of corporate sovereignty.

[111] See *The Savage Republic*, chapter five, for a fuller discussion.

into corporate guilds and waging a form of 'class warfare'[112] against both the Spanish occupiers and the urban *regenten*.[113] The essential 'balancing act' that must be performed is to secure the unquestioned benefits of national independence while self-consciously authoring the constitutional foundations of political stability in the face of the constant threat of democracy, or 'the rule of the mob'.[114] The final solution, hit upon almost as though by 'trial and error' over the course of the long eighty years of political violence, was the renowned 'mixed constitution' a republican frame incorporating elements of a weak but clearly discernible absolutism embodied within the ubiquitous but shadowy figure of the stadholder. The inchoate nature of early Dutch republicanism comes from its repeated attempts to express in the fixed terms of formal constitutional discourse what was a fluid and rapidly shifting political reality.

Grotius's experimental republicanism not only inhabits the sub-textualspace of *De iure praedae*, linking the apologetic Historica with the speculative Dogmatica; it is the meta-narrative thread that invests all of the juvenilia with an underlying discursive unity. However, unlike the other early works, such as *De rebus Belgicis* or the *Commentarius in theses XI*, the republican content of *De iure praedae* remains invisible. The reason is obvious: the discursive object of the text, as Ittersum has quite rightly shown, is the VOC. But because the company is essentially a 'private' corporation, Grotius scholars have largely failed to consider the various ways in which a private entity can adequately serve as the formal subject of 'public' political theory. As I have shown here, such a conceptual failure is the direct result of a wider failure to consider the

[112] Intriguingly identified by Boone and Prak as 'the Little Tradition' of urban revolt. See Marc Boone and Maarten Prak, 'Rulers, Patricians and Burghers: the Great and the Little Traditions of Urban Revolt in the Low Countries', in Karel Davids and Jan Lucassen (eds), *A Miracle Mirrored: The Dutch Republic in European Perspective* (Cambridge: Cambridge University Press, 1995), pp. 99–134, (*passim*). We know that during the early-sixteenth century, a specifically Catholic form of urban republicanism had developed. Karin Tilmans, 'Republican Citizenship and Civic Humanism in the Burgundian-Habsburg Netherlands (1477–1566)', in Gelderen and Skinner (eds), *Republicanism and Constitutionalism in Early Modern Europe*, pp. 107-25 (*passim*). 'It appears, therefore, that there is a strong continuity of civic or republican discourse extending from the sixteenth- to the seventeenth-century Netherlands. The ideological force of sixteenth-century civic humanism in state formation seems so far to have been underestimated'. Ibid., p. 124.

[113] Boone and Prak, 'Rulers, Patricians and Burghers', 100–1 and 103–4. See also Parker, *The Dutch Revolt*, pp. 146–7, 194 and 245–7, describing the centrality of the 'Little Tradition' of urban revolt.

[114] On the inherent political conservatism of the constitutional arrangements resulting from the Dutch Revolt, see Herbert H. Rowen, *The Rhyme and Reason of Politics in Early Modern Europe: Collected Essays of Herbert H. Rowen*, ed. Craig E. Harline (Dordrecht: Kluwer, 1992), pp. 45–59.

complex and shifting grounds between republicanism, corporatism, property regimes, and the divisibility of sovereignty. The radical, if not subversive, potential of this argument for future scholarship is tremendous, as it may provide us with a new means by which to reconceptualize the nebulous relationship between civil society and process of republican state formation in the seventeenth century. Prima Facie, *De iure praedae* maintains the orthodox hierarchy between public and private by classifying the VOC – the private commercial body – as the juridico-political inferior of the Estates-General, the public political entity.

> It is a generally accepted fact that the individuals who compose the East India Company are subject to the said Estates General. For all persons within the territory in question have pledged allegiance by oath to that assembly, or else tacitly give adequate assurance, by making themselves a part of the political community governed by the latter, of their intention to live in accordance with the customs of this community and to obey the magistrates recognized by it.[115]

What the text elides, at precisely this juncture, is the social context of its own discursive production; because of the extreme oligarchic nature of the Dutch Republic, the Estates-General and the VOC constituted a unified *de facto* organizational entity. The political oligarchy and the *Heeren XVII* were 'one and the same, indistinguishable from each other and indeed often consisting of the same people. This was the reason for the apparent autonomy from metropolitan political control that the VOC enjoyed; because the VOC was identical with the state, this was really no abdication by the state'.[116] The corporatist discourse of the text renders the presumed hierarchy between the 'political' and the 'economic' precarious. But by the same token, international space is transformed, *in potentia*, into that which is of the *respublica*.

[115] Grotius, *De iure praedae*, p. 296.

[116] Pearson, 'Merchants and States', pp. 85–6. See Peter Burke, 'Republics of Merchants in Early Modern Europe', in *Merchants, Companies and Trade: Europe and Asia in the Early Modern Era*, ed. by Jean Baechler, John A. Hall and Michel Morineau (Cambridge: Cambridge University Press, 1999), pp. 220–33, *(passim)*.

Natural Rights and Roman Law in Hugo Grotius's *Theses LVI*, *De iure praedae* and *Defensio capitis quinti maris liberi*

Benjamin Straumann*
New York University
E-mail: benjamin.straumann@nyu.edu

Abstract
Roman property law and Roman contract law as well as the property centered Roman ethics put forth by Cicero in several of his works were the traditions Grotius drew upon in developing his natural rights system. While both the medieval just war tradition and Grotius's immediate political context deserve scholarly attention and constitute important influences on Grotius's natural law tenets, it is a Roman tradition of subjective legal remedies and of just war which lays claim to a foundational role with regard to his conception of subjective natural rights. Grotius made use of Roman law and Roman ethics in order to submit a normative case for a rights-based just war in the East Indies. His conception of a law of nature was originally conceived to apply a theory of compensatory justice to the high seas of Southeast Asia, envisaged as a natural state lacking political authority. Eventually, however, this argument was to reveal its anti-absolutist implications, and contributed—by virtue of its applicability to individuals, private entities and commonwealths alike—to the emergence of a rights-based constitutionalism. This article discusses Grotius's early treatise *De iure praedae commentarius* (1604-1606) and its offshoot *Mare liberum*, which already contained an inchoate version of subjective natural rights, as well as the elaborate natural rights doctrine which can be found in Grotius's early *Theses LVI* and in the *Defensio capitis quinti maris liberi*, a defense of the fifth chapter of *Mare liberum*, written around 1615 and directed against the Scottish jurist William Welwod's attack on *Mare liberum*.

Keywords
Hugo Grotius; Roman law; Natural rights; Roman ethics; Natural law; State of nature

Modern liberty rests on individual rights. A classic expression of this view can be found in Benjamin Constant's famous 1819 lecture 'De la liberté des anciens comparée à celle des modernes', where Constant, drawing on

* The author would like to thank David Armitage for his comments, and Lauren Benton, Peter Borschberg, Benedict Kingsbury, Jon Miller, Beat Näf, and Laurens Winkel for helpful discussions and criticism. Many thanks to Ossai Miazad for her editorial help.

Condorcet, had developed a rights-based notion of 'modern' liberty by contrasting it with the 'liberty of the ancients':

> The ancients, as Condorcet says, had no notion of individual rights. Men were, so to speak, merely machines, whose gears and cog-wheels were regulated by the law. The same subjection characterized the golden centuries of the Roman republic; the individual was in some way lost in the nation, the citizen in the city.[1]

The crucial force credited by Constant for the development of the rights-based, 'modern' conception of liberty is commerce, which not only 'inspires in men a vivid love of individual independence'[2] and 'emancipates' the individual, but also helps to make individuals 'stronger than the political powers'.[3]

This tenacious view of an 'ancient' version of liberty, lacking any notion of subjective rights and lacking therefore what Isaiah Berlin has called 'negative' liberty,[4] seems to be informed mainly by an interest in the constitutional structures of the societies of classical antiquity, and nourished by the bias against democracy expressed by most of classical political philosophy. It is a view that has appealed to rights-friendly liberals such as Constant and Berlin and to nostalgic adherents of a 'back to Aristotle' ethics such as Michel Villey or Alasdair MacIntyre alike,[5] and sometimes, as in MacIntyre's case, the historical record has also been made to carry some philosophical weight.[6]

Hugo Grotius's (1583-1645) doctrine of subjective natural rights may serve to rectify the above-mentioned historical record. The Dutch humanist made a crucial contribution to the development of a modern, rights-based natural

---

[1] Benjamin Constant, 'The Liberty of the Ancients Compared with that of the Moderns', in Id., *Political Writings*, ed. by B. Fontana (Cambridge: CUP, 1988), p. 312.

[2] Ibid., 315.

[3] Ibid., 325. For this tradition of thought, see W. Nippel, 'Antike und moderne Freiheit', in *Ferne und Nähe der Antike*, ed. by W. Jens and B. Seidensticker (Berlin: De Gruyter, 2003), pp. 49-68. Nippel shows a line of argument ranging from Constant over Fustel de Coulanges, Jacob Burckhardt and Lord Acton to Max Weber, and influencing twentieth century historians such as Moses Finley and Paul Veyne.

[4] Isaiah Berlin, 'Two Concepts of Liberty', in Id., *Four Essays on Liberty* (Oxford: OUP, 1969).

[5] See M. Villey, 'Les origines de la notion de droit subjectif', in Id., *Leçons d'histoire de la philosophie du droit*, 2nd edn (Paris: Dalloz, 1962), pp. 221-250; Id., 'Déformations de la philosophie du droit d'Aristote entre Vitoria et Grotius', in *Platon et Aristote à la Renaissance*, ed. by Maurice de Gandillac et J.-C. Margolin, XVIe Colloque International de Tours (Paris: Vrin, 1976), pp. 201-215; A. MacIntyre, *After Virtue*, 2nd edn (Notre Dame: University of Notre Dame Press, 1984), *passim*. In MacIntyre's view, modern ethics is internally incoherent and composed of misunderstood residua of the Aristotelian tradition, making a return to Aristotelian ethics inevitable.

[6] See MacIntyre, *After Virtue*, 51ff.; see the excellent criticism in E. Tugendhat, *Vorlesungen über Ethik*, 3nd edn (Frankfurt/M.: Suhrkamp, 1995), pp. 208-225.

law advocating the freedom of trade,[7] clearly driven by a desire to promote that which Constant thought to be the force behind 'modern liberty', namely commerce. Yet Grotius developed his conception of natural rights out of materials stemming from a time that had allegedly 'no notion of individual rights' and when '[m]en were, so to speak, merely machines, whose gears and cog-wheels were regulated by the law'. It is not the ambition of this article to investigate the question of whether or not the ancients actually did have a notion of individual rights[8] – although a better understanding of Grotius's reading of his ancient sources might very well help the understanding of these sources as well –, but rather to show that Grotius, in developing his conception of just causes of war and the corresponding subjective natural rights, depended heavily on certain classical traditions.

Roman property law and Roman contract law as well as the property-centered Roman ethics put forth by Cicero in several of his works were the traditions Grotius drew upon in developing his natural rights system, or so I argue in this article.[9] While both the medieval just war tradition[10] and Grotius's

[7] Grotius's contribution to the development of a doctrine of natural rights is well known and has received a lot of scholarly attention; see M. Villey, 'Les origines'; R. Tuck, *Natural Rights Theories: Their Origin and Development* (Cambridge: CUP, 1979), pp. 58-81; B. Tierney, *The Idea of Natural Rights* (Cambridge: CUP, 1997), pp. 316-342; P. Haggenmacher, 'Droits subjectifs et système juridique chez Grotius's, in *Politique, droit et théologie chez Bodin, Grotius et Hobbes*, ed. by L. Foisneau (Paris: Kimé, 1997), pp. 73-130; R. Tuck, *The Rights of War and Peace* (Oxford: OUP, 1999), pp. 78-108.

[8] Michel Villey has vehemently argued against a subjective Roman notion of right (an argument that has influenced Isaiah Berlin's 'Two Concepts of Liberty') and has attributed an important role to Grotius in the development of such a subjective notion; see Villey, 'Les origines'. But see, for a Greek origin of rights, F. D. Miller, *Nature, Justice, and Rights in Aristotle's Politics* (Oxford: Clarendon, 1995); P. Mitsis, 'The Stoic Origin of Natural Rights', in *Topics in Stoic Philosophy*, ed. by K. Ierodiakonou (Oxford: Clarendon, 1999), pp. 153-177. The question of whether the Greek Stoics possessed a concept of rights remains open, and need not concern us here. For an overview, see J. Miller, 'Stoics, Grotius and Spinoza on Moral Deliberation', in *Hellenistic and Early Modern Philosophy*, ed. by J. Miller and B. Inwood (Cambridge: CUP, 2003), pp. 117-120. Arguing convincingly for a subjective use of *ius* in Roman law is C. Donahue, 'Ius in the Subjective Sense', in *A Ennio Cortese*, ed. by D. Maffei, 3 vols (Rome: Galilei, 2001), I, pp. 506-535; see also M. Kaser, 'Zum "Ius"-Begriff der Römer', in *Essays in Honor of Ben Beinart*, ed. by Wouter de Vos et al., 3 vols, *Acta Juridica*, 1-3 (1976-78), II, pp. 63-81.

[9] For a more general account of Grotius's dependency on a Roman tradition in developing his conception of a state of nature, with special attention to his use of rhetoric and his interpretation of the Roman just war tradition, see B. Straumann, ' "Ancient Caesarian Lawyers" in a State of Nature: Roman Tradition and Natural Rights in Hugo Grotius's *De iure praedae*', *Political Theory*, 34 (2006), 328-350.

[10] See the authoritative work by P. Haggenmacher, *Grotius et la doctrine de la guerre juste* (Paris: PUF, 1983).

immediate political context – his 'experience of international relations'[11] – certainly deserve ample scholarly attention and constitute important influences on Grotius's natural law tenets,[12] it is a Roman tradition of subjective legal remedies and of just war which lays claim to a foundational role with regard to Grotius's conception of subjective natural rights.

Of the four natural rights that may give rise to a just cause of war – the right to self-defense, to property, to exact debt, and to punish –, the right to private property and the right to exact debt are given most attention in the present article,[13] because these two rights are most intricately tied to what has been acknowledged as the driving force behind the modern concept of rights, that is to say commerce and free trade.[14] The right to punish on the other hand lies beyond the scope of this article. Suffice it to say that Grotius's right to punish is a secondary right of sorts, derivative of the primary rights of self-defense, property and exaction of debt, and designed to prevent these rights from being invaded.[15]

The article proceeds in four sections. The first section gives an account of how Grotius in his early natural law works developed a conception of subjective natural rights by reference to Roman law remedies. The second section provides a brief discussion of Grotius's right to self-defense and its Ciceronian foundation. Sections three and four deal with the right to private property and the right to enforce contractual claims, respectively.

---

[11] C. G. Roelofsen, 'Some Remarks on the "Sources" of the Grotian System of International Law', *Netherlands International Law Review*, 30 (1983), 73-79 (p. 79).

[12] For the political context see P. Borschberg, 'Hugo Grotius, East India Trade and the King of Johor', *Journal of Southeast Asian Studies*, 30 (1999), 225-248; Id., 'The Seizure of the Sta. Catarina Revisited: The Portuguese Empire in Asia, VOC Politics and the Origins of the Dutch-Johor Alliance (1602-ca. 1616)', *Journal of Southeast Asian Studies*, 33 (2002), 31-62; Martine Julia van Ittersum, *Profit and Principle: Hugo Grotius, Natural Rights Theories and the Rise of Dutch Power in the East Indies, 1595-1615* (Leiden: Brill, 2006); see also Borschberg's and Ittersum's contribution to this volume. I am very grateful to Martine van Ittersum for sharing her manuscript with me.

[13] For Grotius's right to property, see R. Brandt, *Eigentumstheorien von Grotius bis Kant* (Stuttgart: Fromman-Holzboog, 1974); S. Buckle, *Natural Law and the Theory of Property. Grotius to Hume* (Oxford: Clarendon, 1991). For contractual rights, see M. Diesselhorst, *Die Lehre des Hugo Grotius vom Versprechen* (Köln: Böhlau, 1959).

[14] See Constant, 'Liberty of the Ancients', p. 325: 'The effects of commerce extend even further: not only does it emancipate individuals, but [...] it places authority itself in a position of dependence'.

[15] But see for the right to punish G. van Nifterik's contribution to this volume; see also B. Straumann, 'The Right to Punish as a Just Cause of War in Hugo Grotius's Natural Law', *Studies in the History of Ethics*, 2 (2006), at www.historyofethics.org

Roman Law Remedies as Natural Rights

The concept of a state of nature constitutes the foundation of Hugo Grotius's law of nature as well as of his law of nations, both resting on a doctrine of the just causes of war.[16] The legitimate *causae belli* consist on Grotius's account in a violation of rights inhering naturally in every inhabitant of the natural state,[17] rights which in turn correspond to the natural rights pertaining to the individual in the state of nature according to natural law, and to a certain degree even to individuals in lawfully constituted commonwealths. Grotius's early treatise *De iure praedae commentarius* (1604-1606)[18] and its offshoot *Mare liberum*[19] already contained an inchoate version of such subjective natural rights, and a still more elaborate natural rights doctrine can be found in Grotius's early *Theses LVI*[20] and in the *Defensio capitis quinti maris*

[16] Grotius tries to render the cause of war as an Aristotelian *causa materialis*. This terminology, however, does not carry any substantive weight and in *De iure belli ac pacis* is abandoned entirely; for Grotius's use of the Aristotelian doctrine of causes in *De iure praedae*, see P. Haggenmacher, *Grotius et la doctrine*, pp. 63ff.

[17] Grotius's doctrine of the just war is also reflected in the early *Commentarius in theses XI*, where only public wars are being discussed, however, and where Grotius does not posit a natural right to punish; see P. Borschberg, *Hugo Grotius 'Commentarius in Theses XI'. An Early Treatise on Sovereignty, the Just War, and the Legitimacy of the Dutch Revolt* (Bern: Lang, 1994), pp. 237ff., 263.

[18] The following edition has been used: Hugo Grotius, *De iure praedae commentarius. A Collotype Reproduction of the Original Manuscript of 1604*, ed. by J. B. Scott, The Classics of International Law 22, 2 vols (Oxford: Clarendon, 1950), vol. 2; when *De iure praedae* (henceforth abbreviated as *IPC*) is cited in English, this translation will be used: Hugo Grotius, *De iure praedae commentarius. Commentary on the Law of Prize and Booty*, tr. by G. L. Williams, with W. H. Zeydel, ed. by J. B. Scott, The Classics of International Law 22, 2 vols (Oxford: Clarendon, 1950), vol. 1. Some of the translations have on occasion been modified.

[19] The twelfth chapter of *IPC*, published anonymously in 1609; the following edition has been used, containing both the text and a translation: Hugo Grotius, *Mare liberum, The Freedom of the Seas*, tr. by R. van Deman Magoffin, ed. by J. B. Scott (New York: OUP, 1916), henceforth abbreviated as *ML*. In the following, when *IPC* or *ML* are cited in English, the translation of *IPC* will be used; the translation in *ML* will be used for passages not contained in *IPC*. Some of the translations have on occasion been modified. For a historical interpretation of *ML*, see P. Borschberg, 'Hugo Grotius' Theory of Trans-Oceanic Trade Regulation: Revisiting *Mare Liberum* (1609)', *IILJ Working Paper* 14 (2005), History and Theory of International Law Series (www.iilj.org).

[20] The manuscript is at Leiden University Library, Ms. BPL 922 I, fols 287-292: *Theses sive quaestiones LVI* (henceforth abbreviated as *TQ*). Citations refer to folio and thesis number, translations are my own. I would like to thank Professor Peter Borschberg for discussing the *TQ* with me and for generously sharing his unpublished draft 'Grotius and the Social Contract Theory: A Preliminary Study of the Unpublished *Theses LVI* and their Relation to his Principal Political-Legal Works, approx. 1602-1625', a paper to which my interpretation of the *TQ* is heavily indebted.

liberi,[21] a defense of the fifth chapter of *Mare liberum*, written around 1615 and directed against the Scottish jurist William Welwod's attack on *Mare liberum*.

Grotius developed his conception of subjective rights against the backdrop of the system of Roman private law remedies. In a passage aimed to show that the justification of war, private or public, hinges on the justness of the war's cause, Grotius compares the possible material causes of war with the legal remedies provided by the Roman law of the *Digest*. Having enumerated the four genera of just causes of war, Grotius goes on to simply identify them with the different kinds of Roman legal actions:

> [I]n both kinds of warfare, [public and private,] one must consider the causes involved. Of these there are four kinds, as we have pointed out: for the authorities who hold that there are three just causes of war (defence, recovery, and punishment, according to their classification), fail to mention the not uncommon cause that arises whenever obligations are not duly discharged. Indeed, *in so far as we are concerned with subject-matter, which is the same in warfare and in judicial trials, we may say that there should be precisely as many kinds of execution* [*exsecutiones*] *as there are kinds of legal action* [*actiones*] [italics mine]. To be sure, legal judgements are rarely rendered in consequence of causes of the first class, since the necessity for defending oneself does not admit of such delay; but interdicts against attack [*interdicta de non offendendo*] properly fall under this head. The actions relating to property [*actiones in rem*] which we call recovery claims [*vindicationes*], arise from the second kind of cause, as do also injunctions obtained in behalf of possession [*interdicta possessionis gratia*]. The third and fourth classes give rise to personal actions, namely, claims to restitution [*condictiones*], founded upon contract [*ex contractu*] or upon injury [*ex maleficio*].[22]

---

[21] Hugo Grotius, '*Defensio capitis quinti Maris Liberi oppugnati a Guilielmo Welwodo*', in S. Muller, *Mare Clausum: Bijdrage tot de Geschiedenis der Rivaliteit van Engeland en Nederland in de Zeventiende Eeuw* (Amsterdam: Muller, 1872), pp. 331-361 (henceforth abbreviated as *DCQ*). Translations from *DCQ* are taken from Hugo Grotius, *The Free Sea, translated by Richard Hakluyt with Wiliam Welwod's critique and Grotius's reply*, ed. by D. Armitage (Indianapolis: Liberty Fund, 2004), pp. 77-130.

[22] *IPC*, VII, fols 30a'f.: *Spectandae igitur in utroque causae, quas esse quatuor diximus. Nam qui tres statuunt iustas bellorum causas, defensionem, recuperationem et punitionem, ut loquuntur, illam non infrequenter omittunt, quae locum habet, quoties quae convenerint non praestantur. Totidem enim esse debent exsecutionum, quot sunt actionum genera, quod ad materiam attinet, quae in bello et iudiciis eadem est. Et ex primo quidem genere raro iudicia redduntur, quia moram istam se tuendi necessitas non permittit. Attamen interdicta de non offendendo huc pertinent. Secundo ex genere sunt in rem actiones, quas vindicationes dicimus: interdicta etiam possessionis gratia comparata. Ex tertio et quarto actiones personales, condictiones scilicet ex contractu et ex maleficio.* Punishment constitutes a cause of war, because guilt (*culpa*) itself creates an obligation; see *IPC*, XII, fols 119. This doctrine of punishment as a natural cause of war gave rise to Grotius's famous theory, anticipating Locke's 'very strange doctrine', that the private individual in the state of nature has a right to punish; *IPC*, VIII, fols 40f. See R. Tuck, *Rights of War*, p. 82. See G. van Nifterik's contribution to this volume.

Grotius maintained that the prohibition of navigation and trade imposed by the Portuguese constitutes an injury according to Roman law.[23] If the matter in question between the Portuguese and the Dutch were taken into court, there could be, according to Grotius, 'no doubt what opinion ought to be anticipated from a just judge'. But if such a judgment cannot be obtained, 'it should with justice be demanded in a war'.[24] The crucial point to be considered was that, as Pomponius in the *Digest* had decided, 'the man who seized [*usurpere*] a thing common to all [*res communis*] to the prejudice of every one else must be forcibly prevented [*manu prohibendus*] from so doing'.[25] That this applies to the sea also follows from an interdict granted by Labeo, cited by Grotius, which is designed to prevent anything from being done in the sea by which shipping could be obstructed.[26] Most importantly, the violation in question does not have to concern just corporeal things, such as an attack on property – rights can be violated as well.

> The defence [*rerum defensio*] or recovery of possessions [*rerum recuperatio*], and the exaction of a debt [*debitum*] or of penalties due, all constitute just causes of war [*iustae bellorum causae*]. Under the head of 'possessions' [*res*], even rights [*iura*] should be included.[27]

The use of common goods (*res communes*), i.e. the high seas, is exactly such a right that can be defended in a just war. Grotius, true to his Roman law sources, treats the right to use the sea as a quasi-possession under Roman law,[28] in that he treats it as an interest that is, although strictly not capable of being possessed – since *usus* in Roman law is as an incorporeal interest not capable of *possessio*, just of *quasi possessio*[29] – , still enjoying the protection of the remedy designed to protect possession. According to Grotius, the right to the use of the high seas can be enforced by means of a prohibitory interdict, which

---

[23] *IPC*, XII, fol. 119 (=*ML*, XIII, p. 74), adducing Ulp. *Dig.* 43.8.2.9; 47.10.13.7.

[24] *ML*, XIII, p. 75: *Quod autem in iudicio obtineretur, id ubi iudicium haberi non potest, iusto bello vindicatur.*

[25] *ML*, XIII, p. 75: *Et quod proprius est nostro argumento, Pomponius eum qui rem omnibus communem cum incommodo ceterorum usurpet, MANU PROHIBENDUM respondit.* The adduced passage (Pomp. *Dig.* 41.1.50) reads: *Quamvis quod in litore publico vel in mari exstruxerimus, nostrum fiat, tamen decretum praetoris adhibendum est, ut id facere liceat: immo etiam manu prohibendus est, si cum incommodo ceterorum id faciat: nam civilem eum actionem de faciendo nullam habere non dubito.* The conclusion by J. Ziskind, 'International Law and Ancient Sources: Grotius and Selden', *The Review of Politics*, 35 (1973), 545 that the use of force was not mentioned by Pomponius, is baffling.

[26] *IPC*, XII, fol. 119 (=*ML*, XIII, p. 74); the citation is from Ulp. *Dig.* 43.12.1.17.

[27] *IPC*, XII, fol. 116' (a passage omitted from *ML*).

[28] *IPC*, XII, fol. 116' (omitted from *ML*): *Si quis igitur ius tale quasi possideat* [...].

[29] The terminology is probably post-classical; see W. W. Buckland, *A Text-Book of Roman Law from Augustus to Justinian*, 2nd edn (Cambridge: The University Press, 1932), pp. 196f.

usually prohibits the use of force against the last rightful possessor. In *De iure praedae*, however, this turns into a *right* of the last rightful possessor, i.e. the Dutch, to assert their claim to the use of the high seas by force given the absence of courts: 'For in all cases to which prohibitory interdicts are properly applicable in court procedure, armed prohibition is proper outside the courts'.[30]

The above illustrates a most important way in which Grotius used private Roman law, viz. how he couched the procedural remedies provided by that law in a language of subjective natural rights. In the *Defensio* of chapter five of *Mare liberum*, Grotius elucidates his notion of right in a subjective sense, a notion already applied in the subtitle of *Mare liberum*: 'The Right [*ius*] Which Belongs to the Dutch to Take Part in the East Indies Trade'.[31] Grotius, who in *De iure praedae* had used the term 'right' (*ius*) in an equivocal way to denote both objective law and subjective rights, ten years later explicitly introduced the notion of a subjective right in his defense of the fifth chapter of *Mare liberum*, directed against William Welwod's attack.[32] In the *Defensio*, Grotius moved to impute to the Roman lawyers the notion of exactly such a claim-right:[33]

> Now add the fact that the sea is not only said by the jurists to be common by the law of nations, but without any addition it is said to be of the right (*ius*) of nations. In these passages 'right' (*ius*) can not mean a norm of justice, but a moral faculty over a thing, as when we say 'this thing is of my right' (*ius*), that is, I have ownership over it or use or something similar.[34]

To what a degree can it be said that the Romans possessed the notion of a subjective claim-right? Fortunately, this is not something we will have to decide in the present article, where exclusively Grotius's use of the Roman

[30] *IPC*, XII, fol. 116' (omitted from *ML*): *Nam quoties in iudiciis interdicta competunt prohibitoria, toties extra iudicia prohibitio competit armata.*

[31] *Mare liberum, sive de iure quod Batavis competit ad Indicana commercia, dissertatio.*

[32] For an excellent discussion of the gradual development of the notion of subjective rights in Grotius's work, see Haggenmacher, 'Droits subjectifs', pp. 73-130.

[33] For the notion of a claim-right, see W. Hohfeld, *Fundamental Legal Conceptions, as Applied in Judicial Reasoning, and Other Legal Essays Essays*, ed. by W. W. Cook (New Haven: Yale University Press, 1919), p. 36.

[34] Grotius, *Free Sea*, p. 107; *DCQ*, p. 348: *Adde iam quod Mare non tantum dicitur a Iurisconsultis esse commune gentium iure, sed sine ulla adiectione dicitur esse Iuris gentium, quibus in locis ius non potest significare normam aliquam iusti, sed facultatem moralem in re: ut cum dicimus haec res est iuris mei id est habeo in ea dominium aut usum aut simile aliquid.* The notion of *ius* as a *facultas* had already been developed by Jean Gerson in the early fifteenth century; see R. Tuck, *Natural Rights*, pp. 25f; but see B. Tierney, 'Tuck on Rights. Some Medieval Problems', *History of Political Thought*, 6 (1983), 429-441; Id., *The Idea of Natural Rights* (Atlanta: Scholars Press, 1997), pp. 207-235.

sources is open for debate, and here it seems that Grotius translated, as it were, the technical Roman law terms for the various remedies with the term 'right' (*ius*), something that is in any case hard to avoid, as Alan Gewirth[35] and more recently Charles Donahue have pointed out: 'A legal system like the Roman that conceives of rights and duties in terms of what one can bring an action for, must have the concept of subjective right, even if it never uses the term'.[36]

Such a rendering of the various *actiones* and *interdicta* as *iura*, and especially the view that doing a wrong consists in a breach of a subjective right, was most probably inspired by the humanists of the *mos Gallicus*, particularly by Donellus.[37] In *De iure praedae*, Grotius still used the term iridescently both in its subjective and its objective sense, but in the *Defensio*, in the passage cited above, Grotius unambiguously attributed a subjective sense to the notion of right, asserting that *iuris gentium esse* had in fact assumed a subjective sense already in the *Digest*,[38] and suggesting that the genitive *iuris gentium esse* is using the term *ius* in a subjective sense, as in *iuris mei esse*, in order to be able to present the sea as a subjective '*right* of nations'. Such a subjective interpretation of the formulation *mare iuris gentium esse*, as it appears in the *Digest*, is certainly untenable – the only thing the Roman jurists meant by that phrase was that the sea was governed by the rules of the *ius gentium*. It is not even sure that Grotius himself, when composing *De iure praedae*, understood the phrase *mare iuris gentium* in a subjective sense.[39] Not later than with the *Defensio*, however, this version was convenient for Grotius both because it supported his subjective use of *ius* in other passages and because it sat comfortably with his rendering of the various *actiones* and *interdicta* as rights.

---

[35] See A. Gewirth, *Reason and Morality* (Chicago: University of Chicago Press, 1978), p. 100.

[36] Donahue, 'Ius', p. 530. Most Roman law textbooks cannot do without the notion of right; see, e.g., Buckland, *Roman Law*, *passim*.

[37] For Donellus and his subjective conception of *ius*, see H. Coing, 'Zur Geschichte des Begriffs subjektives Recht', in Id., *Gesammelte Aufsätze*, 2 vols (Frankfurt a. M.: Klostermann, 1982), I, pp. 251-254; P. Haggenmacher, *Grotius et la doctrine*, pp. 178-180; Id., 'Droits subjectifs', p. 113.

[38] Grotius probably alludes to *Dig.* 1.8.4, where it is said that nobody could be denied access to the seashore, provided he keeps clear of houses and buildings, *quia non sunt iuris gentium sicut et mare*. Cf. *Inst.* 2.1.1.

[39] Grotius refers in *DCQ* back to the following passage in *IPC*, XII, fol. 100' (=*ML*, V, p. 22): *De mari autem prima sit consideratio, quod cum passim in iure aut nullius, aut commune, aut publicum iuris gentium dicatur*. In the manuscript, the words *iuris gentium* look as if they had originally read *iure gentium*, according to the law of nations, and were changed only later to the genitive.

In the early, hitherto unpublished manuscript *Theses LVI*, a very important source for the development of Grotius's thought on rights in a state of nature, Grotius already used the term *ius* in an obviously subjective and individuated sense.[40] In the second thesis, Grotius gives the following description of the rights that belong naturally to man:

> A human being naturally [*naturaliter*] has a right [*ius*] to his actions [*actiones*] and his possessions [*res*], a right both to retain them and to alienate them: regarding life and body, only to retain them. This right, flowing from the law of God [*ius Dei*], is restricted by the law of God, by the law of nature [*per legem naturalem*], and by the Bible and the revelation.[41]

Subjective natural rights on this account are rights that one can 'have', different from the objective norms of law,[42] norms that restrict the subjective rights bestowed on human beings in the state of nature.[43] The rights vested in the subjects of the law of nature according to the *Theses LVI* are of a universal character, insofar as they pertain to everyone *naturaliter*. Moreover, they are rights that can be described as claims *in rem* in the Roman law sense, insofar as they oblige everybody else to respect these rights. The natural, universal subjective rights in the *Theses LVI* constitute a quasi-sovereign territory of the individual subject of law in the state of nature, and are an absolute barrier to the claims of all the other subjects of natural law:

> Human beings do not have a natural right [*ius non habet naturaliter*] to the life, body, actions and possessions of another man, insofar as the other's life, body, actions or possessions are ordinary means to the self-interested [*ad bonum suum*] pursuit of the right [*ius*] to life, body, actions, and possessions [*res*] that everybody

---

[40] The dating of the manuscript remains tentative; Professor Peter Borschberg holds that based on an analysis of the paper's watermarks, the manuscript appears to have been written in the first decade of the seventeenth century, presumably between 1602 and 1605. Based on an analysis of the concepts used, however, I would date the work rather around the *DCQ* (1615), both because of the clear-cut subjective use of *ius* and because of a marginal note denying a natural right to punish (see below, n. 44), which would be more in line with later works such as *Defensio fidei catholicae de satisfactione Christi* and *De imperio summarum potestatum circa sacra*, both written between 1614 and 1617. See also G. van Nifterik's contribution to this volume.

[41] *TQ*, fol. 287 recto, thesis 2: *Homo naturaliter ius habet in actiones et res suas tum retinendi tum abdicandi: vita autem et corpus retinendi tantum. Hoc tamen ius a iure Dei dimanans ab eodem restringitur, per legem naturalem et per verbum tum extrinsecum tum intrinsecum, id est Scripturam et Revelationem.*

[42] See Haggenmacher, 'Droits subjectifs', pp. 81f., who assumes that Grotius only later came to differentiate strictly between subjective and objective *ius*.

[43] In a similar way as natural liberty in the *Institutes* is restricted by law (*ius*); Flor. *Inst.* 1.3.1: *Et libertas quidem est, ex qua etiam liberi vocantur, naturalis facultas eius quod cuique facere libet, nisi si quid aut vi aut iure prohibetur.*

> has [*quod quisque habet*]. Consequently, human beings do not have a [natural] right to punishment.[44]

The idea of a *numerus clausus* of rights that one can have, as put forward in *De iure praedae* as well as in *De iure belli ac pacis*, can be seen in the *Theses LVI* too. The rights here are comparable to the rights enumerated in *De iure praedae*; the right to one's own actions points to the freedom of contract, which constitutes the premise of the right to enforce contractual claims. The right to one's own things foreshadows the right to private property, as well as to contractual claims arising out of contracts of sale, while the right to one's life and body corresponds to the right to self-defense. It is remarkable that, as opposed to both *De iure praedae* and *De iure belli ac pacis*, the right to one's own life and body is not alienable.

In concluding the general discussion of *ius* as subjective right, I submit that subjective rights claims clearly do not hinge on the language of rights and the *ius* terminology, but must be conceived as already inherent in the remedies granted under the law of the *Digest*. The intellectual history of natural rights can consequently be seen as an extension of the remedies granted by Roman procedure – Grotius casting subjective *iura* in actions and injunctions granted by the Roman lawyers of the *Digest*. Grotius's originality lies in the fact that he identified an already existing tradition of natural rights with Roman law remedies, internalizing these remedies by making them a subjective moral quality of each individual, or each individual group of people.

The Right to Self-Defense

The right to self-defense emanates from Grotius's first so-called law (*lex*), as formulated in the 'Prolegomena' to *De iure praedae*: 'It shall be permissible to defend [one's own] life and to shun that which threatens to prove injurious'.[45] In the marginal note, Grotius referred to passages out of Cicero's works *De officiis* and *De finibus* as the sources of that first law, which indeed constitutes a paraphrase of the adduced Ciceronian passages wherein the natural appetite for self-preservation is being portrayed, in a Stoic tradition, as

[44] *TQ*, fol. 287 recto, thesis 6: *Homo autem ius non habet <naturaliter> in <vitam corpus> actiones et res alterius hominis, insiquatenus illae <vita corpus> actiones aut res alterius sunt media ordinata ad consequendum <ad bonum suum> ius quod quisque habet in vitam, corpus, actiones et res suas. <Ergo non habet ius puniendi>* The bracketed words are marginal notes inserted by Grotius.

[45] *IPC*, II, fol. 6: *VITAM TUERI ET DECLINARE NOCITURA LICEAT.*

common to all living creatures.[46] What Cicero had described as natural and therefore desirable in a Stoic sense,[47] Grotius formulated as a permissive norm of the law of nature. Moreover, Grotius in the marginal note to his 'first law' also referred to Cicero's forensic speech *Pro Milone*, where Cicero himself, writing in a time ridden with lawlessness and bound for civil war, had rendered self-preservation as a legal principle.[48] Self-help was lawful in the absence of judicial authority and in a context of diminishing sovereign power, Cicero held, under a 'law which is a law not written, but created by nature'.[49]

In the seventh chapter of *De iure praedae*, Grotius, setting forth the right to self-defense, drew again on Cicero's *Pro Milone*. Every just war according to Grotius has its origin in one of four just causes of war, self-defense (*sui defensio*) being the first of these just causes. Grotius then justifies self-defense with an argument out of *Pro Milone*, according to which 'the act of homicide is not only just but even necessary, when it represents the repulsion of violence by means of violence'.[50] The right to self-defense according to Grotius inheres naturally not only in commonwealths, but also in individuals: 'The examples afforded by all living creatures show that force privately exercised for the defence and safeguarding of one's own body is justly employed'.[51] Grotius supports this contention with various Roman law passages, the following passage from Florentinus out of the *Digest* among them:

> [It belongs to the law of nations] to repel violent injuries. You see, it emerges from this law that whatever a person does for his bodily security he can be held

[46] Cic. *off.* 1.11: *Principio generi animantium omni est a natura tributum, ut se, vitam corpusque tueatur, declinet ea, quae nocitura videantur, omniaque, quae sint ad vivendum necessaria anquirat et paret, ut pastum, ut latibula, ut alia generis eiusdem.* Cic. *fin.* 4.16: *Omnis natura vult esse conservatrix sui, ut et salva sit et in genere conservetur suo.* Cic. *fin.* 5.24: *Omne animal se ipsum diligit, ac simul ortum est id agit ut se conservet, quod hic ei primus ad omnem vitam tuendam appetitus a natura datur, se ut conservet atque ita sit affectum ut optime secundum naturam affectum esse possit.*

[47] For the Stoic background (*oikeiosis*) of Cic. *off.* 1.11, see A. R. Dyck, *A Commentary on Cicero, De Officiis* (Ann Arbor: University of Michigan Press, 1996), pp. 86ff.

[48] Cic. *Mil.* 10.

[49] Ibid.; cited in *IPC*, I, fol. 4'.

[50] *IPC*, VII, fol. 29': *Bellum igitur omne quatuor causarum ex aliqua oriri necesse est. Prima est sui defensio, ex lege prima. Nam ut Cicero inquit, illud est non modo iustum, sed etiam necessarium, cum vi vis illata defenditur.* The citation is from Cic. *Mil.* 9.

[51] *IPC*, VII, fol. 30a: *Ad defensionem tutelamque corporis sui privata vis iusta est omnium animantium exemplo.*

> to have done rightfully; and since nature has established among us a relationship of sorts, it follows that it is a grave wrong for one human being to encompass the life of another.[52]

Defense against an unlawful attack constitutes, according to the law of the *Digest*, a justification for an encroachment on somebody else's rights. Grotius adduces a further passage from the *Digest* which excepts the bearing of weapons 'for the purpose of protecting one's own safety' from the general prohibition under the *lex Julia* on *vis publica* to collect or carry weapons.[53] Clearly, Grotius's just cause of self-defense is modeled on the notion of self-defense as emerging from the *Digest* and some of Cicero's works, with the background of Cicero's speech *Pro Milone* – the civil war like circumstances of the fading Roman republic with its crumbling institutions – providing the paradigm for Grotius's concept of a natural state, characterized by the absence of judicial organs and the norms of a natural law.

The Right to Private Property

The second of Grotius's so-called 'laws' that he expounds in the 'Prolegomena' to *De iure praedae* reads: 'It shall be permissible to acquire for oneself, and to retain, those things which are useful for life'.[54] Citing from Cicero's *De officiis*, Grotius then writes:

> The latter precept, indeed, we shall interpret with Cicero as an admission that each individual may, without violating the precepts of nature, prefer to see acquired for himself rather than for another, that which is important for the conduct of life.[55]

---

[52] Flor. *Dig.* 1.1.3: *ut vim atque iniuriam propulsemus: nam iure hoc evenit, ut quod quisque ob tutelam corporis sui fecerit, iure fecisse existimetur, et cum inter nos cognationem quandam natura constituit, consequens est hominem homini insidiari nefas esse.*

[53] *Dig.* 48.6.11.2: *Qui telum tutandae salutis suae causa gerunt, non videntur hominis occidendi causa portare.*

[54] *IPC*, II, fol. 6: *ADIUNGERE SIBI QUAE AD VIVENDUM SUNT UTILIA EAQUE RETINERE LICEAT.*

[55] *IPC*, II, fol. 6: *quod quidem cum Tullio ita interpretabimur: concessum sibi quisque ut malit, quod ad vitae usum pertinet, quam alteri acquiri id fieri non repugnante natura.* Grotius is citing from Cic. *off.* 3.22, where we read: *Nam sibi ut quisque malit, quod ad usum vitae pertineat, quam alteri adquirere, concessum est non repugnante natura* [...]. In *De iure belli ac pacis*, Grotius cited the whole paragraph from *De officiis*.

Grotius explains that among the ancient schools of philosophy there had been unity in this regard, backing up this contention with a reference to Cicero's portrayal of the various ethical doctrines in *De finibus*.[56]

In *Mare liberum* (chapter twelve of *De iure praedae*), Grotius explains the origin of the *institution* of private property by paraphrasing Cicero's explanation of the *acquisition* of private property in *De officiis*, an explanation that is based on the Roman law concept of long occupancy (*vetus occupatio*).[57] In the 'Prolegomena', Grotius writes that use of certain things requires the acquisition (*apprehensio*) and possession (*possessio*) of these things, and that hence the institution of private property (*dominium*) had originated.[58] In the marginal note, Grotius refers to a passage by Paulus out of the 41st book of the *Digest*, where the origin of private property is traced back to 'natural possession', i.e. the acquisition of possession of an unowned thing *ab initio*.[59] Grotius's is an account of private property that does not take private property to be an original institution of natural law, but, once constituted, private property is protected by the natural legal rules – there are, on Grotius's view, principles of natural justice governing property holdings. Property, then, is not constituted by government.[60] This is very similar to Cicero's account in *De officiis*,[61] although it seems that both Cicero and the account in book 41 of the *Digest* in fact presuppose the notion of private property as an institution rather than explaining its origin, and explain merely the *acquisition* of private property.

Grotius holds that the institution of private property is not the result of a sudden decision, but was brought about by slow change that started under the guidance of nature (*monstrans natura*).[62] There are certain things, Grotius writes, which are consumed by use, a fact making it impossible to distinguish

---

[56] *IPC*, II, fol. 6: *Hac enim de re et Stoicis et Epicureis et Peripateticis convenit, ne Academici quidem videntur dubitasse.*

[57] *IPC*, XII, fol. 101' (=*ML*, V, p. 25), adducing Cic. *off.* 1.21.

[58] *IPC*, II, fol. 6f.

[59] *Dig.* 41.2.1.1: *Dominiumque rerum ex naturali possessione coepisse Nerva filius ait eiusque rei vestigium remanere in his, quae terra mari caeloque capiuntur: nam haec protinus eorum fiunt, qui primi possessionem eorum adprehenderint.*

[60] A view very similar to John Locke's in his *Second Treatise of Government*; see J. Locke, *Two Treatises of Government*, ed. by P. Laslett, 2nd edn, (Cambridge: CUP, 1967; 1st edn 1960), *Second Treatise*, sects. 3, 124, 134, 136. See also J. Waldron, 'Locke, Tully, and the Regulation of Property', *Political Studies*, 32 (1984), 98.

[61] See Cic. *off.* 1.21. For the status of private property in Cicero's political thought, see N. Wood, *Cicero's Social and Political Thought* (Berkeley: University of California Press, 1988), pp. 111-115.

[62] For the conception of private property in *Mare liberum*, see the survey in J. Tully, *A Discourse on Property. John Locke and his Adversaries* (Cambridge: CUP, 1980), pp. 68-70.

between use and property.[63] Grotius predicates this view on a passage of the *Digest*, where usufruct (*ususfructus*) of money and other consumables is being dealt with.[64] With regard to these things, the usufructuary under Roman property law becomes the full owner. The thing belongs to him in an exclusive way, belonging to nobody else at the same time – the concept of private property as the most comprehensive right somebody can have in a thing is therewith formulated. This concept was then, according to Grotius, extended to clothes and gradually to immovable things.[65] As the institution of private property had thus been 'invented' (*reperta proprietas*), the law codifying that institution was stipulated in order to imitate nature.[66] Private property, then, is on Grotius's account an institution of the state of nature, perfectly possible apart from civil society and government. Although not existing by nature, the institution nevertheless came into being in a natural way. Grotius adduces the famous theater analogy, which originally stems arguably from Chrysippus,[67] citing it from Seneca's *De beneficiis*: 'The equestrian rows of seats belong to *all* [*omnes*] the Roman knights; yet the place that I have *occupied* [*occupavi*] in those rows becomes my *own* [*proprius*]'.[68]

---

[63] *IPC* 12, fol. 101 (=*ML*, V, p. 24): *Ad eam vero quae nunc est dominiorum distinctionem non impetu quodam sed paulatim ventum videtur initium eius monstrante natura. Cum enim res sint nonnullae quarum usus in abusu consistit, aut quia conversae in substantiam utentis nullum postea usum admittunt, aut quia utendo fiunt ad usum deteriores, in rebus prioris generis, ut cibo et potu, proprietas statim quaedam ab usu non seiuncta emicuit.*

[64] *Dig.* 7.5: *De usu fructu earum rerum, quae usu consumuntur vel minuuntur.* This corresponds to the argument used by Pope John XXII against the Franciscans in the 14th century; Grotius in the marginal note refers both to John XXII and to Thomas Aquinas. See Tierney, *Idea*, pp. 330f., who ascribes Grotius's reasoning solely to the canonistic tradition, ignoring that John XXII himself had argued in a way influenced by Roman law.

[65] *IPC*, XII, fol. 101 (=*ML*, V, p. 24): *Hoc enim est proprium esse, ita esse cuiusquam ut et alterius esse non possit: quod deinde ad res posterioris generis, vestes puta et res mobiles alias aut se moventes ratione quadam productum est. Quod cum esset, ne res quidem immobiles omnes, agri puta indivisae manere potuerunt* [...].

[66] *IPC*, XII, fol. 101' (=*ML*, V, p. 25): *Repertae proprietati lex posita est quae naturam imitaretur.*

[67] See Cic. *fin.* 3.67, where the following statement is imputed to Chrysippus: *Sed quemadmodum, theatrum cum commune sit, recte tamen dici potest eius esse eum locum quem quisque occuparit, sic in urbe mundove communi non adversatur ius quo minus suum quidque cuiusque sit.* See A. A. Long, 'Stoic Philosophers on Persons, Property-Ownership and Community', in *Aristotle and After*, ed. by R. Sorabji (London: University of London, 1997), p. 24f., who takes Cicero at his word, ascribing this moral justification of private property not very plausibly already to the Greek Stoa from Chrysippus. See thereto the criticism in Mitsis, 'The Stoic Origin of Natural Rights', pp. 171f.

[68] *IPC* 12, fol. 101' (=*ML*, V, p. 25): *Equestria OMNIUM equitum Romanorum sunt: in illis tamen locus meus fit PROPRIUS, quem OCCUPAVI.* The citation is from Sen. *ben.* 7.12.3.

In the *Defensio capitis quinti*, his defense of chapter five of *Mare liberum* against William Welwod, Grotius describes the emergence of private property in a concise passage dedicated to the interpretation of Cicero's statement in *De officiis* that 'no property is private by nature'.[69] Welwod had wrongly ridiculed this statement by Cicero, Grotius argues: Cicero should not be read as saying that nature contradicts private property, he had rather been of the opinion that nature in itself did not make anything private property:[70]

> Therefore, in order that this thing become the property of that man, some deed [*factum*] of the man should intervene [*intercedere*], and therefore nature itself does not do this by itself. Hence it is evident that community [*communitas*] is prior to property [*proprietas*]. For property does not occur except through occupation [*occupatio*], and before occupation, there must precede the right of occupation [*ius occupandi*]. Now this right [*ius*] is not competent to this man or that man, but to all men equally, and is rightly expressed under the term 'natural community' [*communitas naturalis*]. And hence it happens that what has not yet been occupied by any people or by a man is still common, that is, belongs to no one, and open equally to all. By this argument it is surely proved that nothing belongs [*proprium*] to anyone by nature.[71]

Everyone therefore has at least potentially a right to acquisition in the sense of occupation and in this sense a right to private property. Unlike in the *Theses LVI*, private property here in the *Defensio* (as already in *De iure praedae*) is not simply presupposed as natural, but its emergence as an institution is explained, and at the same time the emergence of the existing, concrete property regime is explained as well. The explanation is clearly taken from Roman law, especially book 41 of the *Digest*,[72] and from Cicero,[73] who himself had obviously absorbed the Roman law tenets regarding the natural acquisition of

[69] Cic. *off.* 1.21: *privata nulla natura*. Translations of *De officiis* are taken from Cicero, *On Duties*, ed. by M. T. Griffin, E. M. Atkins (Cambridge: CUP, 1991).

[70] *DCQ*, 336: *Inter quae Ciceronis illud irrideri maxime miror, nihil esse privatum natura, cum sit apertissimae veritatis. Non enim hoc vult Cicero, repugnare naturam proprietati et quasi vetare ne quid omnino proprium fiat, sed naturam per se non efficere ut quicquam sit proprium* [...]. Grotius's interpretation of Cicero is in line with the standard one; see M. Wacht, 'Privateigentum bei Cicero und Ambrosius', *Jahrbuch für Antike und Christentum*, 25 (1982), 35-38.

[71] *DCQ*, 336: *ergo ut res ista fiat istius hominis, factum aliquod hominis debet intercedere, non ergo hoc facit ipsa per se natura. Unde etiam illud apparet, communitatem priorem esse proprietate. Nam proprietas non contingit nisi occupatione, ante occupationem vero praecedat necesse est ius occupandi; hoc autem ius non huic aut illi, sed universis omnino hominibus ex aequo competit, ideoque communitatis naturalis nomine recte exprimitur. Et hinc evenit, ut quae nondum occupata sunt aut a populo ullo aut ab homine etiamnunc sint communia, hoc est nullius propria omnibus ex aequo exposita: quo argumento certissime evincitur nihil a natura cuiquam esse proprium.*

[72] See *Dig.* 41.1.1-41.9.2; the passages are taken mainly from Gaius.

[73] Cic. *off.* 1.21.

property. The main idea consists in every human being having *ab initio* just a general right to be *eligible* to acquire property by occupation, i.e. a right to the *possibility* of being a property-owner,[74] and not a general right to private property as such. It would be correct to describe Grotius's right to property as a special right,[75] having come into being by virtue of certain contingent transactions, and giving the right-bearer an exclusive right *in rem* against everyone else, while only his right to be eligible to acquire property could be adequately described as a general right *in rem* inhering in every human being *ab initio*.[76]

The process of acquisition itself, or rather the normative principles that apply to that process, are not Grotius's main concern. The *distribution* of property is left largely to coincidence. The origin of concrete claims to property, characterized by no moral restrictions, stands vis-à-vis the completed institution of private property, which serves in Cicero as well as in Grotius as the main yardstick for a natural justice of *compensatory* character. Apart form the Roman law requirement that the thing to be acquired as property be *res nullius*, i.e. not yet in anybody else's property, the original acquisition and distribution of property are not subject to any further normative criteria,[77] neither on Cicero's nor indeed on Grotius's account; once emerged, however, private property serves as the pivotal criterion of natural justice. In speaking of the existing property claims of his time, Cicero says, immediately after the passage cited by Grotius: 'If anyone else should seek any of it [i.e. already existing, distributed property] for himself, he will be violating the law of human fellowship'.[78] This is a passage Grotius refers to in the marginal note to his fourth so-called law, which indeed should be read as a paraphrase of Cicero: 'Let no one seize possession of that which has been taken into the possession of

[74] See J. Waldron, *The Right to Private Property* (Oxford: Clarendon Press, 1988), pp. 382f.

[75] For a conceptual discussion of such special rights *in rem*, see Waldron, *Private Property*, pp. 106-109.

[76] In the *TQ*, all the rights described are protected absolutely in that the holders of the rights hold an absolute claim-right against everyone else, entailing a correlative duty of non-interference on the part of everyone else; the subjective rights in *TQ* are all general rights *in rem*, inhering in everyone *ab initio*.

[77] Although the criteria are meager, it is not justified to speak of 'no criterion for deciding whether an entitlement is just', as Julia Annas does; J. Annas, 'Cicero on Stoic Moral Philosophy and Private Property', in *Philosophia Togata*, ed. by M. Griffin and J. Barnes (Oxford: Clarendon, 1989), p. 170. In Cic. *off.* 1.21, victory in a war is mentioned as a further possibility of acquiring property, without clarifying whether it is required that the war be just, which would obviously constitute a further normative criterion. See the discussion of this passage in Dyck, *Commentary*, pp. 110f. Annas, 'Cicero', p. 170n25 describes conquest as unjust acquisition, without considering conquest in a just war.

[78] Cic. *off.* 1.21: *e quo si quis sibi appetet, violabit ius humanae societatis.*

another'.[79] It is probable – although he does not say explicitly in *De iure praedae*[80] – that Grotius also has an example by Chrysippus in mind, handed down by Cicero in *De officiis*, which may serve as a normative principle for the process of acquisition by first occupancy:

> Among Chrysippus' many neat remarks was the following: 'When a man runs in the stadium he ought to struggle and strive with all his might to be victorious, but he ought not to trip his fellow-competitor or to push him over'.[81]

According to one critic, this concept has introduced an 'economic individualism' into political thought, which had been 'alien to the speculations of Plato and Aristotle'. The Ciceronian view of the just original acquisition of property is thus convincingly being seen in a tradition that leads up to John Locke.[82]

Grotius clearly is an important element of that tradition. Natural justice with regard to the original distribution of property is both in Cicero and in Grotius not predicated on the justness of the *result* of the distribution, but exclusively on the *procedure* governing the distribution. Only this procedure must be compatible with natural law in order for the original distribution of property to qualify as legitimate.[83] Grotius does not endeavor to argue morally for his preference of procedural over result-oriented natural justice, which is the obvious conceptual consequence of Grotius's developing a theory of the origin of the *institution* of private property out of the Roman law theory of natural *acquisition* of private property, without even trying to challenge the latter ethically. Given the function of *De iure praedae* as a legal apology of the military expansion of the Dutch East India Company in Southeast Asia, this is not surprising – the Roman law doctrine allowed Grotius to refer the rules

---

[79] *IPC*, II, fol. 7: *NE QUIS OCCUPET ALTERI OCCUPATA. Haec lex abstinentiae* [...].

[80] In *De iure belli ac pacis* Grotius referred to it; see *IBP*, II.2.2.5, note 6.

[81] Cic. *off.* 3.42: *Scite Chrysippus, ut multa, 'qui stadium', inquit, 'currit, eniti et contendere debet quam maxime possit, ut vincat, supplantare eum, quicum certet, aut manu depellere nullo modo debet; sic in vita sibi quemque petere, quod pertineat ad usum, non iniquum est, alteri deripere ius non est'.*

[82] N. Wood, *Cicero's Thought*, p. 114: 'Cicero, like John Locke much later, sees no contradiction between the imperative of morality and the demand of self-advancement as long as the latter is accomplished in a reasonable fashion and not at the expense of others, although both have a rather broad interpretation of what this means'. Similar A. A. Long, 'Cicero's Politics in *De officiis*', in *Justice and Generosity*, ed. by A. Laks and M. Schofield (Cambridge: CUP, 1995), pp. 213-240 (p. 233). See also Waldron, *Private Property*, pp. 153-155, who describes this account of the state of nature as 'negative communism'.

[83] This makes Grotius's theory very similar to John Locke's and, more recently, Robert Nozick's. For interesting criticism of these arguments of procedural justice, see Waldron, *Private Property*, pp. 253-283.

concerning private property solely to land, without having to abandon the idea of natural acquisition, and to exclude the sea from the things that are subject to the right to acquire by occupation (*ius occupandi*), making therewith the Portuguese claims to the seaway to the East Indies appear as unlawful encroachments on property common to everyone (*res communis*).[84]

Contractual Rights

The concept of private property implies the idea of a right to alienate property,[85] and therewith the idea of trade. In reference to the 18th book of the *Digest*, which deals with the contract of sale, Grotius explains the origin of trade as the necessary consequence of the abolishment of common property and regards commerce as the natural and universal foundation of contracts.[86] Citing from Aristotle's *Politics*, Grotius writes that freedom of trade is part of natural law and for this reason cannot be abrogated, unless with the 'consent of all nations',[87] a sentence Grotius himself would be reproached with during the Anglo-Dutch colonial conference in 1613 in London.[88]

---

[84] See R. Brandt, *Eigentumstheorien*, p. 37 not paying attention to the historical context of Grotius's doctrine; see also F. Wieacker, *Privatrechtsgeschichte der Neuzeit*, 2nd edn. (Göttingen: Vandenhoeck & Ruprecht, 1967), p. 292.

[85] Which is best described in Hohfeldian terms as a power to alter existing legal arrangements; see Hohfeld, *Legal Conceptions*; for a summary, see J. Feinberg, *Social Philosophy* (Englewood Cliffs: Prentice-Hall, 1973), chapter 4.

[86] *IPC*, XII, fol. 114 (=*ML*, VIII, p. 62): *Sed cum statim res mobiles monstrante necessitate quae modo explicata est in ius proprium transissent, inventa est permutatio, qua quod alteri deest ex eo quod alteri superest suppleretur.* [...] *Postquam vero res etiam immobiles in dominos distingui coeperunt, sublata undique communio* [...] *neccessarium fecit commercium* [...]. *Ipsa igitur ratio omnium contractuum universalis, ἡ μεταβλητικὴ a natura est* [...]. Grotius refers to *Dig.* 18.1.1 pr.: *Origo emendi vendendique a permutationibus coepit.*

[87] *IPC*, XII, fol. 114' (=*ML*, VIII, p. 63f.): *Commercandi igitur libertas ex iure est primario gentium, quod naturalem et perpetuam causam habet, ideoque tolli non potest, et si posset non tamen posset nisi omnium gentium consensu* [...]. Previously, Grotius cites Aristot. *pol.* 1.1257a15-17.

[88] For the argument of the English delegation, referring to *ML*, VIII, p. 63f., see G.N. Clark and W. J. M. Eysinga, *The Colonial Conferences between England and the Netherlands in 1613 and 1615*, vol. 1, Bibliotheca Visseriana 15, (Leiden: Brill, 1940), Ann. 38, pp. 115f.: *Nec enim latere vos arbitramur quid in hanc sententiam scripserit assertor Maris liberi: 'Commercandi (inquit) libertas, quae ex iure est primario gentium et quae naturalem et perpetuam causam habet, tolli non potest et, si posset, non tamen nisi omnium gentium consensu'.* See also ibid., Ann. 39, p. 120; for the colonial conference in general see G.N. Clark and W. J. M. Eysinga, *The Colonial Conferences between England and the Netherlands in 1613 and 1615*, vol. 2, Bibliotheca Visseriana 17 (Leiden: Brill, 1951), pp. 59-81.

Contractual relations are in Grotius's view derived from freedom of action, forming the origin of any positive arbitrary law that deviates from the law of nature. In the *Theses LVI,* Grotius renders the freedom of action as 'the right to one's own actions' (*ius in actiones suas*), a right alienable by an indication of will (*indicium voluntatis*):

> Both natural law [*lex naturalis*] and the Bible relate the restriction that man, by an indication of his will [*indicio voluntatis*], is being obliged [*obligetur*] to his fellow man and insofar gives up his right [*ius*], both with regard to his actions [*actiones*] and his possessions [*res*].[89]

This means that the *Theses LVI* do not merely state a freedom of action, but they posit a natural right to one's action, implying the recognition of a *power*[90] to do something which is given legal effect under the law of nature. In *De iure praedae*, this power or right to one's actions is being described as analogous to the Roman conception of private property; liberty[91] to actions is what private property is to things – natural liberty consists in the faculty to do what everyone wants to do, Grotius holds in reference to a passage in the *Institutes.*[92] Unlike private property, which in *De iure praedae* is not originally natural, the power or right to one's action is – as in the *Theses LVI* – a natural institution in the strict sense. Both actions and private property, however, can be alienated according to *De iure praedae*, which extends the commerce-friendly aspect of the right to private property to one's own actions, and, in *De iure belli ac pacis* at the latest, to one's own person and body.[93]

Breaches of contract constitute, like violations of property rights, just causes of war. Grotius derives this formally from his sixth so-called law that 'Good deeds must be recompensed'.[94] Substantively, however, Grotius derives this

---

[89] *TQ*, fol. 287 recto, thesis 3: *Lex naturalis simul et Scriptura hanc restrictionem tradunt, ut Homo indicio voluntatis <alteri> facto obligetur, et eatenus amittat ius cum in actiones tum in res suas.*

[90] A power to alter existing legal arrangements in the Hohfeldian sense; see for a discussion in the context of free trade Waldron, *Private Property*, p. 296.

[91] I use 'liberty' and 'freedom' interchangeably.

[92] *IPC*, II, fol. 10: *Quid enim est aliud naturalis illa libertas, quam id quod cuique libitum est faciendi facultas? Et quod libertas in actionibus idem est dominium in rebus.* Grotius refers to Flor. *Inst.* 1.3.1: *Et libertas quidem est* [...] *naturalis facultas eius quod cuique facere libet* [...]. The passage had already been used by Fernando Vazquez de Menchaca for the identification of *dominium* and *naturalis libertas* in his *Controversiae illustres* (I.17.4-5). See Tuck, *Natural Rights*, p. 51; Haggenmacher, 'Droits subjectifs', p. 92.

[93] In the *Theses LVI*, alienation is restricted to *res* and *actiones*, while later Grotius extends freedom of contract congruously to body and life.

[94] *IPC*, II, fol. 8: *BENEFACTA REPENSANDA.*

just cause of war from the necessary condition for just war under the Roman fetial law (*ius fetiale*) that redress be demanded (*rerum repetitio*). Grotius attaches importance to the statement that breach of contract gives rise to an independent just cause of war, substantiating his claim by reference to the fetial formula handed down by Livy:

> A third cause [of just war] – one that a great many authorities neglect to mention – turns upon debts arising from a contract or from some similar source. To be sure, I presume that this third group of causes has been passed over in silence by some persons for the reason that what is owed us is also said to be our property. Nevertheless, it has seemed more satisfactory to mention this group specifically, as the only means of interpreting that well-known formula of fetial law: 'And these things, which ought to have been given, done or paid, they have not given, paid or done'.[95]

The addition of breach of contract to the traditional causes of war constitutes a clear deviation from the medieval tradition of just war jurisprudence, which had not acknowledged the violation of an obligation as a just cause of war. Grotius's novel systematics of the law of war is best seen in light of the private law terminology of the law of the *Digest*, and of the parallel between individuals and polities, private and public war that goes along with that terminology.[96] The use of force for the exaction of debt is in Grotius's view just under the law of nature,[97] a stance characteristically substantiated by reference to the law of the *Digest*.[98] Grotius makes it clear that the right to wage war

[95] *IPC* 7, fol. 29': *Tertia, quae a plerisque omissa est, ob debitum ex contractu, aut simili ratione. Sed idcirco praeteritum hoc puto a nonnullis quia et quod nobis debetur nostrum dicitur. Sed tamen exprimi satius fuit cum et Iuris illa Fecialis formula non alio spectet: Quas res nec dederunt, nec solverunt, nec fecerunt, quas dari, fieri, solvi oportuit.* The rendering of the fetial formula is taken from Liv. 1.32.5.

[96] See Haggenmacher, *Grotius et la doctrine*, pp. 178-180, who intimates with regard to the distinction between absolute rights *in rem* and personal rights at the influence exerted by Donellus and his *Commentarii de iure civili* (1589). See also Haggenmacher, 'Droits subjectifs', p. 113; Coing, 'Zur Geschichte', pp. 251-254. Grotius in 1618 had in his library a copy of Donellus' commentary on the title *De pactis et transactionibus* of the *Codex Justinianus*; see P. C. Molhuysen, 'De bibliotheek van Hugo de Groot in 1618', *Mededeelingen der Nederlandsche Akademie van Wetenschappen*, Afdeeling Letterkunde, n.r., 6 (1943), Nr. 246.

[97] *IPC* 7, fol. 30a: [...] *privata vis iusta est omnium animantium exemplo* [...] *ad consequendum id quod nobis debetur.*

[98] *Dig.* 42, 8, 10, 16: *Si debitorem meum et complurium creditorum consecutus essem fugientem secum ferentem pecuniam et abstulissem ei id quod mihi debebatur, placet Iuliani sententia dicentis multum interesse, antequam in possessionem bonorum eius creditores mittantur, hoc factum sit an postea: si ante, cessare in factum actionem, si postea, huic locum fore.* Grotius does not cater to the differentiation made here in terms of the moment of the bankruptcy proceedings, which in absence of a judge is not relevant.

corresponds to a claim against a person under a contract in Roman law, or rather to the relevant remedy, the *actio in personam*. If according to Roman law there lies an *actio in personam* for the enforcement of a contractual claim, then in the state of nature everyone can under the law of nature legitimately enforce his contractual claims by the use of force, Grotius holds – the institution of contract is for Grotius an institution of natural law, emanating from the natural liberty of action human beings in the natural state enjoy.[99]

These causes of war, corresponding to the *actiones in personam* under a contract in Roman law, are the same causes that Grotius in the 'Prolegomena' had identified with the voluntary (*hekousia*) legal transactions described by Aristotle in the *Nicomachean Ethics* under the heading of compensatory justice.[100] The conception of contract, however, is understood in a wide sense and extended beyond the *numerus clausus* of Roman law types of contract to include, as in *De iure belli ac pacis*, promises (*pacta nuda*); for support of his conception, Grotius hints at those passages in the *Digest* and in Cicero's *De officiis* which emphasize the element of mutual consent and give less weight to form.[101]

This conception corresponds to the account in the *Theses LVI*; Grotius compares the relations among the inhabitants of the natural state with the relations between a physician and a patient, where the physician only has consultative power (*consilii potestas*), not entitling him to hold any claims against the patient.[102] It is only through the means of consent, i.e. contract, that rights can be forfeited. Thus no one has any natural right of coercion (*ius exsecutionis*). Such a right can be created only through voluntary transactions that may give

---

[99] See Haggenmacher, 'Droits subjectifs', p. 92; see also Diesselhorst, *Die Lehre vom Versprechen*, who however refers almost exclusively to *De iure belli ac pacis*.

[100] *IPC* II, fol. 8, referring to Aristot. *eth. Nic.* 5.1131a1ff. See the discussion of Grotius's use of Aristotle's theory in K. Haakonssen, 'Hugo Grotius and the History of Political Thought', *Political Theory*, 13 (1985), 239-265 (pp. 254ff). Haakonssen errs, however, in thinking that Grotius's compensatory justice is to be identified with Aristotle's particular justice, which would include distributive justice; Grotius in fact identifies his compensatory justice only with Aristotle's justice *en tois sunallagmasi*. See also *IBP* I.1.8.1.

[101] Grotius cites – as later in *IBP* – Cic. *off.* 1.23 on *fides* and *Dig.* 2.14.1 on *pacta*. This is evidence against the view, held by Nörr, that Grotius's *fides* is a notion pertaining specifically to the law of nations, and is not derived from the *bona fides* of Roman private law; see D. Nörr, *Die Fides im römischen Völkerrecht* (Heidelberg: Müller, 1991), pp. 45f. For *fides* in Grotius's *Parallelon rerumpublicarum*, see W. Fikentscher, *De fide et perfidia. Der Treuegedanke in den 'Staatsparallelen' des Hugo Grotius aus heutiger Sicht* (Munich: Bayerischen Akademie der Wissenschaften, 1979).

[102] *TQ*, fol. 287 recto, thesis 7: *Quatenus autem eadem illa sunt media ordinata ad bonum cuique suum, eatenus homo alter in ea ius non habet; atque ita sapiens et medicus consilii habent potestatem non imperii: quod iure exsecutionis demonstratur*. The example can be attributed to Plato's *Gorgias*, where Gorgias illustrates the alleged necessity of rhetoric with the example of the physician who has to coax the patient into taking his medicine; see Plat. *Gorg.* 456b.

rise to rights in another subject.[103] These transactions are clearly modeled upon the Roman consensual contracts (*obligationes consensu contractae*) as described by Gaius,[104] where an agreement, entirely free of form, is enough to produce enforceable contracts.

Conclusion

This article may be seen against the background of the ongoing debate on the origins of the modern notion of political freedom and individual rights. As is well known, the perception of a dualism between what came to be called negative and positive liberty, that is to say between rights-based and participatory liberty, started only after the French Revolution and was put forward most influentially in the first half of the nineteenth century by Benjamin Constant.[105] The view has found a famous and equally influential expression in the twentieth century in the writings of Isaiah Berlin, especially in his 'Two Concepts of Liberty', and has become a foundational tenet in liberal political thought.

Those arguing from an anti-liberal, so-called communitarian point of view, such as the legal historian Michel Villey or the philosopher Alasdair MacIntyre, seem to have adopted this originally liberal view of a dualism between modern and ancient liberty and made what had been described by Constant as the ancient 'positive' liberty the starting-point of their normative considerations. The crucial point seems to be that ancient so-called positive liberty allegedly did without the concept of subjective rights, which made the positive conception of liberty acceptable to the Aristotelians Villey and MacIntyre. Quentin Skinner, in his work on what he calls the 'neo-roman' conception of liberty, seems to be inclined to make a broadly similar point, by referring to the fact that the 'neo-roman writers on the *vivere libero* from the Italian Renaissance', Machiavelli, for example, never employed the language of rights,[106] an observation which leads Skinner to the conclusion that theories

[103] *TQ*, fol. 287 recto, thesis 8: *Quod ita ver(um) est nisi consensus accesserit: cuius virtute alter ius habet ad eliciendi media ad bonum alterius.*

[104] Gai. *inst.* 3.135f.

[105] See Constant, 'Liberty of the Ancients', p. 316: '[T]he liberty of the ancients [...] consisted in an active and constant participation in collective power'. Modern liberty on the other hand is rights-based; see ibid., 321: 'But amongst us individuals have rights which society must respect [...]'.

[106] See Q. Skinner, *Liberty before Liberalism* (Cambridge: CUP, 1998), p. 18; see also Q. Skinner, 'The Idea of Negative Liberty', in *Philosophy in History*, ed. by R. Rorty, J. B. Schneewind, Q. Skinner (Cambridge: CUP, 1984), p. 203.

of liberty in principle can do without presupposing any kind of subjective individual rights – even theories of negative liberty, since the 'neo-roman' concept on Skinner's view counts as a version of the concept of negative liberty.

Grotius, in constructing his rights-based natural law system, did not look to the actual constitutional makeup of ancient societies. Unlike Constant, who was using historical material on Athenian democracy and the Roman republic as a contrast for the presentation of the rights-based liberty he was interested in, Grotius made use of certain normative sources, viz. Roman law and Roman ethics, in order to submit a normative case for a rights-based just war in the East Indies. Grotius's conception of a law of nature was of course conceived to apply a theory of compensatory justice to the high seas of Southeast Asia, envisaged as a natural state lacking political authority.[107] Eventually, however, this argument revealed its anti-absolutist implications, and contributed – by virtue of its applicability to individuals, private entities and commonwealths alike – to the emergence of a rights-based constitutionalism.[108]

There are thus considerable ramifications of Grotius's use of and dependency on a Roman tradition in developing a doctrine of subjective rights, since it seems to suggest that some of the crucial features of modern liberalism, such as deontological individual rights, were in fact derived explicitly from a Roman tradition. Apart from what that tells us about Grotius and his time, it might also tell us something about classical antiquity. Grotius and his predecessors of the *mos Gallicus*, such as Donellus, were good humanists, and the fact that they believed that a notion of subjective rights (*iura*) could be gained from certain Roman traditions should make us look at those traditions more closely than we would be inclined to after having read Constant, Berlin, or MacIntyre. Such a closer look could very well reveal what the early modern humanists, perhaps better equipped than Constant and his followers for this task, already saw: that there is a distinct Roman tradition of a rights-based system of rules. The lessons to be drawn from such an account of Grotius's doctrine of rights, then, are both of a conceptual and a historical nature.

[107] Which is why only a small part of Aristotle's theory of justice, compensatory justice, is imposed on a polis-less natural state that is far more susceptible to the normative sources of Roman origin, which place little emphasis on distribution.

[108] For Grotius's influence on political theory, see Haakonssen, 'Hugo Grotius'; Id., *Natural Law and Moral Philosophy* (Cambridge: CUP, 1996), p. 30; Id., 'The Moral Conservatism of Natural Rights', in *Natural law and civil sovereignty. Moral right and state authority in early modern political thought*, ed. by Ian Hunter and David Saunders (Basingstoke: Palgrave, 2002), pp. 27f.; emphasizing Grotius's role in the pre-history of human rights is Haggenmacher, 'Droits subjectifs', p. 114n1.

Conceptual in that this account of Grotius's doctrine of rights suggests that anything deserving the label 'negative liberty' seems difficult to conceive of without a notion of subjective rights, and historical in that it may direct the ongoing search for the origins of modern human rights[109] towards the normative texts of Roman law and Roman ethics.

[109] See T. Kammasch, S. Schwarz, 'Menschenrechte', in *Der Neue Pauly. Enzyklopädie der Antike*, vol. 15, 1, ed. by M. Landfester (Stuttgart: Metzler, 2001), pp. 383-391, who deny an ancient origin of subjective natural rights.

Tuck's Grotius: *De iure praedae* in Context

George Wright
Professor of Political Science, University of Wisconsin-Superior
e-mail: GWright@uwsuper.edu

Abstract
This paper explores Richard Tuck's account of Grotius as the key innovator in the history that leads to the invention both of the free individual, protective of his or her rights, and of the modern liberal state, respectful of individuals' rights. Contextualism as a method for dealing with texts is discussed by way of a recent interview given by Tuck's teacher, Quentin Skinner. The attempt is made to see contextualism in context.

Keywords
contextualism, Tuck, Skinner, Hobbes, Grotius, liberalism

Hugo Grotius has been fortunate in his recent critics, particularly Richard Tuck, for whom he stands at the head of the most influential thinkers in our modern political tradition.[1] Tuck's interpretation, by which Grotius enjoys a prominence not recently accorded him, has met with stiff and persistent resistance,[2] but, rather than detail that resistance, this essay will have as its focus a few of the conditions which make Tuck's interpretation possible. That is, I seek to set Tuck's interpretation in the context not only of seventeenth-century political philosophy but also of present-day historiography regarding that philosophy. For, Tuck is associated with contextualism, a theory or method of

[1] Tuck has produced three major statements of his understanding of the role which Hugo Grotius played in the development of modern, liberal rights theories: first, *Natural Rights Theories*: Their Origin and Development (Cambridge: CUP, 1979); second, *Philosophy and Government*: 1572-1651 (Cambridge: CUP, 1993), and, third, *The Rights of War and Peace*: Political Thought and the International Order from Grotius to Kant (Oxford: OUP, 1999).

[2] See, for example, Perez Zagorin, 'Hobbes without Grotius', *History of Political Thought*, 21 (2000), pp. 6-40.

interpretation which has challenged and to an extent eclipsed other approaches to the history of ideas.[3]

My purpose is thus to describe the grounds of the possibility of Tuck's interpretation of Grotius, that is, to locate that interpretation in its own context and thereby to contextualize the contextualizer.

Tuck is of course the student of Quentin Skinner, to whom I turn in the thought that teachers sometimes make an impact upon their students[4] and because Skinner has written a good deal about contextualism,[5] whereas Tuck, to my knowledge, has not. Thus, in a recent, engaging interview,[6] Skinner explained that he took up this approach to texts as a result of reading Peter Laslett's edition of Locke's *Two Treatises on Government.* Laslett had shown that Locke wrote some years before the Glorious Revolution of 1688, whose justification the *Treatise* had been thought to be. The *Treatise* putatively celebrated the establishment of a balanced parliamentary constitution, whereas in fact this obviously could have had nothing to do with what Locke thought he was doing in writing it years earlier. What the author had intended was not what we, his readers, had received.

Of course, this discrepancy between authorial intention and reader reception happens all the time. *Habent sua fata libelli.* An author's intentions never exhaust and cannot determine the meaning of a text for its readers. For one, he or she may be, or is likely to be, unaware of the text's full implications.

---

3 For an exchange regarding the forms of reasoning appropriate to the history of ideas, see the Institute of Historical Research seminar on Mark Bevir's *The Logic of the History of Ideas* (Cambridge: CUP, 1999), with Alun Munslow, Siep Stuurman, Allan Megill, Kari Palonen and Frank Ankersmit as commentators, found on December 8, 2006 at: http://www.history.ac.uk/discourse/munslowAlun.html#muns, originally found in 'Rethinking History', *The Journal of Theory and Practice* 4 (2000), available on December 8, 2006, at http://www.tandf.co.uk/journals/routledge/13642529.html. These issues came up at the 2006 Philosophy and Historiography conference of the British Society for the History of Philosophy, held at Cambridge University, April, 2006; the conference program was available on December 9, 2006, at http://www.york.ac.uk/depts/phil/bshp/confs/historio/historio.htm.

4 The adoption of contextualism as a common method has not prevented teacher and student from reaching contrasting conclusions regarding the thought of Thomas Hobbes; while Tuck plumps for the modern skeptical tradition, especially as described by the late Richard Popkin, Skinner stresses the impact of the rhetorical tradition on Hobbes's thought. See Quentin Skinner, *Reason and Rhetoric in the Philosophy of Hobbes* (Cambridge: CUP, 1996). On this divergence, see below, p. 8.

5 See his recent, three-volume collection of methodological essays, *Visions of Politics* (Cambridge: CUP, 2002).

6 See Maria Lúcia Pallares-Burke, 'Quentin Skinner', *The New History* (Cambridge: Polity Press in association with Blackwell, 2002), pp. 212-40. I owe this reference to the kindness of Peter Burke.

The author may be self-deluded. Nor is any author free of the background assumptions and practices that make communication possible; we all stand within a given horizon of understanding.[7] This is true even of contextualism and its practitioners.

Skinner deflects these post-modernist criticisms by agreeing with them and by making a distinction:[8]

> [T]here has been so much postmodernist criticism of my work, in which my critics have emphasized that authors are not necessarily the best authorities on their own texts, that the meaning of their works is a public matter and separable from what they may have intended, that one has to take on board Derrida's points about the polysemic character of virtually all our utterances, etc, etc. Well, I have never doubted any of that and I'm pretty much a postmodernist in relation to these issues. So all these critics of my work have been attacking a position I've never defended.
>
> What I have defended is a completely different position. I am interested in intentionality not with respect to meanings but with respect to speech acts. I am interested, that is, in trying to recover what may have been the meaning of the act of writing particular texts.

He then cites his 1996 book on Hobbes to exemplify this point:

> The question that underpins the book is not so much what Hobbes means in his various texts, but what he is *up to*, what he may have *meant* by writing as he did.

Whether this answer meets the postmodernist criticism of his work or not, we find a basic interpretive assumption expressed here, namely, that texts are ways in which authors do things with words,[9] and we can recognize a debt to Austin, Strawson, Grice and others in the analytical school, a debt which Skinner avows.[10] In that action is key, we should not be surprised to find that

---

[7] This reflection recalls the hermeneutic theory and practice of Hans-Georg Gadamer as an alternative in method and goal to the contextualism advanced by Skinner, Tuck, J. G. A. Pocock and others. See Hans-Georg Gadamer, *Truth and Method*, 2nd edn., revised by Joel Weinsheimer and Donald G. Marshall (New York, NY: Continuum, 2004); Idem, *Reason in the Age of Science*, tr. by Frederick G. Lawrence (MIT Press: Cambridge, MA, 1996), and Idem, *Philosophical Hermeneutics*, tr. and ed. by David E. Linge (Berkeley, CA: University of California Press, 1976).

[8] See Skinner, *Interview*, p. 232.

[9] Texts of course also send messages by way of diagrams, frontispieces, devices, etc. For an account of the visual strategies used by Thomas Hobbes in *Leviathan*, see Horst Bredekamp, *Thomas Hobbes Visuelle Strategien der* Leviathan: *Urbild des modernen Staates: Werkillustrationen und Portraits* (Berlin: Akademie Verlag, 1999).

[10] See his 'On Performing and Explaining Linguistic Actions', *The Philosophical Quarterly*, 21 (1971), pp. 1-21.

political theories, when they are contextualized, are seen as authors' means of achieving specific ends; that is what they are 'up to'.[11]

Given this assumption, we should not be surprised to find that political theorists, when they are contextualized, are constantly trying to achieve specific, tangible ends through their texts and determining what these ends are is the goal of the contextualizer. There is thus no canon of texts we might specify independent of their contexts which might lead us to better understandings regarding what action we might take today. At least, the job of the contextualizer has ended when he or she has identified an appropriate context and reduced a theorist to whatever goals appear salient within its limiting horizons.[12]

This focus on action as the goal of thought encompasses a theorist's use of moral argument, and here Skinner draws a comparison between his contextualist approach and the familiar Marxist theory of ideology. Marx's view, as Skinner describes it, is that 'people's beliefs can be explained not just as causal products but as mere epiphenomena of their social circumstances'.[13] For Skinner, successful theory may require the employment of a moral language that can make concerted action possible. But, such languages are made available only insofar as they are 'historically embedded and available in consequence as recognizable weapons of debate'.[14] That is, 'they are given to us, not made by us', and hence not epiphenomenal but in fact 'causal conditions of social change'. Or, as he says in *Liberty before Liberalism*:

> What it is possible to do in politics is generally limited by what it is possible to legitimize. What you can hope to legitimize, however, depends on what courses of action you can plausibly range under existing normative principles. But this implies that, even if your professed principles never operate as your motives, but only as rationalizations of your behavior, they will nevertheless help to shape and limit what lines of action you can successfully pursue.[15]

Notice that Skinner understands the employment of a given moral language from the point of view of its utility as well as the possible constraints it may place upon the action which an author seeks to produce as well as the possibilities for joint action which such languages open up. This certainly responds to the Marxist view that moral languages have no causal impact in that they

---

[11] In his *Persecution and the Art of Writing*, Leo Strauss points to the possible further complication that authors may seek to send different messages to different audiences.

[12] For a programmatic discussion of these issues, see Skinner, *Liberty before Liberalism* (Cambridge: CUP, 1998), pp. 105ff.

[13] See Skinner, *Liberty*, pp. 220ff.

[14] Ibid.

[15] Ibid.

are merely epiphenomenal to material relations. But, notice also that Skinner focuses on moral thinking largely as a form of social behavior or interaction, whose meaning resides in its use in a given context, that is, as presented to a given audience.[16]

To the stress on action as the goal of thought, we may add another characteristic attitude regarding the role of the exemplary in political philosophy. It is apparent in Prof. Skinner's criticism of Laslett, who failed to see the deeper implications of his own work. For Laslett, the fact that the *Treatise* witnessed to its author's call to action within a specific configuration of identifiable interests disqualified it from consideration as a serious contribution to political thought; that is, it did not truly belong in the canon.[17] It was merely an occasional piece of slight value, failing to address the so-called 'perennial questions definitive of political thinking itself',[18] as Skinner characterizes them. This criticism could not be brought against *Leviathan*, which remained for Laslett a work of lasting value.

Skinner's goal instead has been to extend Laslett's procedure, though not his evaluative criteria, to all texts of political thought. Rather than exclude from the canon that which is occasional, he has sought to draw into question the notion of canonicity itself,[19] that is, the very idea that there is or should be a canon of leading texts, whose meaning extends 'timelessly' beyond their immediate impacts[20] and widely regarded as the only proper objects of research in the history of political thought. Laslett erred, Skinner says, in that 'he still seemed to think of Hobbes as the author of a system of politics capable of being appraised independently of its historical context'.[21]

---

[16] For Skinner's defense of the concept of authorial intention, see Skinner, 'On Performing'. For a discussion of Skinner's interpretive assumptions, see Mark Bevir, 'Mind and Method in the History of Ideas', *History and Theory*, 36 (1997), pp. 167-89.

[17] For an analysis that endorses much of the current critique of both the canon of texts in political thought as well as the concept of canonicity itself, see Siep Stuurman, 'The Canon of the History of Political Thought: Its Critique and a Proposed Alternative', *History and Theory*, 39 (2000), 147-66. See also the Website of the Paradoxes of De-canonization Study Group at Erasmus University, Rotterdam, found December 8, 2006, http://www.fhk.eur.nl/onderzoek/paradoxes/. The team's project is to analyze processes of de-canonization in national historiography and memory.

[18] See Skinner, *Liberty*, p. 102.

[19] Ibid.

[20] See Skinner, *Interview, passim.*

[21] See Skinner, *Liberty*, p. 218. Laslett's criteria of canonical status need not engross our attention, and 'timelessness' will likely not suit the 'temper of the times'. But, that some well-considered standards and evaluative criteria might be applied broadly to the texts of political thought seems a desirable outcome, for teaching and learning purposes if for no other, as does retaining the process by which we adopt, apply and debate these standards and criteria.

By contrast, Skinner set out to do to Hobbes what Laslett had done to Locke, that is, by linking him to his historical context, to give an interpretation of Hobbes from within his given historical circumstance, thereby to render an account of his thought whose accuracy no merely textual reading of his thought could hope to achieve.[22] The tendency of his work is thus to shift the researcher's focus away from textuality, that is, the careful and close reading of exemplary texts, to intertextuality, the reading of texts among texts to recreate the contexts of their production.[23]

We may summarize: contextualism entails an unremitting insistence on action as the ground and significance of expression and communication. Skinner wants to know what Hobbes is 'up to'. Second, there is the desire to render impossible, or at least highly questionable, a purely textual approach to texts and, along with this, the desire to tie all texts to the specific historical contexts in which they arose. Finally, this entails both opposition to the notion of a fixed canon of classic texts, standing above their times,[24] and a tendency towards iconoclasm, that is, the mooting and destruction of criteria for determining what one may deem exemplary in the past. Canons are, of course, continually made, unmade and re-made; indeed, they function best if understood as essentially contested concepts.[25] That is their great pedagogical value, allowing those taking part in the contestation to do so in the knowledge both of the elenchus and of its bearing on their lives. But, what is notable about contextualism, at least in Skinner's practice of it,[26] is its tendency

[22] Ibid.

[23] For several illuminating insights regarding the role of context in interpretation, see Peter Burke, 'Context in Context', *Common Knowledge*, 8 (2002), pp. 152-177.

[24] Gadamer's work provides the best, most comprehensive explanation and defense of the role of tradition in interpretation in general. For differing views of the relation of the individual to tradition within literature, see T. S. Eliot, 'Tradition and the Individual Talent', in Idem, *The Sacred Wood: Essays on Poetry and Criticism* (London: Methune, 1920), and Harold Bloom, *The Anxiety of Influence: A Theory of Poetry*, 2nd ed. (New York: OUP, 1997).

[25] On Gallie's seminal essay, see http://en.wikipedia.org/wiki/Essentially_contested_concept, available December 8, 2006. While, as we have seen above, p. 3, Skinner allows for the polysemy of words, he does not acknowledge possible application of this concept to the canon itself. Moreover, focusing only on single, highly particularized contexts of meanings would tend to dispossess us of the rich insights and broadened perspectives which comparative study can bring to the understanding of political philosophy.

[26] This effect of his work is desired; as he says:

> [I]ntellectual historians will do well to focus not merely or even mainly on a canon of so-called classic texts, but rather on the place occupied by such texts in broader traditions and frameworks of thought.

See Skinner, *Liberty*, pp. 101ff.

both to make canon formation and maintenance impossible or meaningless in given instances and more generally to undermine their value as pedagogical devices.[27] This is unfortunate if we consider the power which certain canonical texts exercise over current political discourse, that is, their ability to become embedded *in* or, better, *as* 'common sense', that which Gramsci once described as those things we presumptively hold in common,[28] that which typically grounds political consent and makes arguments of one kind presumptively superior to those of another.[29]

Both Skinner and Tuck believe that Hobbes is pivotal in the stories they tell about the development of modern political thought, but they differ as to how this is so. Skinner discusses the influence of the rhetorical tradition, whereas Tuck cites the skeptical tradition as a factor of overriding importance. The disagreement is crucial in that the story that Tuck tells has Grotius as the originator of a characteristic post-skeptical political theory leading to Hobbes. And, it is in the Grotius of the *De iure praedae*[30] that Tuck finds support

[27] Taken to an extreme, this attitude is obscurantist, self-denying and self-defeating. For, the effect of 'contextualization' is likely, if it is not meant, to change the repute accorded political theorists of the past; in part as a result of Skinner's work, Hobbes receives far more attention today than ever in the past and surely out of proportion to his value as a political thinker. A flaw in Skinner's interpretive practice and theory seems thus to be its inability to see and understand itself in its effects and thus to thematize the grounds of its own possibility and operation. For a somewhat analogous view of method, see Gadamer's criticism of Habermas, 'The Scope and Function of Hermeneutical Reflection', in Idem, *Philosophical Hermeneutics*, pp. 18ff. For a description of Hobbes's elevation to canonical status, see Roberto Farneti, *Il Canone moderno. Filosofia politica e genealogia* (Turin: Bollati Boringhieri, 2002).

[28] See Antonio Gramsci, *Selections from the Prison Notebooks*, tr. by Q. Hoare and G. Nowell Smith (London: Lawrence & Wishart, 1971), pp. 321-43, discussed by David Harvey, *A Brief History of Neoliberalism* (Oxford: OUP, 2005), p. 39.

[29] On the process by which 'liberalism' has ousted all other languages of modern political discourse, see Farneti, *Canone moderno*, passim, and Skinner, *Liberty.*

[30] The *De iure praedae*, also known as *De Indis*, grew out of Grotius's attempt to justify the seizure of a Portuguese merchant ship, the Santa Catarina, by Jacob van Heemskerck, captain and later vice admiral with the Dutch East India Company (the *Vereenigde Oostindische Compagnie* or *VOC*). On his second voyage to the East Indies in 1603 in the area around modern-day Singapore, van Heemskerck seized the ship in revenge for Portuguese mistreatment of Dutch merchants in the East Indies, as he asserted in a letter written to the VOC directors. Grotius adopted and developed the captain's justification for his action, defending the individual's right to punish transgressors of the natural law in the absence of an independent and effective judge. The Amsterdam Admiralty Court confiscated the Santa Catarina on September 4, 1604, and authorized the sale of contents. See Peter Borschberg, 'The Seizure of the Sta. Catarina Revisited. The Portuguese Empire in Asia, VOC Politics and the Origins of the Dutch-Johor Alliance (1602 c.1616)', *Journal of Southeast Asian Studies*, 33 (2002), pp. 31-62; Martine van Ittersum, 'Hugo Grotius in Context: Van Heemskerck's Capture of the Santa Catarina and Its Justification in *De Jure Praedae* (1604-1606)', *Asian Journal of Social Science*, 31 (2004), pp. 511-548, and Edward Keene, *Beyond the Anarchical Society: Grotius, Colonialism*

for the hypothesis that the precocious and brilliant Dutchman is the truly innovative figure in laying down the outlines of rights theory in modern Western political thought.[31]

Tuck wants to correct a misperception in the modern history of ideas that he traces to Kant, who, he says, 'despised the answer to relativism found in Grotius and his successors and who wished to rewrite the history of ethics in such a way as to make his own innovations the climax of the story'.[32] Tuck presents his work as an exploration of a theory of government and the individual that lies at the root of present-day political institutions, for whose merits he feels more than nostalgia or antiquarian interest.[33] For, Grotius's theory of rights, he says, rests on an understanding of individual autonomy that is the product of a specific configuration of events, interests, understandings and justifications.[34] Thus, he quotes Weber on the connection in early-modern Europe between 'liberal politics at home', wherein conceptions of individual rights developed and came to dominate political discourse, and the 'expansion of Europe' abroad through voyages and actions like those of Captain Heemskerck in the Straits of Singapore.[35] Weber asks:

---

and Order in World Politics (Cambridge: CUP, 2002). Grotius chose not to publish his text except, later, its twelfth chapter, entitling it *Mare Liberum*, which was both influential and controversial; among others, the Englishman John Selden published a critical reply entitled *Mare Clausum*. See also Benjamin Straumann, '"Ancient Caesarian Lawyers" in a State of Nature: Roman Tradition and Natural Rights in Hugo Grotius's *De Iure Praedae*', *Political Theory*, 34 (2006), pp. 328-350, and by the same author, 'The Right to Punish as a Just Cause of War in Hugo Grotius' Natural Law', *Studies in the History of Ethics* (2006), available only on-line, December 11, 2006, at: http://www.historyofethics.org/022006/022006Straumann.html.

[31] According to Tuck, Hobbes merely generalized to the level of society what Grotius had conceived regarding the skepticism and precaution which one rightly experiences regarding the motives and interests of others. As he states:

> Grotius...was probably more original; but Hobbes saw deeper into the issues of relativism than any philosopher of his time, and perhaps even than any philosopher since. For that reason he must remain the foundational philosopher of our political institutions: the state structures which came into being in his time persist down to our time, and his summation of the political arguments about their emergence is still a textbook for us.

See Tuck, *Philosophy*, p. xvii. See below, note 38.

[32] See Tuck, *Philosophy*, p. xv.

[33] Prof. Skinner is particularly sensitive to the criticism that his work is antiquarian; see Skinner, *Liberty*, pp. 106ff.

[34] For an account that largely agrees with Tuck's thesis regarding the Grotius-Hobbes connection, though it departs in several other particulars, see J. B. Schneewind, *The Invention of Autonomy: A History of Modern Moral Philosophy* (Cambridge: CUP, 1998).

[35] Tuck emphasizes the analogy between the individual's life and personality and the character of the modern state.

> The question is: how are freedom and democracy in the long run at all possible under the domination of highly developed capitalism … The historical origin of modern freedom has had certain unique preconditions which will never repeat themselves. Let us enumerate the most important of these: First, the overseas expansions. In the armies of Cromwell, in the French constituent assembly, in our whole economic life even today this breeze from across the ocean is felt … but there is no new continent at our disposal.[36]

Tuck's work then presents what he calls the 'richest tradition we have for thinking about human freedom',[37] referring presumably to the line that leads from Grotius to Locke, though not to Kant.[38] While we might not want to encounter such buccaneer figures as Captain Heemskerck in daily life today, Tuck says that 'it is important that we are clear about what autonomy meant in the days when it became the central virtue, so that we can be clear about what we may be losing in our own time'.[39]

In place of Kant's faulty history of ethical thought, Tuck reverts to the assessment, made by such figures as Barbeyrac (1674-1744), that a 'truly modern and "scientific" way of thinking about ethics and politics had come into being in the seventeenth century and that the novelty of its approach consisted in its new response to the problem of skeptical relativism'.[40] This was the train of

---

[36] See Tuck, *The Rights of War*, pp. 14-15.

[37] See Tuck, *The Rights of War*, p. 234.

[38] Tuck does not extend the line to Rousseau, Kant, Hegel and Marx, though in these thinkers, certainly in Hegel, freedom is the 'central virtue'. Tuck may prefer the analysis of freedom given in English liberalism, but it is question begging to assert or imply that its answers establish evaluative criteria which in any sense disqualify or oust from out attention the line from Rousseau to Marx and beyond. That conclusion must rest upon a prior political and/or moral judgment that is not explicitly thematized in his work. It is not enough merely to claim that our current political institutions took their origins in the period under discussion; the techniques, mechanisms and competences of representative government in modern democracies reflect the progressive effects of centuries' thought and experience beyond those formative years. To ignore these effects, to return us in theory to the site of their productive ground as though nothing had happened in the interim, is a remarkable interpretive leap. Similarly, the Hobbes whom we study today is not *simpliciter* the Hobbes of the seventeenth century. He is the product of quite different histories of reception, in different national contexts, from which we cannot escape without making those histories explicit subjects of inquiry. On this point, see essays in *The History of Political Thought in National Context*, ed. by Dario Castiglione and Iain Hampsher-Monk (Cambridge: CUP, 2001). This is to say that the position of the intellectual historian should in some way be an explicit theme in our study; the adoption of a given method does not free us of this obligation. In my view, the current, Anglo-American Hobbes, even as contextualized in the accounts of Skinner and Tuck, remains that, in broad outline, of the Utilitarians and of those, following them, who established him as a canonical figure. On the members of the Sunday Walking Club, see Farneti, *Canone moderno*, pp. 96ff. On the multiple 'liberalisms' of Europe, see Guido de Ruggiero, *The History of European Liberalism*, tr. by R. G. Collingwood (Boston: Beacon Press, 1959).

[39] See Tuck, *The Rights of War*, p. 234.

[40] Ibid.

such thinkers as Grotius, Selden, Hobbes, Pufendorf and Locke, and, among them, it was Grotius who first 'broke the ice'.[41]

Tuck's overarching thesis is that, though it was resisted in Germany, which was unable to build a modern state, the seventeenth century saw the transformation of the language of political thought from what he calls *raison d'etat* theory into a fully articulated natural jurisprudence. Its foundational idea, expressed as a natural right, was self-preservation, both on the part of the individual and of the collectivity to which he or she belonged; hence, the link between the new *raison d'etat* Humanism and state-building in the early modern period.[42]

Grotius, Hobbes and Locke did not use the language of *raison d'etat*; they spoke of natural law and natural rights and on the surface resembled scholastic writers from the thirteenth century on. And, some modern writers have been fooled by this, Tuck says, into thinking that they do not represent as great a break with tradition as those who immediately succeeded them perceived.[43]

But, the background they assumed and the tendencies of their work were not scholastic, but Humanist, of the *raison d'état* type. This Humanism had burgeoned in the late sixteenth century as an explicitly anti-constitutional and often anti-ethical literature, seeking the replacement of constitutionalism by what Tuck calls a 'modern, instrumental and often unscrupulous politics'. It had grown up in the Renaissance, with Machiavelli and Guicciardini as precursors, but, instead of taking Cicero as their ancient exemplar, as had republican Humanism, *raison d'etat* writers preferred Tacitus, whose *Annales* described how Tiberius, a ruthless and manipulative ruler, used techniques to crush his equally ruthless and manipulative opponents.

Thus, by the 1570's, the Frenchman Pibrac was composing a defense of the St. Bartholomew's Day Massacre. Some emergencies, Pibrac argued, require 'major and extreme remedies', applied without judicial process, especially if the unruly mob is engaged.

The two Humanisms, the earlier Ciceronian one, and the later Tacitean one, also differed as regards their attitudes to skepticism, with large consequences for politics. For, if, Tuck argues, behind *raison d'état* lay skepticism, then politicians, acting under the impulses of both Stoic and skeptical ethical theory, would see their political role as that of disciplining and manipulating

---

[41] See Tuck, *Natural Rights Theories*, p. 4; *The Rights of War*, p. 6, and *Philosophy*, p. xiv.

[42] There is a consistent subtext in Tuck's work on political theory, namely, that the changed circumstances of Renaissance military history, especially the advent of standing armies, lies at the root of early-modern state-building and hence of its theoretical development.

[43] See Tuck, *Philosophy*, p. xivff.

a population in the interests of its own security, much as they themselves as individuals contained and controlled their passions.[44]

And, here is another major feature of Tuck's argument, namely, that Grotius conceived of governing not merely as regulation of the affairs of a state but also of the individual, so that one became an analogy of the other, as he says:

> Since ... [Grotius's] general theory then involved him in attributing comparable rights to *private* individuals, he equipped the modern liberal rights theories which he had launched with a far-reaching account of what agents can do to one another, both in a state of nature and in the international arena.[45]

While Grotius's moral and political doctrine springs from skeptical, *raison d'état* theory, it is intended as an adequate answer to that theory's skepticism. This is to say that it retains the skeptical case regarding self-preservation as universally true but develops out of it a fundamental human right, with a set of consequential rights such that it could provide a theory of ethical conduct, including a theory of justice. Tuck says, 'He proposed in effect to use the skeptics' vision of how a life should be led in order to refute their initial skepticism about the possibility of a moral science'.[46] 'Grotius sought quite explicitly to render in terms of natural law some of the main insights of the modern humanists and to answer the skeptic not with some countervailing dogma but by the manipulation of the skeptic's own beliefs'.[47]

This he accomplished in *De iure praedae* by stating a 'minimalist theory of natural law', namely, that, in addition to the laws of self-preservation and self-interest, there are two other laws, namely, the laws of inoffensiveness and abstinence, with self-preservation the prior and overriding obligation. Helping one's neighbor follows upon securing one's own preservation, and in nature such help consists in no more than returning like for like, including the individual's duty to return injury for injury, that is, to punish those who transgress the principles of inoffensiveness and altruism.[48]

More richly developed societies derive only from explicit, originary contractual undertakings among free individuals in local circumstances. Thus, it was only with a civil society or state, constituted by an explicit or tacit agreement, that considerations of general utility could begin to weigh against

[44] For an account of the economic ramifications of this view of politics and human nature, see Albert O. Hirschman, *The Passions and the Interests: Political Arguments for Capitalism before Its Triumph*, 20th anniversary ed. (Princeton: Princeton University Press, 1996).

[45] See Tuck, *The Rights of War*, p. 108.

[46] See Tuck, *Philosophy*, p. 173.

[47] Ibid.

[48] See Tuck, *The Rights of War*, pp. 86ff.

individual self-preservation. The power of the state then is the result of collective agreement among individuals, including the right of the magistrate to punish, and here Tuck finds evidence of Grotius's innovation, namely, that any powers claimed by the state can only have come from the prior possession of such powers by individuals. Thus, the state's right to punish stems from individuals' suppression of wanton injury that would take place before the creation of civil societies.[49] And, the right to overthrow a tyrant stems from the breach of the contractual terms by which government is instituted among free individuals.[50]

Given this focus on the role which individuals' rights play in making possible the rights of states, it is of central importance to know the source(s) of right and of rights, and this is where the question of subjective right, especially as it developed in the context of Europe's recovery of Roman law, enters into Tuck's account.[51]

The rights of free individuals in the state of nature make possible political rights in civil societies. This move is the basis and warrant for Tuck's claim as to Grotius's striking originality:

> There was something natural in the development into the institution of private property of the basic and inherent human right to use the material world, and no agreement was ever necessary. Rather, all that was necessary was labor of some kind. Men had physically to take possession of the material object or to alter or define it in some way....It is easy to see how Grotius was able to argue from these premises that the sea was not yet private property in the modern sense, but equally that men did have rights of a kind over it and on it....they could take what they wanted, knowing that they had a definite right to do so. This right was also something which they had the further right to protect against threats: by putting forward this theory of property, Grotius had provided a useful ideology for competition over material resources in the non-European world, and had clearly begun the intellectual process that was to culminate in the competitive rights of the Hobbesian state of nature.[52]

This then is Tuck's explanation of how the theory of individual rights stated by Grotius in *De iure praedae* led not only to Hobbes and others but also to present-day political institutions.

---

[49] See Tuck, *Philosophy*, p. 177.

[50] See Tuck, *The Rights of War*, p. 96. Tuck claims Grotius would somewhat modify this point in editions of *De iure belli* later than 1625, as a means of facilitating his return to Holland.

[51] It seems clear that Tuck's explanation of the medieval development of Roman legal concepts, especially the idea of subjective right, may be in need of revision due to its inclusion of certain erroneous conclusions drawn from the work of Michel Villey. See Charles Donahue, Jr., '*Ius* in the Subjective Sense in Roman Law: Reflections on Villey and Tierney', *A Ennio Cortese* ed. by D. Maffei et al. (Rome: Il Cigno, 2001), pp. 505-35.

[52] See Tuck, *Natural Rights Theories*, p. 61.

In conclusion, I would like to offer a comment regarding contextualism in political context. Tuck has followed Weber in drawing a connection between the free, rights-possessing, entrepreneurial individual and the free, enterprising nation, seeking profit in faraway lands through commercial exploitation, and he worried with Weber that the absence of new continents to conquer would imperil freedom. Recall Weber's question:

> [H]ow are freedom and democracy in the long run at all possible under the domination of highly developed capitalism…The historical origin of modern freedom has had certain unique preconditions which will never repeat themselves. Let us enumerate the most important of these: First, the overseas expansions. In the armies of Cromwell, in the French constituent assembly, in our whole economic life even today this breeze from across the ocean is felt…but there is no new continent at our disposal.

The invention of autonomy, that is, the historical construction of the personality of the enterprising individual, protective of his or her rights and willing to resist and punish those who infringe them, together with the development of the modern liberal state, has led to what Tuck describes as the 'richest tradition we have for thinking about human freedom'.[53]

But, this tradition's concept of freedom is only one among a number of political options and not necessarily the most attractive. Certainly, it is question-begging to denominate it as 'freedom' and as the sole alternative to the iron cage of regimentation and bureaucracy, as Tuck so dramatically suggests. Tuck has presented a work of history with an evident political message, but one that is, in my view, both politically backward-looking, not to say regressive, and based on an overly restrictive and therefore false dichotomy.

---

[53] See Tuck, *The Rights of War*, p. 234.

Beyond the Law. The Image of Piracy in the Legal Writings of Hugo Grotius

Michael Kempe
Assistent für Geschichte Universität St. Gallen
e-mail: Michael.Kempe@unisg.ch

Abstract
It is still underestimated to what extent in his main works Hugo Grotius not only sketched and developed a system of private, state and international law; but also outlined a general philosophy or theory of law. By asking questions concerning the law of property, the law of prize and booty, the law of peace and war or the legal status of sovereignty he did not only refer to the 'right side', i.e. to actions that can be labelled as rightful and legal. He also dealt with many aspects of what is not right and unlawful, not limiting himself to just give mere examples of crossing the border to the 'non right side'. It was a part of Grotius's methodological approach to systematically reflect on the law from the perspective of its violations. One example of such a violation is the act of piracy and the figure of the pirate. To outline this is the aim of the following article. By showing that the pirate and his 'legal twin', the privateer, were belong together as two sides of the same coin, they come to symbolise in an exemplary way the differentiation between 'right' and 'non right' as the unity of law in the legal philosophy of Grotius.

Keywords
piracy, privateering, freebooters, bellum iustum, ius postliminii, ius praedae

'While these events were taking place, a rumour reached the neighbouring Chinese city of Canton, to the effect that, "foreigners sent ashore from their ships, had been seized by the Portuguese". [...] From the whole throng of Dutchmen, they selected six men unacquainted with any language other than that of their native land [...]. Now, when the six Dutchmen [...] prostrate at the feet of the Chinese envoy, [...] The envoy demanded an answer to the accusations of the Portuguese, who were charging these poor sailors with piratical savagery [*piraticae feritatis*], and when the latter could make no response even to these charges, the Portuguese insisted that their silence should be regarded as a confession. [...] Thus it came to pass that six men of Holland – O fatherland! O justice and law, and liberty vainly defended at home! – were subjected to the cruellest and most hideous punishment, suited to robbers and pirates [*latronum et piratarum*], by Portuguese sojourners in that Kingdom of China which the Hollanders had sought amid so many hardships and perils, and where their presence was in turn desired. The Chinese looked on pityingly at this spectacle and afterwards prayed, with averted faces, that these men might not be unavenged, whatsoever race and whatsoever region of the earth had sent them as guests to Chinese waters and shores, if they worshipped any divinity or had any native land'.[1]

Here, Hugo Grotius reported about members of the crew of the Dutch Admiral Jakob Corneliszoon van Neck, landed off the coast of Canton and charged and executed for piracy and robbery by the Portuguese in 1602. With this episode Grotius's endeavour in *De iure praedae* to stigmatise the cruelty and treachery of the Portuguese against the Dutch in Asia reached one of its climaxes. In this way, Grotius has linked these events with the justification of the seizure of 'Santa Catarina' by the Dutch Admiral Jakob van Heemskerk in February 1603. In fact, it was particularly the execution of members of Admiral van Neck's men as pirates in Canton and Macao that played a significant role in fuelling the anger of Heemskerk and his crew against the Portuguese.[2] However, Grotius's conceptualisation of natural rights and natural law in *De iure praedae* is based to a large extent on Van Heemskerck's own justification of privateering.[3]

By blaming the Portuguese for their harsh treatment of Hollanders as *illegal* pirates and by defending a Dutch captain as a *legal* privateer Grotius gives us an example of his understanding of the borderline between lawfulness and unlawfulness. The distinction between piracy and privateering exemplifies the unity of justice and injustice and, thus, becomes a major instigation of Grotius's efforts towards a sound foundation of a theory of law. Historians of natural and international law have so far failed to recognise this.[4] In *De iure praedae*

---

[1] Hugo Grotius, *Hugo Grotii De Iure Praedae Commentarius. Ex Auctoris Codice descripsit et vulgavit Hendrik G. Hamaker* (The Hague: Nijhoff, 1868) [= *IPC*], XI, pp. 189-190; *English*: Grotius, Hugo, *De Iure Praedae Commentarius. Commentary on the Law of Prize and Booty*, tr. Gwladys L. Williams and Walter H. Zeydel (New York: Oceana, 1964; repr. Buffalo N.Y.: Hein 1995) [= *Commentary*], pp. 199-200.

[2] See Peter Borschberg, 'The Seizure of the *Sta. Catarina* Revisited: The Portuguese Empire in Asia, VOC Politics and the Origins of the Dutch-Johor Alliance (1602-c.1616)', *Journal of Southeast Asian Studies*, 33 (2002), 31-62 (pp. 44-45).

[3] See Martine Julia van Ittersum, 'Hugo Grotius in Context: Van Heemskerck's Capture of the *Santa Catarina* and its Justification in *De Jure Praedae* (1604-1606)', *Asian Journal of Social Science*, 31 (2003), 511-548.

[4] For the early history of the myth of Grotius as 'the father of the law of nations', see Michael Kempe, 'Der Anfang eines Mythos. Zum grotianischen Natur- und Völkerrecht in der

(1604) and *De iure belli ac pacis* (1625) Hugo Grotius has not only sketched and developed a system of private, state and international law; but furthermore he has outlined a general philosophy or theory of law. His treatments of the law of property, the law of prize and booty, the law of peace and war and the legal questions of sovereignty refer to the basic questions of the foundation of law itself. By dealing with these questions the Dutch lawyer and philosopher did not only treat the meaning of what is right and lawful, but also the meaning of what is *not* right and *un*lawful.

One important aspect on the latter side – on the side *beyond the law* – can be identified as the discussion of the problem of piracy. By analysing how Grotius has dealt with this topic we observe some fundamental elements and features that constitute the frame of his theory of law, because in Grotius's discourse on booty and seizure different, but not yet separated fields or disciplines of law, i. e. natural law, international law, private and state law and even political theory were interlinked with each other. As we discuss in the present article, against this background the juridical treatment of piracy and privateering enabled Grotius to specify and sharpen the border of the law.[5] The article is divided into seven parts. I shall begin with Grotius's definition of piracy as part of his typology of dishonourable seizure of spoils (1). In the next part I will focus on the question of who are identified by Grotius as pirates (2). The third part investigates the topic of sea-robbery as part of the discussion on *bellum iustum* (3). Afterwards, I follow the attempt to reconstruct the debate of the difference between a sovereign state and a gang of sea-robbers (4). Then, the focus will be on piracy as a phenomenon to historicise natural and international law (5). After touching the treatment of piracy and property (6), I will finally analyse the difference between privateering and piracy as a main tenet within the framework of the legal theory of Grotius (7).

Definition and Typology

To individuals 'who despoil others through privately exercised force and without urgent reasons to do' 'we give the name "pirates" when their activities take

europäischen Aufklärung', in *Staat bei Hugo Grotius*, ed. by Norbert Konegen and Peter Nitschke (Baden-Baden: Nomos, 2005), pp. 139-157.

[5] The article is part of my Habilitation project 'Curse of the Sea. Piracy, International Law and Interntaional Relations in early modern times'. For a general discussion and helpful hints and comments I would like to thank the fellows of the Max-Planck-Institute for European Legal History (Frankfurt/Main, Germany), especially Marie Theres Fögen(†), Karl-Heinz Lingens and Michael Stolleis, and also Birgit Biehler, Peter Borschberg, Fabio Crivellari, Daniel Damler,

place upon the sea [*quos in mari piratas dicimus*]'.[6] What is remarkable of Grotius's definition of pirates in *De iure praedae* are not the juridical relevant features – the form of violence, the motive and the scene of crime – because these features are common in legal definitions of piracy since antiquity, although there is no authoritative definition of piracy in International Law until today.[7] Remarkable, instead, is that Grotius has developed this definition within a fourfold typology of *dishonourable* seizure of spoils. Besides the pirates as the first type Grotius identifies three other types of dishonourable seizure of spoils: The second applies to 'acquisitions made by persons who without any legitimate cause usurp authority to wage public war. [...] To despoilers of this kind we refer (and not unjustly) as 'freebooters' [*praedones*]'.[8] Here, Grotius gives us the examples of ancient peoples, testified by Homer, or the Normans in more recent times. The third type embrace those persons 'who snatch away property prior to the execution of the measures required in order that war may be lawfully taken. Such attacks upon property are severely censured by writers on the subject as acts of "robbery" [*quas invasiones latrocinii nomine scriptores exgitant*]'.[9] While these three types of dishonourable seizure would be obvious, the fourth type could not be as easily and directly identified. This type of seizure occurs 'when, in the course of a just war or a war believed to be just, someone grasps at profit in a way which indicates that he has been mindful only of profit for its own sake and not of the true objective of war, namely, the attainment of rights'.[10]

Due to his basic distinction between private and public wars Grotius distinguishes consequently between *private* see-robbery by *piratae* and *public* see-robbery by *praedones*. From this he further distinguishes two forms of unlawful seizure, before and during a justly waged and legitimate war. All types together represent the *four* forms of how prize and booty are unjustly acquired. The interesting point here is not only that Grotius defined piracy and other illegal forms of raiding within the context of the question of who has the right to

---

Dieter Groh, Thomas Maissen, Jürgen Osterhammel, Rudolf Schlögl, Frank-Steffen Schmidt, Rolf Peter Sieferle and Stefan Siemer.

[6] *IPC*, XIV, p. 307; *Commentary*, pp. 325-326.

[7] See Barry Hart Dubner, *The Law of International Sea Piracy* (The Haag: Nijhoff, 1980).

[8] *IPC*, XIV, p. 307; *Commentary*. p. 326. The *English* translation of *praedones* as freebooters is misleading because in early modern times the term "freebooter" was mostly used for lawful privateering and not for unlawfully plundering.

[9] *IPC*, XIV, p. 307; *Commentary*, p. 326.

[10] *Commentary*, XIV, p. 326. For this category Grotius gives us the example of "the despoilers of fishermen or of ship-masters who have been caught by chance upon a sea where the assailants themselves fear to be seen." Ibid.

wage war; so did already, for instance, Alberico Gentili in his *De iure belli* (1588/89). More interesting is that Grotius presented these forms as primarily a question of *honour*. In a long passage Grotius mentions the war of the Dutch against the Hanseatic and other states in the year 1438 as an example of how one's enemies can be treated in a most honourable way while executing a just vengeance.[11] In *De iure praedae* the phenomenon of piracy is defined within a framework in which the distinction between *right* and *not right* has been supplemented and congruently reshaped by the distinction between *honour* and *dishonour*. When Grotius here uses a concept of *honestas* which refers to *virtus* and *meritum* and in which it is granted that, speaking with Cicero, *non posse non honestum esse quod justum est omni ex parte*,[12] then Grotius's philosophy of law is far from being a mere *legalistic philosophy*.

However, the fourfold typology has not been picked up, again, by Grotius in *De iure belli ac pacis* in 1625. Here, the terms *piratae*, *praedones* and *latrones* are used in different contexts but not in as systematic and coherent a way as in *De iure praedae*. We miss, for example, a sharp distinction between *piratae* and *praedones*, although Grotius speaks in one case of a people of maritime plunderers.[13] The expression *latrocinium maris* stands for piracy or see-robbery. In cases where Grotius treats robbery (*latrocinium*) in general and where the scene of crime – land or sea – is not of any matter, he mostly uses the double term *piratae et latrones*, for instance when it comes to the problem of authority to wage war or to mark the difference between a sovereign state and a community of plunderers.

Identification and Perspective

Whom has Grotius in mind when he speaks of pirates? Most examples are taken from Antiquity: Reports about piracy and the fights against them by Homer, Thucydides, Polybius, Cicero, Strabo or Plutarch, the story of the Pompeian pirate war or Caesar, been captured by Mediterranean pirates, later putting his vengeance on them. One individual sea-robber Grotius mentions from his ancient sources, at least implicitly, is the pirate Demetrius, who once,

---

[11] *Commentary*, XIV, pp. 328-329.

[12] *IPC*, XIV, p. 300.

[13] Hugo Grotius, *De Iure Belli ac Pacis, Libri Tres in quibus ius naturae et gentium: item iuris publici praecipua explicantur*, ed. B.J.A. De Kanter-Van Hettinga Tromp (Leiden: Brill, 1939) [= *IBP*], III.9.19, p. 730.

according to Augustine, had put Alexander the Great in the same class with himself.[14] As to the *praedones* he counts, for instance, the Cretans, the Cilicians and even the ancient Greeks.[15]

But Grotius does not only refer to ancient cases, he also gives some examples of piracy in more recent times, e.g. where he mentions the Normans and the North Africans of the 'Barbary' coast as two raiding maritime peoples. Consulting his huge correspondence we do not find substantial discussion of any of the famous or notorious contemporary pirates like for example the English privateer and 'see-dog' Walter Raleigh. Although there is some reference to privateering 'heroes' Francis Drake and Piet Heyn.[16]

When treating more recent examples of maritime seizures the 'discourse on piracy' immediately turned into a highly explosive object of political and ideological partisanship. Before Grotius began to justify the capture of the Portuguese carrack 'Santa Catarina' he had launched his argument with a long polemic against the Lusitanians. Grotius reproached them for their discrimination of the Dutch as pirates in order to bring them into an disrepute among the 'East Indian tribes'. Grotius stated: as long as the Dutch were unfamiliar to the 'native rulers and kingdoms' the Portuguese had told the latter the malicious lie 'that pirates had come [*venisse piratas*], whose home was the sea, whose trade was robbery, and who had no peaceful dwelling-place'.[17] Grotius's interest in the views and legal standpoints of the inhabitants of India and Asia was limited to the question of whether they would accept the seamen from the Low Countries as their trading partners. Concerning the prize case 'Santa Catarina' Grotius had based his view almost only on some testimonies by Dutch sea-captains on their encounters with the Portuguese.[18] Although some scholars have maintained a strong non-European influence on the Grotian law

[14] *IBP*, II.1.1.3, p. 169. With reference to Augustine, *De Civitate Dei*, IV.4. Here reference to Cicero, *rep*. III.14. Concerning robbers Grotius cites Dio Cassius telling the story of Augustine who paid to the brigand Corocotta, who had delivered himself up, the reward placed on his head. See Grotius, *IBP*, III.19.2.2, p. 816.

[15] We can take his predilection for antiquity as an example of Grotius's method to use illustrations from 'better times and better peoples', thus, preferring 'ancient examples, Greek and Roman', as he pointed out in his 'Prolegomena' of *IBP*. See Hugo Grotius, *The Law of War and Peace. De Jure Belli ac Pacis Libri Tres*, tr. Francis W. Kelsey (Oxford: Clarendon Press, 1925; repr. Indianapolis [1962]) [= *Law of War and Peace*], Prolegomena 46, p. 26.

[16] See, for instance, Hugo Grotius, *Briefwisseling van Hugo Grotius*, ed. P. C. Molhuysen, et al., 17 vols (The Hague: Nijhoff, 1928 – 2001) [= *BW*] 3, 4, 6, 8, 17.

[17] *IPC*, IV, p. 176; *Commentary*, pp. 182-183.

[18] See W. Ph. Coolhaas, 'Een bron van het historische gedeelte van Hugo de Groots de Jure Praedae', *Bijdragen en Mededelingen van het Historisch Genootschap*, 79 (1965), 415-540.

of nations[19] it is, after all, rather unlikely that Grotius had any deeper knowledge of Indian or Asian legal systems.[20]

However, Grotius did not only blame the Iberians for stigmatizing the Dutch seamen as sea robbers. He also called them villains and bandits and used his above mentioned fourfold typology of dishonourable seizure of spoil to identify the Portuguese, who, by turning the tables, were not far away from acting like pirates.[21]

> If we apply the foregoing observations to our present purpose, recalling at the same time the events that have already been narrated, we shall plainly perceive that the Portuguese, though they assume the guise of merchants, are not very different from pirates.[22]

Saying that the Lusitarians were not much better than sea robbers was definitely one climax of picking up directly or indirectly the ideological patterns of the *leyenda negra* in Grotius *De iure praedae*.[23] Of course, the mutual accusation of piracy by both the Dutch and the Portuguese was used on each side to impair and isolate the competing opponent. Therefore, it is no wonder that a third power could profit from the freebooting battle between the two. So, one long-term development of the 'Santa Catarina' seizure was that the kingdom of Johor managed to secure its status as an independent regional power in Asia.[24]

Identifying 'the other' as a sea brigand and murderer implies the latter's criminalisation as well as delegitimation as an equal combatant in war. By naming each other 'pirates', the Portuguese as well as the Dutch would both have agreed to label the native resistance against their conquest as 'piracy' too. To delegitimise the resistance of the Kunjalis as an irregular use of military force, the Portuguese have treated theirs adversaries on the Malabar coast of India in the

---

[19] See C. H. Alexandrowicz-Alexander, 'Grotius and India', *The Indian Year Book of International Affairs*, (1954), 357-367; or Ram Prakash Anand, *Development of Modern International Law in India* (Baden-Baden: Nomos, 2005).

[20] Cornelis Gerrit Roelofsen, 'The Sources of Mare Liberum; the contested origins of the Doctrine of the Freedom of the Seas', in: W. P. Heere (ed.), *International Law and its Sources* (Deventer: Kluwer, 1988), pp. 93-124.

[21] *IPC*, XIV, p. 308.

[22] *Commentary*, XIV, p. 327.

[23] On Grotius and the Spanish black legend see Martine Julia van Ittersum, *Profit and Principle. Hugo Grotius, Natural Rights Theories and the Rise of Dutch Power in the East Indies (1595-1615)* (Leiden: Brill, 2006), pp. 53-104.

[24] See Borschberg, 'The Seizure'; and Peter Borschberg, 'Luso-Johor-Dutch Relations in the Straits of Malacca and Singapore, c. 1600-1623', *Itinerario*, 28 (2004), 15-43.

sixteenth century as 'cossarios'.[25] Consequently, Grotius did not differ from the standpoint of the Spaniards or the Portuguese in calling the Indian leader Cunala 'the pirate chief of the Malabar Indians [*Cunalam Indorum Malabarum archipiratam*], notorious for his fifty years of freebootery [...]'.[26]

Piracy and *Bellum Iustum*

As the fourfold typology in *De iure praedae* clearly shows, all types of dishonourable seizure of booty were interpreted by Grotius as forms of an unjustly waged war: the *piratae* fight an unjust private sea war, the *praedones* an unjust public sea war; the *latrones* seizure spoils *prior* to the execution of a just war; while the less obvious *latrones* of the fourth type would raid for their own sake and profit *during* a just war. All four types have in common, according to Grotius, that they lack any *iusta causa*. If all the robbers and plunderers wage an unjust war, they violate the law and, thus, give reason for fighting a just war against them.[27] As *subjects* of an unjust war they are, at the same time, *objects* of a just war.

Wars can, as Grotius put it in *De iure belli ac pacis*, be 'justly waged against those who act with impiety towards their parents [...]; against those who feed on human flesh'; and – as Grotius has added in the edition of 1631 – *in eos qui piraticam exercent*.[28] With Aristotle he agrees 'that war against them was sanctioned by nature'.[29] Grotius in these cases broadens the concept of just war beyond war undertaken by who have directly suffered injury or have jurisdiction over the person who was attacked. Thus, Grotius has allowed, what we today would called 'a humanitarian intervention'.

At the same time piracy is for Grotius an example *par excellence* of a violation of the law of all nations and peoples. If no public authority exists or if it would fail to prosecute and punish pirates, the *ius gentium* guaranties every single person a private jurisdiction over pirates. In *De iure praedae* Grotius gives us the example of Gaius Julius Caesar who as a private citizen had prosecuted and crucified pirates after the official authority had failed to do so:

---

[25] See Anne Pérotin-Dumon, 'The pirate and the emperor: power and the law on the seas, 1450-1850', in *The political economy of merchant empires*, ed. by James D. Tracy (Cambridge: CUP, 1991), pp. 196-227 (p. 204).

[26] *IPC*, XI, p. 196; *Commentary*, p. 206.

[27] Because, as Grotius stated in *IBP*: 'No other just cause for undertaking war can there be excepting injury received'. *IBP*. II.1.1.4; *Law of War and Peace*. p. 170.

[28] *IBP*, II.20.40.3 [since the additions of the editions of 1631, 1632, 1642, 1646] p. 510; *Law of War and Peace*. p. 505.

[29] *IBP*, II.2040.3, p. 510; *Law of War and Peace*, p. 506.

> When Caesar (he who afterwards became Dictator) was still a private citizen, he pursued with a hastily raised fleet the pirates by whom he had been captured on earlier occasion. Some of their boats he put to flight, some he sank; and when the Proconsul neglected to punish the guilty captives, Caesar himself put out to sea again and crucified the culprits, influenced undoubtedly by the knowledge that the judge to whom he had appealed was not fulfilling the functions of the judicial office, as well as by the consideration that it was apparently possible to take such action guiltlessly upon the seas, where one is governed not by written precepts but by the law of nations.[30]

Later, in his defense of the fifth chapter of *Mare liberum*, Grotius argued against the criticism of William Welwod that it makes no difference that the shore is more easily occupied than the sea;

> Plutarch, Vellius and others relate that pirates on the sea were captured by Gaius Julius Caesar while still a private citizen and that when the proconsul neglected to punish them, Caesar sailed back on the sea and there the pirates were crucified by him. Caesar would no more have dared this on the sea than in the province, indeed would have committed *lese majesty*, if the sea had been as much the territory of the Roman people as the province itself.[31]

But from the right to punish pirates we cannot, according to Grotius, derive ownership of or sovereignty over the sea.[32] Grotius denied that from the suppression of piracy would follow the right to occupy the sea as it was traditionally maintained by many imperial sea powers like, for instance, Venice and Genova each claiming maritime dominion over parts of the Mediterranean.[33] Even the so-called *mare nostrum* of the ancient Romans could not be interpreted in that way. Reformulating the twelfth chapter of *De iure praedae* Grotius wrote in his *Mare liberum* in 1609:

> Now those who say that a certain sea belonged to the Roman people explain their statement to mean that the right of the Romans did not extend beyond protection and jurisdiction [*protectionem et iurisdictionem*]; this right they distinguish from ownership [*a proprietate*]. Perchance they do not pay sufficient attention to the fact that although the Roman People were able to maintain fleets for the protection of navigation and to punish pirates captured on the sea, it was not done by private right, but by the common right which other free peoples also enjoy on the

---

[30] *IPC*, VIII; *Commentary*, p. 95

[31] Hugo Grotius, *Defense of Chapter V of the Mare Liberum which had been attacked by William Welwod, Professor of Civil Law, in Chapter XXVII of that book written in English to which he gave the title 'An Abridgement of all Sea-Lawes', in Some less known Works of Hugo Grotius*, tr. by Herbert F. Wright, Bibliotheca Visseriana Dissertationum Ius Internationale Illustrantium, 7 (Leiden: Brill, 1928), pp. 144-205 (pp. 204-205).

[32] *IPC*, XII, p. 104; *Commentary*, p. 237.

[33] See Pitman B. Potter, *The Freedom of the Seas in History, Law, and Politics* (New York: Longmans, Green & Co., 1924), p. 351.

> sea. We recognize, however, that certain peoples have agreed that pirates captured in this or in that part of the sea should come under the jurisdiction of this state or of that, and further that certain convenient limits of distinct jurisdiction have been apportioned on the sea. Now, this agreement does bind those who are parties to it, but it has no binding force on other nations, nor does it make the delimited area of the sea the private property of any one. It merely constitutes a personal right between contracting parties.[34]

Even Seraphim de Freitas, one of Grotius's adversaries in the controversy of *mare liberum* versus *mare clausum*, recognized that jurisdiction and ownership are two different things, so that strictly speaking no one can be said to occupy the sea.[35] For all their fundamental differences they both held that freedom of the seas could never mean a total absence of law on the sea because, at least, a universal right to prosecute and punish pirates has to be presupposed in any case.

The universal jurisdiction over pirates culminates in the classical formula of the pirate as the 'common enemy of all mankind' (*hostis generis humani*). Already in antiquity Cicero had called pirates *communis hostis omnium*; but in a literal sense the phrase *hostis generis humani* can be dated back to the fourteenth-century jurist Bartolus of Sassoferrato.[36] In his *De iure belli* Gentili combined for the first time the definition of pirates as universal enemies with the notion of international law. Indirectly Grotius used this definition too, after identifying the Portuguese as pirates, calling them persons that 'were worthy objects of universal hatred in that they were harmful to all mankind'.[37] From the standpoint of criminal law and in accordance with Roman law, Grotius did not make any distinction between highwaymen and sea-robbers, between *latrones* and *piratae*. Yet, from the standpoint of international law it is the pirate and not the highwayman who potentially threatens all nations because he plunders on the high seas as the connecting 'highway' of the peoples and all nations.

[34] Hugo Grotius, *The Freedom of the Seas or the Right which belongs to the Dutch to take part in the East Indian Trade*, tr. by Ralph van Deman Magoffin, ed. by James Brown Scott (New York: OUP, 1916), V, p. 35.

[35] See Mònica Brito Vieira, '*Mare Liberum* vs. *Mare Clausum*: Grotius, Freitas, and Selden's Debate on Dominion over the Seas', *Journal of the History of Ideas*, 64 (2003), 361-377.

[36] See Emily Sohmer Tai, 'Marking Water: Piracy and Property in the Pre-Modern West', in: *Seascapes, Littoral Cultures, and Trans-Oceanic Exchanges*, ed. by Debbie Ann Doyle and Brandon Schneider (= Conference Proceedings, 12th-15th February 2003, Library of Congress, Washington, D.C.), Internet, URL: www.historycooperative.org/proceedings/seascapes/benton .html.

[37] *IPC*, XIV, p. 308; *Commentary*, p. 327.

However, from the global enmity it follows for both Gentili and Grotius that the laws of war cannot be applied to the pirates.[38] This implicates that a declaration of war to them is not required.[39] A war against pirates is always a *bellum iustum* without being a *bellum solenne*. As an enemy to everybody the pirate was no regular combatant to anybody. Pirates could never be *iusti hostis*. The piratical raid is, thus, not only a *bellum iniustum* in an objective, but also in a *subjective* sense, because the see-robber cannot even think that he is waging a just war. Therefore, when Grotius applied the label of piracy to the Portuguese to justify the capture of the 'Santa Catharine', it was the harshest thing he could do within his theory of *bellum iustum*.

Sovereign States and See-Robber Gangs

Although pirates and robbers were defined as standing on the side of unlawfulness, they were not understood as standing *outside* the law. Agreements with them are binding, because as human beings *piratae et latrones* also have a common share in the law of nature.[40] Furthermore, for practical reasons robbers and pirates who have become strong and frightful should be justly received and defended, because 'it is to the advantage of mankind that they should be brought back from their wicked ways through confidence in their freedom from punishment'.[41] Nevertheless, they do not have any legal status as a community. They have, for example, no right to send ambassadors, because: 'Pirates and brigands, who do not constitute a state, cannot avail themselves of the law of nations'.[42]

The last statement shows that the problem of piracy and robbery was not only interlinked with international law but also with the parallel discipline of constitutional law and political theory. When Jean Bodin defined political sovereignty in *Les six livres de la République* (1576) he started his argument with a discussion on whether or not we can distinguish a sovereign state from

---

[38] See Alberico Gentili, *De ivre belli, libri III* (Hannover: Guilielmus Antonius, 1598), I.25, p. 202.

[39] *IPC*, VIII, 44, *Commentary*, p. 97: 'For it is not customary, nor is it necessary, to declare a civil war; and this statement is also applicable to warfare against tyrants, robbers, pirates, and all persons who do not form part of a foreign state.' See also *IBP*, III.3.1.

[40] Pompey, as Grotius writes, 'finished the war with the Pirates in great part by means of treaties, promising to them their lives, and places in which they might live without plundering.' *IBP*, III.19.2.2; *Law of War and Peace*. p. 794.

[41] *IBP*, II.21.5.5; *Law of War and Peace*, p. 533.

[42] *IBP*, II.18.3.2.3; *Law of War and Peace*, p. 440.

a community of robbers or pirates. In doing so he mentioned Chaireddin Barbarossa and Dragut Reis, two of the most notorious 'Barbary' pirates of the North African coast in the sixteenth century. Grotius, too, takes up this discussion in *De iure belli ac pacis* and compares a state with a gang of *piratae et latrones* – referring to the *locus classicus* of this comparison in Augustine's *De civitate Dei* (IV.4). On the one hand, Grotius distinguished a lawfully constituted community, although acting unjustly, from a gang of brigands and sea-robbers, although acting according to their own rules; the latter 'are banded together for wrongdoing', while the former 'even if at times they are not free from crime, nevertheless have been united for the enjoyment of rights'.[43]

On the other hand, Grotius conceded that a transformation may take place not merely when certain individuals 'instead of being leaders of brigands became lawful chiefs, but also in the case of groups, so that those who have only been robbers upon embracing another mode of life become a state'.[44] Thus, power could constitute law. In this way, Grotius tried to evade the 'Anfangsproblem' (Niklas Luhmann) of law, i.e. the suspicion that right and law were originally non-right and non-law. Since Grotius admitted that a group of *piratae ac latrones* can, indeed, be legally transformed into a lawful state, he accepts that the state could have originated in a crime.

Piracy and Legal History

The question of robbery and plunder is used by Grotius for the purpose of a *historisation* of international law and law of nature. Due to this he did not only take up the above mentioned examples of classical antiquity; he even went further back to more archaic times by developing a kind of *history of decay* in which the law of nature and the natural bond between men had been forgotten by moral depravation and evil customs *before* and for some time *after* Noah's deluge; in those times it was considered lawful to rob and plunder foreigners without a declaration of war.

> In consequence the question in Homer, "Are you plunderer?" is a friendly inquiry [...]. In the ancient law of Solon there are companies "of those who go out for booty". Indeed, as Justin says, up to times of Tarquin piracy was considered an honour.[45]

---

[43] *IBP*, III.3.2.1; *Law of War and Peace*, p. 631.

[44] *IBP*, III.3.3; *Law of War and Peace*, pp. 632-633.

[45] *IBP*, II.15.5.1-2; p. 392: 'ut Iustinus ait, ad Tarquinii tempora latrocinium maris gloria habebatur.' *Law of War and Peace*, p. 394.

By using, again, the terms *honestas* and *gloria* we can now understand why Grotius had first defined piracy within a typology of dishonourable seizure: defining piracy, raiding and unlawful plundering as an act of dishonour implicates that our times can clearly be distinguished form the time when the precepts of *ius naturae* had been forgotten. In this way, the reading of Homer's Odyssey and other early Greek sources created a certain kind of legend, the *myth* of an honourable or even heroic past of piracy. This myth was hardly questioned over the centuries; and even in modern times it still continues to exist. Otto Eck, e.g., wrote in his *Seeräuberei im Mittelmeer* – a book that has strongly influenced the image of piracy in Ferdinand Braudel's *monde méditerranéen* –:

> Religionshaß, Völkerhaß, politische Intrigen, Raub und Mordlust sind die wirklichen Triebfedern der Seeräuberei gewesen, wenn man von den allerersten Zeiten absieht, da sie noch heroischen Charakter besaß.[46]

In a similar way Carl Schmitt has maintained in *Der Nomos der Erde*:

> Keiner der Helden Homers hätte sich geschämt, der Sohn eines solchen wagemutigen, sein Glück erprobenden Piraten zu sein. [...] Erst als große See-Reiche [...] entstanden, wurde auf dem Meere Sicherheit und Ordnung hergestellt. Die Störer der so geschaffenen Ordnung sanken jetzt zu gemeinen Verbrechern herab.[47]

However, things were not so simply. If we e.g. look like Grotius at the poems of Homer, we find in fact an ambivalent image of piracy, indicating that all depends on the point of view, as the historian Philip de Souza has shown recently:

> Pirates and their activities can be, and are, looked upon with disapproval in the Homeric poems. Piracy is an evil business from the victims' point of view, yet for the heroic practitioners it brings high status and prestige, largely because of the fighting involved and the booty that is obtained.[48]

Piracy and Property

Does a piratical spoil lead to a change of ownership? Grotius answered this question in the context of the discussion about the postliminy. The Roman *ius*

---

[46] Otto Eck, *Seeräuberei im Mittelmeer. Dunkle Blätter europäischer Geschichte* (München: Oldenbourg, 1940), p. 2.

[47] Carl Schmitt, *Der Nomos der Erde im Völkerrecht des Jus Publicum Europaeum* (Köln: Greven, 1950; 2nd edn Berlin: Duncker & Humblot, 1974), pp. 14-15.

[48] Philip de Souza, *Piracy in the Graeco-Roman World* (Cambridge: CUP, 1999), p. 21.

postliminii had originally granted a person who was enslaved as a captive of war the full recognition of his former legal status if he returns back home. With reference to Ulpian Grotius maintains that the captives taken by a brigand will never be his property.[49] Transferring the *ius postliminii* from persons to things he states: 'things which pirates or brigands have taken from us have no need of postliminy [...]; the reason is that the law of nations does not concede to pirates or brigands the power to change the right of ownership'.[50] Goods recaptured from pirates, thus, have to be returned to the original owner.

This conclusion could, indeed, implicate serious practical problems since the raiding activities of the 'Barbary' corsairs had rapidly increased in the Mediterranean in the sixteenth century. Grotius was aware of the many problems caused by the corsairs of the North African coasts, as we learn from his correspondence.[51] The problem was that the Moslem see-raiders, defining themselves as *ghâzis* or *mudjâhid*, fighters of the *djihād* against the Infidels,[52] neither could be seen as mere pirates, raiding for their own sake, nor as mere privateers spoiling with an official commission of the state. Furthermore, it was not clear whether the 'Barbary' cities Algiers, Tripoli and Tunis are to be seen as sovereign states or only as parts of the Ottoman Empire.

From the above difficult questions follow. For instance, what if goods from an English merchant vessel seized by a Moslem see-fighter have been recaptured by a Spanish ship? If the raiding *mudjâhid* were seen as pirates, these goods have to be transferred back to their original owner; if they were seen – on the contrary – as part of a regular naval force, the captor could claim the goods as his own property. Grotius seems to tend to the latter; he referred to a particular judgement of the highest chamber at Paris by saying: 'The decision held that goods which had belonged to French citizens, and had been captured by the Algerians, a people accustomed in their maritime depredations to attack all others, had changed ownership by the law of war, and therefore, when recaptured by others, became the property of those who had recovered them'.[53] The approval with that court decision implicates the acknowledgment of the North African corsairs as lawfully fighting sea-warriors equivocal to European state-sponsored 'privateers' (Engl.), 'kaapvaarder' or

[49] *IBP*, III.3, § 2, 3; *Commentary*, p. 632.

[50] *IBP*, III.9.16, p. 728; *Law of War and Peace*, p. 713.

[51] E.g. *BW*, 17, p. 438.

[52] For the Moslem perspective see Daniel Panzac, *Barbary Corsairs. The End of a Legend 1800 – 1820* (Leiden: Brill, 2005).

[53] *IBP*, III.9, § 192; *Law of War and Peace*, p. 715. See also Jörg Manfred Mössner, *Die Völkerrechtspersönlichkeit und die Völkerrechtspraxis der Barbareskenstaaten (Algier, Tripolis, Tunis 1518-1830)* (Berlin: de Gruyter, 1968).

'commissievaarder' (Dutch), 'capteur' (French) or 'Kaperer' (German). From this analogy follows the recognition of the 'Barbary' cities as sovereign authorities owning the right of waging war.

Piracy and Privateering

The main goal of *De iure praedae* was not, of course, to blame piracy but to justify the seizure of foreign goods as a lawful booty, as a 'good prize'. In doing so Grotius had to face a case with two sides that had to be separated from each other through a strict borderline that would mark the difference between the just and the unjust, between right and wrong. Both sides had to be defined in a distinct way to establish a sound law of prize and booty. On the side of the unlawful seizure of spoils we find the pirate, on the other side the privateer, his lawful brother.[54] The latter has been authorized either by a general prize act or by a prize-taking commission – in his letters Grotius uses the Dutch term 'commissie'[55] – by a sovereign authority to wage war serving at his own charge.[56] To legitimise his seizure of spoils the engagement must somehow take part of a just war. For Grotius (self-)defence, recovery of the captured and punishment are the main just causes of a *bellum iustum*. In general, a war is just for the reason that it tends toward the attainment of rights; 'and in seizing prize or booty, we are attaining through war that which is rightfully ours'.[57] Three just causes for prize taking were identified by Grotius: 1. compensation for our property unjustly taken by the enemy whether by recovering our own property or an equivalent to the extent of the said property; 2. punishment of offences; 3. indemnity for all losses and expenses of the war.[58] This can only take place in cases where the law has been violated. While the pirate permanently violates the law, the just captor of spoils defends it instead. And in this way, the frontier of the law has been constituted from both sides, inside and outside the law.

The legal side, the sphere of *ius praedae*, can be understood as structured from the inside by the regulations on prize-taking[59] and by the complicated

[54] For the semantic history of the term "privateer" see, for instance, David J. Starkey, *British privateering enterprise in the eighteenth century* (Exeter: University of Exeter Press, 1990).

[55] See, for instance, *BW* 17, p. 16.

[56] See *IBP*, III.18.2.1-2.

[57] *Commentary*, IV, p. 43.

[58] *Commentary*, IV, p. 46-49.

[59] In general, properties of the enemy could be taken under the condition of making restitution. Absolute ownership may be acquired to compensate a state waging a lawful war to

discussion of how to balance the rights of the belligerents and the rights of the neutrals. Privateers are distinguished from those who receive payment like the naval soldiers or mercenaries. In contrast to the latter the former serve at their own charges and 'support a part of the war with their own expenditures, such as those who fit out and maintain ships at private cost'.[60] To defend the expanding privateering policy of the Vereenigde Oostindische Compagnie (VOC) the legal side of taking booty has been extended by Grotius to a considerable dimension. Not only could the state give all its subjects the right of plundering the enemy even without a prize-taking commission [*etiam sine codicillis*]. Thus, the state can not be bound to require a bond or a caution. Furthermore, the state would be under no obligation when one of its privateers turns to piracy. The government is only liable to an injured party in case of the latter fails to punish the culprits.[61] Grotius's rule echoed the decision of the Amsterdam Admiralty court 1617 in favour of the General States after the Dutch privateer Dirck Dircksz had seized a ship of the Pomerian Jacob Lange.[62] On the other hand, the state's authorities would indeed be responsible and liable for neglect when they fail to take measures for the prevention of robbery and piracy.[63] While the lawful side of bootery is extended to a wide scope, its unlawful side remains a zone of severe jurisdiction to prevent and harshly punish piracy and robbery. For their persecution Grotius even concedes the risk to involve and endanger innocent people: '[...] we may bombard a ship full of pirates, or a house full of brigands, even if there are within the same ship or house a few infants, women, or other innocent persons who are thereby endangered'.[64]

With his large-scale prize law Grotius marked the transformation of what Ivo van Loo has described as the change from a *defensive* privateering, practised by the 'watergeuzen' in the early years of the Dutch revolt to defend their new

---

a certain amout that was fixed by the beginning of a war or from a later act. Furthermore, the property of the guilty can be taken away as a means of imposing a penalty. Up to the defined limit enemy goods could become property of the captor. Captured booty above the limit ought to be restored to the state. See *IBP*, III.18.2.2; 3; *Law of War and Peace*, p. 789-790.

[60] *IBP*, III.18.2.1; *Law of War and Peace*, p. 789.

[61] *IBP*, II.17.20.1, pp. 432-433; *Law of War and Peace*, p. 436.

[62] See Cornelis Gerrit Roelofsen, 'The Claim of some Citizens of Stettin against the Dutch Republic and its Adjudication (1609-17) State-responsibility in early modern Europe; *Apropos* of de iure belli ac pacis II.17.20', in *Reflections on Principles and Practice of International Law. Essays in Honour of Leo J. Bouchez*, ed. by Terry D. Gill and Wybo P. Heere (The Hague: Nijhoff, 2000), pp. 175-189.

[63] *IBP*, II.17.20.1, pp. 432-433; *English* p. 436. See also *IPC*, VIII, 47; *Commentary*, p. 106.

[64] *IBP*, III.1.4.1, p. 613; *Law of War and Peace*, p. 601.

freedom, to a more *offensive* Dutch privateering to establish a powerful naval force and to encourage a massive colonial expansion.[65] Keeping in mind Grotius's story of the six Hollanders in China we should add that, in the years after 1624, the Dutch tried to instrumentalise different groups of Chinese pirates to attack and smash the Ming Empire in China.[66] However, prize-taking, as it was justified by the young Grotius, became a significant economic activity in the Indian Ocean.[67]

In conclusion: the debates on *piratae* and *latrones* give us a good example of how Grotius systematically reflects on law and legal order from the perspective of their violation.[68] By focusing on the discussion of sea-robbery – and robbery in general – we cast a light on the 'dark side' of Grotius's prize law. As the reconstruction shows: this side, while yet included by *ius naturae*, may be excluded from positive law, yet forms, at the same time, a constitutive and inseparable part of it. While the privateer legally participates as a state-sponsored private man in a lawful public war, the pirate always wages an unlawful private war. Like the two sides of a coin privateering and piracy represent both halves of the maritime *ius praedae* concerning private sea-war engagement. It is an example of the 'Einheit der Differenz von Recht und Unrecht' (Niklas Luhmann). If we take the famous slogan of the seventeenth century, 'No peace beyond the line', not in a geographical but in a metaphorical sense, we could apply this slogan to the status of the illegal booters determining as outcasts of the sea the law beyond its line.

---

[65] Ivo van Loo, 'For Freedom and Fortune: the rise of Dutch Privateering in the first half of the Dutch Revolt, 1568-1609', in *Exercise of Arms: Warfare in the Netherlands, 1568-1648*, ed. by Marco van der Hoeven (Leiden: Brill, 1998), pp. 173-195.

[66] See Tonio Andrade, 'The Company's Chinese Pirates: How the Dutch East India Company tried to lead a Coalition of Pirates to War against China, 1621–1662', *Journal of World History*, 15 (2004), 415-444.

[67] See Ileana Porras, 'Constructing International Law ind the East Indian Seas: Property, Sovereignty, Commerce and War in Hugo Grotius' De Iure Praedae – The Law of Prize and Booty, or on how to distinguish Merchants from Pirates', *Brooklyn Journal of International Law*, 31/3 (2006), pp. 741-804.

[68] In so far this example could confirm Hasso Hofmann, 'Hugo Grotius', in *Staatsdenker*, ed. by Michael Stolleis (München: Beck, 1995), pp. 52-77 (p. 68).

Grotius and the Origin of the Ruler's Right to Punish*

Gustaaf van Nifterik
Faculty of Law, University of Amsterdam
g.p.vannifterik@uva.nl

Abstract
An important aspect of any constitutional theory is the state's power to punish transgressions of the law, or the *ius gladii*. Although Grotius never formulated a complete, comprehensive constitutional theory, traces of such a theory can be found in many of his writings not explicitly devoted to constitutional law. Punishment even plays an important role in his books on war (and peace), since to punish transgressions of the law is ranked among the just causes of war.
Given the fact that a state may punish transgressions of the law – transgressions by individuals within and even outside the state, but also transgressions of the law by other states – the question may arise concerning the origin of such a right to punish. It will be shown that Grotius did not give the same answer to this question in his various works. As the right to punish is concerned, we find a theory that seems to be akin to the one of John Locke in the *De iure praedae* (around 1605), one akin to the theories of the Spanish late-scholastics in *De satisfactione and De imperio* (around 1615), and a theory coming close to what Thomas Hobbes had said on the ruler's right to punish in the *De iure belli ac pacis* (around 1625).
Of course, Grotius can only have been familiar with the theory of the Spanish late-scholastics, since those of Locke and Hobbes were still to be written by the time Grotius had passed away.

Keywords
right to punish, civil society, constitutional theory, criminal law, natural law

Introduction

Both in his *De iure praedae commentarius* (chapter 7) and his *De iure belli ac pacis* (section II.1.2) Grotius distinguishes several causes of a just war.[1] One of

* Based on a lecture held in Wassenaar at the conference 'Piracy, Property, Punishment. Hugo Grotius and De iure praedae' NIAS, Wassenaar, The Netherlands, June 9-11, 2005. I want to thank the participants in the discussion for their contribution and Peter Borschberg for his information on Grotius's unpublished *Theses LVI*.

[1] See for a short introduction to this well known doctrine J. Barnes, 'The just war', in *The Cambridge History of Late Medieval Philosophy. From the rediscovery of Aristotle to the disintegration*

them is punishment, which will be the central focus of this paper. Punishment as a cause of war is elaborated in chapter 8 of the *De iure praedae*, and treated much more extensively in chapter II.20 (*De poenis*) of the *De iure belli ac pacis*.[2] In this paper I intend to deal with Grotius's ideas on the origin of the right to punish and on punishment as a *causa belli* as being part of a constitutional theory, to be grasped from his legal and theological texts. The competence of a state, or a ruler, to fight a penal war against another state or actor on the international level, rests on the same fundaments as the competence of a state to use the sword (*ius gladii*) against its own subjects. Therefore, the arguments on punishment as a *causa belli* contribute to the discussion on the power of the state as such at the same time.

In the past few decades Richard Tuck pointed out several times the similarities between the theories on the origin of the right to punish of Hugo Grotius as can be found in the *De iure praedae* and the one of John Locke,

of scholasticism, 1100-1600, ed. by N. Kretzmann, A. Kenny and J. Pinborg (Cambridge: CUP, 1984), pp. 771-784 and Duane L. Cady, 'Just war', in: *An Encyclopedia of War and Ethics*, ed. by Donald A. Wells (Westport: Greenwood, 1996), p. 255-259. Concerning Grotius also Peter Haggenmacher, *Grotius et la doctrine de la guerre juste* (Paris: Presses Universitaires de France, 1983). Also many of the articles in *Grotius*, Great Political Thinkers 7, ed. by John Dunn and Ian Harris, 2 vols (Cheltenham: Elgar, 1997) [= *Great Political Thinkers. Grotius*], deal with Grotius and the just war doctrine.

[2] For Grotius on punishment see D. Beaufort, *La guerre comme instrument de secours ou de punition*, The Hague: Nijhoff, 1933), especially pp. 156-177; W.C.L. van der Grinten, 'De opvatting van Grotius over straf', *Tijdschrift voor Strafrecht*, 51 (1941), 155-176; H.J.A. Nolte, 'Eenige rechtsfilosofische opmerkingen naar aanleiding van het strafbegrip bij Hugo Grotius', *Tijdschrift voorStrafrecht*, 55 (1947), 73-94; André Langui, 'Grotius et le droit pénal', *XVIIe Siècle*, 32 (1980), 37-58; Gerhard Simson, 'Hugo Grotius und die Funktion der Strafe', in *Festschrift Günter Blau zum 70. Geburtstag am 18. Dezember 1985*, ed. by Hans-Dieter Schwind (Berlin: De Gruyter, 1985), pp. 651-663; Robert Legros, 'Une lecture pénale de Grotius', *Bulletin de la classe des lettres et des sciences morales et politiques*, Académie Royale de Belgique, 5th series, 63 (1987), 424-457; Furukawa Teruni, 'Punishment', in *A Normative approach to war. Peace, War and Justice in Hugo Grotius*, ed. by Onuma Yasuaki (Oxford: Clarendon Press, 1993), pp. 221-243. Two articles by Peter Haggenmacher, 'Sur un passage obscur de Grotius. Essai de réponse à Cornelis van Vollenhoven', *Tijdschrift voor Rechtsgeschiedenis*, 51 (1983), 295-315 (repr. in *Great Political Thinkers. Grotius*, II, pp. 165-185) and 'Droits subjectifs et système juridique chez Grotius', in *Politique, droit et théologie chez Bodin, Grotius et Hobbes*, ed. by Luc Foisneau (Paris: Kimé, 1997), pp. 73-130 deal to a great extent with Grotius on the right to punish. Recently on Grotius and punishment: Hans W. Blom, 'Grotius and Socinianism', in *Socinianism and Arminianism. Antitrinitarians, Calvinists, and cultural exchange in seventeenth-century Europe*. ed. by Martin Mulsow and Jan Rohls, Brill's studies in the intellectual history, 134, (Leiden: Brill, 2005), pp. 121-147. I want to thank Blom for sending me his final draft before publication. See also Joannes van Riet, *Dissertatio juridica inauguralis de Hugonis Grotii in jure criminali meritis*, Diss. Leiden (Amsterdam: Martin, 1828).

written some decades later, and today known to scholars as the 'very strange doctrine'.[3] Tuck also pointed out that Locke cannot have taken his theory from Grotius, since the text of the *De iure praedae* will not have been available to him, and the theory cannot be found in the *De iure belli ac pacis*, which was available to him. Therefore, Tuck concludes this is 'one of the most striking examples of intellectual convergence'.[4] Although it will be shown that there are some fundamental similarities in Grotius's thoughts on the right to punish in *De iure praedae* and *De iure belli ac pacis*, I think Tuck is right in saying that Locke did not find the very strange theory in *De iure belli ac pacis*.

De iure praedae

In his *De iure praedae*,[5] written around 1605, Grotius tried to justify the capture of the richly laden Portuguese carrack *Santa Catarina* in 1603 by Jacob van Heemskerck, admiral in service of the Dutch East India Company (VOC).[6] Grotius presented the seizure as an act of war, to be judged by the law governing war (so in the first chapter of *De iure praedae*). The argument that follows focuses on the just causes of war, the just ways to fight a war and on questions of whom is licensed to undertake a war and to carry out acts of war. In answering these questions Grotius treats public war and private war (the use of force by private individuals against private individuals) as essentially the same. If not subjected to civil law and human jurisdiction, that is: in a non-civil society, private individuals hold the same position towards each other, and are governed by the same laws, as states and rulers do on the international level (at the end of the second chapter). These laws are the law of nature, together with the rules accepted by all humans (*consensus hominum*),

[3] Richard Tuck, *Natural rights theories. Their origin and development* (Cambridge: CUP, 1979), pp. 62-63; Id., *The Righs of War and Peace. Political Thought and the International Order From Grotius to Kant*, (Oxford: OUP, 1999), pp. 82.

[4] Tuck, *The Rights of War and Peace*, p. 82.

[5] I have made use of the edition by H.G. Hamaker (ex auctoris codice descripsit et vulgavit), *Hugonis Grotii De jure praedae commentarius*, The Hague 1868 [= *IPC*]. Many of the topics touched upon in this paper can be found in Haggenmacher, *Grotius et la doctrine de la guerre juste*, première partie.

[6] On the seizure and Grotius's justification of it, see Martine Julia van Ittersum, 'Hugo Grotius in Context: Van Heemskerck's Capture of the *Santa Catarina* and its Justification in *De Jure Praedae* (1604-1606)', *Asian Journal of Social Science*, 31 (2003), 511-548 and the contribution of Martine van Ittersum and Peter Borschberg in this volume.

the so-called secondary law of nature, or the primary *jus gentium*.[7] These laws are (still) in force where there are no civil laws, no civil courts and human jurisdiction, whether it be temporary or permanent. Men are governed by natural law wherever the original, natural laws are not set aside by civil laws.[8]

Grotius discusses the natural law causes of a just war in chapter 7 of *De iure praedae*. One of them is the reaction against any form of criminal or unjust behavior (*ob maleficium injuriamque omnem, quae iniquo animo tam facto quam verbis infertur*). Concerning this cause Grotius in chapter 8 discusses a difficulty. A private person cannot legitimately wage war as a punishment without a verdict of some court, unless he would posses a natural right to punish. Most scholars however, says Grotius, deny the individuals such a natural right, and ascribe the competence to punish exclusively to the state and its officials. This position would undermine Grotius's starting point that there is no fundamental difference between the law governing private individuals in a non-civil (natural) society and the law states are governed by in their mutual relationship.

To solve this paradox Grotius sketches the state of affairs before men came to the establishment of civil societies (states) and courts. The civil law and its courts, says Grotius, are established to discourage and prevent the excesses that may occur when every individual can judge for himself and enforce his own right. Now the right to punish wrongdoers (Grotius quotes Cicero, Tacitus, the Holy Bible and more to support his view) is natural and of an earlier date than civil society and civil laws. It must of necessity have its roots in natural law. It is the same natural right to punish as is confirmed, or restated by God in Genesis 9.6. Grotius shows by quotations from antiquity that the causes for punishment are natural too. The offender by his wrongful act brings about his degradation and subjection,[9] so that he is on a par with pests who may be killed by anybody if necessary. Would then not every state, Grotius rhetorically asks, have the competence to punish offenders of the law?

---

[7] Thus in chapter II, ad rule II; see under rule VII for the secondary *ius gentium*, '*jus gentium quod recte ac proprie secundarium dicetur*'. On the sixteenth-century history of the division of the *ius gentium*, see Merio Scattola, *Das Naturrecht vor dem Naturrecht. Zur Geschichte des 'ius naturae' im 16. Jahrhundert*, Frühe Neuzeit 52 (Tübingen: Niemeyer, 1999), especially the second part on jurisprudence. On Grotius see also Peter Haggenmacher, 'Genèse et signification du concept de "ius gentium" chez Grotius', *Grotiana*. 2 (1981), 44-102, and 631-643 (also published in *Great Political Thinkers. Grotius*, II, p. 21-93). See also in Haggenmacher, *Grotius et la doctrine de la guerre juste*.

[8] Chapter II, ad law 13 and at the beginning of chapter 8.

[9] See also in chapter II, under rule IX: *quod ab omnibus traditum est, alteram rempublicam alterius subditam fieri delinquendo*.

Of course they have and, as a consequence of Grotius's other basic assumption that all competences of the state come from the individuals who have established the state, it leads to the conclusion that originally the individuals must have had a competence to punish transgressions of the law.[10] This last conclusion is inevitable indeed, since Grotius also holds to the Roman law rule that one cannot transfer to another a greater right than he has himself (as a *regula iuris* to be found in Digest 50.17.54).[11]

As an argument in favor of the natural right to punish Grotius in chapter 8 points out that nobody would deny a state's official the right to punish foreigners if they have offended the state's laws (p. 91). Now the competence to punish foreigners cannot be based upon their voluntary subjection to the state's officials and the state's laws do not bind foreigners. Therefore, the competence to punish foreigners must have its source elsewhere, in a law preceding human voluntary law, i.e. the natural law. Again, since the state's powers are deduced from those of the individuals, and since the individuals cannot transfer a right they do not have themselves, the right to punish must originally have been a natural right of the private individuals. By setting up a state the individuals transfer their right to punish to the state. In places where, temporarily or permanently, no state or any form of civil power exists (as, for instance, on high sea), natural law is still in force without any restriction; this includes the right of private individuals to punish transgressions of the (natural) law.

Grotius is not very detailed on the question of who actually would inflict punishment in the natural state of affairs. It seems natural to him that dispensation of justice, both within and outside the family, is a task of the *patresfamilias* (p. 92). A little below (p. 94) Grotius concurs with Plutarch, saying that in a natural course of things the just and practical men endorsed with a public spirit will be appointed to this task. In the same manner, those of whom one could expect they would exceed the just measure (*justus modus*) are ruled out (p. 93-94).

In chapter 8 of the *De iure praedae* Grotius says that both the urge and the right to punish transgressions of the law are natural and that by nature the individuals have this right to punish. Punishment is taken as a necessary instrument to protect (the well being of) the community. Wherever there is no civil jurisdiction, temporary or permanent, the protection of the human

---

[10] Haggenmacher, *Grotius et la doctrine de la guerre juste*, p. 228: 'Voilà où Grotius dépasse la tradition scolastique, attentive toujours à refuser le pouvoir vindicatif au particulier.'

[11] *Dig.* 50.17.54 (Ulpianus): *Nemo plus iuris ad alium transferre potest, quam ipse habet.*

community is the responsibility of all of its members, irrespective of whether the executor of the punishment was himself a victim or not.[12] For in chapter 6 (p. 60) Grotius had already said that men are always associated in the *totius humani generis societas* so that that a *malum* done to another man also affects us. It is the offender, who – by committing the crime – has made himself fit to undergo punishment, since by the very act he demoted himself to a rank below the other members of the community. As a consequence, the one who punishes the offender, even if he is a private person, by the law of nature does not sin (p. 95). In a civil society normally the civil law forbids the private members to exact punishment.

This of course in outline is the same theory as can be found in John Locke's second *Treatise on Government*, of which he, some decades after Grotius, said that 'this will seem a very strange Doctrine to some Men'.[13] Whereas Locke used the theory to ground political power upon the rights inherent in the individuals, Grotius came to it from the opposite direction. Given the purpose of the *De iure praedae*, he wants the individuals in a state of nature (as on high sea) to have the same rights as civil states. However, he seems to have forgotten the whole theory for long, since he only partly returns to it in his *De iure belli ac pacis* (1625). We now turn to some works written in between.

De Satisfactione

The right to punish is extensively discussed in chapter 2 of the *Defensio fidei catholicae de Satisfactione Christi*, hereafter referred to as the *De Satisfactione*.[14] This work, written from 1614 on and first published in 1617, is a juridical-philological response to the work of the Italian protestant Faustus Socinus (Fausto Sozzini) on the true meaning of Christ's suffering and death, *De Iesu*

[12] See also conclusion 7 in *IPC*, VIII, p. 93.

[13] John Locke, *Two treatises of government*, ed., intr. and notes by Peter Laslett, Cambridge texts in the History of Political Thought (Cambridge: CUP, 1988), II.9. See also above, footnote 3 on Tuck.

[14] I have used the following edition: *Defensio fidei catholicae de Satisfactione Christi adversus Faustum Socinum Senensem*, ed., intr. and notes by Edwin Rabbie, English tr. by Hotze Mulder, Hugo Grotius Opera Theologica, 1, (Assen: van Gorcum, 1990). See on this work and on Socinus and Socinianism the 'Introduction' by Edwin Rabbie; further Haggenmacher, *Grotius et la doctrine de la guerre juste*, p. 512 ff and Jacqueline Lagrée, 'Droit et théologie dans le De Satisfactione Christi de Hugo Grotius', in *Politique, droit et théologie*, ed. by Luc Foisneau, pp. 193-212. See also Blom, 'Grotius and Socinianism', who, on p. 122, says: '...it will become evident that the opinion of the modern editor of this text that *De Satisfactione* is essentially a work in theology is misguided'.

Christo servatore. Socinus does not take Christ's suffering as a punishment for the sins of men, but 'as an example inspiring faith into sinful man and as a prelude to his resurrection, inspiring hope'.[15] Grotius, on the other hand, from a Calvinistic perspective takes it as a punishment for men's sins against God, washing of our sins at the same time.[16]

In the second chapter of *De Satisfactione* Grotius turns to the question of Gods role, or capacity, in punishing Christ and liberating mankind from punishment at the same time. God can only have inflicted punishment, he says in the chapter's first section, as a ruler, since both to inflict and to liberate from punishment are a prerogative of a ruler as such (*qua talis primo et per se*). Punishment is a form of compulsion, and compulsion is the exclusive competence of a ruler, as is the father in a family, a king in a state, and God in the universe (II.2).

Socinus' basic error, says Grotius in II.4, is that he holds that the offended party as such (*qua tali*) would have the competence to punish, or even have the right that the offender is punished. Grotius denies this right all together, since in punishment the offended party is not a creditor. To the offended party only restitution is due, and nothing else (II.10). The cause of punishment, says Grotius, is the moral wrongness of the act of the offender, not that anything is lacking to the offended party.

If the offended party were the creditor in punishment, rulers would not have the competence to punish transgressions of the law without themselves being offended by it (this argument is found in II.6). Grotius rejects the view that the ruler may punish breaches of his laws because all offences in some way injure the state of which the ruler is the head, so that the ruler could always be seen as an injured party. He argues against this view that it cannot explain the rightly and laudably punishment of subjects who have committed crimes outside the territory and against foreigners.[17] Grotius's discussion concerning the liberation of the offender (II.17) points in the same direction. If the offended party were a creditor in punishment, only payment made to him would liberate the offender. But in punishment it does not matter by whom it

---

[15] Rabbie, in the 'Introduction' of the above mentioned edition of *De Satisfactione*, p. 6.

[16] In *IBP*, I.4.4.6, however, quoting I Peter 2.20 '*Sed si bene agentes, et tamen male habiti subsistitis, hoc cedit vobis gratiae apud Deum*'. *Confirmat mox hoc a Christi exemplo*. For *IBP* see footnote 32.

[17] This is not the same argument as we have seen above in *De iure praedae*. The point made in *De iure praedae* is that a ruler can rightly punish foreigners, even without their voluntary subjection to the ruler's power; the point made in *De Satisfactione* is that a ruler can punish transgressions of the law (by his subjects) without being offended himself. The same argument as in *De Satisfactione* can be found in *IBP*, II.20.40.1 to which we turn below; see also *IBP*, II.20.8.2.

is inflicted; the punished will be liberated before all. And so it is only on account of similarity when we say that the order of things and the public good function as creditor, and that the ruler has the *ius puniendi* since dispensing of this order and good has been committed to him (II.19 and 23).

It is now clear that God must have acted as a ruler (*ut rectorem*, as in the chapter's title) when he punished Christ, and at the same time liberated men from their sins. A superior, says Grotius (II.6), has the right to punish in his capacity as superior authority; if you assume 'superior authority' you also assume the right to punish, and if you do not assume the former you neither assume the latter. The ruler's right to punish is neither a real right nor a personal right (*non est aut ius absoluti dominii aut ius crediti*, II.16).[18] It does not exist for the sake of him who punishes (as do the *iura dominii* and *crediti*), but for the sake of a community. And when we say 'I owe punishment' (*debeo poenam*), this should be understood as 'I deserve punishment and I am held to undergo it' (II.17). It is a *debere* not in relation to a particular person, but it is *absolute*, a *debere* without a creditor. The offence does not create a relation between two persons, but one between two things: a crime and the punishment. Equality suitable to order and the public good should be established between these two things (V.15).[19]

Concerning the (in)justice of the particular punishment of Christ for our sins, Grotius in chapter four amply argues that it is not essential of punishment that it is suffered by the offender himself. The punishment is not essentially related to one's own sin (*non esse de essentia poenae relationem ad peccatum proprium*, IV.7), although it is essentially inflicted on account of sin (IV.10: *esse essentiale poenae, ut infligatur ob peccatum, sed non item essentiale ei esse ut infligatur ipsi qui peccavit*). What matters is that there is a bond between the offender and the punished; this bond can either be natural (as between father and son), or mystical (as between king and people), or voluntary (as between defendant and surety, IV.11). The very act of punishing someone (*actus poenalis*, the actual use of force) can be licit in three cases (IV.11): by previous right of him who punishes, by consent of him who is to be punished, or by a delict of the one to be punished.[20]

---

[18] Compare his three types of (subjective) right in *IBP*, I.1.5: power (*potestas*), real right (*dominium*) and personal right (*creditum*).

[19] *De Satisfactione* V.15: *[...] iuris dominici et crediti proximum fundamentum est relatio quaedam rei ad personam; poenae autem relatio rei ad rem, nimirum aequalitas delicti cum nocumento aliquo conveniens ordini et bono communi.*

[20] I think the three cases in IV.22 can be taken as examples of what Grotius says in IV.11. The first case is that a ruler refuses public offices to children of public enemies; second, the case that someone is guilty of some crime while someone else of his own free will takes upon himself the

Attention is paid in chapter five to the question of why God wanted to punish Christ for our sins and liberate us. The reason is that God wanted to show both His clemency and severity (*clementia et severitas*). He needed to show severity in order to make clear that He was not pleased by the transgressions of His laws, but He also wanted to show clemency to those who believe in Him and His son. Christ was perfectly fit for both purposes. With much emphasis, punishment is shown in chapter five of *De Satisfactione* to be a useful instrument in the hands of rulers.

Interesting as all this may be, our question on the origin of the right to punish is not answered in *De Satisfactione*. As a compulsive act, punishment is the exclusive (and useful) competence of a ruler, such as a father, a king, and God. Our question of course is, where rulers get their competence from. For an answer that fits well into what we have just seen from the *De Satisfactione* we can turn to Grotius's work from roughly the same period, *De Imperio*.

De Imperio

De Imperio summarum potestatum circa sacra, on the authority of the supreme powers in matters of religion, was conceived in 1614 and finished in 1617, but only published in 1647.[21] In discussing church government, the book deals with supreme power as such, with a strong tendency towards absolutism.[22] As in *De Satisfactione* we find the sword exclusively in the hands of the supreme powers.[23] The right to punish itself is hardly discussed in this book, but it does contain important thoughts on the origin of power as such, especially in section 2 of chapter ten (*De electione pastorum*).

Concerning the institution of priests Grotius in that section distinguishes between the actual *facultas praedicandi* (or *mandatum*) of a priest and the

obligation to go in exile; and third, the decimation usual in the Roman legions, where someone who had committed a crime was punished not only for his own crime, but also for that of all the others. On the decimation of a legion in antiquity, see also *IBP*, I.4.7.10-15.

[21] I have made use of the critical edition with introduction, English translation and commentary by Harm-Jan van Dam, Studies in the History of Christian Thought, 102-3, 2 vols (Leiden: Brill, 2001). On the book, see the 'Introduction' and Haggenmacher, *Grotius et la doctrine de la guerre juste*, pp. 510 ff.

[22] See for instance sections I.3, II.4, III.3, IV.3, VI.13 and 14, IX.21; see I.3 and III.8 for references to Bodin.

[23] As in III.14: *Haec ostendunt quam alte christianorum animis haeserit vox illa Domini quae* gladium *vetat* arripere. *Arripit autem qui non a Deo accipit. Dedit autem Deus soli summae potestati, aliis non nisi per illam*. In IV.9 the sword is called the instrument of power: *imperii instrumentum gladius*.

applicatio (or *ordinatio*) of it to a particular person.[24] To clarify his point he gives some examples in which the same distinction between the *facultas* and the *applicatio* can be made. The first is the power of the husband (*potestas maritalis*).[25] The power itself comes from God (*a Deo*), says Grotius, only the application of this power to a particular person happens by consent of the wife. This is demonstrated by pointing out that consent itself is not sufficient to dissolve a marriage, and that husband and wife cannot by agreement lay down that he shall not rule over her. The wife's consent does not create the husband's power, it is only needed to attribute this power to a particular person. In the same way the imperial power (*imperatoria potestas*) is never possessed by the Electors, so that they cannot give this power to anybody, but that it is only applied by them to the person they have chosen. Third and last the right of life and death (*ius vitae et necis*) is mentioned, a right the people do not and cannot posses before they join together in a state. For a private person, says Grotius, does not have the right to punish: *privatus enim ius vindictae non habet*.[26] Still, after the formation of a state this power is applied by the people to a particular person or assembly.

In comparison with *De iure praedae* Grotius seems to have changed his mind considerably. We no longer find the idea that the state's competences are deduced from those of the private individuals in their pre-civil state. In *De imperio* the power comes from God[27] and consent is only needed to

[24] Also I.1, where he differentiates between the exercise of authority and the person exercising it; and II.2 between authority and the functions which authority has at its command.

[25] In I.3 Grotius calls the paternal authority *naturale et antiquissimum*; II.4 clearly shows that domestic authority is older than civil authority; IV.6 makes clear that the power of the *pater familias* is not derived from supreme power, although it is subjected to it (*Imperium sub supremo collocatum et non ex supremo ortum habens*).

[26] In Grotius's manuscript *Theses sive questiones LVI de iure hominis in actiones et res suas* (Leiden University Library, BPL 922 I), according to Peter Borschberg written in the first decade of the seventeenth century (a publication by Borschberg on the *Theses LVI* will follow soon), we find a discussion on the *ius* men have to their own life, body, actions and possessions and the lack of such a right in those of another men. For the texts see in section 1 and 4 of the contribution of Benjamin Straumann to this volume. In the margin of the manuscript we find a line, according to Borschberg (judged on the color of the ink) more or less contemporary to the main text, saying: *Ergo non habet ius puniendi*. However, I am not convinced of Straumann's reading of the texts and this marginal insertion, since the insertion on the *ius puniendi* is written in the margin of thesis 7 (where we read that *sapiens et medicus consilii habent potestatem non imperii: quod iure exsecutionis demonstratur*), although marked by a line to belong to thesis 6 (on the *ius in vitam, corpus, actiones et res alterius hominis*). Below the sentence we find a reference to Genesis 4.15. Before drawing my conclusions I think the manuscript and its context need to be studied more carefully.

[27] Van Dam in the 'Introduction' (p. 3-4) to the edition I have used: '*De Imperio* can, in fact, be summarized by two arguments, one scriptural and one logical: In Romans 13 it is said that

attribute it to a certain ruler. The same theory can in essence be found in many of the political theories of scholars, both catholic and protestant, from the same period and from the decades before Grotius. Important controversies arose concerning the consequences of such a consensual attribution, which need not be treated here.[28]

Inleidinge

The thought that the offended party is entitled to restitution and no more than that – a thought not found in *De iure praedae* but clearly set out in *De Satisfactione* – is worked out in the *Inleidinge tot de Hollandsche rechtsgeleerdheid*, the introduction to the jurisprudence of Holland that Grotius wrote during his captivity in the castle of Loevestein (1618-1621).[29]

In III.32.7 Grotius describes the two obligations a wrong can give rise to: one is the obligation to make restitution, the other to suffer punishment. Both obligations come from the law of nature and need to be determined more precisely by civil law. As concerns the obligation to suffer punishment, it is reason that teaches us that fear is the only way to prevent (too many) wrongful acts in this wicked world; the way to produce this fear is punishment. The right to punish belongs to the government, the right to claim redress belongs to those who have suffered the wrong.[30]

Grotius in III.32.7 mentions 'onze voor-ouders' (our ancestors) who after having suffered a wrong could demand punishment of the wrongdoer by the government, and who could even in default of a legal process ('by

---

the supreme power is placed above other men by God; and Aristotle teaches that there cannot be more than one supreme power'.

[28] See Quentin Skinner, *The Foundations of Modern Political Thought*, 2 vols (Cambridge: CUP, 1978), II, part II and III. See also my *Vorst tussen volk en wet. Over volkssoevereiniteit en rechtsstatelijkheid in het werk van Fernando Vázquez de Menchaca (1512-1569)* (s.l. 1999), especially chapter 6, pp. 96-104 and J.W. Sap, *Paving the way for Revolution. Calvinism and the struggle for a democratic constitutional state* (Amsterdam: VU, 2001), an English translation of the earlier, Dutch edition *Wegbereiders der revolutie. Calvinisme en de strijd om de democratische rechtsstaat* (Groningen: Wolters-Noordhof, 1993).

[29] I have used the *Inleidinge tot de Hollandsche Rechts-geleerdheid. Met de te Lund teruggevonden verbeteringen, aanvullingen en opmerkingen van den schrijver en met verwijzingen naar zijn andere geschriften*, ed. by F. Dovring, H.F.W.D. Fischer en E.M. Meijers (Leiden: Universitaire pers, 1952) and the English translation by R.W. Lee, *The Jurisprudence of Holland*, 2 vols (Oxford: Clarendon Press, 1926-1936). The legally more sophisticated distinction between the obligations to restitution and punishment in the *Inleidinge*, is also pointed out by Haggenmacher, 'Droits subjectifs'.

[30] See also *Inleidinge* III.5.4, III.20.32 and 35, and III.24.20.

rechts-gebreck') execute punishment themselves. In the manuscript found in Lund references are made to the *De republica Anglorum* by Thomas Smith.[31] Thomas Smith in III.3 mentions the '*duellum*, or the campe' as a reaction to blood violently shed: 'However it be, this kinde of triall of longe time hath not beene used. [...] Neverthelesse the Lawe remaineth still, and isnot abolished, and if it shall chaunce the murderer or mansleer if he that hath slaine the man, hath his pardon of the prince [...] yet the partie grieved hath these two remedies, I say to require justice by grande assise, or battle upon his appeale and private revenge, which is not denyed him' (ed. p. 124-125). Grotius takes the aforementioned right of our ancestors to arise from custom, which, says Grotius, forms part of the civil law; execution of punishment by private individuals was a right conferred by the government.

As in *De iure praedae*, both punishment and the obligation to suffer punishment are said to be natural. But an individual natural right to punish cannot be found in the *Inleidinge*.

De iure belli ac pacis

In his three books on the law of war and peace from 1625, *De iure belli ac pacis*, Grotius deals with both the *ius ad bellum* and the *ius in bello*, war being defined as the condition of those contending by force (*status per vim certantium*, I.1.2.1).[32] As in *De iure praedae*, war can either be public, or private. In the second book the justifiable causes of war are discussed, being as numerous as those from which lawsuits spring, since war begins where judicial settlement fails (II.1.2.1). The justifiable causes of war are defense, the obtaining of that which belongs to us or is our due, and, finally, the inflicting of punishments. Chapter 20 of the second book (*De poenis*) deals with punishment as a cause of war. The chapter is rather long and attracted attention from different disciplines.[33]

---

[31] Thomas Smith, *De Republica Anglorum. The maner of Government or policie of the Realme of England* (London: Printed by Henrie Midleton for Gregorie Seton, 1583; ed. and intr. by Mary Dewar: Cambridge: CUP, 1982). I used the edition (with an Introduction). The hand-written notes by Grotius in the manuscript found in Lund can be found in the edition of the *Inleidinge* I have made use of.

[32] I have made use of the edition Hugo Grotius, *De iure belli ac pacis libri tres*, ed. by B.J.A. de Kanter-van Hettinga Tromp, new annot. by R. Feenstra, C.E. Persenaire, and E. Arps-de Wilde (Aalen: Scientia, 1993) [= *IBP*] and the English translation *De jure belli ac pacis by Hugo Grotius, Volume two: The Translation Book I-III*, tr. by Francis W. Kelsey, The Classics of International Law (Oxford: Clarendon Press, 1925).

[33] See footnote 2 above.

Before we turn to punishment as a cause of war, it is useful to turn to the second chapter of the first book, on the question whether it can ever be lawful to wage war. Grotius's first conclusion is that nature itself is not opposed to the use of force to settle disputes. Our first and natural tendencies (*prima naturae*, translated by Kelsey as the 'first principles of nature'),[34] preservation of life and limb and of things useful to this end, even are in its favour (I.2.1.4). Neither do reason and our social nature prohibit all use of force,[35] but only the use that by taking away the right of another is in conflict with society (I.2.1.5). As a consequence, the use of force that does not violate the right of another is not unjust (I.2.1.6). Grotius next points out that neither the *ius gentium voluntarium* (I.2.4), nor the *ius divinum voluntarium* (I.2.5) reject war altogether. As the *ius divinum* is concerned, he argues that Genesis 9.6 and the Commandment 'Thou shalt not kill' turn against the unjust shed of blood, the shed of blood as a crime, not against shed of blood as a punishment. They merely repeat the rule of natural law stated above. Neither in natural law, nor in divine law, it is unjust to shed the blood of him who first shed the blood of an innocent person (or committed a crime no less serious).[36] It is not unjust that he who does evil, suffers evil; this is the so called Law of Rhadamanthus (I.2.5.3).

Grotius opens his chapter on punishment saying there is a lack of a clear understanding as to the origin and nature of it. Punishment, he says is a *malum passionis quod infligitur ob malum actionis* (II.20.1.1). It is a return for a crime (*malum ob malum*) that is not unjust since it is not in conflict with society that he who did evil, suffers evil. The wrongdoer is obligated to

---

[34] See also *IPC*, p. 9: *Cum igitur res conditas Deus esse fecerit et esse voluerit proprietates quasdam naturales singulis indidit, quibus ipsum illud esse conservaretur et quibus ad bonum suum unumquodque, velut ex prima originis lege, duceretur.*

[35] Characteristic of man is his desire for a social life and his faculty of knowing and of acting in accordance with general principles (Prolegomena 6 ff.). I agree with B.P. Vermeulen and G.A. van der Wal, 'Grotius, Aquinas and Hobbes. Grotian natural law between *lex aeterna* and natural rights', *Grotiana*, 16-17 (1995-1996), pp. 55-83, saying: 'Therefore, when Grotius calls the laws of self-preservation the first principles of nature he does not imply that these laws have priority over those regarding the well-being of other persons: he merely means to say that these principles are 'first according to nature' because they impel every animal (man included) instinctively from the moment of its birth to have regard for itself and preserve itself. The other principles, flowing from right reason, though they become manifest later, have preference over the first principles' (pp. 79-80). Basically the same ideas can be found in the *Controversiae illustres* of the Spaniard Fernando Vázquez; see my *Vorst tussen volk en wet*, pp. 41 ff. See also Scattola, *Das Naturrecht vor dem Naturrecht*, pp. 178 ff for other examples.

[36] Crimes against things of equal value as life, such as reputation, maidenly chastity, and conjugal fidelity, or against things without which life cannot be safe, such as respect for the governing power which maintains the social order (I.2.5.7).

undergo punishment by his own will, since he who wills to sin by consequent wills to deserve punishment also: *qui delinquit sua voluntate se videtur obligasse poenae ... qui directe vult peccare, per consequentiam et poenam mereri voluerit* (II.20.2.3).[37] A serious crime cannot go without punishment. In punishment expletive (i.e. commutative) justice is exercised.[38]

In II.20.3 Grotius turns to the question of who is the subject of this right to punish (*iuris subiectum*), to whom this right is due (*cui ius debetur*). This question is not easy to answer, since, as Grotius says, it has not definitely been fixed by nature. Our reason declares that the criminal may be punished, because punishments are indispensable to protect the (human) society. It does not, however, say who ought to inflict the punishment. It only says that it is most suitable (*convenientissimum*) that punishments are inflicted by someone who is superior.[39] But even this is not altogether necessary, unless we say that he who has done wrong by the very act made himself inferior to all others and demoted himself from the class of men into the class of beasts. Seen thus, all others not guilty of a crime no less serious can be said to be superior to the wrongdoer. Elsewhere in *De iure belli* we find that compulsion (remember that Grotius in *De Satisfactione* II.2 wrote that *poena sit ultimum in coactione*) is inconsistent with the position of inferiority so that at least a recognition of parity is required.[40]

In the chapter on punishment emphasis is laid on the person who is under obligation to undergo the punishment. *Deberi poenam* is the term Grotius uses, the same as in *De Satisfactione*, meaning it is proper for him to be punished (*aequum esse ut puniatur*, II.20.2.2),[41] that he deserves punishment. Just for the argument, Grotius in *De Satisfactione* called the order of things and the public good the creditor of punishment; in Prolegomena 8 of the

[37] Karl Olivecrona, *Law as Fact* (London: Stevens, 1971), p. 294: 'Grotius mentions a criminal act (*delictum*) as a cause of subjection without consent. But in the chapter on punishment he actually derives the right of punishing from the implied consent of the culprit'. See *IBP*, II.5.32 for a crime as a cause of subjection without consent. Although the difference is quite subtle, one could say that the obligation to undergo punishment is based on the implicit will of the offender, but that the subjection as the actual penalty is not.

[38] See on the different forms of justice chapter I.1, in particular paragraph 8.

[39] See II.20.10.1 for those who have the right to inflict punishment according to the laws of men: parents, guardians, masters and magistrates (*quibus leges humanae id permittunt puta a parentibus, tutoribus, dominis, magistris*).

[40] I.3.17.1: *Et cogere non est quidem semper superioris: nam et naturaliter quisque ius habet cogendi debitorem, sed cum inferioris natura repugnat. Itaque ex coactione saltem paritas sequitur.*

[41] Also John Salter, 'Sympathy with the poor: theories of punishment in Hugo Grotius and Adam Smith', *History of Political Thought*, 20 (1999), pp. 205-224.

De iure belli ac pacis we find the maintenance of the social order as the source of human law, including criminal law. In II.20.4.2 we read that one man is so bound to another by ties of common blood that he ought not to do harm to another save for the sake of attaining some good. This also counts in punishment.

The good to be expected from punishment is discussed in II.20.6-9, after having done away with vengeance just for the enjoyment of seeing the other suffer as incompatible with reason and the law of nature.[42] Reason should always govern our desires and make us use them to attain a useful end. In punishment the useful end can either be the good of the wrongdoer (II.20.7: admonition or correction), or the good of him who has been wronged (II.20.8: vengeance as form of prevention), or the good of mankind (II.20.9: to prevent the same crime to take place). All these ends may by nature be strived for by all individuals; in a state only as far as it is permitted by its laws.[43] Although in civil societies the right to punish may be exclusively in the hands of the judges, the old natural liberty (*naturalis libertas*, II.20.8.5),[44] i.e. the primitive right (*priscum ius*, II.20.9.5) persists wherever there are no judges and courts. This follows from Grotius's ideas on the origin and function of civil power, this power being nothing else than the power to make use of our human nature by those who are not subjected to anyone, within the bonds set by reason and natural law. Subjection entails the loss of the natural right to punish and to defend what is ours, and the highest authorities rule over men exactly because they are subject to no one and thus still can use their natural powers according to natural law.[45] It is left to the authorities to use it on behalf of the subjects who, because (and as long as) they are subjects can no longer make use of their liberties to defend what is theirs and to punish transgressions of the laws.

[42] In II.20.10.6 Grotius distinguishes between revenge as retaliation for the past and as a preventive for the future; see also II.20.8.2 in which paragraph the preventive form of vengeance is taken as part of the law of self-defense if it is employed within the bonds of right.

[43] II.20.9.2: *Huius* [...] *iuris potestas naturaliter penes unumquemque est* [...] *Quae tamen in republica intelligenda sunt quatenus eius leges id ferunt.*

[44] Also II.20.40.1: *libertas humanae societati per poenas consulendi.* In II.21.3.1: *Poenas* [...] *naturaliter cuivis cui nihil simile obiici potest exigere licet*; II.20.7: *Punitionem* [...] *natura cuivis esse licitam.*

[45] II.20.40.1: *Nam libertas humanae societati per poenas consulendi, quae initio ut diximus penes singulos fuerat, civitatibus ac judiciis institutis penes summas potestates resedit, non proprie qua aliis imperant, sed qua nemini parent. Nam subjectio aliis id jus abstulit.* See also I.2.5.5 where we read that originally it was not *iniquum* to kill a murderer, but that after the establishment of courts this was restricted solely to the courts. In other words: from then on only state officials are licensed to do what naturally all men were at liberty to do.

Whoever is not, or no longer subjected to civil authorities is at liberty to exploit his human nature within the bounds of natural law.[46]

If I am right the argument runs as follows: the subjects did not give the sovereign that right to punish; but only in laying down theirs, strengthened him to use his own, as he should think fit, for the preservation of them all; so that it was not given, but left to him, and to him only; and (within the limits set him by natural law) as entire, as in the condition of mere nature. Note well that these lines are not my own, but that they are – with a slight adaptation-taken from Thomas Hobbes, *Leviathan* (1651), chapter 28, 'Of Punishments, and Rewards'.[47] Of course, Hobbes did not mean to express Grotius's theory on punishment, but his own. However, I think his words are totally appropriate to summarize Grotius's thoughts on punishment as set out in *De iure belli ac pacis*.[48]

What we find here in II.20.40.1 is important, since Grotius in chapter I.3 is not very clear on the origin of civil power (*potestas civilis*, I.3.6) of the people; a power that may, or may not, but in most cases will come into the hands of one or few persons (I.3.8). It can be deduced from chapter II.20 that civil power consists of those competences – in the sense of natural liberties – that the subjects have been willing to renounce for the sake of social well-being.

---

[46] This includes, it may be good to point out once more, the right to punish any transgressions of the law (of nature), wherever and by whomever. In II.20.40.4 Grotius himself says he so far follows the opinion of Pope Innocent IV (1243-1254) as can be found in his Decretal *Quod super his* and of others such as Antoninus Florentinus (15th Century) and Sylvester Prierias (16th Century), saying war may be waged upon those who sin against nature. Grotius turns against the contrary view of some influential sixteenth century (Spanish) authors such as Francisco de Vitoria and Fernando Vázquez de Menchaca. The important question in the sixteenth and early seventeenth century of course was the right to wage war upon the American infidels; the Spaniards mentioned above said it requires jurisdiction to wage a penal war, Grotius held a contrary opinion. On this paragraph, and on two difficulties the text of the paragraph contains: Haggenmacher, 'Sur un passage obscur de Grotius', especially pp. 300f. and 304ff. See also Richard Tuck, *The Rights of War and Peace*, pp. 60 ff. ('Scholasticism') and pp. 68 ff. ('Thomism'), and Joseph Höffner, *Christentum und Menschenwürde. Das Anliegen der spanischen Kolonialethik im Goldenen Zeitalter*, (Trier: Paulinus, 1947).

[47] Thomas Hobbes, *Leviathan* (London: Andrew Crooke, 1651); in the Pinguin-edition I have used (with an introduction by C.B. Macpherson, (London: Penguin, 1985) the text can be found on p. 354.

[48] On the similarities between Hobbes and Grotius, see Richard Tuck in his publications mentioned earlier, and more, as in his 'Grotius, Carneades and Hobbes', *Grotiana*, 4 (1983), pp. 43-62 (also published in *Great Political Thinkers. Grotius*, II, pp. 263-282); on the differences between Grotius and Hobbes, however, see Perez Zagorin, 'Hobbes without Grotius', *History of Political Thought*, 21 (2000), pp. 16-40 and Haggenmacher, 'Droits subjectifs', pp. 118-121.

The same can be deduced from I.4.2.1[49] were we read that the natural right to protect ourselves and our possessions is set aside by the greater right of the civil society in the interest of public peace and order, to the extent necessary for this end.[50] And so the real question is: the use of which natural liberties have the founders of a civil society[51] been willing to renounce in order that they may exclusively be used by the civil authorities for the sake of them all?

Grotius seems to have changed position again. In *De Satisfactione* punishment, as an *actus nocivus*, necessarily had to fall within the limits of the power (*sit in potestate*) of the *puniens* and therefore assumed a relationship between a superior and an inferior. Punishment can be licit on three grounds: a previous right to punish, consent to undergo punishment (for someone else's crime), or the crime of the one to be punished. In *De iure belli ac pacis* emphasis is laid on the duty to undergo punishment; the corresponding *ius* to inflict punishment is the moral quality to use force against somebody else without injustice (see I.1.4: *Qualitas moralis personae competens ad aliquid iuste habendum vel agendum*). The use of force to attain the goals set by reason and our social nature and within the limits of natural law, is not unjust.[52] It is enough that he

[49] On this paragraph and the Grotian notion of sovereignty, see Yves Charles Zarka, 'The Mutation of the Right of Resistance in Grotius and Hobbes. From the collective right of the people to the right of the individual', *Grotiana*, 20-21 (1999-2000), pp. 35-47.

[50] I think the view of Knud Haakonssen, 'Hugo Grotius and the History of Political Thought', *Political Theory*, 13 (1985), pp. 239-265 (also published in *Great Political Thinkers. Grotius*, II, pp. 338-364), on p. 245 is too narrow, where he says: 'What is it precisely that is given up by individuals in the contract which forms the explicit or implicit basis for a sovereign civil society? Grotius says clearly that it is the right to resist other people if they transgress on our rights [...]', followed on the next page by 'When [Grotius] says that it is the right of resistance that we give up, I suggest that he means simply the right to punish others'. Punishment is the only cause of just war that does not (only, or directly) aim to defend our rights, but rather to defend the law. I think it is more appropriate to say that generally speaking in constructing a civil society the individuals give up their liberty to wage a private war on one of the four causes of just war, including the right to punish. I think Haakonssen is right where he on p. 246 rejects the reading 'according to which all rights are surrendered to the sovereign'.

[51] On the law of non-resistance, Grotius in I.4.7.2 says: *Haec autem lex de qua agimus pendere videtur a voluntate eorum, qui se primum in societatem civilem consociant, a quibus ius porro ad imperante manat.*

[52] Haggenmacher, 'Droits subjectifs', p. 108 concludes that the right to punish, as being part of the commutative justice, is 'un droit subjectif qui répond à l'obligation encourue par le délinquant'. I think Knud Haakonssen, 'Hugo Grotius and the History of Political Thought', is right where he on p. 242 calls the natural right to punish 'a kind of second-order right' (cf. also Olivecrona, *Law as Fact*, pp. 294-5). The right to punish is not (primary) to be used for one's own benefit, but for the well being of society.

who punishes and he who undergoes the punishment are equal to each other; for it is against nature that an inferior punishes a superior. The offender himself voluntarily renounced his (natural) right to resist against punishment: by his crime he willingly took upon himself the obligation to undergo the punishment. Therefore, different from *De iure praedae*, Grotius in *De iure belli ac pacis* no longer needs to say that the offender by his offence has made himself inferior to all other humans; he mentions the idea in II.40.3.1, but only as a second thought.[53]

The (exclusive) power of the state to punish transgressions of the laws is the result of the renouncement of this right (liberty) by the founders of the civil society, and the retention of it by the sovereign, who – as in the state of nature – is subjected to no one.

Conclusion

In conclusion we can say that Grotius's ideas on the origin of the ruler's right to punish as set out in *De iure praedae* come close to those of John Locke some decades later. In the natural society men are governed by natural law and have the individual right to punish transgressions of the (natural) law. Men transfer this right when they form a civil society to the community and from the community it is transfered to the ruler. Outside the civil societies the natural right (including the individual right to punish) still governs human interactions.

In *De Satisfactione* and *De imperium* the individuals are denied the (natural) right to punish. A right to punish is always part of the power of a ruler or superior. As part of the natural scheme, punishment cannot do without superiority (and superiority not without punishment). Whoever grants superiority to somebody (as for instance to a husband, king or emperor), grants to him a bundle of competences, among which the competence to punish licitly.

In *De iure belli ac pacis* Grotius holds that men are governed by natural law in the pre-civil society and that those who construct a civil government can choose which natural liberties they want to retain, and which they are willing to renounce; natural law is only partly set aside. But the natural individual right (*ius*) to punish is no longer taken as a (subjective) right that can be transferred at will (as it was in *De iure praedae*), but as a liberty, a license to inflict

[53] See what Coccejus (Henrici de Coceji, *Grotius illustratus seu commentarii ad Hugonis Grotii de jure belli et pacis libros tres*, (Bratislava: Johannis Jacobi Korn, 1746)) had to say on this idea in his comment on II.20.3.1: *Nemo unquam vocem* superioris *hoc modo intellexit.* Neither did Coccejus like the idea that the offender had willed the punishment.

a *malum* without acting unjust in certain cases. Someone only has a *ius* to punish if his act is not unjust according to natural law. Reason and our social nature determine in which cases force may be used against another human being. Subjection to a civil government means to give up (part of) our natural liberties to use our physical human possibilities, needed in the pre-civil society to take care of ourselves and our associates. Transformed into the (civil) power to do so for the sake of the community as a whole, this liberty is left to the sovereign ruler, who is subjected to nobody and who is still only governed by natural law.

Can the difference between those works concerning the individual right to punish be explained,[54] or is it simply that Grotius did not 'need' such a right in his *De Satisfactione* and *De Imperio* as he did in his works on the right of war? Or maybe the difference is not that big after all. For, firstly, Grotius in *De iure praedae* thought of the *patresfamilias* and the just and practical men endorsed with a public spirit as the dispensators of justice in the pre-civil society. In *De Satisfactione* Grotius explicitly says that punishment is a form of compulsion and that compulsion is the competence of a ruler, such as a father; in *De Imperio* however, a private person is denied the *ius vindicate*. In *De iure belli ac pacis* it is the wise man who naturally should be the one to inflict punishment. The idea that it takes superiority to inflict a punishment justly is never completely abandoned, but no longer needed in *De iure belli ac pacis* since the obligation to undergo punishment is now based on the (implicit) will of the offender. To inflict punishment equality is required. Secondly, Grotius nowhere seems to have thought of the individual right to punish as a right to be used for the individual's own good (as in my opinion is a core meaning of a subjective right). He probably came closest to this thought in *De iure praedae*, which can be explained by pointing out that in this early work he did not clearly distinguish between punishment and restitution. In the course of time Grotius seems to have refined his juridical understanding of punishment as such. In *De Satisfactione* and *De Imperio* the natural individual right to punish is denied. In *De iure belli ac pacis* it is a *ius*, but only to be used for the welfare of society. Indeed, thirdly, both in *De iure praedae* and in

[54] For an insight in the purposes of Grotius in *De iure praedae*, *De Satisfactione*, and *De iure belli ac pacis* see Blom, 'Grotius and Socinianism', especially on pp. 128-131, where Blom distinguishes between the 'republican argument for public virtue', introducing just punishment 'on the basis of the priority of the commonwealth over *amour propre*', and another 'on the basis of the moral value of faithfulness'. On p. 130: 'From the former perspective punishment is the prerogative of authority, from the latter perspective punishment is everyone's business'. Also pp. 136-137.

De iure belli ac pacis a private individual who punishes can and should be seen as acting on behalf of the (human) society; Grotius in *De Satisfactione* on account of similarity said that the order of things and the public good function as creditor in punishment.

So, I think Tuck is right when he says that Locke did not find the very strange theory in *De iure belli ac pacis*.[55] In *De iure belli ac pacis* the natural individual right to punish is not a right that is transferred to the society – as it was in *De iure praedae* and as it is in Locke's theory – but a natural liberty of those that are not subject to anyone, such as a individual in the natural state and a sovereign in the civil state. This last theory on the right of punishment of the ruler is closer to Hobbes than to Locke.

---

[55] See above, footnotes 3 and 4.

Index